HIGHLANDS

+ Ardsmuir

+ Castle
  Leoch

Moray Firth

Beauly + St. Kilda
  Inverness   Culloden

Lallybroch

*Atlantic
Ocean*

Fort
William   + Craigh na Dun

SCOTLAND

Stirling
Glasgow   Prestonpans

Falkirk   Edinburgh
Wentworth Prison

Carlisle

York

*Irish
Sea*   ENGLAND

IRELAND

Derby

Ludlow

London

*Celtic
Sea*

English Channel

+ Abbey of Ste.
  Anne de Beaupré

Le Havre   Rouen
           Amiens
           Compiègne
Versailles Paris

N
Fontainebleau

FRANCE

+ *location is approximate*

0   MILES   200

✦ THE ✦
OUTLANDISH
COMPANION

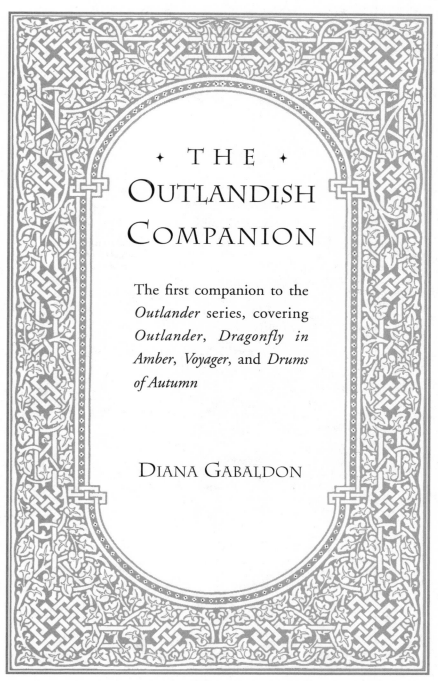

✦ THE ✦
OUTLANDISH
COMPANION

The first companion to the
Outlander series, covering
Outlander, *Dragonfly in
Amber*, *Voyager*, and *Drums
of Autumn*

DIANA GABALDON

DOUBLEDAY CANADA

Doubleday Canada and colophon are registered trademarks of Random House of Canada Limited.

Library and Archives Canada Cataloguing in Publication data is available upon request.

ISBN: 978-0-385-68524-5
eISBN: 978-0-385-68525-2

Custom illustrations: Running Changes, Inc. Photographs: Barbara Schnell
Endpaper maps: James Sinclair

Book design by Virginia Norey

Printed and bound in the USA

Published in Canada by Doubleday Canada,
A division of Random House of Canada Limited,
A Penguin Random House Company

www.penguinrandomhouse.ca

10 9 8 7 6 5 4 3 2 1

Penguin
Random House
DOUBLEDAY CANADA

ACKNOWLEDGMENTS

The author would, as usual, like to acknowledge

. . . Her husband, who keeps saying, "Yes, but when are you going to finish the next *real* book?" (I'm working on it. Them. Whatever. Soon. Well, as soon as I can, anyway. Time is relative, isn't it?)

. . . Her children, who still make witty remarks from time to time, but who are now old enough to register objections to having these quoted in public (what they said [collectively] was "You've been putting *us* in your books? MOTHER! Our *friends* read these books!" To which I replied in some consternation, "Well, tell your friends I think they're all *much* too young to be reading these books!")

. . . the Usual Suspects: the longtime and ever-changing array of electronic friends (and many passing acquaintances of kindly intent) who provide me with interesting factoids, entertaining questions, vital information, scintillating conversation, and fascinating raw material.

•

. . . the Readers, who both instigated this book and supplied me with a great deal of its content by asking questions, suggesting Things They Would Like to Know, and providing all sorts of interesting miscellanea, like the Celtic discography (music to be listened to while reading the novels). To say nothing of those who argued with me about the actions of characters in the books—as though I had anything to do with it!

This book has been somewhat different from the novels that I write, not only in its content, but in its form and substance. Normally, the only really important thing in a book is the story, and while the mechanical details such as design and copyediting are certainly not unimportant, they aren't vital. This particular volume is much more than the sum of its words, though, and much more the product of dedication on the part of a great many talented (and long-suffering) people besides myself, including:

. . . Barbara Schnell, my delightful (and faithfully accurate) German translator, who provided many of the photographs of the Highlands near Lallybroch.

. . . Carlos and Deborah Gonzales, who used their artistic magic to transform visions into reality.

. . . Dr. James Brickell, who emigrated from Scotland to North Carolina in 1733, and went to the trouble of drawing pictures of the flora and fauna encountered *en route.*

. . . Kathy Pigou, the Australian astrologer who cast the horoscopes for Claire and Jamie.

. . . Iain MacKinnon Taylor (and his brother Hamish and his aunt Margaret), who has done his bit to prevent the extinction of the Gaidhlig tongue, by providing me with Gaelic translations, pronunciations, definitions, and grammar notes.

. . . Michelle LaFrance, another devoted to the perpetuation of Gaidhlig/Gaelic/whateveryouwanttocallthebeastlylanguage, who provided me with reams of useful resource material.

. . . the staff and habitués of the CompuServe ROOTS Forums, who helpfully provided all kinds of reference material on genealogy.

. . . The Scottish Trustees of the *Carmina Gadelica,* for permission to quote assorted Celtic blessings and invocations in their entirety.

. . . the anonymous editor of The Baronage Press, for his erudite and authoritative assistance in preparing the heraldry and genealogical notes that accompany the Family Trees.

. . . Judie Rousselle, Diane Schlichting, Fay Zachary, Tabbak, BCMaxy, Sassenak, and the others who have so kindly given Jamie and company a continuing online presence through their Web sites—and in particular, Rosana Madrid Gatti, who designed and maintains the Official Diana Gabaldon Home Page, to the delight of all who see it.

. . . Virginia Norey (whose name ought really to be presented here with illuminated capitals, at least), for the stunning design of this book, to say nothing of the subsidiary illustrations.

. . . Mark Pensavalle, the production manager, whose blood and sweat stain the pages of this volume (I would say tears, but I don't think it's been bad enough to make him actually cry yet).

. . . Johanna Tani, chief copyeditor, who has provided the ever-necessary vigilance against those hordes of errors that breed in the gutters of books, hatching out into the light of day when the covers are opened.

. . . Susan Schwartz, without whose herculean efforts this book would simply not exist.

. . . Jennifer Prior, copyeditor, one of the normally unsung heroes of book production, and

. . . the many other people who have contributed so much to this book: Ann Fraser, for details of the Fraser of Lovat family tree; Elaine Smith, for the ring patterns; Stephen and Anne McKenzie, and Karen Jackson, for the photographs of Castle Leod, and all the other helpful souls whose many contributions have made this book what it is (i.e., large).

Thank you all!

Diana Gabaldon
www.dianagabaldon.com

For Jackie Cantor,
My companion on this long Outlandish journey

CONTENTS

· THE ·
OUTLANDISH
COMPANION

PROLOGUE

Well, it was all an accident, is what it was. I wasn't trying to be published; I wasn't even going to *show* it to anyone. I just wanted to write a book—any kind of book.

Not actually *any* kind of book. Fiction. See, I'm a storyteller. I can't take any particular credit for this—I was born that way. When my sister and I were very young and shared a bedroom, we stayed up far into the night, nearly every night, telling enormous, convoluted, continuing stories, with casts of thousands (like I said, I was born with this).

Still, even though I knew I was a storyteller from an early age, I didn't know quite what to do about it. Writing fiction is not a clearly marked career path, after all. It's not like law, where you do go to school for X years, pass an exam, and *bing!* you can charge people two hundred dollars an hour to listen to your expert opinions (my sister's a lawyer). Writers mostly make it up as they go along, and there is no guarantee that if you do certain things, you will get published. Still less is there any guarantee that you'll make a living at it.

Now, I come from a very conservative background (morally and financially, not politically). My parents would take my sister and me out for dinner now and then, and while waiting for the food to be served, would point out the oldest, most harried looking waitress in the place, saying sternly, "Be sure you get a good education, so you don't have to do *that* when you're fifty!"

With this sort of nudging going on at home, it's no wonder that I didn't announce that I was moving to London to become a novelist right after high school. Instead, I got a B.S. in zoology, an M.S. in marine biology, a Ph.D. in ecology, and a nice job as a research professor at a large university, complete with fringe benefits, pension plans, etc. The only trouble was that I still wanted to write novels.

Now, I have had rather a varied scientific career, featuring such highlights as the postdoctoral appointment where I was paid to butcher seabirds (I can reduce a full-grown gannet to its component parts in only three hours. Oddly enough, I have yet to find another job requiring this skill), or the job where I tortured boxfish and got interrogated by the FBI (they didn't care about the civil rights of the boxfish; it was the Russian exchange scientist grinding up clams in my laboratory they were after). At the time when my desire to write novels resurfaced, though, I was working at Arizona State University, writing Fortran programs to analyze the contents of bird gizzards.

This was really an accident; I was supposed to be developing a research program dealing with nesting behavior in colonially breeding birds. However, I was the only person in my research center who had (and I quote the director) "a background in computers." At the time, said "background" amounted to one Fortran class, which I had taken in the College of Business in order to keep my husband company. However, as the director logically pointed out, this was 100 percent more computer knowledge than anyone *else* in the place had. I was therefore drafted to help with the analysis of ten years' worth of avian dietary data, using punch cards, coding sheets, and the university's mainframe computer. (In other words, this was long before the term "Internet" became a household word.)

At the conclusion of eighteen months of labor—which resulted in a gigantic eight-hundred-page coauthored monograph on the dietary habits of the birds of the Colorado River Valley—I said to myself, You know, there are probably only five other people in the entire world who care about bird gizzards. Still, if they knew about these programs I've written, it would save each one of those five people eighteen months of effort. That's about seven and a half years of wasted work. Why is there no way for me to find those five people and share these programs with them?

The net result of this rhetorical question was a scholarly journal called *Science Software,* which I founded, edited, and wrote most of for several years.[1] A secondary result was that when my husband quit his job to start his own business and we needed more money, I was in a position to seek freelance writing work with the computer press.

I sent a query letter to the editors of *Byte, InfoWorld, PC,* and several other large computer magazines, enclosing both a recent copy of *Science Software* and a copy of a Walt Disney comic book I had written.[2] The query said roughly, "As you can see from the enclosed, you'll never find anyone better qualified to review scientific and technical software—and at the same time, capable of appealing to a wide popular audience."

By good fortune, the microcomputer revolution had just bloomed, to the point where there actually *was* a fair amount of scientific and technical software on the market. And as one of perhaps a dozen "experts" in the newly invented field of scientific computation (it's really pretty easy to be an expert, when there are only twelve people in the world who do what you do), I got immediate assignments. It was in the course of one of these that a software vendor sent me a trial membership to CompuServe, for the purpose of mentioning a support forum that the vendor maintained for the software I was reviewing.

I spent half an hour checking out the software support forum, and then—finding myself with several hours of free connect time in hand—set out to see what else might be available in this fascinating new online world. This being the mid-1980s, there was not nearly so much online as there is today (there was no World Wide Web; only the subscription services, such as CompuServe, GEnie, and Prodigy. America Online didn't even exist yet). Still, among the resources available then (on CompuServe) was a group called the Literary Forum.

This was a fascinating group of individuals who all liked books. That was the only common denominator; the group included people of every conceivable background and profession—among them, a few published writers, a good many aspiring writers, and a great many nonwriters who simply liked to discuss books and writing. Finding this congenial gathering to be the ideal social life for a busy person with small children—something like a twenty-four-hour electronic cocktail party—I promptly

---

[1] *The university and I later sold this publication to John Wiley & Sons, Inc., though I continued to serve as editor. It eventually was sold again, to a small British publisher, who merged it with an existing publication called* Laboratory Microcomputer. *Last time I looked, I was still listed as a contributing editor, but that was some time ago.*

[2] *Oh, the comic books. Well, my mother taught me to read at an early age, in part by reading me Walt Disney comics. What with one thing and another, I never stopped. At the age of twenty-eight or so, I was reading one of these, and said to myself, You know, this story is pretty bad. I bet I could do better myself!*

I found out the name and address of the editor in charge, and sent him a medium-rude letter, saying in essence, "I've been reading your comic books for twenty-five years, and they're getting worse and worse. I don't know *that I could do better myself, but I'd like to try."*

Fortunately the editor—Del Connell—was a gentleman with a sense of humor. He wrote back and said, "Okay. Try." He didn't buy my first attempt, but did something much more valuable; he told me what was wrong with it. He bought my second story—one of the Great Thrills of my life—and I wrote for him and for another Disney editor, Tom Golberg, for some three years, until their backlog obliged them to stop purchasing freelance scripts.

Between them, Del and Tom taught me most of what I know about story structure. I acknowledge the debt with great gratitude.

signed up with CompuServe, and began logging on to the Literary Forum several times a day, to read and exchange posted messages with the kindred spirits there.

At this point in my life, I had a full-time job with the university, I was writing part-time for the computer press, and I had three children, ages six, four, and two. I'm not sure quite why I thought this was the ideal time to begin writing my long-intended novel—mania induced by sleep deprivation, perhaps—but I did.

I didn't intend to show this putative novel to anyone. It wasn't for publication; it was for practice. I had come to the conclusion—based on experience—that the only real way of learning to write a novel was probably to write a novel. That's how I learned to write scientific articles, comic books, and software reviews, after all. Why should a novel be different?

If I didn't mean to show it to anyone, it wouldn't matter whether what I wrote was bad or not, so I needn't feel self-conscious in the process of writing it; I could just concentrate on the writing. And, if it was just for practice, I needn't worry too much about what kind of novel it was. I made only two rules for myself: One, I would not give up, no matter how bad I thought it was, until I had finished the complete book, and two, I would do my level best in the writing, at all times.

So . . . what kind of novel should this be? Well, I read everything, and lots of it, but perhaps more mysteries than anything else. Fine, I thought, I'd write a mystery.

But then I began to think. Mysteries have plots. I wasn't sure I knew how to do plots. Perhaps I should try something easier for my practice book, then write a mystery when I felt ready for a *real* book.

Fine. What was the easiest possible kind of book for me to write, for practice? (I didn't see any point in making things difficult for myself.)

After considerable thought, it seemed to me that perhaps a historical novel would be the easiest thing to try. I was a research professor, after all; I had a huge university library available, and I knew how to use it. I thought it seemed a little easier to look things up than to make them up—and if I turned out to have no imagination, I could steal things from the historical record.[3]

Okay. Fine. Where to set this historical novel? I have no formal background in history; one time or place would do as well as another.

Enter another accident. I rarely watch TV, but at the time I was in the habit of viewing weekly PBS reruns of *Doctor Who* (a British science-fiction serial), because it gave me just enough time to do my nails.[4] So, while pondering the setting for my hypothetical historical novel, I happened to see one very old episode of *Doctor*

Who featuring a "companion" of the Doctor's—a young Scottish lad named Jamie MacCrimmon, whom the Doctor had picked up in 1745. This character wore a kilt, which I thought rather fetching, and demonstrated—in this particular episode[5]—a form of pigheaded male gallantry that I've always found endearing: the strong urge on the part of a man to protect a woman, even though he may realize that she's plainly capable of looking after herself.

I was sitting in church the next day, thinking idly about this particular show (no, oddly enough, I *don't* remember what the sermon was about that day), when I said suddenly to myself, Well, heck. You want to write a book, you need a historical period, and it doesn't matter where or when. The important thing is just to start, *somewhere*. Okay. Fine. Scotland, eighteenth century.

So I went out to my car after Mass, dug a scrap of paper out from under the front seat, and that's where I began to write *Outlander;* no outline, no plot, no characters—just a time and a place.

The next stop was plainly the Arizona State University library, where I went the next day. I began my research by typing SCOTLAND HIGHLANDS EIGHTEENTH CENTURY into the card catalog—and one thing led to another.[6]

I had not the slightest intention of telling my online acquaintances in the Literary Forum what I was up to. I didn't want even the best-intentioned of advice; I wanted simply to figure out how to write a novel, and was convinced that I must do this on my own—I'd never asked anyone how to write a software review or a comic book script, after all, and I didn't want anyone telling me things before I'd worked out for myself what I was doing.

So I didn't say anything. To anybody. I just wrote, a bit every day, in between the other things I was doing, like changing diapers and writing grant proposals.

Some eight months along in this process I found myself one night having an argument with a gentleman in the Literary Forum, about what it felt like to be pregnant.[7] He asserted that he knew what this was like; his wife had had three children.

---

[3] *This is a really sound technique, by the way.*

[4] *Doctor Who is unfortunately no longer on our local PBS channel, but luckily I can still do my nails on Saturday nights, while watching* Mystery Science Theater 3000—*which is, in fact, the only TV I do watch on a regular basis. No doubt this explains something, but I couldn't tell you what.*

[5] *It was "War Games," for those interested in trivia.*

[6] *See "Research."*

[7] *Via posted messages, left bulletin-board style; I've never been in a "chat room" in my life, save as an invited guest for a mass public interview.*

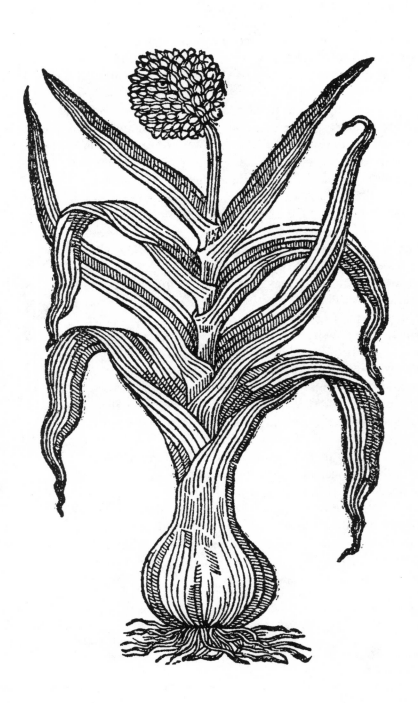

I laughed (electronically) and replied, "Yeah, buster. *I've* had three children!"

To which his reply was, "So tell me what you think it's like."

Now, among the fragments of the story that I had so far was one short piece in which a woman (Jenny Murray) tells her curious brother (Jamie Fraser) what it feels like to be pregnant. Since this piece seemed to sum up the experience with more eloquence than I could manage in a brief posted message, I told my correspondent that I had a "piece" explaining the phenomenon, and that I'd put it in the Literary Forum Library.[8]

Most conversations on CompuServe forums are public; that is, posted messages are visible to everyone, unless they've been marked as private (in which case, they're visible only to the participants). Anyone may enter a "thread" (a series of bulletin-board-like messages and replies on a given topic) as they like.[9] A number of people had been following the pregnancy argument, and so when I posted my "piece" in the library, they went and read it.

Several of them came back and left messages to me, saying (in effect), "This is great! What is it?"

To which I cleverly replied, "I don't know."

"Well, where's the beginning?" they asked.

"I haven't written that yet," I answered.

"Well . . . put up more of it!" they said.

So I did. Let me explain that I not only don't write with an outline, I don't write in a *straight* line. I write in bits and pieces, and glue them together, like a jigsaw puzzle. So whenever I had a "piece" that seemed to stand on its own, without too much explanation, I'd post it in the library. And gradually, people began to talk about my pieces, and to ask me about the book that was taking shape. Eventually, they said to me, "You know, this stuff is good; you should try to publish it."

"Yeah, right," I said. "It's just for practice, and I don't even know what kind of book it *is*." (What with the time travel and the Loch Ness Monster and a few other things, I sort of didn't think it was a historical novel anymore, but I had no idea what it might be instead.) "On the other hand . . . if I wanted to publish it, what should I do?"

"Get an agent" was the prompt response from several published authors with whom I had become friendly. "An agent can get you read much faster than if you

---

[8] *"Libraries" are electronic spaces set aside within CompuServe forums for members to post—semipermanently—things they'd like to share: stories, poems, essays, articles, shareware files, etc.*

[9] *Chat rooms and live-time interactions did not exist at the time. CompuServe messages, unlike those of AOL, exist only temporarily, with new messages essentially "pushing" old ones off into the ether.*

submit the manuscript yourself, and if it does sell, an agent can negotiate a much better contract than you can."

"Fine," I said. "How do I find an agent?"

"Well . . ." they said, "you're nowhere near finished with the book, you say, so you have plenty of time. Why don't you just ask around? Find out which agents handle what, who has a good name in the industry, who you should keep away from, and so on."

So I did. I listened to the stories of published authors, I asked questions, and after several months of such casual research, I thought I had found an agent who was a good prospect. His name was Perry Knowlton, and he appeared to be both reputable and well-known in publishing. Still better, he appeared to have no objection either to unorthodox books or to very long books—both of which, it dawned on me, I had.

However, I had no idea how to approach this man. I had heard that he didn't accept unsolicited queries, and he wasn't available online. Still, I was a long way from finished with the book, so I didn't worry about it; just kept asking questions.

I was conversing one day (via posted messages) with an author I knew casually, named John Stith, who writes science fiction/mysteries, and asked him if he could tell me about his agent, if he had one.

John replied that he did have representation—Perry Knowlton. "Would you like me to introduce you to him?" John asked. "I know you're nearly ready to look for an agent."

Presented with this gracious offer, I swallowed hard, and said weakly, "Er . . . that'd be nice, John. Thanks!"

John then sent a note to Perry, essentially saying that I might be worth looking at. I followed this with my own query, explaining that I had been selling nonfiction (and comic books) for some years, but that now I was writing fiction and I understood that I really needed a good agent. He had been recommended to me by several writers whose opinions I respected; would he be interested in reading excerpts of this rather long novel I had? (I didn't tell him I wasn't finished writing the thing yet; "excerpts" were all I had.)

Perry kindly called and said yes, he'd read my excerpts. I sent him the miscellaneous chunks I had, with a rough synopsis to bind them together[10]—and he took me on, on the basis of an unfinished first novel.[11]

At any rate, I went on writing, and six months later finally finished the book. I sent Perry the manuscript, and also mentioned that I would be in New York the next week, for a scientific conference—perhaps I could come by and meet him face-to-face?

When I went up to Perry's office, I was rather apprehensive, since I knew that he had by this time read the manuscript—but I didn't know what he thought about it. Perry himself turned out to be a charming gentleman who did his best to put me at my ease, taking me back to his office and chatting about various of his other clients. It was at this point that I discovered that—in addition to those electronic acquaintances from whom I'd learned of him—Perry also represented such eminent writers as Brian Moore, Ayn Rand (granted, she was dead, but still . . .), Tony Hillerman, Frederick Forsyth, and Robertson Davies.

If these revelations were not enough to unnerve me, he had my manuscript sitting on his desk, in the enormous orange boxes in which I'd mailed it. I was positive that at some point in the conversation he was going to cough apologetically and tell me that having now seen the whole thing, he was afraid that he really didn't think it was salable, and give it back to me.

However, as I was sitting there listening to him (meanwhile thinking, If you have the nerve to call Robertson Davies "Robbie," you're a better man than I am, Gunga Din), he said instead, "You know, the thing about Freddy Forsyth and Robbie Davies is that both those guys are great storytellers." Then he laid a hand on my manuscript, smiled at me, and said, "And you're another one."

At this point, I really didn't care whether we sold the book or not. I felt as though I'd been beatified. As it was, though, I gathered sufficient presence of mind to ask what he planned to do with the book.

"Oh," he said casually, "I'm sending it to five editors today," and proceeded to tell me about the editor who he thought was the best prospect.[12]

"Really," I said, swallowing. "And . . . er . . . how long do you think it might take to hear back?" I had, like most aspiring writers, read all the publishing information in *Writer's Market,* and knew it often took six, nine, even twelve months to hear from an editor.

"Oh," Perry said, even more casually, "I've told them I want an answer in thirty days." At this point, I decided that I had probably picked the right agent.

---

[10] *A slightly altered version of this synopsis appears in Part Two.*

[11] *Ignorant as I was at the time, I hadn't realized that agents (and editors) normally want to see a complete manuscript before making a judgment on it—just to be sure that the writer can actually* finish *the book. Perry, fortunately, was willing to gamble that I could.*

[12] *Who, interestingly enough, rejected the manuscript. "It's a great story," she said, "but it's not really a standard romance novel, and that's what we publish."*

So I went home to wait—as patiently as possible—for thirty days. Four days later, though, I came home to find a message waiting on my answering machine. "This is Perry," said a calm voice. "I've just called to update you on your manuscript."

Uh-oh, I said to myself. One of the five took one look at the box and said, "I'm not reading a ten-pound manuscript, take it back." So I called Perry, expecting to hear this.

Instead, he said, "Well, of the five I sent it to, so far three of them have called back with offers."

"Oh," I said, and paused, feeling as though I'd been hit on the head with a blunt instrument. "Ah. That's . . . uh . . . good. Isn't it?"

Perry assured me that it was. He then negotiated among the various editors for two weeks, emerging at that point with comparable offers from two publishers. Everything else being equal, he said, it came down to a choice of editor—and he recommended that we go with Jackie Cantor, at Delacorte Press. Knowing absolutely nothing about editors, I said, "Okay, fine." Which turned out to be the best choice I ever made—other than choosing my husband and my agent.

I had told Perry when I gave him the book that there seemed to be more to this story, but I thought that perhaps I should stop while I could still lift the manuscript. Being a good agent, Perry emerged with a three-book contract. After that . . . well, after that, things got out of hand, and here we are, eight years later.

So where *are* we, exactly? As I said above, I don't write with an outline—if I knew what was going to happen, it wouldn't be any fun to write the book, now, would it? However, as I go along, merrily gluing pieces together, I do sometimes get a vague idea as to *some* events that may take place in the story. So, as I finished *Cross Stitch* (my working title for what later became *Outlander*),[13] I could see that there was more to the story.

With a three-book contract in hand, I started in on the second book, *Dragonfly in Amber.* A little over halfway through, though, I began to get this uneasy feeling that perhaps I wouldn't be able to cram the entire American Revolution into one more book, and there would have to be four volumes. I confided this fear to Perry, who said, "Don't tell them *that.* Not until the first one is on the shelves, anyway."

---

[13] See "Where Titles Come From (and Other Matters of General Interest)". *I just love footnotes, don't you?*

Fortunately, by the time we decided to reveal the Awful Truth, the first books had come out and sold decently, and the publisher was happy to make us an offer for the fourth (and presumably final) book in the series. Feeling that this was perhaps the only chance I might get to induce someone to pay me to write a mystery, I got bold and said they could have the fourth book if they'd also give me a contract to write a contemporary mystery. Rather to my surprise, they gave me a contract for *two* mysteries—and the fourth of the *Outlander* books.

So I set in to write. I wrote, and I wrote, and I wrote, and after a year and a half of this, I said, I've got a quarter-million words here; why the heck am I not nearly done with this? A little thought revealed the answer; I had (once again) too much story to fit into one book.

Attending a writers' conference at which my editor was also present, I leaned over during the awards banquet and hissed in her ear, "Guess what? There are five of them." To which Jackie, a woman of great presence and equanimity, replied, "Why am I not surprised to hear this?"

Actually, it was worse than I thought. When I removed all the pieces that belonged in the fifth book, I finally realized that what I was looking at was a double trilogy—six books in all. The first three books—*Outlander, Dragonfly in Amber,* and *Voyager*—are centered around the Jacobite Rising of 1745. The second three books are centered in a similar way around the American Revolution, which was, in a way, a greatly magnified echo of the earlier conflict that ended at Culloden.

And that leads us in turn to a consideration of just what's going on in these books. Once I realized that I really was a writer, and that I had not one, but a series of books, I had two main intentions.

One was a desire to follow the great social changes of the eighteenth century. This was a time of huge political and social upheaval that saw the transition of the Western world from the last remnants of feudalism into the modern age, in terms of everything from politics and science to art and social custom. The tide of history was changing, flowing from the Old World to the New, borne on the waves of war, and what better way to look at this than through the eyes of a time-traveler?

Now, this is great stuff for the background of a novel, to be sure, but the fact is that good novels are about people. A book that doesn't have an absorbing personal story in the foreground may be good history, or have good ideas—but it won't be good fiction. So what about the personal angle of this story?

The first book was originally marketed as a historical romance because, although the book didn't fit neatly into *any* genre (and at the same time was certainly

not "literary fiction"), of all the markets that it might conceivably appeal to, romance was by far the biggest. However . . .

Other considerations aside, romance novels are courtship stories. They deal with the forming of a bond between a couple, and once that bond is formed, by marriage and sexual congress (in that order, we hope)—well, the story's over. That was never what I had in mind.

I didn't want to tell the story of what makes two people come together, although that's a theme of great power and universality. I wanted to find out what it takes for two people to *stay* together for fifty years—or more. I wanted to tell not the story of a courtship, but the story of a marriage.

Now, to handle adequately themes like the Age of Enlightenment, the fall of monarchy, and the nature of love and marriage, one requires a certain amount of room. One also requires rather a complex story. People now and then say to me, "But aren't you getting tired of writing about the same old characters?" I certainly would be, if these *were* the same old characters—but they're not. They grow, and they change. They get older, and their lives become more complex. They develop new depths and facets. While they do—I hope—remain true to their basic personalities, I have to rediscover them with each new book.

And that leads to another question I'm often asked: What is it that people find interesting about the books? For a long time, I replied (honestly), "Beats me," but after years of getting letters and E-mail, I now have some idea of the things readers *say* they like.

Many of them enjoy the sense of "being there"; the vicarious experience of another place and time. Many like the historical aspects of the books; they enjoy (they say) "learning something" while being entertained. Many like the sense of connection, of rediscovering their own heritage. A good many enjoy the curious details: the botanical medicine, the medical procedures, the how and why of daily life in another time. But by far the most common element that people enjoy in the books is simply the characters—readers care for these people, are interested in them, and want to know more about them.

So, this companion is intended for the readers: a quick reference for those who don't necessarily want to reread a million and a half words in order to refresh their memories as to Who or What; a source of information and (maybe) insight on the characters, a companion for those with an interest in backgrounds and trivia; an auxiliary guide for those with an interest in the eighteenth century and Things Scottish, and finally—a brief glimpse into the working methods of a warped mind.

> *"True. I have heard the point made, though, that the novelist's skill lies in the artful selection of detail. Do you not suppose that a volume of such length may indicate a lack of discipline in such selection, and hence a lack of skill?"*
>
> *Fraser considered, sipping the ruby liquid slowly.*
>
> *"I have seen books where that is the case, to be sure," he said. "An author seeks by sheer inundation of detail to overwhelm the reader into belief. In this case, however, I think it isna so. Each character is most carefully considered, and all the incidents chosen seem necessary to the story. No, I think it is true that some stories simply require a greater space in which to be told."*
>
> —*VOYAGER, chapter 11: "The Torremolinos Gambit"*

PART ONE

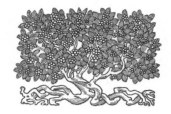

SYNOPSES

These synopses are provided for the benefit of those readers who send me letters saying "Who the heck is Archie Hayes?" or "I don't remember exactly how they got from Falkirk to the Duke's house, can you clear that up for me?" and an assortment of other questions easily answerable by anyone with the books sitting in front of them. Still, in the rush and hurry of modern life, who has time to go back and thumb leisurely through a million and a half words of print? Not me, I'll tell you.

So, for the use of those who have lent out their books and don't want to drive to the library to check a plot detail or a character name, or for those who merely wish to refresh their memories . . .

Flying Squirrel

Racoon

Pan ther

OUTLANDER

I T's 1946,[1] the Scottish Highlands are in bloom, and Claire Randall, an English ex-army combat nurse, has come to Scotland on a second honeymoon with her husband, Frank, from whom she's been separated by the war.

While she doesn't share Frank's passion for genealogy, she's looking forward to starting the next branch on the family tree. Meanwhile, she occupies her spare time in exploring the countryside, pursuing an interest in botany. On one such expedition, she discovers an ancient circle of standing stones—made the more interesting by Frank's having heard that the circle is still in use by a local group of women who celebrate the "old ways" there.

In the dawn of the ancient Feast of Beltane—May 1—Claire and Frank creep up to the circle, to see the women dancing and chanting, calling down the sun. The couple steal away unseen, but later Claire returns to the circle to get a closer look at an unusual plant she's seen growing there.

She touches one of the standing stones and is enveloped in a sudden vortex of noise and confusion. Disoriented and half-conscious, she finds herself on the hill outside the circle, and slowly makes her way down—to find what she assumes is a film shoot in progress at the bottom; a prince-in-the-heather epic, with kilted Scotsmen being pursued by red-coated British soldiers.

Claire carefully skirts the scene, so as not to ruin the shot, and making her way through the woods stumbles into a man in the costume of an eighteenth-century English army officer. This doesn't disturb her nearly as much as does the man's striking resemblance to her husband, Frank.

The resemblance is quickly explained; the man is in fact Frank's ancestor, the notorious "Black Jack" Randall, of whom Frank had often told her. While very similar in appearance, however, Jack Randall unfortunately does not share his descendant's personality—the former-day Randall being a sadistic bisexual pervert rather than a mild-mannered history professor.

Claire is rescued from Black Jack's clutches by one of the Scotsmen she had seen earlier, who takes her to the cottage where his fellows are hiding, waiting for darkness to escape. One of the men has been wounded, and Claire treats his wound—as best she can—meanwhile trying to come to terms with the apparent truth of where—and *when*—she is.

Bemused not only by Claire's peculiar

---

[1]*See note following "Titles" "Outlander vs. Cross Stitch."*

dress—or lack of it—but by the sheer impossibility of her presence—English ladies simply aren't found in the Highlands in 1743—the Scotsmen decide to take her with them when they decamp under cover of darkness.

As Claire remarks, *"The rest of the journey passed uneventfully; if you consider it uneventful to ride fifteen miles on horseback through rough country at night, frequently without benefit of roads, in company with kilted men armed to the teeth, and sharing a horse with a wounded man. At least we were not set upon by highwaymen, we encountered no wild beasts, and it didn't rain. By the standards I was becoming used to, it was quite dull."*

Arriving at dawn at Castle Leoch, seat of clan MacKenzie, Claire meets The MacKenzie, Colum. A courtly man deformed by a hideous genetic disease, Colum is both intrigued and suspicious. He can think of no conceivable reason for an Englishwoman to have been wandering the Highlands, and makes no pretense of believing Claire's thin story of having been beset by robbers. Not knowing who she may be, or what her purposes are, he makes it plain that he intends to keep her as his guest for the time being—willing or not.

While laying plans for her escape and return to the stone circle, Claire becomes

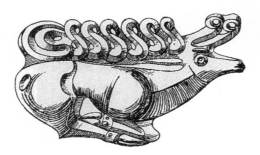

better acquainted with the young man whose wound she had dressed, a clansman named Jamie, whom she at first takes for a groom at the castle.

She discovers her mistake; Jamie is in fact the nephew of Colum and his brother, Dougal (the clan's war chieftain, who leads the men to battle in place of his crippled brother), though his father belonged to clan Fraser. He is also an outlaw, wanted by the English for offenses ranging from theft to unspecified "obstruction"—offenses that have left his back webbed with the scars of flogging.

Relations between uncles and nephew appear oddly strained, and the reason is explained following a clan Gathering, at which Colum demands an oath of loyalty from Jamie—and fails to get it. Colum has one son, Hamish, age eight. As Jamie explains to Claire, if Colum should die—as is likely, given the nature of his disease—before young Hamish is of an age to lead the clan, who will inherit the chieftainship?

Dougal is the obvious candidate, but there are those among the clan who feel that while he is an able warrior, he lacks the cool head and intelligence a chief should have. Hamish is plainly too young—but there is another candidate: Jamie. While Jamie himself professes no desire to usurp the chieftainship, Colum and Dougal are not so sure his protestations are sincere, and are inclined to take steps—some of them lethal—to prevent any such attempt.

Claire has so far failed twice in her attempts to escape from Leoch, so she is delighted to hear Dougal announce that he intends to take her with him on his journey to collect rents from the tacksmen of

the district. His professed intention is to take her to the captain of the English garrison, who may either be able to shed light on her presence or take charge of her. Or both.

Claire is highly in favor of this, feeling sure that she can persuade the English captain to send her back to the stone circle, from which she may be able to get back to her own time. Her hopes vanish abruptly upon her discovery that the captain of the garrison is Jack Randall.

For his part, Jack Randall is delighted to see Claire again, and determined to find out who and what she is. Englishwomen simply don't go to the Highlands; if she is here, alone, she must undoubtedly be a spy—but for whom, and why? His notions of interrogation are not gentle, and even Dougal MacKenzie is appalled. Refusing to leave her with the Captain, Dougal takes Claire away with him, and after a pause for thought, tells her that he has conceived a plan: The Captain has the right to compel the person of an English citizen, but cannot arrest a Scotswoman in her own country without legal formalities. So, Dougal announces triumphantly, he will make her a Scot; she must marry his nephew Jamie without delay.

Nearly as horrified by this notion as by the Captain's behavior, Claire does her best to resist, but can find no alternative. Convinced at last

that if she marries Jamie, she will have a better chance of escape, she consents, finding her horror tempered with bemusement at her prospective bridegroom's inexperience:

"Does it bother you that I'm not a virgin?" He hesitated a moment before answering.

"Well, no," he said slowly, "so long as it doesna bother you that I am." He grinned at my drop-jawed expression, and backed toward the door.

"Reckon one of us should know what they're doing," he said. The door closed softly behind him; clearly the courtship was over.

However, there is no immediate chance of escape, and Claire is obliged to consummate her marriage with Jamie—under Dougal's firm orders. Dougal, it appears, is killing two birds with one stone; while he has sufficient humanitarian instincts to wish to keep Claire away from Randall (and is still curious enough about her to want to find out for himself what she's doing there), his principal motive is to stifle any chance of his nephew attaining the chieftainship of clan MacKenzie—for the clan will never accept Jamie as leader with an English wife.

Realizing that Jamie is as much under duress as is she, Claire accepts the inevitable—and finds herself becoming very fond of her new young husband. Much too fond; for she still means to escape and return to Frank, as soon as she can.

Soon enough, she finds her chance, and steals away while Jamie is occupied elsewhere. However, her attempt fails when she falls once more into the hands of a prowling Jack Randall and is taken to his inner sanctum in Fort William, where she discovers more than she wanted to know about the Captain's recreational proclivities. This time, she is rescued by Jamie, who escapes with her from the fort while the other Scots create a diversion by blowing up the powder magazine.

During the angry confrontation that follows their escape, Claire learns that there is more to Jamie's antipathy toward Randall than his recent behavior. She already knows that the scars on Jamie's back were inflicted by Randall, who had taken the young Scotsman prisoner several years before. Now she learns that the vicious flogging was the result of Jamie's refusal to yield his body to Randall, who gratifies his inclinations with the readiest victims: the Scottish prisoners under his control, who have no recourse or means of escape.

Returning, perforce, to Leoch, Claire does not give up searching for a way back to the stones—and Frank—but becomes increasingly aware of how wrenching such a return would be, tearing her away from the man she has come to love.

One small difficulty shows some hope of resolution, though; Colum—now secure in the knowledge that his nephew is no threat to his son Hamish's chieftainship—offers to intercede for Jamie with an English noble of his acquaintance, the Duke of Sandringham. Perhaps, Colum thinks, the Duke could be induced to gain a pardon from the Crown for Jamie, removing the continuing danger of outlawry.

Arrangements are made for Jamie and Dougal to accompany the Duke on a hunting trip, where the delicate negotiations for a pardon might be accomplished.

Tiger

As Jamie remarks wryly to Claire, *"It goes against the grain a bit, to be pardoned for something I've not done, but it's better than being hanged."*

Meanwhile, Claire has formed a friendship with the wife of the local Procurator Fiscal, a woman named Geillis Duncan, with whom she shares a knowledge of herbs and healing. But at a dinner to honor a visiting duke, the Fiscal dies—probably poisoned.

Rumors spread like wildfire, fueled with hysteria and superstition, and in Jamie's absence Claire finds herself on trial for witchcraft, in company with Geillis Duncan. On the verge of condemnation, Claire discovers Geilie's secret—she is pregnant, and clearly not by her impotent late husband. She is indeed a poisoner, if not a witch—but proves also a good friend; she creates a distraction that allows Jamie to rescue Claire.

Jamie and Claire flee from the castle on horseback, but once safely away he confronts her—he will love her forever, and stand by her no matter what, but for his own peace of mind, he must know—is she a witch?

Hysterical from her recent ordeal, Claire tells him that it's much worse than *that,* and confesses the truth, explaining to him about the stones—and about Frank.

Road to Lallybroch.

Clearly not believing her, but shaken by her obvious emotion, Jamie takes her through the Highlands to the stone circle. The truth of her story proven by events in the circle, he says she must make her choice—to stay with him, or to go back to her husband in the future—and leaves her alone by the stones to decide.

Agonizing through most of an afternoon, she finally stands, makes her way slowly toward the cleft stone that is her passage back to her own time—and then finds herself running the other way, stumbling and falling down the hillside, her body having decided what her mind cannot—running toward Jamie.

Reunited, Claire asks, *"Do you really believe me, Jamie?"*

He sighed, and smiled ruefully down at me.

"Aye, I believe ye, Sassenach. But it would ha' been a good deal easier, if you'd only been a witch."

With the truth clear between them, they make their way through the Highlands to Jamie's home at Lallybroch, where they are made welcome by his remaining family, his sister Jenny, with her husband, Ian, and son, Young Jamie. Their idyll is short-lived, though; Jamie is waylaid by the local Watch, an unofficial police force in the pay of the English, who will deliver him to his enemies.

Assisted by Jamie's godfather, Murtagh, Claire sets out to rescue him. Jamie has escaped from the Watch, she learns, but is now somewhere afoot in the Highlands. Plainly he cannot return to Lallybroch; the place is watched. How to find a man who might be anywhere in a desolate countryside?

Murtagh and Claire work their way north, thinking that Jamie might be heading for Beauly, where his Fraser grandfather, Simon, Lord Lovat, might offer him help. Before they reach Beauly, though, they encounter someone else—Dougal MacKenzie, who has brought disastrous news: Jamie has been captured, tried, and condemned to hang. He has been sent to Wentworth Prison, near the border, where the sentence of execution will be carried out.

Insisting that it is not possible to free Jamie, Dougal (a recent widower) instead promises to take care of Claire, proposing marriage to her. Instantly, a number of things become clear to Claire; by the terms of Jamie's inheritance, a woman can own Lallybroch estate. If Jamie is executed, Lallybroch will belong to her—or to whoever marries her.

During the ensuing confrontation with Dougal, Claire verifies what she previously suspected; young Hamish is not Colum's son—Colum's disease renders him sterile, and largely impotent as well. Hamish was sired by Dougal, as an act of loyalty to the brother he loves, to give Colum an heir.

The tête-à-tête is interrupted by Murtagh, armed with pistols, who politely suggests that they have more pressing business: getting to Wentworth while Jamie is still alive to save. Under duress, Dougal reluctantly supplies them with money and a few men—and a surprising bit of information.

Geillis Duncan, he tells Claire, was indeed burned as a witch, after the birth of her child—who was also sired by Dougal.

Before being taken to the stake, though, she gave Dougal a message to be passed on to Claire, should Dougal ever meet her again. The message, to be repeated verbatim: *"Tell her that I do not know for certain, but I think it is possible."* That sentence, and four numbers: one, nine, six, and eight.

Claire, Murtagh, and their companions leave at once on the long ride to Wentworth, which gives Claire time to ponder the meaning of Geillis's message—clearly, what Geillis meant was that she herself thought it possible to return through the stones to Claire's own time. And the numbers? *"She had told them to him separately, for the sake of a secrecy which must have gone bone-deep in her by that time, but they were all part of one number, really. One, nine, six, eight. Nineteen sixty-eight. The year of **her** disappearance into the past."*

Arriving at Wentworth, Claire inveigles her way into the prison on the eve of the execution, searching for Jamie—and finds him in the dungeon, at the mercy of Jack Randall. Unable to exercise his inclinations to the fullest, Randall must content himself with such brutality as will pass without comment—bruises and broken bones are within the realm of official toleration; homosexual rape is not.

Claire succeeds in freeing Jamie from

his shackles, but is interrupted by the return of Randall, in company with his hulking, mentally deficient—but terribly obedient—orderly, Marley. Delighted to see Claire again, Randall declares his intention of giving her to Marley to enjoy, allowing Jamie to watch as his final entertainment before hanging.

Jamie attacks Marley, and after a bone-crushing fight, succeeds in overpowering him. Randall, though, has a trump—a knife at Claire's throat.

Desperate, and feeling that he has nothing left to lose, Jamie makes a devil's bargain—his body, and his silence, in return for Claire's freedom. Unable to resist the temptation of a victim at once completely unwilling but completely compliant, Randall agrees. After all, Claire is quite helpless—he thinks.

Thrown out into the snow, Claire makes her way frantically in search of help. She has a plan—if only she is in time. Randall has put her out by a small rear door, concealed in a narrow declivity that forms the prison's garbage dump. Randall doesn't know about Claire's companions; if she can find them in time, they can perhaps force the rear door and enter the prison. Unfortunately, Claire meets not her companions, but the dump's inhabitants—a small pack of degenerate wolves.

Claire manages by luck and desperation to kill one wolf, but is stalked relentlessly through the winter twilight by the others. Suddenly an arrow whizzes out of nowhere—one of the woodsmen of Sir Marcus MacRannoch, whose estate adjoins Wentworth, has been attracted by the wolves' howling, and is astonished to find Claire, tattered, bloodstained, and in a state of desperate hurry.

Reaching Sir Marcus, she implores his help in freeing Jamie from the prison. He is sympathetic, but adamant; there is nothing he can do. Claire offers to pay him, bringing out the string of freshwater pearls that Jamie gave her on their wedding day: pearls that had belonged to his mother, Ellen.

MacRannoch is shaken by the sight of the pearls; as a young man, he had paid court to Ellen MacKenzie, and when she chose elsewhere had insisted nonetheless that she keep his gift—the freshwater pearls. Still, much as he would wish to help Ellen's son, he tells Claire, he dares not risk an assault on the prison; the prison's governor would be sure to take revenge on Eldridge Manor, MacRannoch's estate.

Driven to despair, Claire collapses, only dully noticing the entry of another of MacRannoch's men, who reluctantly reports that he and his companions have managed to find only a small fraction of MacRannoch's purebred herd of Highland cows—and there is a snowstorm coming on.

Hearing this, Claire begins cautiously to hope. For one of her companions is Rupert MacKenzie, a man with a great reputation for "cattle-lifting"—and one unlikely to resist the temptation offered by a straying herd. Rising to her feet, she informs MacRannoch that she has a plan that will protect him from suspicion in Jamie's escape—and if he wants to see his cattle again, he'd better agree to it.

Finding her companions, Claire tells them her plan, leads them to the door—and then is forced to wait, as they drive head af-

Castle Leoch.

ter head of shaggy Highland cattle down the alley and into the prison's dungeons.

Meanwhile, Sir Marcus MacRannoch, to whom the cattle belong, has stormed into the Governor's office, claiming that the garrison soldiers have stolen his herd and insisting that he be allowed to search for them. Under cover of the bellowing confusion in the dungeon, his men have orders to find and rescue Jamie, spiriting him out through the rear door.

As Sir Marcus reports to Claire, a man emerged from the dungeon cell to investigate the racket and was trampled to death beneath the cattle's hooves, *"nay more than a rag-doll, rolled in blood."* Jack Randall is dead, then, and Jamie rescued—but hours have passed; hours spent in an airless dungeon with a monster.

Claire can heal Jamie's external wounds, but how can she deal with the damage to his soul? She and Murtagh manage to get Jamie safely across the Channel to France, where one of Jamie's uncles is the abbot of the Abbey of Ste. Anne de Beaupré.

Taking refuge in the abbey, Claire faces her last and most important fight. With nothing but her healing skills and her own courage, she risks both her life and Jamie's, using opium to resurrect and exorcise the ghost of Jack Randall, that Jamie might reclaim his manhood through the same violence by which it was taken from him.

At the last, they both find healing in the grotto of a hot spring, in a cave far under the abbey.

We struggled upward, out of the womb of the world, damp and steaming, rubber-limbed with wine and heat. I fell to my knees at the first landing, and Jamie, trying to help me, fell down next to me in an untidy heap of robes and bare legs. Giggling helplessly, drunk more with love than with wine, we made our way side by side, on hands and knees up the second flight of steps, hindering each other more than helping, jostling and caroming softly off each other in the narrow space, until we collapsed at last in each other's arms on the second landing.

Here an ancient oriel window opened glassless to the sky, and the light of the hunter's moon washed us in silver. We lay clasped together, damp skins cooling in the winter air, waiting for our racing hearts to slow and breath to return to our heaving bodies.

The moon above was a Christmas moon, so large as almost to fill the empty window. It seemed no wonder that the tides of sea and woman should be subject to the pull of that stately orb, so close and so commanding.

But my own tides moved no longer to that chaste and sterile summons, and the knowledge of my freedom raced like danger through my blood.

"I have a gift for you, too," I said suddenly to Jamie. He turned toward me and his hand slid, large and sure, over the plane of my still-flat stomach.

"Have you, now?" he said.

And the world was all around us, new with possibility.

THE END

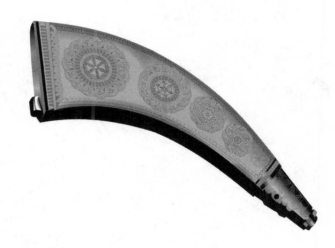

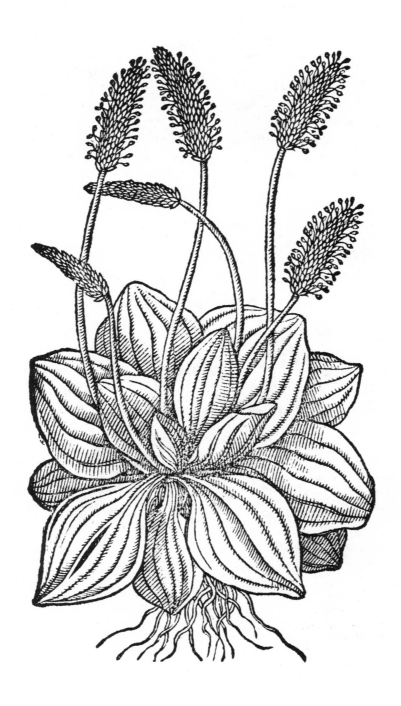

Dragonfly in Amber

I T is the spring of 1968 in Inverness, Scotland, and Roger Wakefield is going slowly mad. Faced with the task of clearing up the tons of historical debris left by his late adoptive father, the Reverend Wakefield, Roger thinks longingly of jumping into his car and heading back to Oxford, leaving the manse and its bulging contents to the mercies of rats, mildew, and the ladies of the Church Guild. When the doorbell rings, Roger is ready to invite in the devil himself—anyone and anything that offers distraction from his current situation.

"Distraction" is putting it mildly. The visitors are Dr. Claire Randall, widow of an old friend of the Reverend's—and her very striking daughter, Brianna. Reeling from the impact of a six-foot-tall redhead at close range, Roger pays only minor attention to Claire's request: She has a list of names, Jacobite soldiers who fought at Culloden; can Roger find out for her how many survived?

Motivated as much by a desire to impress Brianna as by historical curiosity and the inclination to oblige a family friend, Roger agrees to help. Besides, it will get him out of the house and away from the sagging bookshelves, the crammed-to-bursting desk, and the impenetrable murk of the Reverend's garage, filled from floor to ceiling with boxes of cryptic papers.

As Roger embarks on Claire Randall's project, though, small things begin to bother him. Why does Claire not want him to take Brianna near the standing stone circle at Craigh na Dun? Why does she blanch at the name of the leader of her troop of Jacobites—and ask Roger not to mention the name James Fraser to her daughter?

Suspicion is succeeded by shock late one night when Roger finds a roll of newspaper clippings in the Reverend's desk; pictures of Claire Randall, taken twenty years before, over a headline: KIDNAPPED BY THE FAIRIES? Twenty-three years before, Claire Randall had disappeared in the Scottish Highlands, leaving no trace. Three years later, she had been found, malnourished, ragged, and half-crazed, wandering near the standing stones at Craigh na Dun.

A picture shows Frank Randall, her husband, rushing to her bedside. A hell of a shock, Roger thinks, to find your wife after having given her up for dead.

A greater shock awaited Frank, though—and now awaits Roger. Noticing the date of the clippings, Roger recalls Brianna's birthday, mentioned in casual conversation. Counting rapidly backward, the blood drains from his face as he realizes that Claire Randall had returned from her disappearance bruised, disoriented, starving—and pregnant.

What to do? Plainly Brianna regards Frank Randall as her father; she doesn't know the truth, and Roger cannot bring himself to tell her. The mystery surrounding Claire Randall deepens; perhaps, Roger surmises, Brianna's real father was a Highland Scot. James Fraser is a common enough name in the Highlands—if the unknown man was called that, it would be enough to account for Claire's extraordinary reaction to hearing the name. Has Claire brought her daughter to Scotland in order to reveal the truth of her parentage? Perhaps even to meet the mysterious James Fraser?

Increasingly fond of both women, Roger is uncertain what to do in order to

prevent either of them being hurt. There seems nothing he *can* do, save stick close to them, and be ready to help, whatever happens.

Meanwhile, his quest is bearing unexpected fruit. He has found her Jacobites, he tells Claire; the odd thing is that none of them appears to have been killed at Culloden—extraordinary, in view of the great slaughter that took place there. Nearly one man in two on the field was killed; it's remarkable that none of the thirty men on Claire's list was among them.

Claire's response to this news is as puzzling as her other reactions; she turns pale and nearly collapses with relief. What difference can the fate of men dead two hundred years make to her? Roger wonders.

The mystery deepens when Brianna helps Roger disinter some of the Reverend's journals from the garage—journals that refer obliquely to Claire's reappearance, to some dreadful secret that she seemed to be hiding—and to a mysterious request made by Frank Randall. The Reverend writes that he has done as Frank wished with regard to the gravestone—but of James Fraser, there is no record. Who *is* this mysterious James Fraser—and what has he to do with Claire?

In an effort at distraction, Roger has taken Brianna to view the battleground at Culloden, with its mute and moving testament to the slaughter of the Highland clans; Claire, pleading a spurious illness, stays home. She agrees, however, to go along on another jaunt, to an old and long-deserted church some distance out of town.

Claire plans to enjoy the Highland scenery, collect a few plants, and keep an eye on the budding relationship between

St. Kilda's Cemetery.

Roger and her daughter. Brianna and Roger have other plans; looking through the Reverend's papers, Roger has found a mention of a Captain Jonathan Randall, an ancestor of Brianna's father—or supposed father—Frank. Thinking to surprise Claire, they lead her to Randall's grave—and are not only surprised, but shocked, at Claire's reaction, which is one of sudden and irrational fury.

Leaving Claire to collect herself, the two baffled young people go into the deserted church, only to be yanked outside almost at once by the sound of a scream. They find Claire, incoherent and shaking, standing over a grave in the shadow of the yews. The stone on the grave is a "marriage stone"; a quarter-circle of granite, meant to be paired with another, forming a semi-circle to mark the resting place of husband and wife.

Only the husband lies here, though; the other half of the stone is missing.

"What is it?" Roger said urgently, trying to rouse her from the staring trance she had fallen into. "What is it? Is it a name you know?" Even as he spoke, his own words were ringing in his ears.
No one's been buried here since the eighteenth century, *he'd told Brianna.*

Viper

No one's been buried here in two hundred years.

Claire's fingers brushed his own away and touched the stone, caressing, as though touching flesh, gently tracing the letters, the grooves worn shallow, but still clear.

"JAMES ALEXANDER MALCOLM MACKENZIE FRASER," she read aloud. "Yes, I know him." Her hand dropped lower, brushing back the grass that grew thickly about the stone, obscuring the line of smaller letters at its base.

"Beloved husband of Claire," she read.

"Yes, I knew him," she said again, so softly Roger could scarcely hear her. "I'm Claire. He was my husband." She looked up then, into the face of her daughter, white and shocked above her. "And your father," she said.

In the wake of Claire's revelation, the three return to the manse, where Claire reveals the bare bones of her secret: that twenty-three years before, she had stepped through the stones of Craigh na Dun—and disappeared into the past. Struggling to survive in the barbarous Scotland of 1743, she had found her chief enemy to be Jack Randall; her husband Frank's distant ancestor, and a man unsettlingly like his descendant in appearance, if not in character—"Black Jack" being a predator of marked and unusual tastes.

In order to stay out of Randall's hands, she had been obliged to marry a young clansman—Jamie Fraser—only to find her difficulties deepening as she fell in love with him. Brianna is less than sympathetic to this account, caught between feelings of disbelief and betrayal.

In the course of events, Claire tells the young people, Jamie discovered the truth

Green Lizard

about her and insisted that she must return to her own time—and to Frank. However, brought at last to the stone circle she had struggled so long to reach, she found she could not take the final step through the cleft stones—but made the choice to remain in the past, with Jamie.

They had returned to Jamie's home, Lallybroch, but their idyll there was brief; Jamie was arrested by the Watch, and fell into the hands of Jack Randall. Claire had succeeded in rescuing him from Wentworth Prison, though not in time to prevent his being tortured and brutalized by Jack Randall. Seeking safety, the Frasers had sailed for France, taking refuge in the Abbey of Ste. Anne de Beaupré, where one of Jamie's uncles was abbot. Here Claire undertook her greatest challenge—healing Jamie's wounds of mind and body—and in the process became pregnant.

Brianna refuses utterly to countenance any of this, insisting that her mother must be suffering from shock or delusion. Roger, seeing no choice, gives her the newspaper clippings; if they don't verify her mother's claims that James Fraser was Brianna's father, they do at least prove that Frank Randall *wasn't.*

If Brianna is shocked and horrified by her mother's story, Roger is enthralled. While sympathetic to both women, it is the historian in him that is uppermost at the moment.

*"Then those men whose names you gave me, the ones who fought at Culloden—you **knew** them?"*

I relaxed, ever so slightly. "Yes, I knew them." There was a grumble of thunder to the east, and the rain broke in a spatter against the long windows that lined the study from floor to ceiling on one side. Brianna's head was bent over the clippings, the wings of her hair hiding everything but the tip of her nose, which was bright red. Jamie always went red when he was furious or upset. I was all too familiar with the sight of a Fraser on the verge of explosion.

"And you were in France," Roger murmured as though to himself, still studying me closely. The shock in his face was fading into surmise, and a kind of excitement. "I don't suppose you knew . . ."

"Yes, I did," I told him. "That's why we went to Paris. I'd told Jamie about Culloden—the '45, and what would happen. We went to Paris to stop Charles Stuart."

Abbot Alexander of Ste. Anne de Beaupré is Jamie's uncle—and a Jacobite supporter, strongly in favor of restoring the Catholic Stuarts to the throne of Scotland. He urges his nephew—newly recovered from his ordeal in Wentworth—to go to Paris, where the young Prince Charles Edward Casimir Maria Sylvester Stuart has just arrived. Jamie's mission—should he choose to accept it—is to lend his prince aid and succor, and assist him in forming the political and business connections that will help him to regain his throne.

This assignment suits the young Frasers very well; Jamie is outlawed, under sentence of death, and they cannot return to

Scotland. At the same time, Claire knows the shape of the future there: that Charles Stuart will lead a rebellion that will end in slaughter at Culloden and leave the Highland clans in smoking ruins.

They must find a way to stop the deadly march of events toward Culloden—how better to subvert an attempt at a Stuart restoration than by befriending the Bonnie Prince? Jamie has a relation, Jared Fraser, now a wealthy and respected wine merchant with warehouses and ships in Le Havre, and a residence in Paris. Jared also has Jacobite sympathies, and is more than willing to employ his younger cousin, thus giving him entree into the circles where he might be of most use—or obstruction—to Charles Stuart.

While Jared and Jamie toast the successful conclusion of their business arrangement onboard one of Jared's ships in the harbor at Le Havre, Claire is on deck, watching as another ship is unloaded. Seeing a man carried off, obviously ill, she hurries down to lend assistance, and is in time both to diagnose a case of smallpox—and to see the man die in front of her.

Unfortunately, the harbormaster has arrived in time to hear her diagnosis, and in accordance with French maritime law declares that the ship from which the sailor came must be towed out into the harbor and burned, in order to prevent contagion being spread through the port.

Still more unfortunately, the Comte St. Germain, the owner of the ship in question, is present—and strongly inclined to blame Claire for the loss of his ship and cargo. Jamie arrives in time to prevent harm, but the Comte St. Germain, Claire is given to understand, is not a good enemy to have. Shadowed by the flames of the burning ship, the Frasers leave Le Havre, bound for Paris and what seem the lesser perils of Royal politics.

With Jared gone to Germany on business, Jamie takes over the French affairs of the House of Fraser, and takes his place in the circle of Jacobites that surround Charles Stuart. Near in age to the Prince, he quickly becomes Stuart's boon companion and confidante, unwillingly privy to the Prince's affairs—including an affair of the heart with the married Princesse Louise de Rohan.

Blissfully married himself, and looking forward to the birth of his first child, Jamie views the carryings-on of Charles Stuart with a jaundiced eye. Still, duty calls, and many a night sees him coming home to Claire's bed with the scent of wine and strange women clinging to his skin.

"Who looks on a woman with lust in his heart hath committed adultery with her already. Is that how ye see it?"

"Is it how **you** *see it?"*

"No," he said shortly. "I don't. And what would ye do if I **had** *lain wi' a whore, Sassenach? Slap my face? Order me out of your chamber? Keep yourself from my bed?"*

I turned and looked at him.

"I'd kill you," I said through my teeth.

Both eyebrows shot up, and his mouth dropped slightly with incredulity.

"Kill **me***? God, if I found you wi' another man, I'd kill* **him***." He paused, and one corner of his mouth quirked wryly.*

"Mind ye," he said, "I'd no be verra pleased wi' **you** *either, but still, it's him I'd kill."*

"Typical man," I said. "Always missing the point."

He snorted with a bitter humor.

"Am I, then? So you dinna believe me. Want me to prove it to ye, Sassenach, that I've lain wi' no one in the last few hours?" He stood up, water cascading down the stretches of his long legs. The light from the window highlighted the reddish-gold hairs of his body and the steam rose off his flesh in wisps. He looked like a figure of freshly molten gold. I glanced briefly down.

"Ha," I said, with the maximum of scorn it was possible to infuse into one syllable.

"Hot water," he said briefly, stepping out of the tub. "Dinna worry yourself, it won't take long."

"That," I said, with delicate precision, "is what **you** think."

Fighting jealousy, Claire is reassured to hear that Jamie has conceived a scheme to prevent his carousing comrades from pressing him to join in their debauches; he has told them that Claire is La Dame Blanche—the White Lady, a sorceress whose powers will shrivel his private parts, should he ever be unfaithful to her. Sodden with drink and strongly superstitious, the men believe him, and rumors of La Dame Blanche are soon circulating through Paris—much to Claire's amusement.

Between the demands of business and Royal intrigue, Jamie is thoroughly occupied. Between morning sickness and dinner parties, Claire is not. Seeking useful occupation, she volunteers her medical services at L'Hôpital des Anges, a convent hospital run by the redoubtable Mother Hildegarde and her assistant, the dog Bouton.

Jamie also has acquired an assistant: a French lad met—by accident—in a brothel.

"He's to be called Fergus," Jamie explained. "His name is really Claudel, but we didna think that sounded verra manly."

"But we already have a stable-lad, and a lad to clean the knives and boots," I objected.

"Oh, aye," Jamie replied. "But we havena got a pickpocket."

With the aid of Fergus's light touch with a mailbag, Jamie keeps a thumb on the secret pulse of Royal politics and learns encouraging news: The Old Pretender, the ex-King James, harbors no hopes for the restoration of his throne. His motive in sending Charles to France was instead a hope of shaming Louis into providing a secure future for the young man, possibly as a general in the French army.

Perhaps, Jamie and Claire think, with the beginnings of hope, their mission is unnecessary?

Charles, the Young Pretender, harbors higher aspirations than the French army, though. The Frasers learn with alarm of Charles Stuart's new venture: an investment in a shipload of port, the proceeds of which might be sufficient to finance the rebellion Stuart dreams of. Still more alarming is Charles's choice of business

partner in this venture—the Comte St. Germain.

Jamie begins a delicate game, probing among the bankers and nobles, the merchants and diplomats, to find a way to stop this venture from succeeding. Accompanying him to social events despite her growing bulk, Claire does her part in tracking rumor—and in starting it.

Among Claire's new acquaintances is a young girl, met at one of Louise de Rohan's parties: Mary Hawkins, the fifteen-year-old niece of one of Jamie's business acquaintances. Shy, pretty, and afflicted with a stammer, Mary is ignorant of men in general—and blissfully ignorant of her uncle's plan to marry her to an elderly and degenerate member of the French aristocracy.

At first sorry for the girl, and then befriending her, Claire finally realizes why Mary Hawkins's name seemed so familiar—Claire has seen the name on a genealogical chart; Mary is—or will be—the six-times-great-grandmother of Frank Randall—the wife of Black Jack Randall.

But how? Jack Randall died at Wentworth Prison, trampled under the hooves of a herd of Highland cattle during Jamie's rescue months before. And yet . . . Claire still wears the gold ring of her marriage to Frank, cool and secure on her left hand. How can that be, with the man who sired Frank's line dead before any child of his could be conceived?

Jonathan Randall may be dead, but his ghost walks Jamie's dreams. With the scars of Wentworth Prison still raw on his back, he wakes in a cold sweat, with Randall's voice in his ears, Randall's touch on his skin. Refusing to let Claire share the horror of his memories, he fights his demons alone at night, and rises in the morning with his memories clamped tight in a steel box of will.

Seeking herbal remedies that might ease his sleep, Claire makes the acquaintance of a small, mysterious apothecary, Master Raymond, who warns her both of the dangers of Royal intrigue, and of the Comte, whose sinister reputation is further clouded by rumors of his occult associations. Is the Comte behind the attempt on Jamie's life in the Paris streets—or Claire's near-poisoning at Versailles?

Within the widening circles of intrigue and uncertainty, the Frasers find refuge only within the security of their marriage. As the baby that is the tangible evidence of their love for each other grows in Claire's womb, she and Jamie draw ever closer together, protecting each other from the shadowy dangers that surround them.

"Doesn't it make you feel a bit nervous?" I asked as we went up the stairs. *"Never being able to trust anyone?"*

He laughed softly. "Well, I wouldna say **anyone,** *Sassenach. There's you—and Murtagh, and my sister, Jenny, and her husband, Ian. I'd trust the four of you wi' my life—I have, for that matter, more than once."*

I shivered as he pulled back the drapes of the big bed. The fire had been banked for the night, and the room was growing cold.

"Four people you can trust doesn't seem like all that many," I said, unlacing my gown.

He pulled his shirt over his head and tossed it on the chair. The scars on his back shone silver in the faint light from the night sky outside.

"Aye, well," he said matter-of-factly. *"It's four more than Charles Stuart has."*

In spite of the intrigues and rumors that surround them, the King has taken a liking to both Claire and Jamie, and their presence is often required at Royal functions. Claire's presence is requested at a luncheon held to honor a visiting English nobleman—an old acquaintance of the Frasers', the Duke of Sandringham. It's neither the Duke nor Claire's continuing nausea that causes her to faint in the gardens at Versailles, though; it's the sudden appearance of a man she knows twice dead.

Then I saw him. I could feel all of the blood draining from my head as my eye traced disbelievingly over the elegant curve of the skull, dark-haired and bold amid the powdered wigs around it. Alarms rang in my head like air-raid sirens, as I fought to accept and repel the impressions that as-

*sailed me. My subconscious saw the line of the nose, thought "Frank," and turned my body to fly toward him in welcome. "Not-Frank," came the slightly higher, rational center of my brain, freezing me in my tracks as I saw the familiar curve of a half-smiling mouth, repeating, "You **know** it's not Frank" as the muscles of my calves knotted. And then the lurch into panic and the clenching of hands and stomach, as the slower processes of logical thought came doggedly on the trail of instinct and knowledge, seeing the high brow and the arrogant tilt of the head, assuring me of the unthinkable. It could not be Frank. And if it were not, then it could only be . . .*

"Jack Randall." It wasn't my voice that spoke, but Jamie's, sounding oddly calm and detached. Attention attracted by my peculiar behavior, he had looked where I was looking, and had seen what I had seen.

He didn't move. So far as I could tell through the increasing haze of panic, he didn't breathe. I was dimly aware of a nearby servant peering curiously upward at the towering form of the frozen Scottish warrior next to me, silent as a statue of Mars. But all my concern was for Jamie.

To draw arms in the presence of the King was death. Murtagh was on the far side of the garden, much too far away to help. Two more paces would bring Randall within hearing distance. Within sword's reach. I laid a hand on his arm. It was rigid as the steel of the swordhilt under his hand. The blood roared in my ears.

"Jamie," I said. "Jamie!" And fainted.

The new arrival is not Jack Randall, though, but rather his younger brother, Alexander Randall, who shares a striking family resemblance, but appears to be quite the opposite of his vicious brother in personality and temperament. Jack was a soldier and a sadist; Alex is a curate, a gentle, intellectual young man who serves as the Duke's chaplain and secretary. He is also, Claire learns, Mary Hawkins's secret love, though it seems impossible for the young couple ever to marry, given Alexander's impoverished state and Mary's (as yet unannounced) engagement to the Vicomte Marigny.

Jamie has nothing against Alexander Randall—save his physical resemblance to his brother. Alexander's arrival in Paris triggers further nightmares, though, in which Jamie feels the touch of Jack Randall on his skin, and hears his dead voice, murmuring obscenity in the dark. He wakes from these dreams sweating and ill, but will not let Claire comfort him, choosing instead to fight the ghost of Jack Randall within his own mind.

At an outing to the Royal stables at Argentan, the Duke of Sandringham approaches Claire with an interesting proposition; if Jamie will agree to return to Scotland and abandon Charles Stuart, a pardon can be arranged.

Why? Jamie wonders. The Duke owes him nothing, and can hope for nothing from him. Does the Duke—or possibly the English Crown, using the Duke as agent—intend to deprive Stuart of his allies, in the hope of thwarting his efforts?

Claire and Jamie plan a dinner party, at which they hope both to divine the Duke's purposes—is he a secret Jacobite, or the opposite?—and to gain a clue as to whether the Comte St. Germain is behind the attempts on their lives. As night falls, Claire hurries home from L'Hôpital des Anges to dress for the party, in company with Mary Hawkins, Fergus, and Murtagh, Jamie's godfather and companion.

Night is falling, though, and the group is attacked in the darkness of the Rue du Faubourg St.-Honoré. With Murtagh bound and helpless, Mary is thrown to the ground and raped. Claire seems likely to suffer a similar fate when her hood falls back and a shaft of lantern-light illuminates her face.

"Mother of God!" The hands clutching my arms slackened their grip, and I yanked loose, to see Spotted-shirt, mouth hanging open in horrified amazement below the mask. He backed away from me, crossing himself as he went.

*"**In nomine Patris, et Filii, et Spiritus Sancti,**" he babbled, crossing and recrossing. "La Dame Blanche!"*

"La Dame Blanche!" The man behind me echoed the cry, in tones of terror.

Within moments the assailants have fled, leaving the street empty and disaster in their wake.

Fergus has run to fetch Jamie. With him comes Alex Randall; too shy and too conscious of his impecunious state to approach her directly, he has been following Mary about the city, hoping for occasional glimpses of his beloved. Freeing Murtagh,

Jamie takes them all home—and then, with Claire, must make hasty preparations for a very ill-omened dinner party.

What I wanted at the moment was peace, quiet, and total privacy in which to shake like a rabbit. What I had was a dinner party with a duke who might be a Jacobite or an English agent, a Comte who might be a poisoner, and a rape victim hidden upstairs.

The dinner party is the event of the season—one that will be talked about for months, as Claire wryly observes—though not for the usual reasons. The inopportune appearance of a drugged and disheveled Mary Hawkins in the middle of dinner triggers confrontation, fistfights, and general hysteria, ending with Mary Hawkins removed to her uncle's house, Silas Hawkins and Alex Randall laid out cold, the Comte St. Germain gloating, and Jamie in the hands of the Paris police.

Released at dawn, Jamie returns to the house in the Rue Tremoulins, wanting nothing but clean clothes and Claire's arms. One more conversation awaits him, though—Murtagh kneels at his feet, his dirk held out hilt-first, and asks Jamie formally to take his life. He cannot live, he says, with the shame of having failed in his duty to protect his chief's wife and unborn child.

Rather than grant his godfather's request, Jamie instead lays an oath on Murtagh:

Jamie's voice dropped still further, but it was not a whisper. Holding the middle three fingers of his right hand stiff, he laid them together over the hilt of the dirk, at the juncture of haft and tang.

"I charge ye, then, by your oath to me and your word to my mother—find the men. Hunt them, and when they be found, I do charge ye wi' the vengeance due my wife's honor—and the blood of Mary Hawkins's innocence."

He paused a moment, then took his hand from the knife. The clansman raised it, holding it upright by the blade. Acknowledging my presence for the first

time, he bowed his head toward me and said, "As the laird has spoken, lady, so I will do. I will lay vengeance at your feet."

Jamie decides to conduct his own investigation in other directions—affairs at the dinner party and the interception of a mysterious musical cipher promising aid to the Stuart cause have made it still more urgent to determine where the Duke of Sandringham's loyalties actually lie.

Claire accompanies Jamie to the Duke's house, meaning to find an opportunity to steal away and find Alexander Randall. With the attack in the Rue du Faubourg St.-Honoré a matter of public knowledge, Mary's marriage to the Vicomte is definitely off. Alex and Mary cannot meet publicly, but Claire means to invite Alex to her house, where he can talk to Mary privately.

Stealing away from Jamie's conversation with the Duke, she finds not Alex, but Mary—who has in turn stolen away from her uncle's house and come to find the man she loves. A sympathetic footman tells the women that they are too late; as a result of the scandal at the dinner party, Alexander Randall has been dismissed from the Duke's service and is already en route for England.

Shocked and disbelieving, Mary rushes into the hall, pursued by Claire, eager to prevent the scandal that will result if Mary is found. Dashing around a corner in pursuit, though, Claire forgets Mary entirely,

when she crashes headfirst into a man coming the other way.

He let out a startled "Whoof!" as I struck him amidships, and clutched me by the arms to keep upright as we swayed and staggered together.

"I'm sorry," I began, breathlessly. "I thought you were—oh, Jesus H. Fucking Christ!"

My initial impression—that I had encountered Alexander Randall—had lasted no more than the split second necessary to see the eyes above that finely chiseled mouth. The mouth was much like Alex's, bar the deep lines around it. But those cold eyes could belong to only one man.

The shock was so great that for a moment everything seemed paradoxically normal; I had an impulse to apologize, dust him off, and continue my pursuit, leaving him forgotten in the corridor, as just a chance encounter. My adrenal glands hastened to remedy this impression, dumping such a dose of adrenaline into my bloodstream that my heart contracted like a squeezed fist.

He was recovering his own breath by now, along with his momentarily shattered self-possession.

"I am inclined to concur with your sentiments, madam, if not precisely with their manner of expression." Still clutching me by the elbows, he held me slightly away from him, squinting to see my face in the shadowed hall. I saw the shock of recognition blanch his features as my face came into the light. "Bloody hell, it's you!" he exclaimed.

"I thought you were dead!" I wrenched at my arms, trying to free them from the iron-tight grip of Jonathan Randall.

He let go of one arm, in order to rub his middle, surveying me coldly. The thin, fine-cut features were bronzed and healthy; he

*gave no outward sign of having been
trampled five months before by thirty
quarter-ton beasts. Not
so much as a hoofprint on his
forehead.*

Claire is shocked by the revelation that Jack Randall still lives, but even more distressed by the effects of this revelation on Jamie—and its possible repercussions.

Jamie sends her home in the carriage, and disappears. What has he done, what is he doing? He cannot challenge Randall openly at Sandringham's house—but a challenge is certainly what he intends.

Desperate with fear and worry, Claire arrives back at Jared's house, only to find an unexpected visitor—Jamie's uncle, Dougal MacKenzie. An ardent Jacobite, Dougal is visiting Paris for undisclosed reasons of his own, but is concerned to hear of his nephew's impending duel. Duelling is illegal, and likely to get the participants locked up in the Bastille—a development that would certainly put a damper on Jamie's abilities to help Prince Charles.

Claire has a plan, conceived in desperation, and enlists Dougal's help in carrying it out. She will go to the police and denounce Jack Randall as one of the men who attacked her in the Rue du Faubourg St.-Honoré. He is, of course, innocent of the charge, but the police will lock him up until he can prove his innocence—giving Claire time to find Jamie.

The scheme works, and Jamie returns to the house, thwarted of his prey and cold with fury. Jamie is bent on vengeance;

nothing will quench the fires of his rage save Jack Randall's blood. Claire understands, and would be more than willing not only to help, but to kill Randall herself—were it not for one thing: Frank.

Jack Randall is Frank's six-times-great-grandfather; the child who will be next in the line of descent that leads to Frank has not yet been conceived. Claire implores Jamie to delay his vengeance only a little while—only a year; time enough for Randall to marry and sire a son. Then, with Frank safe . . . Jack Randall can die.

Jamie meets this request with an outburst of fury. How can she expect him to wait, to let a man live who has done to him what Jack Randall has done? Still, his love for Claire—and his sense of obligation to Frank Randall—win out at last, and he grudgingly agrees to wait for the satisfaction of his outraged honor.

ALL THE REASONABLE WAYS of stopping Charles Stuart's venture had so far failed, and the situation is growing more threatening; Charles has ordered two thousand broadswords from Holland, and eyes the ships at anchor with the covetous gaze of a would-be invader. Desperate to stop him, Jamie conceives a bold plan.

If the ship bearing Stuart's port is found to have smallpox aboard, the French authorities will destroy it. Ergo, if pox is discovered aboard before the ship reaches port, the Captain will change course for Spain, which does not have such stringent restrictions. And, with a shipload of port on his hands, the Captain may well be persuaded to dispose of it to a handy buyer—Jamie, armed with gold borrowed from the bankers he has cultivated. Murtagh, armed with several of Claire's herbal concoctions, will play the smallpox victim; Jamie the Captain's savior. Cargo in hand, Jamie can sell the port in Spain, recover the money, and return to France to pay his debts—leaving Charles Stuart fundless and fuming, but safely stranded, far from Scotland.

Plans in place, Jamie sets about leaving Jared's business in good order, only to be interrupted by a note from the warehouse foreman, apologetically informing him that that gentleman has run into financial difficulties in a brothel, and would Jamie kindly come to his assistance. Torn between amusement and irritation, Jamie goes, taking Fergus with him.

Claire's pregnancy has meanwhile shown some signs of danger, and she has reluctantly given up her work at the Hôpital, the entertaining, and all exertion, in order to protect the child she carries. Her Parisian friends call at the house, though, in order to keep her abreast of all the gossip. Informed by the butler that she has two such visitors one afternoon, Claire makes her way slowly downstairs to receive them—only to overhear news that makes her reel with shock.

One of the women has heard of a fight that occurred that morning, at one of the better-known Parisian brothels; Jamie has attacked an English soldier, thrown him downstairs, and been heard to issue a challenge to a duel! The ladies are delightfully shocked at such scandal; Claire is prostrated.

Something has made Jamie break his word to her. Perhaps only the sight of Jack Randall, perhaps something else—but whatever it is, he means to meet Randall at dawn the next day, and plainly means to

kill him. Such a duel can have only two outcomes, either one disastrous; either Jamie will indeed kill Randall, which results in Frank's line being extinguished, and Frank himself not existing—or Randall will kill Jamie.

Claire deduces where the duel will take place, and despite her advanced state of pregnancy, goes there at dawn, hoping to stop the duel. She is too late, though; the sound of clashing swords greets her as she enters the clearing.

Both men are excellent swordsmen, but Jamie is driven by fury that lends wings to his sword. Claire dares not call out, for fear of distracting Jamie from his fatal endeavor. A slip on wet grass, the flash of a blade, and Jack Randall lies on his back, at Jamie's mercy. Claire opens her mouth to scream at Jamie not to kill Randall—but is seized by pain, as something rips loose within her. She sees no more than Jamie's sword descending, piercing the fawn of Randall's breeches—and then is on the ground herself, drenched in her own blood, with the approach of death blinding her to what is happening nearby.

A week later, Claire lies in L'Hôpital des Anges, hovering near death from infection following her miscarriage. Jamie has not been seen since the duel in the Bois de Boulogne. With body and soul empty of the love she once carried, Claire does not care. Whether it is guilt at having broken his

word to her—and thus having destroyed at once Frank Randall's line and his own—that keeps him from her, or something else, she has no wish to see him.

A visit from Raymond the apothecary saves her life, however, and a convalescent Claire is taken to Fontainebleau, where her friend Louise hopes that the country air will help restore her health and spirits.

While Claire's body heals, though, her spirit languishes. There is no word from Jamie. He has gone to Spain, Claire thinks, forced by necessity to carry out their plan. Surrounded by a numbing gray fog of bereavement, she does not care if he returns.

The fog is lightened, if not relieved, by a chance discovery. She learns from Fergus what it was that made Jamie break his word to her and go to fight Jack Randall; completing his own business at the brothel, he had found Randall in the act of brutalizing Fergus, and in an excess of rage, challenged him. Claire understands—but cannot forgive. Too much has been lost.

Sometimes I found myself wondering when—or whether—I would see him again, and what—if anything—we might say to each other. But for the most part, I preferred not to think about it, letting the days come and go, one by one, avoiding thoughts of both the future and the past by living only in the present.

This walking trance is broken one day, though, by the arrival of a note at Fontainebleau—a note that makes it clear that Jamie is *not* in Orvieto, as Claire has thought. But then . . . where is he?

"He's in the Bastille," Louise said, taking a deep breath. "For dueling."

My knees felt watery, and I sat down on the nearest available surface.

"Why in hell didn't you tell me?" I wasn't sure what I felt at this news; shock, or horror—fear? or a small sense of satisfaction?

"I—I didn't want to upset you, chérie," Louise stammered, taken aback at my apparent distress. "You were so weak . . . and there was nothing you could do, after all. And you didn't ask," she pointed out.

"Jesus H. Roosevelt Christ," I muttered, wishing I had something stronger to say.

"It is fortunate that le petit James did not kill his opponent," Louise hastened to add. "In that case, the penalty would have been much more . . . eek!" She twitched her striped skirts aside just in time to avoid the cascade of chocolate and biscuits as I knocked over the newly arrived refreshments. The tray clanged to the floor unregarded as I stared down at her. My hands were clasped tightly against my ribs, the right protectively curled over the gold ring on my left hand. The thin metal seemed to burn against my skin.

"He isn't dead, then?" I asked, like one in a dream. "Captain Randall . . . he's alive?"

"Why, yes," she said, peering curiously up at me. "You did not know? He is badly wounded, but it is said that he recovers. Are you quite well, Claire? You look . . ." But the rest of what she was saying was lost in the roaring that filled my ears.

There is no choice. Whatever Claire's feelings for Jamie—and she herself is not sure what they are—she must free him from the Bastille. Only days remain; Charles Stuart's ship will be sailing soon—and with it, all hope of stopping the disaster of the Rising.

Claire returns to Paris, frantically seeking help. Only one avenue presents itself, though—a personal appeal to the King himself. The King is susceptible to the charms of women—but such appeals have their price.

"He will expect to lie with you," Mother Hildegarde said bluntly.

I stared down at the inlaid table, scarcely seeing the complex curves of enamel that swept through abstractions of geometry and color. My forefinger traced the loops and whorls before me, providing a precarious anchor for my racing thoughts. If it was indeed necessary for Jamie to be released from prison, in order to prevent the Jacobite invasion of Scotland, then it seemed that I would have to do the releasing, whatever the method, and whatever its consequences.

At last I looked up, meeting the music master's eyes. "I'll have to," I said softly. "There's no other way."

"I will pray for you," Mother Hildegarde said, smiling what would have been a tremulous smile on a face less solidly

carved. Her expression changed suddenly to one of deep consideration.

*"Though I do wonder," she added meditatively, "exactly **who** would be the proper patron saint to invoke in the circumstances?"*

Going to the palace to keep her rendezvous with the King, Claire is torn between revulsion at the prospect—and a bone-deep rage against Jamie, who has inadvertently forced her to prostitute herself. The only minor consolation is that he has not, in fact, killed Jack Randall—at least Frank is safe, somewhere in the future.

But it is the present that concerns Claire, as the equerry opens the door of the King's boudoir. Much to Claire's astonishment, though, she finds that the King requires a different service from her. Two men stand trial before the King's secret council, accused as sorcerers. They accuse each other; only one can judge between them—La Dame Blanche.

One man is Raymond the apothecary; the other, the Comte St. Germain. Claire stands helpless in the midst of the sorcerors' duel, unsure what to do or say, as each man defends himself against the charge of magic—until the Comte turns

the accusation of sorcery against her.

"You see?" he said triumphantly. "The woman shrinks away in fear! She is a witch!"

Actually, compared to one judge, who was huddling against the far wall, I was a monument of fortitude, but I must admit that I had taken an involuntary step backward when the snake appeared. Now I stepped forward again, intending to take it away from him. The bloody thing wasn't poisonous, after all. Maybe we'd see how harmless it was if I wrapped it around his neck.

Before I could reach him, Master Raymond spoke behind him. What with all the commotion, I'd rather forgotten him.

"That is not all the Bible says, Monsieur le Comte," Raymond observed. He didn't raise his voice, and the wide amphibian face was bland as pudding. Still, the buzz of voices stopped, and the King turned to listen.

"Yes, Monsieur?" he said.

Raymond nodded in polite acknowledgment of having the floor, and reached into his robe with both hands. From one pocket, he produced a flask, from the other a small cup.

"'They shall handle serpents unharmed,'" he quoted, "'and if they drink any deadly poison, they shall not die.'"

Raymond gives the cup to Claire, who drinks from it, trusting him. He then takes the cup and drinks himself—then gives the cup to Claire, to hand to the Count. In the process of drinking, though, Raymond has poisoned the contents by sleight of hand.

I did know that the cup I held in my hands was death. The white crystal hung around my neck, its weight a reminder of poison. I hadn't seen Raymond add anything to it; no one had, I was sure. But I didn't need to dip the crystal into the blood-red liquid to know what it now contained.

The Comte saw the knowledge in my face; La Dame Blanche cannot lie. He hesitated, looking at the bubbling cup.

"Drink, Monsieur," said the King. The dark eyes were hooded once more, showing nothing. "Or are you afraid?"

The Comte might have a number of things to his discredit, but cowardice wasn't one of them. His face was pale and set, but he met the King's eyes squarely, with a slight smile.

"No, Majesty," he said.

He took the cup from my hand and drained it, his eyes fixed on mine. They stayed fixed, staring into my face, even as they glazed with the knowledge of death. The White Lady may turn a man's nature to good, or to destruction.

Claire returns to Fontainebleau, leaving—she thinks—everything behind her. Everything is gone: both love and danger. The fog creeps in again, and she embraces the grayness, living only from day to day, afraid even to think of the future. Jamie is free—she has bought his freedom, at a price she does not care to contemplate. Presumably he has gone to Orvieto, to carry out their plan. When he succeeds—*if* he succeeds . . . Claire doesn't want to think that far.

But the future reaches out to us, as does the past, and all times are the present. One rain-streaked afternoon, the footman announces the Lord Broch Tuarach, and Claire's fog is rent by panic. Jamie pursues her through the gardens, and at last confronts her in the grape arbor, where they are forced to face their losses—and choose whether to cling to what is left.

He had risen, was standing over me. His shadow fell across my knees; surely that meant the cloud had broken; a shadow doesn't fall without light.

"Claire," he whispered. "Please. Let me give ye comfort."

"Comfort?" I said. "And how will you do that? Can you give me back my child?"

He sank to his knees before me, but I kept my head down, staring into my upturned hands, laid empty on my lap. I felt his movement as he reached to touch me, hesitated, drew back, reached again.

"No," he said, his voice scarcely audible. "No, I canna do that. But . . . with the grace of God . . . I might give ye another?"

His hand hovered over mine, close enough that I felt the warmth of his skin. I felt other things as well: the grief that he held tight under rein, the anger and the fear that choked him, and the courage that made him speak in spite of it. I gathered my own courage around me, a flimsy substitute for the thick gray shroud. Then I took his hand and lifted my head, and looked full into the face of the sun.

A condition of Jamie's freedom is that he must leave France. A pardon has been secured; he can return to Scotland. With Charles Stuart's plans effectively thwarted, and with painful memories behind him, the Frasers are only too happy to leave—to go home, to Lallybroch.

The solitude of the Highlands and the peaceful, busy life of the farm are a refuge for both Jamie and Claire. They have succeeded, they think; Stuart is penniless, discredited with every banker in France and Italy—he has no hope of raising the money for an army. They are free to turn to each other, to rebuild their life together, to wrap themselves in the cloak of their love, warm against all future winds.

But fate—and Charles Stuart—is capricious. The peace of Lallybroch is shattered by the arrival of a letter. Stuart has landed at Glenfinnan to claim his throne, with no more than a few companions and a dozen casks of brandy. With these, he hopes to charm the Highland chiefs to join his cause. The letter holds far worse news, however; to strengthen his show of support, Charles has published the names of the Highland chieftains pledged to follow him—and blithely added Jamie's name to the list, sure of his friend's allegiance.

There is no choice. They have failed to stop Charles Stuart, and now, branded a traitor by Stuart's list, Jamie finds himself with only one action open to him—to help Charles Stuart win.

With thirty men, Jamie and Claire march to join the Highland army near Preston. On the way, though, they encounter a stranger: a sixteen-year-old boy, a young English soldier who is also marching toward the meeting at Preston with his regiment. Jamie captures the boy, and be-

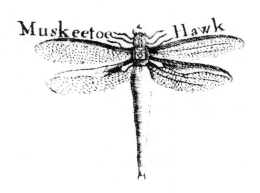

Muskeetoe—Hawk

fools him into giving away the number and position of his regiment's artillery—which Jamie and his men neatly disable, under cover of darkness.

The boy—John William Grey—swears bitter vengeance on Jamie before being taken away to be safely returned to his companions. This mildly comic interlude is succeeded by one of deadly purpose; the Highland army faces its first test, against the vastly superior English force under General Jonathan Cope.

Claire waits in fear, with the other women who travel with their men in the army. Foresight is no reassurance; she knows that the Highlanders will win, with only thirty casualties—but which of those thirty will be men she knows—or a man she loves?

The battle is won, though, and Jamie survives. The victorious Highlanders march on to Edinburgh, where Charles Stuart is hailed a hero. The city celebrates with balls and parties at Holyrood Palace—despite the presence of an English garrison, safely ensconced behind the brooding walls of Edinburgh Castle. There is a brief and giddy excitement; several lords and chieftains are coming to Stuart's side—foreign envoys are arriving, cautiously assessing the prospects of victory.

Among those who come to see for themselves is Colum MacKenzie, chief of the MacKenzies of Leoch. Meeting privately with Jamie, he asks his nephew bluntly for his advice; shall he commit the men of Leoch to the Prince's cause—or turn back, and keep clear of what may be folly? His brother Dougal is strongly committed to the Jacobite cause, but it is Colum's to say what the clan will do.

Jamie hesitates in his advice; would the withdrawal of the MacKenzies of Leoch prevent a victory that might otherwise be won? But if there is no victory, there will be no clan—and the men of Leoch are his mother's people, his own blood. No, he tells Colum at last. Keep clear; turn back. And if disaster comes, there will be that many fewer souls on Jamie Fraser's conscience.

Claire meets her own moment of decision at Holyrood; answering the door late one night, she comes face-to-face with the one man she least expects to see—Jack Randall. Leaving Jamie asleep, lest he wake and find the man, she goes with Randall to the ruined abbey church, to hear a startling proposal.

Alexander Randall is in the city, very ill. Believing Claire to have some supernatural power, Jack desires her to come and give the benefit of her healing abilities to his younger brother; in exchange, he will give her intelligence of the English army's movements, obtained from his colleagues in the Castle garrison.

Reluctantly agreeing to this, Claire finds Alex Randall in dire straits—very ill

with consumption and the first stages of congestive heart failure—but she is able to assist him in some small degree, and the intelligence gained from Jack Randall further brightens the prospects for Charles Stuart.

The Stuart prospects brighten further with the unexpected—and presumably natural—death of Colum MacKenzie. With Colum dead, leadership of clan MacKenzie passes to Dougal—and Dougal is all too willing to commit his men and resources to the Rising.

With his support solidifying, Charles Stuart sets out to gain as much as he can—and in pursuit of the rest of the Highland clans, sends Jamie and Claire to Beaufort Castle, to seek the support of the Old Fox—Simon, Lord Lovat, chieftain of clan Fraser—and Jamie's grandfather.

As Jamie tells Claire, *"My grandfather has the sort of character that would enable him to hide conveniently behind a spiral staircase."* This is not the first time the Old Fox has played both ends against the middle, and Lord Lovat is too old and canny to let himself be persuaded one way or another by a young—and illegitimate—grandson. However, Simon convinces himself that his best chance for gain lies with the Stuarts, and he dispatches a sizable body of men to return to Edinburgh with Jamie, under the command of his son, Young Simon.

In Edinburgh, things are growing grimmer, despite the infusion of men. Support from the Lowlands has failed to materialize; some of the chieftains are growing disaffected. Highlanders are farmers; the winter is drawing in, and they feel the need to return to their crofts, to ready their

homes and their crops before the cold. But needs must when the devil drives, and the Highland army will meet the English once more—at Falkirk.

Among the furor surrounding the imminent hostilities, Claire visits Alexander Randall, whose condition has deteriorated to an alarming extent. One thing brings Alex comfort; the unexpected arrival of Mary Hawkins, who—upon learning of Alex's whereabouts—has tricked her father into sending her to stay with an aunt in Edinburgh.

Claire knows that once more the Highlanders will be victorious, but this knowledge is hollow comfort; all around her she sees the beginnings of the dreaded end, the small signs of crumbling confidence, of poor leadership, of scarce resource, that will—perhaps—doom the Stuart cause and those who follow it. But for the moment, victory is once more near; marching on Falkirk at night, the Highlanders meet with a small troop of English soldiers, and the sound of gunfire rends the night.

Hurried away into a deserted church for shelter, Claire finds herself trapped with a few of the MacKenzies of Leoch—including both Dougal and his lieutenant, Rupert, who has been fatally wounded in the skirmish. Jamie joins the group, but not in time to get Claire away before the church is surrounded. In imminent danger of being burned alive inside the church, Dougal seizes the only expedient: Claire must pretend to be an Englishwoman taken hostage by the Scots. The Highlanders will exchange her for their freedom; once safely away, Jamie can circle back to aid her escape from the English.

The plan works, at least initially. But things go quickly wrong when Claire discovers that the battle she thought already over has in fact not yet begun. With all the English officers engaged in preparations, no one has time to spare for her—and she is quickly sent South, under guard as a suspicious person. Trying and failing to escape, she is delivered at last to an unexpected destination in northern England—a manor called Bellhurst. Her host is also unexpected: the Duke of Sandringham.

Hearing of the astonishing case of the Englishwoman held hostage, the Duke has shrewdly guessed who the Englishwoman must be, and arranged to have Claire delivered to him, to serve as bait for Jamie Fraser. In an edgy interview with the Duke, Claire learns the truth—or part of it. It was the Duke who arranged the attacks on Jamie's life and on Claire's, in Paris, in an effort to remove an influential source of support for the Stuart cause. The man who led the attack in the Rue du Faubourg St.-Honoré was Albert Danton, the Duke's valet—an attack that ironically prevented the marriage of the Duke's goddaughter, Mary Hawkins.

Jamie does follow Claire, but succeeds in sneaking into the mansion undetected, where he kills Danton and releases both Claire and Mary. The expedition is not without cost: Hugh Munro, a friend of Jamie's who sought to warn him, is taken by the Duke's men and hanged. Accompanied by Murtagh, who carries away a bag of loot from the mansion, Jamie and his men head north, pausing for the melancholy duty of delivering Hugh's body to his wife.

Murtagh laid the bag on the floor at my feet, then straightened up and looked from me to Mary, to Hugh Munro's widow, and at last to Jamie, who looked as puzzled as I felt. Having thus assured himself of his audience, Murtagh bowed formally to me, a lock of wet dark hair falling free over his brow.

"I bring ye your vengeance, lady," he said, as quietly as I'd ever heard him speak. He straightened and inclined his head in turn to Mary and Mrs. Munro. "And justice for the wrong done to ye."

Mary sneezed, and wiped her nose hastily with a fold of her plaid. She stared at Murtagh, eyes wide and baffled. I gazed down at the bulging saddlebag, feeling a sudden deep chill that owed nothing to the weather outside. But it was Hugh Munro's widow who sank to her knees, and with steady hands opened the bag and drew out the head of the Duke of Sandringham.

Returning north with all speed, the Frasers reach Edinburgh. While Jamie is impatient to push on and join the Highland army—where the men of Lallybroch

are—Mary Hawkins has one small request: that he and Claire will attend as witnesses to her marriage.

A marriage not to the dying Alexander Randall, but to his brother, Jonathan. Mary is with child, and Alex wishes her to have the protection of name and family—a protection that he cannot give her himself. As a curate, though, he can perform the marriage between his lover and his brother; a final act of desperation before his death.

So the mystery of Frank Randall's descent is solved; but Claire has no time to contemplate it. Disaster is approaching like storm clouds over the Highland peaks. The Highland army is headed for Culloden, and destruction—threatening

to take with it the men of Lallybroch. The Frasers hurry northward, hiding, starving, pressing on to their final confrontation with history.

The Frasers arrive at Culloden House on the eve of battle, to find chaos and despair. Starving men lie in mud and rags, sleeping in exhaustion from a long and futile march. Tomorrow they will stand on the moor, to be cut down by English cannon fire.

Taking refuge in a small attic at the top of the house, Claire tells Jamie that there is one last, desperate measure that can be taken: Charles Stuart is the focus of the rebellion, the leader of the Highland forces, at whose behest the ragged survivors of his army will take the field at Drumossie

Moor. If Charles Stuart were to die—here, tonight—the final battle at least could be averted.

Both struck with horror at the suggestion, nonetheless they contemplate the possibility—Claire has poison, and access to the Prince; it might mean her own life, but is that not worth the lives of the hundreds who will die on the field tomorrow? At last, though, they face the truth—neither Jamie nor Claire can commit murder in cold blood, even knowing what lies at stake.

This conclusion comes too late; Dougal MacKenzie, seeking Jamie, has overheard their conversation. Denouncing Claire as a treacherous witch who has seduced his nephew, he draws his dirk, intending to kill her on the spot. A desperate fight ensues between Jamie and Dougal, ending with Dougal dead on the floor, Jamie's dirk socketed at the base of his throat.

Fleeing from Culloden House, Jamie finds his godfather, Murtagh, and his servant, Fergus. Pulling out a document that he had prepared long before in case of disaster, he asks Murtagh to witness it: a deed of sasine, passing ownership of Lallybroch to his own nephew, James Murray. Antedated, the deed will keep the estate from being seized by the Crown as the property of a traitor.

The deed is entrusted to Fergus, who is sent with it to Lallybroch, removing him from the danger of the oncoming battle. Jamie then instructs Murtagh to gather the men of Lallybroch; he, Jamie, will see Claire safe—and then return to command his men and see them safely off the field before the battle.

Arriving at the stone circle the evening before the battle, Claire refuses to leave Jamie; if he dies on Culloden, she will die with him.

"If you're not afraid, I'm not either," I said, firming my own jaw. "It will . . . be over quickly. You said so." My chin was beginning to quiver, despite my determination. "Jamie—I won't . . . I can't . . . I bloody won't live without you, and that's all!"

He opened his mouth, speechless, then closed it, shaking his head. The light over the mountains was failing, painting the clouds with a dull red glow. At last he reached for me, drew me close and held me.

"D'ye think I don't know?" he asked softly. "It's me that has the easy part now. For if ye feel for me as I do for you—then I am asking you to tear out your heart and live without it." His hand stroked my hair, the roughness of his knuckles catching in the blowing strands.

*"But ye must do it, **a nighean donn**. My brave lioness. Ye must."*

"Why?" I demanded, pulling back to look up at him. "When you took me from the witch trial at Cranesmuir—you said then that you would have died with me, you would have gone to the stake with me, had it come to that!"

He grasped my hands, fixing me with a steady blue gaze.

"Aye, I would," he said. "But I wasna carrying your child."

I tried to fight down the waves of nausea—so easily attributable to fright and starvation—but I felt the small heaviness, suddenly burning in my womb. I bit my lip hard, but the sickness washed over me.

Jamie let go my hands, and stood before me, hands at his sides, stark in silhouette against the fading sky.

Cormorant

"Claire," he said quietly. "Tomorrow I will die. This child . . . is all that will be left of me—ever. I ask ye, Claire—I beg you . . . see it safe."

I stood still, vision blurring, and in that moment, I heard my heart break. It was a small, clean sound, like the snapping of a flower's stem.

At last I bent my head to him, the wind grieving in my ears.

"Yes," I whispered. "Yes, I'll go."

It was nearly dark. He came behind me and held me, leaning back against him as he looked over my shoulder, out over the valley. The lights of the watchfires had begun to spring up, small glowing dots in the far distance. We were silent for a long time, as the evening deepened. It was very quiet on the hill; I could hear nothing but Jamie's even breathing, each breath a precious sound.

"I will find you," he whispered in my ear. "I promise. If I must endure two hundred years of purgatory, two hundred years without you—then that is my punishment, which I have earned for my crimes. For I have lied, and killed, and stolen; betrayed and broken trust. But there is the one small thing that shall lie in the balance. When I shall stand before God, I shall have one thing to say, to weigh against the rest."

His voice dropped, nearly to a whisper, and his arms tightened around me.

"Lord, ye gave me a rare woman, and God! I loved her well."

One final night together, in the ruined cottage on the hill below Craigh na Dun—and the two prepare in the morning to part, forever.

"They say . . ." he began, and stopped to clear his throat. "They say, in the old days, when a man would go forth to do a great deed—he would find a wisewoman, and ask her to bless him. He would stand looking forth, in the direction he would go, and she would come behind him, to say the words of the prayer over him. When she had finished, he would walk straight out, and not look back, for that was ill-luck to his quest."

He touched my face once, and turned away, facing the open door. The morning sun streamed in, lighting his hair in a thousand flames. He straightened his shoulders, broad beneath his plaid, and drew a deep breath.

"Bless me, then, wisewoman," he said softly, "and go."

Claire's blessing is interrupted, though, by the sudden arrival of English soldiers.

He kissed me once more, hard enough to leave the taste of blood in my mouth. "Name him Brian," he said, "for my father." With a push, he sent me toward the opening. As I ran for it, I glanced back to see him standing in the middle of the doorway, sword half-drawn, dirk ready in his right hand.

The English, unaware that the cottage was occupied, had not thought to send a scout round the back. The slope behind the cottage was deserted as I dashed across it and into the thicket of alders below the hillcrest.

There was a crashing in the brush behind me. Someone had seen me rush from the cottage. I dashed aside the tears and scrabbled upward, groping on all fours as the ground grew steeper. I was in the clear space now, the shelf of granite I remembered. The small dogwood growing out of the cliff was there, and the tumble of small boulders.

I stopped at the edge of the stone circle, looking down, trying desperately to see what was happening. How many soldiers had come to the cottage? Could Jamie break free of them and reach his hobbled horse below? Without it, he would never reach Culloden in time.

All at once, the brush below me parted with a flash of red. An English soldier. I turned, ran gasping across the turf of the circle, and hurled myself through the cleft in the rock.

1968

And that, Claire tells her daughter, was the final part of Jamie Fraser's story; the thing she came to Scotland to learn; whether he had succeeded in his final quest—in saving his men before returning himself, to die in battle. Having done that, he would not have felt his life entirely wasted. And knowing now the end of his story, she is able at last to tell his daughter the truth.

Hearing the conclusion of her mother's story, Brianna Randall bursts into angry denial. It can't be—Frank Randall is her father! Furious at what she sees as Claire's betrayal, and refusing to believe her story, Brianna storms out, leaving Claire and Roger in stunned silence.

With the evidence to hand, and no emotional stake in disbelief, Roger *does*

believe Claire's story. In answer to her tentative questions, he tells her the final chapter—what happened to the men she knew: those who died at Culloden. Knowing what disaster she left behind, and seeking to build a new life with Frank and Brianna, Claire has tried never to look back; never sought to know the details of the death of the Highland clans. But now the time of denial is over—she can mourn the fallen, make peace with the past.

And the present. As she and Roger walk together through the rain-drenched evening, she tells him that there is one final part to her story—something she must tell him, for his own sake. And a decision that only he can make.

Roger bent over the genealogical chart, then looked up, moss-green eyes thoughtful.

"This one? William Buccleigh MacKenzie, born 1744, of William John MacKenzie and Sarah Innes. Died 1782."

Claire shook her head. "Died 1744, aged two months, of smallpox." She looked up, and the golden eyes met his with a force that sent a shiver down his spine. "Yours wasn't the first adoption in that family, you know," she said. Her finger tapped the entry. "He needed a wet nurse," she said. "His own mother was dead—so he was given to a

King Fisher

family that had lost a baby. They called him by the name of the child they had lost—that was common—and I don't suppose anyone wanted to call attention to his ancestry by recording the new child in the parish register. He would have been baptized at birth, after all; it wasn't necessary to do it again. Colum told me where they placed him."

"Geillis Duncan's son," he said slowly. "The witch's child."

"That's right." She gazed at him appraisingly, head cocked to one side. "I knew it must be, when I saw you. The eyes, you know. They're hers."

Claire tells Roger that the decision must be his; this is 1968, the year of Geillis Duncan's disappearance into the past, and the feast of Beltane is fast approaching. Shall they try to find the woman, and stop her? For if she goes, she goes to meet a fiery death in the past, condemned as a witch. But if she does *not* go—

"I'll leave it to you," Claire said quietly. "It's your right to say. Shall I look for her?"

Roger lifted his head off the table and blinked at her incredulously. "Shall you look for her?" he said. "If this—if it's all true—then we have to find her, don't we? If she's going back to be burned alive? Of course you have to find her," he burst out. "How could you consider anything else?"

"And if I do find her?" she replied. She placed a slender hand on the grubby chart and raised her eyes to his. "What happens to you?" she asked softly.

If Geilie Duncan returns to the past, she will bear the child who is Roger's ancestor—and she will die in a barrel of pitch, burned as a witch. If she does not go back through the stones, presumably she will be saved from a ghastly death . . . but what then of her child . . . and of Roger?

Reeling from the shocks of the day, Roger is staggered by this final, personal revelation. Still, he decides that they must find the woman known as Geillis Duncan—find her, talk to her, and—perhaps—prevent her return to a deadly past.

Accompanied by a reluctant and suspicious Brianna, Roger sets out to help Claire find Geillis Duncan—known in this time as Gillian Edgars. As they search out the trail of the mysterious witch whose green eyes look mockingly out of Roger's mirror each day, he realizes Claire's stake in the matter: not just a feeling of obligation toward Geillis Duncan, who saved her life in the past. Geillis/Gillian is the only real proof of the truth of Claire's story—for seeing someone actually disappear through the standing stones would convince even Brianna.

Roger and Brianna find Gillian's husband, Greg Edgars, but too late—Gillian has left home a week before, and no one knows where she is. With her friends, the Scottish Nationalists and neo-Jacobites, Greg gloomily suggests; his wife's obsession with Scotland's past has led her away from home before.

Claire has traced the missing woman to a local school, where she finds Gillian's notebooks—a mixture of raving lunacy and reasoned logic.

The notebook suggests what Claire has suspected; that the door to the past stands widest open on the ancient feasts of sun and fire—and one such feast is hard upon them; it is Beltane, the date upon which Claire herself disappeared in 1946.

Going to the sinister hill of Craigh na Dun at night, they find Gillian/Geillis's car, but no sign of the woman. Climbing

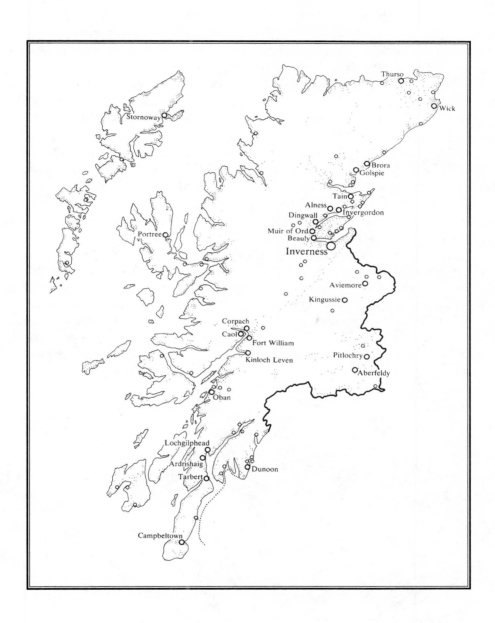

the hill to the circle of standing stones, Roger smells petrol—and a sudden whiff of fire illuminates the circle. Gillian Edgars has lured her husband to the hill, and in the belief that a blood sacrifice will open the door to the past, has killed him and set fire to the body.

He pushed past Brianna, focused only on the tall, slim girl before him, and the image of a face that mirrored his own. She saw him coming, turned and ran like the wind for the cleft stone at the end of the circle. She had a knapsack of rough canvas, slung over one shoulder; he heard her grunt as it swung heavily and struck her in the side.

She paused for an instant, hand outstretched to the rock, and looked back. He could have sworn that her eyes rested on him, met his own and held them, beyond the barrier of the fire's blaze. He opened his mouth in a wordless shout. She whirled then, light as a dancing spark, and vanished in the cleft of the rock.

At once, Roger is struck by a wave of noise and chaos like nothing he has ever experienced. Dazed, blinded, deafened, he is crawling toward the cleft himself when Brianna succeeds in rousing him. Deeply shaken by the experience, he is unhurt. But where is Claire?

Knocked unconscious by the shock wave of Gillian Edgars's passage through the stones, Claire lies in the grass of Craigh na Dun. Roger and Brianna get her back to the manse, where she slowly regains consciousness, to meet her daughter's questions.

"It was true, then?" Brianna asked hesitantly. "Everything was true?"

*Roger felt the small shudder that ran through the girl's body, and without thinking about it, reached up to take her hand. He winced involuntarily as she squeezed it, and suddenly in memory heard one of the Reverend's texts: "Blessed are those who have not seen, and have believed." And those who **must** see, in order to believe? The effects of*

belief wrought by seeing trembled fearful at his side, terrified at what else must now be believed.

Even as the girl tightened, bracing herself to meet a truth she had already seen, the lines of Claire's tensed body on the sofa relaxed. The pale lips curved in the shadow of a smile, and a look of profound peace smoothed the strained white face, and settled glowing in the golden eyes.

"It's true," she said. A tinge of color came back into the pallid cheeks. "Would your mother lie to you?" And she closed her eyes once more.

Himself shaken by the events of the night, Roger leaves mother and daughter to recover quietly together. It is only the next day, when the police have come, made their futile enquiries, and left, that Roger faces his final decision.

It had taken some time, but he had found it—the short passage he remembered from his earlier search on Claire Randall's behalf. Those results had brought her comfort and peace; this wouldn't—if he told her. And if he were right? But he must be; it accounted for that misplaced grave, so far from Culloden . . .

"Claire?" His voice felt scratchy from disuse, and he cleared his throat and tried again. "Claire? I . . . have something to tell you."

She turned and looked up at him, no more than the faintest curiosity visible on her features. She wore a look of calm, the look of one who has borne terror, despair, and mourning, and the desperate burden of survival—and has endured. Looking at her, he felt suddenly that he couldn't do it.

But she had told the truth; he must do likewise.

"I found something." He raised the book in a brief, futile gesture. "About . . . Jamie."

Speaking that name aloud seemed to brace him, as though the big Scot himself had been conjured by his calling, to stand solid and unmoving in the hallway, between his wife and Roger. Roger took a deep breath in preparation.

"What is it?"

"The last thing he meant to do. I think . . . I think he failed."

Her face paled suddenly, and she glanced wide-eyed at the book.

"His men? But I thought you found—"

"I did," Roger interrupted. "No, I'm fairly sure he succeeded in that. He got the men of Lallybroch out; he saved them from Culloden, and set them on the road home."

"But then . . ."

"He meant to turn back—back to the battle—and I think he did that, too." He was increasingly reluctant, but it had to be said. Finding no words of his own, he flipped the book open, and read aloud:

"After the final battle at Culloden, eighteen Jacobite officers, all wounded, took refuge in the old house and for two days, their wounds untended, lay in pain; then they were taken out to be shot. One of them, a Fraser of the Master of Lovat's regiment, escaped the slaughter; the others were buried at the edge of the domestic park.

"One man, a Fraser of the Master of Lovat's regiment, escaped . . ." Roger repeated softly. He looked up from the stark page to see her eyes, wide and unseeing as a deer's fixed in the headlights of an oncoming car.

"He meant to die on Culloden Field," Roger whispered. "But he didn't."

THE END

Flying
Fish

Old Wife

Sea
Tortoise

VOYAGER

He was dead. However, his nose throbbed painfully, which he thought odd in the circumstances. While he placed considerable trust in the understanding and mercy of his Creator, he harbored that residue of elemental guilt that made all men fear the chance of hell. Still, all he had ever heard of hell made him think it unlikely that the torments reserved for its luckless inhabitants could be restricted to a sore nose.

On the other hand, this couldn't be heaven, on several counts. For one, he didn't deserve it. For another, it didn't look it. And for a third, he doubted that the rewards of the blessed included a broken nose, any more than those of the damned . . .

*His hand struck something hard, and the fingers tangled in wet, snarled hair. He sat up abruptly, and with some effort, cracked the layer of dried blood that had sealed his eyelids shut. Memory flooded back, and he groaned aloud. He had been mistaken. This **was** hell. But James Fraser was unfortunately not dead, after all.*

He isn't dead, and he isn't in hell. Where Jamie Fraser *is* is lying wounded on Culloden Moor, the body of his enemy, Jack Randall, on top of him, and the English army all around him, dispatching those Highlanders unlucky enough not to be already dead.

Rescued—temporarily—by friends, he takes refuge with other wounded Jacobite officers in a farmhouse by the moor. Here they wait for two days, hearing the crack of gunshots on the field, smelling the fires built to consume the bodies of the Highland dead—whom they will soon join.

The other Highlanders do indeed go to join their comrades in death, executed by the English. Jamie, though, is saved by chance; the commanding officer who visits the farmhouse is Harold, Lord Melton; elder brother of John William Grey, whose life Jamie had spared a few months earlier, during an encounter on the road to Prestonpans. Unable to disregard what he considers a debt of honor, Melton discharges his unwelcome obligation by removing Jamie secretly, sending him home to Lallybroch. He is badly wounded, and may die on the journey—but that, Melton thinks, is hardly his concern. For the moment, Jamie Fraser is alive.

MEANWHILE, BACK IN the future (1968) . . .

Claire Randall and her daughter, Brianna, have just learned from Roger Wakefield that, contrary to Claire's long-held belief, Jamie Fraser survived the battle of Culloden. Claire is staggered by this news—but when Roger asks whether she wants him to find out what happened to Jamie Fraser, she agrees.

A detective hunt through history ensues, with Brianna Randall at first reluctant, but then increasingly absorbed in the story of the man who was her father—and the three-cornered love affair among her parents: Claire and Jamie, her real father—and Frank Randall, the man she has loved as her father all her life.

Given Brianna's complex feelings about her two fathers, Claire cannot talk to her daughter about her two husbands—or her own complex feelings. She does talk to Roger, who is equally fascinated but lacks Brianna's emotional involvement. As the hunt for Jamie Fraser goes on, Roger gradually learns more and more about what happened when Claire returned from the past, starving, half-demented with grief at the loss of her lover—and pregnant.

He hears the story of Claire's struggle back to life, for the sake of Jamie's child—and then of her struggle to fulfill the other half of her destiny, as a healer. Torn between the roles of mother and doctor, she finds a balance made possible only by the actions of her husband, Frank—who, torn between rage and love, finds it in himself to support a destiny he cannot share, for the sake of the woman who is—again—his wife; and for the sake of another man's child, now his own.

Roger feels himself delicately balanced between two women he cares for: Claire, whose personality and story fascinate him—and Brianna, with whom he is falling ever more deeply in love. As he talks with Claire, and searches with Brianna, he feels more and more strongly the unseen presence of the third member of this family—Jamie Fraser.

MEANWHILE, JAMIE'S OWN story unwinds, punctuated by Claire's memories, as told to Roger, and Roger's own investigations with Bree.

Reaching Lallybroch safely, Jamie survives his wound but is forced to hide in a cave on the estate, to avoid the notice of the English patrols that cross the district after Culloden, looting, burning, and killing. Apart from his family, but near them, he survives hardship and loneliness, solitude and grief, taking some comfort in being able to provide for and protect those he loves, if only in a small way. He does not speak Claire's name, and lets it be assumed that she is dead. Only in his heart does he speak his daily prayer—*Lord, that she may be safe. She and the child.*

Life is perilous in the Highlands, and not only for those who fought with Charles Stuart. Between marauding English soldiers and near famine, hardship and danger are a way of life for the inhabitants of Lallybroch. When Jamie's presence comes close to exposing his sister and his newborn nephew to English wrath, Jamie determines to carry out a bold

Ground Squirrel

Trail to Jamie's Cave.

Humming Bird

course of action. He arranges to have one of his tenants "betray" his presence to the English, thus collecting the price on his head, the gold to be used to feed and care for the people of Lallybroch.

Jenny rubbed her fist hard against her lips. She was quick; he knew she had grasped the plan at once—and all its implications.

"But Jamie," she whispered. "Even if they dinna hang ye outright—and that's the hell of a risk to take—Jamie, ye could be killed when they take ye!"

His shoulders slumped suddenly, under the weight of misery and exhaustion.

"God, Jenny," he said, "d'ye think I care?"

There was a long silence before she answered.

"No, I don't," she said. "And I canna say as I blame ye, either." She paused a moment, to steady her voice. "But I still care." Her fingers gently touched the back of his head, stroking his hair. "So ye'll mind yourself, won't ye, clot-heid?"

The ventilation panel overhead darkened momentarily, and there was the tapping sound of light footsteps. One of the kitchen-maids, on her way to the pantry, perhaps. Then the dim light came back, and he could see Jenny's face once more.

"Aye," he whispered at last. "I'll mind."

Lord John Grey is in disgrace. Exiled from London as the result of a scandalous affair, and sent to the wilds of the Scottish Highlands as governor of a small prison fortress, he finds his new surroundings remote, uncomfortable, and unpleasant. He finds the prisoners worse than unpleasant; among the roll of grim and dour Scots is a name he hoped never to hear again—that of Jamie Fraser, Laird of Broch Tuarach.

Writhing in shame at the memory of his encounter with Jamie Fraser during the Rising, Grey is torn between a desire for revenge and a sense of honor that makes revenge impossible. Fraser, once his enemy, is now his prisoner, a ward of his care. Abuse of his position and power is unthinkable—whatever else they may be, the Greys have always been men of honor. Grey resolves never to see Fraser alone, never to speak to him. With luck, the man will in time become one of the faceless mass of prisoners.

This scheme is short-lived; the appearance in the nearby village of a mysterious stranger, wet with seawater and raving of gold, forces Grey to summon James Fraser—the only man available who speaks both French and Gaelic, and who, as a prisoner, cannot make use of information for himself. The mention of gold is enough to prick any man's ears in this part of the Highlands, where rumors abound of a fortune in French gold, sent—some say—by the French king, Louis, to aid his Stuart cousin; but sent too late, and lost in the final days of the Rising.

A bargain is struck; Grey will have Jamie's irons removed, if Jamie will agree to translate the stranger's ravings, and keep them secret between Grey and himself. Jamie abides by his bargain, but does not tell Grey that he recognizes the man—Duncan Kerr—nor that the man's ravings hold a kind of sense beyond their words.

Duncan spoke of "the white witch." To Jamie, the white witch is the woman he has lost: Claire, his wife. He cannot imagine what she might have to do with the islands or the treasure Kerr describes, and yet . . . he cannot ignore the man's words. Three days following the stranger's death, Jamie Fraser escapes from Ardsmuir Prison.

Recaptured, Jamie refuses to speak of his reasons—or of his discoveries, if any. Determined to find out whether the treasure exists, Grey overcomes his personal feelings and invites Jamie to resume the custom followed with the previous governor: weekly dinners, at which Jamie, as chief and spokesman for the prisoners, would present requests and problems. Grey learns little regarding the treasure—until he thinks of blackmailing Jamie with threats against his family. Forced to reveal the truth—or part of it—Jamie confesses that he did find a treasure: not French gold, but a small cache of ancient coins and gems. This treasure, he informs Grey, he threw into the sea; unable to make use of it himself, he saw no reason why the English should have it.

Grey reluctantly accepts Jamie's story—but continues their meetings, gradually coming to the realization that his own feelings are changing; far from regarding Jamie Fraser with suspicion and anger, he is becoming attracted to the man, both physically and mentally. Worse—he is falling in love. When Grey steels himself to make a tentative approach, though, he is rejected with bruising finality, and all cordial relations between them are severed. The severance is made final when Jamie takes responsibility for possession of a bit of clan tartan—a crime, by the English law passed after Culloden. The penalty is flogging, and Grey—sick at the thought—is obliged to have it carried out.

ROGER IS GETTING CLOSER; he and Claire have found the proof of Jamie's survival, found the record of his name on the prison rolls at Ardsmuir. He did survive, he was alive—for how long? What became of him then?

THE PRISONERS OF ARDSMUIR are transported to the American Colonies, there to serve as indentured labor—with one exception. As a convicted traitor, Jamie's sentence cannot be commuted, save at the King's pleasure. Instead of transportation, he is sent to Helwater, a farm in the Lake District, there to serve as a groom. At first convinced that this is Lord John's revenge—to have him sentenced to menial work, where Grey can see him and gloat—Jamie finally comes to realize what Grey has really done: saved him from the deadly hardships of transportation and slave labor, and given him the nearest thing to freedom that could be managed.

If it is not true freedom, he does at least have light and air, free movement and the

A Jay

company of horses. For the first time since leaving Lallybroch, Jamie begins to find some small measure of content, living under an alias, as Alex MacKenzie.

This relative peace is threatened by the daughter of the house, Geneva Dunsany. A spoiled, headstrong girl with little regard for anyone's feelings but her own, she has taken a liking to Jamie—much to his alarm. Alarm becomes outrage when Geneva informs him that she is to be married, against her will—but before submitting to a marriage with the elderly Earl of Ellesmere, she is determined to have her virginity taken by someone more attractive—Jamie.

Nothing, he informs Geneva, will induce him to come to her bed. Nothing? Nothing, save the threat she smilingly produces—an intercepted letter from his sister, containing information that would provoke an English inquiry into affairs at Lallybroch. Faced with the prospect of having his entire family questioned and imprisoned, and their property confiscated, Jamie takes a deep breath and agrees.

He held her against his chest, not moving until her breathing slowed. He was conscious of an extraordinary mixture of feelings. He had never in his life taken a woman in his arms without some feeling of love, but there was nothing of love in this

encounter, nor could there be, for her own sake. There was some tenderness for her youth, and pity at her situation. Rage at her manipulation of him, and fear at the magnitude of the crime he was about to commit. But overall there was a terrible lust, a need that clawed at his vitals and made him ashamed of his own manhood, even as he acknowledged its power. Hating himself, he lowered his head and cupped her face between his hands.

With the deed well past, and Geneva safely married, Jamie breathes easier; until word comes from Ellesmere that the new Countess is with child. Jamie counts backward, curses Geneva, and tries to dismiss the thought; he was with her only a few days before her marriage; it's impossible to say.

However, six months later, word comes to Helwater; the Countess is delivered. Further word; the Countess's life is in danger, and her father and sister are summoned—Jamie being called to accompany the coach. Upon arrival, all is in chaos. Geneva is dead, the baby—a son—is alive and healthy, and the Earl of Ellesmere is in his study, drunk and raging. The servants know the reason; the Earl has claimed from the first that the child is not his.

Jeffries, well along with his second glass, snorted in contemptuous amusement. "Old goat with a young gel? I should think it like enough, but how on earth would his Lordship know for sure whose the spawn was? Could be his as much as anyone's, couldn't it, with only her Ladyship's word to go by, eh?"

*The cook's thin mouth stretched in a bright, malicious smile. "Oh, I don't say as 'ed know whose it **was** now—but there's one sure way 'ed know it wasn't 'is, now isn't there?"*

Jeffries stared at the cook, tilting back on his chair. "What?" he said. "You mean to tell me his Lordship's incapable?" A broad grin at this juicy thought split his weatherbeaten face. Jamie felt the omelet rising, and hastily gulped more brandy.

A crisis occurs; Jamie and the coachman, Jeffries, are summoned to the study at once, to lend aid to their employer. Dunsany is wrestling with the Earl of Ellesmere, who has been casting aspersions on Geneva's purity and her father's honesty. The inopportune arrival of Lady Dunsany with the child affords the maddened Ellesmere a chance to vent his rage; he seizes the child and threatens to drop him from the window to the stones of the courtyard, thirty feet below. Jeffries, who has arrived with his coachman's pistols, hesitates, unsure what to do.

Past all conscious thought or any fear of consequence, Jamie Fraser acted on the instinct that had seen him through a dozen battles. He snatched one pistol from the transfixed Jeffries, turned on his heel, and fired in the same motion.

The roar of the shot struck everyone silent. Even the child ceased to scream. Ellesmere's face went quite blank, thick eyebrows raised in question. Then he staggered, and Jamie leapt forward, noting with a sort of detached clarity the small round hole in the baby's trailing drapery, where the pistol ball had passed through it.

He stood then rooted on the hearthrug, heedless of the fire scorching the backs of his legs, of the still-heaving body of Ellesmere at his feet, of the regular, hysterical shrieks of Lady Dunsany, piercing as a peacock's. He stood, eyes tight closed, shaking like a leaf, unable either to move or to think, arms

wrapped tight about the shapeless, squirming, squawking bundle that contained his son.

In gratitude for his saving her grandchild, Lady Dunsany offers to try to have Jamie pardoned. The thought of leaving the damp confinements of the Lake District for the free air of the Highlands is a temptation almost beyond bearing. But to leave would mean abandoning his child, likely never to see him again. Jamie declines Lady Dunsany's offer—for the present.

The next several years are a time of surprising peace and contentment. If life is still lonely, there are compensations; chief among these being Jamie's son, William. Adored and spoiled by his female relatives, Willie is still a bonny lad, and much attached to "Mac," his groom, with whom he spends a great deal of time, riding or working in the stables.

All good things come to an end, though; as Willie grows, his face—at first round and pudding-shaped—begins to take on an alarming resemblance to Jamie's own bold features. While a casual eye might still pass over it, it's clear to Jamie that soon the resemblance will cause comment—and worse. It's time to go.

A pardon is arranged, through the offices of Lady Dunsany and Lord John Grey, whose family has influence at Court.

Grey comes to bid farewell to Jamie—in the process revealing that he has guessed the secret of William's parentage. Jamie's alarm at the revelation is tempered by Lord John's further news; he is marrying the Lady Isobel, Geneva's younger sister, and will thus become William's guardian.

Aware that Lord John's chief reason for undertaking this marriage is his desire to guard the boy for Jamie's sake, Jamie steels himself to offer—awkwardly—the only thing he has to give John Grey in return.

"I . . . would be obliged to you." Jamie sounded as though his collar were too tight, though in fact his shirt was open at the throat. Grey looked curiously at him, and saw that his countenance was slowly turning a dark and painful red.

"In return . . . If you want . . . I mean, I would be willing to . . . that is . . ."

Grey suppressed the sudden desire to laugh. He laid a light hand on the big Scot's arm, and saw Jamie brace himself not to flinch at the touch.

"My dear Jamie," he said, torn between laughter and exasperation. "Are you actually offering me your body in payment for my promise to look after Willie?"

Fraser's face was red as the roots of his hair.

"Aye, I am," he snapped, tight-lipped. "D'ye want it, or no?"

While strongly tempted, Lord John is entirely aware of Jamie's feelings—or lack of them. Realizing that Jamie cannot give him a love he doesn't possess, he is willing to settle instead for Jamie's friendship; that, both men can share with sincerity.

Leaving Willie to the care of Lord John, Jamie takes a painful farewell from his son, and turns his face toward the mountains of Scotland—going home, at last, to Lallybroch.

In 1968, the year is drawing toward Samhain, the November Feast of All Souls—and Claire is drawing closer to the moment of decision. All through their search, she has asked herself—what if he is alive? What then? Now, Roger and Brianna have traced Jamie—they think—to a printer's shop in Edinburgh, where an "A. Malcolm" printed commercial matter and political pamphlets that match handwritten documents in Jamie's writing.

If time works as they think it does, then Claire may return to a time twenty years past her departure on the eve of Culloden; she may be able to find "A. Malcolm." But should she? Her daughter is grown; a college student living on her own. But to leave, with no prospect of return through the perilous stones—not only to risk her life, but to accept never seeing her daughter again . . . is the chance of finding Jamie worth such a sacrifice?

Claire searches her heart, and the past, seeking an answer with Roger Wakefield's help. Roger, in love with the daughter—and not a little with the mother—promises Claire that he will keep Brianna safe; she will not be left alone. Brianna urges her mother to go—but the bond between mother and child is strong, and cannot be broken easily.

In the end Claire is still undecided, even as she climbs the hill of Craigh na Dun. Should she go? Can she go? Her questions are answered by the sight of Roger and Brianna, waiting for her in the stone circle—Brianna dressed in eighteenth-century-style clothes. If Claire will not go, she firmly informs her mother, then *she* will. Someone must find Jamie, and tell him that his sacrifice was not in vain; his wife survived, his child was safely born.

She was holding my hands tight between her own, squeezing hard.

"He gave you to me," she said, so low I could hardly hear her. "Now I have to give you back to him, Mama."

The eyes that were so like Jamie's looked down at me, blurred by tears.

"If you find him," she whispered, "when you find my father—give him this." She bent and kissed me, fiercely, gently, then straightened and turned me toward the stone.

"Go, Mama," she said, breathless. "I love you. Go!"

From the corner of my eye, I saw Roger move toward her. I took one step, and then another. I heard a sound, a faint roaring. I took the last step, and the world disappeared.

The journey through the stones is dangerous and draining—but successful. Recovered from the passage, Claire makes her way to Edinburgh, filled with fear and anticipation. Is "A. Malcolm" truly James Alexander Malcolm MacKenzie Fraser? And if he is . . .

Another minute and I would lose my nerve. I shoved open the door and walked in.

There was a broad counter across the front of the room, with an open flap in it, and a rack to one side that held several trays of type. Posters and notices of all sorts were tacked up on the opposite wall; samples, no doubt.

The door into the back room was open, showing the bulky angular frame of a printing press. Bent over it, his back turned to me, was Jamie.

"Is that you, Geordie?" he asked, not turning around. He was dressed in shirt and breeches, and had a small tool of some kind in his hand, with which he was doing something to the innards of the press. "Took ye long enough. Did ye get the—"

"It isn't Geordie," I said. My voice was higher than usual. "It's me," I said. "Claire."

Their reunion is both tender and joyous, tinged by shock, and enhanced by the pictures Claire has brought with her: photographs of Brianna, at every age from babyhood to young womanhood. Glancing around Jamie's spartan rooms, Claire is reassured; no woman tends this house. Hours are spent, lost in the simple miracle of each other's presence—until Jamie is brought to a realization of the time.

Exclaiming that he has forgotten "Mr. Willoughby," he springs to his feet and

rushes out with Claire, to a nearby local tavern. Here she meets Mr. Willoughby— a Chinese "associate," whom Jamie had found on the Edinburgh docks two years earlier and rescued from freezing. Jamie's explanation of the nature of the "association" is delayed when Mr. Willoughby's appearance provokes a small riot at the tavern, causing Claire, Jamie, and Mr. Willoughby (aka Yi Tien Cho) to flee through the backstreets and wynds of the city, finding refuge at last in a brothel— whose female proprietor seems to be on very familiar terms with Jamie.

Alone at last in an upper room, partial explanations emerge; Jamie is a printer, indeed, but derives a good part of his income from smuggling liquor on the side; Madame Jeanne provides both a hiding place for the smuggled goods and an outlet for their sale. Claire still has questions— many of them—but further explanations can wait; the night is upon them, and they are alone, together.

After the blissful reunion of the night, Jamie rises early. He has urgent business, he explains, but will be back soon. Before Jamie can leave, though, an unexpected visitor arrives at the brothel—Jamie's brother-in-law, Ian.

"Wife?" Forgetting to look away, Ian goggled at Jamie in horror. "Ye've marrit a whore?" he croaked.

"I wouldn't call it that, exactly," I said. Hearing my voice, he jerked his head in my direction.

"Hullo," I said, waving cheerily at him from my nest of bedclothes. "Been a long time, hasn't it?"

I'd always thought the descriptions of what people did when seeing ghosts rather exaggerated, but had been forced to revise

my opinions in light of the responses I had been getting since my return to the past. Jamie had fainted dead away, and if Ian's hair was not literally standing on end, he assuredly looked as though he had been scared out of his wits.

Eyes bugging out, he opened and closed his mouth, making a small gobbling noise that seemed to entertain Jamie quite a lot.

"That'll teach ye to go about thinkin' the worst of my character," he said, with apparent satisfaction. Taking pity on his quivering brother-in-law, Jamie poured out a tot of brandy and handed him the glass. "Judge not, and ye'll no be judged, eh?"

Ian has come in search of his youngest son, Young Ian. Chafing under the restrictions of life at Lallybroch, and longing for adventure, Young Ian has run away, leaving word that he has gone to Edinburgh— presumably to join his adored uncle. Jamie disclaims knowledge of Young Ian's whereabouts, but promises to go with his brother-in-law at once, to make inquiries and to carry out his own mysterious business. Claire's dress was damaged in the riot at the tavern; with nothing to wear, she has little choice but to remain in bed, awaiting both breakfast and Jamie's return.

Instead of breakfast, she receives more visitors: first Mr. Willoughby, who tells her the story of how "Tsei-mi" saved his life— and then a very unexpected Young Ian, Jamie's fourteen-year-old nephew, in search of his uncle. Finding what he assumes is Jamie's mistress abed, he blushes, stammers, and disappears.

In the wake of these visitations, Claire determines to find some clothes and venture forth; wrapped in a quilt, she has breakfast with a number of amiable pros-

titutes, who mistake her for Madame Jeanne's newest recruit.

"Tsk!" murmured Mollie, seeing the proprietor. "An early customer. I hate it when they come in the middle o' breakfast," she grumbled. "Stop ye digesting your food proper, it does."

"Ye needn't worry, Mollie; it's Claire'll have to take him," Peggy said, tossing her dark plait out of the way. "Newest lass takes the ones no one wants," she informed me.

"Stick your finger up his bum," Dorcas advised me. "That brings 'em off faster than anything. I'll save ye a bannock for after, if ye like."

"Er . . . thanks," I said. Just then, Madame Jeanne's eye lit upon me, and her mouth dropped open in a horrified "O."

Hastily removed to a small room to dress, Claire overhears a conversation between the Madame and her doorman; there has been a murder in Edinburgh—*another* murder. The Edinburgh Fiend has claimed another victim; this one, a chambermaid from the brothel, who has just been found beheaded in her lodgings nearby.

Hearing this, Claire is seized by uneasiness; Jamie still has not returned from his mysterious errand, and his nephew Ian is also evidently wandering about the city, alone. Meanwhile, an air of urgency pervades the brothel. Where is everyone, and what's going on?

Her questions are interrupted by the sudden arrival of a handsome man with dark hair, a hook replacing his missing hand—and a very familiar face. Recognition comes to both of them, and Claire is overjoyed to be reunited with Fergus, whom she had last seen as a boy. The rapture is short-lived:

"There ye are! What in the name of God are ye doing up here, Fergus?" Jamie's tall figure loomed suddenly in the doorway. His eyes widened at the sight of me in my embroidered shift. "Where are your clothes?" he asked. "Never mind," he said then, waving his hand impatiently as I opened my mouth to answer. "I havena time just now. Come along, Fergus, there's eighteen ankers of brandy in the alleyway, and the excisemen on my heels!"

And with a thunder of boots on the wooden stairs, they were gone, leaving me alone once more.

Coming cautiously downstairs in her borrowed shift and a shawl, Claire meets a strange man in the doorway to the kitchen. He accosts her, asking about contraband and mentioning rewards; an exciseman, she thinks, and backs away from him, wondering how to escape and warn Jamie. The exciseman seizes her by the arm, but is in turn accosted by Mr. Willoughby, standing on the stairs—with a loaded pistol.

The Chinese, still much the worse for drink, shoots the supposed Customs agent, who promptly dies in Claire's lap. Fergus reappears, followed by Jamie, who quickly takes charge of the situation, bundling the body into Claire's shawl and leading Claire downstairs, into the cellar of the brothel, where a false wall conceals the site of Jamie's brandy-smuggling operations.

A closer inspection of the supposed exciseman's body leads to puzzlement; the man has no warrant of office, but instead—and more alarming—has a copy of the New Testament in his pocket: a copy printed at the shop of A. Malcolm. Someone has made the dangerous connection between the respectable A. Malcolm, printer, and the smuggler "Jamie Roy"—but who?

Leaving disposal of body and distribution of brandy to Fergus, Jamie and Claire seek a moment's peace at Moubray's, one of Edinburgh's better eating establishments. Peace is momentary, though; their luncheon is interrupted by Sir Percival Turner, a local Crown official, who offers smiling congratulations on (what he assumes to be) their new marriage—and sinister warnings.

Sir Percival knows him as a smuggler, Jamie explains; however, Sir Percival assumes that Jamie—along with a good proportion of the population of Scotland—is dealing with contraband dry goods from Holland: cambric, velvet, and the like, rather than the much more profitable—and dangerous—liquor trade. A delivery from France is expected in the next few days; Sir Percival's warning makes it apparent that the meeting place is known. However, there is a fallback system arranged; Jamie and his men will repair to the alternate location, on the cliffs above Arbroath.

Before Jamie can leave on this errand, though, there are a few loose ends to be attended to—Claire, and his nephew Young Ian. Young Ian's whereabouts are revealed in dramatic manner; returning to the print shop after their "wedding" luncheon, Jamie and Claire discover it in flames, with Young Ian trapped inside.

Rescued from the conflagration, Young Ian is confronted by a wrathful father and uncle, back at the brothel. His father's wrath is not assuaged by Young Ian's refusal to accompany him home to Lallybroch at once; both infuriated and hurt by his son's behavior, the elder Ian takes his leave, alone.

JAMIE IS SHOCKED and troubled by Ian's treatment of his father, but more shocked by Ian's revelations of his motives. The boy had spent the morning in shadowing a mysterious one-eyed seaman whom he had overheard in a tavern asking for Jamie—by his real name, which no one in Edinburgh should know, Jamie being known as "Malcolm the printer" under his legitimate cover, and "Jamie Roy" among the smugglers and brandy merchants.

Having lost the man, Ian had eventually made his way back to the print shop, only to find the one-eyed man in the back room, in the act of taking away some newly printed pamphlets—these of a deeply incriminating nature, having been printed for a small group of illegal seditionists. In his effort to stop the man from getting away, Ian set the shop on fire by overturning the lead-forge, and—he thinks—killed the one-eyed man in the process. Unable

to face his father with the confession that he is a murderer, he thought perhaps his uncle Jamie would understand.

Jamie, groping hastily in his sleeve for a handkerchief, looked up suddenly, struck by a thought.

"That's why ye said ye must tell me, but not your da? Because ye knew I've killed men before?"

His nephew nodded, searching Jamie's face with troubled, trusting eyes. "Aye. I thought . . . I thought ye'd know what to do."

"Ah." Jamie drew a deep breath, and exchanged a glance with me. "Well . . ." His shoulders braced and broadened, and I could see him accept the burden Young Ian had laid down.

Jamie recommends prayer for the moment, confession on the morrow—and the comfort of his reassurance that Ian had no choice in the matter, and is not damned as a murderer. The process of healing continues with supper, and bed. The latter, however, is complicated by Fergus, who has thoughtfully arranged with Madame Jeanne that Ian shall not be left to brood alone in bed. Horrified, Jamie is unable to prevent Ian's retiring with a young prostitute; in resignation, he admits to Claire that in fact the best remedy for the soul-sickness of killing is often to be found in a woman's arms.

Be that as it may, Jamie bustles his charge off to confession first thing in the morning, leaving Claire to reacquaint herself with Edinburgh, as she visits the apothecary's shop for fresh herbs. While there, she meets another customer, a Free Church minister named Archibald Campbell, who—upon learning of her experience as a healer—begs her to come and see his sister, who suffers from strange silences and "fits."

Miss Margaret Campbell does indeed have "fits," staring and screaming—and when not so engaged, lives peacefully in the past, before the traumatic experience with English soldiers after Culloden that has deprived her of her wits. Claire is unable to offer more than nutrition and sedatives, but holds some hope that the Reverend's intention to remove his sister to the Indies may make some difference in her condition.

Returning to the brothel, Claire finds Jamie and Fergus deep in conference. There is a fallback arranged for the rendezvous with the French smuggling ship; the details are arranged by letter between Jamie and Jared, with the smugglers informed only just before each rendezvous, so the secret seems safe. Jamie reluctantly decides to take Claire and Ian with him, as it is necessary to take Ian home to Lallybroch. However, he adds sternly, they are *not* to come anywhere near the actual rendezvous, but instead to remain safely at the inn on the road above the beach.

This plan is scotched when they find upon arrival that the inn has burnt to the ground. Left to themselves on the cliffs, with strict instructions to keep out of the way, Ian and Claire have a ringside seat as events below unfold. What unfolds, in fact, are excisemen, who have lain hidden in the sand, awaiting the smugglers. In the resulting melee, Claire and Ian flee to the road, where Claire nearly runs into another pair of excisemen, these waiting to trap any fleeing smugglers.

From the Customs officers conversation, it's apparent that this was not only an arranged ambush, but one designed specifically to trap Jamie Fraser. Claire steals away to warn Jamie, who has managed to escape and is giving his smugglers directions to fade quietly away to their homes. Returning along the road, they find only one Customs officer—hanging from a tree.

With the print shop in ashes, dead excisemen at every turn, and the obvious fact that someone—and possibly more than one someone—is aware of Jamie's multiple identities and his less-legal activities, a return to Edinburgh seems unwise. Jamie is not looking forward to a return to Lallybroch, either, but it *is* necessary to take Young Ian home.

For her part, Claire is wondering how she will be received by Jenny, the woman who was once her friend. The initial reception is strained, owing to Young Ian's behavior, and his parents' hurt at his apparent rejection of them in favor of his uncle. Jamie finds a way for both Young Ian and himself to make atonement, though, and the situation is resolved in warmth.

Claire rejoices at waking next morning in a place that has been for her the closest thing to home. Rising in the cold to light the fire, though, she sees three riders—all women—coming toward the house. She wonders who they might be, but finds her curiosity distracted by Jamie's attentions.

He was interrupted by a sudden bang as the door flew open and rebounded from the wall. Startled, we turned to look. In the doorway stood a young girl I had never seen before. She was perhaps fifteen or sixteen,

with long flaxen hair and big blue eyes. The eyes were somewhat bigger than normal, and filled with an expression of horrified shock as she stared at me. Her gaze moved slowly from my tangled hair to my bare breasts, and down the slopes of my naked body, until it encountered Jamie, lying prone between my thighs, white-faced with a shock equal to hers.

*"Daddy!" she said in tones of total outrage. "**Who** is that woman?"*

Claire is wondering much the same thing, but her curiosity is soon satisfied. The young woman is named Marsali; the daughter of Laoghaire, who meets Claire's appearance with a horror equal to Claire's own. Jamie is hers, Laoghaire declares; they were married upon his return to Lallybroch from Ardsmuir. She doesn't know where Claire has come from, but she ought to return there at once!

Staggered by this revelation, Claire's shock is succeeded by fury. Stunned and dismayed by news of the marriage, she is infuriated by Jamie's failure to tell her of it. He intended to tell her, he insists—but was afraid that her reaction would be exactly what it is. There is a dreadful fight, concluding with Jamie's stamping out of the house—and Claire's flight away from Lallybroch and back toward the stones.

Her steps grow slower and slower, though, as she approaches the end of her dreams.

*Only with Jamie had I given everything
I had, risked it all. I had thrown away caution and judgment and wisdom, along with
the comforts and constraints of a hard-won
career. I had brought him nothing but myself, been nothing but myself with him,
given him soul as well as body, let him see
me naked, trusted him to see me whole and
cherish my frailties—because he once had.*

*I had feared he couldn't, again. Or
wouldn't. And then had known those few
days of perfect joy, thinking that what had
once been true was true once more; I was
free to love him, with everything I had and
was, and be loved with an honesty that
matched my own.*

*The tears slid hot and wet between my
fingers. I mourned for Jamie, and for what
I had been, with him.*

Do you know, *his voice said, whispering,*
***what it means, to say again "I love you,"
and to mean it?***

*I knew. And with my head in my hands
beneath the pine trees, I knew I would
never mean it again.*

Sunk in miserable contemplation,
Claire is suddenly roused by the unexpected appearance of
Young Ian. He has, he
says, been sent by
Jamie to ask Claire to
come back to Lally-
broch. Further infuri-
ated by this evidence
of Jamie's callous-
ness—he doesn't care
enough to come him-
self!—Claire indig-
nantly refuses, trying
to free her horse's
reins from Young
Ian's stubborn grip.

But she *must* come, he insists. It's not
like she thinks; Jamie really needs her.

"Let go!"

"But Auntie Claire, it's not that!"

"What's not that?" Caught by his tone of
desperation, I glanced up. His long, narrow
face was tight with the anguished need to
make me understand.

*"Uncle Jamie didna stay to tend
Laoghaire!"*

"Then why did he send you?"

*He took a deep breath, renewing his grip
on my reins.*

*"She shot him. He sent me to find ye, be-
cause he's dying."*

Claire's initial response to this revelation is, *"If he isn't dying when I get there, I'll
kill him myself—and you, too, Ian Murray!"*
but this doesn't lessen her anxiety as they
hasten back toward Lallybroch. Upon arrival there, she finds Jamie battling infection and high fever, groggy enough with
pain and heat to think her appearance a
hallucination. He has, he tells her, come
close to death from fever twice before; this
time it will finish him, and is welcome to
do so.

Claire, however, has brought one other
thing from the future besides Brianna's
photographs; a small case, holding hypodermic syringes and penicillin tablets. Informing Jamie that eighteenth-century
germs are no match for a modern antibiotic, she tends briskly to his wounds, in-
jects him with the drug, and then sits
down to watch over him—at last reluctantly ready to hear what he had tried to
tell her before: the story behind his marriage to Laoghaire.

It was a marriage made of loneliness;
a mismatch born of hope and compassion.
Jenny, fearing for her brother's sanity and

aching for his need, had tried again and again to induce him to take a wife after Claire's disappearance. He had refused, again and again—not only because no one could replace her, but because his circumstances did not admit of taking a wife; living in a cave, hiding, endlessly on the run—what sort of life could that be for any woman?

But now . . . returning from his long exile in England, he found himself free of the threat of law, but rootless, a stranger in his own place. The estate had passed to Ian's son; the responsibility and obligation that had sustained Jamie for so long had vanished. His own son was miles away, forever unacknowledged, forever lost to him. With no one and nothing to bind

him, he wandered ghostlike through the rooms of the house that had once been his.

And so, when Jenny once more forced the possibility of marriage upon him, he was at last obliged to listen. Laoghaire was a widow, with two daughters to support. She was also one of the few links remaining to his own youth. And so, he tells Claire, they wed—with no sense of love, but thinking that they might be able at least to help each other.

It was a mismatch, though; instead of being comfort to one another, there was nothing but misunderstanding and misery, and within a year, Jamie had left to work in Edinburgh, sending back money for the care of Laoghaire and her girls.

Guard Fish

Despite her anger, Claire is moved to understanding; she, too, has had a marriage of obligation, and knows too well the pitfalls of a bond without love.

"Do ye know?" he said softly, somewhere in the black, small hours of the night. "Do ye know what it's like to be with someone that way? To try all ye can, and seem never to have the secret of them?"

"Yes," I said, thinking of Frank. "Yes, I do know."

"I thought perhaps ye did." He was quiet for a moment, and then his hand touched my hair lightly, a shadowy blur in the firelight.

"And then . . ." he whispered, "then to have it back again, that knowing. To be free in all ye say or do, and know that it is right."

"To say 'I love you,' and mean it with all your heart," I said softly to the dark.

"Aye," he answered, barely audible. "To say that."

His hand rested on my hair, and without knowing quite how it happened, I found myself curled against him, my head just fitting in the hollow of his shoulder.

"For so many years," he said, "for so long, I have been so many things, so many different men." I felt him swallow, and he shifted slightly, the linen of his nightshirt rustling with starch.

"I was 'Uncle' to Jenny's children, and 'Brother' to her and Ian. 'Milord' to Fergus, and 'Sir' to my tenants. 'Mac Dubh' to the men of Ardsmuir and 'MacKenzie' to the other servants at Helwater.

'Malcolm the printer,' then, and 'Jamie Roy' at the docks." The hand stroked my hair, slowly, with a whispering sound like the wind outside. "But here," he said, so softly I could barely hear him, "here in the dark, with you . . . I have no name."

I lifted my face toward his, and took the warm breath of him between my own lips.

"I love you," I said, and did not need to tell him how I meant it.

Jamie's recovery is uneventful, save for the appearance of Hobart MacKenzie, Laoghaire's brother. Charged with wiping out the stain on his sister's honor, Hobart has brought not the expected sword or pistol, but something far more dangerous—a lawyer. Claire is delighted to find her old friend Ned Gowan still alive and vigorous—though somewhat less pleased at the arrangement he suggests; in dismissal of all claims and charges, Jamie agrees to pay Laoghaire an annual sum for maintenance of her household, and to provide dowries for her two daughters, Marsali and Joan.

While all right in principle, this arrangement has a slight drawback in practice, insofar as Jamie has no funds with which to meet the obligation. There is, however, a way.

Jamie tells Claire the story of his time in prison; the appearance of Duncan Kerr, and Jamie's subsequent escape to find the truth of Kerr's ravings about treasure and "the white witch." He found no trace of Claire, but *did* discover treasure. Not the French bullion of legend, but a box of gemstones and ancient coins, hidden on a rocky isle guarded by seals.

Returning to Ardsmuir in order to care for his men there, he had concealed the truth from the prison's governor, swearing to him that the treasure "lies in the sea." Since then, the existence of the treasure has been held as a secret trust by the Murrays of Lallybroch; in time of great need, one or another of the older boys would journey to the coast with Ian, and then swim out to the seals' isle in order to abstract a single gem from the hoard. The jewel would then be sold secretly in France, with their cousin Jared's assistance, and the money used for the help of Jacobite exiles or the support of the Lallybroch tenants.

These secret journeys had been rites of passage for the two older Murray boys; now it is Young Ian's turn. Jenny and Ian are hesitant at first, but consent to the expedition. Jamie's wounded arm makes it impossible for him to make the arduous swim, and Young Ian's thirst for adventure makes him restless on the farm. The lad would like nothing better than to accompany his beloved uncle on an exciting mission; at the same time, he would be safely under Jamie's eye. And, as Ian says, *"Better to give him his freedom while he still thinks it's ours to give."*

The expedition to the seals' isle is a good bit more exciting than even Young Ian could have hoped. Young Ian's arrival on the fog-shrouded rock coincides with another—a tough-looking bunch of seamen, who abscond with both the treasure and Ian while Jamie and Claire look on helplessly from the cliffs above.

Jamie is stricken; beyond his own deep love for his nephew is horror at the thought of having to go back to Lallybroch and tell Jenny what has happened to her youngest son. Vowing instead to recover the boy, no matter what the cost, he takes Claire at once across the Channel to France. Failing to stop the kidnappers, the Frasers had managed to catch a glimpse of the pirates' ship. With this scanty information, perhaps Cousin Jared, with his contacts among the shipping trade, can find out the ship's destination—and provide another ship in which to pursue it.

Fuming at every second's delay, Jamie has no time to worry over the prospects of seasickness. Instead, once the ship is prepared, he hastily returns to Scotland to gather a small band of men: his companions in smuggling, including Duncan Innes, an ex-prisoner from Ardsmuir, and Mr. Willoughby.

His foster son, Fergus, is meant to accompany the rescue expedition, but barely makes the sailing—accompanied by Marsali, Laoghaire's daughter. They are in love, the girl defiantly tells Jamie, and they mean to elope—with him.

The ship has already left shore; there is no turning back. Jamie, keeping a tight rein on his temper, tells Fergus and Marsali that they will sleep apart on the ship; if, once arrived in the Indies, they are still convinced that they wish to be married, he will find a priest to bless their union. Until then—hands off.

North
Sea

Inverness

HIGHLANDS

SCOTLAND

Stirling
Edinburgh
Glasgow Falkirk
Carlisle

York

IRELAND

ENGLAND

NETHERLANDS

Ludlow

London

BELGIUM

English Channel

Le Havre

Atlantic
Ocean

Paris
Versailles

FRANCE

0   MILES   200

Boulogne

SPAIN

Fergus and Marsali agree to abide by this dictum, which is as well, since Jamie has little strength left to enforce it. Felled by seasickness, he lies helpless in his bunk, Claire's herbal remedies useless to combat it. Mr. Willoughby, though, has a suggestion—and Jamie once more appears on the deck of the *Artemis,* glowering beneath a prickling of gold acupuncture needles.

The wind is fair and the voyage quick and mostly uneventful, save for Mr. Willoughby's acquisition of a pelican named Ping An (the Peaceful One), whom the Chinese poet tames and teaches to fish. The tedium of sailing is broken by a chance meeting at sea with an English man-of-war, the *Porpoise,* who poses a substantial danger to the success of the *Artemis*'s voyage. While England and France are not at war, and the *Artemis* sails under French colors, half her crew are English or Scottish—and the man-of-war may impress any English subjects, should she prove to be shorthanded. The fact that this would cripple the *Artemis,* leaving her with insufficient crew to do more than limp slowly westward, is of no concern to His Majesty's Navy.

Shorthanded she is; the *Porpoise*'s very young Captain stumbles aboard, begging for help. An epidemic has broken out onboard; half his crew are dead, dying, or falling sick. Thomas Leonard is himself no more than Third Lieutenant, acting Captain by default, all senior officers having perished. He must have help; does the *Artemis* boast a surgeon?

Against Jamie's wishes, but impelled both by pity for the young lieutenant and by her Hippocratic oath, Claire goes aboard the *Porpoise,* where she finds conditions much worse even than Captain Leonard's description; there is a full-fledged typhoid epidemic and the crew quarters are full of dying men. Claire issues such directions and instructions as are possible, all the while knowing that the available measures are largely futile; she cannot save most of the sick, but can only try to prevent the spread of infection.

Her apparent expertise has an unforeseen consequence; the young acting Captain of the *Porpoise,* desperate for any help and with an important political passenger aboard, informally impresses Claire, taking her to Jamaica with the promise that he will return her to Jamie and the *Artemis* upon their arrival—assuming that enough of the crew survive to make such an arrival possible.

Both frightened and infuriated by this kidnapping on the high seas, Claire has no choice but to do her best to fight the epidemic, with no weapons to hand save distilled alcohol and a basic knowledge of hygiene. In the course of the fight, drained

Porpoise

and exhausted by the futility of her efforts, the prevalence of death, and her own isolation from Jamie, she finds consolation from an unexpected source—Lord John Grey, the newly appointed governor of Jamaica. Twenty years past their first meeting in a dark wood, neither recognizes the other, but Claire takes comfort from the meeting with the quiet, compassionate stranger.

The epidemic at last burnt out, the *Porpoise* limps toward Jamaica. What should seem deliverance to Claire, though, is instead a new danger; in the course of her stay aboard the *Porpoise,* she has found a sinister entry in the Captain's log, and met with one Harry Tompkins, the one-eyed seaman who had—after all—escaped the conflagration of the burning print shop in Edinburgh. With a mixture of brandy and threats, Claire extracts the truth from Tompkins; Jamie's identity is known—both to Sir Percy Turner, who has political aspirations that would be helped by the apprehension of an important seditionist and smuggler—and to Captain Leonard, who has learned of Jamie's identity from Tompkins, and who—regretting the necessity imposed by duty—intends to arrest Jamie upon their rendezvous in Jamaica.

Escape is imperative, but Claire's attempts to leave the ship at various stops before Jamaica are foiled by the Captain's watchfulness. At last, desperate to escape, she enlists the help of the gunner's wife and slips overboard during the night into the Mouchoir Passage, supported by empty brandy casks, to float ashore on the nearby island of Hispaniola. From here, perhaps she can reach Jamaica in time to meet the *Artemis,* and to warn Jamie of the danger from the *Porpoise.*

Arriving wet, hungry, thirsty, and cold, Claire makes her way painfully inland, with no clear idea what to do next—only knowing that she must find water, food, and Jamie, in that order. What she finds is a Jewish naturalist named Lawrence Stern, who provides water and takes her in search of food at the house of a nearby friend: a defrocked—and not quite sane—English priest named Fogden.

Meanwhile, the *Artemis* has been in hot pursuit, urged on by Jamie's fear for Claire's safety. Catching up to the crippled man-of-war at one port of call, the *Artemis* hides out of sight, while Jamie crosses a spit of land and boards the *Porpoise,* unseen, to search for Claire—who has, of course, already left the ship, herself unseen.

Combing the ship with increasing desperation, Jamie fails to find his wife, but is discovered and imprisoned, left alone in a small cell with the horrifying news that Claire is dead, lost overboard. His presence is noted by the gunner's wife, though, who deduces his identity and liberates him.

He remembered the last thing she had said, though, as she pushed him toward the tilting taffrail.

"She is not dead," the woman had said. "She go there"—pointing at the rolling

Sun Fish

seas—*"you go, too. Find her!"* And then she had bent, got a hand in his crutch and a sturdy shoulder under his rump, and heaved him neatly over the rail and into the churning water.

Thus informally arriving himself on Hispaniola after a frantic swim, Jamie makes the acquaintance of a group of creole children playing near the shore, who take him to their mother's *taverna,* next door to the military garrison in Cap-Haïtien.

A Dolphin

MEANWHILE, CLAIRE HAS been enjoying the hospitality of Father Fogden. The delights of conversation regarding hidden caves, maroons (escaped slaves), blind fish, and dead sheep are interrupted, however, by the priest's revelation that a ship has run aground during the recent storm, quite nearby. Catching a reference among his imprecations to the "one-handed" man captaining the ship, Claire realizes that the ship in question cannot be the *Porpoise*— but just might be the *Artemis.*

It is indeed the *Artemis,* captained by Fergus, the original captain having been washed overboard during the shipwreck. Claire's delight in being reunited with her companions fades considerably upon her realization that Jamie is not with them. Anxiety as to his whereabouts is relieved shortly, though; the repairs to the *Artemis* are interrupted by a visit from troops sent from the garrison in Cap-Haïtien to inspect—and "salvage"—the wreck, under the command of one Captain Alessandro—a tall soldier with a red beard and a remarkably familiar aspect.

The bewildered garrison soldiers are

overpowered and imprisoned in the hold (to be put ashore once the *Artemis* is safely afloat), and the bedraggled company reunited once more—save for Young Ian. Seizing the opportunity offered by circumstance, Marsali presses Jamie to keep his promise; they are ashore in the Indies, with a priest to hand—he must keep his word and allow her and Fergus to be married, she says.

Seeing the young couple's devotion and determination, Jamie reluctantly assents, and a wedding takes place.

"I've told Marsali she must write to her mother to say she's wed," Jamie murmured to me as we watched the preparations on the beach go forward. *"But perhaps I shall suggest she doesna say much more about it than that."*

I saw his point. Laoghaire was not going to be pleased at hearing that her eldest daughter had eloped with a one-handed ex-pickpocket twice her age. Her maternal feelings were unlikely to be assuaged by hearing that the marriage had been performed in the middle of the night on a West Indian beach by a disgraced—if not actually defrocked—priest, witnessed by twenty-five seamen, ten French horses, a small flock of sheep—all gaily beribboned in honor of the occasion—and a King Charles spaniel, who added to the generally festive feeling by attempting to copulate with Murphy's wooden leg at every opportunity. The only thing that could make things worse, in

Laoghaire's view, would be to hear that I had participated in the ceremony.

Taking command of the *Artemis*, Jamie resumes the interrupted search for his nephew among the islands of the West Indies, making inquiries of the network of Scottish Freemasons on the islands, and acquiring in the process a profitable cargo of bat guano, much prized among the planters for use as fertilizer.

With the hold full of this valuable substance, the *Artemis* presses on toward Jamaica. En route, though, they are rammed at night by a strange ship, and boarded by pirates. Claire and Marsali take refuge in the hold, but are surprised by a marauding pirate. Claire attacks the pirate with a blade from her surgical kit, cutting off one of his toes and allowing Marsali to escape. Fleeing out of the hold and upward into the ship's shrouds, she is pursued and trapped; waiting with eyes closed for the final slash of the cutlass, she hears a strange sound:

There was a sort of thump, a sharp grunt, and a strong smell of fish.

I opened my eyes. The pirate was gone. Ping An was sitting on the crosstrees, three feet away, crest erect with irritation, wings half-spread to keep his balance.

"Gwa!" he said crossly. He turned a beady little yellow eye on me and clacked his bill in warning. Ping An hated noise and commotion. Evidently, he didn't like Portuguese pirates, either.

The fight below is over; the pirate ship is moving away. Clinging to the shrouds, Claire can see men on the deck below, beginning to tend the wounded and put things to right. Dizzy and light-headed from her flight, she begins to make her way slowly down.

She is feeling sick and cold when she hits the deck, but makes her way at once to Jamie, relieved to find him suffering from no more than a small cut on the head—or so she assumes.

There were stains of dark, drying blood on the front of his shirt, but the sleeve of his shirt was also bloody. In fact, it was nearly soaked, with fresh bright blood.

"Jamie!" I clutched at his shoulder, my vision going white at the edges. "You aren't all right—look, you're bleeding!"

My hands and feet were numb, and I only half-felt his hands grasp my arms as he rose from the cask in sudden alarm. The last thing I saw, amid flashes of light, was his face, gone white beneath the tan.

"My God!" said his frightened voice, out of the whirling blackness. "It's no my blood, Sassenach, it's yours!"

Narrowly saved from bleeding to death from a cutlass slash down her arm, Claire is doctored by Jamie and Mr. Willoughby, and uses a bit more of her precious penicillin to cure an incipient fever. Jamie stays close to her at night, waking by her bed from dreams of fire and slaughter; stirrings of the dormant memories buried in his mind since Culloden.

Claire dozes next day, recovering, to be wakened by Jamie in search of healing lotion for a prisoner rescued from the sea. As the *Bruja* drew off, he explains, a black man—evidently an escaped slave, from the scars on his back—dived off the pirate ship into the ocean. Having discovered an apparent link between the *Bruja* and the seals' treasure—a dead pirate, wearing a rare fourth-century tetradrachm from the hoard—Jamie is now sure that it was the *Bruja* that took Ian, and is eager to interrogate the prisoner.

Accompanying him to the orlop, Claire meets a slender man with tribal scars on his face, the scars of slavery on his back—and the larger scar of an obliterated brand on one shoulder. This is Ishmael, one-time cook, and once something more than a cook, from his bearing.

Ishmael is understandably cautious, fearing that the Frasers might either restore him to his previous owner or enslave him themselves. Still, from what he tells them and from clues obtained from the papers Claire was given with the one-armed slave she bought, Temeraire, it seems that Mrs. Abernathy, of Rose Hall on Jamaica, may hold the next piece of the puzzle that will lead them to Ian.

Indian Nut Tree.

Upon arrival at Jamaica, Ishmael claims his reward; rather than the offered gold, though, he chooses something different—Temeraire. The one-armed slave consents to go with him, and the two men are put ashore, disappearing into the uninhabited jungle.

The *Artemis* sails around the island to Kingston Harbor, only to discover an unwelcome sight: the *Porpoise* at anchor.

"It's persecution!" Jamie said indignantly. "The filthy boat's pursuing me. Everywhere I go, there it is again!"

Claire's explanation of the man-of-war's presence—naturally the *Porpoise* would be in Kingston Harbor, since she is delivering the new Governor of the island—changes Jamie's attitude significantly, though. Hearing the name of the new Governor, he is first surprised, then pleased; Lord John Grey is a friend of his, he says, and may be of help in locating Ian.

Claire is mildly surprised that he should choose to approach the Governor first, rather than going directly to Rose Hall, but after all, if they meet resistance in their inquiries, it's as well to have a friend in high places. Leaving Fergus to discharge the *Artemis*'s cargo, the Frasers go at once to Jared's plantation, Blue Mountain House, where the overseer and his wife—Mr. and Mrs. MacIver—make them welcome, and help with their preparations.

In search of information, Jamie and Claire attend the new Governor's reception, with Mr. Willoughby in tow. Claire is pleased to see Lord John Grey again, and assumes that his look of shock in the reception line is due to his sight of Jamie, disguised—in full wig, powdered face, and red-heeled shoes—as M. Alexandre de Provac, French immigrant from Martinique. The Reverend Campbell is unexpectedly present at the reception, too; while disapproving mightily of the occa-

sion, he has come to seek information and help in locating his sister Margaret, who has disappeared.

Despite this unsettling encounter, things seem to be progressing well; Mr. Willoughby charms the ladies, Claire is introduced and makes the social rounds, and Jamie eventually retires discreetly to the Governor's office, with Lord John. Following him, Claire is detained by the crowd, and reaches the office a few minutes later—only to find Jamie holding Lord John Grey in fervent embrace.

The Governor's shock at learning that I was Jamie's wife was now at least partially explained; that one glimpse of unguarded, painful yearning had told me exactly how matters stood on his side. Jamie was another question altogether.

He was the Governor of Ardsmuir Prison he had said, casually. And less casually, on another occasion, D'ye ken what men in prison do?

I did know, but I would have sworn on Brianna's head that Jamie didn't; hadn't, couldn't, under any circumstances whatever. At least I would have sworn that before tonight. I closed my eyes, chest heaving, and tried not to think of what I had seen.

Shocked, and trying to make sense of what she has seen, Claire retreats, unseen, and makes her way back through the crowd. Unwilling to face Jamie immediately, she heads for the ladies retiring rooms. What she finds there, though, is not refuge—but murder.

Mina Alcott, a local widow with something of a reputation, lies with her throat cut, blood puddling beneath her head. And beyond the body is a line of footprints, leading toward the open window—

Pelican

the small neat prints of a felt-soled foot, outlined in blood.

The reception dissolves in hue and cry; soldiers are sent in instant pursuit of Mr. Willoughby, the militia is roused, and all the guests are questioned—particularly M. Alexandre de Provac, who appeared to be a close associate of the murderer. Left alone in the Governor's office after her own questioning, Claire is not particularly pleased to be joined by the Governor himself.

Lord John had discovered the fan Claire had dropped in the hall; realizing that she had seen the embrace between himself and Jamie, he does not pretend that matters are not as they are—on his side, at least. But in the ensuing discussion, Claire learns what lies on Jamie's side of the relationship, and exactly why Jamie insisted on coming first to see the Governor.

It was a portrait, an oval miniature, set in a carved frame of some fine-grained dark wood. I looked at the face, and sat down abruptly, my knees gone to water. I was only dimly aware of Grey's face, floating above the desk like a cloud on the horizon, as I picked up the miniature to look at it more closely.

He might have been Bree's brother, was my first thought. The second, coming with the force of a blow to the solar plexus, was "My God in heaven, he is Bree's brother!"

The edgy conversation that follows leaves Claire with various bits of unwelcome information: the fact that Jamie has an illegitimate son, about whom he has not told her, the fact that he shares an intimate history with John Grey—and the fact that she feels an altogether unwilling sympathy with Grey. Both John and Claire love Jamie; both have, in a way, given him

Parekeetoe

a child—and each of them is slightly jealous of the other.

Both jealousy and shock fade, though, when Jamie emerges from a long night of questioning and takes Claire home to Blue Mountain House. Drawn close together by fatigue and the shocking events of the night, they talk intimately, and Jamie confesses to Claire the fact of Willie's existence, showing her a miniature of the boy; the twin of the one John Grey had shown her.

"I was afraid to tell ye," he said, low-voiced. "For fear ye would think that perhaps I'd gone about spawning a dozen bastards . . . for fear ye'd think that I wouldna care for Brianna so much, if ye kent I had another child. But I do care, Claire—a great deal more than I can tell ye." He lifted his head and looked directly at me.

"Will ye forgive me?

"Geneva—Willie's mother—she wanted my body," he said softly, watching the gecko's pulsating sides. "Laoghaire needed my name, and the work of my hands to keep her and her bairns." He turned his head then, dark blue eyes fixed on mine. "John—well," he lifted his shoulders and let them drop. "I

*couldna give him what he wanted—and he
is friend enough not to
ask it.*

*"But how shall I tell ye all these things,"
he said, the lines of his mouth twisting.
"And then say to you—it is only you I have
ever loved? How should you believe me?"*

*The question hung in the air between us,
shimmering like the reflection from the
water below.*

"I'll believe you, if you say it."

*I pressed my own wrist against his, pulse
to pulse, heartbeat to heartbeat.*

"Blood of my blood," I whispered.

*"Bone of my bone." His whisper was deep
and husky. He knelt quite suddenly
before me, and put his folded hands in
mine; the gesture a Highlander makes
when swearing loyalty to his chieftain.*

*"I give ye my spirit," he said, head bent
over our hands.*

*"'Til our life shall be done," I said softly.
"But it isn't done yet, Jamie, is it?"*

*Then he rose and took the shift from me,
and I lay back on the narrow bed naked,
pulled him down to me through the soft yellow light, and took him home, and home,
and home again, and we were neither one
of us alone.*

United again, Jamie and Claire pursue
the search for Ian to Rose Hall. Arriving

at the remote plantation, they are admit-
ted and sit down to wait for Mrs. Abernathy, the owner. Her appearance, though,
comes as more than a surprise, for "Mrs.
Abernathy" is no stranger.

*I took a deep breath, and got my voice
back.*

*"I trust you won't take this the wrong
way," I said, sinking slowly back onto the
wicker sofa, "but why aren't you dead?"*

*She laughed, the silver in her voice as
clear as a young girl's.*

*"Think I should have been, do you? Well,
you're no the first—and I daresay you'll no
be the last to think so, either."*

Geillis Duncan—as the mistress of Rose
Hall was once known—explains her escape
from burning, in the aftermath of the witch
trial at Cranesmuir, twenty-odd years before. Reprieved from execution until after
the birth of her child, Geillis blackmailed
the child's father, Dougal MacKenzie, by
threatening to kill the child, and forced him
to help her escape. The body of an elderly
woman who had died of natural causes was
substituted for her own presumably strangled body, and sent to heaven in a pillar of
fire. Geillis herself had escaped to France,
and come by various paths to her present estate. And what, she asks with avid curiosity,
of Claire?

The two women, once friends, are wary
of each other, but consumed by curiosity.
Alone of all the world, they think, they
have the gift of travel through the stones.
Geilie remarks that she has met "one
other" like them, but is still insistent on
learning all she can of Claire's experiences—the more so when she finds the
photographs of Brianna in Jamie's coat
pocket and realizes the truth; that Claire

has traveled through the stones not once, but *three* times! How was it done?

In return to Claire's vague answers, Geilie reveals the results of her own research; she has concluded that travel through the stones can be controlled—to some degree, at least—by use of gemstones, and to this end, has collected many large and flawless jewels. Her casual reference to using "blood" as a means of protection passes with no more than a slight shudder; Claire knows about the murder of Geillis's first husband, Greg Edgars—and the second, Arthur Duncan.

Claire's heart beats faster at sight of the box Geilie produces, showing off the gems; it is the box that Jamie found on the seals' island—sure proof of a connection between Geillis Duncan and the pirates of the *Bruja;* proof, she thinks, that despite Geilie's denials, Young Ian must be hidden somewhere on the estate.

Geilie firmly denies all knowledge of the boy, though, and hurries them away, claiming that an important visitor is expected. Leaving, the Frasers see the visitor: the Reverend Archibald Campbell. They also realize, once away from Rose Hall, that Geilie has stolen one of Brianna's pictures. Why? A person like Geillis Duncan can have no good intentions, Jamie thinks; at the same time, he is too intent on finding his nephew to spend much time in worry. Convinced from his investigations that Young Ian is concealed in a cellar beneath the sugar refinery on the estate, Jamie lays his plans for rescue.

A few days later, the Frasers and several of Jamie's Scottish smugglers sail quietly up the Yallahs River toward Rose Hall, in a small ship provided by Lord John Grey.

Arriving at night, they mean to steal ashore, attack the refinery by surprise, and retrieve Young Ian—liberating any of the other Scottish captives in the process.

Jamie leaves Claire near the boat, armed with a pistol and with strict instructions to stay put and wait for them. However, within minutes of his departure, Claire sees a tall, thin shadow in the window of Rose Hall; it can't possibly be Geilie, but may very well be Young Ian. The men are already too far away to catch; she will have to go and see herself. Creeping up onto the veranda, Claire finds the front door standing open, and noises of someone in the study. She goes quietly in, hoping to find Young Ian, but instead discovers that the owner of the shadow is the Reverend Campbell. Geillis herself is nowhere to be found; the Reverend complains that she has disappeared, leaving him alone.

In the ensuing confrontation, a number of things are revealed, including the fact that the Reverend is convinced that Jamie was responsible for the traumatic events that stole his sister's wits; Jamie, he thinks, was "the Hieland man" whom his sister left her home to find, in the midst of the Rising. Despite Claire's assurances that Margaret's lover was in fact a friend of Jamie's, Ewan Cameron, the Reverend is adamant in his hate.

This is sufficiently disturbing to Claire. Somewhat more disturbing is the knowledge that Geillis Duncan has been in correspondence with the Reverend as a scholar of Celtic prophecies, with particular reference to the "Fraser Prophecy," a mysterious prediction left by the Brahan Seer, to the effect that a ruler "of Lovat's line" will one day lead Scotland.

Obsessed as Geillis Duncan is with the rulers of Scotland, this knowledge gives Claire a sickening feeling that she knows where Geilie might have gone—at least in general terms. "Lovat's line" consists of the descendants of Simon, Lord Lovat, chief of clan Fraser, who was executed following the Rising. While Lovat left a number of children, the direct line died out in the 1800s—or so Geilie thought, until she saw the pictures of Brianna, and realized that Lovat did indeed have a direct descendant, living in the future.

Whether Geilie wishes to find Brianna for some sinister purpose, or only to use her photograph as an anchor point for her travel through the stones, the conclusion that the witch of Rose Hall is embarked on a journey to the future seems inescapable.

Claire's questions are interrupted, though, by the unexpected appearance of Mr. Willoughby. Considerably the worse for wear from days of hiding in the jungle, the Chinese man has not emerged to seek assistance from Claire— but to confront the Reverend.

"Most holy fella," he said, and his voice held a tone I had never heard in him before; an ugly taunting note.

The Reverend whirled, so quickly that his elbow knocked against a vase; water and yellow roses cascaded over the rosewood desk, soaking the papers. The Reverend gave a cry of rage, and snatched the papers from the flood, shaking them frantically to remove the water before the ink should run.

"See what ye've done, ye wicked, murdering heathen!"

Mr. Willoughby laughed. Not his usual high giggle, but a low chuckle. It didn't sound at all amused.

"I murdering?" He shook his head slowly back and forth, eyes fixed on the Reverend. "Not me, holy fella. Is you, murderer."

"Begone, fellow," Campbell said coldly. "You should know better than to enter a lady's house."

"I know you." The Chinaman's voice was low and even, his gaze unwavering. "I see you. See you in red room, with the woman who laughs. See you too with stinking whores, in Scotland." Very slowly, he lifted his hand to his throat and drew it across, precise as a blade. "You kill pretty often, holy fella, I think."

In the confrontation that follows, the Reverend draws a case knife, and is killed by Mr. Willoughby, who strikes him on the head with the bag containing his heavy jade "healthy balls."

Yi Tien Cho disappears into the Caribbean night, and Claire, unable to stay in the room with Campbell's body, goes upstairs to Geilie's workroom, looking for clues as to her whereabouts—or Ian's. What she finds there is sinister: the stolen photograph of Brianna, in the center of a charred pentacle. Is Geilie intending merely to use the image as a focus for her time travel—or has she some more threatening motive? In either case, plainly the witch of Rose Hall has left, and Claire needs to find Jamie, as soon as possible.

Stumbling through the blackness outside, Claire returns to the shore, hoping to

find Jamie and his men near the boat. Instead, she meets with something else—a crocodile, from which she is rescued by several slaves, who kill the beast. Given the stress of recent events, Claire is only mildly taken aback to find that the leader of the slaves is Ishmael—the man rescued from the *Bruja;* the slave kidnapped—from Rose Hall, evidently—by the pirates.

The connection between the *Bruja* and Rose Hall is more or less clear; evidently the pirate captain had retrieved and delivered the seals' treasure for Geillis, along with a consignment of young Scottish boys. Whether as part of the agreed-upon price, or only by whim, the *Bruja* had taken Ishmael—Geilie's cook—as the ship departed. Why, though, has he come back?

The answer to that question emerges quickly. Half-fainting, Claire is taken to one of the slave huts to recover from her encounter with the crocodile, and wakes to find a voodoo ceremony beginning—featuring an oracle: the missing Margaret Campbell.

This is why Ishmael has come back; to retrieve his oracle, the thing that gives him power over the other slaves. For an oracle Margaret Campbell truly is; as Claire listens in horrified fascination, she hears the *loas*—the spirits of the dead, the avatars of voodoo deities—speak through the lips of the Scottish woman. Among the *loas* summoned is that of Bouassa, a famous ma-

roon, who raised a slave rebellion—and died for it, tortured to death. Ishmael asks the *loa*'s blessing on some enterprise—and Bouassa grants it, with a bitter laugh.

Her mouth closed, and her eyes resumed their vacant stare, but the men weren't noticing. An excited chatter erupted from them, to be hushed by Ishmael, with a significant glance at me. Abruptly quiet, they moved away, still muttering, glancing at me as they went.

Ishmael closed his eyes as the last man left the clearing, and his shoulders sagged. I felt a trifle drained myself.

"What—" I began, and then stopped. Across the fire, a man had stepped from the shelter of the sugarcane. Jamie, tall as the cane itself, with the dying fire staining shirt and face as red as his hair.

He raised a finger to his lips, and I nodded. I gathered my feet cautiously beneath me, picking up my stained skirt in one hand. I could be up, past the fire, and into the cane with him before Ishmael could reach me. But Margaret?

I hesitated, turned to look at her, and saw that her face had come alive once again. It was lifted, eager, lips parted and shining eyes narrowed so that they seemed slightly slanted, as she stared across the fire.

"Daddy?" said Brianna's voice beside me.

Shocked and mesmerized, Claire and Jamie listen to the voice of their daughter, speaking through Margaret Campbell's blood-smeared lips. *"Don't let Mama go alone,"* she tells Jamie. *"Go with her."*

But go where? With the vanishing of the *loa,* Ishmael sends Margaret away in the care of his women, and tells Jamie and Claire to leave themselves, at once. Jamie informs him that they are going nowhere without Ian.

Ishmael's brows went up, compressing the three vertical scars between them.

"Huh," he said again. "You forget that boy; he be gone."

"Gone where?" Jamie asked sharply.

The narrow head tilted to one side, as Ishmael looked him over carefully.

"Gone with the Maggot, mon," he said. "And where she go, you don' be going. That boy gone, mon," he said again, with finality. "You leave, too, you a wise man."

Pressed for the whereabouts of Mrs. Abernathy (the Maggot) and Ian, Ishmael reluctantly reveals that they have gone to Abandawe—a name Claire recognizes. It is a secret cave on the island of Hispaniola, carved by an underground river—a magic place, Ishmael assures them.

"You ain' gone do the magic, what the Maggot do. That magic kill her, sure, but it kill you, too." He gestured behind him, toward the empty bench. "You hear Bouassa speak? He say the Maggot die, three days. She taken the boy, he die. You go follow them, mon, you die, too, sure."

Despite this chilling warning, there is no choice; they must go to Abandawe, and hope they are not too late.

Jamie turned, then stopped suddenly, and I whirled about to see what he had seen. There were lights in Rose Hall now. Torchlight, flickering behind the windows, upstairs and down. As we watched, a surly glow began to swell in the windows of the secret workroom on the second floor.

"It's past time to go," Jamie said. He seized my hand and we went quickly, diving into the dark rustle of the canes, fleeing through air suddenly thick with the smell of burning sugar.

Leaving the scene of the crocodile's fire, they sail downriver with their helpers, leaving in their wake a bloody slave uprising. Rose Hall is burning, and the lights of distant fires at other plantations wink into life against the dark mountains.

The trip to Hispaniola is undertaken at once, leaving the confusion of Jamaica, its slave risings and manhunts, behind. Arriving on Hispaniola with Lawrence Stern and the Scottish smugglers, Jamie and Claire take Stern as a guide to the hidden cave of Abandawe, leaving the others to sail a short distance away in order to avoid attracting attention.

Outside the cave, Claire hears the sound of standing stones, of a time passage, and has a sudden vision of Geillis Duncan, eyes green and gleaming in sardonic welcome. The Frasers leave Stern on guard outside the cave, and go down into darkness, after the witch and her hostage.

They are in time—but barely; Geillis is completing her elaborate preparations, gemstones laid out in a pentagram of protection, a glittering trail of diamond dust joining the points of her pentacle—and Ian, bound and gagged, laid across the pattern, ready for sacrifice.

Neither bargaining nor confrontation is of any use; telling Claire that she will have to "take the girl" but will leave her the man, Geilie sprinkles Ian with brandy, holding Jamie and Claire at bay with a loaded pistol. Jamie lunges at her, and she fires; Jamie drops, his face a mask of blood.

Moved beyond any thought of self-preservation, Claire seizes the ceremonial axe Geillis has brought for her sacrifice— and swings.

The shock of it echoed up my arm, and I let go, my fingers numbed. I stood quite still, not even moving when she staggered toward me.

Blood in firelight is black, not red.

She took one blind step forward and fell, all her muscles gone limp, making no attempt to save herself. The last I saw of her face was her eyes; set wide, beautiful as gemstones, a green water-clear and faceted with the knowledge of death.

Jamie is not dead, as Claire feared. He is wounded, but able to walk. With Young Ian, they make their stumbling way back out through the cave's labyrinth, pursued by a rising wind that seems to make the cave behind them breathe.

Finding Lawrence outside, they find their way through the island's jungles, toward the beach where they mean to rendezvous with their friends. Along the way, Young Ian tells them what little he knows of his own experience; Geillis Duncan apparently had been hunting a mythical stone "that grows in the innards of a boy." One catch, though; the boy must be a virgin, unsullied by carnal touch.

Thanks to his earlier experiences in Edinburgh, Ian no longer qualified for this distinction—a failing that had saved his life, so far. A thrifty Scot, though, Geillis saw no reason for waste; first taking him to her bed, she had then saved him for later use as a sacrifice to protect her travel.

AT THE BEACH, the Frasers find not only their friends, but a scene of desperate pursuit; the rebellious slaves of the Yallahs River had swarmed aboard the ship *Bruja,* taking it for their escape. Succeeding in reaching the open sea, they were spied— and pursued—by the *Porpoise,* on watch for any such attempt.

Unskilled in navigation and seamanship, the slaves have managed to reach Hispaniola, but panicked by the *Porpoise's* pursuit, have run the *Bruja* aground. The man-of-war is shelling the wreck and its fugitives; fleeing slaves disappear into the jungle, others are blown to bloody fragments on the sand.

The melee is taking place some distance from the Frasers' rendezvous, but they cannot escape unseen. Their only hope is to run for it, hoping that the *Porpoise* will be delayed sufficiently by its engagement to allow them to get away. Too late, though; the *Bruja* has been destroyed, and the man-of-war seeks other prey.

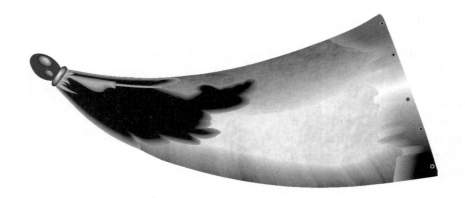

Fleeing before a rising wind, the smaller boat is more agile, and manages to stay ahead of the *Porpoise* for some time. They cannot outrun the man-of-war, though; especially with the increased wind filling the big ship's sails. More than bad weather is in store; the greenish sky and howling wind portend a Caribbean hurricane. In the maelstrom, the *Porpoise* is swamped; losing her topmast, she heels over and is dragged down, with the loss of all hands.

The smaller boat does not escape unscathed, though; coming through the hurricane, she limps along with a damaged superstructure. A broken spar falls from above, knocking Claire overboard, unconscious. She comes to herself, choking and gagging, with Jamie supporting her, clinging to a bit of drifting spar. Injured, and drifting in and out of consciousness, Claire has no idea where they are, and no means of saving herself—save Jamie's grip on her hands.

The wave subsided and the wood rose slightly, bringing my nose above water. I breathed, and my vision cleared slightly. A foot away was the face of Jamie Fraser, hair plastered to his head, wet features contorted against the spray.

"Hold on!" he roared. "Hold on, God damn you!"

I smiled gently, barely hearing him. The sense of great peace was lifting me, carrying me beyond the noise and chaos. There was no more pain. Nothing mattered. Another wave washed over me, and this time I forgot to hold my breath.

The choking sensation roused me briefly, long enough to see the flash of terror in Jamie's eyes. Then my vision went dark again.

"Damn you, Sassenach!" his voice said, from a very great distance. His voice was choked with passion. "Damn you! I swear if ye die on me, I'll **kill** *you!"*

Fortunately, Claire's waking impression that she is in fact dead is quickly dispelled; regaining consciousness in a white room filled with light, she finds Jamie by her side. They have been washed ashore, where they were found and rescued, taken to a nearby house and cared for. But where are they?

The appearance of their hostess, Mrs. Olivier, doesn't help; an Englishwoman married to a Frenchman, she tells them they are on a plantation called Les Perles. But is Les Perles on Martinique? On Jamaica or one of the other English-owned islands, where they will be in danger from the Crown? On St. Thomas, on the Dutch-owned Eleuthera?

Mrs. Olivier kindly inquires what their names might be, causing Jamie and Claire to exchange cautious glances; just *where* they are will determine *who* they are—that is, which island they are on will determine which of Jamie's various identities will be safest. But—

Mrs. Olivier smiled indulgently. "You are not on an island at all. You are on the mainland; in the Colony of Georgia."

"Georgia," Jamie said. "America?" He sounded slightly stunned, and no wonder. We had been blown at least six hundred miles by the storm.

"America," I said softly. "The New World." The pulse beneath my fingers had quickened, echoing my own. A new world. Refuge. Freedom.

"Yes," said Mrs. Olivier, plainly having no idea what the news meant to us, but still smiling kindly from one to the other. "It is America."

Jamie straightened his shoulders and smiled back at her. The clean bright air stirred his hair like kindling flames.

"In that case, ma'am," he said, "my name is Jamie Fraser." He looked then at me, eyes blue and brilliant as the sky behind him, and his heart beat strong in the palm of my hand.

"And this is Claire," he said. "My wife."

THE END

DRUMS OF AUTUMN

 I heard the drums long before they came in sight. The beating echoed in the pit of my stomach, as though I too were hollow. I saw heads turn as the people fell silent, looking up the stretch of East Bay Street, where it ran from the half-built skeleton of the new Customs House toward White Point Gardens.

The drums are attending a procession to the gallows. Among the spectators are Claire and Jamie Fraser, there not from morbid curiosity, but as moral support for one of the condemned—Gavin Hayes, who was once a fellow prisoner with Jamie in Ardsmuir Prison, in Scotland. Transported as a felon and later released from indenture, Gavin has fallen afoul of the English Crown for the last time.

The attention of the onlookers is drawn from the noose and its dangling burden by something more exciting; another of the condemned prisoners has seized the distraction of Gavin's death to make a run for his life, dodging away among the palmettos and the crowds on the thronged seafront.

With all of Charleston roused in the hunt for the escaped man, circumstances seem too dangerous for the Frasers to linger. Jamie's association with a condemned man is known, and he wants to invite no official curiosity—not with what the Frasers carry. Shipwrecked in Georgia two months before, they arrived in the New World with nothing save the remnants of their clothing—and a fortune in gemstones, salvaged from the cave of Abandawe on Hispaniola.

While the Frasers are technically wealthy, the gems "might be beach pebbles, for all the good they were to us," as Claire notes. Trade in the Colonies is conducted mostly by means of barter; there are few merchants or bankers in the South with the available capital to turn the Frasers' fortune into money. With no more than a few shillings in ready cash, they must decide whether to stay in Charleston to look for a buyer, or head north immediately, toward the Cape Fear region of North Carolina, where there are many Highland immigrants—and where Jamie has kinfolk.

Deciding that the path of wisdom lies north, the Frasers and their companions—Jamie's nephew Ian, his French foster son, Fergus, and his friend Duncan Innes—pause only long enough to bury Gavin Hayes. Coming out of the churchyard at night, though, they are startled to find a stowaway in their wagon: the Irish prisoner who fled the gallows earlier in the day.

Introducing himself as Stephen Bonnet, the man begs their mercy and their help to escape the city. The roads out will be pa-

trolled, he says; will Jamie help him, for the sake of Gavin Hayes, who was his friend as well?

Jamie is skeptical; Bonnet is personable, but as Jamie later tells Claire privately, *"The Crown doesna* always *hang the wrong man; most of those at the end of a rope deserve to be there."* Duncan is moved by drink and sentiment, though, and urges Jamie to help the Irishman, for Gavin's sake. With some reluctance, Jamie agrees, and they smuggle Bonnet out of the city, parting from him in the dark near a distant creek, where he plans to meet with unknown associates.

Seeking solitude, Jamie and Claire find respite from the day's adventures on the banks of the creek, and amid speculations about their uncertain future in this strange new land, find a temporary comfort in each other's arms.

MEANWHILE, BACK IN the future . . .

A phone rings in the dark in Boston, awakening Brianna Randall. Roger Wakefield is calling from Scotland with news and a question: He will be in Boston next month for a historical conference; does she want to see him?

The question is hesitantly asked, but promptly answered. Despite his unanswered letters, Roger has been much on Brianna's mind—yes, she wants very much to see him. Hanging up with a pounding heart, Brianna is unable to go back to sleep. Roger is her chief link with the past; a past she is at once unable to forget and unwilling to contemplate.

Roger shared with her the morning when her mother disappeared forever through the stone circle on Craigh na Dun; Roger, too, hears the stones. In the aftermath of that shocking bereavement, she found herself falling in love with Roger—and then tore away, both from necessity and from doubt. Her mother had confided her to Roger's care; but Brianna would not bind him to her with the strands of obligation. If it were something more than that, though . . .

If there might be a future for them . . . and that was what she couldn't write to him, because how could she say it without sounding both presumptuous and idiotic?

"Go away, so you can come back and do it right," she murmured, and made a face at the words.

But now Roger *is* coming back—with luck, to do it right.

Their first sight of each other is enough to prove that the attraction still exists; a week spent in each other's company merely reinforces the conviction, while still not solving their basic problem. Roger is a don at Oxford, Brianna still at university. Beyond the temporary separation imposed by their careers, Roger wonders whether they can find a way to be together, given the basic differences in their outlooks.

Might there be common ground for them, a historian and an engineer? He facing backward to the mysteries of the past, she to the future and its dazzling gleam?

Then the room relaxed in cheers and babbling, and she turned in his arms to kiss him hard and cling to him, and he thought perhaps it didn't matter that they faced in opposite directions—so long as they faced each other.

IN 1767, CLAIRE AND JAMIE and their small party of companions have reached Wilmington, North Carolina. Given the choice of trudging inland for two hundred miles, or making the journey up the Cape Fear River by boat, Jamie opts reluctantly for the faster journey over water, leaving Duncan to follow with the wagon, under the guidance of John Quincy Myers, a mountain man and local guide whom Claire encounters in the street in Wilmington.

Myers informs Jamie that Jamie's uncle by marriage, Hector Cameron, has died within the last year—but that his aunt Jocasta still lives at River Run, a plantation that lies north of Cross Creek. Deducing Claire's expertise at healing, Myers's attention then turns to his own difficulties.

"Big purple thing," he explained to me, fumbling his loosened thong. "Almost as big as one o' my balls. You don't think it might could be as I've decided sudden-like to grow an extry, do you?"

"Well, no," I said, biting my lip. "I really doubt it." He moved very slowly, but had almost got the knot in his thong undone; people in the street were beginning to pause, staring.

"Please don't trouble yourself," I said. "I do believe I know what that is—it's an inguinal hernia."

Unable to deal adequately with Mr. Myers's medical problems in Wilmington, Claire promises to see what she can do surgically at a later date, and escapes to keep a date for dinner with the Governor of the

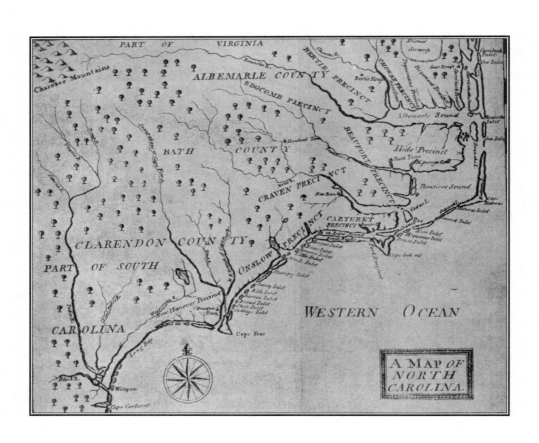

Colony. Taking advantage of a distant family connection, Jamie has wangled the invitation in the hope of finding a buyer for one of their gemstones; he has no desire to present himself at his aunt's door in rags.

The dinner is successful in more ways than one; another of the guests, Baron Penzler, agrees to buy a ruby, thus providing the Frasers with much-needed capital—money both to supply their own needs, and to send back to Scotland, in partial payment of Jamie's promise to Laoghaire, the woman he had (reluctantly) married, under the conviction that Claire was lost to him forever.

Beyond the sale of the stone, though, the dinner party results in another interesting—and alarming—development. Governor Tryon, new to the Colony, but an able administrator, is actively seeking "men of worth" to settle the dangerous and unexploited backcountry of the Colony, by taking land grants from the Crown and sponsoring the settlement of the land by emigrants. Tryon offers Jamie such a grant, putting aside the minor consideration that Jamie is a Catholic—and as such, technically ineligible; only white male Protestants are allowed to hold land grants.

"The offer is one of considerable interest," Jamie said formally. "I must point out, however, that I am not a Protestant, nor are most of my kinsmen."

The Governor pursed his lips in deprecation, lifting one brow.

"You are neither a Jew nor a Negro. I may speak as one gentleman to another, may I not? In all frankness, Mr. Fraser, there is the law, and then there is what is done." He raised his glass with a small smile, setting the hook. "And I

am convinced that you understand that as well as I do."

"Possibly better," Jamie murmured, with a polite smile.

Initially bewildered by the alacrity of the Governor's offer, Claire quickly grasps Jamie's explanation of Tryon's reasoning: Jamie is closely connected with the Camerons, a wealthy and influential family in the Colony. At the same time, Jamie himself is an "incomer," with no existing ties or loyalties—save to the Governor, who is offering him land. Tryon knows Jamie for a soldier, and a man accustomed to command; who better to settle a part of the colony alive with unrest and the discontented agitations of the Regulators, an association of backcountry men with strong—and often violent—objections to the capricious and sometimes illegal behavior of the Crown's appointees?

"The trouble is damped down but not settled," Jamie said, shrugging. "And damp powder may smolder for a long time, Sassenach, but once it catches, it goes off with an almighty bang."

Would Tryon think it worth the investment, to buy the loyalty and obligation of an experienced soldier, himself in turn commanding the loyalty and service of the men under his sponsorship, all settled in a remote and troublesome area of the colony?

I would myself have called the prospect cheap, at the cost of a hundred pounds and a few measly acres of the King's land. His Majesty had quite a lot of it, after all.

The proposal bears little risk for Tryon; if Jamie doesn't perform as the Governor desires, Tryon need only "discover" Jamie's Catholicism, and a Royal court would revoke the grant.

The risk to Jamie is substantial—even more than he himself realizes, or so Claire fears. She has seen his gravestone in Scotland; presumably this means he will die there. So long as he remains in the New World, then, he must be safe? Intriguing as the Governor's proposal is, she feels it's not worth the risk of losing Jamie. If he goes to Scotland to raise a band of emigrants to settle his land, he may never come back.

At the same time, the prospect is undeniably tempting; to be once again what he once was—a laird, with land and tenants to care for and be sustained by. Claire decides to keep her silence—for now.

If Jamie is tempted, he is also cautious. He wishes to see the land the Governor proposes to give him, and assess its prospects before making a decision. Besides, he is anxious to visit his aunt Jocasta—his mother's widowed sister, the last survivor of the MacKenzies of Leoch. Jocasta Cameron may be able to tell him more of conditions in the Colony, and give him enough information to decide on his course of action.

Jocasta Cameron's estate, River Run, lies some two hundred miles north of Wilmington. Gritting his teeth, Jamie agrees to make the journey by river—much faster than the overland route. His dread of seasickness fades as the *Sally Ann* makes its way up the Cape Fear—but *mal de mer* is not the only danger on the river.

Aligator

The Fraser party is wakened at dawn by an unwelcome intrusion: river pirates, led by their erstwhile acquaintance, Stephen Bonnet. Bonnet's goal is the gems that they carry—but one of his associates spies Claire's wedding rings, and tries to take them by force. Claire succeeds in swallowing her silver ring and thus preserving it, but the gold band that once linked her to Frank Randall is gone.

Arriving before his only kinswoman penniless and ragged with travel is galling to Jamie's pride, but they now have little choice. As it is, Jocasta's welcome is more than warm—and their raggedness passes unremarked, for Jocasta Cameron is blind.

The Widow Cameron greets her long-lost nephew with joy, making him welcome to her house and lands. While some part of her generosity is undoubtedly due to family feeling, Claire quickly realizes that Jocasta is also the last of the MacKenzies of Leoch—a family *"charming as the larks in the field—but sly as foxes with it,"* as Jamie once remarked of his kin.

Jocasta's ulterior motives are slowly revealed. Widowed and blind, she must depend on the help of two men to run her large and thriving plantation: Ulysses, the black butler who serves as her eyes and runs her household, and Byrnes, the white overseer who acts as her hands, running the slaves, who do the profitable work of timbering and producing the valuable stores of turpentine, tar, pitch, and spars that River Run sells to the Royal Navy. Ulysses is a devoted and able servant; Byrnes is a violent, drunken sot, whose ineptitude has jeopardized the lucrative Naval contracts on which River Run depends.

A terrible incident at the sawmill demonstrates Byrnes's unfitness; an altercation with one of the slaves ends with the slave attempting to remove Byrnes's head with a timber knife. Succeeding only in depriving the overseer of an ear, the slave is automatically condemned to death under the Colony's law of bloodshed; any slave who sheds the blood of a white person must die, regardless of circumstance.

Farquard Campbell, another plantation owner, has come in haste, to tell Jocasta what has happened, and to summon Jamie. As Jocasta's nearest male relative, neither Jocasta, Campbell—nor Jamie himself—questions his responsibility to go and deal with the situation. Claire, though, has considerable reservations about the whole affair.

"Execution? Do you mean to say you intend to execute a man without even knowing what he's done?" In my agitation, I had knocked Jocasta's basket of yarn over. Little balls of colored wool ran everywhere, bouncing on the carpet.

"I do know what's he done, Mrs. Fraser!" Campbell lifted his chin, his color high, but with an obvious effort, swallowed his impatience.

"Your pardon, ma'am. I know you are newly come here; you will find some of our ways difficult and even barbarous, but—"

"Too right I find them barbarous! What kind of law is it that condemns a man—"

"A slave—"

"A man! Condemns him without a trial, without even an investigation? What sort of law is that?"

"A bad one, madame!" he snapped. "But it is still the law, and I am charged with its fulfillment. Mr. Fraser, are you ready?" He clapped the hat on his head and turned to Jamie.

Arriving at the sawmill, the Frasers find they are too late, a lynching has already

Beaver

taken place. Jamie goes at once to deal with Byrnes and his assistants; Claire's attention is for the gruesomely injured slave.

Hastily assessing the situation, she realizes that while the man is terribly injured, there is a faint possibility that she might save his life—at least temporarily.

No one was paying any attention to the true object of the discussion. Only seconds had passed—but I had only seconds more to act. I placed a hand on Jamie's arm, pulling his attention away from the debate.

"If I save him, will they let him live?" I asked him, under my breath.

His eyes flicked from one to another of the men behind me, weighing the possibilities.

"No," he said softly. His eyes met mine, dark with understanding. His shoulders straightened slightly, and he laid the pistol across his thighs. I could not help him make his choice; he could not help with mine—but he would defend me, whichever choice I made.

"Give me the third bottle from the left, second row," I said.

The third bottle from the left contains aconite, a quick and deadly poison.

One-fiftieth grain will kill a sparrow in a few seconds. One-tenth grain, a rabbit in five minutes . . . I tried to hear nothing, feel nothing, know nothing but the jerky beat beneath my fingers. I tried with all my might to shut out the voices overhead, the murmur nearby, the heat and dust and stink of blood, to forget where I was, and what I was doing.

Claire returns to River Run with Jamie, troubled not only by the experience at the sawmill but by her growing realization that Jamie's bonds of kinship make him indeed a part of this society, with all its capacity for injustice, violence, and terror, as well as its promises of wealth and adventure. What Farquard Campbell has told them is true; Jocasta needs a man to deal with the harsh exigencies of the plantation's affairs—and Jamie is, by blood and obligation—the natural choice.

To complicate matters further, Lieutenant Wolff, who negotiates the quarterly Naval contracts, has offered marriage to Jocasta—not, as she tartly observes, from desire of her person, but rather in order to become master of River Run. So far, she has evaded the Lieutenant's attempts, with the help of her old friend Farquard Camp-

Saffafras Tree.

bell—but the Lieutenant is pressing hard, pointing out that Jocasta cannot run the plantation without a man, and threatening loss of the valuable Naval contracts.

Caught in this delicate situation, Jocasta perceives Jamie's arrival as the answer to prayer—and soon forms a plan. She will have a great party, she declares, to make her nephew and his wife known to the Scottish community of Cape Fear. To this end, every influential person in the area is summoned to River Run, and Claire and Jamie are outfitted with great splendor—though not without arousing some suspicions.

Jamie clearly suspects that Jocasta is up to something; he tells Claire to stay alert, ready to create a diversion, should he signal to her during the dinner. However, Jocasta's arrival forestalls his explanation, leaving Claire alert—but not knowing why.

In the event, a diversion is provided, but not by Claire; the dinner party is interrupted by the dramatic arrival of Duncan Innes with John Quincy Myers—the mountain man having achieved a majestic state of drunkenness in anticipation of Claire's performing surgery on his hernia. Faced with the prostrate form of her prospective patient, Claire is dubious about the wisdom of doing surgery with the assistance of whisky-induced anesthesia, but is persuaded. As Jamie observes, *"He may ne'er have the nerve or the money to get that drunk again."*

Performing a hernia repair on the dinner table, before the cream of Cape Fear society, may possibly not have been precisely what Jocasta Cameron had in mind by way of presenting her new niece socially, but it does make an impression—and effectively, if only temporarily, prevents the announce-

Wild Turkey

ment of whatever scheme Jocasta may have had in mind herself.

That scheme is shortly revealed; Jamie takes Claire outside to talk, leaving the unconscious Mr. Myers recovering in the care of a slave. The butler, Ulysses, had told Jamie what his mistress intended, just before dinner; with Jamie garbed in his dead uncle's Highland dress, and sitting in Hector Cameron's place at the head of the table, Jocasta meant to rise and announce before the assembled company that she was making Jamie her heir—laird of River Run.

The prospect is glittering . . . but also daunting. River Run's prosperity depends on the work of slaves, and Claire recoils from the prospect of being a slave owner—the more so when Jamie explains that they could not legally free the slaves of River Run, even after Jocasta's death; in fear of an armed uprising, the North Carolina As-

sembly allows slaves to be manumitted only one at a time, and only by approval of the Assembly.

Claire doesn't see how she can possibly live as a slave owner, but keeps quiet for the moment, unwilling to impose her own moral concerns on Jamie as he wrestles with the problem. He is, however, quite aware of her reservations—and has his own doubts about Jocasta's offer, as well.

"Her husband is dead. Whether she was fond of him or no, she is mistress here now, with none to answer to. And she enjoys the taste of power too well to spit it out."

He was plainly correct in this assessment of Jocasta Cameron's character, and therein lay the key to her plan. She needed a man; someone to go into those places she could not go, to deal with the Navy, to handle the chores of a large estate that she could not manage because of her blindness.

At the same time, she patently did not want a husband; someone who would usurp her power and dictate to her. Had he not been a slave, Ulysses could have acted for her—but while he could be her eyes and ears, he could not be her hands.

No, Jamie was the perfect choice; a strong, competent man, able to command respect among peers, compel obedience in subordinates. One knowledgeable in the management of land and men. Furthermore, a man bound to her by kinship and obligation, there to do her bidding—but essentially powerless.

Reaching the edge of the river, Jamie helps Claire into a small boat and rows up to the creek where the sawmill stands—taking a troubled survey of the kingdom he is invited to rule, and reminding both himself and Claire of the difficulties that rule entails.

Disembarking at the sawmill, the Frasers find it standing eerie in the darkness, disquieting with the memory of blood. The mill is haunted by more than ghosts, though, and the smell of blood is real. A dying girl lies in the overseer's bed, evidently the victim of a botched abortion . . . or of deliberate murder.

Investigations into the girl's identity and her presence reveal that she is an army laundress, without family or connections. The public assumption is that, finding herself inconveniently with child, she would have sought to rid herself of the burden—but alone, or with someone's help?

A step ahead of the investigation, Claire deduces the presence of a slave-woman known for her medical skills—a woman named Pollyanne, who has fled from her shack to hide in the woods, obviously afraid that she will be blamed for the death of the girl—and die in turn, a victim of the bloodshed law.

Jamie's efforts to establish the girl's identity take him into Cross Creek, to the garrison headquarters there, where he meets an old enemy—Sergeant Murchison, who, with his twin brother, was once an officer at Ardsmuir Prison. The Sergeant is no more pleased by the meeting than is Jamie, and his temper grows no better when he finds what errand has brought the Frasers to his office.

Returning from this acrimonious encounter, the Frasers discover that Duncan and Ian have succeeded in finding the slave-woman Pollyanne, whom they have hidden in a remote tobacco barn. Still, there is an urgent need to smuggle her away from the district, and Myers, nearly recovered from his public surgery, suggests a plan: He has friends among the Tuscarora tribe, and is sure that the Indians would accept the woman into one of their villages, where she would be safe.

Myers's plan offers not only safety for Pollyanne, but advantages for Jamie—he can remove himself from his aunt's scheming long enough to make up his own mind without pressure, he can avoid the antagonistic presence of Sergeant Murchison—and in the process of delivering Pollyanne to her refuge, he can survey the mountainous backcountry land offered to him by Governor Tryon, in order to weigh the possibilities afforded.

A small expedition accordingly sets off for the mountains: Myers, Pollyanne, Jamie, Claire—and Young Ian, who is keen to see adventure and Red Indians. Duncan remains behind to help Jocasta with the business of the estate.

Once into the mountains, the party separates; Myers and Young Ian make their way into the Tuscarora's territory, to deliver Pollyanne, while Claire and Jamie make their way upward into the mountains.

As they travel, Claire is torn between joy in Jamie's evident delight—he is at home in the free air of the mountains, as he is nowhere else—and fear of what that joy might mean. She has seen his tombstone in Scotland; so long as he stays in America, she thinks, he will be safe. But if he should decide to take up the Governor's offer, he will need men to settle the land—and where else should he get them, save in Scotland?

At last, they come to a high ridge, covered in wild strawberries, which Jamie takes as a sign. The strawberry plant is the emblem of clan Fraser—the white flower for courage, green leaves for constancy, and the fruit for passion, shaped like a heart. It is a good place, one that speaks to the Highlander. What would she think? Jamie asks. Would she be willing to settle here with him? Plant crops, raise beasts, build a cabin—establish their new life here, high in the mountains, free of the obligations and uncertainties of life in the valley?

Claire sees the hope and the joy in him, but cannot share it for fear. At last, she breaks down and confides what she fears; that if he goes to Scotland to raise men for the land, he will die there.

Apprised of her fears, Jamie is incredulous. How, he demands, does she expect him to go to Scotland and raise men—walking on the water? While they have some capital now, from the sale of one stone, they are a long way from rich. Besides, he adds reassuringly, he does not in-

tend to go to Scotland. *If* he should be so foolhardy as to take up the Governor's invitation, he would instead seek out the men of Ardsmuir—his men, transported to the Colonies.

And why, Claire demands, should these men follow him? Those who survived will have worked out their indenturement; many will have begun new lives. Why should they abandon everything, risk everything, to follow him?

"You did, Sassenach," he said.

IN THE INVERNESS of 1969, Roger Wakefield is waiting impatiently for the arrival of Brianna. Beyond the joy of seeing her again, there is an extra dimension to his anticipation; he means to ask her to marry him.

The arrival of the postman with a forwarded letter for Brianna exposes a certain complication, though; Brianna has—without telling Roger—begun searching the historical record for any mention of her parents. Roger is at first hurt that she didn't tell him, but understands her ambivalence; the fear of finding out versus the fear of never knowing. In fact, he may be the only person in the world who truly does understand.

He will help her, he says. Beyond a simple desire to assist the girl he loves lies both personal curiosity and a certain personal concern; he fears that she cannot or will not give herself fully to a life with him in the present, if her questions of the past remain unanswered.

The two continue with the long job of clearing up the Reverend Wakefield's effects, and the business of dismantling his childhood home increases Roger's longing for a home and family of his own—and for Brianna as his wife, always by his side. For her part, Brianna makes it clear that she wants him, too, and so emboldened, Roger asks her to marry him as they walk home from the midnight services on Christmas Eve.

"I want you, Brianna," he said softly. "I cannot be saying it plainer than that. I love you. Will you marry me?"

She didn't say anything, but her face changed, like water when a stone is thrown into it. He could see it plainly as his own reflection in the bleakness of a tarn.

"You didn't want me to say that." The fog had settled in his chest; he was breathing

ice, crystal needles piercing heart and lungs. "You didn't want to hear it, did you?"

She shook her head, wordless.

"Aye. Well." With an effort, he let go her hand. "That's all right," he said, surprised at the calmness in his voice. "You'll not be worried about it, aye?"

Brianna *is* worried about it, though; what worries her is not doubt of her feelings for Roger, nor his for her—what troubles her is the possibility that they won't last. They can't be wed at once, she points out; she has another year of schooling, Roger has his position at the university to think of. What if something were to happen in the meantime, what if one of them was to meet someone else?

She leaned against the lamppost, hands behind her, and met his eyes directly. "I think I love you, too."

He didn't realize he had been holding his breath until he let it out.

"Ah. You do." The water had condensed in his hair, and icy trickles were running down his neck. "Mmphm. Aye, and is the operative word there 'think,' then, or is it 'love'?"

She relaxed, just a little, and swallowed. "Both."

She held up a hand as he started to speak.

"I do—I think. But—but I can't help thinking what happened to my mother. I don't want that to happen to me."

"Your mother?" Simple astonishment was succeeded by a fresh burst of outrage. "What? You're thinking of bloody Jamie Fraser? Ye think ye cannot be satisfied with a boring historian—ye must have a—a— great passion, as she did for him, and you think I'll maybe not measure up?"

"No! I'm not thinking of Jamie Fraser! I'm thinking of my father!" She shoved her

hands deep in the pockets of her jacket, and swallowed hard. She'd stopped crying, but there were tears on her lashes, clotting them in spikes.

"She meant it when she married him—I could see it, in those pictures you gave me. She said 'better or worse, richer, poorer'—and she meant it. And then . . . and then she met Jamie Fraser, and she didn't mean it anymore."

Her mouth worked silently for a moment, looking for words.

"I—I don't blame her, not really, not after I thought about it. She couldn't help it, and I—when she talked about him, I could see how much she loved him—but don't you see, Roger? She loved my father, too—but then something happened. She didn't expect it and it wasn't her fault—but it made her break her word. I won't do that, not for anything."

IF SHE TAKES A VOW, Brianna says stubbornly, she'll keep it—no matter what. But she will not take that vow until she's positive she can keep it. She loves him, she wants him; she'll sleep with him, if he likes—but she won't marry him; not yet. Seeing that there is no moving her, Roger reluctantly accepts her decision—though with his own warning. He will have her all, he says . . . or not at all.

And so matters rest between them, symbolized by Roger's Christmas gift— a plain silver bracelet, engraved in French:

"JE T'AIME . . ." it says. "Un peu, beaucoup, passionement, pas du tout." I love you. A little, a lot, passionately . . . not at all.

HAVING FOUND a place he feels his own, Jamie asks Claire to stay and begin their life on the mountain at once; not even returning to Cross Creek, where Jocasta spreads her tempting nets of obligation. The cost of labor and hardship seems small, measured against the prospect of freedom.

Ian stays with them to help in the building of their first simple shelter, Myers returning to Cross Creek to deliver Jamie's letter of acceptance to the Governor, apprise Jocasta of her nephew's decision—and bring back with him such supplies as may be needed to build a cabin and plant a small crop in the spring.

In the course of exploring, Claire and Jamie have met some of the Indians whose hunting territory lies nearby; the Tuscarora chief, Nacognaweto, and two of his sons, who were most impressed by Jamie's prowess in killing a bear with his dirk. As

Palmeto Tree

the Frasers work on their new habitation, Nacognaweto returns, bringing with him his womenfolk—his wife, his stepdaughter, and his grandmother, Nayawenne, who is a singer and a healer—bearing gifts of food.

Nayawenne recognizes Claire as a kindred spirit, and shows her many of the useful plants that grow nearby. The old woman seems to know her, and eventually tells her that they have met before, in a dream; a dream in which Claire appeared as a white raven—rather a sinister omen. In parting, the old woman makes a cryptic prophecy, telling Claire not to worry: "Sickness comes from the gods. It won't be your fault."

IT IS A FRAGILE and tenuous foothold that they have upon the mountain as winter sets in—but a foothold, for all that. As the snows come down, the Frasers turn inward, to each other, taking pleasure in their close companionship and the warmth of their small cabin. They talk now and then of their daughter, Claire telling Jamie stories of Brianna, he confiding his dreams of her, and his curiosity about this child he's never seen.

Bear

"If she goes on wi' the history—d'ye think she'll find us? Written down somewhere, I mean?"

The thought had honestly not occurred to me, and for a moment I lay quite still. Then I stretched a bit, and laid my head on his shoulder with a small laugh, not altogether humorous.

"I shouldn't think so. Not unless we were to do something newsworthy." I gestured vaguely toward the cabin wall and the endless wilderness outside. "Not much chance of that here, I don't imagine. And she'd have to be deliberately looking, in any case."

"Would she?"

I was silent for a moment, breathing the musky, deep scent of him.

"I hope not," I said quietly, at last. "She should have her own life—not spend her time looking back." The fire crackled softly to itself, casting red and yellow highlights on the wooden walls of our snug refuge, and we lay in quiet peace, not bothering to sort out whose limbs were whose. On the very verge of sleep, I felt Jamie's breath, warm on my neck.

"She'll look," he said, with certainty.

BRIANNA IS LOOKING, searching history for traces of her parents, seeking identity and reassurance. Roger, unsure of her wisdom and afraid of what she might find, still is helping with the search, understanding her need as only a man raised without a father could.

Roger's fears are borne out, though, when he discovers a small announcement in an eighteenth-century newspaper, reporting the deaths by fire of one James Fraser and his wife, Claire, in North Carolina in 1776. Shocked and grieved himself, he hesitates to show the clipping to Brianna—not only out of reluctance to hurt her, but from a deeper fear; there is still time. If Brianna were to risk the journey through the standing stones, she might reach her parents before the date of the fire. If he tells her what he has found, she may well insist on going, whether in an attempt to save them—or only to seize the last chance of seeing the father she has never known.

Roger is himself convinced that history cannot change; Brianna cannot save her parents or alter their fate. He understands an orphan's longing for knowledge and connection, all too well. If she goes through the stones, though, she may be lost to him forever. Wracked by pangs of guilt, Roger reaches his conclusion; he will not show Brianna the announcement. Lest she find it herself, he makes up his mind that he must now try to dissuade her gently from her search, telling her that he has found nothing, trying to persuade her, bit by bit, that it is both fruitless and unhealthy to look backward too much; better that she turn her thoughts to the future—with him.

But knowledge once gained cannot be unlearned, and Roger cannot turn his own thoughts so easily away from his visions of fire and haunting loneliness.

ON FRASER'S RIDGE, the tiny homestead is slowly prospering and Claire's reputation as a healer is spreading to the far-flung farms of the nearby countryside. She makes her medical rounds on horseback, traveling—mostly—unafraid through the mountains. The wilderness has its dangers, though; returning from attendance at a birth, she is thrown from her horse during a thunderstorm and stranded miles from anywhere, lost, wet, and completely alone.

Taking refuge from the storm beneath the upflung roots of a giant red cedar that has toppled in the wind, she sinks into the troubled sleep of cold, hunger, and exhaustion, waking to a sense of someone nearby. Searching in the darkness for her shoes, she makes instead a bizarre discovery: a buried skull, and with it a smooth rock with an incised petroglyph. More disturbing still, the skull shows clear evidence of violence; the man—whoever he was—had been beheaded.

Waiting out the hours of the night, with nothing but this macabre companion, she sees a light coming down the slope toward her refuge.

THERE WAS A LIGHT *on the ridge. A small spark, growing to a flame. At first I thought it was the lightning-blasted tree, some smoldering ember come to life—but*

then it moved. It glided slowly down the hill toward me, floating just above the bushes.

I sprang to my feet, realizing only then that I had no shoes on. Frantically, I groped about the floor, covering the small space again and again. But it was no use. My shoes were gone.

I seized the skull and stood barefoot, turning to face the light.

I CLUTCHED THE SKULL *closer. It wasn't much of a weapon—but somehow I didn't think that whatever was coming would be deterred by knives or pistols, either.*

It wasn't only that the wet surroundings made it seem grossly improbable that anyone was strolling through the woods with a flaming torch. The light didn't burn like a pine torch or oil lantern. It didn't flicker, but burned with a soft, steady glow.

It floated a few feet above the ground, just about where someone would hold a torch they carried before them. . . .

It is an Indian who holds the torch; a man dressed in breechclout and war paint, a man with his face painted black.

I was invisible, completely hidden in the darkness of my refuge, while the torch he held washed him in soft light, gleaming off his hairless chest and shoulders, shadowing the orbits of his eyes. But he knew I was there.

I didn't dare to move. My breath sounded painfully loud in my ears. He simply stood there, perhaps a dozen feet away, and looked straight into the dark where I was, as though it were the broadest day. And the light of his torch burned steady and soundless, pallid as a corpse candle, the wood of it not consumed.

"WHATEVER DO YOU WANT?" *I said, and only then realized that we had been in some sort of communication for some time. Whatever this was, it had no words. Nothing coherent passed between us—but something passed, nonetheless. . . .*

"What do you want?" I said again, feeling helpless. "I can't do anything for you. I know you're there; I can see you. But that's all."

Nothing moved, no words were spoken. But quite clearly the thought formed in my mind, in a voice that was not my own.

That's enough, *it said.*

With the disappearance of the mysterious apparition, Claire sinks gradually back into a troubled sleep, waking again to the welcome realization of daylight and of rescue: Jamie, Ian, and Ian's dog Rollo have found her.

Once past the relief of reunion, Claire asks how they found her, so far from home and with no knowledge that she was lost in the first place. Jamie replies that they had been asleep the night before, but were suddenly awakened by Rollo's baying, flinging himself at the cabin door, insistent on a pursuit of some kind. Catching up their plaids and mounting their horses, they had followed the wolf-dog to Claire's refuge.

Delighted to be rescued, but still puzzled by the means, Claire wonders how Rollo could have led them to her.

"We searched the clearing," Jamie said, "from the penfold to the spring, and didna find a thing—except these." He reached into his sporran and drew out my shoes. He looked up into my face, his own quite expressionless.

"They were sitting on the doorstep, side by side."

Every hair on my body rose. I lifted the flask and drained the last of the brandy-wine. The brandywine was buzzing in my ears, swaddling my wits in a warm, sweet blanket, but I had enough sense left to tell me that for Rollo to have followed a trail back to me . . . someone had walked all that way in my shoes.

RETURNED TO THE SAFETY of home on the Ridge, Claire tells Jamie of her experience on the mountain, and shows him the stone that was buried with the skull; it is a large opal, the rocky matrix incised in the shape of a spiral, showing the fiery stone beneath.

If the stone and the apparition were mysterious, the skull is more so. Examining it for the first time in the light of day, Claire notes both the severed vertebrum that indicates the victim was beheaded, and the shattered teeth that further betokened a violent end. The real shock, though, lies in the teeth that are whole—the molars of the skull have silver fillings.

*"My God," I said, all tiredness forgotten. "My God," I said, to the empty eyes and the lopsided grin. "Who **were** you?"*

BACK IN THE FUTURE, Roger is grimly wrestling with his own mysteries; his campaign of discouragement is bearing sour fruit. Brianna's letters keep coming, but the tone is changed—friendly, but increasingly distant. Has his attempt to keep her from looking for her parents succeeded only in driving her away from *him*?

ON FRASER'S RIDGE, the peace of daily life has been disrupted; first, by the arrival of a Tuscaroran hunting party, one of whose members is ill with measles, and then by the appearance of a rattlesnake in the privy. Such mundane considerations are overshadowed, however, by another unexpected arrival—Lord John Grey and his son, William.

Or rather, his stepson. The boy is the son of his wife's dead sister and the late Earl of Ellesmere. William is now Viscount Ashness, ninth Earl of Ellesmere—so far as the world is concerned.

Claire is shocked, both by the boy's appearance—(*He did look quite a bit like Jamie, but it was my memories of Brianna that had caused that instant jolt of recognition when I saw him. Only ten years her junior, the childish outlines of his face were much more similar to hers than to Jamie's*)—and by his presence. What has possessed Grey to bring the boy here? For that matter, what is Grey himself doing here?

Grey's explanation is plausible enough; his wife, Isobel, en route to join him in Jamaica, has died aboard ship. In consequence of her death, Grey had decided not to remain in Jamaica, but to take Willie—naturally much distressed by the loss of his mother—to Virginia, where his late wife

had property. Grey must decide what to do with the property, and hoped that the diversions of the journey might distract William from his grief.

Claire is not convinced by this; even if it is, as Grey claims, no more than a slight diversion to visit Fraser's Ridge, it involves some risk. What if William remembers a groom named MacKenzie—or worse, notices the resemblance that is so clear to Claire? While Grey might possibly have meant only to allow Jamie a glimpse of his son, she thinks it much more likely that his purpose is more personal. *"Always diffi-cult to harbor warm feelings for a man with a professed homosexual passion for one's husband, after all,"* as she says.

The visit is uneventful, though, until the Indian in the corncrib dies of his illness. Beyond natural distress at the event, his death presents the Frasers with a delicate problem: how to inform his people of his demise. Claire insists that they cannot take the body to his people for burial; to do so would risk infecting them. But to bury it themselves might arouse suspicion that the Frasers have had a hand in his death, and are concealing it.

The problem is both compounded and resolved by Lord John's coming down with measles himself. William cannot be exposed to the illness, Claire says; best for Jamie to take the boy with him to the Tuscarora village. Jamie can enlist Nacognaweto's help in informing the dead man's family of his death, and at the same time, remove Willie from danger. The fact that this plan would also give Jamie a few days in the company of his son is one that passes unremarked—though not unnoticed.

Willie objects fiercely to leaving his beloved stepfather, desperately afraid that John Grey will die, too—like both his mothers, and like the Indian in the corncrib, whose death Willie has witnessed. Still, he is obliged to go with Jamie, and the two establish wary respect and a tentative liking for each other on the journey—as much, Jamie thinks, as he may ever have with this boy, and a gift for which he is grateful; or tries to be.

It wasn't stubbornness, or even loyalty, that had made Willie insist on staying at the Ridge. It was love of John Grey, and fear of his loss. And it was the same love that made the boy weep in the night, desperate with worry for his father.

An unaccustomed weed of jealousy sprang up in Jamie's heart, stinging like nettles. He stamped firmly on it; he was fortunate indeed to know that his son enjoyed a loving relationship with his stepfather. There, that was the weed stamped out. The stamping, though, seemed to have left a small bruised spot on his heart; he could feel it when he breathed.

Back on Fraser's Ridge, Claire is nursing two sick men—Young Ian having also contracted the measles—and wrestling with her own resentments of John Grey. She finds these tempered, though, by a reluctantly growing liking for the man that is answered by his own for her—equally reluctant.

Edgy and jealous of each other, Lord John and Claire at last come to a grudging recognition of what they have in common; not only a love for Jamie Fraser, but a deep honesty that forces each to admit the other's virtues, and see what it is that Jamie values in each of them. Presuming on this honesty, Claire asks bluntly why Lord John has come.

"You asked me why I came; you questioned my motives; you accused me of jealousy. Perhaps you don't want to know, because if you did, you could not keep thinking of me as you choose to."

"And how the hell do you know what I choose to think of you?"

His mouth twisted in an expression that might have been a sneer on a less handsome face.

"Don't I?"

I looked him full in the face for a minute, not troubling to hide anything at all.

"You did mention jealousy," he said quietly, after a moment.

"So I did. So did you."

He turned his head away, but continued after a moment.

"When I heard that Isobel was dead . . . it meant nothing to me. We had lived together for years, though we had not seen each other for nearly two years. We shared a bed; we shared a life, I thought. I should have cared. But I didn't."

He took a deep breath. I saw the bed-clothes stir as he settled himself.

"You mentioned generosity. It wasn't that. I came to see . . . whether I can still feel," he said. His head was still turned away, staring at the hide-covered window, grown dark with the night. There was plenty of the infusion left. I poured another cup and held it out to Lord John. Surprised, he sat upright and took it from me.

"And now that you've come, and seen him—do you still have feelings?" I said.

He stared at me for a moment, eyes unblinking in the candlelight.

"I do, yes." Hand steady as a rock, he picked up the cup and drank. "God help me," he added, so casual as almost to seem offhand.

Jamie and Willie reach the Tuscarora village of Anna Ooka, but something is wrong; the village is in flames, the houses half-burnt and the people gone. Leaving Willie in hiding, Jamie goes cautiously in search of the inhabitants, who he finds encamped not far away. It is not a raid, not war; they have packed their belongings for an orderly withdrawal.

Sickness, replies Nacognaweto, when asked what has happened. Measles has

come into the village, killing nearly half the people. The survivors are leaving, intending to take refuge in another village to the north. Without their *shaman,* their singer, there was no cure for the sickness. Has Jamie seen her, Nacognaweto asks? Nayawenne had gone to the forest, seeking a vision to help the stricken village, attended by Gabrielle and her daughter, Berthe; none of the women has returned.

Jamie has no knowledge of the women; there is nothing he can do to help, and his original mission has been lost in the enormity of the catastrophe that has overtaken the Indians.

He went, the grief of the place clinging to him like the smoke that permeated clothes and hair. And within his charred heart as he left the camp sprang a small green shoot of selfishness, relief that the grief was—for this time—not his own. His woman still lived. His children were safe.

OR AT LEAST he thinks they are. Willie will go on to his new life in Virginia with Lord John, but in the future, Brianna has been making her own plans.

A letter from Bree cancels plans for the summer, telling Roger she intends instead to go to Sri Lanka for a conference, and nearly convincing him that all is lost. At once enraged and depressed at the news, he accepts an offer himself, to lead a seminar in Oxford, rather than returning to the Highlands, where Brianna's absence would be even more painfully felt.

Returning to his rooms at the end of the seminar, though, Roger finds unexpected hope. Four heavy boxes, filled with memories: the family silver, old photographs, ancient toys, and jewelry. The note with

them reads, "You once told me that everybody needs a history. This is mine. Will you keep it with yours?" The note is signed simply "B," in Brianna's strong black hand.

Roger's puzzlement increases and his elation abates as he grasps the implications of this delivery. Consternation changes to alarm when he dumps out the contents of Brianna's jewelry box to find two items missing: his silver bracelet, which she always wears—and her grandmother's pearls . . . which she never wears.

Rushing to the phone, he calls Boston, hoping against hope that his apprehensions are unfounded.

It took forever to get the international operator on the line, and a longer time yet of vague electronic poppings and buzzings, before he heard the click of connection followed by a faint ringing. One ring, two, then a click, and his heart leapt. She was home!

"We're sorry," said a woman's pleasant, impersonal voice, "that number has been disconnected, or is no longer in service."

A quick call to Joseph Abernathy, Claire's friend and Bree's informal guardian, reveals that Brianna *has* come to the Highlands, and Roger at once heads for Inverness, hot on her trail. The trail leads, as he feared, directly to the stone circle on Craigh na Dun. She has gone back in search of her parents—without telling him.

Fear for her safety is mixed with rage at her abandonment—and guilt at his own betrayal. Whether she has found the news item he tried to conceal from her, or whether her flight into the past has been impelled by something else, the fact remains: Brianna is gone, and there is only one way to follow—if he can.

Roger finds unexpected help in Inverness. The granddaughter of Mrs. Graham,

the Reverend's old housekeeper, Fiona has inherited more from her granny than a talent for scones and clotted cream. She is the leader of the group of women who dance on Craigh na Dun at dawn on the Feast of Beltane; she is the caller of the sun. More important, she knows something of Gillian Edgars, the woman who vanished into the past and transformed herself into the witch Geillis Duncan.

Gillian has left behind her *grimoire,* her book of magic—or in this case, her speculations as to the means of time travel. Fiona has read it, and knows what Roger means to attempt. A loyal friend, she offers her help and goes with him to the circle on Midsummer's Eve, the ancient sun feast of Litha. If Geillis was right in her specula-

tions, the door of time stands widest open on fire feast and sun feast—and the stones are buzzing as Roger approaches.

His first attempt ends in failure—and near death. Entering the time passage, Roger is thinking of his own father, long dead, and wondering whether . . . The result of this is a brief and ghostly meeting with his father, and an almost catastrophic meeting with himself; by inadvertence, he has crossed his own lifeline, and the impossibility of existing twice in the same time has blown him out of the stones to lie unconscious on the grass, his clothes in flames, where his mother's garnet-crusted locket, carried for luck, has vaporized in his pocket.

Still, he is not dead—and many previous time-travelers have ended up that way.

The Bridge at Inverness.

Evidently, Geillis's injunctions regarding the protective benefit of gemstones have merit. Fiona gives him her diamond engagement ring, insisting that he take it. Summoning strength and resolve for another try, he takes farewell of Fiona and walks back through the stones, clinging tightly to his thoughts of Brianna.

BRIANNA HAS INDEED reached her destination—at least the first leg of it. Not knowing exactly where her parents may be, she goes to Lallybroch in search of information, and finds more than she bargained for: an unexpectedly large, warm family—and Laoghaire MacKenzie Fraser, her father's second wife.

Reeling from Laoghaire's bitter accusations against her father, she is supported and reassured by Ian and Jenny, who tell her that her parents are both well and safe, though very distant, in the wilds of North Carolina. She insists that she will go to them, no matter how far or how difficult the journey. Eager to help, but dubious about her safety, her uncle and cousin insist that she engage a servant to accompany her.

The servant is not precisely what Ian and Young Jamie had envisioned; far from the protectively muscular manservant they had in mind, Brianna's choice falls on a wispy young girl, Elizabeth Wemyss, whose father begs Brianna to buy his daughter's contract of indenture, in order to save her from the hands of a man whom he fears has dishonorable intentions.

Sure of her ability to take care of herself *and* Lizzie, Brianna insists that the girl will be her maid, and the two embark for North Carolina, with Brianna assuring her new servant that they will find Lizzie's fa-ther—himself sold as a bondsman in the Colonies—as soon as they find Brianna's.

ROGER'S SECOND ATTEMPT to pass through the stones is successful. Seeking traces of Brianna, he heads at once for Inverness, to consult the shipping registers and—if he can determine where she has gone—to make arrangements to follow her himself.

She is there—or rather, her name is there, inscribed as a passenger on the *Phillip Alonzo,* headed for the southern Colonies. Roger takes the first opportunity to follow, shipping as a hand on the *Gloriana,* bound for the Carolinas—captained by one Stephen Bonnet, who has the reputation of a fair but ruthless man.

Embarked on the long sea journey, Roger finds his loneliness slightly assuaged by watching the Scottish passengers—themselves embarked on a passage no less hazardous than his own, but willing to forsake home and country for the chance of a better life for themselves and their children.

This hope will prove vain for some. One night Roger is waked by a terrible commotion near the hold; smallpox has broken out among the passengers, and in an effort to prevent the disease from spreading the sailors are throwing the victims—many of them children—overboard to drown.

Joining the melee, Roger sees two dark figures crouched in the shadow near the cargo hold; one attacks him—a tall, fair man, whom he had noticed before. Not for the man's own sake, but for the sake of his wife, a bonny wee girl named Morag MacKenzie, who has a nursing child.

The passengers' revolt is subdued and the survivors clapped under hatches. But what of the second figure Roger has seen? He goes unobserved to the cargo hold next day, to make his own investigation. What he finds is what he suspected: Morag MacKenzie, hidden with her child. The boy has a rash on his face; in the panic over the pox he would certainly be dispatched with the rest. But it is not smallpox, Morag insists; nothing but a teething rash. It will clear within a few days; until then she must hide, to save baby Jemmy's life. Surely Roger will not give her away? Moved by her plight, he promises to keep her secret, and to bring her food, until she can safely come out.

But a ship is a small place, and little happens that does not come to the attention of the Captain. Coming from the hold in a dense fog next day, Roger meets Stephen Bonnet, who demands to know his reason for hiding the girl—and offers Roger a dreadful gamble: the toss of a coin for the infant's life.

Roger wins the toss, and hears the strange story of Bonnet's early life, and the death of a beggar man who lies under the foundation of a great house in Inverness, killed in Bonnet's stead by the toss of a coin. A coin the Captain still holds— along with Roger's fate.

He opened the hand that held the coin, and held it cupped thoughtfully before him, tilting it back and forth so the silver gleamed in the lantern light.

"Heads you live, and tails you die. A fair chance, would yez say, MacKenzie?" . . .

As in a dream, Roger felt the weight of the shilling drop once more into his hands. He heard the suck and hiss of the water on the hull, the blowing of the whales—and

the suck and hiss of Bonnet's breath as he drew on his cigar. . . .

The fog had closed over the deck. There was nothing visible save the glowing coal of Bonnet's cigar, a burning cyclops in the mist. The man might be a devil indeed, one eye closed to human misery, one eye open to the dark. And here Roger stood quite literally between the devil and the deep blue sea, with his fate shining silver in the palm of his hand.

"It is my life; I'll make the call," he said, and was surprised to hear his voice calm and steady. "Tails—tails is mine." He threw, and caught, clasped his one hand hard against the back of the other, trapped the coin and its unknown sentence.

He closed his eyes and thought just once of Brianna. **I'm sorry,** *he said silently to her, and lifted his hand.*

A warm breath passed over his skin, and then he felt a spot of coolness on the back of his hand as the coin was picked up, but he didn't move, didn't open his eyes.

It was some time before he realized that he stood alone.

Safely arrived in Wilmington, Brianna faces one more obstacle on her journey to find her parents; her maid, Lizzie, has contracted a mysterious fever that Brianna fears may be malaria; it comes and goes,

leaving Lizzie sweat-drenched and shaking with chills. While the recurrent fever traps them in Wilmington for the moment, Lizzie's sickness merely reinforces Brianna's urgent need to find the Frasers—she must find her mother, who will know what to do for the fever, before Lizzie dies.

Leaving Lizzie in the care of the landlady, Brianna goes to sell their horses, in preparation for the journey upriver to Cross Creek; Jocasta Cameron will know where to find Claire and Jamie, she hopes. The fever breaks, as it has before, and Lizzie—weak but clear-eyed—greets Brianna upon her return to the inn with news that she has learned of Jamie Fraser's whereabouts; he will be in the town of Cross Creek, a week's travel upriver, come Monday week.

Fired by excitement, Brianna makes the arrangements to travel by canoe to Cross Creek—and returns to the inn in the evening, where she is found by Roger, who has jumped ship in Edenton, made his way to Wilmington, and has been searching the inns and taverns of the town.

His greeting is not quite what he might have hoped; Brianna's initial joy at seeing him turns at once to shocked dismay. What, she demands to know, is he doing *here*? Looking for her, he heatedly replies, and what was her notion in rushing off through the stones without a word to him?

She arranged to deceive him, she informs him, because she was convinced that if he discovered what she was about to do, he would have tried his best to stop her. Roger can hardly deny the truth of that— he *did* in fact try to stop her, and can only hope she never finds out how.

But now what are they to do? she asks in evident distress. So far as she could deter-

mine, the only way of navigation through the currents of time is to have a point of attachment—a person whose presence in a time can draw the traveler to a safe haven.

"GETTING BACK! *You have to have somebody to go to—somebody you care for. You're the only person I love at that end—or you were! How am I going to get back, if you're here? And how will you get back, if I'm here?"*

He stopped dead, fear and anger both forgotten, and his hands clamped tight on her wrists to stop her hitting him again.

"That's why? That's why you wouldn't tell me? Because you love me? Jesus Christ!" She reached up and took hold of his wrist, but didn't pull his hand away. He felt her swallow.

"Right," he whispered. "Say it. I want to hear it."

"I . . . love . . . you," she said, between her teeth. "Got it?"

"Aye, I've got it." He took her face between his hands, very gently, and drew her down. She came, arms trembling and giving way beneath her.

"You're sure," he said.

"Yes. What are we going to do?" she said, and began to cry.

"We." She'd said we. She'd said she was sure.

Roger lay in the dust of the road, bruised, filthy, and starving, with a woman trembling and weeping against his chest, now and then giving him a small thump with her fist. He had never felt happier in his life.

It will be all right, Roger assures her; there is another way—Geilie Duncan's way. He has seen gemstones, in Stephen Bonnet's possession aboard the *Gloriana*. He knows roughly where the *Gloriana* was going—he will find the ship, and get the gems, by whatever means are necessary.

Brianna is more than dubious; beyond the simple difficulties of finding the gems is the risk entailed. As she says, *"They* hang *people for stealing in this time, Roger!"*

He is insistent, though; he must act now, while the gems can be found—for what other chance might there be, in a place like this? One thing he wants, though, before he leaves.

Handfasting is an old and honorable Highland tradition; a couple may wed by this means, for a year and a day. At the end of that time, if they are well-suited, they may wed more formally, by kirk and Book; if not, they may part. Both Roger and Brianna are sure of themselves and their love—but with no minister at hand, and time so short . . .

If I make a vow like that, I'll keep it— no matter what it costs me. Was she thinking of that now?

She brought their linked hands down together, and spoke with great deliberation.

"I, Brianna Ellen, take thee, Roger Jeremiah . . ." Her voice was scarcely louder than the beating of his own heart, but he heard every word. A breeze came through the tree, rattling the leaves, lifting her hair.

". . . as long as we both shall live."

The phrase meant a good bit more to each of them now, he thought, than it would have even a few months before. The passage through the stones was enough to impress anyone with the fragility of life.

There was a moment's silence, broken only by the rustle of the leaves overhead and a distant murmur of voices from the tavern's taproom. He raised her hand to his mouth and kissed it, on the knuckle of her fourth finger, where one day—God willing—her ring would be.

A BRIEF AND PASSIONATE wedding night, spent in a shed behind the inn, comes to an even more passionate end, when Brianna discovers accidentally just what it was that led Roger to find her in North Carolina. Finding that he had learned of the death notice months earlier, and had suppressed it, Brianna is enraged. How dare he presume to keep such a thing from her? she demands. He might have deprived her of the only chance ever to find the father she has never known!

Given that this was precisely what Roger intended to do, he finds himself with no defense but the—in her eyes, quite inadequate—truth: He wished to protect her from the dangers of the stones, from the risks of the past. At its simplest and most ignoble—he was afraid to lose her. Beyond that, he wished to save her pain; the future can't be changed, he is convinced of it. She cannot save her parents.

Brianna's response to this is immediate and furious. She *will* find her parents, she *will* save them from the fire—and as for Roger . . . he can bloody well go and get hanged if he wants to!

Stomping back into the inn, Brianna dashes the candlestick to the floor, flings off her clothes, and crashes closed the shutters, as her terrified maid cowers in bed, hearing a voice outside roar, "Brianna! I *will* come for you!"

Brianna says nothing of what has passed, and after a long time, falls asleep, leaving Lizzie wide-eyed in the dark. The dark wicked man named MacKenzie took her mistress out of the inn with him, and now she has come back, disheveled and upset, with MacKenzie outside, vowing to return. What in the name of God has happened?

Unable to sleep, Lizzie creeps out of bed at dawn, and tries to order her mind by setting the tumbled room to rights. Picking up Brianna's discarded, dirtied clothing, Lizzie is appalled to find the rank scent of a man upon it—and the stain of fresh blood in the breeks. But with the daylight, Lizzie's fever comes once more, and she cannot ask her mistress anything; only shiver and moan, and hope not to die in this strange place.

For her part, Brianna's turbulent feelings are further exacerbated by this delay. She wants nothing but to leave this place, put aside all thought of Roger and his perfidy, to go upriver at once to find Jamie Fraser. But here she is, and here she must stay, chafing and fuming, until Lizzie mends enough to travel.

Going down to the inn's kitchen to fetch up tea for Lizzie, though, she sees a sight that drives impatience and anger from her mind at once, to replace them with fear. Men are gambling in the taproom, and one man has among his stake a wide gold band—a woman's wedding ring, with an inscription inside that Brianna knows well: *From F. to C. with love. Always.*

Whatever the strains of her marriage to Frank Randall, nothing would cause Claire willingly to give up that band. What has happened to her mother, and where did this man—this Bonnet, as he is called—come by that ring?

Her hand was trembling as she gave it back.

"It's very pretty," she said. "Where did you get it?"

He looked startled, then wary, and she hastened to add, "It's too small for you—won't your wife be angry if you lose her ring?" How? she thought wildly. How did he get it? And what's happened to my mother?

The full lips curved in a charming smile.

"And if I had a wife, sweetheart, sure I'd leave her for you." He looked her over once more closely, long lashes dropping to hide his gaze. He touched her waist in a casual gesture of invitation.

"I'm busy just now, sweetheart, but later . . . eh?"

The jug was burning through the cloth, but her fingers felt cold. Her heart had congealed into a small lump of terror.

"Tomorrow," she said. "In the daylight."

He looked at her, startled, then threw his head back and laughed.

"Well, I've heard men say I'm not a one to be met in the dark, poppet, but the women seem to prefer it." He ran a thick

finger down her forearm in play; the red-gold hairs rose at his touch.

"In the daylight, then, if ye like. Come to my ship—Gloriana, near the naval yard."

With no other way to discover what may have happened to Claire, Brianna goes to meet Bonnet next day, offering to buy the ring from him, and inquiring as to its past history. He tells her that the previous owner of the ring is in good health, so far as he knows, and agrees to sell her the ring. The price he has in mind, however, isn't money.

LIZZIE'S FEVER BREAKS and then recurs on the journey upriver, and Brianna has neither time nor thought to spare for anything but the struggle to keep Lizzie alive until they reach Cross Creek.

Tired and grubby from the agonizing trip, Brianna cannot rest; Jamie Fraser is meant to be in town, and she *must* find him. Leaving Lizzie in safe hands, she ventures into Cross Creek—and finds what she is seeking in the backyard of a tavern.

She could scarcely breathe. His eyes were dark blue, soft with kindness. Her eyes fixed on the open collar of his shirt, where the

curly hairs showed, bleached gold against his sunburnt skin.

"Are you—you're Jamie Fraser, aren't you?"

He glanced sharply at her face.

"I am," he said. The wariness had returned to his face; his eyes narrowed against the sun. He glanced quickly behind him, toward the tavern, but nothing stirred in the open doorway. He took a step closer to her.

"Who asks?" he said softly. "Have you a message for me, lass?"

She felt an absurd desire to laugh welling up in her throat. Did she have a message?

"My name is Brianna," she said. He frowned, uncertain, and something flickered in his eyes. He knew it! He'd heard the name and it meant something to him. She swallowed hard, feeling her cheeks blaze as though they'd been seared by a candle flame.

"I'm your daughter," she said, her voice sounding choked to her own ears. "Brianna."

Jamie Fraser is all that Brianna had hoped for. Overwhelmed with emotion at finding her, he takes her and Lizzie to River Run, where Jocasta makes much of them.

Jamie has come down from Fraser's Ridge to testify at a trial; Fergus has been arrested on false charges of attacking and defrauding a tax collector. Both charges and trial are the result of Sergeant Murchison's machinations—a malicious attempt to damage Jamie both by imprisoning Fergus and by compelling Jamie to leave his land in the midst of harvest in order to help his foster son.

The charges are proved false, though, and Jamie and Brianna are allowed to leave for Fraser's Ridge—and Claire.

THE REUNION IS EVERYTHING Claire might have dared to wish; her beloved daughter is with her again, and Jamie and Brianna take a shy but obvious delight in each other, that delights Claire as well. The only fly in the ointment is the absence of Roger Wakefield. Brianna has told her parents about Roger's following her, their argument, and about his quest for gemstones to ensure safe passage. But days—and weeks—pass, and there is no sign of Roger.

Has something happened to him? Or has he decided not to come back, angered and wounded by Brianna's words? There is no telling—and no word of the missing Wakefield, though Jamie has made inquiries everywhere.

One day a visitor *does* come to the Ridge, though. Young Ian and Lizzie are at the flour mill when a man comes asking for directions to Fraser's Ridge—a man Lizzie recognizes as the man called Mac-Kenzie. Terrified that he has come to claim Brianna, Lizzie tells Young Ian, and the two young people take steps to delay Roger, then rush home to warn Jamie of the danger.

Lizzie tells a shocked Jamie of their encounter with the "wicked MacKenzie" in Wilmington, of her discovery that Brianna had—she thinks—been assaulted by Mac-Kenzie, and her much more recent discovery—that Brianna is pregnant.

Thus it is that when Roger reaches a clearing below the Ridge, he finds a welcoming party, composed of Jamie and Young Ian. Confused by their evident hostility, Roger admits that his name is indeed MacKenzie, and tells them that he has come for his wife. Further, upon Ian's taunting, Roger is stung into admitting that he has indeed taken Brianna's maidenhead. This being all Jamie needs to hear, he promptly beats Roger insensible, and takes further steps to be sure that this threat to his daughter is safely removed.

Meanwhile, Claire has taken Brianna mushroom-hunting, in order to gain sufficient privacy to question her daughter. Observing small physical changes, Claire has reached her own conclusions, which Brianna verifies. She is indeed pregnant.

Claire's immediate concern for Brianna's well-being gives way to another pressing worry; it is well into the autumn now, nearly past the time of year when ships will set sail for Europe. Brianna must leave at once, Claire exclaims, putting aside her own fear and grief. She must go back to Scotland now; she can return through the stones pregnant—Claire herself did it while pregnant with Brianna—but no one in their right mind would

undertake the journey through the stones with a small child. Brianna has only three choices—go back through the stones at once, without waiting for Roger to appear; bear her child in the dangerous conditions of the eighteenth century and then abandon it there—or stay forever, trapped in the past.

Brianna rejects the first two possibilities, insisting that she must stay and find Roger; if he is in trouble, she can't leave him alone in the past. Claire reluctantly concedes, only to face further shock when Brianna reveals that there is in fact another small problem—the baby is quite possibly not Roger's.

With a firm grip on her own shaky emotions, she tells her mother what happened aboard Stephen Bonnet's ship in Wilmington. Bonnet callously raped her, but did then carelessly give her the thing she had come for—Claire's wedding ring, which Brianna now returns to her shocked and grieving mother. She will tell Jamie, Brianna agrees, but in her own time.

When Jamie arrives that evening, with his hands scraped and damaged—from building a chimney, he says—he forestalls her confession, making it clear that he already knows about the child. She need not worry, he tells Brianna, he will take care of her, and her baby. However, as the days pass and there is still no sign of Roger Wakefield, Jamie becomes worried about Brianna's prospects, and goads Young Ian into proposing marriage to her—at least she will have a kind husband, and one who will have the means to take care of her and her child.

During the escalating arguments resulting from this proposal, Brianna furiously rejects Jamie's attempts to find her a husband, insisting that she will have Roger—or no one. Jamie protests that he has done everything he can think of to find Wakefield—but pressed further by Brianna's evident distress, comes up with a fresh inspiration: He will have a broadsheet printed, he declares, and published throughout the Colony, with particulars of Wakefield. Perhaps *someone* has seen the man, and will come forward.

Heartened by this suggestion, Claire suggests that Brianna might draw a picture of Roger Wakefield, to be published with his description; Brianna is a great hand with a likeness, she tells Jamie. Brianna eagerly agrees, and sits down, charcoal in hand—whereupon the picture of Roger MacKenzie Wakefield emerges before the horrified gaze of Jamie and Young Ian.

*Ian was leaning over the table, looking as though he might be going to throw up any minute. "Coz—d'ye mean honestly to tell me that . . . **this**"—he gestured feebly at the sketch—"is Roger Wakefield?"*

"Yes," she said, looking up at him in puzzlement. "Ian, are you all right? Did you eat something funny?"

He didn't answer, but dropped heavily onto the bench beside her, put his head in his hands, and groaned.

During the resulting scene, in which Brianna upbraids Jamie for "disposing" of Roger by selling him to the Iroquois, and Jamie reproaches Brianna for telling him that she was pregnant as the result of rape, Bree reveals to her father that indeed she *was* raped, by Stephen Bonnet—and Claire, horrified by the vicious way in which Bree and Jamie are attacking each other, throws down her gold wedding ring on the table in proof of Bree's word.

This puts an immediate stop to the argument, but does not improve relations, and it is in a strained condition that the small family makes its next preparations.

Jamie instructs Claire to pack Brianna's things; they will take the girl to River Run, to stay with Jocasta, while he, Claire, and Young Ian head north, to rescue Roger MacKenzie Wakefield, and bring him back to his wife—and possible child.

Conditions between Claire and Jamie are strained as well, with the weight of the gold ring and guilt over Brianna's secrets hanging between them. The journey north is lightened only by an encounter with Pollyanne, the ex-slave whom Jamie and Claire had helped to escape. Now ensconced in a new life with the Tuscarora, she has married and has a child. In the course of conversation, she tells the Frasers what happened on the night that the girl died in the sawmill; hiding in the shadows, Pollyanne saw a heavyset man enter the mill, and leave a few minutes later, just before the Frasers' arrival. The firelight fell upon his face as he passed close to her, however, and she saw that he was pockmarked. She didn't recognize the man, but Claire does—Sergeant Murchison.

Seeing the constraint between his beloved uncle and aunt, Young Ian takes a hand, and the situation is resolved in the dark intimacy of an Indian longhouse.

Reconciled and encouraged by each other's strength, the little party pushes on toward Snaketown, the distant Mohawk village where they hope to find Roger and ransom him with whisky. Young Ian, with his appreciation and knowledge of Indian ways and his skill with the Tuscaroran tongue—closely related to the tongue of the Mohawk, the *Kahnyen'kehaka*—is an invaluable ambassador. His budding relationship with a Mohawk girl promises help in their endeavor—if Roger is, in fact, captive in Snaketown.

In fact, he is. Enslaved by the Mohawk, he has not been badly mistreated, but life as an Indian slave is no bed of roses, and the constant hard work is not eased by a continuing infection in his foot, injured while trying to escape. Beyond physical injury and hardship, though, is the burden of questions that he bears: Was it by Brianna's doing that he is here? Was she so angered at his betrayal that she has in turn betrayed him?

Returning to the village after a hunting trip, burdened with moose meat, he is surprised to be taken and hustled away to a small hut containing a young Jesuit priest. Roger has no notion what may be happening, but is relieved beyond measure to have another white man to talk with. The other man, Père Alexandre Ferigault, is a missionary, who has lived some years with the Mohawk, converting some—alienating others. As he observes, "One

is *Kahnyen'kehaka,* or one is—other." In spite of his years with the Indians, Père Ferigault is still "other."

His current status as captive is the result of a schism precipitated by a love affair with one of his converts. Not the affair as such—as he explains to Roger, the Mohawk do not practice marriage in the European fashion, and have no objection to cohabitation by willing partners—but rather his repudiation of it. Learning that his lover was pregnant, Father Alexandre experienced what he thinks was a heavenly message revealing the error of his ways, whereupon he promptly removed himself from the girl's longhouse.

However, he had established a policy of not baptizing children unless their parents were both practicing Catholics in a state of grace, fearing that otherwise the Indians might—as they did elsewhere—view baptism as merely a superstitious charm against evil, rather than a sacrament. Bound by his own policy, therefore, he cannot baptize his child—his lover remained a convert, in spite of considerable reason to renounce her faith, but he cannot absolve himself of sin—and thus achieve a state of grace—because he cannot bring himself to stop loving her.

It is this delicate situation that has caused his present difficulties; the nonconvert population has never been fond of him, and tolerated him only

for the sake of a high-ranking man who was one of his converts. This man, the grandfather of the infant in question, is now infuriated at the priest's refusal to baptize his own child, and has withdrawn his protection. The priest has been brought to Snaketown to face the judgment of the Council there—and Father Alexandre is not hopeful of his prospects.

Père Ferigault's story distracts Roger from his own misery, but adds to his fear, as the Indians remove the priest temporarily in order to torture him. Why is Roger held here? Is he meant to face a similar fate?

Roger is, in fact, merely being hidden in order to prevent the Frasers from catching sight of him until a bargain has been concluded for his ransom. Jamie has come with his entire stock of whisky, prepared to give it for Roger's release, but—no more trusting than the Indians—has cached it in the woods until the bargain is made.

For their part, some of the Indians are willing to accept the bargain, others—wary of the effects of liquor on the people—are not. Some women of the village show a disposition to keep Roger and adopt him into the tribe—a Mohawk custom with some captives.

In order to show goodwill and demonstrate the quality of the goods offered, Young Ian arranges—through the offices of the young woman with whom he has formed a relationship—a small *ceilidh,* a whisky-tasting party at which stories are told and songs sung, involving several of the more prominent men of the village. Claire is invited to share the fire of Tewaktenyonh, an elderly woman of some importance in the village, sister to both the war chief and the *sachem* of the village.

Claire has with her the opal unearthed with the skull she found on the mountain a year earlier—an opal that makes the Indians very uneasy indeed. While the men are drinking, Tewaktenyonh asks to see the stone, and upon hearing Claire's story of its discovery, tells a story of her own—the story of Otter-Tooth, a strange man who came to the village some forty years before.

Urging the Mohawk to attack and drive out the white settlers, Otter-Tooth made a name for himself as a warrior, but incurred the villagers' uneasiness. The Mohawk do not make war for no reason, and there was neither treaty nor friction requiring it— yet Otter-Tooth urged war with greater and greater urgency. Finally he so disturbed the village that he was ordered to leave—but would not. Cast out, he kept returning, always preaching doom for the Mohawk, foretelling their destruction if they would not heed his words.

Concluding that Otter-Tooth harbored a malign spirit, and was likely a sorcerer himself, the Mohawk tried once more to thrust him out of the village, and failing this, decided to kill him. Tortured and left bound, Otter-Tooth succeeded in escaping, and was pursued to the south by the men of the village, who eventually caught up with him and killed him.

To prevent his spirit from following them home, the men cut off his head and buried it, together with the great opal that Otter-Tooth carried. He called the stone his *tika-ba,* Tewaktenyonh tells Claire. The Indians have no notion what this term meant, but Claire thinks she does— the opal was his "ticket back"—the means of return for a time-traveler.

Meanwhile, Jamie and Young Ian have celebrated a successful *ceilidh,* and the

Frasers retire, hopeful of an early escape from the village.

AT RIVER RUN, Brianna is physically thriving, abloom with pregnancy. Her emotions are in a less flourishing state, however. Fear for her parents and Roger, loneliness and guilt, give way to astonishment and anger, when she learns that Jocasta, eager to protect River Run, has decided both to make Brianna her heir— and to find her a suitable husband, to be enticed by the rich promise of her inheritance.

Brianna protests that she cannot possibly own slaves, does not want to marry in any case . . . but as Jocasta's body servant, Phaedre, observes, "Well, like I say—it ain't so much what you want. It's what Miss Jo wants. Now, let's try this dress."

Successful in rebuffing the advances of the local suitors, Brianna is slightly more wary of a new arrival—Lord John William Grey, of Mount Josiah plantation in Virginia, who is, she is informed, not only a rich man and a lord—eminently suitable, in other words—but an old friend of her father's.

To her surprise, Lord John is kind, personable, witty, and honorable. He is also homosexual, a fact she discovers by accident one night. The discovery supplies her with a means to solve the problem plaguing her.

She cannot in good conscience marry a man she doesn't love; at the same time, she doesn't want Roger to marry her out of a sense of obligation—feeling that even though his sense of honor may compel him to stay with her, he will resent being permanently trapped in the past. This, added to the doubt about the impending baby's paternity, seems too much to ask of him, and an unfair burden with which to begin a marriage. If he returns to find her unmarried, though, he may feel that he has no choice.

Brianna therefore implements her plan—blackmailing Lord John into marriage. She explains her reasoning to him; since he would not in any case desire her in a wifely fashion, she wouldn't be depriving him of the physical love she can't give. At the same time, Roger would be relieved of both choice and obligation. And if Lord John does not choose to acquiesce . . . she takes a deep breath and threatens to expose him as a pederast.

Lord John's response to this remarkable threat is, *"Child, you would make an angel weep, and God knows I am no angel!"*

Reluctantly, he is obliged to reveal the background of his relationship with Jamie Fraser, a tale to which Brianna listens with mingled horror and fascination. Lord John convinces her that she must at least allow Roger to make his own choice, and further, that she must forgive her father for his part in her troubles. Firmly declining to go along with her plan, he suggests that they pretend to an engagement that will at least temporarily relieve her of the unwanted attentions of Jocasta's horde of suitors.

IMPRISONED IN HIS SMALL HUT, Roger has no inkling of the arrival of a ransom party. He has no notion what the Indians mean to do with him, but his fears are not allayed by their treatment of the priest. Father Alexandre is stripped, removed from the hut, and returned some hours later, minus one ear. The priest tells Roger that he is sure the Mohawk mean to kill him, and asks Roger—the son of a minister—both to hear his confession and to pray for him, telling him that "in time of need, any man may do the office of a priest."

When the Indians come at nightfall to remove the priest, Roger is sure the worst is happening. Still, he has no choice but to sit and listen to the beating of the drums, and the sound of upraised voices outside.

The yelling escalates, though, and it becomes clear that whatever is happening outside, it's out of control. A fight is raging in the center of the village, and among the shouts and screams, Roger hears an undeniably Scottish voice, shouting in Gaelic. Inspired by the thought that rescue is at hand, Roger seizes the absence of the guard from his doorway to rush out, armed with a makeshift spear broken from a bedframe.

Outside, everything is confusion. Men are fighting, stumbling to and fro in the darkness amid a reek of whisky—and in the huge firepit, the flames are roaring high, consuming the body of the priest. Roger is attacked and strikes back with his spear, felling his opponent, but then is attacked himself from behind, clubbed into near-insensibility.

Waking back in the confines of the hut, he finds another senseless body lying on the ground nearby—Jamie Fraser, the man he has been itching to get his hands on for

The Fraser stone.

the last several months. Faced with Fraser at last, though, his response is neither fury nor alarm, but joyful relief—Fraser can be here only because Brianna has sent him.

Dying with the assurance that Brianna loves him is better than dying without it—but he hadn't wanted to die in the first place. Luckily, Fraser is not dead, either, and only slightly injured. Restored to his senses, Jamie is less than thrilled to see Roger, being more concerned with the whereabouts of Claire. He tells Roger what he knows of events outside; the Indians had tortured the priest and hung him in the flames, when quite unexpectedly, a girl standing in the crowd had handed a cradleboard with a baby to Claire and walked steadily into the fire herself.

An uproar immediately began, apparently exacerbated by drunkenness—some of the Indians having discovered the cache of whisky barrels. Caught up in the maelstrom, Jamie found himself fighting, along with Young Ian, to protect Claire and the baby, but was overcome.

The rest of the story is supplied by Claire, who arrives near daybreak. She has spent the night in a longhouse, under the

Kill Deer

protection of Tewaktenyonh, and is able to tell the men what has happened—or most of it.

Some of the younger braves had taken the whisky, assuming the bargain for Roger to be concluded. However, one man has perished in the fighting—the man Roger pierced with his spear. Since the whisky was given as the price for Roger's life, the Indians do not intend to kill him in revenge—but rather intend to forcibly adopt one member of the ransom party, in replacement of the dead man. The only things Claire doesn't know at this point are who will be selected—and where Young Ian is.

Jamie insists that he will remain with the Indians; Roger must return with Claire, for Brianna's sake. Besides, as he points out logically, if he and Claire are to die in a fire in 1776, neither of them can be killed in the meantime. He will be safe enough in Snaketown, and so soon as an opportunity presents itself, he will escape and head south by himself.

Claire is more than reluctant to agree to this, but has no choice. Neither has Jamie; later in the day, the door flap opens to admit Ian, his scalp plucked to a war lock, and the marks of fresh tattooing blood-crusted on his cheeks. He has made his choice, he says quietly—he will remain, with the young woman he calls Emily. The others are free to go.

Remonstrance and objection are useless; Ian is now *Kahnyen'kehaka,* allowed to speak in no tongue but the Mohawk, scrubbed clean of the taint of white blood, named Wolf's Brother in a ceremony that claims him forever as an Indian. Heartsick, Claire and Jamie take leave of Ian and Rollo, turning to go south with Roger.

They haven't gone far when Jamie's grief over Ian turns to fury with Roger. He reveals to Roger the truth about Brianna's pregnancy—that it is likely the result of rape by Bonnet—and demands to know whether Roger intends to stand by his daughter. If not, he says, Roger can bloody well go back through the stones at once.

Roger is taken completely by surprise, and deeply shocked. After a brief and violent altercation, Jamie abandons him, insisting that Claire accompany him. He flings the opal at Roger's feet, leaving Roger to make up his mind whether he can accept the coming child as his own, and be a decent husband to Bree—or whether he will go back through the stones of the circle he discovered on his way north with the Indians.

Bald Eagle

In River Run, Lord John has arrived with news—Stephen Bonnet has been captured, and condemned to hang. Momentarily shocked by the news, Brianna comes to a decision; she must see Bonnet, she tells Lord John, and speak to him. Upon Lord John's objection to this notion, she shows him the note Jamie left her upon his departure—urging her to find some way by which to forgive Bonnet, for the sake of her own peace. At first too angry with Jamie to listen to him, she has spent enough time alone to realize the wisdom of his words. So far she has found no way to forgive; if she sees the man, perhaps she can make peace with both him and herself.

Reluctantly, Lord John agrees, and takes her to the warehouse on the river—where the Crown stores imported liquor, as well as the turpentine, pitch, and other naval stores intended for the naval yards at Charleston—where Bonnet is held prisoner, in an underground cell.

His gaze stayed on her face, mildly curious. "Have we business still to do then, darlin?"

She took a deep breath—through her mouth, this time.

"They told me you're going to hang."

"They told me the same thing." He shifted again on the hard wooden bench. He stretched his head to one side, to ease the muscles of his neck, and peered up sidelong at her. "You'll not have come from pity, though, I shouldn't think."

"No," she said, watching him thoughtfully. "To be honest, I'll rest a lot easier once you're dead."

He stared at her for a moment, then burst out laughing. He laughed hard enough that tears came to his eyes; he wiped them carelessly, bending his head to swipe his face against a shrugged shoulder, then straightened up, the marks of his laughter still on his face.

"What is it you want from me, then?"

She opened her mouth to reply, and quite suddenly, the link between them dissolved. She had not moved, but felt as though she had taken one step across an impassable

abyss. *She stood now safe on the other side, alone. Blessedly alone. He could no longer touch her.*

"Nothing," she said, her voice clear in her own ears. "I don't want anything at all from you. I came to give you something."

She opened her cloak, and ran her hands over the swell of her abdomen. The small inhabitant stretched and rolled, its touch a blind caress of hand and womb, both intimate and abstract.

"Yours," she said.

He looked at the bulge, and then at her.

"I've had whores try to foist their spawn on me before," he said. But he spoke without viciousness, and she thought there was a new stillness behind the wary eyes.

"Do you think I'm a whore?" She didn't care if he did or not, though she doubted he did. "I've no reason to lie. I already told you, I don't want anything from you."

She drew the cloak back together, covering herself. She drew herself up then, feeling the ache in her back ease with the movement. It was done. She was ready to go.

"You're going to die," she said to him, and she who had not come for pity's sake was surprised to find she had some. "If it makes the dying easier for you, to know there's something of you left on earth—then you're welcome to the knowledge. But I've finished with you, now."

Her departure is prevented, though, by the sudden appearance of Sergeant Murchison. Creeping down to the dungeon to join Bonnet, he has come upon and killed—evidently—Lord John, who lies in a boneless heap, facedown on the dank bricks of the passageway. His plain intent is to murder Brianna as well, but the close quarters prevent his raising the musket to shoot her. He lifts the gun instead, to club her with the stock, but he has bargained without the protective fury of a mother-to-be—and the strength of a tall and muscular woman. She seizes the gun from him, strikes him in the head, and watches him fall unconscious.

With the strength of her outburst fading fast, she steps back far enough to get Bonnet at gunpoint, and forces him to tell her what has been going on. Prior to his capture, he had been running cheap contraband alcohol up the river, exchanging it for expensive brandy and wine stocked in the warehouse, which Murchison had abstracted. The cheap alcohol was stored in casks marked with the Crown's stamp, the good liquor sold off quietly. But since Bonnet's capture, one of Murchison's soldiers, a Private Hodgepile, had gotten wind of the scheme and had been asking questions.

The plan was therefore that Murchison would release Bonnet, after setting fuses in the warehouse and spilling several barrels of highly flammable turpentine. The warehouse would go up in flames, concealing all evidence of the smuggling—and Bonnet would escape, being assumed dead in the conflagration.

Dancing with impatience, Bonnet urges her to let him go. The fuses have been set and lit, he tells her; the warehouse is going to explode overhead at any moment! She steps back, a little dazed, but motions to the unconscious Murchison, insisting that Bonnet cannot mean to leave him behind—the man is still alive.

Pragmatic as always, Bonnet takes the knife from Murchison's belt and cuts his throat. Observing that he is no longer alive, and thus presents no moral dilemma, he strides to the door, urging Brianna to leave as well—and promptly.

Her first impulse is to do just that—but she cannot go without finding out whether Lord John is truly dead. A frantic search for a pulse reveals him to be badly injured, but not quite dead. A smallish man, he is still too much for her to carry by herself, but she cannot, will not, leave him.

At this point, though, Bonnet returns, exhorting her to leave, and quickly! Shocked, but still retaining her presence of mind, Brianna brings up her musket, and insists that he bring Lord John to safety. Bonnet is not pleased, but is as always practical, and does as she says. They exit onto the riverbank below the loading ramp of the warehouse, and scramble to safety as the flames of the burning warehouse roar into the night sky.

Dumping Lord John on the ground, Bonnet turns to escape, but pauses to invite Brianna to accompany him. She declines, and as Bonnet leaves, he reaches into his mouth and extracts something he had hidden there—the black diamond, originally stolen from the Frasers on the river.

"For his maintenance, then," he said, and grinned at her. "Take care of him, sweetheart!"

And then he was gone, bounding long-legged up the riverbank, silhouetted like a demon in the flickering light. The turpentine flowing into the water had caught fire, and roiling billows of scarlet light shot upward, floating pillars of fire that lit the riverbank bright as day.

Lord John survives, much to Brianna's relief. Claire and Jamie return safely, to her even greater relief, and she and Jamie are reconciled, though Roger has not yet returned.

Brianna's child is born—a lusty boy, who resembles neither of his putative fathers. But, as Jamie states, *"If I dinna ken who his father was, at least I know who his grandsire is!"* and the family returns—with its new addition—to the house on Fraser's Ridge.

It is a bright summer's day soon thereafter when a ragged figure limps slowly into the dooryard—Roger, who has made his choice.

"I don't imagine it pleases you any more than it does me," he said, in his rusty voice, "but you are my nearest kinsman. Cut me. I've come to swear an oath in our shared blood."

I couldn't tell whether Jamie hesitated or not; time seemed to have stopped, the air in the room crystallized around us. Then I watched Jamie's dirk cut the air, honed edge draw swift across the thin, tanned wrist, and blood well red and sudden in its path.

To my surprise, Roger didn't look at Brianna, or reach for her hand. Instead, he swiped his thumb across his bleeding wrist, and stepped close to her, eyes on the baby. Roger knelt in front of her, and reaching out, pushed the shawl aside and smeared a broad red cross upon the downy curve of the baby's forehead.

"You are blood of my blood," he said softly, "and bone of my bone. I claim thee as my son before all men, from this day forever."

But nearly a year has passed since the night when Roger and Brianna took each other for better or for worse, and who can say which of them has changed the most in the time since then? Unsure whether Roger has come back only from obligation, or because he truly loves her, Brianna is hesitant.

Jamie decrees that Roger will stay; they are married, if only by handfasting. However, the traditional span of handfasting is for a year and a day. Roger has that long to convince his wife of his motives; Brianna has that long to make up her mind. In the meantime, they will live as husband and wife—though if Roger seeks to sleep with Brianna against her will, Jamie asserts that he will cut out Roger's heart and feed it to the pig.

For his part, Roger is more than willing to try to convince Brianna of his devotion—the difficulty is getting to talk to her for more than a few moments at a time, with the interruptions caused by the baby, and the fact that Roger is temporarily immobilized by Claire's treatment of his foot injury. One night, though, he comes to Brianna's cabin, and forces her to listen to him.

Be careful, her mother said, and **my daughter doesna need a coward,** *said her father. He could flip a bloody coin, but for the moment he was taking Jamie Fraser's advice, and damn the torpedoes.*

"You said you'd seen a marriage of obligation and one of love. And do you think the one cuts out the other? Look—I spent three days in that godforsaken circle, thinking. And by God, I thought. I thought of staying, and I thought of going. And I stayed."

"We have time," he said softly, and knew suddenly why it had been so important to talk to her now, here in the dark. He reached for her hand, clasped it flat against his breast.

"Do you feel it? Do you feel my heart beat?"

"Yes," she whispered, and slowly brought their linked hands to her own breast, pressing his palm against the thin white gauze.

"This is our time," he said. "Until that shall stop—for one of us, for both—it is our time. Now. Will ye waste it, Brianna, because you are afraid?"

"No," she said, and her voice was thick, but clear. "I won't."

There was a sudden thin wail from the house, and a surprising gush of moist heat against his palm.

"I have to go," she said, pulling away. She took two steps, then turned. "Come in," she said, and ran up the path in front of him, fleet and white as the ghost of a deer.

AT THE END of October 1770, the Frasers go to the great Gathering on Mount Helicon—the largest Gathering of Scots in the New World. Here marriages are made, children are christened, news is exchanged, and business is done.

The new baby will be christened here—if Roger and Brianna can ever agree on a name for him. Jeremiah, Roger suggests; it is an old family name. In fact, his father's first name was Jeremiah, and it is Roger's middle name—his mother once called him "Jemmy," for short. It is the memory of this nickname that brings back to Roger other memories, of the days of terror on the *Gloriana,* with his vivid images of the woman, Morag MacKenzie, and her child—named Jemmy—whom he helped to save.

With a disturbing notion blossoming in his brain, Roger asks Claire whether she perhaps recalls the details of his own genealogical record—she had examined it in some detail. She does, she replies; why? Does she also recall, he asks carefully, the name of the woman who married William Buccleigh MacKenzie—the "changeling," the illegitimate child born to Dougal MacKenzie and the witch Geillis Duncan? Indeed she does, Claire answers—the woman's name was Morag, Morag Gunn.

Thanks, Roger murmurs, and settles back to deal with the realization that he has—quite unknowingly—saved his five-times-great-grandfather from drowning, and thus ensured his own survival; at least for the moment.

The Gathering brings John Quincy Myers, down from the north with an important message—a brief note from Young Ian, written on the torn-out flyleaf of a book. He is well, Ian writes. He has married, in the Mohawk way, and his wife expects a child in the spring. He is happy—but he will never forget them.

Another bit of news comes by way of a letter, though delivered less directly. Roger seeks out Jamie one evening by their family fire, to tell him of the contents of a letter he had discovered in Inverness, while waiting to go through the stones after Brianna. Unsure whether to share this with Claire—and feeling that, in fact, Jamie might be the intended recipient—he has finally decided to relate it to Jamie, and let him decide whether Claire—and Brianna—should be told.

The import of the letter is that Frank had asked the Reverend Wakefield to erect a gravestone in the abandoned kirkyard at St. Kilda's. Unable to dismiss Claire's assertions about the past—and likewise unable to accept them—Frank had done the only thing he could: looked for James Fraser in the historical record. Finding a man whose connections matched those Claire had recounted, he was forced to accept Jamie's reality—but in accepting it, was faced with

a desperate choice; whether or not to tell Claire that James Fraser had survived the Battle of Culloden.

On the one hand fearing to lose Claire, and on the other, fearing that she might remain with him for Brianna's sake and yet still pine for Fraser, he chose to keep his silence—and Claire. He cannot help but feel guilt, though, at the sight of Brianna, with her father's face.

He is her father, he feels; and yet, she has another. He has, in effect, stolen Claire from Jamie, or at least kept her with him by deceit. He feels he owes Brianna the knowledge of her other father—at the same time, he knows himself too weak ever to tell her himself. His compromise with conscience is the false gravestone, bearing Jamie's full name—JAMES ALEXANDER MALCOLM MACKENZIE FRASER—and the name of his wife. That, he tells the Reverend Wakefield, must suffice. If Brianna should be interested in her past—in *his* history—then she will go to St. Kilda's, and find Black Jack Randall's grave. If she sees the nearby stone for Jamie, she is bound to ask Claire—and the truth will be known, with Frank Randall safely dead and buried. As for Fraser himself . . . *"Hadn't thought of this before—do you suppose I'll meet him in the sweet by-and-by, if there is one? Funny to think of it. Should we meet as friends, I wonder, with the sins of the flesh behind us? Or end forever locked in some Celtic hell, with our hands wrapped round each other's throat?"*

If Frank Randall had chosen to keep secret what he'd found, had never placed that stone at St. Kilda's—would Claire have learned the truth anyway? Perhaps; perhaps not. But it had been the sight of that spurious grave that had led her to tell

her daughter the story of Jamie Fraser, and to set Roger on the path of discovery that had led them all to this place, this time.

Jamie Fraser stirred at last, though his eyes stayed fixed on the fire.

"Englishman," he said softly, and it was a conjuration. The hair rose very slightly on the back of Roger's neck; he could believe he saw something move in the flames.

Jamie's big hands spread, cradling his grandson. His face was remote, the flames catching sparks from hair and brows.

"Englishman," he said, speaking to whatever he saw beyond the flames. "I could wish that we shall meet one day. And I could hope that we shall not."

Among the bits of business still to be decided, then, is the matter of Claire's ring. Jamie still has the gold wedding band, flung down during the confrontation with Brianna months ago. Knowing now what he does of Frank, his motives, his thoughts, and his actions, Jamie comes to Claire by the fire, and asks her—will she have it back?

"And will ye choose, too?" he asked softly. He opened his hand, and I saw the glint of gold. "Do ye want it back?"

I paused, looking up into his face, searching it for doubt. I saw none there, but something else; a waiting, a deep curiosity as to what I might say.

"It was a long time ago," I said softly.

"And a long time," he said. "I am a jealous man, but not a vengeful one. I would take you from him, my Sassenach—but I wouldna take him from you."

He paused for a moment, the fire glinting softly from the ring in his hand. "It was your life, no?"

And he asked again, "Do you want it back?"

I held up my hand in answer and he slid the gold ring on my finger, the metal warm from his body.

From F. to C. with love. Always.

"What did you say?" I asked. He had murmured something in Gaelic above me, too low for me to catch.

"I said, 'Go in peace,'" he answered. "I wasna talking to you, though, Sassenach."

And then the final bit of business is accomplished, the final news exchanged:

Across the fire, something winked red. I glanced across in time to see Roger lift Brianna's hand to his lips; Jamie's ruby shone dark on her finger, catching the light of moon and fire.

"I see she's chosen, then," Jamie said softly.

Brianna smiled, her eyes on Roger's face, and leaned to kiss him. Then she stood up, brushing sand from her skirts, and bent to pick up a brand from the campfire. She turned and held it out to him, speaking in a voice loud enough to carry to us where we sat across the fire.

"Go down," she said, "and tell them the MacKenzies are here."

THE END

PART TWO

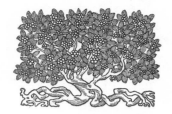

CHARACTERS

"It was . . . a lady novelist who remarked to me once that writing novels was a cannibal's art, in which one often mixed small portions of one's friends and one's enemies together, seasoned them with imagination, and allowed the whole to stew together into a savory concoction."

—*J. Fraser,* Voyager

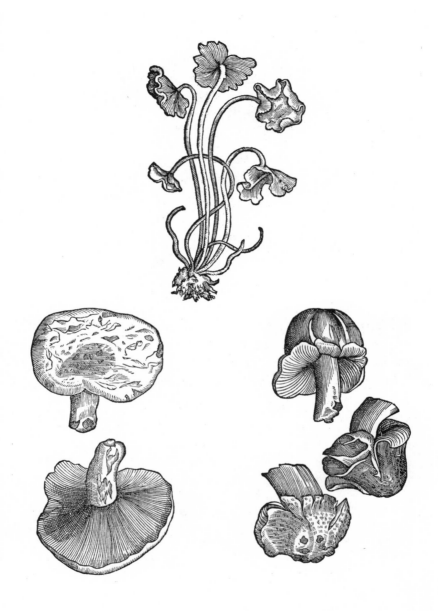

WHERE CHARACTERS COME FROM: MUSHROOMS, ONIONS, AND HARD NUTS

HENEVER one talks about writing—writing fiction, at least—the conversation always turns to character, for obvious reasons. All good stories are built on, or by, good characters. Characters are defined in a story on the basis of what they *want*. What they want, of course, depends a lot on who they are, and so does the manner in which they go about getting it.

Readers seem as interested in questions of character as do writers, though they ask slightly different questions. "Where do you get your characters?" readers ask. "Do you plan them, or do they pop up ad-lib?"

Writers ask, "If you *do* plan a character, and he (or she) just lies there like a corpse on a slab, how do you bring him to life?" And finally: "What do you do if your characters won't stick to your plan, and insist on going off and doing things on their own?"

FICTIONAL CHARACTERS

Mushrooms

The answers to these questions are, of course, as many and various as are the writers who ask them. For myself, I've found that a lot of characters *do* pop up like mushrooms: Geillis Duncan, Master Raymond, Fergus, and Murphy the sea cook, to name a few from my own books.

I'll be slogging along, hoping to dig myself into the day's work, and all of a sudden this . . . *person* shows up out of nowhere and walks off with the whole scene. No need to ask questions, analyze, or consciously "create"; I just watch in fascination, to see what he'll do next.

I have no idea where these characters come from, but I'm delighted and grateful when one shows up.

Onions

Other characters were conceived before I wrote them, and were consciously intended to serve some specific purpose in the story. However, once I began to write them, they obligingly came to life and started acting on their own. Mother Hildegarde in *Dragonfly in Amber* was one such "built" character—I needed someone who could decode a musical cipher, and I needed a hospital for Claire to work in. Fine, I thought, let's have the abbess of a convent hospital, and give her a musical avocation, thus saving my having to make up an additional character. The moment I began to write Mother Hildegarde, though, I could see her ("a face of an ugliness so transcendent as to be grotesquely beautiful"), and within a couple of paragraphs, I could hear her talk.

Likewise, Mr. Willoughby, in *Voyager*, was a "made" character. Simply put, I needed to find a way to get Jamie Fraser across the Atlantic Ocean without killing him. Ergo, I needed a method of curing seasickness that would be reliable and that could plausibly exist in the eighteenth century. Aha, acupuncture! Perfectly plausible, but only if I had a Chinese person to administer it or instruct Claire in its uses. Enter Yi Tien Cho, aka Mr. Willoughby. ("Mr. Willoughby," by the way, was entirely Jamie's notion; I have no idea why he thought that a suitable name, but that's what he insisted on calling him.)

Now, Mother Hildegarde and Mr. Willoughby are what I call "onions"; characters who develop slowly through the addition of multiple layers of personality, rather than popping up full-fledged as the "mushrooms" do. Mother Hildegarde was an onion, but her dog, Bouton, was a pure mushroom.

*"Is that a **dog**?" I asked one of the orderlies in amazement, when I first beheld Bouton, passing through L'Hôpital at the heels of his mistress.*

He paused in his floor-sweeping to look after the curly, plumed tail, disappearing into the next ward.

"Well," he said doubtfully, "Mother Hildegarde says he's a dog. I wouldn't like to be the one to say he isn't."

One may not know everything about an onion all at once, but rather discover him little by little, by writing multiple scenes involving him, or by thinking about him and figuring out bits of his personal history. Claire and Jamie both developed in this way; even though I had a good grasp of their essential characters from the beginning, I gradually found out more about them as I deduced their personal histories and became well acquainted with them.

(I have writer friends who do this formally—give characters a history, before they even begin writing scenes involving them. Michael Lee West—who's one of the best "character" writers around—often draws up extensive genealogical charts for her characters, including generations of people who never appear in the story. She also says that she knows what kind of peanut butter her characters prefer—smooth or crunchy. This would drive me crazy, but as long as it works for Michael Lee . . .)

What do you do when your characters don't adhere to a plan, but go off and do things on their own? Ha! One should be so lucky *all* the time!

Hard Nuts

Beyond mushrooms and onions are the hard nuts (onions, mushrooms, and nuts; this is beginning to sound like an exotic recipe for turkey stuffing. Oh, well; cookery and writing have quite a bit in common, after all). These are the most difficult characters for me to animate; the characters whose function in the story is structural—they're important not because of personality or action, but because of the role that they play.

One example of a hard nut is Brianna, Jamie and Claire's daughter. She existed in the first place only because I had to have a child. The fact of her conception provides the motive for one of the major dramatic scenes in *Dragonfly*, but it didn't matter at all at that point *who* this kid was or what she would be like; the fact that Claire was pregnant was the only important factor.

Still, once having created this kid—even in utero—there she was. I couldn't just ignore her. Her existence—rather than her personality—dictated quite a bit about the structure of the third book, and thus, the second as well; I decided to use her as an adult, creating a "framing story" for the main action of the second book. Here again, though, it was her existence as a structural element that was important, rather than the girl herself. That is, I needed a grown daughter to whom Claire would confess the secret of her past, said confession leading to the future events of the third book.

But who the heck *was* this character? And having created her purely for plot purposes, how was I to give her a personality? She didn't talk to me for quite a long time, and it was difficult to crack the puzzle of her personality. She plainly wasn't a clone of either parent, but someone unique. Who, though?

Well, there are various ways and means of giving a character reality, none of which necessarily works all the time, but all of which may be worth trying sometimes.

PHYSICAL DESCRIPTION

This tends to be easy for me; I "see" people very easily. Other writers have told me that they deliberately visualize popular actors or people they know as the original basis for their characters. With the exception of the Real People (see p. 140), I never do this. In fact, I was actually rather appalled by the idea when I heard this; it seemed rather like body-snatching. Still, whatever works . . .

Some writers write out the physical description of the character separately from the story itself—rather like the police description of a suspect. This description may grow to involve more than the purely physical, including things such as mannerisms and incidental characteristics (e.g., this person bites her nails, sunburns easily, smokes like a chimney—but only mentholated Super 100s—and is so overweight her thighs are chronically chafed). I don't do this, either—I seldom write down anything at all, other than the actual text of the book itself—but many good writers do.

I could in fact "see" Brianna quite easily; the physical part of her persona was there from the beginning. I happen to have a tall, redheaded husband, and two redheaded daughters, so I had some experience to draw on, in terms of appearance and resemblances. Still, appearance is only a beginning.

IDIOSYNCRASY

One may also develop a character by supplying him or her with a striking idiosyncrasy of some kind. Mr. Willoughby began to assume a personality for me when

I purchased a sprightly little volume from a remainder table, titled *The Sex Life of the Foot and Shoe.* This went into every variety of foot fetishism one could imagine (and several that would *never* have occurred to me, I having led a sheltered life before I began writing novels), including a section on foot-binding and ancient Chinese attitudes toward the perfect "lotus foot."

Having a Chinese man in the story already—and foot-binding being in fact an aspect of Chinese culture in the eighteenth century (as well as earlier)—I couldn't resist the notion of letting Mr. Willoughby have a "thing" for feet—with the concomitant notion of a strong attraction toward women in general—which in turn led me to the story of his escape from China, and his true vocation as a poet.

Brianna, though, seemed not to have any striking idiosyncrasies. Part of the difficulty there, of course, was that she was quite young, with a sheltered upbringing. Parts of her emerged slowly—she had a feel for objects, the ability to make a space her own, manual dexterity, and a flair for building—but none of that was sufficiently striking as to illuminate her character for me.

CULTURAL BACKGROUND

One can also develop a character by supplying her with an Exotic Background. If a character comes from a different culture or society than the writer does, or than the story's main characters do, one can sometimes understand her or round her out by reading about social customs, fairy tales (you learn as much about people from the stories they tell as from their more "official" histories), or other cultural attributes.

Mr. Willoughby, the *houngan* Ishmael, Louis XV—all these characters drew on elements of an exotic cultural background. But Brianna? English by descent, American by upbringing, thoroughly contemporary in outlook. Nothing helpful there, I'm afraid.

BACK STORY

One can also tell the character's "back story." That is, what led this character to his involvement in the situation where the writer has placed him? Even though this information may not be included in the story, knowing it may give one substantial insight into the character. (And then again, some of us write the back story and can't keep it *out* of the main story, which is one of the things that leads to thousand-page books.)

Brianna's back story, though, was really her *parents'* story (all three of them). She found herself in situations as the result of actions that certainly had an effect on her—but in which she had had no active part.

THE RATIONAL APPROACH

I once heard a talk on character development in which an author advocated using a standard psychological test (the Minnesota Multiphasic Personality Inventory, in fact) to figure out what characters were like, and get a grip on them before writing. I'm not a rational writer at all, so this notion does nothing for me (though I suppose I wouldn't really like to think of myself as an irrational writer).

THE INTUITIVE APPROACH

And finally . . . you can just live with characters for a while, put them in different situations inside your head (not story situations, necessarily; just things like "Character A cuts his toenails. Does Character B offer to help, watch closely, turn away in disgust?"), and gradually get a feel for them.

Similarly, you can learn about the characters by the way the other characters regard them. Brianna finally began to come to life for me when Roger, watching her in church, thought to himself, *Though capable of the most tender expressions, hers was not a gentle face.* Aha! I thought. At last I know something about her; she doesn't have a gentle face. And from that, I began to intuit *why*, and the conflicts that might underlie someone ungentle but at the same time capable of tenderness.

Returning to the basic story question: What does this person want? That's where the complexity of Brianna Randall Fraser lies, I think. The superficial answer would

be "She wants her father." But that's not quite it.

If she were a teenager or a younger girl, then yes. But she is an adult young woman, well-educated, fairly self-confident, and on her own. Of course she has the deep-seated yearning for a father that all girls have— but at the same time, she's *had* a father's love . . . and returned it.

So she may want to know Jamie Fraser out of a sense of curiosity, loneliness, obligation, etc.—but it's not the same feeling as that of a woman who had never had a father at all. She feels complete in herself; and yet there is that urge to know the truth about herself—and about her parents' relationship.

The urge to find out, though, is complicated by her feelings of attachment to Frank. Many adopted children refrain from searching for a birth parent out of feelings that this is somehow a betrayal of a beloved "real" parent. Add to this the feelings of abandonment caused by Claire's disappearance into the past, and you have a young woman with greatly conflicted feelings: the urge to find out battling with the urge to avoid the whole issue, love for her mother versus subconscious anger at her departure, and finally—curiosity about Jamie Fraser, warring with feelings of filial love for Frank.

The general result of all this is to cause her to become rather secretive; she deals with her conflicting urges by concealing them. Only Roger—adopted himself, but with a firm grounding in his own history— understands.

And so gradually I "found" Brianna, mostly by watching Roger as he fought his way through Brianna's layers of self-protection.

Are You Claire?

Evidently there are a great many people under the impression that all fiction is essentially autobiographical; I think these are the same people who want to see a movie made of the *Outlander* books because they want to *see* "what Claire and Jamie look like."

But to answer the question . . .

Physically? Well, disregarding such small matters as height, hair and eye color, hair texture, skin pigment, and build, of course—I mean, we're both obviously female.

In terms of personality and attitude . . . well, as the result of having been raised in a conservative Catholic home and school, I am completely unable to swear. I will say, "Damn!" in situations of extreme stress, such as dropping an iron skillet on my foot, but that's it. Consequently, Claire swears for me. Being a person of great courage and forthrightness—attributes I admire, whether I share them or not—she's also able to do things that I personally would be much too shy to attempt.

Still, on one level, the answer to the question must obviously be yes. *All* of an author's characters must in some way be manifestations of the author's psyche and experience; after all, where else would you get them?

There is a local group of readers who invite me to a formal tea once a year, for the purpose of picking my brains about what I'm writing. On one such occasion, the ladies present got onto the subject of Jack Randall, and began denouncing him with heat and passion. "He's just *loathsome*!" went the refrain. "He's such *scum*, such a

horrible human being. I just despise him!" And so forth and so on.

During all of which I sat quietly, sipping my cup of Earl Grey, and thinking, You don't have any idea that you're *talking* to Black Jack Randall, do you?

Where do characters come from? Sometimes I think it's better not to know.

Names

Naming fictional characters has never seemed to be a problem for me; most of them simply *have* names, from the moment of creation. Still, sometimes I'm able to recognize the ground from which my subconscious mined a particular gem.

This process started early on. When I decided that I should have a female character, I simply introduced her, knowing nothing about her other than the fact that she was an Englishwoman. She walked into a cottage full of Scotsmen, who all stared at her in some consternation. The leader got to his feet and introduced himself courteously as Dougal MacKenzie.

"Dougal," because at that point I knew very few appropriate Scottish names, but did know that my husband's name—Douglas—was Scottish in origin, meaning "dweller by the dark water." I got "MacKenzie" off a tartan-patterned cooler I'd seen in the grocery store (well, look, I'd only been writing for two or three days; I hadn't had a lot of time to do research yet).

So, Dougal MacKenzie stood up and introduced himself, asking—with furrowed brow—who this visitor might be?

To which she replied, speaking quite clearly, "Claire Elizabeth Beauchamp—and who the hell are you?"

Now, in retrospect, I think "Claire" was the result of my having just read Isabel Allende's *House of the Spirits,* which has a significant character named Clara. Allende had a recurrent riff on this name, repeating "Claire, Clara, clairvoyant" at intervals throughout the story (the character having a certain amount of supernatural talent). This created a nice rhythm, which was likely still ringing in my inner ear—so when Claire spoke up and identified herself, the name was there on the surface of my mind.

"Beauchamp" because the minimal amount of research I'd done to that point had referred to the French link with Scotland and its importance in the Jacobite Rising. It seemed vaguely desirable to give her a French name, so that I could later invoke French connections for her, if that seemed useful (at this point, I still thought she was an eighteenth-century woman). Anyway, Beauchamp was the name of a math teacher at my high school, and I'd been struck—in high school—by the fact that it was pronounced "Beechum," in spite of the obviously French spelling. If I

wanted a patently English lady, but with a French name, Beauchamp seemed a good choice.

"Elizabeth"? Well, it fit, that's all. Whereupon Claire Elizabeth Beauchamp promptly took over the story and began telling it herself. Being in no position to argue with her, I took the path of least resistance, and went along to see what would happen next.

Jamie was originally named in compliment to the *Doctor Who* character who inspired the setting and time period of the book(s). This character, a young Scots lad acquired as a companion by the doctor, was named Jamie MacCrimmon—and while he had nothing in common with my character other than nationality and a certain pigheaded notion of male gallantry, I liked the name Jamie.

So Jamie he was, but with a blank for a last name. Knowing nothing about Scotland when I began, I was reluctant to give him a last name until I knew more about the history of the Highlands and its clans. He remained "Jamie [ ]" for several months, in fact—until I happened in the course of my research to read *The Prince in the Heather,* by Eric Linklater.

This book told the story of what happened to the Bonnie Prince and his followers after the disaster at Culloden. Included in the description of those harrowing days was the poignant quote which I later used in *Dragonfly in Amber: After the final battle at Culloden, eighteen Jacobite officers, all wounded, took refuge in the old house and for two days, their wounds untended, lay in pain; then they were taken out to be shot. One of them, a Fraser of the Master of Lovat's regiment escaped the slaughter;*

the others were buried at the edge of the domestic park.

Now, by this point I had "seen" enough of the story to think that it should end at Culloden—but I had the feeling that there was more to the story than that. So, on the off chance that there might one day be a sequel to this book (cough), I thought it might be advisable for Jamie [ ] to survive that battle—and if that were the case . . . well, plainly his last name should then be Fraser.

As to the other characters in the books, some name themselves without apparent reference to anything, some names I pick from the mists of memory or the ragbag of whimsy, and others I select quite consciously—though these latter names tend to belong to minor characters.

Colum MacKenzie (Callum, in *Cross Stitch*) was another character who arrived early on. Groping for a Scottish-sounding name, I picked "Colum" from one of James Clavell's novels (*Noble House*, I think), in which a Scottish family had a son so named. Much, much later, when we sold the book to a U.K. publisher, and I asked them to have a Scot read it, Reay Tannahill (who read the manuscript and made many helpful comments) informed me that while this was a Gaelic name, the usual Scottish spelling was "Callum"; "Colum" is, evidently, Irish.

Ah, well. We changed it for the U.K. edition, but since the U.S. edition had already reached the galley-proof stage, we didn't change it there—on the grounds that the spelling would be immaterial to U.S. readers—and given the extreme variations in Gaelic spellings that I had so far encountered, Colum/Callum seemed minor.

I WATCHED **DOCTOR WHO** as reruns on our local PBS channel. Owing to the differences of format between British shows and American programming, the credits of imported shows were sometimes cut off, to allow time for PBS announcements following the show. Consequently, it was not until I had finished writing **Outlander** that I discovered the name of the actor who had played Jamie MacCrimmon—one Frazer Hines.

As I went on doing research through the course of the novels, I came across the legend of the Dunbonnet—the survivor of Culloden who returned to his estate, and lived seven years in hiding in a cave, protected by his loyal tenants. This struck me as a most romantic and suitable story, so—in the larcenous fashion of novelists—I snatched it and adapted it to my own purposes.

Many months later, I came across the story of the Dunbonnet, repeated by another source. This one, more complete, gave the real name of the man known as the Dunbonnet— one James Fraser.

Colum's son (or not, as the case may be), Hamish, was named in compliment to the hero of M.C. Beaton's delightful comic novels, the Highland policeman Hamish MacBeth.

Where did I get names like Letitia and Maura? Heaven knows: I don't.

Geillis Duncan was a conscious choice, though. In the course of the research, I had discovered a Scottish witch, executed in the late sixteenth century, named Geillis Duncan. I liked the name—and had also seen a passing reference in one of Dorothy Dunnett's novels (which I much admire) to Geillis as "a witch's name." Little did I realize that the woman who bore it in *Outlander* had also chosen it deliberately, and for the same reason! She so informed me, sometime later, when she chose to reveal her real name—or what I must presently assume to be her real name—Gillian Edgars.

Mother Hildegarde was another who named herself. Having decided upon her profession and avocation, I set out to write her, and found the name "Hildegarde" being insistently shoved under my nose. Nonsense, I said, I don't think Hildegarde is even a French name. Surely she ought to be Berthe or Matilde or something. But no, it was "Hildegarde" and nothing else.

Fine, I said, already used to argumentative characters. Have it your way, Hildegarde. We can always change it later, if the copy editor tells me it isn't French.

A year or two later, I found myself in London, in a store called Past Times, which specializes in the reproduction of art and artifacts from . . . er . . . past times. They had a rack of musical recordings, compositions dating from the tenth century to the twentieth, performed on period instruments and according to the performance conditions appropriate to the time of the composition. Finding this interesting, I thumbed through the rack, only to find a tape of songs composed by . . . one Mother Hildegarde.

Hildegarde von Bingen, to be exact (as I recall, my actual exclamation at the time was, "Ha! So it *isn't* French!"). A mystic, a composer—and an abbess—from the twelfth century. But Mother Hildegarde, nonetheless.

As for the minor characters who don't speak up for themselves, I often rely on a book titled *Scottish Christian Names,* by Leslie Alan Dunkling. This is really a rather misleading title, since a good many popular Scottish names are not "Christian" at all, coming from much more ancient Celtic roots. The author of the book really means simply "first" names, as opposed to surnames, and the general derivation, meaning, and alternative forms of each name are included.

HISTORICAL CHARACTERS

Names are, of course, not a problem when dealing with characters who are real historical persons. The chief difficulty in these instances is to do justice to the actions and personality of the dead (or at least to treat them with such respect as they seem to deserve), while still ruthlessly subverting them to the purposes of the story.

This is an ethical as well as a technical problem, though one luckily has the advantage of not needing to worry about being sued for defamation. Any novelist who deals with historical characters has to determine how to handle them—and the handling of course grows somewhat easier if little is written about those characters, since this allows the author maximum flexibility.

The principal historical character with whom I was dealing was, of course, Charles Stuart, a person about whom much has been written—most of it glamorized, inaccurate, and wildly misleading.

A major difference in doing real historical research, versus that required for writing a historical novel, is that with the latter, one need not be quite so picky about the reliability of the sources. Still, a sense of obligation and respect toward the historical characters—who were, after all, real people—dictates that one should try to obtain at least fairly accurate information as to who they really were, and then to do nothing to discredit them, beyond the bounds of their known reputations.

I was fortunate enough to find a book titled *Bonnie Prince Charlie,* by Susan Mac-Lean Kybett, on a remainder table (one of a writer's greatest resources). It appeared to be by far the best description of Charles Stuart available; the book is scholarly (Kybett being a respected British historian), thorough, and—luckily—very readable, and presented an excellent picture both of

Stuart and of the political situation surrounding the circumstances of the Rising.

I've found that when doing historical research, while one may consult hundreds of books, normally only a few prove to be extremely useful. *Bonnie Prince Charlie* was one such book, and I used Kybett's portraits of Charles Stuart and the other prominent Jacobites as the basis for my own fictional portrayals.

While it was, of course, necessary to invent incident and dialogue involving Stuart and other historical persons, I tried to make sure that such descriptions fit with what was known of each character's real persona and actions. Hence, Charles Stuart's speech; while he did speak English, he spoke it badly, and with a pronounced Italian accent. While the incident of the rooftop excursion and the monkey bite (in *Dragonfly in Amber*) is invented, the affair with Louise de Rohan was not. The affair of the cargo ship full of port is invented; the negotiations with Manzetti the banker and the purchase of the Dutch broadswords were not.

With Simon Fraser, Lord Lovat (the Old Fox), I played somewhat more loosely. Though I saddled him with a thoroughly fictitious illegitimate grandson,[1] the general depiction of his personality as wily, sensual, and politically astute is based soundly on a good many accounts of his life and behavior—even though those accounts vary considerably in detail and reliability.

At the same time, the prostatitis that served as his ostensible excuse for not joining Charles Stuart was purely my inven-

---

[1] *However, the existence of bastard sons is quite consonant with what's known of Lovat's character*

tion. I had been reading an article at the local health club about the symptoms of prostate enlargement and prostatitis, which included a remark about how common this problem was in men over sixty-five. I at once exclaimed "Eureka!," went home, and wrote the scene at Beaufort Castle (the Castle also had to be invented, as the original was leveled after the Rising, and thus wasn't available for research) in which Claire performs her dinner table diagnosis.

Young Simon (the Young Fox) is also a real historical character, about whom a fair amount is known. Most of the actions for which he was known, though, took place in the latter years of his life—a span that falls outside the constraints of the story so far. However, I rather think we haven't seen the last of Young Simon.

Louis XV was—obviously—a real historical person. The descriptions of his levee and Court customs, his sexual behavior (exchanging political patronage for the favors of the wives of those seeking advantage), and his deep interest in the occult were taken from various historical sources.

Dr. Fleche and his servant, Plato, are likewise real historical characters; the Doctor, in fact, is widely credited with having caused the premature demise of a good many of the French Royal Family.

The Comte St. Germain was a real character of the times, and one with a reputation for being involved in occult matters—but very little else seemed known for sure about him. I consequently took nothing but his name and his unsavory associations, and beyond that, invented wholesale. (I note in passing that another author—Chelsea Quinn Yarbro—evidently took the Comte and used him fictionally; as a vampire, whose immortality allows

him to live in various interesting time periods.)

Monsieur Forez was a professional hangman, operating in Paris at roughly the time of *Dragonfly in Amber.* I found mention of him with a description of the perquisites of the hangman's trade, and—being quite unable to resist including "hanged-men's grease" in the book—included Monsieur Forez, too.

Governor Tryon of North Carolina is naturally a real historical personage. While his dialogue with Jamie is of course invented, he did in fact pursue an aggressive policy of land grants in an effort to settle and civilize the backcountry of the Colony. The language of the land grant—and of the oath required of the defeated Jacobites—is taken word for word from historical documents of the time.

Farquard Campbell, Jocasta's friend in *Drums of Autumn,* was likewise a real person, prominent in the affairs of the Cape Fear River area and very influential among the Highlanders who settled there. His personal life, however—wives, children, etc.—is invented.

Other minor characters taken from the pages of history are marked in the Cast of Characters for each novel.

REAL PEOPLE

There is a second classification of Real People who serve as characters in my own books; these are the beloved and long-suffering friends whose forebearance has allowed me to exercise my sense of humor at their expense, by writing them into my stories.

John Simpson Sr. and John Simpson Jr.

John E. Simpson Jr. was one of my earliest electronic friends, distinguished by his gentle wit and beautiful prose, as much as by the rather unusual style of his name. Having shared a close relationship with his father, John sometimes used the "Jr." style, both professionally and personally. (He writes wonderful literary short stories and computer books [*Just XML*], and has just published a mystery novel.)

I was therefore astonished and delighted when, in the course of my research into Scottish weaponry, I came upon a mention of the historical Simpsons—a father and son team of sword makers, operating in Scotland during the mid–eighteenth century, and famed for the quality of their blades. Both, coincidentally, named John. I therefore wrote a small piece for *Dragonfly in Amber* featuring the sword makers, but giving them—with John's permission—the approximate physical characteristics of the contemporary Simpsons.

Labhriunn MacIan

Labhriunn MacIan was an early electronic acquaintance, who helpfully supplied my first lesson in Gaelic pronunciation, with regard to his name: Lay-vree-AHN. While I didn't know Labhriunn well, have

never met him, and have long since lost all contact with him, we shared one very long telephone conversation, in which he told me a great deal about Celtic heritage, the Shetland Islands (from which he hailed), and other things that proved indirectly inspirational in the writing of the books. He also told me the story of his grandfather, a blind piper who practiced on the seashore, bouncing the sound of his pipes off the sea cliffs. I therefore wrote Labhriunn himself into *Dragonfly in Amber* in a small walk-on role as a piper, incorporating the story of his grandfather in the process.

Margaret Campbell

As is evident, this process of character cannibalization began with online conversations. In one such conversation, Margaret Campbell (a longtime friend and duct-tape dilettante)[2] confided that she had harbored a childhood ambition to be a carnival geek—the person in old-time carnival sideshows whose "act" was to bite the heads off live chickens.

Someone jokingly responded that—given the SPCA and modern attitudes toward performance art—her only chance of achieving this particular ambition was likely to be "if Diana writes you into one of her books that way."

Now, I wish to state for the record that I am, too, capable of resisting insidious random suggestions. Just not all of them.

Well, I *did* intend to write a section of the book located in the West Indies. Ergo, I might quite reasonably have a small voodoo ceremony, at which it would be

---

[2]*Look, don't blame me; I asked her how she wished to be described here and that's what she said.*

entirely appropriate to have the sacrifice of a black cock, and so . . . enter the Scottish voodoo oracle, Miss Margaret Campbell, sweetheart of Captain Ewan Cameron, and sister to the Edinburgh Fiend.

Barry Fogden

Likewise, another electronic friend, Barry Fogden, made the mistake of mentioning in casual conversation that his grandfather had been a shepherd, and that he, Barry, had often helped with lambing and other chores in his wanton youth. Human nature being what it is, this revelation led to a predictable outbreak of sheep jokes among the inhabitants of the CompuServe Literary Forum.

Consequently—a writer's mind being what it is—the notion of sheep led to the notion of "flock," which in turn suggested a priest. And I did need some way for Fergus and Marsali to get married. Thus B. Fogden, erstwhile shepherd, reputable and eminent British poet, became the disreputable and outcast Father Fogden, accompanied into the pages of *Voyager* by his dog, Ludo, and his . . . er . . . flock (Ludo is real; the sheep are fictional).

John (Quincy) Myers

One of my oldest electronic friends is the novelist John L. Myers, who—among his other notable attributes—possesses a striking physical appearance, being six-feet-seven in height. John also hails from North Carolina, and was most helpful in supplying incidental information, ghost stories, and other arcana having to do with his home territory (I am indebted to John for the story of the Brown Mountain Lights, which loosely inspired the ghost story in *Drums*).

I repaid this kindness by creating Johnnie Lee Myers, Mountain Man, and—as is my custom—forwarding the fictional creation to his namesake for approval prior to publication, asking whether there were any changes that I ought to make before JLM appeared in print.

John replied that the fictional creation was really amazingly similar in appearance—beard, snaky locks, and all—to his own grandfather Quincy Myers, who had been a revenuer in the North Carolina mountains. He requested that I change the character's name slightly, to include "Quincy," as a small tribute to his grandfather—and thus, the character emerged into publication in *Drums of Autumn* as John Quincy Myers.

Cast of Characters

I now and then get letters or E-mail from people who cannot recall quite who one or another of the characters in the books is[1]—or recall the name, but not which book the character occurred in—or recall name and book, but not what the character was doing in the story. After considering for some time how best to organize a list of characters in order to make them easy to look up, and most effective in jogging errant memories, I finally decided to provide a simple alphabetic listing, giving a capsule description of the character and his or her relationships, and noting the book or books in which each character occurs.

On the other hand, there's nothing really "simple" about an alphabetical listing, given the number of characters and the variety of their names. Still, that seemed the only reasonable approach, so I've adopted the following conventions, for the sake of consistency:

All characters are listed alphabetically 1) by their last name (if they had one), 2) by first name (if they were referred to by only one name), or 3) by the main word describing them (if they were nameless)—like "ghost."

Characters who appear under different names at different points in the story (e.g.,

Claire Beauchamp Randall becomes Claire Fraser; James Alexander Malcolm Mac-Kenzie Fraser appears as Alexander Malcolm, Captain Alessandro, and a variety of other aliases; Roger Wakefield reclaims his original family name of MacKenzie, etc.) are listed under all their names, though only the main listing (the name by which the character is most commonly known) gives a description of the character; aliases merely refer the reader to the original name.

Characters who were real people existing in historical times (or at least my fictional version of them) are marked with a dagger(†). Characters who are real people, and friends of mine (or at least were *before* I began putting them—liberally embellished by my imagination—in books) are marked with a double dagger (††).

Many characters do not appear directly in one book or another, but are mentioned with some significance—such as the ghost in *Outlander.* We never actually *see* the ghost, and yet Frank's description of meeting him is sufficient to make the ghost a significant character. Likewise, Jamie's par-

---

[1] *Not surprising, given the sheer staggering number of them. I hadn't realized quite how many characters there were, myself, until I began compiling this list. You'd think these were Russian novels, rather than Scottish ones.*

ents, Brian and Ellen Fraser, never appear directly in the story, but are important figures, nonetheless. Ergo, characters who are mentioned in the story (and important to it in some way), but who do not appear directly, are listed with an (m) notation following their names.

Very Minor Characters, who are named individually, but appear only as members of a group and have no great importance to the story, are listed collectively at the end of the alphabetical listing (e.g., Dougal's men, Monks at the Abbey of Ste. Anne de Beaupré, etc.). Minor characters who have no names, but are identified only by their office (e.g., "Le Havre harbormaster"), are also listed here.

A

Barnabas Abernathy (m)—last husband of Geillis Duncan, who died under mysterious circumstances, leaving her Rose Hall. [*Voyager*]

Mrs. Abernathy of Rose Hall—the last known alias of Gillian Edgars/Geillis Duncan. [*Voyager*]

Dr. Joseph Abernathy—Claire's best friend, whom she met at medical school, and whom she later leaves in charge of her daughter. [*Dragonfly, Voyager, Drums*]

Leonard Abernathy—son of Joseph Abernathy; a friend of Brianna's. [*Dragonfly, Drums*]

Abigail—one of Jamie's small great-nieces; a red-haired lassie with outspoken opinions. ("*We* call him Snot-rag," she informed me.) [*Voyager*]

Absalom—MacRannoch's cowherd. [*Outlander*]

Don Armando Alcantara (m)—the betrayed and deserted husband of Ermenegilda. [*Voyager*]

Ermenegilda Ruiz Alcantara y Meroz (m)—the young woman for whom Father Fogden abandoned his priestly vows. [*Voyager*]

Mina Alcott—merry widow of Kingston; murdered by the Reverend Campbell at the Governor's reception. [*Drums*]

Judge Alderdyce—a prominent Justice, a friend of Jocasta Cameron's, and (Jocasta thinks) a good potential husband for Brianna. [*Drums*]

Mrs. Alderdyce—the widowed mother of Judge Alderdyce, eager to see her son wed to Brianna, in hopes of obtaining a grandchild. [*Drums*]

"Auld Alec"—see "Alexander MacMahon MacKenzie."

Captain Alessandro—Jamie's alias, when he temporarily joins the Spanish garrison on Hispaniola. [*Voyager*]

"Young Alex"—serving boy at Castle Leoch. [*Outlander*]

Etienne Marcel de Provac Alexandre—one of Jamie Fraser's aliases, used in Jamaica, where he attends the Governor's reception disguised as a French planter from Martinique. [*Voyager*]

Aline—Simon Fraser's sister-in-law. [*Dragonfly*]

Dame Aliset (m)—a legendary figure; the "White Lady" of the Highlands. [*Dragonfly*]

Rufus Allison—innkeeper of the Lime Tree tavern, where Lord John Grey and Jamie go to question Duncan Kerr. [*Voyager*]

† **Richard Anderson,** of Whitburgh—the man who showed the Highland army a secret way across the field at Preston-

pans, thus allowing them to take the English by surprise. [*Dragonfly*]

"L'Andouille"—"The Sausage." A French courtier, known for his sexual proclivities. [*Dragonfly*]

Mrs. Andrews—secretary to Dr. McEwan at the Institute for Highland Studies, where Gillian Edgars began her research into the standing stones. [*Dragonfly*]

Sister Angelique—a nun at L'Hôpital des Anges. [*Dragonfly*]

Uncle Angus—a stuffed Aberdeen terrier, companion of Roger's youth. [*Drums*]

Angus Mhor ("Big Angus")—Colum's body servant, bodyguard, and general factotum of justice. NB: "Mhor" is not a last name, but rather a Gaelic adjective. [*Outlander, Dragonfly*]

Anne—Geillis Duncan's serving woman. [*Outlander*]

Father Anselm—a priest visiting Ste. Anne de Beaupré, who counsels with Claire on the morality of time travel. [*Outlander*]

M. and Mme. (Marie) d'Arbanville—social acquaintances of the Frasers in Paris. [*Dragonfly*]

Arnold (and Harry)—English deserters, who come upon and attack Jamie and Claire. [*Outlander*]

† M. Arouet (aka Voltaire) (m)—eighteenth century philosopher and critic. [*Voyager*]

Atlas and Hercules—twin slaves, belonging to Geillis Abernathy at Rose Hall. [*Voyager*]

B

Father Bain—the local priest in Cranesmuir, who condemns Claire as a witch and a Sassenach. [*Outlander*]

Mrs. Baird—landlady of the bed-and-breakfast where Claire and Frank stay in Inverness. [*Outlander*]

Mr. Bainbridge (m)—an Inverness solicitor with an interest in history; friend of Frank Randall. [*Outlander*]

† "Balhaldy" (William MacGregor, or Drummond of Balhaldies)—a seedy Jacobite hanger-on, who frequented the company of Prince Charles in Paris. [*Dragonfly*]

Father Balmain—the young priest who attends L'Hôpital des Anges. [*Dragonfly*]

† Lord Balmerino—one of the prominent Jacobite earls; later executed at Tower Hill for his part in the Rising. [*Dragonfly*]

The Baronet—Mary Hawkins's father; Silas Hawkins's brother. [*Dragonfly*]

Bear Killer—the name given to Jamie Fraser by the Tuscarora, in consequence of his having killed a black bear singlehanded, with a knife. [*Drums*]

Davie Beaton (m)—the late physician of Castle Leoch; Claire inherits his stock and casebook. [*Outlander*]

Henry Montmorency Beauchamp (m)—Claire's father. [*Dragonfly*]

Quentin Lambert Beauchamp (aka "Uncle Lamb") (m)—Claire's paternal uncle, who raised her from childhood following the death of her parents in a car accident. [*Outlander*]

Father Beggs—pastor of St. Finbar's, the parish church in Boston that Frank attends, and where Claire goes in the middle of the night, seeking peace and comfort. [*Voyager*]

† Pope Benedict—supporter of the Catholic Stuarts; succeeded Clement. [*Dragonfly*]

Father Benin—a priest accompanying the Jacobite troops at Prestonpans. [*Dragonfly*]

Hugh Berowne—a tax collector who, at the instigation of Sergeant Murchison, falsely accuses Fergus of nonpayment of tax, and confiscates his horse, saddle, and bridle in payment. [*Drums*]

Berta—one of Louise de Rohan's servants at Fontainebleau; a secret Huguenot, and one of Pastor Laurent's parishioners. [*Dragonfly*]

Berthe—Gabrielle's daughter by her first husband, a French trapper. [*Drums*]

Betty—one of Jocasta Cameron's house-slaves. [*Drums*]

"Black Jack" Randall (aka Jonathan Wolverton Randall)—see under "R."

Colonel Bogle (m)—Harry Quarry's predecessor as Governor of Ardsmuir Prison; put Jamie Fraser in irons. [*Voyager*]

Madame Bonheur (m)—a midwife at L'Hôpital des Anges. [*Dragonfly*]

Stephen Bonnet—an Irishman orphaned young, Stephen Bonnet made his way in life by any means possible, consulting no one's desires save his own. Condemned to hanging for piracy, he escaped the gallows in Charleston, and fell in with the Frasers by hiding in the wagon bearing the body of Gavin Hayes. Prevailing upon their kindness to aid his escape, he later repaid their generosity by ambushing their party on the river, stealing both their gemstones and Claire's gold wedding ring. Bonnet uses one of the gems to finance his acquisition of the *Gloriana,* a small cargo ship on which Roger MacKenzie later sails to America. He meets Brianna Randall Fraser in an inn in Wilmington, where she spots her mother's ring. When Brianna goes to the *Gloriana* to try to buy back the ring—and learn what has happened to her mother—Bonnet gives her the ring, but at his own price—rape. Later, when Bonnet is captured, Brianna—believing him about to be executed—tells him that the child she is carrying is his; Bonnet escapes, giving Brianna a black diamond for the maintenance of the child he thinks is his. [*Drums*]

Gayle Bosworthy—Brianna's best friend in college. A great admirer of men in kilts. [*Drums*]

† Bouassa—a notorious maroon; executed for rebellion. His *loa* comes, summoned by Ishmael, to give his blessing to the slaves who plot escape from Jamaica. [*Voyager*]

Comtesse de Brabant—member of the court at Versailles. [*Dragonfly*]

Edwina Briggs—dean of the college at Oxford where Roger Wakefield is employed. [*Drums*]

Bruno (aka Theobald)—doorkeeper and bouncer at Madame Jeanne's brothel in Edinburgh. [*Voyager*]

Mrs. Buchanan—the Inverness postmistress; member of the dancing ladies on Craigh na Dun. [*Outlander*]

Corporal Brame[2]—one of Lord John Grey's soldiers at Ardsmuir. [*Voyager*]

bridie seller—old woman who sells Brianna hot pasties ("bridies") at the hiring-hall in Inverness. [*Drums*]

Brutus—the horse Brianna acquires after traveling through the stones, to carry her to Lallybroch. [*Drums*]

Ernie Buchan—Fiona's fiancé, who views her relationship with Roger Wakefield MacKenzie with considerable suspicion. [*Drums*]

---

[2] *Named in compliment to Gloria Brame, a poet friend of mine.*

Maisri Buchanan—A mother whom Claire counsels on nutrition, at the Gathering. [*Drums*]

Mr. Buchanan—a Scottish plantation owner in North Carolina, a social acquaintance of Jocasta Cameron. [*Drums*]

Vicomte de Busca (m)—young man rumored to be one of Les Disciples de Mal. [*Dragonfly*]

Davie Byrnes—the incompetent and drunken overseer of the timber camp and sawmill operations at River Run. Responsible for the gruesome lynching death of a slave at the sawmill, Byrnes dies himself of tetanus as a result of wounds sustained in the precipitating incident. [*Drums*]

C

† **Archie Cameron** (m)—brother to Lochiel; a physician who attended the Highland army; later executed for his part in the Rising. [*Dragonfly*]

Ewan Cameron—a Jacobite soldier; one of Jamie's friends during the Rising; lover of Margaret Campbell. [*Dragonfly, Voyager*]

Hector Cameron—Jamie Fraser's uncle by marriage; husband to Jocasta MacKenzie Cameron, Jamie's aunt. [*Drums*]

Hugh Cameron (m)—chief of clan Cameron; a Jacobite. [*Dragonfly*]

† **Jenny Cameron**—sister of the chief of clan Cameron; hearing of Prince Charles's landing at Glenfinnan, she raised three hundred Camerons and led them to join the Stuart Rising. [*Dragonfly*]

John Cameron (m)—first husband of Jocasta MacKenzie. [*Outlander*]

Reverend Archibald Campbell—an ex-soldier (for the English Crown) turned clergyman; also turned murderer (see "Edinburgh Fiend"). Devoted brother of the demented Miss Margaret Campbell, whom he takes to the West Indies in hopes of restoring her senses. [*Voyager*]

† **Farquard Campbell**—a prominent member of Cape Fear's Scottish community, and a close friend to Jocasta Cameron. A law-abiding man with a scrupulous conscience, he is a county magistrate, as well as a planter. [*Drums*]

Margaret Campbell—sister of Archibald Campbell. A devoted follower of the Jacobite cause, she leaves home to join the Highland soldier with whom she is in love (Ewan Cameron), but falls afoul of Government troops, who brutalize her and leave her for dead. Surviving the assault, she has lost her wits—but the vacant housing of her mind provides the necessary vessel for the *loas*, voodoo spirits summoned by Ishmael, the *houngan*. [*Voyager*]

Ronnie Campbell—one of Farquard Campbell's numerous offspring, who comes to inform Jamie of Byrnes's death. [*Drums*]

Angus Walter Edwin Murray Carmichael—one of Ian and Jenny's grandsons; son of their daughter Maggie. [*Voyager*]

† **du Carrefours** (m)—a sinister French figure, with a reputation for involvement in the occult, burned for witchcraft in Paris some years prior. [*Dragonfly*]

Duc di Castellotti—a dissipated Italian nobleman; companion to Charles Stuart on his drunken ramblings through Paris. [*Dragonfly*]

Sister Cecile—a nun at L'Hôpital des Anges. [*Dragonfly*]

Sister Celeste—a nun at L'Hôpital des Anges. [*Dragonfly*]

"Bonnie Prince Charlie"—see "Charles Stuart."

Mr. Cheesewright (m)—Roger Wakefield's tutor at Oxford. [*Voyager*]

Corporal Chisholm (m)—a patient of Claire's, nursed during World War II. [*Outlander*]

Geordie Chisholm (m)—an ex-prisoner from Ardsmuir, desiring to take up residence at Fraser's Ridge. Jamie and Duncan Innes discuss whether to accept Geordie Chisholm or Ronnie Sinclair. [*Drums*]

Bart Clancy (m)—small, obnoxious son of Mrs. Clancy, the history department secretary. [*Voyager*]

Mrs. Clancy (m)—secretary in the history department where Frank works in Boston. [*Voyager*]

Clarence—Jamie's mule; a sociable creature, given to loud greetings. [*Drums*]

Claudel—see "Fergus."

Duchess of Claymore (m)—an English noblewoman, visiting the French Court. [*Dragonfly*]

† **Clanranald** (m)—a prominent Jacobite chief. [*Dragonfly*]

† **Pope Clement** (m)—supporter of the Catholic Stuarts. [*Dragonfly*]

Clotilda—Geillis Abernathy's door slave at Rose Hall. [*Voyager*]

Mrs. Coker (m)—mentioned as the cook at Lallybroch, though she is also referred to as Mrs. Crook. [*Dragonfly, Voyager*]

† **General Jonathan Cope** (m)—commander of the English army at Prestonpans;

defeated by a numerically vastly inferior Highland force. [*Dragonfly*]

M. Clouseau[3] (m)—Louise de Rohan's doctor, whom she had summoned to attend Claire, but whom Claire escapes.

Brodie Cooper—one of the crew of the *Artemis*. [*Voyager*]

Mr. Justice Conant—magistrate of the court where a tax collector brings false suit against Fergus for nonpayment of tax. [*Drums*]

Nellie Cowden—woman engaged by the Reverend Campbell to be abigail (serving-woman) for his sister Margaret on the voyage to the West Indies. [*Voyager*]

Mr. Crook—an elderly acquaintance who takes Claire botanizing in the Highlands, and in the process shows her the stone circle at Craigh na Dun. [*Outlander*]

Mrs. Crook (aka Mrs. Coker—see "Errata")—cook at Lallybroch, who dies during the difficult conditions after Culloden. [*Voyager*]

† **William Augustus, Duke of Cumberland** (m)—leader of King George's forces, bent on subduing the Jacobite Rising and stamping out its remains. [*Dragonfly, Voyager*]

D

Daft Joey (m)—a witless beggarman, lured into the cellar of a great house being built in Inverness, crushed to death with the cornerstone to serve as a blood sacrifice for the foundation. [*Outlander, Drums*]

---

[3] *"There ees a quastion as to whether ze man or e's minkey was brakking ze leaw."*

Myra Dalrymple (m)—resident gossip in Kingston. [*Voyager*]

Albert Danton—the Duke of Sandringham's valet; leader of the gang that attacks Claire and Mary Hawkins in the Rue du Faubourg St.-Honoré. [*Dragonfly*]

Danu (m)—the Celtic goddess of luck. [*Drums*]

Daphne (m)—Edinburgh prostitute whose dress Claire borrows, after her own is damaged in a pub brawl. [*Voyager*]

Reverend Davis (m)—a Kingston minister. [*Voyager*]

Corporal Dawes (m)—the soldier at Ardsmuir, charged with flogging Jamie Fraser for possession of contraband tartan. [*Voyager*]

Mr. Dixon—paymaster of the *Gloriana*.

Mr. Justice Dodgson (m)—a corrupt justice, the victim of violence imposed by a gang of Regulators. [*Drums*]

Drusus—one of Jocasta's slaves. [*Drums*]

Duff—a hand on the *Gloriana*. [*Drums*]

Arthur Duncan—the Procurator Fiscal in Cranesmuir; Geillis Duncan's husband; a murder victim, he is poisoned with cyanide at Colum's dinner party. [*Outlander*]

Geillis Duncan (aka Gillian Edgars)—wife of the Procurator Fiscal in Cranesmuir; Claire's friend; a suspected witch. Sentenced to burning, she was temporarily reprieved by reason of pregnancy, and bore a child to Dougal MacKenzie. Later escaped to Paris with Dougal's help, and made her way by various means to the West Indies, where her attempt to travel back to her own time led her to a final confrontation with Claire in the cave of Abandawe. [*All*]

† **Dundas** (m)—Sir Henry Dundas, an important figure in Scottish politics during the latter half of the eighteenth century. [*Voyager*]

Geneva Dunsany—eldest daughter of the Dunsany family of Helwater; taking a fancy to Jamie Fraser, she forces him to her bed by means of blackmail, and bears a son (William) to him, dying soon after giving birth. [*Voyager*]

Gordon Dunsany (m)—son of Lord Dunsany and heir to Helwater; killed in the Rising. A friend of Lord John Grey's. [*Voyager*]

Isobel Dunsany—younger daughter of Lord and Lady Dunsany of Helwater, younger sister to Geneva Dunsany. Following the death of her sister in childbed, she becomes foster mother to her sister's child, William, and later marries Lord John Grey, who thus becomes the boy's stepfather and guardian. [*Drums*]

Lady Dunsany—mother of Geneva and Isobel, grandmother of Willie, whose parentage she may suspect. She offers to arrange Jamie's pardon, so that he can leave Helwater. [*Drums*]

Lord Dunsany—a minor—and rather impoverished—aristocrat, who accepts Jamie Fraser (under the alias Alexander MacKenzie) as a groom on his estate, Helwater, as a favor to Lord John Grey. He arranged his daughter Geneva's marriage to the elderly Earl of Ellesmere, hoping that this would ensure her shortly becoming a wealthy young widow—and a countess. [*Drums*]

Corporal Dunstable—one of John Grey's soldiers at Ardsmuir, responsible for searching the prisoners' quarters for contraband. [*Voyager*]

Mrs. Dunvegan (m)—wife of the minister of the Old Church in Inverness; an acquaintance of Roger Wakefield. [*Drums*]

† **M. Duverney the elder**—Louis XV's Minister of Finance. [*Dragonfly*]

† **M. Duverney the younger**—son of Duverney the elder; a successful banker. [*Dragonfly*]

E

Gillian Edgars (aka Geillis Duncan)—A mysterious young woman with a monomania, and the ability to travel through the stones. [*All*]

† **Lord Elcho** (m)—one of the Jacobite earls.

Madame Elise—proprietor of the brothel in which Fergus was born. [*Dragonfly*]

Lord Ellesmere—husband to Geneva Dunsany; putative father of William, Viscount Ashness. Killed by Jamie Fraser while threatening the life of the newborn infant whom he knows to be the result of cuckoldry. [*Voyager*]

Eutroclus—a black freeman, serving as hand on the riverboat *Sally Ann*. [*Drums*]

George Everett (m)—John Grey's ex-lover, the cause of the scandal that exiled him to Ardsmuir. [*Voyager*]

Lord and Lady Everett (m)—parents of John Grey's ex-lover. [*Voyager*]

F

Dr. Charles Fentiman (m)—a surgeon from Cross Creek. [*Drums*]

Father Alexandre Ferigault—a young Jesuit priest. Coming to preach to the Mohawk, he succeeded in converting part of the village, but then fell in love with one of his parishioners, getting her with child. His subsequent behavior leads to a serious schism in the village, and finally results in his torture and death, and the death of his lover. He leaves behind an infant daughter, whom Roger baptizes Alexandra. [*Drums*]

Fergus (aka Claudel)—a young pickpocket, hired by Jamie to steal confidential political documents, who later becomes Jamie's foster son. Fergus loses his left hand in an encounter with English soldiers at Leap o' the Cask, and marries Jamie's erstwhile stepdaughter, Marsali, on a beach in the West Indies. Father of Germain. See also Claudel, Fergus Fraser. [*Dragonfly, Voyager, Drums*]

the Edinburgh Fiend—a killer of women, later revealed to be the Reverend Archibald Campbell. [*Voyager*]

Mrs. FitzGibbons (Glenna)—Chatelaine at Castle Leoch; Murtagh's aunt by marriage. [*Outlander*]

† **M. Fleche**—the Royal Doctor who attends Louis XV and his Court.

Father Fogden—a defrocked, disgraced priest who lives on Hispaniola. He offers hospitality to Claire when she is marooned, and later marries Fergus and Marsali. [*Voyager*]

Gerald Forbes—a lawyer, prominent inhabitant of Cross Creek; he brings four gemstones to assist his suit when paying court to Brianna. [*Drums*]

Miss Forbes—the sister of Lawyer Gerald Forbes, who praises her brother's accomplishments to Brianna. [*Drums*]

† **M. Forez**—the official hangman for

the Fifth Arrondissement,[4] who also volunteers his services as a bonesetter at L'Hôpital des Anges, where he befriends Claire. [*Dragonfly*]

Mrs. Forrest (m)—woman giving lodging to Margaret Campbell in Kingston. [*Voyager*]

Abbot Alexander Fraser—brother to Brian Fraser; uncle to Jamie Fraser; abbot of Ste. Anne de Beaupré priory. An ardent Jacobite, the abbot arranges for Jamie and Claire to live in Paris and assist Charles Stuart in his attempt to regain the throne of Scotland. [*Outlander, Dragonfly in Amber*]

Annie Fraser (m)—a young inhabitant of the village of Broch Mordha, whose death of the bloody flux is reported by the elder Ian Murray in one of his letters to Jamie. [*Drums*]

Brian Fraser ("Brian Dubh") (m)—husband to Ellen MacKenzie; father of Jamie Fraser and Jenny Fraser Murray. [*Outlander, Dragonfly, Voyager*]

Claire Elizabeth Beauchamp Randall Fraser—English ex-army combat nurse, who goes to Scotland on a second honeymoon with her husband, Frank Randall, following World War II—only to walk through a circle of standing stones, with surprising results. [*All*]

Ellen MacKenzie Fraser (m)—wife to Brian Fraser; sister to Colum and Dougal MacKenzie; mother to Jamie Fraser and Jenny Fraser Murray. [*Outlander, Voyager, Drums*]

Faith Fraser (m)—Claire and Jamie's first child, stillborn at L'Hôpital des Anges, following a miscarriage as the indirect result of Jamie's duel with Jack Randall. [*Dragonfly*]

Fergus Fraser—see "Fergus."

Lady Frances Fraser—one of Simon Fraser's daughters. [*Dragonfly*]

Geordie Paul Fraser—one of Jamie's followers. [*Dragonfly*]

James Alexander Malcolm MacKenzie Fraser—Laird of Broch Tuarach. Son of Ellen MacKenzie and Brian Fraser; illegitimately descended (though legitimately born) grandson of Simon Fraser (the Old Fox); Claire's second husband, father of Faith Fraser (stillborn), Brianna Ellen Randall (Fraser), and (by Geneva Dunsany) William, Viscount Ashness, ninth Earl of Ellesmere. [*All*]

Jared Munro Fraser—successful expatriate Scottish wine merchant, with ships and warehouses in Le Havre, and a mansion in Paris. Jamie's cousin, and a strong Jacobite. He later lends Jamie and Claire his ship, *Artemis,* to hunt for Young Ian in the West Indies. [*Dragonfly, Voyager*]

Marsali Joyce MacKimmie Fraser—see "Marsali."

Murtagh FitzGibbons Fraser—Jamie Fraser's godfather and companion. [*Outlander, Dragonfly*]

† **Simon Fraser, Lord Lovat** (the Old Fox)—chief of clan Fraser; Jamie Fraser's paternal grandfather. [*Dragonfly*]

† **Simon Fraser, Lord Lovat** (the Young Fox)—son of the executed Lord Lovat (also named Simon, known as the Old Fox); younger half-brother to Jamie

---

[4]*M. Forez is a real historical personage; his association with the Fifth Arrondissement is fictional, since in fact I am not positive that Paris had adopted the Arrondissement system of administration at the time in question.*

Fraser's father, thus half-uncle to Jamie Fraser. He led Fraser clansmen at Culloden, but escaped execution, though suffering the loss of most of his family property—later regained through legal process and as a reward for his efforts in raising a regiment to fight in the Colonies during the French and Indian War. [*Dragonfly, Drums*]

Wallace Fraser—tenant at Lallybroch. [*Dragonfly*]

William Fraser (m)—Jamie's elder brother, dead of smallpox at age eleven. [*Outlander*]

Frank—Claire's first husband; see also Franklin Wolverton Randall.

Captain Freeman—captain of the *Sally Ann,* the riverboat that carried the Frasers up the Cape Fear River from Wilmington to Cross Creek. [*Drums*]

G

Gabrielle—second wife to Nacognaweto, a woman of mixed blood, earlier married to a French trapper. Fluent in French, she translates for Claire and for her grandmother-in-law, Nayawenne. [*Drums*]

Tom Gage—an Edinburgh political agitator and seditionist; hires the printer A. Malcolm to print political pamphlets. [*Voyager*]

Lissa Garver—the pregnant girl whom Jamie and Claire finding bleeding to death in the sawmill, the apparent victim of a botched abortion—in truth, murdered by her erstwhile lover, Sergeant Murchison. [*Drums*]

Charles Gauloise (m)—Jamie's rival for the attentions of Annalise de Marillac. [*Dragonfly*]

Gayle—see "Gayle Bosworthy."

M. Genet—a French banker. [*Dragonfly*]

Geordie—print shop employee. [*Voyager*]

† **George II**, King of England. [*Dragonfly*]

† **George III**, King of England. [*Voyager*]

Germain(e)—firstborn son of Fergus and Marsali; proper French spelling of the masculine is "Germain."

† **Comte St. Germain**[5]—a member of the French Court; a noble with a reputation for dabbling in occult matters. Charles Stuart's business partner. [*Dragonfly*]

Comtesse St. Germain—wife of the Comte St. Germain. [*Dragonfly*]

Johannes Gerstmann—the King of France's Austrian music master. [*Dragonfly*]

a Native American ghost—Claire meets a man on a deserted mountain in North Carolina, his face painted black, holding a torch that burns but is not consumed. [*Drums*]

a Scottish ghost (m)—the spectral figure of a big Highlander, in kilt and running-stag brooch, whom Frank Randall encounters outside the bed-and-breakfast where he and Claire are staying in Inverness. [*Outlander*]

Duncan Gibbons (m)—a crofter on Lallybroch; Jenny's choice to marry Peggy Murray—if Jamie does not want to marry her himself. [*Voyager*]

Lachlan Gibbons (m)—a man saved from drowning by Maisri's Sight. [*Dragonfly*]

Ewan Gibson—Hugh Munro's eldest stepson. [*Dragonfly*]

---

[5]*The Comte St. Germain was a real historical character, an inhabitant of Paris at roughly the time of the story told in* Dragonfly. *The Comte had a sinister reputation, and was rumored to be heavily involved in the occult, but there is very little definite information available regarding him.*

Gideon (m)—Simon Fraser's secretary. [*Dragonfly*]

Gilbert (Gibbie)—a small boy aboard the *Gloriana,* one of the victims of the smallpox outbreak. [*Drums*]

Jonathan Gillette (m)—proprietor of the *Wilmington Gazette,* in which the death notice for Jamie and Claire Fraser appears. [*Drums*]

† **Glengarry**—prominent Jacobite chief. [*Dragonfly*]

† **Gérard Gobelin**—an important French banker, much involved with the financing of political figures. [*Dragonfly*]

Sir Fletcher Gordon—governor of Wentworth Prison. [*Outlander*]

† **Lord Lewis Gordon** (m)—a Jacobite supporter, who raised men for Charles Stuart.

Pastor Gottfried—pastor of a small group of German Lutherans, settled in North Carolina. He comes to Fraser's Ridge to tell Claire of the deaths of Petronella Mueller and her baby, and to warn her that Gerhard Mueller is seeking vengeance upon the local Indians, whom he blames for the deaths. [*Drums*]

Ned Gowan—a lawyer from Edinburgh; legal advisor to clan MacKenzie; helps to rescue Claire from the witchcraft trial in Cranesmuir; later, he handles negotiations resulting from Jamie Fraser's invalid marriage to Laoghaire MacKenzie. [*Outlander, Voyager*]

Fiona Graham—Mrs. Graham's granddaughter. A practical young woman with a domestic touch, she has set her sights on Roger, but abandons this project upon realizing that Roger is in love with Brianna. Fiona succeeds her grandmother, both as housekeeper at the manse, and as the "caller"—the leader of the women who dance on Craigh na Dun, calling down the sun on the Feast of Beltane. A good friend of Roger's, she helps him with his quest to follow Brianna, giving him the grimoire left behind by Geillis Duncan, and later giving him her own engagement diamond, to safeguard his passage through the stones. Engaged to marry Ernie Buchan. [*Dragonfly, Voyager, Drums*]

Master Georgie Graham—Mrs. Graham's small, coach-sick son. [*Voyager*]

Mrs. Graham—the Reverend Wakefield's housekeeper, Roger's foster mother, and grandmother to Fiona, who inherits her grandmother's position as leader of the dancing ladies who call down the sun at Craig na Dun on the Feast of Beltane. [*Outlander*]

Mrs. (Jemima) Graham—passenger in the coach taking Claire to Edinburgh to look for Jamie. [*Voyager*]

Malcolm Grant (m)—chieftain of clan Grant; rejected suitor of Ellen MacKenzie. [*Outlander*]

† **Margaret Grant** (m)—Simon Fraser's second wife. [*Outlander*]

Miss Grant—proprietor of an Inverness pastry shop; member of the dancing ladies. [*Outlander*]

Mungo Grant (m)—assistant cook at Castle Leoch. [*Outlander*]

Sir Greville (m)—the King's Commissioner on Antigua. [*Voyager*]

Lord John William Grey (aka "William Grey," in *Dragonfly*)—fourth son of Countess Melton; a sixteen-year-old who attacks Jamie in the wood, shortly before Prestonpans. He is overpowered, captured, and eventually returned to his companions, swearing vengeance on

Jamie. Later, he is appointed Governor of Ardsmuir Prison, where he makes Jamie's acquaintance once more. He marries Isobel Dunsany, and becomes stepfather to her nephew William. As Acting Governor of Jamaica, he meets Claire and Jamie again, and later befriends their daughter Brianna in North Carolina. [*Dragonfly, Voyager, Drums*]

Mr. Grey (m)—a Jamaican planter, who purchases the *Artemis*'s cargo of bat guano. [*Voyager*]

Mr. Grieves (m)—factor at Helwater. [*Voyager*]

Sergeant Grissom—one of Lord John Grey's officers at Ardsmuir. [*Voyager*]

Griswald—a fourteen-year-old private in the English army, who stops the Frasers on the road from Charleston to Wilmington, as they aid Stephen Bonnet's escape. [*Drums*]

Lady Grozier—friend of Lady Dunsany; remarks the unusual resemblance between the young William and his groom, MacKenzie, thus precipitating Jamie's exit from Helwater. [*Voyager*]

Loch Ness guide—a Highlander who takes Claire and Frank on a boat trip down Loch Ness, recounting many of the local legends. [*Outlander*]

Gwyllyn—Welsh bard, a retainer at Castle Leoch. [*Outlander*]

H

† **Jenny Ha** (m)—proprietor of a well-known tavern on the Royal Mile in Edinburgh. [*Dragonfly*]

Mr. Harding (m)—an agent of the Hand-in-Hand Assurance Society, which insured A. Malcolm's premises in Edinburgh. [*Voyager*]

Mr. Haugh—proprietor of an apothecary's shop on the Royal Mile in Edinburgh. [*Dragonfly*]

Haugh the Younger—proprietor of an apothecary's shop on the Royal Mile, inherited from his father. [*Voyager*]

Louisa Haugh—wife of Haugh the Younger. [*Voyager*]

Father Hayes (m)—priest who hears Jamie's and Young Ian's confession, following the print shop fire and its aftermath at the brothel. [*Voyager*]

Archie Hayes (Leftenant)—son of Gavin Hayes; wounded and captured at Culloden, Archie Hayes joined the English army as an alternative to transportation, and achieved the rank of leftenant. With his regiment of Scottish Highlanders, he arrives at the Gathering at Mount Helicon, in search of Jamie, who—he has heard—"kent my faither." [*Drums*]

Gavin Hayes—one of the Jacobite prisoners at Ardsmuir during Jamie Fraser's imprisonment there. Transported to the American Colonies after the closing of the prison, Gavin was later convicted of theft and hanged in Charleston, South Carolina. In a tavern, following the hanging, Jamie and Duncan tell Claire the story of Gavin's past—of his encounter with a *tannasg* in the Highlands, and of his search for his son, Archie—who took the field with his father at Culloden, but disappeared after the battle. Jamie claims Gavin's body, and buries him by night in the churchyard of St. Michael's, before traveling northward to North Carolina. [*Drums*]

Mrs. Hayes—one of Roger's neighbors at Inverness. [*Drums*]

Corporal Hawkins—aide to Captain Jonathan Randall. [*Outlander*]

Mary Hawkins—daughter of a minor English baronet, niece to Silas Hawkins. Engaged to an ancient member of the French nobility, but in love with Alexander Randall. [*Dragonfly*]

Mrs. Hawkins—Silas Hawkins's wife; Mary Hawkins's aunt. [*Dragonfly*]

Silas Hawkins—uncle of Mary Hawkins, brother of a baronet; a wine-seller, and customer of Jared Fraser. [*Dragonfly*]

† **General Hawley** (m)—an English commander, who led some of the troops that met the Highland army at Falkirk. [*Dragonfly*]

Harry (and Arnold)—English deserters. [*Outlander*]

Hector—MacRannoch's henchman, who finds and assists Claire following her escape from Wentworth. [*Outlander*]

Hector (Dalrymple) (m)—John Grey's first lover; killed at Culloden. [*Voyager*]

Lady Hensley (m)—a friend of the Dowager Countess Melton. [*Voyager*]

Herbert (m)—one of the Reverend Wakefield's dogs, mentioned in his journal. [*Dragonfly*]

Mother Hildegarde—Mother Superior of L'Hôpital des Anges; Claire's friend, and a good amateur musician and composer, who disentangles the musical cipher used by the Duke of Sandringham. [*Dragonfly*]

Dr. and Mrs. Hinchcliffe—dean of the history department and his wife. [*Voyager*]

Arvin Hodgepile[6]—An English soldier, stationed at the Crown warehouse in Cross Creek. Suspecting that someone is substituting cheap contraband for legitimately imported liquor, he ferrets about incognito, making inquiries that lead him as far as Jamie's mountain still, where he loses a button. He is blown up, presumed dead, in the conflagration following Stephen Bonnet's escape from the prison cells under the warehouse. [*Drums*]

Hoechstein (m)—an intern at the hospital where Claire did her medical training. [*Voyager*]

Hugo—Louise de Rohan's footman. [*Dragonfly*]

Hughes—head groom at Helwater. [*Voyager*]

Hughie—Jenny Murray's merino ram. [*Voyager, Drums*]

Mr. Hunter (m)—late surgeon of the *Porpoise,* dead of typhoid. Claire inherits his instruments and medicines. [*Voyager*]

† **Mr. Evan Hunter** (m)—a well-known medical authority and researcher, who wrote extensively on medical topics in the eighteenth century. [*Drums*]

† **James Hunter**—one of the leaders of the Regulator movement in North Carolina. [*Drums*]

† **Hermon Husband**—one of the leaders of the Regulator movement in North Carolina; a Quaker, and thus opposed to violence, but a man of principle who cannot abide the malfeasance of corrupt officialdom. [*Drums*]

Hutchinson—first mate of the *Gloriana.* [*Drums*]

I

the Indian in the corncrib—one of Ian's Tuscarora hunting companions, who

---

[6] *This name was given to me, courtesy of Barry Fogden, who having graciously allowed me to use his own persona, let me snatch his alias, as well.*

falls ill of the measles. Despite Claire's nursing, he dies in the corncrib, thus landing the Frasers with the difficult problem of how best to dispose of his remains, without either infecting his people or giving them the unfortunate notion that the Frasers had somehow caused his death. [*Drums*]

Duncan Innes—a one-time fisherman, part-time smuggler, ex–Ardsmuir prisoner. Jamie's friend and helper, despite the loss of one arm. Later becomes the consort of Jocasta MacKenzie. [*Voyager, Drums*]

Mrs. Innes—the midwife who delivers Young Ian. [*Voyager*]

Mr. Isaacson (m)—a wealthy Jew, interested in marrying Mary Hawkins. [*Dragonfly*]

Ishmael—the ex-cook of Rose Hall; a *houngan* who is kidnapped by pirates, escapes, and is rescued by the *Artemis*. [*Voyager*]

Isobeail—a small girl whom Roger befriends aboard the *Gloriana*. [*Drums*]

J

"Black Jack" Randall (aka Jonathan Wolverton Randall)—see under "R."

Captain Jacobs—militia captain of Kingston, charged with hunting Mr. Willoughby following Mrs. Alcott's murder. [*Voyager*]

Jamie Roy—*nom de guerre* used by Jamie Fraser during his smuggling career. Derived from his nickname during the Rising—"Red Jamie" (*Seaumais ruaid,* in Gaidhlig: pronounced [roughly] as "Jamie Roy"). See "James

Alexander Malcolm MacKenzie Fraser." [*Voyager*]

Madame Jeanne—French Madame of an Edinburgh brothel, partner and customer of "Jamie Roy" in the brandy-smuggling business. [*Voyager*]

Jeffries—Irish coachman, employed by Lord Dunsany; present when Jamie shot Lord Ellesmere. [*Voyager*]

Jenkins—English soldier who searches Lallybroch following Young Ian's birth, when the attention of the English is drawn by pistol shots. [*Voyager*]

Jenny (Janet) Fraser Murray—see under "M."

Joan (MacKimmie)—Laoghaire's younger daughter by Simon MacKimmie. [*Voyager*]

Jocky—Young Ian's dog at Lallybroch. [*Voyager*]

Annekje Johansen—goat-keeper on board the *Porpoise,* who helps both Claire and then Jamie to escape from the ship. [*Voyager*]

Erik Johansen—gunner on the *Porpoise,* Annekje's husband. [*Voyager*]

John—one of Colum's attendants at Castle Leoch. [*Outlander*]

Johnson—Sir Percival Turner's aide. [*Voyager*]

Josephine—Jared Fraser's parlormaid. [*Voyager*]

Josh—Jocasta Cameron's groom; a slave born in North Carolina, but speaking both Gaelic and Scots-accented English, as a result of having been born on a plantation owned by a man from Aberdeen. [*Drums*]

Judas—Claire's horse, who tosses her off a ledge during a thunderstorm, leaving her exposed to the elements and to Indian ghosts. [*Drums*]

K

Kennyanisi-t'ago (m)—a war chief of the Mohawk, converted by Father Ferigault. [*Drums*]

Duncan Kerr—a MacKenzie clansman, found wandering near Ardsmuir, sea-soaked and demented, babbling of white witches and hidden gold. [*Voyager*]

Amyas Kettrick (m)—neighbor who tells Jenny of Hobart MacKenzie's impending arrival to deal with the matter of his sister's honor. Years later, he sees Brianna riding toward Lallybroch at a distance, and mistaking her for her father, tells Laoghaire MacKenzie (Fraser) that Jamie Fraser has returned. [*Voyager, Drums*]

† **Lord Kilmarnock**—one of the Jacobite earls; later executed for treason. [*Dragonfly*]

† **John, Master of Kilmarnock**—Lord Kilmarnock's young son and heir, who had tormented Fergus; later killed on the field at Culloden. [*Dragonfly*]

Alexander Kincaid—one of Jamie Fraser's tenants from Lallybroch, who dies of wounds sustained in the Battle of Prestonpans. [*Outlander*]

Alasdair Kirby (m)—a young inhabitant of the village of Broch Mordha, whose death of the bloody flux is reported by the elder Ian Murray in one of his letters to Jamie. [*Drums*]

Joseph Fraser Kirby (m)—tenant at Lallybroch. [*Dragonfly*]

Mrs. Kirby—widow of one of Jamie's murdered tenants, who took refuge at Lallybroch. [*Voyager*]

L

Laoghaire—see "Laoghaire MacKenzie."

Madame Laserre—a professional groomer of noble ladies. [*Dragonfly*]

† **Pastor Walter Laurent**—an itinerant Swiss preacher, whom Claire encounters hiding in a shed on Louise de Rohan's estate at Fontainebleau. [*Dragonfly*]

Tilly Lawson (m)—woman who first looked after Margaret Campbell; declined to accompany the Reverend and his sister to the West Indies. [*Voyager*]

† **Leiven** (m)—a Danish inventor from St. Croix, who made Geillis Abernathy's concealed box. [*Voyager*]

LeJeune (m)—a renowned French swordmaster. [*Dragonfly*]

Fergus mac Leodhas (m)—Scottish mercenary; in command of a regiment serving in France, where both Jamie Fraser and Ian Murray (the elder) served. Namesake of the young pickpocket Jamie adopts in Paris. [*Outlander, Drums*]

Captain Thomas Leonard—young third lieutenant in HMS Navy, acting captain of HMS *Porpoise,* who impresses Claire as ship's surgeon, to deal with a typhoid epidemic aboard. Later lost with his ship during a hurricane in the Caribbean. [*Voyager*]

Leroi—Stephen Bonnet's closest companion. [*Drums*]

† **Mr. Lillington** (m)—a prominent citizen of Wilmington, at whose house Jamie and Claire meet Governor Tryon. [*Drums*]

Kenny Lindsey—one of Jamie's comrades from Ardsmuir prison, later settled on Fraser's Ridge. [*Drums*]

Rosamund Lindsey—wife of Kenny Lindsey. [*Drums*]

†† **Dr. Eric Linklater**[7]—author of *The Prince in the Heather*. [*Dragonfly*]

†† **Bill Livingstone**[8]—Drum Major of the 78th Fraser Highlanders Pipes and Drums. [*Drums*]

† **"Lochiel"**—Donald Cameron of Lochiel, one of the Highland chiefs who fought at Culloden. [*Dragonfly*]

† **Louis XV,** King of France. [*Dragonfly*]

† **Louise**—see Princesse Louise de la Tour de Rohan, under "R."

† **Dowager Lady Lovat** (m)—Simon Fraser's first wife; rumored to have been married forcibly for her lands and title. [*Dragonfly*]

† **Lord Lovat**—see "Simon Fraser (Old Fox)."

Anthony Brian Montgomery Lyle (m)—son of Kitty Murray and Paul Lyle; grandson to Ian and Jenny Murray. [*Drums*]

M

MacAlpine (m)—an Edinburgh tavern owner who knowingly buys smuggled brandy, and unknowingly accepts the body of a mysterious Customs officer, sealed in a cask of crème de menthe. [*Voyager*]

General MacAuliffe (m)—World War II general, recollected by Claire. Famous for his remark upon being requested to surrender—"Nuts!" [*Outlander*]

Hamish MacBeth—one of Jamie's tenants; a soldier fighting with the Jacobite troops; wounded at Prestonpans, where Claire repairs the injury to his scrotum. [*Dragonfly*]

MacBeth the postie—the Inverness postman who delivers a letter for Brianna, revealing to Roger her interest in tracing her parents' life in the past. [*Drums*]

† **Aeneas MacDonald** (m)—a minor banker who helped to finance the Rising; one of the companions who landed at Glenfinnan with Charles Stuart. [*Dragonfly*]

† **Angus and Alex MacDonald of Scotus** (m)—brothers; prominent Jacobites. [*Dragonfly*]

† **Duncan William McLeod MacDonald, of Glen Richie**[9]—one of the Jacobite officers executed at Culloden by order of Lord Melton. [*Voyager*]

Robert MacDonald—a member of the Glen Elrive Watch; forcibly interrogated by Claire and her sister-in-law,

---

[7] *While Mr. Linklater is unfortunately not a personal friend (I've never met him), he definitely is a real person, and a fairly contemporary person, at that. He is the author of* The Prince in the Heather, *from which the quote about the Jacobite officers in the farmhouse near Culloden was taken ("After the final battle at Culloden, eighteen Jacobite officers, all wounded, took refuge in the old house and for two days, their wounds untended, lay in pain; then they were taken out to be shot. One of them, a Fraser of the Master of Lovat's regiment, escaped the slaughter; the others were buried at the edge of the domestic park").*

[8] *Also, alas, not a personal acquaintance of mine—but definitely contemporary.*

[9] *While created as a purely fictional character, a Duncan MacDonald (of the Master of Lovat's regiment) did in fact die at Culloden, as I discovered some time after writing* Voyager.

Jenny, in their efforts to find and rescue Jamie. [*Outlander*]

Tammas McDonald (m)—one of the Frasers' neighbors in North Carolina; Jamie considers him as a prospective husband for Brianna. [*Drums*]

Mavis MacDowell (m)—the daughter of an Inverness tobacconist; one of Roger Wakefield's early loves. [*Drums*]

†† **Labhriunn MacIan**—a piper with the Scottish forces at Falkirk. [*Dragonfly*]

Martin Mack (m)—resident near Lallybroch, with a horse for sale. [*Outlander*]

Alexander MacMahon MacKenzie "Auld Alec"—Master of Horse at Castle Leoch. [*Outlander*]

Ambrose MacKenzie (m)—one of Roger MacKenzie's distant ancestors, mentioned by the Reverend. [*Drums*]

Colum (Callum) MacKenzie mac Campbell—Chief of the MacKenzies of Leoch, brother to Ellen, Dougal, Jocasta, and Janet; uncle to Jamie Fraser. Father (presumably) to Hamish, heir to the leadership of the clan. Concerned with the shape of future events, Colum debates the wisdom of committing his clan to the support of the Stuarts, and will do anything to protect what he sees as the interests of the clan. [*Outlander, Dragonfly*]

Dougal MacKenzie—war chieftain of Clan MacKenzie, brother to Colum, sister to Ellen; uncle to Jamie Fraser. Father to four daughters: Margaret, Eleanor, Molly, and Tabitha (Tibby). Unacknowledged father of Hamish MacKenzie (who is passed off as the son of Dougal's brother Colum), and secret father of the bastard child (later known as William Buccleigh MacKenzie) born

to Geillis Duncan. [*Outlander, Dragonfly*]

Ellen MacKenzie—see "Ellen MacKenzie Fraser."

Geordie MacKenzie—a MacKenzie clansman, killed by a boar during a *tinchal* at Leoch. [*Outlander*]

Hobart MacKenzie—Laoghaire's brother, who comes to avenge her honor, when he discovers that her marriage to Jamie is bigamous. [*Voyager*]

Hugh MacKenzie of Muldaur—one of Colum MacKenzie's tacksmen; (first) husband of Laoghaire. [*Dragonfly*]

Jacob MacKenzie (m)—late chieftain of clan MacKenzie; father of Ellen, Colum, Dougal, Jocasta, and Janet; grandfather of Jamie Fraser and Jenny Murray. [*Outlander*]

Janet MacKenzie (m)—younger sister to Ellen, Colum, and Dougal. Died of a fever, age twenty-four. [*Outlander*]

Jeremiah MacKenzie (m)—husband to Mary Oliphant, great-great-grandfather to Roger Wakefield. Jeremiah is "an old family name," being borne also by Roger's father and others in the MacKenzie family tree. [*Drums*]

Jeremiah Buccleigh MacKenzie (Jemmy)— son of William Buccleigh MacKenzie and Morag Gunn MacKenzie, five-times great-grandfather to Roger MacKenzie. Emigrating to the American Colonies with his parents as an infant, he narrowly escapes death from smallpox and drowning, on board the *Gloriana*. [*Drums*]

Jerry (Jeremiah Walter) MacKenzie (m)—Roger (Wakefield) MacKenzie's father, a WWII hero who was shot down in his RAF Spitfire over the English Channel in 1941. Married to Marjorie Wakefield MacKenzie, Roger's mother. [*Drums*]

Grannie Joan MacKenzie (m)—old woman whose corpse was burnt in place of Geillis Duncan's. [*Voyager*]

Jocasta MacKenzie—youngest sister of Ellen, Colum, and Dougal; Jamie's aunt. Married three times: to John Cameron, to Black Hugh Cameron of Aberfeldy, and finally to the late Hector Cameron, with whom she fled to America after the failure of the Stuart Rising. The Camerons settled near Cross Creek in the colony of North Carolina, and became prosperous owners of the plantation called River Run. [*Outlander, Drums*]

Letitia (Chisholm) MacKenzie—wife to Colum MacKenzie; mother of Hamish (by Dougal MacKenzie). [*Outlander*]

Laoghaire MacKenzie[10] (pronounced "Leery," "L'heer," or "L'heery," depending on regional usage)—a young girl at Castle Leoch, with designs on Jamie Fraser. Later marries Jamie, following Claire's return to the future and Jamie's release from captivity. Mother of Marsali and Joan. [*All*]

Morag Gunn MacKenzie—wife of William Buccleigh MacKenzie, mother of a son called Jeremiah ("Jemmy"), and Roger MacKenzie's six-times great-grandmother. Attempting to save her son from being drowned during a smallpox scare on board the *Gloriana,* she hides in the hold, where Roger discovers her. Not knowing her identity, he is moved by her plight, and saves her and her child from Captain Bonnet's wrath. [*Drums*]

William Buccleigh MacKenzie—illegitimate son of Geillis Duncan and Dougal MacKenzie; fostered to a family who had lost a child of the same age, and given the same name as the dead child. Married to Morag Gunn, he later emigrates to America with his wife and infant son, Jeremiah. [*Dragonfly, Drums*]

Willie Coulter MacKenzie—one of Dougal's men, who comes unexpectedly on Jamie, Dougal, and Claire at the conclusion of the fight in Culloden House, which has left Dougal dead. Shocked, he allows Jamie to leave with Claire. [*Dragonfly*]

Simon MacKimmie (m)—Laoghaire's second husband; father of Marsali and Joan. Died in prison, following the Rising. [*Voyager*]

†† **Iain (Taylor) MacKinnon**—one of the Jacobite soldiers who helps Jamie off the field at Culloden. [*Voyager*]

Barton MacLachlan (m)—an inhabitant of Cross Creek. [*Drums*]

John MacLeod (m)—a lobsterman found dead in one of the stone circles. Mentioned in the grimoire of Gillian Edgars. [*Drums*]

MacLeod (on Naylor's Creek) (m)—ex–Ardsmuir prisoner, come to settle on Fraser's Ridge. [*Drums*]

† **Cluny MacPherson** (m)—a fugitive Jacobite who lived in hiding in the Highlands, mentioned in Robert Louis Stevenson's *Kidnapped*. [*Voyager*]

Mrs. MacPherson—one of Claire's assistants at Prestonpans; wife of one of the Jacobite soldiers. [*Dragonfly*]

---

[10]*Also known disparagingly as "Loghead" or "Leghair," by various readers who disapprove of the lady.*

Maura (Grant) MacKenzie (m)—Dougal MacKenzie's wife. [*Outlander*]

Rupert MacKenzie—a tacksman of clan MacKenzie, a distant cousin to Dougal and Colum. He helps Claire to rescue Jamie from Wentworth Prison, and later dies by Dougal's hand in an abandoned church, after being wounded during the Battle of Falkirk. [*Outlander, Dragonfly*]

Sarah MacKenzie (m)—a deceased member of clan MacKenzie, who expired following treatment by Davie Beaton. [*Outlander*]

Father MacMurtry (m)—parish priest at Broch Mordha, following the Rising. [*Voyager*]

Grannie MacNab—elderly resident on Lallybroch estate; mother of Ronnie; grandmother of Rabbie. She asks Jamie to take Rabbie onto the estate as stable-lad, to remove him from his abusive father. [*Outlander*]

Mary MacNab—widow of Ronald MacNab, mother of Rabbie. She comes to offer Jamie comfort in his cave, on the eve of his surrender to the English. [*Voyager*]

Rabbie MacNab—abused son of Ronald MacNab; he becomes stable-boy at Lallybroch, later the best friend of Fergus. [*Outlander, Dragonfly*]

Ronald MacNab—a tenant at Lallybroch; a drunken, violent sot. He abuses his son Rabbie, who is rescued by Jamie. Ronald is later suspected of betraying Jamie to the Watch, and dies when someone sets fire to his house, presumably in revenge for the betrayal. He leaves a widow, Mary, who becomes a maid at Lallybroch. [*Outlander*]

Andrew MacNeill—a plantation owner near the Cape Fear, and prominent member of the Scottish community. He leads Jamie and Claire to the sawmill where the lynching takes place, and later meets Lizzie in Wilmington, where he tells her the whereabouts of Jamie Fraser. [*Drums*]

Donald MacNeill—son of Andrew MacNeill. He comes to inform Farquard Campbell of the incident at the sawmill, and summon him to oversee execution of the slave Rufus. [*Drums*]

Nettie and Abby MacNeill—the two elderly, spinster sisters of Andrew MacNeill. [*Drums*]

John MacRae—the village locksman in Cranesmuir, who is obliged to imprison Claire and Geillis in the thieves' hole, and to assist at the witch trial. [*Outlander*]

Lady Annabelle MacRannoch—wife of Sir Marcus MacRannoch of Eldridge Manor, who helped the Frasers to escape from Scotland after Jamie's rescue from Wentworth Prison. [*Outlander*]

Sir Marcus MacRannoch—owner of Eldridge Manor, near Wentworth; early suitor of Ellen MacKenzie. Gave pearl necklace to Ellen; later sends wolfskin and pearl bracelet to Claire. [*Outlander*]

Madeleine—a maid at Madame Jeanne's brothel; sister of one of the Fiend's victims. [*Voyager*]

Sister Madeleine—a nun at L'Hôpital des Anges. [*Dragonfly*]

Magdalen—a woman of Castle Leoch, a minor acquaintance of Claire's. [*Outlander*]

Magdalen—the Frasers' pregnant red cow, whose impending state gives Brianna fears for her own future. [*Drums*]

Maggie—a sometime prostitute, who confronts Jamie and Mr. Willoughby in the World's End, starting a minor riot. [*Voyager*]

Magnus—Jared's butler at the house on the Rue Tremoulins. [*Dragonfly*]

Maisri—a Highland seer, possessed of second Sight. [*Dragonfly*]

Maitland—cabin boy aboard the *Artemis*. [*Voyager*]

Alexander Malcolm—Edinburgh printer; Jamie Fraser's alias. [*Voyager*]

Mamacita—Ermenegilda's mother, who stays to take care of Father Fogden after the death of her daughter. [*Voyager*]

Captain Manson (m)—World War II acquaintance of Claire Randall's. [*Outlander*]

† **Jean-Paul Marat** (m)—important figure of the French Revolution. [*Voyager*]

Annalise de Marillac—an old flame of Jamie Fraser's, for whose sake he fought his first duel, at the age of eighteen. [*Dragonfly*]

† **Signor Manzetti** (m)—an Italian banker, approached for a loan by James Stuart. [*Dragonfly*]

† **(John Erskine) Earl of Mar** (m)—a prominent, elderly Jacobite noble, who took part in both the 1715 and 1745 Risings. [*Dragonfly*]

Marley—Jonathan Randall's mentally deficient but physically powerful orderly at Wentworth Prison. [*Outlander*]

Marguerite—Jared's parlormaid at Rue Tremoulins. [*Dragonfly*]

Marie, Queen of France. [*Dragonfly*]

Vicomte Marigny (of the House of Gascogne) (m)—Mary Hawkins's erstwhile fiancé. [*Dragonfly*]

† **(George Keith), Earl of Marischal**—a prominent Jacobite noble. [*Dragonfly*]

Marsali—Laoghaire's elder daughter by Simon MacKimmie; Jamie's stepdaughter, who marries Fergus on a beach in the West Indies. See "Marsali Joyce MacKimmie Fraser." [*Voyager*]

Charlie Marshall (m)—K-9 Corps sergeant; World War II acquaintance of Claire Randall's, who gives her advice on withstanding a dog attack. [*Outlander*]

Martin the porter—porter and lodgekeeper at the Oxford college where Roger is employed as a history don. [*Drums*]

Mrs. Martins—midwife who delivers Jenny Murray's second child, Maggie (Margaret Ellen). [*Outlander*]

Mary Ann—parlormaid at Ellesmere. [*Voyager*]

Mathilde—Jared Fraser's cook at the house in the Rue Tremoulins. [*Voyager*]

Sorley and George McClure—brothers; tenants at Lallybroch. [*Dragonfly*]

Dr. McEwan—head of the Institute for Highland Studies in Inverness, where Gillian Edgars began her research into the standing stones. [*Dragonfly*]

Kenneth and Rosie McIver—Jared's overseer in Jamaica, and his wife, who live at Blue Mountain House. [*Voyager*]

Giles McMartin—one of the young Jacobites executed after Culloden by Lord Melton's troops. [*Voyager*]

Mrs. McMurdo—one of Claire's assistants at Prestonpans; wife of one of the Jacobite soldiers. [*Dragonfly*]

Mrs. McMurdo—one of Roger's neighbors in Inverness. [*Drums*]

Comte Medard (m)—neighbor of Louise de Rohan, with land adjoining hers at Fontainebleau, on which he hanged three Huguenots. [*Dragonfly*]

Dowager Countess Melton—Lord John Grey's mother. [*Voyager*]

Harold, Lord Melton—eldest brother of Lord John Grey, who found a group of Jacobite officers in a farmhouse near Culloden Field, and ordered them all executed—save for Jamie Fraser, whom he saved in order to repay the debt of honor owed by his younger brother. [*Voyager*]

Graham Menzies—the patient whom Claire helps to die, in Boston. [*Voyager*]

Mickey—one of Jocasta's slaves. [*Drums*]

Millefleurs (aka "Milly")—one of the horses at Helwater. [*Voyager*]

Sister Minèrve—a nun at L'Hôpital des Anges. [*Dragonfly*]

† **Madame Montresor** (m)—one of the King of France's many mistresses. [*Dragonfly*]

Freddy Mueller—Petronella's young husband. [*Drums*]

Gerhard Mueller—patriarch of a large German Lutheran family, with a farm some miles from Fraser's Ridge. The old man is upright and honorable, devoted to his family—but highly intolerant and rigid, given to drawing wrong conclusions and clinging stubbornly to them. Deciding that the deaths of his daughter-in-law and grandchild were the result of a hex put upon his house by Indians, he sets out to take vengeance, and in retribution kills three women whom he comes across in the forest—Gabrielle, Berthe, and Nayawenne, the Tuscarora *shaman*. [*Drums*]

Petronella Mueller—daughter-in-law of old Gerhard Mueller. Claire delivers Petronella's first child, but both mother and child die shortly afterward, in a measles epidemic. [*Drums*]

Tommy Mueller—one of Gerhard Mueller's sons. [*Drums*]

Munro—a clerk in the shipping office in Inverness, who advises Roger Wakefield how to sign on as a seaman. [*Drums*]

Hugh Munro—a longtime friend of Jamie Fraser's; an ex-schoolteacher turned beggar as the result of having lost his tongue at the hands of the Turks. He gave a dragonfly in amber to Claire as a wedding present. Later hanged by the Duke of Sandringham's game-keepers. [*Outlander, Dragonfly in Amber*]

Mrs. Munro (Mrs. Gibson)—Hugh Munro's wife. [*Dragonfly*]

Sergeant Robert Murchison—twin brother to William Murchison. "Wee Bobby" and "Wee Billy" were both stationed at Ardsmuir, where they had a reputation for bullying and sadism. Robert disappeared, presumed drowned in the stone quarry near Ardsmuir. [*Drums*]

Sergeant William Murchison—an old and unfriendly acquaintance from Jamie's days in Ardsmuir Prison. Sgt. Murchison was one of a pair of sadistic twins; his brother Robert met a mysterious death at Ardsmuir, for which the Sergeant holds Jamie at least partly responsible. First implicated in the death of Lissa Garver, the woman in the sawmill, the Sergeant is later involved in a smuggling scheme with Stephen Bonnet, involving the theft of liquor from the Crown warehouse in Cross Creek. [*Drums*]

Aloysius O'Shaughnessy Murphy—cook on the *Artemis*. [*Voyager*]

Benjamin Murray—Young Jamie's fourth child. [*Drums*]

Caitlin Maisri Murray (m)—sixth child of Ian and Jenny Murray; died shortly after birth. [*Voyager*]

Edwin Murray—cousin to Ian Murray (the elder), and secretary to Mrs. Tryon, wife of the governor of North Carolina. Edwin Murray provided the invitation to dinner that allowed Jamie both to meet Governor Tryon (with consequent offer of a land grant), and to sell a ruby to Baron Penzler. [*Drums*]

Frederick Murray—one of the young Jacobites executed by Lord Melton's troops after Culloden. [*Voyager*]

† **Lord George Murray**—chief commander of Charles Stuart's army. [*Dragonfly*]

Henry Murray (m)—eldest son of James Murray (Young Jamie) and his wife, Joan; grandson to Ian and Jenny Murray. [*Drums*]

Ian Murray—Jamie Fraser's best friend and brother-in-law; Jenny Murray's husband; father to Young Ian and his siblings. Factor of Lallybroch. [*All*]

Ian Murray (Young Ian)—Jamie Fraser's youngest nephew, Ian's destiny seems entwined with his beloved uncle's. Linked in danger on the occasion of Ian's birth, when the two narrowly escaped discovery and slaughter by the English army, Ian has been the closest thing to a son that Jamie has ever had. Running away from home to join Jamie in Edinburgh, Ian discovered a mysterious sailor making inquiries, and ended up setting fire to Jamie's print shop, narrowly escaping death himself. Returned to Lallybroch, he later accompanied Jamie to the seals' isle off Coigach, and was kidnapped by pirates while endeavoring to retrieve the hoard of jewels concealed on the island. Taken captive to the West Indies, he fell into the hands of Geillis Duncan (aka Mrs. Abernathy, the witch of Rose Hall), and

is nearly killed as a blood sacrifice, being rescued by Jamie and Claire from the cave of Abandawe. Arriving in North Carolina, he accompanies Jamie and Claire to River Run, and helps to establish the homestead on Fraser's Ridge. Helping to rescue Roger MacKenzie (Wakefield) from the Iroquois, he volunteered to take Roger's place, and allowed himself to be adopted by the Indians, marrying a Mohawk girl. [*Voyager, Drums*]

James Alexander Gordon Fraser Murray—"Young Jamie"; oldest son of Ian and Jenny Murray; Jamie Fraser's nephew. Father of Henry, Matthew, Caroline, and Benjamin. Inherits Lallybroch, as a result of a deed of sasine written by his uncle and namesake. [*All*]

Janet (Jenny) Fraser Murray—Jamie Fraser's sister; wife to Ian Murray, mother of Young Jamie, Margaret Ellen, Katherine, Michael, Janet, and Young Ian (also Caitlin, stillborn). [*All*]

Janet Ellen Murray—daughter of Jenny and Ian Murray, twin sister to Michael, elder sister to Young Ian. [*Voyager, Drums*]

Joan Murray—wife of Young Jamie, mother of Henry and Matthew. [*Voyager, Drums*]

Old John Murray (m)—Ian Murray's father. [*Outlander*]

Kitty Murray—Katherine Mary, third child of Ian and Jenny Murray. [*Dragonfly, Voyager, Drums*]

Margaret Ellen Murray—second child of Ian and Jenny Murray, known as Maggie. [*Outlander, Drums*]

Matthew Murray—second son of James Murray (Young Jamie) and his wife, Joan; grandson to Ian and Jenny Murray.

Michael Murray (m)—second son to Ian and Jenny Murray; twin to Janet Murray (the younger), older brother to Ian Murray (the younger). Sent to France to be apprenticed to Jared Fraser, Michael is making a success of himself in the wine business. [*Voyager, Drums*]

Peggy Murray—widow of one of Jamie's murdered tenants, who takes refuge at Lallybroch after the Rising. [*Voyager*]

Mutt (and Jeff)—Claire's nicknames for ecclesiastical examiners who conduct the witch trial at Cranesmuir. [*Outlander*]

†† **John Quincy Myers**—a hunter and mountain guide who meets the Frasers in Wilmington. Suffering from an inguinal hernia, he becomes a public spectacle when Claire is obliged to repair the hernia on the dinner table in the middle of a formal party at River Run. Back in good form, Myers volunteers to help the Frasers with the escape of a runaway slave, by guiding them into the mountains. [*Drums*]

N

Nacognaweto—a village chief of the Tuscarora. Jamie and Claire meet him and two of his sons by accident, when Jamie kills a bear the Indians have been following. They become friends as a result of this meeting, and Nacognaweto later brings his womenfolk to call, with gifts of food. [*Drums*]

Nayawenne—her name means "It may be; it will happen." Grandmother of Nacognaweto, the Tuscarora woman is a shaman, the "singer" for her village. She tells Claire of a prophetic dream, gives her guidance in finding and using herbs

of the area, and when she is mistakenly killed, leaves her amulet—a leather pouch containing a raw sapphire, among other things—to Claire. [*Drums*]

Duc de Neve—a French noble. [*Dragonfly*]

O

† **O'Brien** (m)—a Jacobite spy. [*Dragonfly*]

† **Lord Ogilvie** (m)—a prominent Jacobite. [*Dragonfly*]

Mary Oliphant (m)—Roger MacKenzie's great-great-grandmother. Married six times, but bore children only with Jeremiah MacKenzie, her "bonny lad." [*Drums*]

Patsy Olivier—the Frasers' inadvertent hostess in Georgia after they are shipwrecked by a hurricane; mistress of Les Perles plantation. [*Voyager*]

Onakara—one of Ian's hunting companions, from the village of Anna Ooka. Entrusted by Jamie and Ian with the disposal of Roger Wakefield, he sells Roger to the Mohawk, and later leads Claire, Jamie, and Ian to Snake-town, where Roger is held. [*Drums*]

† **Duc d'Orléans** (m)—brother of Louis XV. [*Dragonfly*]

Joe Orr (m)—resident near Lallybroch, acquaintance of Ian and Jenny Murray. [*Outlander*]

Osbert—Brianna's private name for her unborn child, later named (officially) Jemmy. [*Drums*]

† **O'Sullivan** (m)—one of Charles Stuart's companions, later put in charge of the Highland army's commissary arrangements, to ill effect. [*Dragonfly*]

Otter-Tooth—see "Ta'wineonawira."

Mr. Overholt—the purser of the *Porpoise*. [*Voyager*]

P

M. Pamplemousse[11]—a minor French official.[*Dragonfly*]

Mrs. Patterson—landlady of the World's End Pub on the Royal Mile in Edinburgh. [*Voyager*]

Paul—pageboy to the Comtesse St. Germain. [*Dragonfly*]

Madame de Pérignon—a member of the French Court. [*Dragonfly*]

† **Duke of Perth** (m)—another commander of Charles Stuart's army. [*Dragonfly*]

Peter—a drover; sees monster at Loch Ness with Claire, and later testifies against her at the witch trial. [*Outlander*]

Phaedre—Jocasta Cameron's body slave. Observant and intelligent, she becomes Claire's secret ally, helping to discover the identity and whereabouts of the runaway slave Pollyanne. [*Drums*]

† **Philip, King of Spain**—the third of the Bourbon monarchs, with ties (reluctantly acknowledged) to the Catholic Stuart dynasty. [*Dragonfly*]

† **Mrs. Pinckney** (m)—a plantation owner in South Carolina, famed for her introduction of domestic silk production. [*Drums*]

Ping An ("Peaceful One")—a tame pelican; Mr. Willoughby's pet fishing bird, who dislikes loud noises. [*Voyager*]

† **Lord Pitsligo** (m)—a Jacobite supporter, who raised men for Charles Stuart. [*Dragonfly*]

† **Plato**—M. Fleche's medical assistant.

Pollyanne—a slave recently acquired from Africa, with a talent for healing and the use of herbs. Living in the slave quarters near the sawmill, she provides both excuse and scapegoat for the murder of Lissa Garver in the mill. In order to save her from execution under the law of bloodshed, the Frasers smuggle her away to the mountains, where John Quincy Myers helps her find a place of refuge among the Tuscarora. [*Drums*]

Pompey—one of the slaves working at River Run's turpentine camp; disfigured in a pitch explosion. [*Drums*]

Captain Portis—captain of one of Jared's ships. [*Dragonfly*]

Elias Pound—the young seaman who helps Claire during the typhoid epidemic on board the *Porpoise*, before dying of the disease himself. [*Voyager*]

M. and Mme. Prudhomme—members of the French Court, who attend the Royal stud at Argentan with Jamie and Claire. [*Dragonfly*]

Q

Colonel Harry Quarry[12]—John Grey's predecessor as Governor of Ardsmuir Prison. [*Voyager*]

Don Francisco de la Quintana—Spanish envoy, sent by Phillip of Spain to assess the Jacobite Rising. [*Dragonfly*]

---

[11] Now and then, a French-speaking reader inquires whether I was aware that this translates to "Mr. Grapefruit." Yes, I was.

[12] Harry Quarry appears again, along with Lord John, in the first solo short story (well, relatively short; it's only eleven thousand words or so) I ever wrote professionally. This is a story titled "Hellfire," which I wrote for an anthology titled Past Poisons: The Ellis Peters Memorial Anthology of Historical Crime published by the U.K. publisher, Headline, in December 1998. While this story is not, strictly speaking, part of the Outlander novels (it doesn't deal with Claire or Jamie Fraser, though Jamie is mentioned indirectly), it is part of the overall oeuvre.

R

Captain Raines—captain of the *Artemis;* drowned in a storm off Hispaniola. [*Voyager*]

Madame de Ramage—friend of Louise de Rohan. [*Dragonfly*]

Georges, Vicomte de Rambeau—a Court fop with an eye for the ladies; husband of the jealous Vicomtesse. [*Dragonfly*]

La Vicomtesse de Rambeau—a noble lady of violent and jealous temperament; much given to the use of spells and poison. [*Dragonfly*]

Alexander Randall—younger brother of Jonathan Randall; a curate in the employ of the Duke of Sandringham. Mary Hawkins's lover, and the father of her child. [*Dragonfly*]

Brianna Ellen Randall—daughter of Claire and Frank Randall—and of Claire and Jamie Fraser. Later married to Roger MacKenzie, mother of John Jeremiah Alexander Fraser MacKenzie. [*Dragonfly, Voyager, Drums*]

Claire Beauchamp Randall—wife of Frank Randall. A nurse during World War II, she later becomes chief of surgery at a large Boston hospital. Later widowed, but a successful doctor and mother, she brings her daughter to the Scottish Highlands, returning after an absence of twenty years, to reveal the secrets of the past. [*All*]

Franklin Wolverton Randall—Claire's husband, Frank; a professional historian with a deep interest in the eighteenth century. [*All*]

Jonathan Wolverton Randall ("Black Jack")—Frank Randall's six-times great-grandfather, a captain in the English army; a man of violence and perverse desires. [*Outlander, Dragonfly, Voyager*]

William Randall (m)—eldest of the three Randall brothers; a minor baronet, from Sussex. [*Voyager*]

Mr. Ransom—a broker who handles the sale of indentured servants in Inverness. [*Drums*]

Dr. Daniel Rawlings—original owner of the medicine chest Jamie gives Claire as an anniversary present. Dr. Rawlings disappeared under mysterious circumstances, leaving his instruments and casebook behind. [*Drums*]

Master Raymond—a small, mysterious apothecary, who seems to know a great deal regarding secret matters, both political and occult. [*Dragonfly*]

Reilly the Leinsterman (m)—fellow prisoner with Jamie Fraser at Wentworth; expert in lock-picking. [*Outlander*]

Roberts—one of Stephen Bonnet's associates, who with his companions, robs the Frasers on their way upriver to Cross Creek. [*Drums*]

Mme. Melisande Robicheaux—Geillis Duncan's alias, while living in Paris following her escape from Cranesmuir. See also "Gillian Edgars," "Geillis Duncan," and "Mrs. Abernathy." [*Voyager*]

Janet Robinson—witness at witch-trial. [*Outlander*]

Roderick (and Willie)—stable-lads. [*Outlander*]

Rodney (m)—a twentieth-century teenage acquaintance of Brianna's, whose appearance in a photograph rouses Jamie's fatherly suspicions. [*Voyager*]

† **Jules de Rohan** (m)—cuckolded husband of Louise, Princesse de Rohan. [*Dragonfly*]

† **Princesse Louise de La Tour de Rohan** (aka Marie-Louise-Henriette-Jeanne de La Tour d'Auvergne). Claire's best friend in Paris; Charles Stuart's lover, and mother of his (supposed) son, Henri. [*Dragonfly*]

Rollo—Young Ian's dog. Rollo is a gigantic wolf-cross, acquired by Ian as a gambling prize in Charleston. Large, fierce, and devoted to his master, he thrives in the wilderness, and accompanies his master to a new life with the Iroquois. [*Drums*]

Sister Marie Romaine—Brianna's fifth-grade teacher.[13] [*Drums*]

Ross the smith—a blacksmith from Broch Mordha. [*Dragonfly*]

† **Mayer Rothschild**[14, 15]—A traveling numismatist and coin dealer from Frankfurt, who meets Jamie and Claire at the house on the Rue Tremoulins in Paris, where he gives them the clue (the gold tetradrachm) that connects the Duke of Sandringham with a Jacobite plot. [*Voyager*]

Duchesse de Rouen—a member of the French nobility. [*Dragonfly*]

Rufus—an obstreperous slave, frequently in trouble, whose calamitous career ends with a fight with Byrnes, the overseer. By the law of bloodshed, the slave is condemned to death, but he is lynched by Byrnes and his companions before the law can deal with him. Arriving too late to prevent the incident, and unable to save the man, Claire administers atropine, a deadly poison, to hasten his death and cut short his suffering. [*Drums*]

S

Clarence Marylebone (Duke of Sandringham)—an acquaintance of Colum MacKenzie's; an English noble whose political sympathies and sexual preferences are highly suspect; he dabbles in coin collecting, murder, and politics, and eventually pays the price of his chicanery, at the hands of Murtagh FitzGibbons Fraser. [*Outlander, Dragonfly*]

a sempstress—makes a dress of cream-colored silk for Claire to wear to dinner with Baron Penzler; *may* then have told one of Stephen Bonnet's associates about the jewels carried by the Frasers. [*Drums*]

Comte Sevigny—French nobleman. [*Dragonfly*]

---

[13]*By coincidence, my fifth-grade teacher was also named Sister Marie Romaine. Requiescat in pace.*

[14]*The founder of the great Rothschild fortune was indeed a traveling numismatist during the latter part of the eighteenth century, but my representation of his age and appearance during this period is fictional, based on general notions of European dress at the time. The history of the Rothschild name is fact, though—or at least is so represented in historical sources.*

[15]*I do in fact occasionally take things* out *of a book. I don't, however, throw them away, since you never know when something will come in handy. The scene in which Jamie and Claire meet Mayer Rothschild was originally written as part of* Dragonfly in Amber, *but I removed it, feeling that, while it was a good scene, it wasn't really necessary to the book. As it was, the scene fit much better—with the small addition of the gold tetradrachms—into* Voyager, *where it finally appeared.*

† **Thomas Sheridan** (m)—Charles Stuart's tutor. [*Dragonfly*]

Geordie Silvers (m)—husband to Katherine Murray; son-in-law to Ian and Jenny Murray; father of Josephine. [*Drums*]

Josephine Silvers—eldest daughter of Katherine Murray Silvers; granddaughter to Ian and Jenny Murray. [*Drums*]

†(††) **John Simpson Jr.**—a famous Scottish swordsmith, son of Simpson Sr.

†(††) **John Simpson Sr.**[16]—a famous Scottish swordsmith.

Ronnie Sinclair—one of the ex-prisoners from Ardsmuir who takes up homesteading on Fraser's Ridge; a cooper, whose skill in making whisky casks earns him his land and shop. The cooper's shop is a focus for gossip and news from the surrounding countryside. [*Drums*]

Junior Smoots—son of the Blue Bull's landlady; a lad with an eye for Lizzie. [*Drums*]

Mrs. Smoots—landlady of the Blue Bull Inn, where Brianna and Lizzie stay in Wilmington. [*Drums*]

Lloyd Stanhope—a landowner from Edenton, who is much taken by Claire at a dinner in Wilmington. [*Drums*]

Georgina and Mr. Stephens (m)—acquaintances of Marcelline Williams; residents of Jamaica. [*Voyager*]

Lawrence Stern—a German Jewish naturalist who meets Claire in the mangrove swamps of Hispaniola. [*Voyager*]

† **Stewart of Appin**—a Jacobite chief. [*Dragonfly*]

† **Charles Edward Casimir Maria Sylvester Stuart, the Young Pretender**—son of the Old Pretender, James III of Scotland, VIII of England. Heir to the exiled Catholic royal dynasty, and a young man bent on glory—no matter what the cost. [*Dragonfly*]

† **James Stuart, the Old Pretender** (m)—James III of Scotland, VIII of England; exiled Catholic monarch. [*Dragonfly*]

Tom Sturgis—gunner aboard the *Artemis*. [*Voyager*]

Sukie—housemaid at Lallybroch. [*Voyager*]

Sykes—one of Lord John Grey's soldiers at Ardsmuir. [*Voyager*]

T

Ta'wineonawira—Otter-Tooth; a rabble-rousing Iroquois, of unknown clan and tribe, who tried to instigate all-out war between the Nations of the Iroquois and the white settlers, only to be killed by the Mohawk as a troublemaker. Possibly the possessor of the skull (with silver fillings) that Claire finds buried under the roots of a red cedar. [*Drums*]

Temeraire—"the Bold One"; a one-armed slave whom Claire accidentally acquires in the slave market in Kingston. [*Voyager*]

Tewaktenyonh—sister of war chief and sachem in the village where Roger is held captive. An elderly woman who befriends Claire, and tells her the story of Otter-tooth. [*Drums*]

Mrs. Thomas (m)—proprietor of the bed-and-breakfast where Claire and Brianna stay in Inverness upon their first visit to the Highlands. [*Dragonfly*]

---

[16] *The Simpsons, famous swordsmiths, were in fact historical persons of the period. By coincidence, my friend John E. Simpson, who kindly allowed me to use his persona, is also a Jr.*

Horace Thompson—anthropologist who brings a decapitated skeleton for Joe Abernathy to identify. [*Voyager*]

Tompkins—a seaman on board the *Porpoise;* he is also discovered to be the one-eyed stranger Young Ian found snooping around the print shop in Edinburgh; a spy for Sir Percival Turner. [*Voyager*]

† **Madame Nesle de La Tourelle**—favorite mistress—at one point—of the King of France. [*Dragonfly*]

† **Francis Townsend**—a Jacobite commander; took and held Stirling Castle for Charles Stuart. [*Dragonfly*]

† **William Tryon**—governor of the colony of North Carolina.

† **Tullibardine**—an elderly Jacobite; one of Charles Stuart's long-time attendants. [*Dragonfly*]

Sir Percival Turner—a corrupt government official, who seeks to improve his political standing by the capture of a major smuggler and ex-Jacobite ("Jamie Roy"), while accepting bribes from the minor smuggler Alexander Malcolm, unaware that these are the same person. [*Voyager*]

Two Spears—war chief of the village where Roger is held captive. [*Drums*]

U

Ulysses—Jocasta Cameron's butler; born a freeman, enslaved as a child, Ulysses was so named by the schoolmaster who bought him. Fluent in French and English, able to read both Greek and Latin, he is a talented man who becomes the eyes of his mistress when she loses her sight. [*Drums*]

† **Mr. Urmstone**—a circuit-riding preacher, famous for his outdoor sermons preached on the Bluffs, near Cross Creek. [*Drums*]

V

Mr. Villiers (m)—a Barbados planter. [*Voyager*]

Jacques Vincennes (m)—friend of Marie d'Arbanvilles, who sees Jamie meet with Jack Randall in a brothel. [*Dragonfly*]

Madame Vionnet—Jared's cook at the house in the Rue Tremoulins. [*Dragonfly*]

Hanneke Viorst—sister of Hans Viorst; she offers temporary shelter and food to Brianna and Lizzie in Cross Creek. [*Drums*]

Hans Viorst—a resident of Cross Creek, who makes a living by transporting passengers and cargo by canoe on the Cape Fear River between Cross Creek and Wilmington. He agrees to carry Brianna and Lizzie upriver to Cross Creek, and takes them home with him when Lizzie falls ill en route. [*Drums*]

M. Voleru—an amateur medico who offers his services at L'Hôpital des Anges. [*Dragonfly*]

W

Wakatihsnore ("Acts Fast")—sachem of the Mohawk village where Roger is held captive. [*Drums*]

Reverend Reginald Wakefield—a Presbyterian minister, friend of Frank Randall. An amateur historian with a preference for the eighteenth century and the instincts of a pack rat, he is great-uncle and adoptive father to Roger MacKenzie Wakefield. [*Outlander*]

Roger Jeremiah MacKenzie Wakefield (aka Roger MacKenzie)—the Reverend Wakefield's great-nephew, adopted by the Reverend following the death of Roger's parents in World War II. Agreeing to help Claire discover the fate of the Highlanders from Broch Tuarach, he finds himself falling in love with Brianna Randall, and being ever more deeply enmeshed in the Randalls' affairs. [*All*]

Wakyo'teyehsnonhsa (aka "Emily")—"Works with her hands"; the Mohawk girl with whom Ian Murray falls in love, and whom he eventually marries. [*Drums*]

Wallace—Lord Melton's aide. [*Voyager*]

Mr. Ambrose Wallace—an Edinburgh lawyer; a passenger in the coach taking Claire to Edinburgh to look for Jamie. [*Voyager*]

Wally (m)—Jamie's employee/accomplice; drives a wagon filled with decoy casks, as part of a brandy-smuggling scheme. [*Voyager*]

Walmisley—butler at Bellhurst (Duke of Sandringham's estate). [*Dragonfly*]

† **Antoine Walsh** (m)—a slave trader; one of the companions who landed with Charles Stuart at Glenfinnan, having supplied the prince with a ship. [*Dragonfly*]

Wan-Mei—second wife of the Chinese Emperor, who wished to take Yi Tien Cho into her household—forcing him to choose between exile and emasculation. [*Voyager*]

Mr. Warren—sailing master of the *Artemis*. [*Voyager*]

Elizabeth Wemyss—known as Lizzie. The daughter of Joseph Wemyss, sold as an indentured servant to Brianna Fraser. Accompanying her mistress to the New World, she falls sick of malaria upon their arrival, detaining them in Wilmington. Drawing conclusions from a meeting between Brianna and Roger, she later informs Jamie Fraser that Roger is a rapist, and the father of Brianna's impending child. [*Drums*]

Joseph Wemyss—a failed shopkeeper from Inverness, forced to sell himself and his daughter Elizabeth as indentured servants. Fearing that Lizzie's contract will be bought by a man who intends to misuse her, he begs Brianna to buy her instead. [*Drums*]

White Raven—the name given to Claire by the Tuscarora medicine woman, Nayawenne, the result of a dream. [*Drums*]

William, Viscount Dunsany, Viscount Ashness, ninth earl of Ellesmere—heir of Lords Ellesmere and Dunsany; illegitimate son of James Fraser and Geneva Dunsany. Assumed by nearly everyone to be the legitimate heir of Geneva's elderly husband, the eighth Earl. [*Voyager, Drums*]

† **William of Orange** (m)—monarch of England; invited to take the throne when the Stuarts were exiled. [*Dragonfly*]

Judah Williams (m)—proprietor of Twelvetrees plantation, on Jamaica, later burned during a slave revolt. [*Voyager*]

Marcelline Williams—a woman who befriends Claire at the Governor's reception in Kingston; sister of Judah Williams, of Twelvetrees. [*Voyager*]

Mary Walker Willis[17] (m)—a woman found dead near one of the Scottish stone circles, mentioned in Gillian Edgars's grimoire.

the Misses Williams—Jacobite supporters from Edinburgh, who danced with Jamie at one of Prince Charles's balls held in that city. [*Dragonfly*]

Mr. Willoughby—Jamie's Chinese associate, picked up on the docks in Edinburgh. A poet and acupuncturist, with a marked weakness for women's feet, he inadvertently betrays Jamie to the Excise, but redeems himself by saving Claire from the Reverend Archibald Campbell (aka the Edinburgh Fiend). See "Yi Tien Cho." [*Voyager*]

Lt. Wolff—A representative of the British Navy, charged with negotiating lucrative naval stores contracts with the timber owners along Cape Fear. An unfortunate choice for the position, given his dislike of Scotsmen. [*Drums*]

Felicia Woolam (m)—one of the daughters of John Woolam the miller. Felicia is involved in a confrontation with Gerhard Mueller, settled by Jamie Fraser. [*Drums*]

John Woolam (m)—Quaker owner of the flour-mill near Fraser's Ridge. [*Drums*]

Sarah Woolam (m)—a Quaker, daughter of John Woolam, the mill owner. [*Drums*]

Wu-Xien (m)—the Mandarin who first recognized Yi Tien Cho's talent as a poet. [*Voyager*]

Judith Wylie—Philip Wylie's sister. A guest at the Governor's dinner, who makes no secret of her disdain for Claire's sense of fashion. [*Drums*]

Phillip Wylie—a prosperous young American plantation owner, who meets Claire at a formal dinner in Wilmington and attempts to flirt with her. [*Drums*]

Y

Yi Tien Cho ("Leans against Heaven")—see "Mr. Willoughby."

Yvonne—Louise de Rohan's maid at Fontainebleau. [*Dragonfly*]

---

[17] *Coincidentally, this is also the name, rearranged, of a popular mystery novelist whose books I happened to see while writing the scene involving the victims of stone circles. The subconscious is a strange and wonderful thing.*

Captain of the *Patagonia*—captain of the doomed ship, burnt in the harbor at Le Havre
a Portuguese pirate

Tenants on the estate at Lallybroch
Tom
Willie
Mrs. Willie
Hugh Kirby
Geoff Murray
Young Joe Fraser

Dougal MacKenzie's men, trapped in the chapel with Claire at Falkirk
Willie Coulter MacKenzie
Gordon McLeod
Geordie
Rupert MacKenzie
Ewan Cameron of Kinnock

English soldiers who take Claire to Bellhurst after Falkirk
[*Dragonfly*]
Corporal Rowbotham
Captain Mainwaring
Colonel Gordon MacLeish Campbell
Private Dobbs
Garvie
Jessie

Four officers of the Master of Lovat's regiment
[*Voyager*]
William Chisholm Fraser
George D'Amerd Fraser Shaw
Duncan Joseph Fraser
Bayard Murray Fraser

Dougal's men
[*Outlander, Dragonfly*]
John Whitlow
Willie MacMurty
Rufus and Geordie Coulter

Monks at the Abbey of Ste. Anne de Beaupré
[*Outlander*]
Brother Bartolome
Brother Polydore
Brother Ambrose
Brother Roger
Brother William
Brother Josef
Brother Eulogius

Parishioners mentioned in Reverend Wakefield's journals
[*Dragonfly*]
Derick Gowan
Maggie Brown
William Dundee

Miscellaneous minor characters
[*Voyager*]
wine seller at inn
patronne at inn in Le Havre
Le Havre port inspector
Le Havre harbormaster

Prisoners at Ardsmuir with Jamie Fraser
[*Voyager*]
Murdo Lindsay
Kenny Lesley
Johnson
MacTavish
Baird
Gavin Hayes
Ogilvie
Angus MacKenzie
Billy Malcolm
Milligan
Morrison (the healer)
Joel McCulloch
Bobby Sinclair
Edwin Murray
Ronnie Sutherland
MacKay

Prostitutes in Madame Jeanne's brothel
Dorcas
Peggy
Mollie
Penelope
Sophie
Josie
the second Mary

Offspring of Ian and Jenny Murray
[*Voyager*]
Young Jamie
Maggie
Kitty
Michael
Janet
Caitlin (deceased)
Young Ian

Smugglers at Arbroath
[*Voyager*]
Joey
Willie MacLeod
Alec Hays
Raeburn
Innes
Meldrum
Hays
the Gordons
Kennedy

Crew members of the Artemis
[*Voyager*]
Picard
Grosman
Manzetti
Russo
Stone
Rogers

Sailors on the Porpoise
[*Voyager*]
Ramsdell Hodges
Holford
Ruthven
Stevens

Attendees at the Governor's reception in Kingston
[*Drums*]
Mrs. Hall
Mrs. Yoakum

I GET LETTERS. . . .

 ince the *Outlander* novels were first published, I've received any amount of mail and other manifestations of interest from readers who find themselves fascinated by the characters, particularly by Claire and Jamie Fraser. By "other manifestations," I mean that people are sometimes kind enough to send me documents, pictures, and objects that they've made, showing me some personal vision of Jamie and Claire, or some special expression of attachment to the books.

Among the items of this sort that I particularly treasure are a) various sketches of Claire, Jamie, or both together, b) assorted pieces of handmade jewelry, approximations of Claire's pearl necklace, or pieces of Celtic-inspired ornament, c) a picture of a racehorse named "Dragonfly in Amber," d) *lots* of beautiful small objects made in cross-stitch, e) pictures of a number of tartan-clad teddy bears named "Jamie," f) pictures of a number of infant children, named (variously) Jamie, Claire, and Brianna (nobody's named a kid Roger or Ian yet—at least not on my account.),[1] g) handmade paper with heather blossoms embedded, h) pressed-flower and photo arrangements, featuring scenes of the Highlands, i) tapes of original songs inspired by the books, j) original poetry, likewise inspired, k) small wooden and pottery objects with a Celtic inspiration, and l) the occasional Really Unique item.

These last include a small, baked-clay figurine, showing a little girl with brown hair, gazing down into a puddle, a fired, glazed ceramic figure of a black-haired woman sitting in an armchair with a book (this one is titled "Lady Reading"), a book of photographs, showing life-size terracotta heads of Jamie, Claire, and Yours Truly (*that* was a shock), a hand-carved wooden "kapertlin'" spoon, made for me by an inmate at a Vancouver prison where I teach a yearly writing class, a cutting board in the shape of the state of Idaho, accompanied by a bottle of potato hand lotion,[2] X-ray films of the covers of all my books (accompanied by an X-ray referral sheet for one James Fraser, showing various diagnosed fractures), and last but not least—personal horoscopes and interpretations for Claire and Jamie.

Now, Jamie's birth date isn't given specifically in any of the novels, and while Claire's birthday is given, she doesn't know

---

[1] *If somebody names their child Murtagh or Laoghaire as a result of reading these books, I'd like to know about it.*

[2] *I have friends in the Boise Convention Center.*

her own time of birth.[3] Kathy Pigou, the reader who did the horoscopes, originally E-mailed me a year or so ago, saying that she was simply curious, and if I would supply her with the necessary data regarding birth dates, times, and places, she would very much like to cast a horoscope for Jamie Fraser, simply for her own interest—though she would be happy to send me a copy.

Finding this fascinating, I did send the data—and was intrigued (more than slightly) by the resulting reading. At my request, Kathy very kindly cast a horoscope and did a reading for Claire as well.

While I unfortunately can't show you *all* of the generous gifts sent to me by readers, I did think that the horoscopes were both suitable for printing in book form and particularly likely to be very interesting to other readers. So, with the kind permission of Kathy Pigou, who constructed the charts and readings, I'm reproducing them here.

—*D.G.*

KATHY PIGOU LIVES IN *Adelaide, South Australia, with her husband (a forensic chemist) and two sons. She has a degree in biology and biochemistry, and while she regards astrology as a hobby, rather than a profession, she does do occasional paid readings. Among her other hobbies, she includes reading, and . . . cross-stitch.* 🌾

A BRIEF GUIDE TO ASTROLOGY

by Kathy Pigou

The horoscope is a geocentric map of the heavens at a particular time and in a particular place. All planets on the lower part of the chart are below the horizon; those on the upper part are above the horizon. Thus, someone born at night will have the sun in the lower half. The signs of the zodiac form a background for the planets, and so each planet is "in" a certain sign. In addition, due to the rotation of the earth, the signs appear to rotate, so that each one rises over the horizon during each twenty-four hours.

The sign that is rising at birth is called the Ascendant, and is an important part of the reading of a chart.

The calculation of the chart is mainly math (unless you use a computer program; I have one, but often like to do the calculations myself, to get a "feel" for the chart). The explanation may make more sense if I describe what I have done on the chart with the calculations on it.

First, the local birth time is expressed in GMT[4] (not necessary for Jamie's chart). This is then adjusted, including factors of longitude of the birthplace, to give a final sidereal or star time, which is expressed on a twenty-four-hour clock.

---

[3] *Fortunately, I do.*
[4] *Greenwich Mean Time*

To get the correct placement of the zodiac signs around the chart, this sidereal time is looked up in a book of Tables of Houses. This gives the right degree of each sign to put on the cusp of each of the twelve segments around the chart, called houses. The degree, and sometimes the sign on each cusp, changes with latitude for the same sidereal time used. The tables are given in whole degrees of latitude, so you have to calculate the difference for the exact latitude with which you are working. You will see on Jamie's chart that the third house contains all of the sign of Capricorn, and all of Cancer is within the ninth house. This is called interception, and happens in latitudes of more than 50 degrees, north or south.

Finally, the positions of the planets need to be calculated, and the planets put on the chart. The planets' positions at midnight (or sometimes midday) for every day are given in a book called an ephemeris. To calculate the correct place for each one, the time of birth (GMT) is expressed as a fraction of twenty-four hours. You work out how far the planet moves in the twenty-four hour period, which includes the birth time, then multiply this answer by the fraction you obtained earlier.

For example, for someone born at 6:00 A.M.—this is .25 of the day. If the planet moves 1 degree in twenty-four hours, the movement at 6:00 A.M. is fifteen minutes. For people born a long way from Greenwich, the birth date used may actually be the day before or the day after the one given. Here in South Australia we are 9.5 hours ahead of Greenwich, so someone born at, say, 2:00 A.M. on October 9, would use a GMT time/date of 4:30 P.M. on October 8.

The erection of the chart is a mathematical exercise, but the reading of it relies on the interpretation of the astrologer. Each planet is associated with a variety of objects and principles, and each sign gives certain qualities to planets in that sign. The house is the area of the person's life in which the planet operates. For example, Mercury represents (among other things) communication, senses, intellect, travel, writing, and speaking. Taurus qualities include being stubborn, patient, thorough, practical, and stable. So someone with Mercury in Taurus likes to have all the facts and think things over before making a decision (thorough and patient, thinking, stable—no quick decisions). This person learns better by doing than by hearing or reading (practical intellect), and rarely gives up on a project (stubborn). Their memory is good and these people are generally good at business and management (practical and thorough in communication).

Of course, the entire chart must be considered, so if there are several other factors indicating this person will be impulsive, the above will be tempered by this.

Finally, if Mercury is in the seventh house, which is the house of relationships, there will be good communication within marriage, and your partner will be an intellectual equal, witty, and talented. This position indicates good communication with the public, in areas such as counseling or law.

The other major consideration is the angle between the planets, called an aspect. The significant aspects are:

0 degrees—conjunction

60 degrees—sextile
90 degrees—square
120 degrees—trine
180 degrees—opposition

The angle doesn't need to be exact. For all except the sextile, the usual orb, or amount of difference from the exact allowed, is 8 degrees; for the sextile it's 4 degrees. These numbers are not absolute. Some astrologers use 10 degrees if the sun or moon is involved, others use 6 degrees for all aspects, but the ones I use are common.

The aspects are shown on the charts as follows. Black rule is either opposition or square, solid gray is trine, and dotted gray is sextile. The conjunctions are shown by a bracket. Before drawing the lines, I mark the aspects on the diagram in the lower right corner of the chart with the calculations on it.

The aspects are considered to be flowing and harmonious (gray) or challenging and stimulating (black). The degree of harmony or disharmony depends quite a lot on the planets involved, as some complement each other and others are less compatible.

The aspects don't always look to be the correct angle when drawn on the chart, but this is because the houses are all drawn the same size; in reality some are larger than others.

So, in reading a chart, the position of the planet by sign and house and the angular relationship to all other planets, plus the Ascendant, must be considered for all the planets one at a time.

I don't usually do predictions, but there are two major types. One is a chart for a year, either a solar return chart, which is a chart for the time the sun returns to exactly the degree it was at your birth, or a progression, which I confess I have never learned about.

The second method is ongoing and is to look at the aspects the planets are currently making to the planets in the birth chart. For example, Jamie's sun is at 11 degrees 12' Taurus, so when the current position of the sun (called the transitting sun) is 11 degrees 12' Virgo, transitting sun is trine natal sun. These transits can be interpreted like the aspects in the birth chart, to give an idea of the likely trends in someone's life at a particular time. That gives a brief overview of how astrology works, and how a chart is read. The rest is a reading of Jamie's and Claire's charts.

It is probably worth mentioning that the horoscope shows a person's basic nature and inclinations, but does not mean a person has no free will. If someone doesn't like a particular part of their behavior, nothing in astrology says it can't be changed. In times of stress, however, people usually revert to their instincts.

Horoscope Reading for James Alexander Malcolm MacKenzie Fraser

Birth date: May 1, 1721
Time of birth: approx. 6:30 P.M.
Birthplace: (near) Inverness, Scotland

Sun in Taurus (The Sun represents the power urge, personality and ego, the inner self.)

This person is persistent, cautious, and determined, and can be stubborn and headstrong. Taureans are slow to anger, but once angry will be furious. He is a loyal and faithful friend, but an implacable enemy. He is very practical and takes his responsibilities seriously. Sense of touch is important, and he is good with his hands.

Sun in Seventh House

This person works best in partnership with another. Marriage is important, and he may have increased success after marriage. His wife will be strong and loyal, as will his friends. He has a self-confident manner and deals well with the public, and is popular and easy to get along with.

Moon in Cancer (The Moon represents the domestic area of life, one's roots, the mother and the emotions.)

This position leads to a great love of home and family, and attachment to the mother. Marriage is important to his emotional well-being. Often his true feelings will be hidden. He will be a good parent but must be careful not to smother chil-

dren with love and must avoid a tendency to want to dominate their lives.

Moon in Ninth House

He is a natural teacher and philosopher who is imaginative and fond of travel, and may live far from his birthplace. His religious beliefs are orthodox, and he has emotional attachment to the values instilled in childhood.

Mercury in Aries (Mercury represents the intellect, expression, and reasoning ability.)

This person is imaginative, with good foresight. He expresses himself easily and can improvise beautifully. He is a competitive thinker and may be headstrong. This position makes Jamie a quicker thinker than most Taureans, who like to deliberate before making a decision.

Mercury in Sixth House

Here the thinking is particularly concerned with practical matters. He is an excellent planner, very observant, efficient, and a hard worker. He can acquire specialized skills and knowledge for work.

Venus in Gemini (Venus represents social urges, sense of values, affection, and the "nice things of life.")

This indicates a generous, friendly person who has wit and conversational ability. He is literate, and likes to roam the world and see what life has to offer. His partner will be intellectual and will share his good sense of humor. He has a great sense of family and gets on well with his siblings. He may marry more than once.

James Alexander Malcolm MacKenzie Fraser

Date of Birth: **5.1.1721**   Time: **18:30**

Place of Birth: Lat: **57 N 20**   Long: **4 W 30**

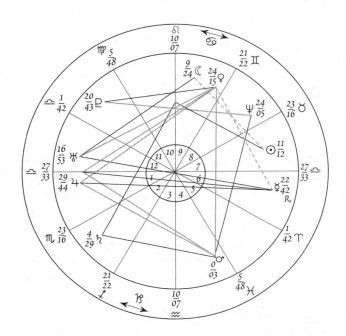

Overall: ♎, ♑   Lacking: ♐, ♓

Aries ♈	Libra ♎
Taurus ♉	Scorpio ♏
Gemini ♊	Sagittarius ♐
Cancer ♋	Capricorn ♑
Leo ♌	Aquarius ♒
Virgo ♍	Pisces ♓

Sun ☉
Moon ☽
Mercury ☿
Venus ♀
Mars ♂
Jupiter ♃
Saturn ♄
Uranus ♅
Neptune ♆
Pluto ♇

Venus in Ninth House

A philosopher who is well educated and has a love of religion. He is likely to marry a foreigner, and may travel widely.

Mars in Pisces (Mars represents action and aggression, initiative and energy.)

This is probably the only part of this chart that doesn't fit well with the personality described for Jamie. It gives excessive emotionalism, and a tendency to brood over past resentments. These people are very sensitive and lack self-confidence. Not J. Fraser at all!

Mars in Fourth House

He is patriotic and may have a military background. He is a handyman and will spend a lot of time around the house. He has a strong constitution and lots of energy, which will last into old age.

Jupiter in Libra (Jupiter represents expansion, education, benevolence, and protection.)

This person is popular and well liked, and deals well with the public, convincing others of the merits of his ideas. He is a good conversationalist. He needs a partner and will have an enduring marriage. He is sincere and concerned with justice.

Jupiter in First House

What a wonderful man! He is optimistic and sociable, and looks on the bright side of life. He is honest, trustworthy, and friendly, with a dignified manner. A leader of others, he has strong moral and religious convictions. He is broad-minded with a good sense of humor. Finally, he has a tremendous vital force and is good at sports. (Hardly believable, but you'll find it in any astrology book.)

Saturn in Sagittarius (Saturn represents the need for security, caution, and learning through experience.)

This position gives good concentration and intellectual discipline. He tries to adhere to honorable and strict morals. He earns what he achieves through hard work and application. His personal reputation is important to him and he is hurt if accused unjustly.

Saturn in Second House

Here there is a need to work hard for a living. He is shrewd in business, and holds on to what money he has. There can be acquisition of property, especially in later years. Material gain through people in positions of power is indicated.

The outer planets were not known in Jamie's time. Because these planets are slow-moving, they spend many years in each sign, so people born over several years will have the same sign for the same planet. This makes the house position more important than usual.

Uranus in Twelfth House

An intellectual who works in unusual ways and often behind the scenes. He may have secret love affairs or belong to secret societies. Likes to break away from convention and restraint.

Neptune in Eighth House

A receptive and intuitive person who has a mysterious charisma that helps to get support from others.

Pluto in Eleventh House

A very loyal person who is interested in reform movements and social improvements. His friends are important to him and he may be a group leader.

Aspects

The sun is trine the moon, which shows a balance between the ego and the emotions, and a person who is comfortable with men and women.

Communication is easy; he can learn from the past and will generally feel happy about himself. This also shows in his ability to be strong (Sun) and gentle (Moon). The Sun is also square the midheaven (the point directly at the top of the chart), which indicates conflict with authority and some difficulties with his public reputation.

The Moon is square Uranus, which may lead to unusual emotional attachments. A restless person, who may have many changes of residence, he has great intellectual ability, but is stubborn. Tends to think of marriage in the old style where the husband is the sole authority.

Mercury is sextile to Venus, a position that gives social grace and charm, and a refined and easygoing personality. He judges fairly, but knows how to compromise. Has a soothing voice.

Mercury is also opposite both Jupiter and Uranus. Here is a case of having to read the whole chart, as these aspects indicate a lack of consideration for others, arrogance, and a person who can't make a decision. As you can see, there are many other factors in Jamie's chart that contradict this, so I would normally consider that he was more prone to say what he thinks straightaway (not like a Taurean), and perhaps to get into trouble through being outspoken.

Mercury is also opposite the Ascendant, which leads him to look for an intelligent spouse, definitely someone he can talk to. He has skill in communicating with the public and is a social wit with good conversational ability.

Venus is trine Mars, indicating an affectionate, warmhearted person. He is faithful in marriage, and the physical side is important to him. He enjoys family life, but also needs independence. This aspect leads to happiness in love and marriage. He also has lots of sex appeal. (I was going to say women find him attractive, but it seems like men do, too!)

Venus is also trine Jupiter. This means he is cheerful and optimistic, but can be serious when necessary. He is graceful, generous, popular, and good with people. He doesn't show his problems, and others may not be aware that he has any. He needs honesty between himself and his lover, and likes harmony in marital and domestic affairs. Again, a pleasant, soothing voice is indicated.

Venus is trine Uranus, which again gives an optimistic outlook, but one who can accept responsibility. He has a magnetic personality and is attractive to women. He will marry well, but possibly to someone in some way unusual, and find mutual trust and understanding. This is an aspect of good fortune.

With Venus square to Pluto, he will have intense emotional and sexual involvements. There can be something fated about his romances, and he may fall in love with someone who is already attached. Social conditions may interfere with his personal happiness.

Finally for Venus, it is trine the Ascendant, once again giving a sociable, charming person who is a good host and enjoys the refined things in life. This position enhances beauty and charm. Friends, siblings and children are all important to him. He has a gentleness of manner that others find appealing, and seems to attract happiness.

Mars is trine Jupiter, which indicates a proud, honorable, and self-confident person who is a good leader, with physical strength and lots of energy. He is interested in sports, travel, and adventure, and is optimistic and enthusiastic. He has strong physical desires, but wants more than this from a relationship—he wants to share in mind, body, and soul.

Mars square Saturn can lead to apathy and setbacks, but all that optimism and energy above tends to cancel that out. This aspect can predispose this person to violence, accidents, and broken bones. There are likely to be dangerous working conditions, and possibly a military career. There may be early loss of a parent.

Mars is trine the Ascendant, giving a strong constitution and lots of willpower. He throws himself into things wholeheartedly, and leads an active life. He inspires confidence in others and is able to persuade others to his point of view.

Jupiter is conjunct the Ascendant, which gives a man who excels at things requiring physical prowess. He is outgoing and friendly, but wants others to respect his moral and ethical standards. He likes to travel and to be outdoors. This position, with Jupiter in the first house, gives increased height and good looks.

Saturn is trine the midheaven, which makes him patient and painstaking, and gives a systematic approach to problems.

The last aspect is Pluto trine Neptune, but this applies to everyone born for quite a few years, so applies to a generation.

I know that it must seem as though I have made a lot of this up to fit, but I was a bit surprised myself and checked through a few books to make sure.

Horoscope Reading for Claire Beauchamp Randall Fraser

Birth date: October 20, 1918
Time of birth: 2:09 P.M.
Birthplace: London

Sun in Libra

This person performs best when part of a partnership, while maintaining her individuality. She is most likely to be married, sometimes more than once. This person is usually diplomatic, social and gregarious, but peace and harmony are important and she will go out of her way to avoid rocking the boat. Librans are interested in psychology and human relationships, like to analyze society and others' behavior, and often make good counselors. They have an intellectual approach to life, but can always see both sides of any question, and thus often find it hard to make decisions.

Sun in Ninth House

This indicates a person who is interested in other cultures and traditions. She is adventurous, likely to travel widely, and may marry a foreigner. She has strong moral convictions, and is a good teacher who is interested in furthering her own education. She may have strong visions of the future, and is certainly open to new experiences.

Moon in Taurus

This shows a person who has stable emotions and is very determined, to the point of being stubborn. She rarely makes a quick decision (if she can make one at all, with her Libra sun!), and thinks carefully before taking action. She is a loyal and lasting friend and marriage partner, who has a lot of common sense and a rather conservative outlook. Her singing and speaking voice will be pleasant, and she is fond of dancing, music, and art. She is affectionate and sentimental, and is particularly sensitive to touch. This position usually indicates a "green thumb."

Moon in Third House

This is an intriguing and intellectually curious person, who learns well by listening, and can express herself well. She is rather restless and likes to travel, even if only on short trips. She has a good memory and finds it easy to relate to others (this is also indicated by the Libran sun).

Mercury in Libra

This position emphasizes many of the features of the Sun in Libra. This person is friendly and broad-minded, logical and rational, and always fair. She will take her time to make a decision, but the outcome will be well thought out. She likes to have a discussion, but will avoid arguments whenever possible. She needs a partner with whom she can have a mental as well as physical relationship, and prefers the company of well-mannered people. Libran influence gives an interest in others and what makes them tick.

Mercury in Ninth House

This gives an intellectual interest in other cultures and countries. She loves to travel and is good at languages. She is interested in higher education, and is an honest and moral person, as well as being intuitive.

Venus in Libra

This shows someone who likes companionship and likes to please others. She is often beautiful, and is certainly charming and attractive to the opposite sex. She remains young at heart. Marriage is important and must be an equal intellectual relationship. Too much disharmony in her life may lead to illness. She may be easily hurt, but doesn't hold a grudge.

Venus in Eighth House

Benefits to this person will come through her partner. She can expect a long life and peaceful death. She is sensual and enjoys good sexual relationships, which are important to her. This person will be more intense than many Librans.

Mars in Sagittarius

This indicates a cheerful and honest person who likes outdoor activities. She has a good philosophy of life and enjoys new experiences. She has natural rhythm and harmony. This position gives lots of energy, and she will use it to fight for what she believes in.

Mars in Tenth House

She is an active and persistent person who is highly motivated to work toward what she wants. She may be controversial if in a public position, and has the ability to achieve in practical ways.

Jupiter in Cancer

This is a good position for public relations, and this person will have grace and sympathy for others. It usually indicates a

Claire Beauchamp Randall Fraser

Date of Birth: **10.20.1918**   Time: **14:09**

Place of Birth: Lat: **15 N 30**   Long: **0 W 5**

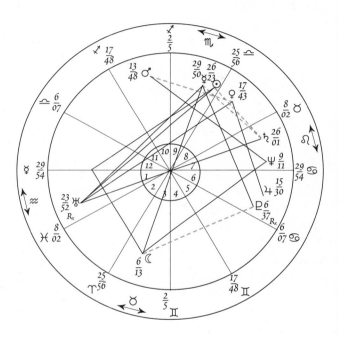

Overall: ♎   Lacking: ♓

Aries	♈	
Taurus	♉	
Gemini	♊	
Cancer	♋	
Leo	♌	
Virgo	♍	

Libra	♎	
Scorpio	♏	
Sagittarius	♐	
Capricorn	♑	
Aquarius	♒	
Pisces	♓	

Sun	☉
Moon	☾
Mercury	☿
Venus	♀
Mars	♂
Jupiter	♃
Saturn	♄
Uranus	♅
Neptune	♆
Pluto	♇

childhood where good values were evident, and in turn this person will pass on these values to her children. It gives great attachment to the home environment, with many people on the domestic scene, and favors working from the home. She has a strong maternal instinct, but the strong Libran influence in this chart means that her partner will always come first once any children are independent.

Jupiter in Sixth House

She is a philanthropic person who prefers to help in a practical way. She has the ability to heal, while enjoying good health herself. She is cheerful and a good organizer who is well respected in her work.

Saturn in Leo

This gives leadership qualities, but she is a person who needs attention and respect from others. She has lots of mental energy, but is strict with herself and others, particularly children.

Saturn in Seventh House

Here is a person who is social and gregarious, but who needs time on her own to recharge her batteries. She may find that her relationships bring many responsibilities, but she is well able to cope with these. There may be a difference in age with her partner.

Uranus in First House

This position gives an independent and original thinker who may appear a bit eccentric to others. She is direct and outspoken (but in a tactful Libran way) and follows her intuition. She may be thought ahead of her time.

Neptune in Seventh House

This position shows a psychic and karmic link to her partner. She is easily affected by the moods of others. She needs

to take care that she is communicating clearly with her partner, and not to assume others know what she thinks.

Pluto in Sixth House

This shows a need to serve others and abilities in the field of healing.

Ascendant in Capricorn

This Ascendant indicates a hard worker who likes material achievements, and to prove her capability to others. Generally this indicates a person mainly concerned with material matters, but other things in the chart show interest in people and a well-developed intuition, so Claire is less worldly than this would suggest. She was never really young as a child, but will age gracefully and not look old. She is dignified and persistent and doesn't suffer fools gladly.

Aspects

Sun conjunct Mercury gives the ability to communicate easily, but a liking to have the last word. This person is good at stimulating those who lack enthusiasm, and has lots of mental energy.

Sun sextile Saturn shows clarity of thought, well-developed concentration, and organizational ability. She is patient and self-disciplined, and learns from experience. This person is a loyal friend who should enjoy a long life with good health.

The Sun is trine Uranus, showing leadership ability and personal magnetism. She is popular and is more interested in others than herself. She is able to use her intuition and creativity to help in humanitarian ways.

With the Sun square to the Ascendant, there is some conflict between how the person feels about herself and how she presents herself to the world. She has a strong personality with lots of drive, but with so much Libran influence in the chart, she knows how to compromise and get along with others.

The Moon is in opposition to Mercury, which sometimes may lead to conflict between the emotions and intellect. She is clever, but may be impatient with those who don't meet her intellectual expectations. She is a loyal friend, and is sensitive and probably easily hurt.

Having the Moon square to Neptune may cause confusion in life. It is very important for her to find out the facts to avoid misunderstandings. She may have psychic tendencies, and will have many people in her life to help through difficulties.

The Moon is square to the Ascendant, showing a sensitive, impressionable person who must break away from the past. She may find it hard to handle anger without getting too emotional.

Mercury makes a sextile to Saturn, which once again confers good memory, good concentration, and disciplined thought. She was comfortable with older people when young, and is responsible and organized. Those with this aspect seek the truth.

Mercury is trine to Uranus, indicating a person who is not bound by tradition and may be ahead of the times. She has an excellent memory and is a good teacher, intuitive and independent.

The trine of Mercury to Pluto once again gives great ability to concentrate and to see to the heart of things. This position favors a career in medicine and/or surgery. She expects a lot from others, but gives a lot in return. She can influence and persuade others with her witty and diplomatic manner.

Mercury is lastly square the Ascendant. This gives ability with the hands, but she may have difficulties with others misunderstanding her. It may indicate a delayed education. Venus is sextile Mars, which shows a person who likes beautiful things, and is warm and affectionate. She is faithful in marriage, and is enriched by it. She has a optimistic and vivacious personality. She likes family life, but likes to retain her independence.

Venus is trine to Uranus, showing a fun-loving person who enjoys life and always looks on the bright side. Her marriage is characterized by trust and understanding, and she knows how best to express her love. She has sex appeal and may be considered unconventional.

Mars trine Neptune is another aspect that favors medicine as a career. She can heal others due to her ability to help with spiritual problems as well as physical ones. She has an exciting love life with honest and sincere lovers. She always looks for the best in others. Saturn is square to the midheaven, showing this person has responsibilities to others that interfere with her personal life.

Other aspects are between slow-moving planets and therefore affect generations rather than individuals.

Magic, Medicine, and White Ladies

Well, it's all Claire Beauchamp's fault, like so many other things about these books. Once she had informed me (by her habits of speech and her unique perceptions) that she was a time-traveler, I had to determine exactly who she was—where she had come from, and her occupation (if any) in her original time.

People commonly say to me, in tones of admiration, "But you write such *strong* women!" This is gratifying, but the simple fact of the matter is that I really don't like weak ones. In other words, Claire is not a competent person because I thought it was my social duty to provide a politically correct role model for young women—I just don't like ninnies and would find it a terrible chore to have to write about one.

Obviously, Claire was intelligent and competent; I could see that with half an eye. So what had she been doing, before fate decanted her into the Highlands of eighteenth-century Scotland? She *might* have been doing all sorts of things, from flying to the moon to competing in triathlons (though she seemed not to be very athletic, given what I'd seen of her so far), but the unfortunate fact is that there would be relatively little scope for the exercise of these talents in eighteenth-century Scotland.[1]

Given the state of things in the Scottish Highlands at the times—i.e., barbaric, violent, and lacking in hygiene—it struck me that doctoring might be a very useful talent indeed. Of all the assorted skills that might aid survival in the eighteenth century, a minimal knowledge of the healing arts certainly seemed one of the most desirable—and the most feasible.

Aside from the fact that it would be helpful to know how to dress wounds and treat minor problems like scurvy, I'd noticed in the course of research that there were in fact almost no "official" physicians at all in the Highlands. There was, of course, no formal program for training and licensing physicians at all, in either Britain or France at the time. There were colleges of medicine, to be sure, in places such as Paris, London, and Edinburgh, but most doctors were trained by apprenticeship, autodidactically, or in many cases they simply declared themselves to be doctors and hung out a shingle, with no training at all.

---

[1] *Though I did once read a book with a time-traveling heroine who listened to motivational business tapes in her own time, and then ended up with a successful business designing silk lingerie for eleventh-century Viking raiders. Neither Claire nor I have that much imagination, I'm afraid.*

However, healing is an art that has traditionally been practiced by women in all historical periods, even in those when social trends have caused an increased reliance on "official" physicians (usually male). The reason for that is obvious to anyone who has a family. Kids get sick. So do pets, domestic partners, and livestock.

In most times and places, there has been no medical assistance save for the wisdom and experience of family and neighbors—and among family and neighbors, those who are most likely to have any knowledge or skill in medical matters are the women because (owing to the undeniable fact that women bear and nourish children) they are the members of the community who are stuck at home, growing plants, feeding all and sundry, and generally keeping things going while the menfolk are out killing mammoths or each other.[2]

In short (well, all right, not *very* short—but I could have gone on a lot longer), it would be entirely reasonable for Claire to have healing skills of some sort, and to be able to use these to her benefit, in a way that would not be feasible for many other modern skills. So . . .

Fine, I thought. She'll be a healer of some kind. Doctor, nurse, EMT? On the whole, I thought a nurse. The main reason for this choice was that I personally am not a doctor,[3] don't have in-depth knowledge appropriate to complex diagnosis and treatment, and didn't at the time have the resources or desire to do sufficient research

to allow Claire to think complicated things about medical conditions.

Another consideration was that a good modern medical training would be rather wasted, given the materials available in the eighteenth century. No matter that Claire recognized diabetes mellitus, for instance, as she did in *Dragonfly*—even though she could make the diagnosis and knew the cure, the cure itself was unavailable. No point in being able to diagnose chronic fatigue syndrome or cystic fibrosis in a time like that, I mean.

It seemed to me, then, that we should be better off with Claire as a nurse. If we came across some interesting condition—such as Colum MacKenzie's degenerative disease—it would be simple enough for Claire to have heard of it somewhere. But on the whole, her expertise would be limited to the fairly simple dressing of wounds and administration of herbal medicines for nonspecific symptoms—interesting, but relatively simple, and hence better suited to a story where the medical details were part of character and setting, but not the

---

[2]*This very equitable division of labor has undergone drastic readjustments with the advent of reliable birth control, but since birth control was not very dependable in the eighteenth century, we really needn't worry about a discussion of gender roles here. In the eighteenth century, women still took care of children and men killed things, the end.*

[3]*I do have a Ph.D. in ecology, and when I taught, my students did usually call me "Doctor"—partially out of respect, no doubt, but mostly because they couldn't pronounce my last name and were too shy to use my first one. My father-in-law called me "Dr.-poo" for a while after I got my degree, but eventually stopped.*

main focus of the story itself (as might be the case in a medical thriller).

RETURN OF THE LEECH

I've been much interested (not to say amused) by recent news reports of medical research involving the use of leeches and maggots in the treatment of wounds. Seems our invertebrate friends actually are very effective in debriding dead tissue and assisting circulation—just as they were used in the eighteenth century (and earlier) by the ignorant physicians of the period, before modern medicine came rushing in with its technological new broom, to sweep away all those cobwebbed superstitions.

In the mid–twentieth century, of course no one would have countenanced the notion of using leeches. Really, one might as well resort to burning herbs under people's noses, and sticking needles in the skin! Smug in the grip of "science," it was plain to society at large that the relevance of all this magical nonsense was long past—and good riddance!

But the wheel of time turns slowly . . .

The dichotomy between magic and science occurs explicitly for the first time in the eighteenth century, as part of the evolution of the Age of Enlightenment. The basis of both magic and science is control of one's personal environment—the body— though magic seeks to do this externally, and science (at least in the sense of medicine) internally.

The Age of Enlightenment—which occurred in the second half of the eighteenth century—was the first period in which great emphasis was placed on rationality as a thoughtful virtue, making it equivalent in importance to the spiritual virtues. This elevation of analytic thought thus paved the way for development of nineteenth-century science, but didn't result in immediate changes.

While science depends ultimately upon rationality (the scientific method) for proof, scientists initially drew material from the old superstitions in their development of theories and hypotheses. In spite of the intellectual ferment of the Enlightenment, the evolution of medicine was thus for a long time still a sort of quasi-science, with a strong metaphysical dimension.

Then—as schools of thought tend to do—things went too far, and any medical practice not rigorously defensible in rational terms was deemed superstitious, unsanitary, and undoubtedly dangerous to the public health.

However, thoughtful people do look back now and then, and thus innovation rediscovers tradition. More things are known in heaven and earth than are dreamt of by many Horatios, and the metaphysical aspects of medicine are returning, with a wholly modern emphasis on "holistic" methods. In fact, the echo between Claire's methods and the present-day interest in holistic and natural healing techniques is purely fortuitous, but it *was* . . . er . . . timely.

"Metaphysical!" is one of those entertaining words with multiple definitions and shades of meaning, but as used in this context, it generally means "of, or relating to, what is perceived as transcendant, supersensible, or transcendental" or "neither analytic nor subject to empiric verification." What one colleague of mine helpfully refers to as "woo-woo stuff."

Modern medicine now generally accepts the notion that there *is* a strong interrelationship between mind and body, even though the precise nature of its operation is unknown—i.e., metaphysical. Since it *is* unknown, there exists an area of mystery in the realm of healing, which in some cultures is called "magic" or "shamanism"—but which is nonetheless an important component of the art of healing, regardless of the forms involved.

For example, a modern doctor may under some circumstances dispense treatment that he or she knows has relatively little therapeutic value, but that nonetheless makes the patient feel better or recover more quickly, owing to the placebo effect—that is, there is a beneficial effect connected with the simple act of treating illness, regardless of the actual physical effects of the treatment. ("Treatment" being loosely defined here, to cover everything from simple attention to the administration of substances or invasive procedures.) By exactly the same token, a person from a shamanistic culture will often be improved by a healing ceremony, whether the ceremony has any directly apparent physical effect or not.

In other words, there is a magical aspect to the practice of medicine, and always has been, though this aspect was decried and ignored for some time, in the excitement (fully justified, by the way; the Germ Theory is no small thing) of scientific discovery.

Given the circumstances of Claire's story—her disappearance through standing stones—there was plainly going to be an air of mystery and magic about it. What occupation could be more appropriate than that of healer—an occupation that has about it the same air of mystery and hint of magic? What better choice of occupation for a time-traveler, whose life itself turns back—and back again—upon itself, with new truths revealed by each change of perspective?

The processes of the body are both intensely personal and highly cryptic, which gives us the sense of significance and mystery that we call "magic." The same mixture of significance and mystery underlies religious feeling, and it is no coincidence that most healers in primitive societies are also priests. Religion and science lie at opposite ends of the spectrum of rationality, with medicine balanced somewhere in the middle. The important thing to note is that it *is* a spectrum; ergo, the elements of it are all connected, even though the extremities may seem so different as to bear no relation to each other.

In fact, healing is an art, and has always been understood as such—at least until the very recent past, when the advent of sophisticated technology has given us the delusion that the miracles of the body are all both explicable and controllable. Many are—but not all. Not yet, anyway!

Consequently, there are echoes throughout all the *Outlander* books—superstition and magic resonating through the practice of rational medicine—that exemplify the unique attitudes of the second half of the eighteenth century. The Age of Enlightenment was a period of transformation, in terms of culture, society, and thought—magic, if you will, brought about by the power of reason.

Claire, with her peculiar perspectives, personifies the practice of medicine, mingling the rational and the metaphysical, the traditional and the modern, in pursuit of the ancient goals of the healing arts: the preservation and restoration of health. Modern as she is, she is herself an echo of the Age of Enlightenment, with its odd mixtures of alchemy and chemistry, its hold on tradition, and its search for innovation. She is, in fact, the Return of the Leech.

White Ladies

If one is looking for entertaining accidents of history, it's worth noting that nurses in modern days have most often been "women in white." Whether chosen for its evident "purity" (and hence the implication of antisepsis), or because blood shows up on it really well, the white uniform worn by many modern nurses evokes the image of earlier "white ladies."[4]

The White Lady is a figure of Celtic myth, known (in varying manifestations) in all Celtic countries, including not only Ireland and Scotland, but Brittany as well (hence the knowledge of "La Dame Blanche" among the rapists Claire meets in the Rue du Faubourg St.-Honoré). Generally speaking, the White Lady is the dryad of death; she is often identified with Macha, Queen of the Dead, and sometimes as the Crone aspect of the Goddess (the Goddess is said to have three forms: Maiden, Mother, Crone—which signify the chief phases of female life).

Looking more particularly, though, legends of "white ladies" don't always portray these as figures of death and destruction—though this depiction is common—but in some places as figures of healing and sorcery. Macha, one of the mythic figures identified as the White Lady, is also the Mother of Life and Death—she (and all lesser white ladies, presumably) presides

---

[4]*I know that not all nurses these days dress in white, nor are they women. I'm speaking generally here of nurses in the twentieth century, for the sake of the point.*

over both birth and death—which, it struck me, was pretty much what a doctor does.

Given Claire's naturally pale complexion, her healing arts (and the ruthlessness which is a natural part of them), and her supernatural connections (both real and perceived), it seemed only reasonable to endow her—via Jamie's fertile imagination and familiarity with Celtic myth—with the title of "La Dame Blanche."[5]

WHY WORLD WAR II?

The decision to make Claire a healer dictated the time period from which she came. There were two reasons for choosing the period right after World War II: one, antibiotics, and two, technology.

World War II marked the emergence of truly "modern" medicine, with the advent of antibiotics—sulfa drugs were put into common usage on the battlefields and in the medical hospitals of World War II, and while penicillin was discovered in 1929, no use was made of it until 1941, when the incidence of wartime injuries and infections made its development both economically feasible and socially imperative.

Prior to this time—and in fact, during a good part of the early days of the war—medical procedures were still very old-fashioned. While techniques such as bleeding and purging had been abandoned, many older techniques—wound-dressing and surgical practices—were still in common use. Therefore, a nurse who had worked under combat conditions in World War II would not find the condi-

tions of the eighteenth-century Highlands to be nearly as strange or unusual as would a more modern medical practitioner. She would be quite accustomed to "hands-on" work, and have no great dependence on modern amenities like indoor plumbing.

The second reason for the choice of World War II is a corollary of the first and a result of the time-travel premise—technology.

Were I to have used a professional healer from contemporary times (the 1980s or 1990s, say), she would have been accustomed to the use of sophisticated equipment and procedures, and—if written with psychological plausibility—would have been missing the use of these acutely, at least in the early stages of exposure to the past.

While Claire is appalled at the lack of hygiene, the ignorance of nutrition, the crudity of surgical procedures, and so on—these are all matters of general medical knowledge that the modern reader also shares. Therefore, a person reading of Claire's perceptions and adventures—bone-setting, wound-stitching, curing fevers—would feel herself (or himself) very much in her shoes. This sympathetic identification would be less if she were

---

[5]*It is quite possibly not coincidental that Ishmael (**Voyager**) asks Claire whether she "still bleeds," explaining that only old women can work real magic—nor is it coincidental that the Tuscaroran seer, Nayawenne, told Claire that she would achieve her full power "when your hair is white (**Drums**).*

On the other hand, it was purely coincidental that Geillis Duncan's hair should have been a blonde so pale as to be "almost white, the color of heavy cream." Or at least I think it was.

constantly thinking how much she'd like to put an epileptic child through an MRI scanner or what a pity it was that she couldn't manage peritoneal dialysis or genetic engineering to correct inborn errors of metabolism.

A third factor in my choice of Claire's time period was the "forward factor." That is, when dealing with time travel, any writer must make decisions as to exactly how the process will be defined; does a traveler age? If a traveler returns to his own time, will he arrive at the same temporal point of departure (i.e., the same hour, day, etc., as when he left), or will some time (spent in the past) have elapsed?

Now, the evolution of the Gabaldon Theory of Time Travel was quite gradual, and in fact is still not yet completely explicated.[6] However, it seemed to me, while writing *Cross Stitch/Outlander,* that time is linear and progressive for an individual; a person is living his or her life in a normal manner, and thus does age normally, no matter which time period he or she occupies while doing so.

That being so, *if* I ever meant Claire to return from the past (and I didn't know whether I did or not, but it struck me as a distinct possibility), she would return to a time farther in the future than the point at which she left it. This in turn meant that if I made her contemporary with myself—set the story in the 1980s or 1990s, that is—her return to the future could well put her in *my* future—she could start in 1990, spend twenty years in the past, and return to 2010—all this in a book that might be published in 1995! (Had I realized at the time how slowly I write, I might have worried less about this.)

I didn't want the books to become dated or seem overtly "wrong" in 2010—as might easily be the case if I tried to project Claire's medical career and daily life in a time later than my own. Looking backward, then, I hit upon World War II as a suitable time period. For one thing, this particular war was the time in which antibiotics were first introduced on a wide scale—the third of the great advances that form the foundation of modern medicine (the first being the notion of asepsis; the second, anesthesia).[7] This was a very important modern medical advance, and one with which most modern readers could identify, but without the need for any technological explanation. Also, if Claire had been a combat nurse, she would naturally be accustomed to hardship—and thus would not find the eighteenth century nearly so much a shock as might the average debutante—and would likewise be independent, self-reliant, and resourceful. Since these were qualities I had already discerned

---

[6] *We discover new refinements and explanations of the Gabaldon Theory as the novels continue. Stay tuned for further developments!*

[7] *Alexander Fleming—a Scot, by coincidence—discovered penicillin in 1929. However, folk remedies involving molds (mostly of bread) are known from as far back as 3000 B.C. (There are in fact hundreds of species of* **Penicillium**, *which grow on substrates from bread to cheeses to rotting melon.)*

in her, my job was only to supply a reasonable explanation as to why she had them. Further, wartime conditions in Britain and France were difficult, austere, and often dangerous. A woman who had lived through nearly a decade of such conditions would not be fazed by the lack of modern amenities—and might be less daunted by the prospect of giving up such things permanently.

And finally, the eighteenth century was rather a violent time. For Claire to be able to deal emotionally and effectively with common conditions—whether she accepted the social basis for them or not—it seemed useful for her to come from a violent time herself. She is—as her daughter notes, considerably *ex post facto*—capable of ruthlessness and great strength in the service of her own ideals. These are not personality traits fostered by soft living.

I didn't realize it consciously at the time, but there was another reason for the choice of World War II as Claire's original time—that being the "echo" between the Jacobite Rising and the Second World War, in terms of the effect of these conflicts on society.

The '45 put an end to the feudal system of the Highland clans, and—as a side effect—threw a large number of Scottish immigrants out into the New World, where they contributed extensively to the development of what would become America. In a similar way, the disruptions and displacements of World War II resulted in a much larger wave of immigrants, who in their turn altered American society and contributed greatly to its modern form.

A side effect of wars is social disruption, and while this is usually unfortunate in individual terms, it not infrequently has unexpectedly beneficial side effects. One result of the Jacobite disaster was the emigration to the New World of numerous Scottish Highlanders—who then contributed greatly to the growth and prosperity of their newly founded country. Results of World War II included the development of the military-industrial complex, which has led to such benefits as space exploration, the development of computers, and the concomitant technological explosion that has transformed modern life.

Major wars invariably lead to rapid developments in medicine—for obvious reasons. The linkage of Claire's occupation to a wartime background, once suggested, became inevitable—and that linkage in turn led to the development of her character and personal history.

MEDICAL BACKGROUND

Where did I get Claire's medical background? Well, that was yet another accident.

As a graduate student, I was fortunate enough to have a full scholarship, and therefore was not given a position as a teaching assistant (a common way for university departments to help students earn their way), the university reasonably feeling that these positions should be reserved for students who needed the income. However, my advisory committee was concerned that I should have at least some slight experience with teaching, since it was likely that I *would* teach at some point in the future.

In consequence, the university awarded me one-eighth of a teaching assistantship; I taught one lab class per week, for which I earned the princely sum of twenty dollars—the low point of my working life, in terms of income. The only class available for me to teach was the lab portion of a class in human anatomy and physiology—and so I taught human anatomy and physiology, in spite of the fact that this class had nothing to do with my own scientific background or aspirations.

Well, time marched on and so did I—to Philadelphia, where my husband was getting an MBA at the Wharton School of Business, and I was trying to find a job so we wouldn't starve. In fact, I found two jobs: The first was a postdoctoral appointment at University of Pennsylvania, where I raised ringdoves and butchered seabirds for a living (this was the low point of my working life in terms of occupational conditions. I couldn't eat fried chicken for nearly a year). The second was a part-time job at Philadelphia Community College, where my "experience" in teaching human anatomy and physiology landed me a job teaching . . . human anatomy and physiology.

This job in turn led to my teaching the same class to nursing students at Temple University, and ultimately, to my teaching the same class—good old human anatomy and physiology—to science students at Arizona State, when I was asked to substitute for a faculty member on sabbatical. In other words, I taught human anatomy and physiology repeatedly, in spite of the fact that none of my degrees or research interests had anything whatever to do with that particular subject.

Since the course was designed for nursing students and for students taking a science elective, the material dealt extensively with clinical medicine—and I thus inadvertently came away with most of what I needed to know to equip Claire Randall to deal with the medical conditions of the eighteenth century.[8]

---

[8]*Coincidentally, the course also exposed me to numbers of nursing students, giving me an appreciation for the mixture of matter-of-factness and dedication so common among them. I still recall one male nursing student I'll call Wally, from my days at Philadelphia Community College.*

My students at PCC were a good deal older than those at the university; most had chosen nursing as a career after several years spent earning a living in other occupations. Wally had been a truck driver, between stints spent in jail for gang and drug-related activities, and was now, at the age of thirty-five, determined to turn his life around and become a nurse. He was one of the best and most attentive students, always asking questions, taking extensive notes, and admonishing the rowdier students to "Shut up and listen to the Doctah!"

All the students were required to take both my class in human anatomy and physiology, and another in "hands-on" clinical nursing, which covered common bedside procedures, among other things. One morning, Wally marched into my class, hair standing on end, his glasses glittering with fury. What happened? I asked, afraid that there might have been some trouble with the law or his former associates.

"What HAPPENED?" he demanded rhetorically. "You want to know what HAPPENED? We just come from the Clinical Nursing final, that's what!"

The Clinical Nursing final was a hands-on exam, in which each student demonstrated expertise in bedside routines such as bathing, dressing, etc., using a lifelike dummy as a subject. It was a very important exam, since all students were required to pass this course in order to stay in the nursing program.

Beyond this accidental preparation, of course, I undertook considerable library research (see Part Twelve: Bibliography), and I began to ask questions of one or two doctors whom I had met online.

I'm greatly indebted to Drs. Gary Hoff and Ellen Mandell, among others—not only for their help and advice in describing and dealing with assorted medical conditions, but particularly for their honesty and openness in letting me see a small part of what it means to be a healer, with all the compassion, dedication, and occasional heartbreak that entails.

(MEDICAL) CONDITIONS AND (PLOT) COMPLICATIONS

One of the plot complications of the first book, of course, revolves around Colum MacKenzie's rather interesting medical condition. People always ask writers, "Where do you get your ideas?" One writer of my acquaintance replies courteously that he orders them in bulk from the Sears catalog, but my own much less imaginative answer is, "Everywhere!" In the case of Colum MacKenzie, I got the idea off the wall of my university office.

At the time, I had a small room in a condemned building on the ASU campus, with crumbling plaster and an ancient air conditioner, which shook like a reducing machine and caused thousands of panic-stricken crickets (who evidently found the crevices of the thing an ideal breeding ground) to leap out into the room whenever I turned it on. To add visual interest to this hole, I fetched in a packet of very cheap cardboard reproductions of Great Paintings, and applied them lavishly to the walls and doors of my sanctum. Each Great Painting had on the back of it a small notice, this containing a brief biography of the artist.

And . . . well, when I sat at my desk, talking on the phone, the painting on the wall directly in front of me was one by Toulouse-Lautrec, that's all. The symptoms of his peculiar disease, including the tendency to impotence and sterility, were included in the biographical note on the back.

You take ideas where you find them.

"8 cont."   *"I did it perfectly!" Wally declared, breathing heavily through bared teeth. "I washed her face and her hands, I combed her hair, I took her vitals, I checked for bedsores—and I kept talkin' to the dummy all the time, callin' it "Mrs. Johnson," sayin' "Now, we'll just take a look here, Mrs. Johnson," just like we're 'sposed to. I did it all just exactly right, right up till I gave Mrs. Johnson the bedpan!"*

He turned to face the class, fists raised in outraged protest to the universe.

"Lookit me!" he yelled. "I'm thirty-five years old! I been divorced three times, I got a wife and two kids! I been in jail, I been in gangs, I lived through stuff would kill most people! And now I'm about to fail my course and ruin my life because I FORGOT TO WIPE A GODDAMN DUMMY'S ASS!!"

I picked up Jamie's dislocated shoulder—and the method of putting back a joint—from a memory of one of Dick Francis's early racing novels (I don't remember which one), in which a jockey described in vivid terms both the pain of the injury and its immediate relief.

The descriptions of several common medical conditions and contemporary treatment methods came from the medical research—the contents of Davie Beaton's surgery was taken from a listing of common medicaments that I found in H. G. Graham's *The Social Life of Scotland in the Eighteenth Century*. The descriptions of procedures in L'Hôpital des Anges in *Dragonfly in Amber* were based on the colorful variety of medical procedures (urinoscopists, truss fitters, bonesetters, *maîtresses sage-femme*) described in *Professional and Popular Medicine in France, 1770–1830* (Ramsey).

Bouton? Well, I looked down, and there he was. I have several dogs myself; Tippy, the smallest and oldest, always goes to my office with me when I work, and guards me faithfully until I go down to bed at three A.M. He lies on the floor near my feet, straight as a compass needle, pink nose on his paws, and a long, fluffy tail laid out behind him.

So as Mother Hildegarde sat down to play her harpsichord, I looked down, and there was Bouton, stretched out faithfully like a compass needle on the floor at her feet. Given Mother Hildegarde's occupation, it seemed only natural for her dog to accompany her on her rounds through the Hôpital—it was his own notion to leap up on the patients' beds and instigate his own form of diagnosis.[9]

Mr. Willoughby's knowledge of acupuncture—in fact, Mr. Willoughby's presence itself—was a matter of sheer necessity; I had to find a way of getting Jamie Fraser across the ocean without having him die of seasickness.

Other bits and pieces of medical lore, conditions, diseases, and cures, were given to me by acquaintances (for instance, the picturesque *loa-loa* worm that Claire encounters in *Voyager* was suggested to me via E-mail by a reader who had noticed that I was writing scenes set in the West Indies), or picked out of the ragbag of memory. The vivid description of death caused by a strangulated hernia was taken (not verbatim, just the notion of it) from a brief excerpt from the writings of Albert Schweitzer, which I encountered in a course in German reading that I took in graduate school (lo these many years ago). I had to translate the passage in which Dr. Schweitzer described the pitiful death of one such patient, and it stuck in my mind. Things do, I'm afraid.

---

[9]*I was therefore pleased—though not surprised—to read, a couple of years ago, of studies being done in which dogs were trained to sniff patients, in order to aid in the detection and diagnosis of certain conditions.*

PART THREE

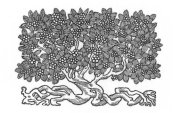

FAMILY TREES

Author's Note: *I am indebted to the Editor of The Baronage Press[1] for great assistance in the research and preparation of the material on the history of the Randall, Beauchamp, and Fraser families, and particularly for the elegant depictions of the arms of these families.*

---

[1] *URL: www.baronage.co.uk*

Claire Elizabeth
Beauchamp

BEAUCHAMP[2]

he Domesday book, compiled some twenty years after Duke William's conquest of England, shows Hugh de Beauchamp to have been well rewarded for his loyalty. Walter, believed to have been his third son, although not so proved conclusively, held Elmley Castle in Gloucestershire and was granted further lands and offices by Henry I, which he was able to pass on to his son William. In the conflict between King Stephen and the Empress Maud, William took Maud's part and suffered the loss of Worcester Castle and much else, but all his honors and estates were restored by Henry II, so that he was able subsequently to bequeath to his son, another William, the office of sheriff in Worcestershire, Warwickshire, Gloucestershire, and Herefordshire.

The second William died early, leaving his son Walter still a minor. Walter was briefly succeeded by his elder son, Walcheline, who died in the same year as his father, and then by Walcheline's only son, William, husband of Isabel, sister and heiress of William Mauduit, Earl of Warwick. The eldest son of this alliance, William, the first Beauchamp Earl of Warwick, founded one of the most powerful English families of the High Middle Ages. The third son, Walter, a crusader, married Alice de Tony, and his third son and eventual heir, Giles, had a son, John, whose elder son, William, was sheriff of Worcestershire and of Gloucestershire. William's son John was elevated to the peerage in 1447 as Lord Beauchamp of Powick.

The brother of William, sheriff of Worcestershire and of Gloucestershire, was Walter, whose elder son, William, married Elizabeth de Braybrooke, heiress to the St. Amand barony, and was subsequently summoned to Parliament in her right as Baron de St. Amand. Their son Richard was attainted in the first year of the reign of Richard III, but was restored immediately Henry VII became king. He had no children other than his illegitimate son, Anthony St. Amand, and as no other heirs were known, the barony of St. Amand has been judged extinct, but his will shows that he bequeathed a cup to his "niece Leverseye," a girl who is assumed to have been his wife's niece but, it has always been accepted, might have been the child of an unknown sister of his own.

It was not until quite recently, when Dr. Quentin L. Beauchamp, the noted historian and archaeologist, examined some old documents found in Warwick Castle, that the existence of Richard's full sister Isabel was revealed, and the consequences of her daughter Leverseye's only child's marriage to the son of Richard's illegitimate Anthony were recognized as continuing the ancient barony. The full facts about the scandal that persuaded the family to keep that marriage secret, and to attempt to eliminate the evidence for the existence of Isabel and Leverseye, have yet to be published by Dr. Beauchamp, but the preparation for his claim to be recognized as Lord St. Amand is currently in the hands of a well-known firm of peerage lawyers, and doubtless the details of the scandal, rumored to be associated with the involvement of Isabel's husband, a close compan-

---

[2]*From the records of The Baronage Press, ca. 1936.*

ion of Henry VII, with the death of the Princes in the Tower "after" the death of Richard III, will doubtless soon be released.

Dr. Beauchamp's sole heir is his niece, Claire Randall, who will be recognized by the Committee for Privileges in the House of Lords as heir presumptive to the title.

RANDALL (IN SUSSEX)[3]

The origins of the Randall family are neither so well known nor so distinguished as those of the Beauchamps. In recent years some of the more imaginative historians have claimed that Randall is but Randolph, and that the origins lie in Scotland with the Randolphs, anciently Earls of Moray, while others write of Rannulf the clerk of Wilkingeston (Wigston) at the end of the twelfth century, whose name was taken as a surname by his great-grandson Adam in 1309. The family continued on the same lands and in the same house until, in 1436, Richard Randolff (also Randull) migrated to Leicester and faded from the records.

Subsequently the name spread wide, many of its owners claiming minor gentility and adopting arms. Most of these arms featured three, four, or five mullets, reminiscent of the arms of the great warrior Freskin, who freed Moray from the threat of the Vikings and whose province passed to the Randolphs. One may assume that the adoption of their mullets was specifically to suggest that origin. Other Randall families took cushions instead of mullets, as three cushions were featured in the Randolph of Moray arms. Yet others, curiously, took martlets (a little bird with no beak and no feet, a notable feature of the Beauchamp of St. Amand arms), one of these being formally granted by the English heralds in 1573 (when the falsification of pedigrees and forgery of armorial histories were so widespread that Queen Elizabeth suggested that if a newly appointed King of Arms was as dishonest as his predecessor it would be no bad thing if he be hanged).

---

[3]*From the records of The Baronage Press, ca. 1940.*

THE ARMORIE OF BEAUCHAMP AND RANDALL

Randall
*First known use by
Sir Denys Randall, Bt
circa 1700*

Sir Richard Beauchamp
*the last Lord St Amand,
died 1508 with no
known legitimate heirs*

Beauchamp Family Tree

David Joubert Beauchamp — Angela Bell

Henry Montmorency Beauchamp
m. Julia Moriston

Quentin Lambert Beauchamp

Claire Elizabeth Beauchamp — Franklin Wolverton Randall

Brianna Ellen Randall
m. Roger Mackenzie

? (son)

The Sussex Randalls emerged from comparative obscurity in the late seventeenth century when Sir Denys Randall was knighted, bought an attractive estate on the South Downs to rear yet more of the sheep that had made his money, and then was awarded a baronetcy by that impecunious monarch George I. (A baronetcy is not an hereditary knighthood, but in many ways its descent behaves as if it is. It was introduced as a title of honor and then degraded by the many kings who treated it as a source of revenue, and who even threatened to inflict fines on candidates who refused the award of the honor.) The subsequent descent of the Sussex Randalls was set out as a neatly illuminated parchment by Dr. Q. L. Beauchamp when his niece Claire married Franklin Wolverton Randall, heir presumptive to the baronetcy held by his fifth cousin, Sir Alexander Randall. (*The Tatler* noted at the time of the wedding the pleasing coincidence of martlets appearing in the arms of both bride and groom.)

Dr Q.L. Beauchamp
*the riband sinister denotes
the descent from Anthony,
bastard son of the last St. Amand*

FRASER OF LOVAT

As with many of the ancient families, scribblers down through the centuries have been ever ready to establish invented or speculative origins for the Frasers. Some have stated categorically that the Scottish Frasers have derived their name from La Fresilière in Anjou, France, while others have insisted that the name was accorded on a hot summer day when the King of France, thirsty from hunting, was presented with a plate of succulent strawberries by one of his companions, who was immediately awarded with a coat of arms bearing three fraises and the command to take the name of Fraser as a surname.

In respect of the heraldic factor it is worth noting that in early heraldry the cinquefoil, sexfoil, and rose are almost indistinguishable, and that only in Scotland has the cinquefoil charge been traditionally recognised as a fraise. And in respect of the Angevin origin, which may perhaps be true, it should be noted also that in the early days of heraldry the cinquefoil, sexfoil, and rose were commonly found among the St. Omer families, when St. Omer was in the Flemish sphere of influence. (Several of the first Fraser Christian names on record—Simon, Bernard, Gilbert, Oliver—are Flemish/Germanic.)

The first of the Scottish Frasers appeared along the River Tweed during the twelfth century. Their origins before this may be disputed, but not their power in Scotland, for they held the most extensive lands in Peebleshire, their names appeared regularly on the rolls of the royal councils, and they became regular benefactors of the religious foundations at Kelso, Newbattle, and Coldingham. Their continued posses-

Randall Family Tree

Denys Randall, Bt. — Jessica Wolverton

Edward (b. 1700)   Jonathan Wolverton   Alexander
m. Stella Adams   (b. Sep. 3, 1705;   (b. 1715,
      d. Apr. 16, 1746)   d. 1746)

- Elizabeth   m. Mary Hawkins
- Daria   (1746)
- Marion

Denys Alexander Randall
m. Sarah Denholm

Alexander   Franklin   Susan
m. Barbara Wormsley

Mary   George Edward — Edith Rysenacht

Sophy Unwin — Peter Franklin   Paul Jonathan

Margaret Ainslie — Alexander

Jonathan Edward — Nora Sheffield

Franklin Wolverton Randall — Claire Beauchamp

Brianna Ellen Randall
m. Roger Jeremiah Mackenzie

? (son)

sion of lands outside Tweeddale is shown in the register of Kelso Abbey, but their first major stronghold was Oliver Castle on the Tweed, perhaps named for Oliver Fraser, whose gift of lands to Newbattle Abbey is noted in its register together with a gift from Adam Fraser, the son of his sister's marriage to Udard Fraser.

The lines of descent from Oliver and Adam are uncertain, but the influence of the Frasers exerted from Oliver Castle was continued through Sir Bernard Fraser and Sir Gilbert Fraser, who held in their turn the hereditary office of Sheriff of Tweeddale. Bernard and Gilbert were probably Adam's brothers, sons of Udard. Bernard was Sheriff of Stirling in 1234, and Laurence, the only known child of his probable brother Adam, was his heir, but as no children of Laurence are recorded as such, this line disappears. The third brother, Gilbert, had four sons, and although from this point the line of descent becomes clearer, the period until Hugh Fraser of Lovat was created Lord Fraser of Lovat in 1464 remains to some extent speculative.

The ancestry of Jamie Fraser

Udard Fraser, shown in the charters of Newbattle Abbey to be living in the second half of the twelfth century, married a sister of Oliver Fraser of Oliver Castle, the son of Kylvert Fraser, and had issue Sir Bernard Fraser, Sheriff of Stirling, Adam Fraser, and Sir Gilbert Fraser of Olivercastle, the direct ancestor of the Frasers of Muchalls and the Frasers of Philorth, and probably the direct ancestor of the Frasers of Lovat, of Strichen, of Inverallochy, and others.

Sir Gilbert was Sheriff of Tweeddale (and described variously as Sheriff of Traquair and Sheriff of Peebles), and died ca. 1263, having had issue John, whose sons were Sir Richard Fraser of Touchfraser and Alexander Fraser of Cornton. (Cornton is in Stirlingshire.) Alexander is claimed as the ancestor of Andrew Fraser of Muchalls, created Lord Fraser 29 June 1633, which title became dormant on the death of Charles, 4th Lord Fraser, 12 October 1716. Although Alexander is traditionally listed as the second son, the royal insistence that the seventeenth-century Lord Fraser should not use a territorial designation—as, for example, Fraser of Lovat—together with the authorized use of the undifferenced arms proclaiming the chiefship of the Fraser Clan, suggest that a good case for seniority had been made and had received royal approval. If this case was valid, then Alexander's name here should be printed before Richard's.

Sir Gilbert's second son was Sir Simon Fraser of Olivercastle, Knight Banneret, Keeper of the Royal Forest of Ettrick, Sheriff of Traquair and of Peebles, who died ca. 1280, leaving issue Sir Simon Fraser of Olivercastle, Sheriff of Traquair and of Peebles, Keeper of the Forests of Traquair and Selkirk, who died in 1291, leaving with other issue Sir Simon Fraser of Oliver and Neidpath, Knight Banneret, a renowned warrior who fought for Edward I in Flanders, served with him at the siege of Carlaverock Castle, joined the war against him in 1301, defeated three English divisions near Roslin in three successive actions on the same day in 1303, and saved the lives of Sir William Wallace at the battle of Hopprew and of King Robert Bruce at the battle of Methven. He was captured in 1306, and hanged, drawn, and quartered in London, leaving two co-heiress daughters, Margaret, who married Sir Gilbert Hay of Locherwort and was ancestor of the Marquesses of Tweeddale, and Joan, who married Sir Patrick Fleming of Biggar and was ancestor of the Earls of Wigton.

Sir Gilbert's fourth son was William, Bishop of St. Andrews, Chancellor of Scotland, who with the Earl of Fife and the Earl of Buchan served as Regent for the North of Scotland and died abroad in 1297.

Sir Gilbert's heir, his eldest son, Richard Fraser of Touchfraser, was apparently the father of an only child, Sir Andrew Fraser, younger of Touchfraser, Sheriff of Stirling, who married Beatrix, an heiress from Caithness, probably of the Le Chen of Duffus family, and died before 1306, leaving several sons: Sir Alexander Fraser of Touchfraser, ancestor of the Frasers of Philorth (now of Saltoun), Chamberlain of Scotland, who married Mary, the sister of King Robert Bruce, and was killed at the battle of Dupplin in 1332, Andrew Fraser, who was killed at the battle of Halidon Hill in 1333, James Fraser, who was killed at Halidon Hill, and Sir Simon Fraser of Brotherton, Sheriff of Kincardine, ancestor of the Frasers of Lovat.

At this point, where the ancestry of the Frasers of Philorth and the Frasers of Lovat divides, it is necessary to stress that the deductions so far have been a little uncertain, owing to the destruction of so many charters during the wars of independence. Another warning must be added. Readers cross-referencing to other records should be aware that many early writers, not understanding the difference between the feudal title "Lord of Lovat" and the peerage title "Lord Fraser of Lovat" (or "Lord Lovat" as it is commonly used since the creation of the new title of Baron Lovat of Lovat), have muddled their numbering of the Lovat succession. Further uncertainty has been created by the forfeit and subsequent restoration of the honors, and by the creation in the nineteenth century of that additional United Kingdom peerage title of Baron Lovat of Lovat. (All editions of Burke's Peerage up to and including 1970 have the Lovat entry hopelessly confused.)

The Gaelic name for the Chief of the Frasers of Lovat, MacShimi (written sometimes as Mac Simi or MacShimidh) means son of Simon, and this Simon is believed to be the Sir Simon Fraser of Brotherton who married the eventual heiress of the Lovat lands previously held by Sir David Grahame of Lovat, and earlier by the Byssets. The Beaufort lands of the Byssets were reunited with the Lovat lands when their eventual heiress, Janet de Fenton, married into the Frasers in 1425.

Sir Simon Fraser of Brotherton, Sheriff of Kincardine, was, as shown above, the third son of Andrew Fraser, Sheriff of Stirling. He married Margaret, the daughter of John, Earl of Orkney and Caithness, whose wife may have been the daughter

and certainly was the eventual heiress of Sir David Grahame, Lord of Lovat, and through Margaret he became the first of the Fraser Lords of Lovat and acquired extensive lands around Loch Ness. (To avoid confusion in numbering, it is important to note that this is a feudal title, not a peerage title.) With his brothers Andrew and James he was killed at the battle of Halidon Hill, having had with other issue Sir Simon Fraser, Lord of Lovat, who was reported by Froissart as having been in the group that captured Edinburgh Castle in 1341 by stratagem, who fought also at the battle of Durham and died unmarried of his wounds in 1346, and Sir Alexander, Lord of Lovat, who married a daughter of Sir Andrew Moray of Bothwell.

The only known child of this marriage was Hugh Fraser, Lord of Lovat, Baron of Kynnell and of Linton, who in 1377, together with the feudal barony of Linton, resigned the last of his lands in Tweeddale and broke the long connection between his highland Frasers and the lowland Frasers along the Tweed. He married Isobel, daughter of Sir John Wemyss of Leuchars by his second wife, Isabel, the daughter of Sir Alan Erskine of Inchmartin, and he died ca. 1409, having with other issue his heir Hugh Fraser, Lord of Lovat.

Hugh Fraser, Lord of Lovat, High Sheriff of Inverness-shire, was born ca. 1376, and married in 1425 as his first wife Janet (who died before December 1429), the sister of William de Fenton of Beaufort. (This is the marriage, mentioned earlier, that brought to the Frasers the other Bysset lands they had not received from the Grahame Lords of Lovat.) Hugh

married as his second wife Isobel, the daughter of Sir John Wemyss of Wemyss and died before July 1440 having had issue by his first wife: Thomas Fraser of Lovat and Hugh Sanctus, his eventual heir.

Hugh Sanctus Fraser, Lord of Lovat, was born in 1417 and married Janet, the daughter of Thomas Dunbar, 2nd Dunbar Earl of Moray. He died ca. 1450, leaving issue Hugh Fraser, Lord of Lovat, who was created before 1464 Lord Fraser of Lovat in the Peerage of Scotland, and in 1464 married Violet, the daughter of John Lyon, 3rd Lord Glamis by Elizabeth, the daughter of Sir John Scrimgeour of Dudhope. Hugh Sanctus Fraser, 1st Lord Fraser of Lovat, died ca. 1500, leaving issue:

A1 Thomas, his heir (see below)
A2 Hugh Fraser, killed 1513 at the battle of Flodden
A3 John Fraser, Rector of Dingwall, a member of the King's Council
a1. Margaret Fraser of Lovat, who married Hector de Kilmalew
a2. Agnes Fraser of Lovat, who married Sir Kenneth Mackenzie of Kintail
a3. Egidia (sometimes known as Marjory) Fraser of Lovat, who married Ferquherd Mackintosh of Mackintosh

Thomas Fraser, 2nd Lord Fraser of Lovat, Justiciary of the North, was born ca. 1461, and married in 1493 as his first wife Janet, the daughter of Sir Alexander Gordon of Abergeldie by Beatrice, the daughter of Sir William Hay, 1st Earl of Erroll, and had issue:

A1 Hugh, his heir (see p. 214)
A2 William Fraser of Teachers

A3 James Fraser of Foyness, who was killed at the battle of Loch Lochy, and was ancestor of the Frasers of Culbokie

a1. Margaret Fraser of Lovat

a2. Isobel Fraser of Lovat

a3. Janet Fraser of Lovat, who married ca. 1527 John Crichton of Ruthven, son of James Crichton of Ruthven by his wife, Janet Ogston. Thomas Fraser, 2nd Lord Fraser of Lovat married 1506 as his second wife, Janet (who married thirdly, as his first wife, David Lindsay of Edzell, later 9th Earl of Crawford), the widow of Alexander Blair of Balthayock and the daughter of Andrew, 2nd Lord Gray, and died 21 October 1524, having by her had further issue:

A4 Robert Fraser, who married Janet Gelly and was the ancestor of the Frasers of Kinnell

A5 Andrew Fraser, reported to have married a daughter of the Laird of Grant, but nothing else is known of him

A6 Thomas Fraser, reported to have married Anna, a daughter of Macleod of Harris

Hugh Fraser, 3rd Lord Fraser of Lovat, Justiciary of the North for Queen Mary, was born in 1494. He married as his first wife Anne, widow of John Haliburton of Pitcur and the daughter of John Grant of Grant and Freuchie by Margaret, the daughter of Sir James Ogilvy of Deskford, and had issue:

A1 Hugh, Master of Lovat, killed with his father at Loch Lochy in 1544 without offspring, after his stepmother, Janet Ross of Balnagowan, had taunted him to make him disobey his father's orders and join the battle (and thus to allow her own son to inherit if he died).

Hugh Fraser, 3rd Lord Fraser of Lovat married secondly Janet, the daughter of Walter Ross of Balnagowan, and with his eldest son was killed fighting the Macdonalds at Loch Lochy on 15 July 1544, having by her had issue:

A2 Alexander, his heir, the beneficiary of his wife's treachery (see below)

A3 William Fraser of Struy, born 1537, married to Janet, a daughter of the Laird of Grant

A4 Hugh Fraser, born circa 1539

a1. Agnes Fraser of Lovat, married before 3 March 1541 as her first husband, William Macleod of Macleod, 9th Chief of Macleod, and married as her second husband, Alexander Bayne of Tulloch.

a2. Margaret Fraser of Lovat

Alexander Fraser, 4th Lord Fraser of Lovat, married Janet (who married secondly Donald McDonald of Sleat) the daughter of Sir John Campbell of Cawdor, third son of Archibald Campbell, 2nd Earl of Argyll, and died at Iona in December 1557, having had issue:

A1 Hugh (see below)

A2 Thomas Fraser of Knockie and 1st of Strichen, whose descendants eventually succeeded to the Lovat titles

A3 James Fraser of Ardachy married and had issue:

a1. Anne Fraser of Lovat married John Fraser of Dalcross.

Hugh Uisdean Ruadh Fraser, 5th Lord Fraser of Lovat, married on 24 December 1567 to Elizabeth (who married secondly 1578 Robert Stuart [previously Bishop of

Some Fraser Arms

Fraser
of that Ilk

Fraser of
Olivercastle

Fraser of
Touchfraser

Fraser
of Philorth

Colour Code

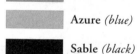

Or *(gold)*

Argent *(silver)*

Gules *(red)*

Azure *(blue)*

Sable *(black)*

Fraser
of Lovat

Fraser
of Strichen

James Fraser
yr of Broch Tuarach

(during the lifetime of his father)

James Fraser
of Broch Tuarach

Caithness], Earl of Lennox and subsequently Earl of March [but divorced him for impotency], and married thirdly in 1581, James Stewart, Earl of Arran) the daughter of John Stewart, 4th Earl of Atholl by his wife, Elizabeth, the daughter of George Gordon, 4th Earl of Huntly, and died 1 January 1577, leaving issue:

A1 Alexander Fraser, Master of Lovat, who died in infancy
A2 Simon, his heir (see below)
A3 Thomas Fraser, Prior of Beauly, died age 8
a1. Elizabeth Fraser of Lovat married Alexander Dunbar of Westfield, Sheriff of Moray
a2. Margaret Fraser of Lovat
a3. Mary Fraser of Lovat, married James Cumming of Altyre
a4. Anna Fraser of Lovat, married Hector Munro of Foulis

Simon Fraser, 6th Lord Fraser of Lovat, Sheriff of Inverness, born ca. 1569, married 1589 as his first wife, Katherine, the daughter of Sir Colin Mackenzie of Kintail by Barbara, the daughter of John Grant of Grant and Freuchie, and had issue:

A1 Simon Fraser, the younger of Lovat, who died young
A2 Hugh, his heir (see below)
a1. Elizabeth Fraser of Lovat, born 1591, married John Dunbar, Sheriff of Morayshire

Simon Fraser, 6th Lord Fraser of Lovat, married 1596 as his second wife Jean, the daughter of James Stewart, 1st Lord Doune, by Margaret, the daughter of Archibald Campbell, 4th Earl of Argyll, and by her had further issue:

A3 Simon Fraser of Inverallochy
A4 Thomas Fraser, who died without issue 1613
A5 Sir James Fraser of Brea, born 1610, married Beatrice Wemyss, and died 6 December 1649 having had issue:
A6 Thomas Fraser, born 1606, died 20 May 1613
A7 James Fraser, baptised 4 June 1612
a2. Anne Fraser of Lovat, died age 8
a3. Margaret Fraser of Lovat, married first as his second wife Sir Robert Arbuthnot of that Ilk, and married 2nd Sir James Haldane of Gleneagles
a4. Jean Fraser of Lovat, died young

Simon Fraser, 6th Lord Fraser of Lovat, married March 1628 as his third wife Catherine, widow of James Grant of Logie and the daughter of William Rose, 11th of Kilravock, by Lilias the daughter of Alexander Hay, 8th of Delgaty, and died 19 September 1658.

Hugh Fraser, 7th Lord Fraser of Lovat, born 1592, married 1614 Isabel, the daughter of Sir John Wemyss of Wemyss by his second wife, Mary, the daughter of James Stewart, 1st Lord Doune, and died 16 February 1646, having had issue:

A1 Simon Fraser, Master of Lovat, born 1621, died unmarried 1640
A2 Hugh, father of Hugh, the heir to the 7th Lord (see p. 219)
A3 Alexander Fraser, took and retained

Fraser of Lovat

Thomas Fraser of Beaufort – Sibylla MacLeod

Dowager Lady Lovat – Simon, Lord Lovat – Kate McBryan
"The Old Fox"

Alexander Fraser

– Davina Porter

Margaret Grant –

Brian Fraser
m. Ellen MacKenzie

Simon Fraser
"The Young Fox"

– William

– Janet

Primrose Campbell –

– James
m. Claire Beauchamp

Archibald Campbell Fraser

Brianna Ellen Fraser
m. Roger Jeremiah Mackenzie

? (son)

title of Master of Lovat after his brother Hugh's death, born 1626, married Sybilla Mackenzie, widow of Ian Mor Macleod, 16th Chief of Macleod and the daughter of Kenneth, 1st Lord Mackenzie of Kintail, and died 27 June 1671, leaving one daughter

A4 Thomas Fraser of Beaufort, de jure 10th Lord Fraser of Lovat (see p. 220)

A5 James Fraser, born 1633, killed in the service of the King of Poland 1657

A6 William Fraser, born 1635, died age 4

a1. Mary Fraser of Lovat, born 1617, married 1635 David Ross of Balnagowan, and died 1659

a2. Anne Fraser of Lovat, born 1619, married 1639 John Gordon, 14th Earl of Sutherland, and died at Dunrobin 23 July 1658

a3. Katherine Fraser of Lovat, born 1622, married as her first husband Sir John Sinclair of Dunbeath, married as her second husband Robert Arbuthnott, 1st Viscount Arbuthnott, and married as her 3rd husband Andrew Fraser, 3rd Lord Fraser (who died 22 May 1674), and died 18 October 1663

a4. Isobel Fraser of Lovat, who died young

Hugh Fraser, Master of Lovat, married Anne, the daughter of Alexander Leslie, 1st Earl of Leven, and died 1643 in his father's lifetime, leaving issue:

A1 Hugh, heir to his grandfather (see below)

a1. Anne Fraser of Lovat

Hugh Fraser, 8th Lord Fraser of Lovat, was born 2 May 1643, married July 1659 to Anne, the daughter of Sir John Mackenzie of Tarbat, Baronet, and succeeded his grandfather 1646. He died 27 April 1672, having had issue:

A1 Hugh, his heir (see below)

a1. Anne Fraser of Lovat, was born 12 March 1661, married Patrick, 2nd Lord Kinnaird, and died 1684

a2. Isabel Fraser of Lovat, born 1662, married Alexander Mackenzie of Glengarry

a3. Margaret Fraser of Lovat, born 1666, married Colonel Andrew Monro

Hugh Fraser, 9th Lord Fraser of Lovat, born 28 September 1666, married Amelia, the daughter of John Murray, 1st Marquess of Atholl, by Amelia Sophia, the daughter of James Stanley, 7th Earl of Derby, and died 14 September 1696, having settled his estates, 20 March 1696, on his cousin and heir male, Thomas Fraser of Beaufort (fourth son of Hugh, 7th Lord), and having had issue:

A1 Hugh Fraser, Master of Lovat, born 1690, died 16 March 1693

A2 John Fraser, Master of Lovat, born 1695, died 10 August 1696

a1. Amelia Fraser of Lovat, assumed the title of Lady Lovat at her father's death and was supported in this by the judgment of the Court of Session 2 December 1702 against her cousin Simon Fraser, the heir male. She married 1702 Alexander Mackenzie of Prestonhall (a Lord of Session as Lord Prestonhall) who adopted the name and designation of Fraser of Fraserdale and died 3 June 1755, age 72. She continued to possess the estates until the Rising of 1715, when her husband was attainted and his life-rent interest in the estate forfeited. In 1730 she was deprived of her peerage title of Lady Fraser of Lovat by a decree of reduction in the Court of Session brought at the instance of the heir male. Her right to the reversion of the estates was not judicially tried but she settled for a money payment. She died 22 August 1763, having had issue:

B1 Hugh Fraser, younger of Lovat, died 9 November 1770
b1. Amelia Fraser of Lovat, died 22 August 1763
a2. Anne Fraser of Lovat, born 1689, married September 1703 as her first husband Norman Macleod of Macleod, 20th Chief, and as her second husband Peter Fothringham of Powrie, and as her third husband John Mackenzie, 2nd Earl of Cromarty, and died 10 August 1734
a3. Katherine Fraser of Lovat, married 25 July 1706, Sir William Murray of Ochtertyre, Baronet, and died 4 March 1771
a4. Margaret Fraser, died unmarried

The cousin and heir male, fourth son of Hugh Fraser, 7th Lord Fraser of Lovat, Thomas Fraser of Beaufort, de jure 10th Lord Fraser of Lovat, married Sibylla, the fourth daughter of Ian Mor Macleod of Macleod, 16th Chief of Macleod. He and his son Simon abducted Amelia, the Dowager Lady Fraser of Lovat, in 1698 and were found guilty of high treason. He died May 1699 having had issue:

A1 Alexander Fraser, Master of Lovat, born ca. 1666 and died unmarried in the lifetime of his father 20 November 1689
A2 Simon, his heir (see below)
A3 Hugh Fraser
A4 John Fraser, was born 1674 and entered the Dutch service as "Le Chevalier Fraser." He died unmarried in 1716.

Simon Fraser, 11th Lord Fraser of Lovat, was famous for his adventurous career. Soon after the death of Hugh, 9th Lord, he induced Hugh's eldest daughter, Amelia, to elope with him. When she returned to her mother, he seized her estates, and for this and other acts of violence he was tried in his absence in 1698, sentenced to death, and attainted. He then forced himself on the widow of the 9th Lord, Amelia the daughter of the Marquess of Atholl, and compelled her to marry him. For this he was tried and outlawed in 1701. In 1715 he supported the Government, and was rewarded with a remission under the Great Seal, and a gift of Fraser of Fraserdale's forfeited life-rent of the Lovat estates. He endeavored to assert his right to the dignity of Lord Fraser of Lovat at elections of Representative Peers in 1721, 1722, and 1727, but objections were made to his vote. In 1729 he brought a reduction before the Court of Session of the decree of 1702, giving the heir female the title, and in virtue of a decree in his favor in 1730, became Lord Fraser of Lovat. He supported the Rising of 1745, was impeached by the House of Lords, and executed on Tower Hill, 9 April 1747. He married as his first wife (discounting the forced ceremony with the Dowager) Margaret, the daughter of Ludovic Grant of Grant, and had with other issue who died unmarried:

A1 Simon Fraser, Master of Lovat (who would, but for the attainder, have become 12th Lord Fraser of Lovat), joined his father in the Rising of 1745, was pardoned 1750, and fought in Portugal and the American war. He was Member of Parliament for Inverness from 1761 until his death. His father's forfeited lands were granted him in 1774, and he died without issue on 8 February 1782.

A2 Alexander (Alistair) Fraser, baptised 1 July 1729, died unmarried 7 August 1762
a1. Janet Fraser of Lovat married Ewan Macpherson of Cluny, and died 14 April 1765
a2. Sybilla Fraser of Lovat, died unmarried 9 February 1755

Simon, 11th Lord Fraser of Lovat, married 1733 as his second wife, Primrose, the daughter of John Campbell of Mamore, son of Archibald Campbell, 9th Earl of Argyll, and had issue a third son:
A3 Archibald Campbell Fraser (who would, but for the attainder, have become 13th Lord Fraser of Lovat), Consul-General at Algiers, member of Parliament for Inverness 1782, married 1763 to Jane, the daughter of William Fraser of Ledeclune, and had issue five sons who all died unmarried in the lifetime of their father.

On the death of Archibald Campbell Fraser on 8 December 1815, the representation of the family in the male line passed to Thomas Alexander Fraser 10th of Strichen, (but for the attainder, 14th Lord Fraser of Lovat), descended, as shown above, from Thomas, second son of Alexander Fraser, 4th Lord Fraser of Lovat.

The descent of the Fraser of Lovat chiefship after the attainder and execution of the 11th Lord would have been different if Brian Fraser, his bastard son by Davina Porter, had been legitimated. He made a good marriage to Ellen, the eldest daughter of Jacob Mackenzie of Leoch, and if his father had enjoyed better relations with Edinburgh the legitimation could have been passed under the Great Seal. The lives of Jamie and his brother William might then have been quite different. Brian Fraser matriculated his father's arms as a bastard, and bore them differenced by a bordure compony Or and Gules. James intended to matriculate as Brian's heir, but the political troubles of the time never allowed him time to complete the petition. The arms he bore in his father's lifetime and those he would have borne later are illustrated on page 215.

Note: There is still some contention among historians as to the exact details of the succession in the 14th and early 15th centuries, some of the early accounts still in circulation having errors unrecognized until the 19th century. The line indicated here is the most probable.

MacKenzie of Leoch

The origins of this particular sept are somewhat obscure. Jacob MacKenzie, who is thought to have been related to the MacKenzies of Torridon, seized Castle Leoch by force in 1690, while the previous Lord of that Castle, Donald MacKenzie of Leoch, was absent from home. Donald died under mysterious circumstances before he could return to defend his property, and Jacob married Donald's widow, Anne Grant, the daughter of Malcolm Grant of Glenmoriston, by whom he had issue:

A1 Colum (see below)
A2 Dougal, who married Maura Grant, daughter of William Grant, younger brother of Malcolm Grant of Glenmoriston and had issue by her, four daughters: Eleanor, Margaret, Molly, and Tabitha
a1. Ellen, who eloped with Brian Fraser, bastard of Simon, 11th Lord Lovat. She bore him three children: William, Janet, and James.
a2. Janet, who married Alexander Hay of Crimond, and died without issue, age 24
a3. Flora, who died in infancy

a4. Jocasta, who married first John Cameron of Torcastle, married secondly Hugh Cameron ("Black Hugh") of Aberfeldy, and thirdly Hector Cameron of Arkaig, with whom she emigrated to America. Jocasta bore one daughter to each of her three husbands: to John Cameron, Seonag, to Hugh Cameron, Clementina, and to Hector Cameron, Morna

Colum MacKenzie married Letitia Chisholm, daughter of Andrew Chisholm of Erchless and had issue:

A1 Hamish, who emigrated to Nova Scotia following the Rising of 1745 and the subsequent razing of Castle Leoch[4]

The petition of Colum MacKenzie for a matriculation of arms was disputed by the heirs of Donald MacKenzie of Leoch, and was the subject of a prolonged legal process. The petition was not granted before the Rising of 1745, and after the Rising (in which the heir of Donald MacKenzie, his son and grandson, were all killed), the emigration of the only heir and the loss of his lands left the matter of the title undecided; the property of the estate reverted to a distant heir of Donald MacKenzie: Jeremiah MacKenzie.

---

[4]*It is thought that various family documents in the possession of Hamish MacKenzie and his heirs may have been preserved, which cast further light upon the antecedents of Jacob MacKenzie. As these documents are presently unavailable, however, nothing further can be adduced at this time.*

MacKenzie of Leoch

Jacob MacKenzie – Anne Grant

— Ellen (b. 1691, d. 1729) m. Brian Fraser (b. 1691, d. 1740) ——

— Colum (b. 1693, d. 1745)
　　m. Letitia Chisolm　——　Hamish

— Dougal (b. 1694, d. 1746)　　　　┌─ Molly
　　m. Maura Grant　　　　　　　　├─ Tabitha "Tibby"
　　　　　　　　　　　　　　　　　├─ Margaret
— Janet (b. 1697, d. 1721)　　　　└─ Eleanor
　　m. Ambrose Mackenzie

— Flora (b. 1700, d. 1700)

— Jocasta (b. 1702)
　　m. John Cameron　——　Seonag *

　　m. Hugh Cameron　——　Clementina *
　　　"Black Hugh"

　　m. Hector Cameron　——　Morna *

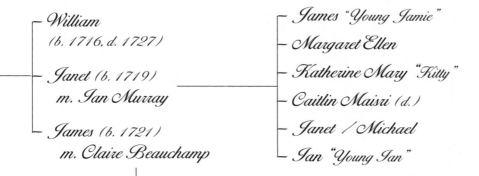

William
(b. 1716, d. 1727)

Janet (b. 1719)
   m. Ian Murray

James (b. 1721)
   m. Claire Beauchamp

James "Young Jamie"
Margaret Ellen
Katherine Mary "Kitty"
Caitlin Maisri (d.)
Janet / Michael
Ian "Young Ian"

Brianna Ellen Fraser
m. Roger Mackenzie

? (son) *

You'll find out.

A GENEALOGICAL NOTE

NOTE ON THE GENEALOGY OF ROGER MacKENZIE (WAKEFIELD)

ow, I don't know whether I haven't explained adequately, or whether perhaps some readers were simply too caught up in the story to notice the details, but I have had letters and questions from a number of people who are confused over the parentage of Roger (MacKenzie) Wakefield.

The questions are most often phrased as follows:

If Roger is the son of Geilie Duncan and Dougal MacKenzie, how did he get into the future? (signed) Confused.

P.S. What's all that stuff about Jeremiah?

This is pretty simple to answer—he *isn't* the son of Geilie Duncan and Dougal MacKenzie, and it beats me how anyone could possibly have concluded that he is, though any number of people evidently have. I can only assume that some readers, in their haste to find out what happens next, overlooked the explanations of Roger's family tree that occur in *every single one of the books,* (sound of author ripping hair out by the roots) or somehow failed to grasp the distinction between "descendant" and "son." (A son is a descendant, all right, but a descendant is not necessarily a son. Got it?)

Roger is in fact the great-great-great-great-great-great-grandson of Geilie and Dougal—a fact that he explains in some detail to Brianna on their wedding night. (I know, I know, you were busy laughing over "Jug-butt," or you were caught up in the . . . er . . . less intellectual aspects of that particular interlude, but pay attention now, and I will explain it to you. Again.)

In *Outlander,* where we first meet Roger, the Reverend Wakefield explains to Claire and Frank that Roger is his great-nephew; the son of his (the Reverend's) niece, who was killed in the Blitz. The Reverend also explains that though he has given Roger his own name (Wakefield), he has drawn up Roger's genealogy—hanging on the corkboard—in order that Roger will not forget his true name (which happens to be MacKenzie) or lineage.

In *Dragonfly in Amber*, Claire uses this same genealogy (still hanging in the Reverend's office) to explain to Roger exactly what happened to the child Geillis Duncan bore to Dougal MacKenzie—and thus why it is a matter of personal concern to Roger whether they find Geilie Duncan in time to prevent her disappearance into the past.

Okay, *about* that son. Geillis Duncan gets pregnant (accidentally) by Dougal MacKenzie [*Outlander*]. She's condemned to burn as a witch, but allowed to live until the child is born. Dougal takes the newborn child and gives it to one of the MacKenzie clansmen to raise as his own (this sort of fostering was common in the Highlands at the time).

As Claire explains to Roger in *Dragonfly*, Dougal gave the boy to a family who had recently lost a new baby to smallpox. This would have been the reasonable thing to do, since the mother of the dead child would be able to feed the adopted child (no formula in the eighteenth century). And, as per the common custom of the times, the family gave the adopted child the same name as that of the child they had lost—William Buccleigh MacKenzie. Claire didn't know this from her own experience, since she had left Leoch before Geillis was (presumably) burned. She did, however, later learn the names of the parents to whom Dougal gave the child (when Dougal visits her in Paris)—and in the process of checking out Roger's family

tree [*Dragonfly*], would have been able to confirm the dead child/adopted child replacement by means of baptismal records, as these would show both baptisms in the same parish, with the same parents, no more than a few months apart.

Allllll right. Now, look at the relevant part of the genealogy that the Reverend wrote out for Roger. See William Buccleigh? He's the changeling. That is, he is *not* the son of William John MacKenzie and Sarah Innes; he is the illegitimate son of Geillis Duncan and Dougal MacKenzie, who was given to William and Sarah to raise. Since the Reverend Wakefield naturally wouldn't have known this (he *may* have known—from the baptismal records—that the child must be adopted, but would have had no way of knowing who the true parents were), William simply appears in the family tree as William and Sarah's son.

Notice also the name of the woman whom William marries—Morag Gunn. Now, you, the reader, have not seen this name before, but Claire certainly has—and remembers it. In *Dragonfly*, she prepares for her quest in part by having Roger's family tree researched. Owing to circumstances, she will have paid particular attention to the changeling and whatever can be found out about him, so it's

not surprising that when Roger asks her much later [*Drums*], she recalls Morag's name.

The important point here is that William Buccleigh is Roger's *direct ancestor*. Likewise, Geillis Duncan is Roger's *direct ancestor* (as is Dougal MacKenzie). If one of these people (or anyone else in this family tree) were to die without having children, that would naturally eliminate all the descendants below them on the chart—including Roger. Hence Claire's concern [*Dragonfly*]; if Geillis doesn't go back and get burned at the stake, she doesn't produce William Buccleigh either—so does Roger cease to exist?

OKAY. Now, in *Voyager,* we don't deal directly with the questions concerning Geillis, but she and her connections with Roger are mentioned, just to keep events in mind for her surprise appearance toward the end of that book. Look. See? There's that genealogy chart again, still tacked to the corkboard in the Reverend's study.

Then we reach *Drums of Autumn.* Now we make a Big Hairy Deal out of Roger's antecedents, in several different places. We mention Geilie and her son (William Buccleigh, remember?), and Roger takes down the genealogical chart with a fair amount of ceremony, as the final act in clearing out his (adopted) father's study. Later, when he takes Brianna to the Celtic Festival, he reminisces about the Reverend, and about his family tree, telling the anecdote about his great-grandmother Oliphant and her "bonny lad," Jeremiah—in the process, getting it across (or so one would think),

that a) Jeremiah is an old family name, recurring several times in the family tree, b) Roger's father was named Jeremiah (called Jerry for short), c) Roger's own middle name is Jeremiah, and d) his mother called him "Jemmy" for short, as a child.

Now, the point of all this is to make the readers more or less pay attention when they later see the names Jeremiah or Jemmy, and I gather most did—they just didn't all make the expected leap: "Jeremiah/Jemmy . . . say, I *wonder* whether this person has anything to do with *Roger's* family?"

So. Now we come to the chapter of *Drums* where Roger finds himself aboard the *Gloriana,* trying to get to the Colonies. He sees an unknown young woman on the dock who attracts him—he envies the closeness between her and her husband, and observes that they have a child (watch that baby). Later, in casual conversation, he learns that her name is Morag MacKenzie (notice the woman who suggests that they might be related ["Perhaps your man is kin to him"]? This is a Clue, awright?).

All right. Some of the passengers—several of them children—contract smallpox. In an effort to keep the contagion from spreading, the crew throw the affected persons overboard (this scene was directly inspired by the story of just such an occurrence, told by an eyewitness). Fearing

that her child's rash will be mistaken for pox, and the baby put over the side, Morag MacKenzie hides in the hold, her escape covered by her husband, who attacks Roger on deck during the melee.

You still watching the baby? Okay. Notice, then, that his mother calls him "Jemmy," hmm? Jemmy MacKenzie. Are we beginning to suspect anything here? Well, that's okay, Roger didn't notice, either. However, moved by compassion, he saves mother and child, risking his own life in the process.

A good deal later, contemplating names for his own son, the name "Jeremiah" is mentioned once again. Roger (finally) makes the connections that have been brewing in his subconscious for lo, these many months (he's seen his own family tree often enough, after all). To confirm his realizations, he asks Claire if she, too, recalls the name of William Buccleigh's wife, which she does—Morag.

A fair-haired man with green eyes, named MacKenzie, with a wife named Morag and a son named Jeremiah. Don't look now; you (and Roger) have just met Geilie and Dougal's son, William Buc-

cleigh, in the process of emigrating to America—and Roger has just saved his great-great-great-great-grandfather Jeremiah from a watery grave (incidentally saving himself from presumed extinction in the process, and giving those readers so inclined food for thought as to why some people time travel, the circular nature of things, and whether history can be changed).

And *that's* why all the fuss about Jeremiah (if you want to observe that Jeremiah was also the name of a rather well-known Biblical prophet with a penchant for unpopular predictions, and make speculations regarding Roger and the oncoming Revolution, that's fine with me, too, but it won't be on the test).

Roger Wakefield MacKenzie's
Family Tree *

William John MacKenzie — Sarah Innes
|
William Buccleigh MacKenzie — Morag Gunn
|
| | | |
Jeremiah   Abigail   Edgar   Andrew
m. Esme McLeod
|
William Jeremiah — Josephine McLennan
|
Jeremiah Gregory — Betsy Oliphant
(widow)
|
Ellis Jeremiah — Emma Watson
|
Jeremiah Walter MacKenzie
m. Marjorie Wakefield
|
Roger Jeremiah MacKenzie
- -
m. Brianna Ellen Fraser
|
? (son)

*This is of course, only part of the complete genealogical chart
that hung on the Reverend Wakefield's wall.

PART FOUR

COMPREHENSIVE GLOSSARY AND PRONUNCIATION GUIDE

When my agent, Perry Knowlton, first read the draft manuscript of *Voyager,* he wrote to tell me that he thought it was a wonderful, adventurous book—noting, however, that there was a small error in one of the French phrases, for which he helpfully gave me the correct usage. I replied with thanks, adding, "One of these days, I will stop writing books involving places I've never been and languages I don't speak—and then where will we all be?"

Why should one use foreign phrases in the first place? Well, for assorted reasons: to give "flavor" to a character or setting, to convey something of the multilingual aspects of European society in the eighteenth century, to add to the atmosphere of unfamiliarity that must afflict a person thrust suddenly into such strange circumstance—and now and then, for humor or suspense.

People occasionally write to me asking how this or that Gaelic phrase is pronounced, or if I can direct them to good courses of study in Gaelic. One or two bold souls have gone so far as to request that *I* teach them Gaelic—by mail, presumably.[1]

Alas, I don't speak Gaelic. Or French. Or German. Or Swedish. Or Mandarin. Or Yoruba. Or Kahnyen'kehaka (Mohawk).

Now, I do speak English (and fairly well, if I do say so myself). I can also make myself understood in Spanish, but not with any real finesse (my Spanish-speaking housekeeper and I have a system of communication involving arm-waving and facial grimaces, which seems to cover any grammatical lapses nicely). I grew up in the Catholic church during the 1950s and 1960s, before the switch of Catholic liturgy to the vernacular, and I sang at the daily 7:30 A.M. Mass for several years in elementary school. Consequently, I have a lot of Latin vocabulary, but no grammar at all. So I'm afraid I have no eclectic linguistic background, in spite of the assorted bits and pieces that appear in the books. What I do have is a nice collection of dictionaries and a lot of obliging bilingual friends.

While the average well-educated reader has no particular trouble with *"Merci beaucoup,"* and similar bits of French, German, Spanish, etc., thrown in for flavor, Gaelic-speakers are thin on the ground in most parts of the world—especially Arizona. I therefore originally intended to include a glossary and pronunciation guide in *Outlander,* to provide background on the Scots and Gaelic terms, but was dissuaded by the publisher. So, along came *Dragonfly in Amber,* and I once again suggested a collective glossary that would cover the Scots and Gaelic terms in both books—pointing out that I was getting quite a few letters from people asking how these words were pronounced. The publisher's reaction? "This book is already so huge, we can't possibly squeeze another *word* into it."

So when *Voyager* came along—some thirty-five thousand words longer than *Dragonfly* (they printed it on special thin paper, to make it look shorter and avoid scaring the paying customers)—I didn't try again. I merely began scheming; the final result of which is this book.

---

[1] *For anyone desiring further information on Gaelic educational programs or materials, please see Appendix II: Gaelic Resources.*

So, with great thanks to Iain and Hamish Taylor (Gaelic), Barbara Schnell (German), Karl Hagen and Susan Martin (Latin and Greek), William Cross, Paul Block, and Chrystine Wu (Mandarin), a great many helpful French-speakers (all with conflicting opinions on idiom), and with deep obligation to the compilers of my multilingual dictionaries . . . here it is. I've provided pronunciations where possible; I'm afraid I didn't have personal sources for all the terms. However, a general guide to Gaelic grammar is included.[2]

A Very Brief Guide to Gaelic[3] Grammar

by Iain MacKinnon Taylor[4]

Some of the simpler, general rules for Gaidhlic reading and writing

This aid to Gaidhlic is a very brief sample of some of the nuances inherent in the language; it is far from complete. The intent in writing it is not to try teaching anyone to read and write Gaidhlic, but to give the reader a small measure of understanding of the challenge facing students of the language in their attempt to learn it. Some do indeed succeed in reading and writing and a few even graduate to speaking Gaidhlic quite creditably.

Proper pronunciation is by no means easy. There are sounds in the language that defy description in English. In the glossary which follows this grammar aid, I have tried to approximate sounds with the letter used in English that seems to be closest. For some readers this may work reasonably well, but for others it will not. For example, "Gh" at the beginning or end of a word, I wrote simply as "G." The real sound is more like a very young baby's gurgle.[5] That's about the only way I can explain it. For "Ch" at the beginning or end of a word, I used the letter "K." The sound is really like in the Hebrew toast, "L'chaim." You will find an attempt at descriptions of the other "Gaidhlic" sounds is made as you read on. Also, in the glossary I have used a hyphen between vowels that should be pronounced separately.

—Iain M. Taylor

---

[2]*NB: While they are not strictly speaking* **foreign,** *I have also included occasional medical terms or colloquial terms in English that seemed sufficiently archaic as not to be easily understood or likely to be found in a dictionary less comprehensive than my own favorite, the massive* **Merriam-Webster's Third New International Dictionary** *unabridged.*

[3]*NB: "Gaelic" is the usual spelling; "Gaidhlig" is the preferred spelling by many current students of the language, and "Gaidhlic" is what Iain says it should be. Iain speaks the bloody language and I don't.*

[4]*Iain MacKinnon Taylor is a native Gaidhlic speaker, born on the Isle of Harris, who has kindly been my main source of information on Gaidhlic (Gaelic) terms for both* **Voyager** *and* **Drums of Autumn,** *and who has also—with the assistance of his brother Hamish, and his aunt, Margaret Beedie— supplied the pronunciation of approximations for the Gaidhlic terms in the glossary.*

[5]*Another Gaelic-speaking friend describes this sound as "the noise made by someone who's just put their bare foot down on a slug."*

The Gaidhlic Alphabet

A,B,C,D,E,F,G,H,I,L,M,N,O,P,R,S,T, U (letter count: 18)

Not Used (From English Alphabet)
J,K,Q,V,W,X,Y,Z

In words where the vowels **A,O,** or **U** precede a consonant, any vowel following the consonant must also be **A,O,** or **U.**

In words where the vowels **E** or **I** precede a consonant, any vowel following the consonant must also be **E** or **I.**

The only exception to this rule is the word "**Esan**" (him).

Aspirated consonants. There are many instances where the letter "H" follows the first letter in a word. This condition is called "aspirated."

Aspirated B, **Bh,** pronounced as "V."

Aspirated C, **Ch,** pronounced as the "Ch" in "L'chaim."

Aspirated D, **Dh,**

Aspirated G, **Gh,** both of these have no equivalent sound in the English language. Try to imitate a baby gurgling. (However, **Gh** followed by **I** is pronounced as "Y.")

Aspirated M, **Mh,** pronounced as "V"

Aspirated P, **Ph,** pronounced as "F"

Aspirated S, **Sh,** the "S" is silent. Pronounce the "H" only.

Aspirated T, **Th,** the "T" is silent. Pronounce the "H" only.

Grammar

Gender. Gaidhlic words have a gender, though this does not necessarily correspond with the gender of the person a given word describes. For example, **duine** (man) is masculine. **Boireanach** (woman) is also masculine. **Bean** (wife), however, is feminine. The easy way to find gender in reading is to see whether the associated adjective is aspirated. Adjectives describing feminine nouns are aspirated, adjectives describing masculine nouns are not. Example: Boireanach **Math** (Good woman). Bean **Mhath** (Good Wife).

The adjective always follows the noun.

Duine math Man good (*Good man*)

Latha math Day good (*Good day*)

Madain mhath Morning good (*Good morning*)

Oidhche mhath Night good (*Good night*)

The adjective follows the adverb.

Tha e gle mhath. It is quite good.

The noun or pronoun follows the verb.

Ruinn mi. Did I.

Ruinn thu. Did you.

Ruinn e. Did he.

The adverb follows the noun or pronoun.

Ruith e luath. Ran he quickly.

Ruith Iain luath. Ran John quickly.

Possessive Case.

Some possessed subjects are aspirated. Examples:

Mo mhàthair (*My mother*)

Do mhàthair (*Your mother*) *singular*

A mhàthair (*His mother*)

Some are not:

A màthair (*Her mother*)

Ar màthair (*Our mother*)

Am màthair (*The mother*)

Bhur màthair (*Your mother*) *plural*

When the spelling for the possessed subject starts with a vowel, as in **athair** (*father*):

"My father" is spoken and written as **M'athair.**

"Your father" *singular* is spoken and written as **D'athair**

Your father *plural* is spoken and written as **Bhur 'n athair.**

"His father" is spoken and written as **'athair.**

"Her father" is spoken and written as **A h'athair.**

"Our father" is spoken and written as **Ar 'n athair.**

Exception.

"Their father" is spoken and written as **An athair.**

The pronoun "you" or "your" is used in the plural form when addressing an elder, as recognition of seniority or a form of respect. Examples:

Ciamar a tha thu? becomes **Ciamar a tha** *sibh?* (*How are you?*)

Bheir ghomh do chòta becomes **Bheir ghomh** *bhur* **chòta.** (*Give me your coat.*)

Vocative case.

A bhalaich. O boy (*This is a form of address, not an exclamation.*)

A dhuine. O man

A bhoireanaich. O woman

A nighean. O girl

A choin. O dog

A charaid. O friend

Proper names starting with a vowel don't get the preceding **A.**

A Thearlaich. O Charles

A Sheaumais. O James

Iain. O Iain

Anna. O Ann

Ealasaid. O Elizabeth

Accents

Generally, vowels are pronounced:

A as in *Arm*

E as in *End*

I as in *Ingot*

O as in *On* or *Onward*

U as in *Ooze*

"Accents" slanting up to the left over a vowel denote a long vowel. (**À È Ì Ò Ù**). An accent slanting up to the right over the vowel **Ó**, indicates a pronunciation of **O** as in **motor.**

COMPREHENSIVE GLOSSARY OF FOREIGN TERMS
(including British slang)

hoovering (*English*)—vacuuming

Sassenach (*Gaelic*) [Sass-uh-nak]—outlander, or foreigner; more specifically an English person; usage generally derogatory. There are multiple spellings of this term: Sassunach, Sassenaich, etc.; I picked one, and stuck with it.

baragh mhor (*Pseudo-Gaelic*)[6]—a large Baragh.

uillean pipes (*Gaelic*) [OOlain]—a small bagpipe, literally, "elbow pipes," as air is supplied by an elbow-pressed bellows, rather than by a mouthpiece. Uillean pipes are generally used for musical entertainments (*as opposed to the Great Northern Pipes—the traditional "bagpipe" most often seen in films—which was used almost exclusively outdoors, and was considered [by the English] a weapon of war*).

---

[6]*Before the welcome advent of Mr. Taylor into my life, I was obliged to resort to such devices as were available for the creation of Gaidhlig terms: dictionaries, historical documents (which often featured highly creative spelling), and imagination. Bear in mind that when I wrote* **Outlander,** *I didn't expect to show it to anyone—let alone anyone who spoke Gaidhlig.*

hurley (*Scots*) "Hurley, hurley round the table . . ." A "hurl" is a short, impromptu journey; "hurly" means either a noise or tumult, or a wheel or handcart; a "hurley" (*modern usage*) is a child's makeshift vehicle, constructed of pram wheels and the like. As used in the original verse, the meaning appears to indicate the passing of food round a table, with concomitant noise and conversation.

pooch nane (*Scots*)—"pouch none"; put nothing in one's sporran; i.e., don't take anything away from the table.

fungas (*Gaelic*) [foongas]—mushrooms; fungus in general.

drammach (*Gaelic*) [dramak]—a mixture of oats and water, uncooked. Very refreshing (*says Iain*) on a hot day while cutting peats, etc.

burke (*English*)—generally dismissive term for an undistinguished male.

tynchal [tinshal]—a hunt. IMT notes that there is no letter "Y" in Gaidhlig, so he doesn't think this is a Gaelic term, preferring "Sealg." (*Sir Walter Scott used it, but he was a Lowlander, what would **he** know?*) It seems to be a Scots (rather than Gaelic) term (*spelt variously*), meaning "a circle formed by sportsmen to encircle deer or other game."

sealg (*Gaelic*) [she-alag]—a hunt.

ballag buachair (*Gaelic*) [Ballag buakair]—mushroom; literally, "manure bubble." (*correct spelling of "balgan-buachrach," as used in **Outlander** is "technically not incorrect" (IMT).*)

quiring (*English, obs.*) [KWI-ring]—singing; choiring.

griss (*Scots*)—nail.

lug (*Scots*)—ear.

swivet (*English*)—state of extreme agitation; "in a swivet" over something.

Luceo non uro (*Latin*)—"I shine, not burn." Motto of clan MacKenzie, appearing on the clan badge with the image of a "burning mountain."

Je suis prest (*French*)—"I am ready." Motto of clan Fraser. NB: This is an ancient form of French; in the modern form, the "s" has been replaced by a diacritical mark, and the word is spelled "prêt." However, the Fraser motto uses the old spelling.

Tulach Ard (*Gaelic*) [Toolak Aarsd]—"The High Hill." Battle cry of clan MacKenzie. I have no idea *what* high hill, but that's what it means.

tarn (*English*)—small pool, commonly found on moorland.

tannasg (*Gaelic*) [tannasg]—spirit or ghost.

sgian dhu (*Gaelic*) [Sgeean duh]—the "black knife"; a small knife carried in stocking-top or armpit.[7]

Stad, mo dhu (*Gaelic*) [Stat, mo ghuh]—"Stay, my black one." (*IMT notes that this is perhaps not the way a native speaker would say it.*)

sguir (*Gaelic*) [sgooir]—stop (*doing whatever you're doing*).

---

[7] *This is given as historical usage; however, neither my Gaelic expert nor my Scottish-born UK editor has been able to discover for me exactly **how** one carries a small knife in one's armpit without a sheath or holster—though the editor, Andy McKillop, helpfully suggests that perhaps the oxter hair was knotted so as to secure the knife in place. This would, of course, involve ripping the hair loose when the knife was drawn, but the ancient Scots were tough auld buggers, so maybe so. Maybe no, too.*

swiving (*English*)—sexual intercourse; vulgar usage.

Buidheachas, mo charaid (*Gaelic*) [Booiakas, a karaid]—roughly, "Thank you, friend"; "buidheachas" indicates thanksgiving or gratitude, or satisfaction. IMT notes that "Taing" is a much more commonly used word for thanks.[8] Easier to spell, too.

donas (*Gaelic*) [DOnas]—devil or demon.

duine (*Gaelic*) [DOOnuh or Du-ine]—a man, an individual.

cobhar (*Gaelic)* [CO-ar]—one dictionary gave this word as "seafoam," which was the meaning I intended. However, another gives it only as "relief or help." IMT says it's help, or refuge.

ciamar a tha thu (*Gaelic*) [Kia-mar a haa u]—greeting; "How are you?"[9]

saft (*Scots*)—literally, "soft." Figuratively, a light drizzle, as in "saft weather," or foolishness/mental deficiency—"saft in the heid."

silkie (*also selkie*) (*Scots*)—a seal.

bassin (*French*) [bah-SEEN]—a basin or shallow dish.

en deshabille (*French*) [ahn day-sha-BEEL]—in a state of undress.

mo airgeadach (*Gaelic*) [mo eregedak]—my silver one. IMT notes that a native speaker would be more likely to say, "Mo nighean bhan." [mo nee-an vaan], meaning "My fair-haired girl." Since Jamie is more likely referring to Claire's skin than her hair, I think perhaps the former is more likely, even if not common usage.

calman geal (*Gaelic*) [calman gi-al]—white dove; "geal" also carries the meaning "bright."

tenebrous (*English*) [TEN-eh-brus]—shadowed.

cullen skink (*Scots*)—As one of my cookbooks remarks, "This is not an offensive small animal, but a traditional recipe for soup from the Moray Firth area." It consists of haddock and mashed potatoes, simmered in milk and cream with onion, butter, mace, parsley, and salt and pepper.

dittay (*Scots*)—a court document; an indictment.

croich gorn (*pseudo-Gaelic*)—your guess is as good as mine—probably better.

philtres (*English, obs.*) [FIL-ters]—potions or formulas, often magical or alchemical in nature.

poofter (*English*)—homosexual; derogatory.

peruke (*English*) [per-OOK]—small wig.

mo buidheag (*Gaelic*) [mo booiak]—my friend. Correct possessive form is "mo bhuidheag."

canty (*Scots*) [CAN-tee]—lively, pleasant, cheerful; implying also something small and neat, or a person in good health.

broch tuarach (*Gaelic*) [BROCK TOO-arak]—north-facing tower.

harled (*Scots*)—plastered.

broch (*Gaelic*) [BROK]—tower. In particular, an ancient round tower, usually either B.C. or very early A.D.

Sheas (*more usually spelled "seas"*) (*Gaelic*) [shais]—stand, or stop.

---

[8]*An early Scottish reader, with a smattering of Gaelic, expressed doubt about this expression, which she thought might mean "Yellow horses, my friend." It isn't right, but it isn't yellow horses, either. Iain Taylor notes he recalls an example of* **Buidheachas** *on the label of a bottle of Drambuie, the name "Drambuie" being a corruption of "Au dram buidheach"— "The drink that satisfies."*

[9]*Fine, thanks. Haa u?*

mo maise (*Gaelic*) [mo vaishe]—roughly, "my beauty." "Maise" means ornament, greaty beauty, elegance. IMT notes that common usage is more likely "mo nighean mhaiseach," meaning "my beautiful girl" [mo nee-an vaisheak]. Also, correct possessive form is "mo mhaise."

mo chride (*Gaelic*) [mo cree or mo kri-e]—my heart. Used as a term of affection.

braw (*Scots*)—literally, "brave," but also implies "fine, splendid, excellent."

cockernonny (*Scots*)—a gathering of hair into a neat bundle.

ruaidh (*Gaelic*) [Rooagh]—red; *a ruaidh,* "the red one." IMT notes that while this does mean red(*haired*), it's commonly applied to the color brown, in general use.

gille (*Gaelic*) [GILL-e; sometimes corrupted in English usage to "gilly"]—a lad, young man, or servant man.

dags (*Scots obs.*)—pistols.

snark (*British and Scots dialect*)—a snore or snort; also, a tangle, as in a noose or snare; also a grumbling, trouble-causing person (*Scots*). As used—as an epithet— "long-nosed snark"—it is probably derogatory, though may also imply something about the entrapping nature of Captain Randall, who is so addressed.

bothy (*Scots*) [BAH-thee]—a small shack or hut.

besom (*Scots*) [BEE-zum]—a woman, generally ill-tempered.

caudle (*English*) [CAW-dul]—a drink, usually made of warm ale or wine, mixed with bread, sugar, eggs, and spices, often administered medicinally.

ogives (*French*)(*ogeev*)—an architectural feature, in which four arches conjoin in a roof.

monstrance (***Latin-English***) [MON-strunce]—an ornamental receptacle (*usually made of precious metal*) in which the consecrated Host (*the Blessed Sacrament*) is placed for display during certain rituals, such as Benediction, or for exposition on an altar.

sortes Virgilianae (*Latin*) [SOR-tees ver-jill-ee-AHN-ee]—an ancient game of fortune-telling, based on the random selection of text from a book.

emerods (*English, obs.*)—hemorrhoids.

scut (*British dialect*)—the tail of a rabbit or deer; in vulgar usage, the female pudenda, by extension, a female servant, or any dirty, mean person.

ma nièce (*French*)—my niece.

ma chère (*French*)—my dear.

ma bonne amie (*French*)—my good friend, my dear friend.

posset (*English*)—a nutritious drink, usually warm milk, curdled with ale or wine, sometimes thickened with bread or egg.

gaberlunzie (*Scots*) [GAB-er-lun-zee]—small lead badge, given to beggars as a license to beg within the borders of a parish.

snuff mull (*Scots*)—a container for snuff, often made from a sheep's horn.

plimsolls (*English*)—sneakers or tennis shoes.

cark it (*English*)—die; be killed.

geyser (*English*) [GEE-zer]—hot-water heater.

Tearlach mac Seamus (*or mac Sheumais*) [Tearlak mac Haamuis]—"Charles, son of James"; Charles Stuart.

rootling (*English*)—to rifle through or dig about.

lych-gate (*English*)—an enclosed passage in the wall of a churchyard, where processions (*such as the coffin, for a funeral*) assemble or rest before entering.

stone (*English*)—a measure of weight. Most often, fourteen pounds, when used as a measure of human weight. Other substances, such as flax, tobacco, etc., were occasionally measured in terms of "stones" of different weights, each type of "stone" being specific to the substance weighed.

oxter (*English*)—armpit.

salope (*French*)—slut; trollop.

femme sans cervelle (*French*) [FAM sahn ser-VELL]—brainless female (*literally "woman without a brain"*).

Non, Monsieur le Comte, je regrette, mais c'est impossible (*French*)—"I'm sorry, Count; it's impossible."

flux (*English*)—diarrhea; any of various forms of intestinal upset resulting in diarrhea.

cozen (*English*) [CUZ-en]—to charm or persuade.

lever (*French*) [leh-VAY]—literally, "rising." Term applied to the ceremonial ablutions of Louis XIV and XV.

de rigueur (*French*) [day ri-GAYR]—literally, "of rigor," but figuratively, "in fashion"; "the way things must be done."

chaise percée (*French*) [Shays per-SAY]—chair set above a commode or chamberpot.

costive (*English*)—constipated.

mo duinne (*Gaelic*)—incorrect form of "my brown one"; correct form should be "mo nighean donn."

crocodile (*French*)—crocodile.

écu (*French*)—unit of French money.

livre (*French*)—another unit of French money.

A la lanterne (*French*)—"To the lamp-post!" Popular cry of the French Revolution, accompanying the hanging of aristocrats.

tumbril (*French*)—wheeled cart in which condemned persons were taken to the guillotine.

gussets (*English*)—tapered panels of fabric, sewn into a seam for ornament, or to adjust the fit of a garment.

silk plissé (*French*)—a fine, light fabric.

Mon petit sauvage (*French*)—"My little savage."

confits (*English*)—small bits of preserved or candied fruit.

Sa Majesté, le Roi Louis! (*French*)—"His Majesty, King Louis!"

Chère Madame (*French*)—"Dear Madam."

ma petite (*French*)—my little one.

C'est un cochon qui vit dans la ville, c'est un cochon qui vit . . . (*French*)—"This little pig lives in the city, and this little pig lives . . ."

ma petite souris (*French*)—my little mouse.

salaud (*French*) [sa-ló]—sloven, dirty person; slut.

appartement (*French*)—apartment.

mon chevalier (*French*)—literally, "my horseman," or "my soldier"—more generally, an honorific meaning merely "gentleman."

parterres (*French*)—flower beds.

skelloch (*Scots*)—a shriek or cry.

servante aux petits soins (*French*)—a "servant of little things"—a body servant or groomer.

mon cher ami (*French*)—my dear friend.

Vite! Dépêchez-vous! (*French*)—"Quick! Stir yourself!"

chirurgeon (*English, obs.*)—surgeon.

les maîtresses sage-femme (*French*) [lay

may-TRESS sahj-FAM]—"the wise-women."

bilboquet (*French*) [bil-bo-KAY]—a handheld game, comprised of a hollow cup, to which a ball is tethered. The object of the game is to catch the ball in the cup.

broken men (*English*)—men affiliated with no specific clan.

charcuterie (*French*) [shar-KOO-ta-ree]—butcher shop.

hurly-burly (*Scots*)—a tempest, a tumult.

angel-makers—French term for abortionists.

la petite Anglaise maladroite (*French*)—"the clumsy (*badly spoken*) English girl."

ma mère (*French*)—my mother.

Volkslied (*German*) [VOHKS-leed]—folk song.

note tonique (*French*) [noht toh-NEEK]—the keynote of a piece of music.

passe-partout (*French*) [pahs par-TOO]—a key (*literally, "passes through everything"*).

clef (*English*)—part of a musical signature, indicating whether a given piece is played in treble or bass. May also indicate the key and tempo of the piece.

Ne vous en faîtes pas (*French*) [Ne voo ahn fayt pah]—"Don't do that."

énorme! (*French*) [ay-NORM]—"enormous!"

c'est tout (*French*) [say TOO]—"That's all."

Bas mallaichte! (*Gaelic*) [Baas malai-hte]—"Black death!" (*used as an exclamation of exasperation*).

une sorcière (*French*) [uhn sorseeayr]—a sorceress.

horloge (*French*) [hor-LOHJ]—a clock; particularly a large, public clock.

havers (*Scots*)—there are several (*wildly divergent*) meanings for this term; as used (*in Dragonfly*), it indicates "to talk at random or incoherently"; "to fuss about nothing."

fiacre (*French*) [Feeaykr]—a carriage, often available for commercial hire.

commissariat de police (*French*)—the police station.

barouche (*French*) [bah-ROOSH]—an open carriage.

les disciples du mal (*French*)—the disciples of evil.

fauteuil (*French*) [fowtooee]—armchair.

Deo volente (*Latin*) [DAY-o voh-LEN-tay]—"God willing."

Allez! Allez! Montez! (*French*) [Allay! Allay! Montay!]—"Come on! Come on! Climb!"

lèse-majesté (*French*) [LEES MA-jes-tee]—the crime of laying hands upon the King; used casually to imply disrespect.

coil (*Scots*)—a difficulty or troublesome circumstance.

Entrez! (*French*) [ahn-TRAY]—Come in!

canaille (*French*) [kah-nay]—rabble, riffraff, mob, scum of the populace; scoundrel.

Non! Ce n'est pas vrai! (*French*) [Suh nay pah vray]—"No! It isn't true!"

les putains (*French*) [lay putanh]—prostitutes.

Que Dieu nous en garde! (*French*) [Kuh Dyoo noo ahn gard]—"May God protect us!"

Au pied, reste! (*French*) [O pyed, rest!]—"To the foot (of the bed), and stay!"

Que Dieu vous bénisse, mon enfant. (*French*) [Kuh Dyoo voo benees, mon enfanh]—"May God bless you, my child."

sans-culottes (*French*)—peasants; the very poor (*the term means literally "without trousers"; i.e., too poor to afford pants*).

Regardez (*French*) [ruh-GARD-ay]—"Look."

putti (*Italian*)—cherubs.

yows (*Scots*)—ewes.

mo luaidh (*Gaelic*) [mo luai]—my beloved, darling.

fricht (*Scots*)—fright.

caurry-fisted (*Scots*)—left-handed.

mo bràthair (**Gaelic**) [Mo vraahair]—my brother. "Mo bhràthair" for correct possessive.

C'est un embarras de richesse! (*French*)—"It's an embarrassment of riches!"

my jo (*Scots*)—my close friend, my dear companion.

mo muirninn (*a muirninn*) (*Gaelic*) [A voornin]—my darling (*NB: IMT gives spelling as "mhurninn," for the possessive.*)

chacun à son gout (*French*) [shah-coon a sohn GOO]—"Each to his own taste."

dunt (*Scots*)—a blow.

Plus ça change . . . (*French*) [ploo sah CHANJ]—The more things change, the more they stay the same.

tierce (*French*)—a fencing parry or guard position.

Ne pétez plus haut que votre cul. (*French*) [Nay paytay ploo ho kay votr cool]—"Don't fart above your arsehole." French proverb, meaning both "Don't get above yourself," and "Don't try to do things you aren't equipped for."

Gu leoir! (*Gaelic*) [Gu leor]—"Plenty, enough!"

burras (*Gaelic*) [Booras]—caterpillars.

mo charaid (*Gaelic*) [mo kharaid]—my friend.

cuir stad (*Gaelic*) [Cuir stat]—put a stop to.

arisaid (*Scots*)—a woman's long shawl.

smoor (*Scots*)—to smother; specifically, to bank a fire.

gomerel (*Scots*)—a fool.

Da nobis hodie . . . (*Latin*) "Give us this day," from the Lord's Prayer.

meachin' (*British dialect*)—slinking or fawning.

mozie auld poutworm (*Scots*)—moldy (*or overripe*) old grub.

proddle (*Scots*)—to prick, goad, or stab.

mumper (*Scots*)—one who chews without teeth, one who gums his food.

nettercap (*Scots*)—spider.

pibroch (*Gaelic*)—IMT says this is English slang for the Gaidhlig "Pi-obairachd." [Peeberakd]. Literally, "piping." "Pibroch" is generally used to describe "classical" pipe music. Gaidhlig speakers call it "Ceol mor"—"big music."

kerfuffle (*English*)—a fuss or flurry.

mo ghràdh (*Gaelic*) [mo graag]—my dear

yeuk (*Scots*)—"the itch"; colloquial expression for any sort of rash or skin inflammation.

Mon Dieu, je regrette . . . (*French*)—"My God, I am sorry . . ."; beginning words of the Act of Contrition.

gowk (*Scots*)—an awkward fool.

dogsbody (*English slang*)—minion or flunky; general assistant.

deed of Sasine (*Scots*)—deed transferring property under Scottish law.

les filles (*French*) (*lay FEE*)—"the girls"; colloquially, prostitutes—"les filles de joie" (*the girls of joy*).

gralloch (*Gaelic*) [grallok]—slaughter, specifically, the knife stroke that disembowels a killed animal.

clot-heid (*Scots*)—clot-head or cloth-head; an idiot or imbecile.

brose (*Scots*)—a broth, often made of barley or kail (*cabbage*). [*IMT notes: "This is not Gaelic, but the brose I and my fellow islanders knew was a stiff mix of the local grain meal—oats or barley, etc.—cooked with water, butter, and salt. Same ingredients as porridge, but much stiffer consistency. Supposed to be 'good for you.' Never liked it myself."*]

hough (*Scots*)—shin of beef.

collops (*English*)—a pan-sized portion of meat, beaten flat.

gomeral (*Scots*)—fool, idiot.

cods (*English*)—slang for a man's genitals.

fiddle-ma-fyke (*Scots*)—a silly, over-fastidious person.

doiters (*Scots*)—blundering fools.

Mon Dieu! C'est bien, ça! (*French*)—"My God! That's good!"

besom (*English*)—derogatory term for a woman, implying a scold or slattern.

fash (*Scots*)—trouble or bother.

girdle (*Scots*)—a flat iron plate set over the fire, used for cooking. Small girdles were often carried by Scottish mercenaries, swung on their belts, enabling them to make oatcakes in the field. Similar in meaning and derivation to the English "griddle."

a mhic an diabhoil (*Gaelic*) [A vihc an diavail]—"You son of the devil." A serious Gaelic curse.

garbel (*Scots*)—to rumble, as an empty stomach.

moil (*Scots*)—a difficulty or trouble.

sark (*Scots*)—a shirt. An ordinary sark was a long, capacious garment, reaching at least to midthigh. A shortened version of this was referred to as a "cutty sark."

blowzabella (*English*)—an attractive woman, not necessarily a whore, but sexually approachable.

wean (*Scots*)—child.

sennight (*English*)—ancient form of "seven nights"—a week.

kine (*Scots*)—cattle.

cockchafers (*English*)—cockroaches.

A charaid, bi sàmhach. (*Gaelic*) [A kharaid, bi saavak]—"My friend, be quiet."

ban-druidh (*Gaelic*) [Ba-un druii]—female sorceror or worker of magic.

coneys (*English*)—rabbits.

mo nighean (*Gaelic*) [Mo nee-an]—my girl, my lass.

codless scut (*English*)—a coward, literally, a "ball-less cunt."

sluire (*Scots; typo—should be "sluit"*)—a sloven or slut.

quim (*English*)—female genital opening (cunt).

ecchymosis (*Latin*) (*medical term*)—an escape of blood into tissue from ruptured blood vessels.

doits (*Scots*)—small copper coins.

Samhain (*Gaelic*) [Savain]—the ancient Scottish equivalent to the feast of All Hallows; Halloween; October 31.

asafoetida (*Latin*)—an aromatic (*very*) compound, worn in a bag around the neck to ward off infection.

ratten (*Scots*)—a rat; also a small person or animal; also a term of endearment.

clattie imp (*Scots*)—variant of "clarty"; "dirty imp."

poolie (*Scots*)—a louse.

neffit qurd (*Scots*)—"neffit" = pigmy, "qurd"; a clot of excrement.

hiddie-pyke (*Scots*)—a miser or niggard.

knivvle (*Scots*)—to beat or thrash.

ked (*Scots*)—a sheep-louse.

whoreson (*English*)—son of a whore.

skrae-shankit skoot (*Scots*)—a spindle-legged braggart; term of contempt.

mo nighean donn (*Gaelic*) [Mo nee-an down]—my brown one; my brown-haired lass.

kittle-hoosie (*Scots*)—whorehouse, brothel.

bubbies (*English*)—breasts.

kivvers (*Scots*)—covers, bedding.

skelloch (*Scots*)—a shout, scream, or cry of alarm.

nez de Cléopatre! (*French*)—"Cleopatra's nose!" Exclamation of alarm or annoyance.

N'est-ce pas? (*French*)—"Is it not so?"

fille de joie (*French*)—prostitute; literally, "girl of joy."

crottin (*French*)—dung, horse dropping.

anker (*English*)—a large, tub-shaped cask, used to ship brandy.

chuckie (*English*)—slang term (*relatively inoffensive*) for a prostitute, used in direct address.

cochon (*French*)—pig. Used in insult, unless you refer to a real pig.

Horreurs! (*French*)—"Horrors!"

spiled casks (*English*)—(*IMT: "I remember in my youth as a sometimes bartender, handling beer in wooden casks, spiling was a step in the process between taking it from storage to dispensing it. A hole was drilled in one of the bungs and a porous wooden spile was driven into the hole to relieve pressure at a controlled rate for a day or two prior to using it. One had to estimate how many 'spiled casks' to have on the rack at any given time."*)

punked wine (*English*)—flavorless or worthless wine.

Post coitum, omne animalium triste est (*Latin*)—"After sex, all animals are sad."

a bhalaich (*Gaelic*) [a valaik]—boy (*vocative case*).

dégustateur de vin (*French*)—a professional wine-taster.

wame (*Scots*)—the belly.

nez (*French*)—"nose"; a professional wine appraiser.

ma petite saucisse (*French*)—my little sausage.

abigail (*Scots*)—a female servant.

"Eirich 'illean! Suas am bearrach is teich!" (*Gaelic*) [Airik illan, sooas am bearrak is tiak]—"Up, lads! Over the cliff and run!"

kebbie-lebbie (*Scots*)—a commotion.

Stramash (*Scots*)—a wrangle or fight.

lang-nebbit (*Scots*)—"long-nosed," figuratively; a nosy person.

collieshangie (*Scots*)—an uproar or squabble.

neb (*Scots*)—nose.

tais-toi (*French*) [tay TWA]—shut up; be quiet.

mo nighean dubh (*Gaelic*) [Mo nee-an dooh]—my black-haired lass; my dark one.

bruja (*Spanish*) [BROO-ha]—witch or sorceress.

bai-jai-ai (*Mandarin*)—mustard seed.

shen-yen (*Mandarin*)—kidneys.

shan-yu (*Mandarin*)—eels.

hôtel de joie (*French*)—literally, "house of joy"; a brothel.

spalpeen (*Irish*)—a low fellow; a scamp or rascal.

an-mo (*Mandarin*)—pressure with fingers.

gwao-fe (*Mandarin*)—foreigner (*derogative*); foreign devil.

huang-shu-lang (*Mandarin*)—weasel.

Ifrinn! (*Gaelic*)—"Hell!"

da-zi (*Mandarin*)—Chinese character.

Komma, komma, komma, dyr get (*Swedish*)—"Come, come, come, dear goat."

Guten morgen (*Swedish*)—"Good morning."

Vous êtes Anglais? (*French*)—"Are you English?"

Hola! (*Spanish*) [OH-la]—greeting; "Hello!"

Quien es? (*Spanish*) [Kee-en es?]—"Who's that?" (*"Who are you?"*)

Mi casa es su casa (*Spanish*) [Mee cahsa es soo cahsa]—"My house is your house"; traditional Spanish invitation, offer of hospitality.

Si, claro (*Spanish*) [See, clahro]—"Yes, certainly" (*literally, "Yes, that's clear"*).

cabron (*Spanish*) [Cah-BROHN]—literally, a male goat. Idiomatically, a major insult, implying incest with the female parent (*i.e., "motherfucker"*).

sala (*Spanish*)—the main room of a house.

Merci aux saints (*French*)—Mercy of the saints, or "Saints have mercy!" Exclamation of surprise and thankfulness.

Vous êtes matelot? (*French*) [Voo etay mahtehlo?]—Are you a sailor?

Je suis guerrier (*French*) [Zhe swee gareeayr]—"I am a soldier" (*literally, "I am a warrior"*).

pistola (*Spanish; corrupt dialect*)—pistol.

"Silence, mes amis. Silence, et restez, s'il vous plaît." (*French*)—"Quiet, my friends. Quiet, and stay where you are, please."

habitant (*French*)—native.

mon enfant (*French*)—my child; used as term of affectionate familiarity or condescension to one younger than the speaker, regardless of age.

C'est bien. Ce n'est qu'un serpent. (*French*)—"It's all right. It's only a snake."

Non. C'est innocent. (*French*)—"No. It's harmless."

Basta, cabron! (*Spanish*)—"That's enough, motherfucker!"

ceo gheasacach (*Gaelic*) [Ceo yasagak] (*Pronounce the first "a" as in "ape"*)—magic mist.

amiki (*taki-taki*)—friend.

bene-bene (*taki-taki*)—it's good; it's okay.

Habla Espanol? (*Spanish*)—"Do you speak Spanish?"

Sprechen Sie Deutsch? (*German*)—"Do you speak German?"

griffon (*French*)—a person of mixed blood; one-quarter black.

An gealtaire salach Atailteach! (*Gaelic*) [An geealtair salak Atailteak]—"Filthy Italian coward!"

weirrit (*Scots*)—strangled; an addition often added to the sentence of burning—a criminal might be allowed the mercy of being strangled before being consigned to the flames.

bhasmas (*Hindi*)—ashes of a gemstone.

nagina (*Hindi*)—stone of high quality.

houngan (*African/creole*)—a medicine-priest; a voodoo practitioner; a witch-doctor.

oniseegun (*Yoruba*)—a priest/practitioner of magic.

Huwe! (*Yoruba*)—"Up!" (*"Lift it up!"*)

egungun (*Yoruba*)—crocodile.

bébé (*French*)—baby; term of endearment.

Ils sont arrivés (*French*) [Eel sohn ahree-vay]—"They have come."

Aya, gado (*Yoruba*)—"Yes, child."

Mana, mana (*Yoruba*)—Thank you, thank you.

grandmère (*French*)—grandmother.

certainement (*French*) [ser-tan-MON]—certainly, surely.

loa (*African dialect*)—spirit, either the spirit of a dead person or a voodoo deity, speaking through an oracle.

buckra (*African/Caribbean dialect*)—disparaging term for a white person.

A Mhicheal bheannaichte, dion sinn bho dheamhainnean (*Gaelic*) [a vi-icheal veanaihte, dion shin vo yoainean]—"Blessed Michael, defend us from demons."

Sionnach (*Gaelic*) [Shionak]—fox.

a shionnach (*Gaelic*) [A hionak]—o fox (*vocative*).

Mar shionnach (*Gaelic*) [Mar hionak]—like a fox.

Pog mo thon! (*Gaelic*) [Po-og mo ho-on]—"Kiss my ass!"

Gabhainn! A charaid! (*Gaelic*) [Gavain! a karaid]—"Gavin! My friend!" (*NB: IMT says "More correctly would be 'A Ghabhainn! A charaid!'"*)

Balach biodheach (*Gaelic*) [Balak bauiak]—beautiful boy.

Mac Dubh (*Gaelic*) [Mac DOO]—"Son of the Black One." Abbreviation of the longer expression (Jamie's formal Gaelic appellation) "Seaumais, an fhearr mac dubh."

Slàinte (*Gaelic*) [Slaainte]—health; also used as a drinking toast; "To your good health." "Slàinte mhath."

tannasg (*Gaelic*) [tannasg]—spirits or ghosts.

tannasgach (*Gaelic*)—ghosts, spirits (*NB:*

IMT says "This takes the adjective form. In this context, should probably be tannasgan—plural noun").

caithris (*Gaelic*) [Cairish]—to be awake all night; a wake over a dead person. Also a formal lament (*also known as a "coronach"*), sung during a funeral procession, recalling the details of the departed person's life.

Tha sinn cruinn a chaoidh ar caraid, Gabhainn Hayes (*Gaelic*) [Ha shinn cruin a kuii ar caraid, Gavain Hayes]—"We are met to weep and cry out to heaven for the loss of our friend, Gavin Hayes!" (Pronunciation tip: "In '**chaoidh**' and '**haou**,' the letters 'ao' are pronounced like the 'ue' in the German name 'Mueller.'" [IMT])

Eisd ris! (*Gaelic*) [Aaishd ris]—"Hear him!" (*"Listen to him."*) Long "a" pronounced as in "hay."

Rugadh e do Sheumas Immanuel Hayes agus Louisa N'ic a Liallainn an am baile Chill-Mhartainn, ann an sgire Dhun Domhnuill, anns a bhliadhna seachd ceud deug agus a haon! (*Gaelic, rather obviously*) [Roogag e do Haamas Immanuel Hayes agus Louisa nihc a Lialain an am bala Kille-Vaartain, an an sgiire Goodn Do-onuil, a-uns a vliana seac ciad diag agus a haon]—"He was born of Seaumais (James) Emmanuel Hayes and of Louisa Maclellan, in the village of Kilmartin in the parish of Dodanil, in the year of Our Lord seventeen hundred and one!"

A Shasunnaich na galladh, 's olc a thig e ghuibh fanaid air bas gasgaich. Gun toireach an diabhul fhein leis anns a bhas sibh, direach do Ifrinn!! (*Gaelic*) [A Hasunaik na gallag, 's olc a hig guiv fanaid air baas gashciak. Gun toireag an diavol haan laish auns a vaas sheev, deerak do Ifrinn]—"Wicked Sassenach dogs, eaters of dead flesh! Ill does it become you to laugh and rejoice at the death of a gallant man! May the devil himself seize upon you in the hour of your death and take you straight to hell!"[10]

Lumen Christi (*Latin*) [LOO-men KREE-stee]—Light of Christ. Sung as a repeated invocation during the procession of an Easter Vigil liturgy.

"Ifrinn an Diabhuil! A Dhia, thoir cobhair!" (*Gaelic*) [Ifrin an Diavuil! A Yia hoir co-ar!]—"Devil's hell! God help us!"

Sacrée Vierge (*French*) [SAC-ray Vee-urj]—"Sacred Virgin!" An invocation of the Blessed Virgin, commonly used as an exclamation of astonishment.

"Arrêtes, espèce de cochon!" (*French*)—"Stop, you species (type) of pig!"[11]

a luaidh (*Gaelic*) [looai]—my dear.

Requiem aeternam dona ei, et lux perpetua luceat ei (*Latin*) [Re-kwee-em ay-ter-nahm do-na ay-ee, et loox per-peh-too-ah loo-chay-aht ay-ee]—"Eternal rest grant unto him, (*O God*) and let perpetual light shine upon him."[12]

craicklin' (*Scots*)—hoarse croaking or snoring sound.

Asgina ageli (*Cherokee*)—person close to the Otherworld.

Miserere nobis (*Latin*) [Mee-say-ray-ray NO-bees]—"Have mercy on us."

ceilidh (*Gaelic*) [KAY-lee]—a festivity or party, often with music and singing.

bodhran (Gaelic) [BOH-ran]—a flat, circular drum, with a stretched skin head over a wooden frame, beaten with a short, double-headed stick.

alagruous (*Scots*)—grim or woebegone.

coccygodynious (*English*) [cok-see-go-DIN-ee-us]—literally, a pain in the region of the coccyx (*the tailbone*).

camstairy (*Scots*)—obstinate, riotous, unmanageable.

Is fhearr an giomach na 'bhi gun fear tighe (*Gaelic*) [Shearr an giomak na vi goon fer taie]—"Better a lobster than no husband" (*Scottish proverb*).

bumf (*English slang*)—a hodgepodge of miscellaneous papers, of dubious use. Abbreviation of "bum-fodder," i.e., toilet paper.

Casteal Dhuni (*Gaelic*) [Casheel Doon]—war cry of clan Fraser

Iain says: "My aunt Margaret (Margaret Beedie) had been to Aberdeen City Library and badgered a young man there to help her research the Fraser war cry. They found no reference so she went for the name of the castle. It showed up as Castle Dounie. This is the same as your research showed and my finding from the Moncrieffe of that Ilk.

"I asked her how the name Downie figured into all this. 'It doesn't.' Quite indignantly, 'Indeed why should it?

---

[10]*I might note that while the Gaelic rendering was given courtesy of Mr. Taylor, the original sentiments expressed in Duncan's **caithris** were mine. When I do things like this, I normally write them out and fax them to Mr. Taylor for translation, though on other occasions, I may simply apply to him for a suitable insult or bit of descriptive invective.*

[11]*Hey, don't blame me; this was supplied by a helpful French speaker from the Literary Forum.*

[12]*The usual form of this prayer includes the word "Domine" (God or Lord), following "dona ei," and when Young Ian repeats the English form, he uses this.*

This was always Fraser property. If this castle was built on or close to a previous fortification as it very likely was, then it's quite obviously Caisteal an Dùin. It just got twisted round, as the English usually do, and the current name got quite separated from the real name.' Bingo!

"Caisteal an Dùin. [Cashte-al an Doo-in] Castle of the fort. You may want to try it out on your neighbors. It's easy to imagine a couple of hundred hairy Frasers charging and sounding 'Casteal an Dùin' in their customary free-for-all, mis-timed discordant manner with hyper-elongated 'OO's.' To the poor helpless little English soldiers, it must surely have been the chorus from hell."

Comme deux chiens . . . aux culs (*French*)—"Like two dogs . . . (*sniffing*) at (*each other's*) backsides."

sehr schön (*German*)—very beautiful.

gute Nacht (*German*)—good night.

Foeda est in coitu et brevis voluptas, Et taedat Veneris statis peracte (*Latin*)—"Doing, a filthy pleasure is—and short. And done, we straight repent us of the sport."[13]

Virtus praemium est optimum. Virtus omnibus rebus anteit . . . (*Latin*)—see Appendix III for complete poem text and translation.

duine uasal (*Gaelic*) [Duine ooasal]—man of worth, a solid citizen, a gentleman; man of means, man of integrity.

kebbie-lebbie (*Scots*)—an altercation where a number of people talk at once.

thole (*Scots*)—to put up with (*"I canna thole that"; "I won't put up with that."*)

ban-lighiche (*Gaelic*) [Ba-un li-ike]—a female physician or healer.

Cha ghabh mi 'n còrr, tapa leibh (*Gaelic*) [Ka gav mi 'n co-orr, tahpa leiv]—"I will have no more, thank you."

a mhic no pheathar (*Gaelic*) [A vihc mo feahar]—nephew; literally, son of my sister (*vocative*) (*there is no single word for nephew; you say "son of my sister" or "son of my brother" [a mhic mo bhràthar]*). ["ao like 'ue' in Mueller"]

taki-taki (*pidgin*)—term for the polyglot pidgin used for trade in the West Indies, this incorporating words from English, French, Spanish, and several African and Polynesian dialects.

Saorsa (*Gaelic*) [Saor-sa]—freedom ["ao" like "ue" in "Mueller"].

droch aite (*Gaelic*) [drok aaite]—bad place.

djudju (*African dialect*)—evil spirits.

Bonsoir (*French*) [bone SWAHR]—"Good evening."

Je suis à votre service (*French*) [zhe swee ah VOTr serVEES]—"I am at your service."

a nighean donn (*Gaelic*) [ah knee-an down]—my brown(haired) lass.

Tempora mutantur nos et mutamur in illis (*Latin*)—"The times are changing, and we with them."

each uisge (*Gaelic*) [Eak uishge]—water horse, a kelpie.

Je m'appelle . . . (*French*)—"I am called . . ."

Grandmère est . . . (*French*)—"Grandmother is . . ."

Pas docteur, et pas sorcière, magicienne. Elle est . . . (*French*)—"Not a doctor, nor a sorceress or magician. She is . . ."

---

[13] *See Appendix III, "Poems and Quotations," for the complete text and translation of this poem.*

Pierre sans peur (*French*)—literally, "stone without fear," though more probably meant to indicate a reassuring talisman.

Ist sie nicht wunderschön? (*German*)—"Is she not wonderfully beautiful?"

Blutwurst (*German*)—blood sausage.

Comment ça va? (*French*)—"How are you?"

greet (*Scots*)—to weep or grieve.

cack-handed (*Scots*)—left-handed; also, awkward or maladroit.

a dhiobhail (*Gaelic*) [a yeavuil]—you devil (*vocative*).

Oidhche mhath (*Gaelic*) [oyke]—"Good night."

meine Dame (*German*)—my good lady, madame.

Ist Euer Mann hier? (*German*)—"Is your husband here?"

Was ist los? (*German*)—"What is the matter?"

Was habt Ihr gesagt? (*German*)—"What have you said?"

Masern (*German*)—measles.

Flecken, so ahnlich wie diese? (*German*)—"Spots, that look like these?"

Ich war dort. Ich habe ihn gesehen. (*German*)—I was there. I saw it.

Rache (*German*)—revenge.[14]

Vielleicht sollen Sie gehen? (*German*)—"Perhaps you should leave?"

Mein junger Mann ist nicht gut (*German*)—Claire's attempt to say that Young Ian (*the younger man on the premises*) is ill; Lord John briskly corrects this to "Ihr Neffe ist krank" (*her nephew is sick*).

Haben Sie jemals Masern gehabt? (*German*)—"Have you ever had the measles?"

Seid gesegnet (*German*)—"Blessings on you." (*literally, "Be blessed."*)

Benedicite (*Latin*)—"Bless you."

Fünf! Es gibt fünf! (*German*)—"Five! I gave (*you*) five!"

Danke, mein Herr (*German*)—"Thank you, sir."

Wie geht es Euch?[15] (*German*)—"How are you?"

Mein Mädchen. Mein Kind. (*German*)—"My lass. My child."

Gnädige Frau (*German*)—Kind lady.

Mein Gott! Er hat Masern! (*German*)—"My God! He has measles!"

Gott sei dank (*German*)—"God be thanked."

Balach math (*Gaelic*) [Balak mah]—"Good boy."

coof (*Scots*)—silly person, idiot.

Slan leat, a charaid choir (*Gaelic*) [Slaan leaht, a karaid koir]—"Farewell, kind friend."

hough (*Scots*)—shin of beef.

a leannan (*Gaelic*) [A le-anan]—sweetheart (*vocative*), with the implication of "baby"—addressed to a daughter or other young person.

lang-nebbit (*Scots*)—literally, "long-nosed"; an interfering, "nosy" person.

mo ghille (*Gaelic*) [mo yille]—my boy, my lad.

---

[14]*Claire's remark—"I know; I've read Sherlock Holmes"—refers, of course, to A. Conan Doyle's "A Study in Scarlet," in which a man's corpse is discovered in a deserted house, with the word "Rache" written in blood on the wall above the body.*

[15]*NB: The German translator for **Drums of Autumn**, Barbara Schnell, took the trouble to use the older forms of some German terms (such as the various forms of "you"), which would have been appropriate to the eighteenth century; hence, some German expressions used in the book will not be exactly the same as modern German.*

teuchter [teukter]—a (*rather derogatory*) term used by Lowlanders for Highlanders. Roughly equivalent to "hick" or "hillbilly."

Cirein Croin[16] (*Gaelic*)—seamonster or sea serpent.

clarty (*Scots*)—dirty, filthy.

arisaid (*Gaelic*) [aarasaid]—a woman's shawl.

deamhan (*Gaelic*) [deoain]—demon or devil.

a bann-sielbheadair {*properly spelt as "a bhan shealbhadair"* (IMT) } (*Gaelic*) [a va-un he-alvadair]—mistress; more literally, owner of a bond of indenture.

each uisge (*Gaelic*) [oorusch]—a water horse.

uisge (*Gaelic*) [uishge]—water.

Oreilles en feuille de chou! (*French*)—literally, "Cauliflower ears!" Meant (*obviously*) as an insult.

bawbee (*Scots*)—a bit of money or a small present.

bree (*Scots*)—either a great disturbance, or a soup (*e.g., partan bree; a crab soup*).

gowk (*Scots*)—an awkward, silly person.

Deo gratias (*Latin*) [DAY-o GRAH-tsee-ahs]—"Thanks be to God."

Ciamar a tha tu, mo chridhe? (*Gaelic*) [Kia-mar a haa u, mo crie-e?]—"How are you, my heart (*darling*)?"

Tha mi gle mhath, athair (*Gaelic*) [Ha Mi glay vah, ahair]—"I am well, father."

An e 'n fhirinn a th'aqad m'annsachd? (*Gaelic*) [An e 'n iirin a h'agad. ansakd?]—"Do you tell me the truth, my love?"

m'annsachd (*Gaelic*)—my best beloved.

Mo gràdh ort, athair (*Gaelic*)—"I love you, Father"; literally, "My love on you, Father." [Mo graag orst, ahair.]

a bheanachd (*Gaelic*) [a ve-anakd]—my blessing (*vocative*).

nighean na galladh (*Gaelic*) [nee-an na Gallag]—literally, "daughter of a bitch"; a very nasty insult.

---

[16]We had quite a bit of difficulty in tracking down this reference. We finally concluded that "Cirein Croin" was originally a big whirlpool or similar such hazard, and that the name had been extended to apply to other seagoing dangers. In the course of the inquiries, though, I received the following message from Iain:

"Taking one word at a time, 'Cirean' is a word used to usually mean a rooster's comb. I've heard breaking waves talked of as 'Cirein' (plural). 'Croin' is an adjective meaning 'harmful.' Again we're left with the possibility of a sea-monster if it had fins or a mane that looked vaguely like a rooster's comb or a whirlpool—'harmful waves.' I would suggest you take your choice or explain both possibilities. I doubt if you're going to find any argument with either.

"Hamish, in his youth (for 'youth' see the movie My Cousin Vinny), before he went to Radio class, worked on a lobster boat out of Tobermory. On one occasion the boat's skipper was absent for some reason and Hamish was elected to deputize for him. The young 'acting captain' decided he'd make a name for himself. The ground round the whirlpool ('Coire Bhreachdain') looked like a really good lobster ground and nobody ever fished it. Our hero promptly went there on, of course, a spring tide and laid all the boat's lobster traps, linked in fleets of twenty, round the whirlpool.

"Next day he went to pick up his gear and pretty soon found out why nobody ever fished 'Coire Bhreachdain.' It took him several days to get his traps out of there, since he could stay there only at slack tide, and a couple of weeks to repair the damage. It didn't take him quite as long to figure out why no lobster live there. He did make a name for himself, however. He is still known, some forty years later, as the only man known to be foolish enough to set lobster traps in Coire Bhreachdain."

Cours! (*French*) [KOORs!]—"Run!"

Yona'kensyonk (*Kahnyen'kehaka*)—dried fish.

Kahnyen'kehaka (*Kahnyen'kehaka*)—the Mohawk, Keepers of the Eastern Gate.

Kakonhoaerhas[17] (*Kahnyen'kehaka*)—dogface.

Kahontsi'yatawi (*Kahnyen'kehaka*)—Black Robe; a Catholic priest, specifically a Jesuit.

Et vous? (*French*)—"And you?"

reposez-vous (*French*)—rest yourself, take it easy.

C'est bien là, c'est bien (*French*)—"That's good; it's all right; everything's all right."

Je suis une sorcière (*French*)—"I am a sorceress."

C'est médicine, là (*French*)—"This is medicine."

O'Seronni (*Kahnyen'kehaka*)—a white person, white people

Hodeenosaunee (*Kahnyen'kehaka*)—the Mohawks' term for the Iroquois peoples.

Do mi! Do mi! (*Gaelic*)—"To me! To me!" (*as in, rally round here and lend a hand!*) (*IMT says: "You probably mean 'To me! To me!' In which case it should be 'Thugam! Thugam!' [Hoogam! Hoogam!]"*)

Parlez-vous français? (*French*)—"Do you speak French?"[18]

Qui est votre Seigneur, votre Sauveur? (*French*)—"Who is your Lord, your Savior?"

Voulez-vous placer votre foi en Lui? (*French*)—"Do you have faith (*do you place your trust*) in Him?"

Oui, certainement. (*French*)—"Yes, certainly."

cuimhnich (*Gaelic*) [cuinik (first "I" longer)]—remember.

an fhearr mac Dubh (*Gaelic*)—translates more or less to "best of the offspring of the Black One"—general meaning, "(*first*) Son of the Black One."

NB: See also Appendix II: Gaelic Resources

———

[17]*I unfortunately didn't have access to a native speaker of Kahnyen'kehaka. I used a rather simple dictionary of Mohawk words and expressions, and therefore some compound terms are my best guess, rather than officially "correct" expressions.*
[18]*Ha.*

PART FIVE

RESEARCH

RESEARCHING
HISTORICAL FICTION:
HOT DOGS AND BEANS

ethods of doing research for a novel are as idiosyncratic as are the methods of writing one. That is, there are general principles that are helpful, and basic skills that apply, but exactly *how* one goes about the process depends on the style and preference of the individual writer.

There's no question that historical novels take lots of research. When I give talks on historical fiction, or the use of details in writing fiction, I usually take along a set of books to use as props: 1) a mystery by Agatha Christie; 2) a contemporary suspense thriller by Martin Cruz Smith, set in the Soviet Union; 3) a contemporary mystery by Elizabeth George, set in England; and 4) a historical novel by Gary Jennings, James Clavell, Colleen McCullough, or one of my own books.

I then display these books one by one and ask the audience whether they notice anything. Since the books are increasing in thickness by roughly one-half inch with each volume, they generally do—and laugh.

Okay. The first type of book—the Agatha Christie—is basically all plot. Setting is familiar, characters are stereotypi-cal, and both are sketchy. Very little descriptive detail is included in an Agatha Christie mystery, because you don't *need* to describe an English village, a vicar, or a train—everyone's seen them often enough (at least in the movies) that you can get away with a bare minimum, and concentrate on the plot.

The thriller set in the Soviet Union is thicker, not only because the plot is more complicated and the characters drawn in more detail, but because the setting is unusual—the average reader has no idea what the streets smell like in Moscow, or what a black-market trading ground looks like, or what a Zil is. Since the setting and social background (also unfamiliar) are necessary elements of the story, a good bit of detail is necessary, in order for the story both to live and to make intuitive sense to the reader.

Elizabeth George books are about the same size as the Russian mysteries; not so much because of an unfamiliar setting—English country and cityscapes are not really offbeat—but because these books are essentially a combination of plot and relationships. There has to be a great deal of detail in the description of character and in the interactions between them, because the relationships among the characters and the development of their personal lives are as important as the overt "mystery" plot.

And then you hit historical novels; subgenre BF ("Big Fat"). These books tend to be huge, not only because they normally cover a substantial span of time and event (i.e., they have a lot of plot and a large number of characters), but because virtually everything in them will be unfamiliar to the average reader, and has to be "drawn"—setting, physical description of city, countryside, homes, details of daily life, social customs, and—most important—the characters. Historical characters are *not* the same as contemporary characters; they will have unusual (and sometimes incomprehensible, unless the author has been skillful) attitudes and relationships, and these too must be detailed carefully, so the reader will understand what's going on.

Aside from the necessity of crafting a convincing historical milieu for the sake of the novel itself, many readers of historical novels are fascinated by historical trivia, and read such books in good part for the tidbits of information and insights they may gain into another time.

So it's legitimate—and desirable—to include detail for the purpose of drawing an unfamiliar milieu, and for the entertainment of the reader. How one includes masses of detail without bogging the reader down in wads of stuff that sound like you cribbed it from the *Encyclopaedia Britannica* is a good question of technique, but the first problem is simply to *find* the stuff.

I mentioned Basic Skills and General Principles in doing research. Basic Skills include: one, knowing how to use a library, and two, how to skim a book for information. General Principles include: one, getting an overview, two, locating specifics, and three, organizing stuff.

BASIC SKILLS

How to Use a Library

Actually, if you don't already have a good notion how to use a library, I strongly recommend that you don't write historical novels. However, beyond a simple familiarity with the card catalog and the nuances of the Library of Congress system, there are a couple of possibly useful things to know.

For really detailed historical research, you will need a large university or college library. Public libraries simply don't stock the sorts of references needed for good research on most periods—for the excellent reasons that most such references are a) fairly old, and b) not what most people want to read for recreation. Public libraries stock books for reading; university libraries stock books for looking up esoteric information.

When I began doing research for my first novel, I was a university professor, and fortunately had a large library available; not everyone is so lucky. Still, if you do live within driving distance of a college or university, go to the library and ask about getting a community borrower's card. Most such libraries have these; for a small annual fee, you can have at least limited borrowing privileges (and if you're a writer, the fee is tax-deductible as a business expense).

If you *don't* live near a good library, it will be a lot harder to do effective research, but luckily these days no one is completely out of touch. Many large collections are accessible online, at least in terms of finding what's available. Getting your hands on a book is another matter, but books can be ordered, or arrangements can be made to borrow material, even at a distance.

Virtually all large libraries have a system called interlibrary loan. This means that if you require, say, a book on Irish costume in the sixteenth century, and have discovered that your local university library doesn't have anything of this nature—but the Boston College library does—you can file a request with your local library for the book, and your library will borrow it from Boston College for you.

This is a wonderful assistance to a researcher; the only real drawback to interlibrary loan is that it's often rather slow, and may take weeks or even months to retrieve a particular volume and get it to your library.

Card Catalog

Most collections these days have been catalogued electronically. This is fast, efficient, and generally a Good Thing. At the same time, the transfer of information from real cards to an electronic version is not always complete; in the interests of efficiency, older volumes that don't circulate

much may not be recorded in the new catalog, or may be put aside for later addition.

The hard copy version of the card catalog also sometimes contains information that isn't included in the new electronic version—handwritten notations by librarians as to book location, related titles, and so on. There isn't much you can do about this, but if your library still has the hard copy card catalog, it's worth consulting that, in addition to the electronic version. Also ask the reference librarian whether your library's collection *has* been completely converted to electronic form, in case some older parts of the collection have not.

The idiosyncrasy of method that I mentioned earlier begins with the first steps of a search—what you type into an electronic card catalog (or a Web search engine). Even here, though, there are General Principles: one, cast your net widely at first, and two, look for call-number patterns.

That is, if you are interested in a specific time-period and a particular place, you would naturally type something like SCOTLAND HIGHLANDS EIGHTEENTH CENTURY as your search parameters. This will give you those titles most closely approximating what you think you're looking for.

However, it's also worthwhile doing another search, simply on SCOTLAND, since you may well find a number of useful books—on geography, history, customs, language, etc.—that *don't* have the keywords HIGHLANDS or EIGHTEENTH CENTURY associated with them.

Casting a wide net, of course, will give you a huge list of titles (this being the point of doing the limited search first; you can be starting with the most relevant

Online Research

OWING TO ONE THING *and another, I seem to have developed an odd reputation as a writer whose career is inextricably intertwined with the Internet. Consequently, many people assume that I must naturally be doing all of my research online, through Web-surfing.*

Frankly, while the Internet is a valuable tool for locating people and resources, I can't imagine doing serious historical research using the Web as a primary source. The depth of information and breadth of detail that one needs just doesn't exist on most Web pages, and the process of searching is much more tedious and time-consuming than is browsing in a good library—with less chance of success.

This is not to say that one can't find very interesting bits and pieces on the Web—and services such as amazon.com and ukbooks.com are invaluable for locating and delivering books conveniently. Likewise, Web-searching can lead you through the holdings of large university libraries and help you find where to go—but Web-surfing is only an adjunct to sound library research, not a replacement for it.

However, one mustn't overlook other aspects of online research; beyond the existence of Web sites, one can locate remarkably helpful people with expertise in various fields, through the large subscription services (like AOL and CompuServe) and various newsgroups.

---

books while looking farther afield). Look through the titles, marking down those that seem as though they might be useful or interesting. Then look at these books, to see whether there are patterns of shared call numbers. That is, do most of the books you've picked out have call numbers beginning "QC 357" or "DA 785"?

If so, stop writing down specific titles (which is a big pain), and simply write down the common call-number prefix. Go to the stack(s) where that call number is located, and browse in person. You will invariably find a number of books that are related in topic to what you were searching for, but which didn't appear in the card catalog search because they weren't entered with the specific key words under which you were searching. (As a small example: *Drums of Autumn* would not come up under a search for NORTH CAROLINA, in spite of the fact that the book is set there, because the person who catalogued it for the Library of Congress evidently didn't read more than the first chapter. Since the first chapter is set in Charleston, the book is catalogued under SOUTH CAROLINA, even though the book itself has nothing to do with that state.)

Another benefit to shelf-browsing is that it enables you to look directly at the book, rather than judging on the basis of title alone whether this is something you need or not. If you're not sure, check the table of contents and the index; that should tell you within seconds whether this book has any information that might be of use to you.

How to Read a Book for Information

Writers occasionally come up to me at conferences and say things like, "Oh, I'd love to do a historical novel. But I just can't bear the thought of all that reeeeeeseeeeearch." ("Research" is always pronounced in a dismal whining tone, when used in this context.)

I suspect that such persons are under the delusion that "reeeeeseeeearch" involves reading every single word of hundreds of terribly boring books, while taking copious notes on eye-glazing topics from "annealing processes used in the early Bronze Age" to "zoofauna of the digestive tract of the Western hoopoe," meanwhile juggling billions of index cards with one hand tied behind one's back.

Well, look. If you can see that a given book is boring, why the heck would you waste hours reading it? There's a major difference between *reading* a book, and gleaning necessary information from it. There's also a major difference between doing research for a historical novel, and doing research for a Ph.D. thesis (ask the woman who's done both).

Say you scan the card catalog and turn up a book that sounds as though it might be useful to you. When you get your hands on the book, look at it. A glance at the first page is usually enough to tell you whether you've got a book written for the edification of the general public, or somebody's dissertation.

What you do then is: one, check the table of contents (if it has one); two, check the index (if it has one); and three, flip hither and yon and browse a few pages. This will tell you what level of detail this book contains, and the scope of the subject matter covered. If it looks hideously boring, close the book and pick up another one. If you think a given library book might contain useful information, take it. Taking it out of the library does not oblige you to read it from cover to cover.

What you are doing here is simply discovering what *kind* of information each book contains. A lot of books may be superficially related to your topic, but not really useful—take them back to the library. Some will be perfect for your purpose—put these aside to be carefully read. Some will have useful information, but not look interesting enough to read. Put these aside to look things up in.

If you know that you will be dealing with a particular battle or political setting, then it makes sense to read detailed accounts of that particular event or setting. But if you need to know what kind of underwear women wore? Nah. You get a good book on costume, but you don't necessary *read* the whole thing, cover to cover. You look up "underwear" in the index, find out what you need to know—and put the book back on the shelf until you need

to know what sort of boots a gentleman would wear for riding.

The odd thing about doing any kind of library research—whether for scientific or literary purposes—is that once you begin searching, things start finding *you*. One thing leads to another; a bibliographic citation in a not-very-relevant paper will lead you to exactly the source you need; browsing in a general section of the library causes books to leap off the shelf at you.

(On one such browsing expedition, I happened to take a very heavy book from the shelf. I sat down on the floor to thumb through it, and when I glanced up from the table of contents—which had nothing very entertaining—what should I see, directly in front of my nose, but a book titled *Muster Roll of Charles Edward Stuart's Army.* That's just what it was, too; a list of all the men known to have fought with the Highland Army in the Rising of 1745. I found this book well after I had written *Voyager,* but out of curiosity, pulled it out and looked up the Master of Lovat's regiment, which—like all the others—listed the officers first. It made the hair rise up on the back of my neck to see LIEUTENANT COLONEL: JAMES FRASER listed—though it rose still more when I turned the page and found Duncan McDonald and Giles McMartin on the next page (see beginning of *Voyager,* and the names of the men who were executed by the English after Culloden).

General Principles of Doing Research

Once you've dug yourself into the library and found a few promising sections of the stacks to mine, how do you proceed? In any way that makes sense to you, really—but in general, you might consider . . .

Overview

First, what do you need to know, in order to start writing? (You don't have to figure this all out ahead of time—you may not *know* what you need to know, until you've been working for a while.) Some writers choose a particular period because they are drawn to it and already know quite a lot about it. Plainly their priorities will be different from those of someone who doesn't know one damn thing about the time or place—like me. I began with total ignorance both of Scotland and the eighteenth century. All I knew was that at some point, men wore kilts—which was at the time a sufficient reason for choosing that period.

One danger of the "I must know everything before I begin" attitude is that it's impossible to know *everything*—and the feeling that one has to know everything before writing is a nifty way of avoiding writing altogether.

As I mentioned above, a disinclination to do the often arduous, and always time-consuming work of research is a major drawback to writing historical novels. If you don't have at least a minor passion for research, you will find the work very difficult.

However, many historical novelists have the opposite problem. They enjoy the research so much that they never get around to actually writing the book. One question that I hear a lot at writers conferences is "How do you know when you've done *enough* research, and are ready to write?"

Well . . . you don't. Or rather, *I* don't. There's always more that could be found out, after all.

Idiosyncrasy and personal preference enter the picture here; some writers feel that they must know almost everything about a time period before they begin writing; others, not so much. Personally, I began doing the writing and the research concurrently, and finding that satisfactory, have kept on doing it that way.

One good, quick way of getting an overview of a time period or geographical location is to check the kids' section of the library. Kids' books are a) usually short, b) always readable, c) present the most salient facts in a condensed space, and d) tend to include the "fun" (i.e., interesting) details of a subject—which are, not incidentally, the sort of details that most appeal to novelists.

Beyond the children's section, look for popular accounts.[1] These overview books are ones that you probably do want to read all the way through (though skimming is perfectly all right; as long as you know what sort of information is in this book, you can always go back later and look up things in more detail). So it's worth choosing texts that are reasonably entertaining.

Take note of more particular or esoteric texts, but as a general principle, put these

aside for later reference, when you have a better idea as to what you really need.

Locating Specifics

Sometimes you will know that you require a great deal of specific information on one or more particular areas of interest. For example, once having cast Claire Randall as a healer, I knew I was going to require quite a lot of information on herbs and botanical medicine—because that was the only effective medical therapy available in the eighteenth century.

Consequently, I began collecting "herbals"—guides to herbs and their uses. I now have some thirty-odd herbals, ranging from Chinese herbal medicine to Native American herbology and beyond (see "Don't Try This at Home"). Have I *read* all these books? Not on your tintype. I have, however, looked at them enough to know when to consult *The Peterson Field Guide to Medicinal Plants* (published in the 1980s) and when to look at *Culpeper's Complete Herbal* (published in the seventeenth century).

That's why such books are called "reference" books; they aren't intended to be read word for word; they're intended to supply specific information easily and quickly.

Luckily, reference books exist on a huge

---

[1] *If you really **want** to know about the economic ramifications of the French-Austrian treaty of 1752, fine, but it's much more entertaining to find out that French ladies at Court did not as a rule retire to the nearest rest room when impelled by urinary urges; instead they simply spread their legs slightly and peed on the floor under cover of their ornate gowns—underwear having yet to become customary. I mean, there's background, and then there's **background**.*

number of topics. Look in the bibliographies of your "overview" books for more specialized references. Browse the relevant sections of libraries and bookstores; always thumb through the stacks on remainder tables.

Another good source of regional or historical references—many of them quite specialized, and not easily available elsewhere—are the bookshops attached to museums and national parks. Particularly in the United States, National Park Service bookshops often stock immensely helpful references on the plant and animal life of the region, plus historical accounts published by local researchers (which may not be available through regular book outlets).

If you're not in a position to visit such places personally, try telephoning; the staffers are often very helpful, and some shops may even have lists or catalogs of available materials which they can send you.

Finally, a useful source of esoteric historical information is the Dover catalog. Dover is a publishing company specializing in reprints of material in the public domain, and they often have inexpensive facsimile reprints of very old material (one of the references on my shelf at the moment is a facsimile reprint of *Baron von Steuben's Revolutionary War Drill Manual*, 1794 edition—which I found in the bookshop at the Saratoga Battlefield National Park).

Sometimes you find Dover reprints in regular bookstores—particularly the coloring books, which are really excellent (and entertaining) reference material. I have a coloring book on "Colonial Trades," for example, that illustrates all the common ob-

jects to be found in the shops of a cobbler, wainwright, tinsmith, silversmith, etc., and another on "Uniforms of the Revolution." But the more obscure materials are usually available only through specialty shops or by catalog order.[2]

Organizing Stuff

Once you are well embarked on your research, the problem arises of organizing and keeping track of it all. Now, here I am afraid you are talking to the wrong person. People often ask me how I organize all the voluminous research required for one of these monstrous books—to which the answer is, "Well, see those three bookcases over there? Most of the stuff I use is in them."[3]

The horrid truth is that I don't organize things, beyond putting all the herbals on one shelf and all the books about magic on another. I don't normally write down anything except the actual text of the novel I'm working on.

I mentioned earlier that there are differences between doing scientific research and novelistic research, and organization of material is one of them—at least for me. When I did scientific research, I kept index card files, and (later) databases of references, because when you write scientific papers, you have to be prepared to back up every single factual assertion with either a) a citation of someone else's work or b) your own data.

---

[2]*The address for Dover Publications, Inc., is 31 East 2 Street, Mineola, NY 11501.*
[3]*And if it's not, it's in one of the piles on the floor. Unless it's downstairs in the kitchen, that is. Or under the front seat of the car. Or maybe . . .*

When you write historical novels, you don't. In fact . . . you can sometimes *make things up*! Which is one of the major inducements for writing fiction, if you ask me.

However. When you write scientific papers, you are normally dealing with a *very* limited and specific set of circumstances: You are interested, say, in the salinity preferences of the Chinese mudskipper, *Periophthalmus chinensis* (Gordon, Gabaldon and Yip, 1987). You will therefore start with a dual search: for general information on Chinese mudskippers and for references on salinity preference experiments.

You will attempt to find *every single reference* locatable in both categories, plus all relevant references to which these lead— and then to read them all carefully. This is necessary, if tedious; scientific research depends on accuracy of observation and replicability of results—and every new bit of knowledge rests upon a firm foundation of what is already known (we disregard for the moment the fact that such foundations shift now and then).

Since someone coming after you may wish to build on your work, you have to leave clearly marked trails and well-built walls; it's a professional obligation. Consequently, you must include citations of all the work that you yourself used as background for your hypothesis and experimental design, and you must make this as complete and well integrated as you can.

You don't do this with a novel. A novel stands alone; no one (other than possibly yourself, if you end up writing a series of books) is coming along after you, depending on your work to support later hypotheses.

ONE OF THE *Ten Favorite Questions Interviewers Ask is:* *"How did you make the transition from being a scientist to being a novelist?"*

"Wrote a book," I reply tersely. *

If it's a formal interview, though, I usually feel obliged to explain that the implied notion that science and art are diametrically opposing poles of human endeavor is mistaken. Many people think that science is logical, rigid, and cold, while art is intuitive, flexible, and touchy-feely. In fact, both processes are simply two faces of the same coin. Intuition feeds logic and vice versa. Science without imagination is useless; art without structure is pointless.

Both science and art ultimately rest on the same foundation: the ability to draw patterns out of chaos. It's just that when you do science, you observe the chaos; when you do art, you get to define it.

---

*That's really all there is to it. They don't make you take a Changing-Careers Exam, you know, or apply for a Novelist's License. Write a book and poof! you're a novelist, just like that. Much easier than becoming a doctor or a firefighter.

Likewise, the purposes of a novel are not those of scientific research, though there *are* similar goals. In both cases, you're constructing a small picture of reality; you are attempting to explain the world and how it works. However, in the case of scientific research, you're doing your explanation via facts, and in the case of a novel, you're doing it with lies—i.e., you're telling a story.

RESEARCH ASSISTANTS— OR NOT

Given the necessity for so much background material, factual trivia, etc., many writers of historical fiction use research assistants—and in fact, I'm often asked how *many* research assistants I use! Actually, I don't use assistants at all. It's not that I don't think they'd be helpful; it's just that I couldn't possibly tell them what to look for.

It's rather like getting groceries for dinner. You *can* send someone to the store with a list—say, hot dogs and beans—and sure enough, they'll come back with hot dogs and beans, and you'll have a fine dinner. Or at least you'll eat.

On the other hand . . . when I go to the grocery store myself, I may have it in mind to buy hot dogs and beans, but as I pass the meat case, I see that there are nice-looking lamb chops in today. Hmm, I think; lamb curry is awfully good, and I already have basmati rice and mango chutney at home. So I add the lamb chops to my basket, and then get a white onion, some garlic, and a six-pack of V-8 to make the curry. And on the way to the vegetable department, I pass the deli, where there is a special on fresh shrimp. Ooh, a shrimp salad to precede

the curry! Get a nice green-leaf lettuce, some spring onions and a cucumber. Oh, and dressing. And then, of course, Mountain Dew, because nothing tastes better with hot curry than cold Mountain Dew. . . .

So I spend a good deal more time (and money) by going to the store myself—but I get a much tastier and more original menu as a result. Novelists who use research assistants tend to get hot dogs and beans.

Translating this into writing—naturally there will be certain things that I find I want or need to know, as necessary ingredients to the story. However, more often than not, when I go looking for these tidbits of information, I come across something much more interesting; some fact whose existence I never dreamed of, and therefore couldn't have sent someone to find.

As a brief example, take Monsieur Forez. I was reading a book on the practice of medicine in France during the second half of the eighteenth century, with the notion that I might pick up tips for Claire to use in her work at L'Hôpital des Anges. I did, in fact, pick up any amount of useful background: small technical trivia, like the art of urinoscopy, but also general information on practitioners of the period.

Licensed physicians were rare, expensive, and not always trusted by the general populace (for good reason; a license didn't always imply either education or effectiveness). "Wisewomen" (*les maîtresses sage-femme*) were not only popular as midwives, but were respected general practitioners, and many people with no medical education also dabbled in the healing arts, while plying a commercial trade for their principal living (e.g., Monsieur Parnelle, the jeweler with a sideline in trusses).

Among the "healers" who were not licensed physicians were—weirdly enough—the public hangmen. Because of the requirements of their trade, hangmen were not only executioners, but torturers, being often required to assist in official investigations by extracting testimony from unwilling witnesses. They were also often skilled bonesetters; you can't disjoint a body easily without knowing quite a bit about how it's put together in the first place.

Likewise, since it was often necessary to keep a victim alive for long periods, the hangmen had considerable knowledge both of gross anatomy and of physiological processes. A Monsieur Forez was cited as one of the best-known of these medically competent executioners, with the casual note that he did a good business in such lucrative sidelines as the sale of victims' bodies (parts of which were used either as dissection room specimens, or as ingredients in magical charms), and the production of "hanged-men's grease": the purified fat rendered from the boiled bodies of executed criminals.

Now, I certainly didn't go looking for a hangman, but having met Monsieur Forez, I was thoroughly charmed. I was also determined to get the hanged-men's grease into the story in *some* fashion. So I got what I'd been looking for—a general picture of French medical practice, plus interesting medical details—and something totally unexpected, besides.

Since I did now have this entertaining hangman, I was obliged to construct a place for him in the story. I could just have used him as part of the background personnel at the Hôpital, and in fact I did this

to begin with. I didn't want to waste the hanged-men's grease in an offhanded way, though; I needed an occasion for its use—someone should be injured or suffer from rheumatism. I had already intended to use the stables at Argentan in some way (another accidental detail; my father-in-law, Max Watkins, a cowboy with a passion for horses, had visited Argentan and told me all about the Percherons and their history), so the notion of some accident involving horses arose—and thence the scene with Fergus and the stable-lads, in which Jamie rescues Fergus, straining a muscle in the process.

Having written the scene in which Claire applies the ointment to Jamie, and in which he makes a nervous joke about having come too close to being one of the ingredients, I began to think (well, actually, I think pretty much all the time when I'm writing, but it helps to have some specific direction).

Hangmen, being hanged, a traitor's death—which is precisely what Jamie was risking by his actions. Enter Monsieur Forez again, for the purpose of pointing out—to Jamie, Claire, and to the reader—that while politics might be played as a game, it was nonetheless one with possibly fatal consequences. (As to Monsieur Forez's scholarly lecture on the details of evisceration—well, I had one postdoctoral appointment in which my main job was butchering seabirds. People always ask me whether my previous education and experience as a scientist is useful to me in writing these books. Not often, but it comes in handy every now and then.)

In terms of the overall book, I thought that Monsieur Forez captured nicely the balance between the farcical aspects of the Rising (which were many), and the deadly serious outcome. He's a minor note in the book, but an important one. And yet, I couldn't have gone looking for him—I didn't know he existed.

The reason I don't take notes on the research I do is that as the story takes shape in my mind, bits and pieces of research material are incorporated into it. Sometimes a piece of research material will trigger a specific scene, or even a subplot; sometimes a particular scene will demand a specific piece of information, which I then go and find. In either case, though, the research information becomes part of the story; and from that point on, it's in my head; I can't forget it. On the other hand, I instantly forget anything that's written down: phone messages, grocery lists, errands . . .

As for the things that I need to know . . . well, some of these simply have to be looked up before a given scene can be written. Most small bits of incidental information, though, aren't really necessary to the shape of a scene or its events. In these cases, when I come to a spot where I need—for instance—to list the herbs that Claire is using for a specific purpose, or the name of a street in Edinburgh, or the height of a mountain—I just put a pair of empty square brackets—"[ ]"—in the text where that information should go. That way, I can continue writing without breaking my stride, and go look up the necessary bits of information later on.

"I took down my mortar and rubbed a handful of [ ] into it. Adding [ ] and [ ], I pounded and ground while thinking what to do next."

The next-to-last thing I do to a book before printing it off to send to the editor is to go through and look up the necessary information to fill in any of the [ ]'s still remaining. (The last thing I do is to break the text into chapters and title them.)

"I've Done My Research, and Now You're Going to Pay"

Don't let the storytelling aspect of the business escape you, by the way. Historical research is fascinating, and many writers fall under its spell; the more you know, the more you want to find out, the more you research, the easier the search becomes—and before you know it, you're in the position of a writer with whom I once shared a panel at the World Fantasy Convention.

The panel was on "Research," and this particular writer was explaining a difficulty she had encountered in her most recent novel. The novel was set in an alternate universe, but involved a caravan, based on those that once traversed the great Silk Road through China. She wished at one point to describe the bells on a camel harness, and had found *exactly* the reference necessary to do this: an exhaustive account of the shapes of camel bells used in caravans of exactly the right kind, taken from precisely the right time period. However . . . the article was unfortunately written in Chinese.

The author held the audience rapt as

DIANA'S CURRY
(with lamb, beef, chicken, or tofu)
   white onion
   garlic
   raisins (optional)
   olive oil
   meat or tofu (about 6 oz. [or one
     medium chicken breast] per person)
   curry powder
   cayenne pepper (optional)
   V-8 juice cocktail

Mince a good handful of white onion and four or five buds of garlic. If you like raisins, add a handful or two. Saute the minced onions and minced garlic and the (whole) raisins in olive oil until the onions are transparent (the raisins will puff up). Add the Main Ingredient (cubed meat or tofu), and brown (or cook through, for shrimp or tofu), stirring frequently. Add curry powder and cayenne to taste, and stir; I prefer enough curry powder to liberally coat the meat, and four or five shakes of cayenne, but the proportions depend on personal taste and on the type of curry powder you use; some brands are much hotter than others.

Add one medium can (12 oz) of V-8 juice per two people. Simmer over low heat. Can be eaten in fifteen minutes, but better if simmered for an hour or two. Even better if simmered for a couple of hours, then allowed to cool and stand overnight, reheated next day. Add additional V-8 if sauce becomes too thick while cooking.

Serve over rice (basmati or jasmine rice is good, as is short-grain white rice). Garnish with chopped cashews, almonds, or coconut; serve with mango chutney and/or fresh pineapple.

---

she described in some detail her struggles to get this article translated, so that she could accurately describe the camel bells. Meanwhile, I had picked up one of the display books sitting in front of her and looked at the spine. FANTASY, it said.

Now, *I* would simply have decided for myself what the bloody camel bells should look like, and got on with writing the story, but . . . methods differ.

Still, this sort of attitude toward historical research all too often leads to a phenomenon which my friend Margaret Ball (who herself writes excellent fantasy novels) describes as: "I've done my research, and now you're going to pay." That is, novels that include mind-numbing masses of detail, because the author can't bear to "waste" any of the effort spent in research.

Don't forget that the purpose of research is to support the story; not the other way around.

BOTANICAL MEDICINE: DON'T TRY THIS AT HOME

O n occasion, the boilerplate clauses in book contracts I've received have included something like the following: (page 2, clause 3) "The author guarantees . . . that any recipes, formulae, or instructions in [the book] will not injure the user."

To which I was obliged to reply (via my agent): "Given that these books are set in the eighteenth century, and make frequent and explicit reference to medical practices of the period, I couldn't reasonably agree to this particular provision. Anyone seeking to abort themselves by means of taking blue cohosh, for instance, would almost certainly be injured. While I think the circumstance unlikely—still less, that someone would treat headache by drinking powdered amethysts, cauterize a wound with boiling water, or treat concussion by trephining the skull—I do think we must delete this phrase."

The British publisher who printed *Cross Stitch* did in fact include an author's note in the book, urging readers *not* to dose themselves with recipes given in the book and warning them about the dangers of practicing uninstructed herbal medicine. This was done at my suggestion, but neither they nor the American publishers have thought it necessary to do this for subsequent books. For what it's worth, I haven't yet heard of any readers succumbing to the effects of any recipe in the books (mind, rubbing the penis with a diamond to ensure potency is likely harmless, but still . . .).

The author's note in *Cross Stitch* reads:

> *I would also like to note that while the botanical preparations noted in the story were historically used for the medicinal purposes indicated, this fact shouldn't be taken as an indication that such preparations are necessarily either effective for such purposes, or harmless. Many herbal preparations are toxic if used improperly or in excess dosage, and should be administered only by an experienced practitioner.*

I suggested to the American publisher that we include a similar note in *Outlander*, just as a precaution. The general reaction was a) "We're trying to sell this as a commercial novel, quit with the footnotes already," and b) "Nobody would be stupid enough to use eighteenth-century medical treatments, anyway."

Well . . . I really *hope* no one would use antiquated medical treatments described in a time-travel novel (I mean, it does say

FICTION on the spine, after all. . . .), but what with the increasing interest in herbal therapies and alternative medicine in general, I do get frequent questions regarding my sources, or requests for recommendations. People want to know how I know all this stuff—am I an herbal practitioner myself? Am I a professional botanist?

Definitely not.

I do grow herbs in my garden, though. I cook with them (I have a very nice recipe for chicken and mushrooms in orange juice with fresh marjoram, which I will include at the end of this section, in case you're interested), and I collect exotic mints (did you know there are varieties of mint that smell like pineapple, bergamot, orange, apple, grapefruit, and chocolate?).

I also grow other herbs for aroma: rue (I'm told you can eat this in sandwiches, like watercress, but since I don't really like watercress, I haven't tried it), lavender, and lemon balm—or as insect repellants: yarrow, pennyroyal, and marigold (pennyroyal is strong enough to repel just about anything, believe me).

Marigolds are also recommended as gopher repellants, under the theory that gophers won't eat them. However, I can state categorically that gophers will *too* eat

Ipeca cuana

marigolds. Of course, I seemed to have unusually stalwart gophers; they even ate the okra plants (no, I don't eat okra. My father-in-law eats okra). Granted, they ate the okra *last,* but they did eat it.

Beyond the culinary and the aromatic, I also grow things now and then for the sake of novelty or curiosity. (I did try growing foxglove once, but it doesn't do at all well in the desert where I live. The birdhouse gourd vine did much better.) And—as the result of having once taught a class called "The Natural History of Arizona," I do have a reasonable idea of which desert plants one should definitely not think of squeezing for water, if marooned in an arid wasteland. (Never, ever ingest a desert plant that doesn't have thorns. Desert plants are a stationary source of water in a dry habitat, and thus in constant danger from bugs, animals, etc. They all protect themselves in one way or another— thorns, spines, thick, waxy skins. If you see a plant that doesn't seem to be using any of these overt forms of defense, the betting is good that it's using something else—poisonous alkaloids.)

But no, I'm not by any means a professional botanist or herbalist. In fact, the sum total of my academic credentials is the six class-hours of botany required to get a B.S. degree in zoology at Northern Arizona University. I can tell a monocot from a dicot, diagram the cross-section of a composite flower, and tell the difference between the basidiomycetes and the ascomycetes (those are different kinds of fungi, in case you were wondering), but what with one thing and another, I've never found any really graceful way to work these bits of information into a fictional scene.

Of Gophers and Gardens

THE ONLY MEANS *I found of peaceful coexistence with the gophers was bribery. If I made a peanut-butter-and-molasses sandwich (on whole-wheat bread; God forbid the gophers should suffer from a lack of dietary fiber) every night, and went and hurled this into the middle of the garden, my plants remained largely untouched. If I forgot the nightly sandwich . . . Whoops! There goes another pelargonium.*

Fortunately, my husband (dear man) built me a gopherproof garden enclosure as a birthday present a few years ago, so the gophers have been reduced to gnawing on the plastic fittings of the irrigation system for their dietary fiber. Now all I have to worry about is dogs with a lust for ripe tomatoes, ants with a passion for my ruby-pearl grapes, and snakes looking for a shady spot to sleep.

However, the furthest I would go in using herbs for medical treatment is to rub crushed lavender on my daughter's temples for a headache, or to pass out my Altoids peppermint tablets to fellow travelers suffering from motion sickness (oil of peppermint relaxes the smooth muscle of the stomach and intestine, relieving indigestion and flatulence. One person to whom I told this said, "I could have lived without knowing that"). It might not help, but it isn't going to hurt anybody.

What I do for the botanical details in my books is what I do for the historical ones—I do research. When I first began to write about Claire Beauchamp Randall Fraser, I thought quite a bit about what skills a time-traveler should ideally have, and concluded that basic medical knowledge might be one of the better things to be well-versed in. This was also a good choice, in purely fictional terms, because it gave her an excellent excuse for being where all the interesting things (like fights, hunts, wars, and epidemics) were going on.

It didn't take much thought or research to realize that in the eighteenth century, prior to the advent of antibiotics and anesthesia, the *only* effective methods of medical treatment were likely to be herbal.

Now, as I say, I have no particular botanical background myself. So, I began looking for information on the use of herbs, whether for domestic purposes like cooking and bug repelling, or for more esoteric medical usage. Luckily, such information was not at all difficult to come by—and in fact, herbal guides and collections have become much more popular in the ten years or so since I began writing *Outlander;* any general bookstore is likely to have several available.

I should point out that a good many of the herbal treatments described in these books are also historical; that is, some uses of herbs have been around for hundreds (and in some cases, likely thousands) of years. The ones that have been around for a long time are *probably* the ones that

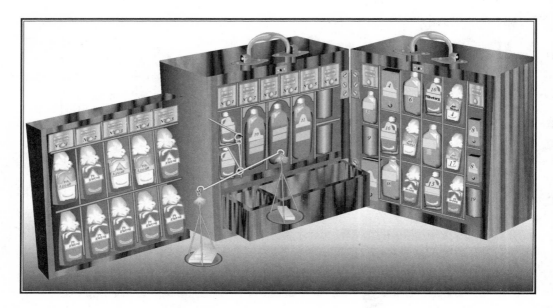

worked, but there's no telling for sure. When I describe herbal treatments in the books, I am always using herbs and preparation techniques that were actually known to have been available at that time, in that place, and for the purpose for which they're described. This doesn't mean they were necessarily effective—but they may have been.

The herbal guides and sources that I have on my shelf currently are all listed in the "Bibliography" section of this book, in a section to themselves, for the convenience of readers with a particular interest in botanical medicine. (I acquired these books over a period of several years, so I didn't necessarily have all of them available to me during the writing of my novels.)

One of the first herbals I acquired was *The New Age Herbal,* which was very helpful indeed, as it included not only general descriptions of various popular herbs and their current uses, but also photographs of the plants, roots, seeds, flowers, etc.

Fairly soon thereafter, I found a copy (a reprint, I hasten to add) of Nicholas Culpeper's *Complete Herbal,* originally published in 1647. This book is also profusely illustrated (with small color drawings), but its chief value to a historical novelist is that it notes the uses to which herbs were put *during historical times.*

Besides providing picturesque details of ailments and treatments, it gives one some notion of the prevailing theories of medicine, and the light in which people saw illness and bodily function. Culpeper's is one of a particular class of book that is particularly useful for historical fiction background, regardless of whether the herbs in question are actually effective. Books of folklore, folk medicine (*American Folk Medicine*), and ethnic medicine (*Indian Herbology of North America*) fall into this category; they may be only picturesque for someone interested in practical applications, but they're invaluable to a writer with an interest in bygone ways.

One other small consideration that affects writers of historical fiction is that plants found in a particular geographical location today might not always have grown there. Of course, one can always manage to acquire anything that's *really* necessary for the plot, via a handy merchant, an Oriental traveler, or a peripatetic naturalist—but it's a good idea to determine whether that's really necessary.

The eighteenth century was a time of considerable global exploration and growth in international commerce; consequently, a good many European plants were imported to the Americas—and vice versa—during this time. Still, most such exotic imports would have been limited to apothecary shops in large cities, or to the ornamental gardens kept by many wealthy (and not-so-wealthy) people with an interest in botany. In other words, a character could *not* reasonably walk into the wildwoods of North Carolina in the mid–eighteenth century and pick horse chestnuts, though they *might* reasonably do so in a coastal town, where this particular English tree had been planted by a homesick emigrant.

COMFREY

Formerly country people cultivated Comfrey in their gardens for its virtue in wound healing, and the many local names of the plant testify to its long reputation as a vulnerary herb—in the Middle Ages it was a famous remedy for broken bones.

Grieve (*A Modern Herbal*)

One drawback to herbal guides is that while some do note that such-and-such a plant is an import from say, Asia or Europe, many don't—and they rarely tell you *when* a plant was imported. There are three things that can help with the problem of geographical plausibility: a) read widely—after a time, you become familiar with where and when the more common plants came into use; b) compare guides with a geographical basis (*The Hamlyn Guide to Edible and Medicinal Plants of Britain and Northern Europe* vs. *A Handbook of Native American Herbs* vs. *Peterson Field Guide to Medicinal Plants*); and c) when in doubt, ask an expert.

I was extremely fortunate, myself, in having as a friend Robert Lee Riffle, an experienced botanist with a good reference library. An excellent literary critic as well as a botanist (and an accomplished author himself—*The Tropical Look: An Encyclopedia of Dramatic Landscape Plants*, Bob was invaluable in helping me find out when and where things grow, and what they look like while doing so. It's a great comfort to a novelist to have a reliable source to whom one can say, "I need a big green bush that grows in the Caribbean and was there during the eighteenth century. It needs to be big enough to hide behind, and it would be nice if you know what it smells like in the rain."

Naturally, not everyone is lucky enough to have a personal botanist on call. However, there are electronic sources of such information: the Garden Forum on CompuServe (also the California and Florida Forums), and similar special-interest areas on America Online. Staffed and patronized by very knowledgeable and helpful people, online reference is one of the best and easiest ways to locate information on specific plants or on the botany of a particular region.

Microbotanicals: Penicillin and Other Antibiotics

I should mention a particular application of botanical medicine—penicillin. The advent of antibiotics was the third great revolution in modern medicine—anesthesia being the first, a general acceptance of the Germ Theory (with the consequent practice of asepsis) being the second. The discovery of penicillin (and other antibiotics) was in fact an outgrowth of research into disease-causing organisms—bacterial pathogens.

I don't imagine there are many people who don't know the basic story: Sir Alexander Fleming discovered penicillin by accident, as the result of poor housekeeping (let's hear it for creative mess!). That is, he noticed that a bacterial culture he was growing had been contaminated—and that the contaminant, whatever it was, had secreted a substance that had killed the bacterial culture around it.

What many people *don't* realize is that Sir Alexander did not immediately pick up a hypodermic and start saving lives right and left. While the original discovery was made in 1929, penicillin didn't become available for general medical use until 1947. This was not because the original discovery was slighted or ignored; it was because it took medical researchers that long to find methods of purifying and stabilizing the product. Prior to that time, penicillin was simply not very useful in a medical sense because it was impossible to tell the strength of a particular batch, to

know what dosage might be effective, or to rely on the medicine maintaining its effectiveness for any set period of time.

I occasionally get letters inquiring why Claire is not slapping moldy bread on wounds throughout the books, since surely she knows about penicillin? Well, actually, she does—which is why she *isn't* slapping moldy bread on people.

What she knows is that a) while there are quite a number of different molds in the genus *Penicillium,* this is far from being the only kind of mold that grows on bread; and b) there's no telling whether a particular piece of moldy bread contains any active penicillin (which is not the mold itself, by the way, but rather a substance secreted *by* the mold); and c) a piece of moldy bread is, in all likelihood, harboring all kinds of other bacterial and chemical contaminants, which it is quite possibly not a good idea to go stuffing into an open wound. Besides . . . rather difficult, I should think, to arrange always to have moldy bread on hand, just in case someone should cut themselves? (Readers don't think of these things; writers have to.)

CHICKEN AND MUSHROOMS *in Orange Sauce with Fresh Marjoram**
  1 chicken breast per person (diced)
  4–5 small mushrooms per person**
  several spears of asparagus (optional)
  orange juice
  chicken broth or bouillon
  onion
  garlic
  marjoram
  flour
  salt
  pepper

Use a deep cast-iron pan, ideally. Mince onion and garlic (I like lots; half an onion and a head of garlic for four breasts), and saute with marjoram in a little butter or olive oil. If using asparagus, break into one-inch pieces and saute with onion and garlic. Add sliced mushrooms and saute till tender.

Add diced chicken, stirring frequently till chicken appears cooked through. Sprinkle flour (about two tablespoons) lightly over chicken and stir in. Add enough orange juice to cover the chicken. Add about half a cup of chicken broth or bouillon (for four breasts). Let simmer until sauce is desired thickness, adjusting with

additional orange juice or broth. Salt and pepper to taste (if you use bouillon, you won't need much salt).

You can serve this on almost anything (rice, kasha, lentils, etc.), but I prefer it on egg noodles, topped with a lot of nice grated Romano cheese.

*Dried marjoram is perfectly all right; I just happen to be able to grow marjoram most of the year here. Quantities? I don't know; how much do you like marjoram? I generally use half a handful of fresh marjoram per four breasts—that would equal roughly a tablespoon of the dried herb.
**If you're using the normal kind of white button mushrooms. I like all kinds of edible fungi, and normally include sliced portobello mushrooms and a few porcinis or shiitakes. If you don't like mushrooms at all, leave 'em out.

Still, since Claire definitely appreciates the role of antibiotics in modern medicine, I rather think that she may make a serious effort to obtain some workable form of penicillin, now that she has a stable home base and (for the time being, at least) is not running around the country pursued by English soldiers and irate clansmen.

I think that some readers are misled by historical fiction, in which herbal remedies are presented as essentially being simply old-fashioned equivalents of modern drugs. Now, in a way, this is quite true; effective herbs (those containing active chemicals that can affect human or bacterial physiology) actually *are* drugs, and modern pharmacology has evolved from them: digitalis is derived from foxglove, diosgenins from wild yams are the basis for the steroid hormones in modern medicines from oral contraceptive to asthma medications, and plant-derived substances from oil of peppermint to ipecac are found in a great many formulations.

PENNYROYAL

"If boiled and drank, it provokes women's courses, and expels the dead child and afterbirth, and stays the disposition to vomit, if taken in water and vinegar mingled together."

Culpeper (*Culpeper's Complete Herbal*)

However, the important words here are "derived from." The fact that you can—with the assistance of a rather large research laboratory and several years' work—eventually produce an oral contraceptive by means of processing chemicals found in wild yams does *not* necessarily mean that a fictional character could prevent pregnancy by eating wild yams. *Au contraire.*

So, while some herbal remedies did (and do) work, the overall effects of these were much less powerful and predictable than those of modern drugs. As Claire herself notes, you might use mashed garlic if you didn't have anything better, but given the choice, one would always opt for iodine.

One has to allow for the warped purposes of the novelist, though. If it is fictionally desirable for a sick person to recover—and it usually is; it slows down a story quite a bit, if you kill all the characters—then the herbal treatments applied will generally work, even if the real-life effectiveness of such a treatment is generally not nearly so spectacular.

Tumble Turd

East India Bat

The poſſum

PENICILLIN ONLINE:
A WRITER'S THREAD

I know I've frequently mentioned my interactions online in the process of writing the *Outlander* novels. Some readers will be familiar with this sort of faceless conversation, but others will have little idea how this fascinating process works. I thought it might be interesting to provide a brief glimpse of one such interaction, both as illustration of the process, and perhaps as a bit of insight into how this sort of "research" contributes to the writing of a book.

There are all kinds of online venues these days, of course, ranging from newsgroups and independent Web sites to the immensity of America Online. While I do now and then visit various such venues (there are five or six groups on AOL alone devoted to discussion of the *Outlander* novels), most of my online time is spent on CompuServe, among the forums of the Readers and Writers Ink Group.

There are several forums in this group: the Writers Forum, the Literary Forum, the Authors Forum, the Romance Forum, the Erotica Forum, the Poetry Forum, and the Book Preview Forum (and by the time this book appears in print, there may well be more). In The Beginning, there was simply the Literary Forum; as membership

increased and online traffic became heavier, though, several new forums evolved from this, offering a broader range and more room for specialized interests among readers and writers.

My own usual electronic hangout is the Writers Forum, where I am a "section leader"[1] in a section called "Research and the Craft of Writing." This section deals with—surprise!—questions of research ("Was peppermint candy available in New York in 1794?" "How do you render someone unconscious quickly, without leaving marks?"), and craft ("How many points of view can you use in a novel?" "Should a writer begin with short stories before tackling a novel?"). Conversations are wide-ranging and always interesting, and I now and then take advantage of the forum's members myself, for expert advice on research questions.

Sometimes, I simply ask a straightforward question ("What does black powder smell like?"); occasionally, I'll post a brief excerpt that I'm working on, to see whether some technical point "comes across" adequately in the context of the story, when read by someone with an expertise in medicine or whatever.

---

[1] *Essentially, this just means I direct traffic, promote conversations, and answer questions where and as I can. All section leaders are unpaid volunteers.*

The following section shows part of a "thread," or conversation, based on one of these excerpts. When a question is asked or a message posted in any of the CompuServe Forums, it may be addressed to a specific person, or to "All," but anyone who reads it is more than welcome to respond.[2] When I occasionally post an excerpt like this, there's no telling who may read it, or what they may have to say about it. The original message(s) and the responses to it are collectively called a "thread."

Most forums have members who participate regularly, as well as those who "lurk," reading messages but rarely responding, and some who simply wander in from time to time. Since the "Research and the Craft of Writing" section is "mine," I'm well acquainted with most of the regular participants and therefore know something of their own interests and backgrounds; other people I know only by name. To give more insight on the following thread, I've provided a quick capsule description of the participants.[3]

Elise Skidmore is an industrial technician by profession, who is section leader for the "Writing Exercises" section of the Writers Forum.

Rosina Lippi-Green is a professor of sociolinguistics and creative writing, and a published historical novelist (writing as Sara Donati).

Mira Kolar-Brown is a Project Manager (Employment Initiatives) based in Manchester, England, presently working on a mystery novel.

Coleen Harman is a veterinarian.

Ellen Mandell, an M.D. with specialties in OB/GYN and epidemiology, was following a trail of breadcrumbs when she plunged down a rabbit hole and hasn't been seen since.

Alan Smithee is a specialist in medical radiology.

Beth Shope is raising a family in Switzerland and working on a fantasy novel.

Barbara Schnell is a German photojournalist and novelist, who also did the (excellent) German translation of *Drums of Autumn* (*Der Ruf der Trommel*).

Marte Brengle is a software expert and technical writer, working on a novel.

Betty Babas is a section leader in the Romance Forum.

Jo C. Harmon is an RN.

Susan Martin is my co-section leader in "Research and the Craft of Writing" and is at work on a historical mystery set in France.

Arlene McCrea is a retired academic.

Eve Ackerman is librarian for several R&WI forums, and is working on a historical novel.

#: 470986 S8/Research & craft [WRITERS]
   23–Aug–97 03:48:21
Sb: SPOILER—Penicillin
Fm: Diana Gabaldon 76530,523
To: All

SPOILER

Whew. Had a migraine all yesterday, and didn't get _anything_ done, but finally fin-

---

[2] *It is possible to post a message privately, in which case only the addressee can read it. Most messages are posted publicly.*

[3] *All messages that appear on CompuServe are the copyrighted property of the people who write them. The messages reproduced here are reprinted by permission of the authors.*

IN ORDER TO GIVE *the flavor of this sort of online exchange, minimal editing has been done, and small conventions of online communication have been left as they appeared in the original messages. These include underscore marks (_) used to indicate italics or other emphasis in the text, abbreviations of commonly used terms, and assorted "emoticons."*

Since it isn't possible to transmit tones of voice, facial expressions, or other nonverbal cues that people normally use in face-to-face conversations, many people use symbols known as "emoticons," to indicate these cues and clarify the meaning of their messages. Such symbols as appear in this thread include:

> *<g> = grin, indicating that the person is smiling, or at least means to be humorous or well-intentioned*
>
> *:) = also a smile (look at the symbol sideways)*
>
> *;) = a wink*
>
> *<d&r> = "ducking and running"; used when the writer has said something that he or she expects might provoke a strong reaction. Used to indicate a humorous intent.*

<< >> = brackets enclose text that is quoted from an earlier message, in order to make it clear when a subsequent message is addressing a particular point from the earlier message.

SPOILER is used at the head of messages that contain excerpts of a to-be-published book or story, or that include discussions of published work (or films) that might give away important material concerning the plot. This is a courtesy warning to people who don't want to know anything about a book, film, etc., prior to seeing the completed work.[4]

IANAD = "I am not a doctor." (also IANAL = "I am not a lawyer") A disclaimer of expert knowledge, preceding an opinion.

LOL = "Laughing out loud"
OTOH = "On the other hand"
FWIW = "For what it's worth"
IOW = "In other words"

---

[4] *The first few messages are reproduced just as they appear online, with all "header" information intact. Beyond the first few, though, most of the header information has been eliminated to improve readability.*

ished this penicillin scene tonight. This is a somewhat longer scene than I'd usually post on the boards, but it's kind of all-of-a-piece, so it didn't seem suitable just to put up the first bit.

It occurs to me that Alan might not want to read this, if he's only beginning with OUTLANDER. But if you're around, Ellen, (or any other of the medically knowledgeable) I'd appreciate any comments on plausibilities and procedures—just so I don't get rashes of letters from People Who Know, later on. <g>

Thanks,—Diana

Excerpt THE FIERY CROSS
Copyright © 1997 Diana Gabaldon

[date]

_Was called from churning to attend Rosamund Lindsey, who arrived in late afternoon with a severe laceration to the left hand, sustained with an axe while girdling trees. Wound was extensive, having nearly severed the left thumb; laceration extended from base of index finger to two inches above the styloid process of the radius, which was superficially damaged. Injury had been sustained approximately three days prior, treated with rough binding and bacon grease. Extensive sepsis apparent, with suppuration, gross swelling of hand and forearm. Thumb blackened; gangrene apparent; characteristic pungent odor. Subcutaneous red streaks, indicative of blood poisoning, extended from site of injury nearly to antecubital fossa.

Patient presented with high fever (est. 104 degrees F, by hand), symptoms of dehydration, mild disorientation. Tachycardia evident.

In view of the seriousness of patient's condition, recommended immediate amputation of limb at elbow. Patient refused to consider this, insisted instead upon application of pigeon poultice, consisting of the split body of a freshly killed pigeon, applied to wound (patient's husband had brought pigeon, neck freshly wrung). Removed thumb at base of metacarpal, ligated remains of radial artery (crushed in original injury) and superficialis volae. Debrided and drained wound, applied approximately ½ oz. crude penicillin powder (source: rotted casaba rind, batch #23, prep. 15/4/71) topically, followed by application of mashed raw garlic (three cloves), barberry salve—and pigeon poultice, at insistence of husband. Administered fluids by mouth; febrifuge mixture of red centaury, bloodroot, and hops; water ad lib. Injected liquid penicillin mixture (batch #23, suspended in sterile water), IV, dosage ¼ oz. in suspension in sterile water.

Patient's condition deteriorated rapidly, with increasing symptoms of disorientation and delirium, high fever. Extensive urticaria appeared on arm and upper torso. Attempted to relieve fever by repeated applications of cold water, to no avail. Patient being incoherent, requested permission to amputate from husband; permission denied on grounds that death appeared imminent, and patient "would not want to be buried in pieces."

Repeated penicillin injection. Patient lapsed into unconsciousness shortly thereafter, and expired just before dawn, [date]._

I dipped my quill again, but then hesitated, letting the drops of ink slide off the sharpened point into the small gourd I used as an inkwell. How much more should I say?

The deeply ingrained disposition for scientific thoroughness warred with caution. It was important to describe what had happened, as fully as possible. At the same time, I hesitated to put down in writing what might amount to an admission of manslaughter—it wasn't murder, I assured myself, though my guilty feelings made no such distinctions.

[continued]

#: 470987 S8/Research & craft [WRITERS]
   23–Aug–97 03:52:01
Sb: #470986-SPOILER—Pencillin
Fm: Diana Gabaldon 76530,523
To: All

[continued]

"Feelings aren't truth," I murmured. Across the room, Brianna looked up from the bread she was slicing, but I bent my head over the page, and she returned to her whispered conversation with Marsali by the fire. It was no more than midafternoon, but dark and rainy outside. I had lit a candle by which to write, but the girls' hands flickered over the dim table like moths, lighting here and there among the plates and platters.

The truth was that I didn't think Rosamund Lindsey had died of septicemia. I was fairly sure that she had died of an acute reaction to an unpurified penicillin mixture—of the medicine I gave her, in short. Of course, the truth also was that the blood poisoning would certainly have killed her, left untreated.

The truth also was that I had had no way of knowing what the effects of the penicillin would be—but that was rather the point, wasn't it? To make sure someone else _might_ know?

I twiddled the quill, rolling it between thumb and forefinger. I had kept a faithful account of my experiments with penicillin—the growing of cultures on media ranging from bread to chewed paw-paw and rotted melon rind, painstaking descriptions of the microscopic and gross identification of the _Penicillium_ molds, the effects of—to this point—very cautious applications.

Yes, certainly I must include a description of the effects. The real question, though, was—for whom was I keeping this careful record? I bit my lip, thinking. If it was only for my own reference, it would be a simple matter; I could simply record the symptoms, timing and effects, without explicitly noting the cause of death; I was unlikely to forget the circumstances, after all. But if this record were ever to be useful to someone else . . . someone who had no notion of the benefits and dangers of an antibiotic . . .

The ink was drying on the quill. I lowered the point to the page. _Age—44_, I wrote slowly. In this day, casebook accounts like this often ended with a pious description of the deceased's last moments, marked—presumably—by Christian resignation on the part of the holy, repentance by the sinful. Neither attitude had marked the passage of Rosamund Lindsey.

I glanced at the coffin, sitting on its trestles under the rain-smeared window. The Lindseys' cabin was no more than half-built; not suited for a funeral in the pouring rain. The coffin was open, awaiting the evening wake, but the muslin shroud had been drawn up over her face.

Rosamund had been a whore in Boston; growing too stout and too old to ply her trade with much profit, she had drifted south, looking for a husband. "I couldn't bide another of them winters," she had confided to me, soon after her arrival on the Ridge. "Nor yet another of them stinkin' fishermen."

She had found the necessary refuge in Kenneth Lindsey, who was looking for a wife to share the work of homesteading. Not a match born of physical attraction—the Lindseys had had perhaps six sound teeth between them—or emotional compatibility, still it had seemed an amicable relationship.

Shocked rather than grief-stricken, Kenny had been taken off by Jamie for medication with whisky—a somewhat more effective treatment than my own. At least I didn't think it would be lethal.

Immediate cause of death—I wrote, and paused again. I doubted that Rosamund's response to approaching death would have found outlet in either prayer or philosophy, but she had had opportunity for neither. She had died blue-faced, congested and bulging-eyed, unable to force word or breath past the swollen tissues of her throat.

My own throat felt tight at the memory, as though I were being choked. I picked up the cooling cup of catmint tea and took a sip, feeling the pungent liquid slide soothingly down. It was little comfort that the septicemia would have killed her more lingeringly. Suffocation was quicker, but not much more pleasant.

I tapped the quill point on the blotter, leaving inky pinpoints that spread through the rough fibers of the paper, forming a galaxy of tiny stars. As to that—there was another possibility. Death might conceivably have been due to a pulmonary embolism—a clot in the lung. That would be a not-impossible complication of the septicemia, and could have accounted for the symptoms.

It was a hopeful thought, but not one I placed much credence in. It was the voice of experience, as much as the voice of conscience,

that bade me dip the quill and write down "_anaphylaxis_," before I could think again.

Was anaphylaxis a known medical term yet? I hadn't seen it in any of Rawlings's notes—but then, I hadn't read them all. Still, while death from the shock of allergic reaction was not unknown in any time, it wasn't common, and might not be known by name. Better describe it in detail, for whoever might read this.

And that was the rub, of course. Who _would_ read it? I thought it unlikely, but what if a stranger should read this and take my account for a confession of murder? That was far-fetched—but it could happen. I had come perilously close to being executed as a witch, in part because of my healing activities. Once almost burnt, twice shy, I thought wryly.

[continued]

#: 470988 S8/Research & craft [WRITERS]
    23–Aug–97 03:52:08
Sb: #470986-SPOILER—Penicillin
Fm: Diana Gabaldon 76530,523
To: All

[continued]

Extensive swelling in affected limb, I wrote, and lifted the quill, the last word fading as the pen ran dry. I dipped it again and scratched doggedly on. _Swelling extended to upper torso, face, and neck. Skin pale, marked with reddish blotches. Respiration increasingly rapid and shallow, heartbeat very fast and light, tending to inaudibility. Palpitations evident. Lips and ears cyanotic. Pronounced exophthalmia._

I swallowed again, at the thought of Rosamund's eyes, bulging under the lids, rolling to and fro in uncomprehending terror. We had tried to shut them, when we cleansed the body and laid it out for burial. It was customary to uncover the corpse's face for the wake; I thought it unwise in this case.

I didn't want to look at the coffin again, but did, with a small nod of acknowledgment and apology. Brianna's head turned toward me, then sharply away. The smell of the food laid out for the wake was filling the room, mingling with the scents of oak-wood fire and oak-gall ink—and the fresh-planed oak of the coffin's boards. I took another hasty gulp of tea, to stop my gorge rising.

I knew damn well why the first line of Hippocrates' oath was, "First, do no harm." It was too bloody easy to do harm. What hubris it took to lay hands on a person, to interfere. How delicate and complex were bodies, how crude a physician's intrusions.

I could have sought seclusion in surgery or study, to write these notes. I knew why I hadn't. The coarse muslin shroud glowed soft white in the rainy light from the window. I pinched the quill hard between thumb and forefinger, trying to forget the pop of the cricoid cartilage, when I had jabbed a penknife into Rosamund's throat in a final, futile attempt to let air into her straining lungs.

And yet . . . there was not one practicing physician, I thought, who had never faced this. I had had it happen a few times before—even in a modern hospital, equipped with every life-saving device known to man—then.

Some future physician here would face the same dilemma; to undertake a possibly dangerous treatment, or to allow a patient to die who _might_ have been saved. And that was my own dilemma—to balance the unlikely possibility of prosecution for manslaughter against the unknown value of my records to someone who might seek knowledge in them.

Who might that be? I wiped the pen, thinking. There were as yet few medical schools, and those few, mostly in Europe. Most physicians gained their knowledge from apprenticeship and experience. I slipped a finger into the casebook, feeling blind between the early pages, kept by the book's original owner, Daniel Rawlings.

Rawlings had not gone to medical school. Though if he had, many of his techniques would still have been shocking by my standards. My mouth twisted at the thought of some of the treatments I had seen described in those closely written pages—infusions of liquid mercury to cure syphilis, cupping and blistering for epileptic fits, lancing and bleeding for every disorder from indigestion to impotence.

And still, Daniel Rawlings had been a doctor. Reading his case notes, as I sometimes did, I could feel his care for his patients, his curiosity regarding the mysteries of the body.

Moved by impulse, I turned back to the pages containing Rawlings's notes. Perhaps I was only delaying to let my subconscious reach a decision—or perhaps I felt the need of communication, no matter how remote, with another physician, someone like me.

Someone like me. I stared at the page, with its neat, small writing, its careful illustration, seeing none of the details. Who was there, like me? No one. I had thought of it before, but only vaguely, in the way of a problem acknowledged, but so distant as not to require any urgency. In the colony of North Carolina, so far as I knew, there was only one formally designated "doctor"—Fentiman. I snorted, and took another sip of tea. Better Murdock MacLeod and his nostrums—most of those were harmless, at least.

I sipped my tea, regarding Rosamund. The simple truth was that I wouldn't last forever, either. With luck, a good long time yet—but still, not forever. I needed to find someone to whom I could pass on at least the rudiments of what I knew.

A stifled giggle from the table, the girls whispering over the pots of headcheese, the bowls of sauerkraut and boiled potatoes. No, I thought, with some regret. Not Brianna.

She would be the logical choice; she knew what modern medicine was, at least. There would be no overcoming of ignorance and superstition, no need to convince of the virtues of asepsis, the dangers of germs. But she had no natural inclination, no instinct for healing. She was not squeamish or afraid of blood—she had helped me with any number of childbirths and minor surgical procedures—and yet she lacked that peculiar mixture of empathy and ruthlessness a doctor needs.

She was perhaps Jamie's child more than mine, I reflected, watching the firelight ripple in the falls of her hair as she moved. She had his courage, his great tenderness—but it was the courage of a warrior, the tenderness of a strength that could crush if it chose. I had not managed to give her my gift; the knowledge of blood and bone, the secret ways of the chambers of the heart. Brianna's head lifted sharply, turning toward the door. Marsali, slower, turned too, listening.

It was barely audible through the thrumming of the rain, but knowing it was there, I could pick it out—a male voice, raised high, chanting. A pause, and then a faint answering rumble that might have been distant thunder, but wasn't. The men were coming down from the shelter on the mountain.

[continued]

#: 470989 S8/Research & craft [WRITERS]
23–Aug–97 03:52:17

Sb: #470986-#SPOILER—Penicillin
Fm: Diana Gabaldon 76530,523
To: All

[continued]

Kenny Lindsey had asked Roger to sing the _caithris_ for Rosamund; the formal Gaelic lament for the dead. "She wasna Scots," Kenny had said, wiping eyes bleared from tears and a long night's watching. "Nor even God-fearin'. But she was that fond o' singin', and she fair admired your way o' it, MacKenzie."

Roger had never sung a _caithris_ before; I knew he had never heard one. "Dinna fash," Jamie had murmured to him, hand on his arm, "all ye need to be is loud." Roger had bent his head gravely in acquiescence, and went with Jamie and Kenneth, to drink whisky by the malting floor and learn what he could of Rosamund's life, the better to lament her passing.

The singing vanished; the wind had shifted. It was a freak of the storm that we had heard them so soon—they would be headed down the Ridge now, to collect mourners from the outlying cabins, and then to lead them all in procession back up to the house, for the feasting and singing and storytelling that would go on all night.

I yawned involuntarily, my jaw cracking at the thought of it. I'd never last, I thought in dismay. I had had a few hours' sleep in the morning, but not enough to sustain me through a full-blown Gaelic wake and funeral. The floors would be thick with bodies by dawn, all of them smelling of whisky and wet clothes.

I yawned again, then blinked, my eyes swimming as I shook my head to clear it. Every bone in my body ached with fatigue, and I wanted nothing more than to go to bed for several days.

Deep in thought, I hadn't noticed Brianna coming to stand behind me. Her hands came down on my shoulders, and she moved closer, so I felt the warmth of her touching me. Marsali had gone; we were alone. She began to massage my shoulders, long thumbs moving slowly up the cords of my neck. "Tired?" she asked.

"Mm. I'll do," I said. I closed the book, and leaned back, relaxing momentarily in the sheer relief of her touch. I hadn't realized I was strung so tightly.

The big room was quiet and orderly, ready for the wake. The girls had lit a pair of candles, one at each end of the laden table, and shadows flickered over the whitewashed walls, the quiet coffin, as the candle-flames bent in a sudden draft.

"I think I killed her," I said suddenly, not meaning to say it at all. "It was the penicillin that killed her."

The long fingers didn't stop their soothing movement.

"Was it?" she murmured. "You couldn't have done any differently, though, could you?"

"No."

A small shudder of relief went over me, as much from the bald confession as from the gradual release of the painful tightness in my neck and shoulders.

"It's okay," she said softly, rubbing, stroking. "She would have died anyway, wouldn't she? It's sad, but you didn't do wrong. You know that."

"I know that." To my surprise, a single tear slid down my cheek and dropped on the blotter, puckering the thick paper. I blinked hard,

struggling for control. I didn't want to distress Brianna.

She wasn't distressed. Her hands left my shoulders, and I heard the scraping of stool legs. Then her arms came around me, and I let her draw me back, my head resting just under her chin. She simply held me, letting the rise and fall of her breathing calm me.

"I went to dinner with Uncle Joe once, just after he'd lost a patient," she said finally. "He told me about it."

"Did he?" I was a little surprised; I wouldn't have thought Joe would talk about such things with her.

"He didn't mean to. I could see something was bothering him, though, so I asked. And—he needed to talk, and I was there. Afterward, he said it was almost like having you there. I didn't know he called you Lady Jane."

"Yes," I said. "Because of the way I talk, he said." I felt a breath of laughter against my ear, and smiled slightly in response. I closed my eyes, and could see my friend, gesturing in passionate conversation, face alight with the desire to tease.

"He said—that when something like that happened, sometimes there would be a sort of formal inquiry, at the hospital. Not like a trial, not that—but a gathering of the other doctors, to hear exactly what happened, what went wrong. He said it was sort of like confession, to tell it to other doctors, who could understand—and it helped."

"Mm-hm." She was swaying lightly, rocking me as she moved, as she rocked Jemmy, soothing.

"Is that what's bothering you?" she asked quietly. "Not just Rosamund—but that you're alone? You don't have anybody who can really understand?"

Her arms wrapped around my shoulders, her hands crossed, resting lightly on my chest.

Young, broad, capable hands, the skin fresh and fair, smelling of fresh-baked bread and strawberry jam. I lifted one, and laid the warm palm against my cheek.

"Apparently I do," I said.

The hand curved, stroked my cheek and dropped away. The big young hand moved slowly, smoothing the hair behind my ear with soft affection. "It will be all right," she said. "Everything will be all right."

"Yes," I said, and smiled, despite the tears blurring my eyes. I couldn't teach her to be a doctor. But evidently I had, without meaning to, somehow taught her to be a mother.

"You should go lie down," she said, taking her hands away reluctantly. "It will be an hour at least, before they get here."

I let my breath go out in a sigh, feeling the peace of the house around me. If Fraser's Ridge had been a short-lived haven for Rosamund Lindsey, still it had been a true home. We would see her safe, and honored in death.

"In a minute," I said, wiping my nose. "I need to finish something, first."

I sat up straight and opened my book. I dipped my pen, and began to write the lines that must be there, for the sake of the unknown physician who would follow me.

[end section]

#: 471087 S8/Research & craft [WRITERS]
   23–Aug–97 12:02:31
Sb: #470988-SPOILER—Penicillin
Fm: Elise Skidmore S/L 6 71576,375
To: Diana Gabaldon 76530,523

Dear Diana,

As usual, this piece of writing from you is wonderfully done. While I don't know any-thing about the medical aspects, the emotional ones ring true. I am always a bit awed when I read these excerpts. You make it look so easy. <s>

Now, I haven't a clue what "cupping and blistering for epileptic fits" is, but I was wondering at your use of "fits." I was always told that term was incorrect, that "seizure" was the "proper" word. I know you're dynamite at research (as this whole excerpt proves), so I'm wondering, would Claire have used "epileptic fits"? When I was around 10–11 ('64–'65), my girlfriend's mother used to have these seizures all the time and I can remember being told about it back then so I don't think it's a PC thing. With Claire being a doctor, I'd think she'd be more sensitive about the wording, but then, I could be wrong. It's happened before. <s> :-)Elise

#: 471147 S8/Research & craft [WRITERS]
   23–Aug–97 15:49:11
Sb: #471087-SPOILER—Penicillin
Fm: Diana Gabaldon 76530,523
To: Elise Skidmore S/L 6 71576,375

Dear Elise—

No, the proper word—and the one Claire would use herself—_is_ "seizure." However, what she's doing there is not contemplating epilepsy _per se_, but thinking of Rawlings's casebook descriptions. And he, being an eighteenth-century practitioner, very likely did say "fits." <g> In other words, she isn't directly quoting him, but she's thinking of the things she read in his case notes.

"Fits," by the way, was common usage in the American South, well into this century. My great-grandmother, from Kentucky, wasn't at all countrified, but she said "fits," and so did most of her family.

Cupping and blistering, by the way, was a process in which small fires were lighted on the skin, to draw evil humours to the surface.

In re "You make it look so easy." Just to put things in perspective, this is just about two weeks' work you're looking at. <g>—Diana

#: 471158 S8/Research & craft [WRITERS]
    23–Aug–97 16:44:19
Sb: #471087-SPOILER—Penicillin
Fm: Elise Skidmore S/L 6 71576,375
To: Diana Gabaldon 76530,523

Dear Diana,

Thanks for explaining the reasoning behind why you used "fits" vs. "seizure." Makes perfect sense to me and I just _knew_ you had good reason for it. <s>
<< In re "You make it look so easy." Just to put things in perspective, this is just about two weeks' work you're looking at. <g> >>
Well, that's the mark of all champions, making what's really tough look like a piece of cake. Kudos to you. I thought the excerpt was very well done. Those two weeks were well spent. :-) Elise

#: 471256 S8/Research & craft [WRITERS]
    23–Aug–97 22:50:22
Sb: #471087-SPOILER—Penicillin
Fm: Marte Brengle 76703,4242
To: Elise Skidmore S/L 6 71576,375

Cupping is exactly what one might think—the application of small, thick-rimmed cups to the skin. The person doing the cupping first lights a bit of some kind of aromatic herb (usually) and tosses the flaming material into the cup, then quickly turns it upside down onto the patient's back. As the flaming material burns up the oxygen, a vacuum forms and the skin rises inside the cup.

My grandmother (Evelyn Eaton) gives a rather vivid description of having this done to her in one of her collections of autobiographical short stories (originally printed in the _New Yorker_). I believe it's "Every Month Was May" but could possibly be "The North Star Is Nearer." My mother's got my copies of the books so I can't check, but the story itself is memorable.—M

#: 471379 S8/Research & craft [WRITERS]
    24–Aug–97 10:36:30
Sb: #471256-SPOILER—Penicillin
Fm: Elise Skidmore S/L 6 71576,375
To: Marte Brengle 76703,4242

So tell me, did this actually help cure anything? Doesn't sound real pleasant to me. :-)Elise

Fm: Marte Brengle 76703,4242
To: Elise Skidmore S/L 6 71576,375

My grandmother had "catarrh" which was an all-purpose term for a heavy chest cold, and yes, apparently the cupping did help. It was about all that was available in rural France in the 1930s.—M—

Fm: Rosina Lippi-Green 102014,1664
To: Diana Gabaldon 76530,532

Diana,

I've read it twice. I'm not surprised it took you a while to write it, it's very, very finely put together.

I can't comment on the medical aspects, of course, but I think the form and rhythm of it—starting with the formal description and moving into the introspection, ending with the conversation—works beautifully.
rosina

Fm: Diana Gabaldon 76530,523
To: Rosina Lippi-Green 102014,1664 (X)

Dear Rosina—

Thanks!—Diana

Fm: Coleen 103361,1003
To: Diana Gabaldon 76530,523

Gosh, Diana, it feels right, emotionally and medically. The medical record is objective, as one would expect, and the doctor is experiencing the mixed emotions during writing that (I think) most healers have experienced. I identified mostly with the emotions and especially the confessional aspect of the situation. Even when you did everything possible, you feel like there must have been something more you could have done. Very well written. The piece has, of course, made me pause to think about possible solutions to Claire's anaphylaxis problem . . . if there were some epinephrinelike plant—ephedra perhaps? Just thinking out loud . . . <g> Coleen

Fm: Diana Gabaldon 76530,523
To: Coleen 103361,1003 (X)

Dear Coleen:

Oh, good; glad it works for you. Re the ephedra—we got it out here in the Southwest, but evidently not in the Eastern/Central region, according to the _Peterson Field Guide to Medicinal Plants_. There's _lots_ of stuff listed as "allergenic," but my general impression is that they mean people are easily allergic to 'em, not that they relieve allergic symptoms. <g>

The only anti-allergenics from the Eastern region are (evidently) wild licorice, chamomile, and wild yam. Wild yam might actually be a possibility, in that diosgenin from yams is the basis for the steroid hormones used in a good many modern drugs—like oral contraceptives and asthma medications—BUT (the book says), such drugs are derived "from elaborately processed chemicals found in the wild yam." Claire wouldn't have anything beyond simple pressing, distilling, extraction, and/or steeping, which might not be sufficient to the purpose. <g>

It's still a thought, but I think one might have procedural problems with administering an antidote to anaphylactic shock—even if you knew of one—insofar as for most such things, you have to steep the herb in boiling water or otherwise do something time-consuming to it, in order to extract the active principle. Judging from the anecdotes I've heard from Kit and others, I don't think you'd have time to do that, if someone went into full-blown anaphylaxis right in front of you—and anaphylactic shock wouldn't be a sufficiently common occurrence in that setting for a physician to keep the remedy always on hand (given that most herbal medicines have to be made fresh at fairly short intervals; they don't keep well).
Thanks!—Diana

Fm: Coleen 103361,1003
To: Diana Gabaldon 76530,523

Hmm . . . interesting dilemma. I also wondered if maybe caffeine from coffee or theophylline from tea would help—but I remember Claire's aversion to the traditional English tea (or even the theobromine from chocolate . . . yum). I know it's not for this patient since it's such a poignant part of Claire's learning experience . . . I'm just doing the typical problem-solving that's been drilled into my head. <g>

No, these probably wouldn't work for acute, severe anaphylactic reactions, only for respiratory signs, or asthma attacks . . . Purified cow's adrenal? LOL—the person she tried that on would probably end up being allergic to cow protein! <g>

Persistent, ain't I?

Coleen

Fm: Diana Gabaldon 76530,523
To: Coleen 103361,1003

Dear Coleen—

Oh, Claire likes tea. <g> However, we are at the moment in a ra-ther remote little settlement in the mountains of North Carolina, it's 1770, and the Townshend Acts have been in effect for the last two years—these being import taxes on British products like . . . er . . . tea? (Boston Tea Party ring a bell? <g>)

Why don't you tell me exactly how to purify a cow adrenal, just in case I ever need to know this? <G>

Diana

Fm: Coleen 103361,1003
To: Diana Gabaldon 76530,523

Hi again, Diana,

<giggle>—I remember her comment about black tea to John Grey in an excerpt from *The King Farewell*—oop! I guess I'm getting a little ahead of the story.

Hmm . . . I remember seeing the TV show dramatizing how the Canadian team discovered insulin . . . I don't think they gave the specifics of how to purify pancreas though <g>. I wonder if it would be the same for adrenal . . . Not quite the same conversation they're having in the Food topic :) I'm afraid school never taught us all those neat recipes. Just poke the vial and suck it out—that's about as much as they thought we could handle <g>.

Coleen (who is actually looking to see if she has anything on the discovery of adrenaline, even if you were being facetious <ggg>)

Fm: Susan Martin/SL8 74101,113
To: Diana Gabaldon 76530,523

Diana,

I can't speak to the medical part—nothing stuck out to me, but then IANAD. As to the emotional part, lovely. Well done!

—Susan

Fm: Diana Gabaldon 76530,523
To: Susan Martin/SL8 74101,113

Dear Susan—

Thank you!

—Diana

Fm: Mira Brown 100425,170
To: Diana Gabaldon 76530,523

Hi, Diana,

Hope the migraine is better. Mountain Dew with avocado and bagels? <g>

To the scene: I echo much of what Rosina has already said. Love the loneliness, the desperate need for contact with the other doctor, the need for reassurance that eventually comes from Brianna.

Also, the "orderly room" filled with the smell of wood and food, complete with the corpse and candles. I've seen it in villages back home—it still makes me shiver a bit but also has that wonderful "life goes on" quality.

However, strictly as a reader <g>, I find it difficult to accept that C. would even consider the woman's death as a murder or her responsibility in such a big way. I repeat here as a lay-reader because in truth it would take a doctor, and the one who had to go through something like that to pass an informed judgment.

Years ago I was involved in a road accident (it wasn't me driving) and between someone's massive incompetence, high snow, ice, etc., I was brought to the hospital having virtually bled to death. Apparently, there's more to blood transfusion than just establishing that I was A+. But, the emergency team had no time for niceties—they grabbed the first A+ to hand. I was very lucky and it happened to be a perfect match, but the boys were still terribly upset when I woke up, because I could have died on them—apparently. The thing is, that was a modern hospital, and they still had no option. Neither did Claire. I could understand her self-recriminations if she had a number of choices and made the wrong one. Even then it would have hardly been a murder. You've tied both her hands behind her back with the state the woman was brought in, the woman's and then her husband's refusal of amputation and insistence on pigeon poultice (pigeon poultice?!—did they really do that?), the absence of any other medication, etc. . . . Would a mature woman and a practicing, experienced doctor really blame herself that much for taking the *only* option open to her? I think I'd rather see anger that she wasn't allowed to do her job as she saw fit, at the futility of the woman's death.

Having said that, I like very much her reluctance to enter the details in her log book. That is very nicely done.

Mira

Fm: Diana Gabaldon 76530,523
To: Mira Brown 100425,170 (X)

Dear Mira—

Well, as you say, the medical people at the hospital were terribly upset, because you _could_ have died, and they felt responsible, even though they had no choice. I've talked with a number of doctors by way of research (and curiosity), and an underlying sense of deep responsibility—that does go beyond reason, now and then—seems to be a trait they share.

One doctor told me about in-house inquiries into patient deaths—a vague variant of which I used in this scene—and mentioned that one of the chief intentions/effects of this was to provide catharsis for the physician who had caused/presided over the death, because there _was_ a deep feeling of guilt attending, no matter whether the physician _could_ have prevented the death or not.

In other words, Claire's feelings of responsibility and guilt are pretty much based on testimony by Real Doctors I Have Known (and read about). They may be slightly complicated here by the use of the penicillin; that is, she _knows_ how chancy the stuff is, though the chanciness would more often have to do with a lack of effectiveness, or an accidental contamination, than with a straightforward hypersensitivity. Still, she knows how desperately valuable an antibiotic can be, and has been making steady efforts throughout the book to find a way to make it reliable enough to be useful.

So, this penicillin is entirely her game, so to speak; naturally, she's going to feel responsible for anything that happens in consequence of using it, no matter what the other circumstances.

As to anger—well, she's been in the eighteenth century for a longish time now, and she's seen one hell of a lot of (what would be by modern standards) unnecessary deaths. I don't think she'd waste a lot of time getting angry at people for ignorance—she never has, if you look back at the other books. She's pretty outspoken about telling people what they _ought_ to do, but she'd lived in primitive places long before her disappearance into the past; she isn't one to look down on people or get mad at them because they don't know what she knows.

Besides. <g> I wanted to make the point about mortality and immortality. For the first time, Claire admits—if offhandedly—that she'll die herself one day. What she knows is very, very valuable in this day and age; she _has_ to find a way to pass it on, if she possibly can. Notes in her casebook are all very well, but what she _really_ needs is to find an apprentice.

Likewise, she realizes—also perhaps for the first time—that she _has_ given part of herself to her daughter, and that will continue, even after Claire herself has gone.

So, the guilt and responsibility flow naturally into that whole mortality/immortality theme (if I dare mention such a word); everything fits—the need for confession, connection, understanding; realization of mortality and the need for continuance; and finally, unexpected absolution. Raging about what had happened wouldn't fit; it would just be a distraction.

See, this scene isn't _about_ Rosamund; it's about Claire.

Glad you liked the "life goes on" part; so did I. <g>
—Diana

Fm: Mira Brown 100425,170
To: Diana Gabaldon 76530,523

Hi Diana,

(In my own case, I should imagine the doctors did get angry with the couple of doctors who failed to stem the bleeding, and with plenty of reason. It wasn't a case of "looking down," just simple, justified expectations from their own profession.)

<<she isn't one to look down on people or get mad at them because they don't know what she knows.>>

Yes, I have noted that before and thought that was really well handled. After I sent the message I realized it would be easy to interpret the "anger" that way and that's not what I meant. I'm talking a more general feeling/ awareness of helplessness and limitations— the anger that's a result of frustration. That's something I can see happening to a doctor over and over again, keeping them from getting de-sensitised (sp?), maintaining the sense of personal responsibility (which is quite different from guilt, far more rational).

You know I get a feeling that we may be hitting yet again the American/European divide. While I don't think there are *any* actual differences, the psychological process is very probably exactly the same on both sides of the Atlantic, interpretation/presentation may be very different. Europeans don't mind being seen as "realistic"; Americans very often wrap it up in emotional tissue paper. Do I need to d&r? <g> Actually, I'd dearly love a British or mainland European doctor to get involved here.

<< Besides. <g> I wanted to make the point about mortality and immortality. For the first time, Claire admits—if offhandedly—that she'll die herself one day. What she knows is

very, very valuable in this day and age; she _has_ to find a way to pass it on, if she possibly can. Notes in her casebook are all very well, but what she _really_ needs is to find an apprentice. Hm? >>

Hm, indeed. You see, until now I've never taken your time travel very seriously. To me it's been just a vehicle, not really very different from a plane or a camel. Now, you are bringing it into a different focus, and at least for the moment, I can't get my head around it. There are questions piling up faster than I can type them: Where is Claire going to die? Does she know she can't change/influence history? How much is anything she does influenced by the fact that she can—at least in theory—pop back to her own time and look up the history records for that time/area? You see, I really can't deal with this imaginatively. <g> How *do* you see it?

<< Raging about what had happened wouldn't fit; it would just be a distraction. See, this scene isn't _about_ Rosamund; it's about Claire.>> Agreed. And a good way of doing it.
Mira

Fm: Diana Gabaldon 76530,523
To: Mira Brown 100425,170

Dear Mira—

Ah, I see. Yes, I had misunderstood your first account of your accident—I thought the doctors who tended you later were upset because the earlier rescuers hadn't done things right. Got it. <g>

Yes, good point regarding American/European methods of expression. That's one reason I gave Claire such a "mixed" background from the beginning; I figured it was inevitable that I would occasionally do some-thing recognizably American, rather than British, but if she had spent a good deal of time in contact with Americans (during the War), or working in America (during her years with Frank), any such cross-cultural lapses would still be believable.
—Diana

Fm: Diana Gabaldon 76530,523
To: Mira Brown 100425,170

P.S. Oh, the time travel. Ah . . . have you read the second book in the series? That begins to deal with these questions—but not nearly on the level that FIERY CROSS will.

Can one change history? Well, yes and no (under the Gabaldon Theory of Time Travel, that is). One usually _can't_ change the outcome of any "large" event, simply because knowledge isn't the crucial factor.

If you _knew_ for an absolute fact that someone was going to assassinate President Clinton tomorrow—what would you do to prevent it? Call the FBI? Sure, and when they ask you how you know, and what you know, and by the way, what is the number you are calling from, please . . . Go to wherever Clinton will be tomorrow (and how do you find that out? And do you have sufficient money to buy a plane ticket to get there?), and try to spot the potential assassin, and/or warn the President himself? Think about it. And then consider that an assassination is a very simple historical event, by contrast to things like battles, wars, major economic movements (how would one go about preventing the Depression of the 1930s, say?), etc.

The thing is, most "large" historical events occur as the result of the cumulative actions (pro, con, and sideways) of dozens, hundreds, _thousands_ of people. _One_ person, no matter how much he or she _knows_, is not likely to be able to exert enough power to sway things.

On the other hand . . . an individual quite possibly _can_ change "small" events, with the assistance of foreknowledge. That is, events that affect only one, or a few people—because those are the sort of events that a single individual normally _does_ affect, with or without specialized knowledge. You probably _could_ keep someone—an ordinary person, whom another ordinary person could easily approach—from getting on a plane you knew would crash; if necessary, you could tackle them physically, or hit them over the head. <g>

You might not always succeed in changing small events—but I think you _could_; whereas an ordinary individual usually wouldn't be in a position where he or she would have the power necessary to change larger events.

That help any?

Fm: Beth Shope 110137,367
To: Diana Gabaldon 76530,523

Diana,
Re: changing history. I have often wondered if Jamie and Claire's efforts to prevent Culloden by ruining Bonnie Prince Charlie financially, did in actual fact ensure that it happened—because the Prince foolishly sailed for Scotland without the necessary resources (which they had so helpfully deprived him of). Beth

Fm: Diana Gabaldon 76530,523
To: Beth Shope 110137,367 (X)

Dear Beth—
Oh, indeed they might have—a thought that occurs to them later on, during heated discussions of time-changing in FIERY

CROSS. As it happens <g>, they didn't, but then, we haven't yet gotten to the revelation of what (and who) really happened to the 30,000 pounds of French gold, either. And one of these days, we might find out whose side the Duke of Sandringham was really on, too. (See above, "cumulative actions of _lots_ of people!" <g>)

One thing we've got going here is the contrast between "large" and "small" historical events. They _couldn't_ change Culloden, which was a large event (and the focus—in that particular plotline—of DRAGONFLY [middle book of the first trilogy]). In FIERY CROSS, the abiding time-change question through the book (middle book of the second trilogy) is a _personal_ question: Can Jamie and Claire avoid their own predicted fate?

They aren't about to try to change the outcome of the American Revolution—aside from the general impossibility of such a thing (there was no climactic battle—though I do have something in mind for Yorktown <g>), they don't have any objection to history continuing in its known pathway. But on a personal level?

Well, as Jamie says, "If ye ken the house is going to burn down, what sort of idiot would stand in it?"

Of course, the interesting thing about time travel, history-changing (or not-changing) etc., is the Moebius twist. <g>—Diana

Fm: Beth Shope 110137,367
To: Diana Gabaldon 76530,523

Diana,
<< And one of these days, we might find out whose side the Duke of Sandringham was really on, too. >>

One of the burning questions of this generation of readers . . . <g>.

<<Can Jamie and Claire avoid their own predicted fate?>>

Well, can they? No, don't answer that. . . . Beth

Fm: Barbara Schnell/SL 7 & 15 70007,6001
To: Diana Gabaldon 76530,523

Dear Diana,

I just started reading THE THIRTY-NINE STEPS this morning, and when Buchan defines his book as "the romance where the incidents defy the probabilities, and march just inside the borders of the possible" in its preface, he echoes very nicely what I thought when reading your excerpt last night.

I don't know how probable Claire's penicillin experiments are (but I do hope the medical experts will give you an all's-clear to let the scene stand), but once again you tie them very nicely with events and questions that are deeply rooted in a doctor's professional life—and, to make them ring even truer, in a mother's life.

That's what kept me reading the later parts of VOYAGER (and keeps me rereading it); that even though the plot sometimes made me think that now Robert Louis Stevenson had finally gotten the better of you <g>, there are always those deeply human elements in it that make this more than "just" entertainment. Same here, on a smaller scale: daring setting, but at the same time something for me to relate to. And to respond to, Kleenex and all <g>.

As you may notice, I've given in to curiosity and read the scene, and I don't think you've spoiled anything for me. So, if you still feel like it, I'd be more than happy if you shared whatever scenes you feel like showing to someone with me.

Thanks for posting this. Baerbel

Fm: Mira Brown 100425,170
To: Diana Gabaldon 76530,523

Hi Diana,

<< Can one change history? Well, yes and no (under the Gabaldon Theory of Time Travel, that is). One usually _can't_ change the outcome of any "large" event, simply because knowledge isn't the crucial factor. >>

Ah, yes, one can't stop the Jacobean uprising but one can tell friends to plant potatoes? I think I've grasped enough of the Gabaldon Theory of Time Travel *not* to expect you to put Mr. Fleming out of business. <g>

OK, I'll try and explain what I mean, but I probably won't do it very well: Even with the accepted perspective on the past and the future, it's fairly normal to have at best limited expectations of one's own impact and contribution. Now, Claire *knows* that penicillin doesn't come into use (other than use of mould in traditional medicine all over the world, I suppose) until WWII. How does, or doesn't it or even shouldn't that affect her "back to the future" view of events? I can understand her desire, even ability, to improve things in whatever small way she can, but somewhere in there must be more doubt than hope, more for her than people who live in their own time. This is where I get lost in all this "backward and forward" stuff.

<<If you _knew_ for an absolute fact that someone was going to assassinate President Clinton tomorrow—what would you do to prevent it? >> Do I have to answer this? <g> Mira

Fm: Eve Ackerman/Librarian 71702,3077
To: Diana Gabaldon 76530,523

Speaking of time travel . . .

I was thinking about your characters the other day. So far, we haven't seen any travel forward in time farther than where he/she would be in "normal" life. IOW, Claire returned to the twentieth century no later than where she would have been anyway, right?

So what does this mean to a baby born in the eighteenth century whose parents can return to their points of departure in the twentieth century? Would he not be traveling forward beyond his biological time?

But of course, being an author, you have godlike powers to do whatever you want. Within reason<g>. Eve Ackerman/Librarian

Fm: Marte Brengle 76703,4242
To: Diana Gabaldon 76530,523 (X)

I think in the event of assassinations and so forth, while one couldn't change the outcome, one *could* use foreknowledge to clear up various and sundry mysteries. Think if you could step through the stones and go back to November 1963 and focus a telephoto lens on that sixth-floor window in Dallas, for example. (And then scoot before the FBI grabbed the film.)

But as for changing small events . . . have you ever read that wonderful science fiction story where the time-traveler steps on the butterfly?—M—

Fm: Betty Babas 76336,113
To: Diana Gabaldon 76530,523

changing events . . .

So, for instance, doing something that assures Hitler dies in WWI wouldn't necessarily prevent WWII. Just that someone else would emerge to take his place?

OTOH, we could (for fictional purposes) alter something in history which, if we *hadn't* interfered, could result in the present being different than it is.

Fm: Diana Gabaldon 76530,523
To: Betty Babas 76336,113

Dear Betty—

Well, there's the rub; _some_ large events really are dependent on the personality of a specified individual—Bonnie Prince Charlie, for example. Eliminate _him_, and sure enough, that particular event (Culloden) probably won't happen (though something else _might_). Thing is—is our putative time-traveler capable of what amounts to cold-blooded murder, even for a larger cause? J & C weren't—and lived to regret it.

Hitler, I dunno. Chances are that_something_cataclysmic would have happened, given all the other circumstances, but it might have taken quite a different shape. Who knows? <g>

That's what makes time travel fun. <G>— Diana

Fm: Alan Smithee 110165,3374
To: Diana Gabaldon 76530,523

Hi, Diana!

You warned me, but I couldn't help reading the penicillin scene. I love the way you use words. It takes me right into the situation, making me feel the pain and sadness that seeing a patient, and a doctor, in this desperate plight always brings.

I think I may need to know more about your intentions and Claire's character to figure how to approach this. After reading the scene I'm unclear about what has caused Rosamund's death. In fact, were I in Claire's position, I don't think I'd conclude that the death could be blamed upon the penicillin—at least not solely upon the penicillin. Is this what you intended? If Claire is the sort of person who would be harder on herself than would her peers, a common tendency among many fine physicians, any mystery, even a slight doubt, about the cause would trouble her because of the unorthodox methods she'd employed.

This is certainly not my bailiwick, but I believe that a fatal drug reaction of this sort would probably occur rapidly, within minutes (possibly even seconds), of the initial injection, though, I suppose, in the patient's already compromised condition, a less catastrophic immune-involved reaction than anaphylaxis could still result in her death over a longer period of time. (I have the impression from the scene that Rosamund's death had required much more time than I would have anticipated.) High fever is not a symptom I'd expect of either anaphylaxis or pulmonary embolic phenomena. (Obviously, severe anaphylaxis would result in high fever were it not for the fact that, without modern forms of intervention, it would most likely result in the patient's immediate expiration.) If Rosamund is already suffering from hyperthermia before Claire gets to her, this obfuscates the cause of death by making it apparent that the sepsis was already advanced and systemic. If high fever occurs following treatment, it actually reduces the likelihood that the penicillin caused the death. High fever would make me think that the surgical treatment of the wound might have spilled an abscess into the patient's bloodstream, thereby leading to anaphylaxis or bacterial embolus or both. That type of accident is always a risk of this type of invasic intervention and is the reason why it would be normal to administer IV antibiotic _before_ attempting it. The risk of sudden systemic introduction of a large colony of pathogens would be greatly reduced by amputation above the affected area, the solution that Claire suggested when she first saw the patient. Before antibiotics, amputation of a gangrenous limb proximal to the infection was the only course with a reasonable expectation of success. (By the way, why does Claire agree to the pigeon poultice? I know that she's working in less-than-ideal social circumstances here, but this is a practice that she might have a really tough time accepting—you know, the "do no harm" thing. Not that a gangrenous wound is likely to become that much more badly infected, I suppose. But the mere mention of it made me flinch in revulsion.)

I would also note that a _single_ (massive) PE causes death by sudden occlusion of major pulmonary arterial supply, resulting in the dramatic onset of anoxia. A strong victim fights violently for a few moments, flailing and gasping desperately for air, before succumbing, a weak patient merely ceases to live. (The problem with pulmonary embolic phenomena is that, however well the patient can move air, it just doesn't do any good. The blood won't be oxygenated because pulmonary circulation has ceased due to the blockage. No heroic measures of any kind can save the victim from massive PE.) A less sudden death from pulmonary embolic phenomena results when there is a more gradual showering of many micro-emboli into the lung-bed capillaries, causing a more gradual reduction in pulmonary circulation. So you might want to refer to pulmonary emboli instead of pulmonary embolus if this is to be the possible cause of a death that doesn't occur suddenly.

Is any of this helpful? I hope I'm expressing my ideas clearly here, and that they may be constructive for you. Ellen and others may have more useful suggestions.

I'm sorry to hear about the migraine. One of my problems in recent months, too. Matter of fact, I had one yesterday—all day. It's a terrible thing when a man feels so bad he can't even whine!!! <bg>

Sincerely, and with best regards, Alan Smithee

Fm: Diana Gabaldon 76530,523
To: Alan Smithee 110165,3374 (X)

Dear Alan—

Thank you! Re your comments, let's see if I can disentangle enough to answer coherently. <g>

Okay. Rosamund is suffering from fever _before_ administration of penicillin (I'd figure anybody who'd had a major wound infection for three days would have some degree of fever, don't you?). So we can probably assume that the septicemia is systemic, thus providing a stronger motive for trying the experimental penicillin. Likewise, we can safely assume that the fever is not caused by the in-

jection. (Claire does write, "Patient presented with high fever . . ." right? Doesn't this mean the patient had a high fever when first seen?)

Rosamund does expire very quickly following the second injection—maybe ten to fifteen minutes? (given that Claire is trying various resuscitory [goodness, is that a word?] techniques, like cricothyrotomy). You (the reader) might not have much idea of the time frame from the original description—which is the result of Claire's caution in writing down a detailed description. If that seems a necessary piece of information, it would be easy to add a line regarding the timing.

If she's writing this purely as her own case notes, it wouldn't be necessary to record a lot of stuff—like the time between injection and expiration, or the failure of resuscitation—because she (Claire) would be unlikely either to forget those details, or to need them later.

On the other hand, if she's writing at least in part for the information of an unknown person who may have nothing to go on _save_ the case notes, she'd better put down every single thing she can, including things like a very detailed description of the anaphylaxis and the steps taken to combat it (ineffective though they might be); an illustrated account of how to perform a cricothyrotomy (with notes on the circumstances in which to employ this procedure); possible causes of complication (including pulmonary emboli, abscess-spilling, etc.), and so on.

However, she hasn't gotten to the point of deciding how much to put down; when the scene opens, she's still in the process of writing. (One thing to consider from a purely novelistic point of view is how much detail will lend that sense of reality to a reader, and how much is overkill <g>. Consequently, I started with the minimum, and let other details—like Rosamund's respiratory distress—

emerge less directly, during the course of Claire's introspection.)

Yes, OK; she should administer the first injection before doing the mechanical intervention—a good point.

Re the pigeon poultice; that's done mostly for the psychological benefit of the patient—that's what the patient is convinced will help. From the description, a thick layer of antibacterial dressing is applied to the wound (which is probably also bandaged—perhaps I should mention that step, too), and then the split pigeon bound over that. As described, the raw pigeon wouldn't actually be in physical contact with the open wound, and while it might be cumbersome, probably_ wouldn't_ do any actual harm.

Many thanks—your comments are _very_ helpful!—Diana

Fm: Alan Smithee 110165,3374
To: Diana Gabaldon 76530,523

Dear Diana,

Yes, I understood that Rosamund presented with high fever. I just wanted to explain that, to me, this sign made it seem less likely that her death was due primarily to anaphylaxis, particularly because death ensued some time later after the second injection. This sequence would make me suspicious that the drug had been ineffective, rather than that it had elicited a fatal reaction in the patient. Normally, to set up anaphylactic reaction with a drug, the patient would have to be exposed to it a week or more before the dose which precipitates

the reaction. I've been assuming that the patient has been sensitized to something besides the penicillin which is present in her environment _and_ in the drug (as an impurity). I believe this to be the most likely scenario for anaphylaxis, given the circumstances. What I'm trying to get at is that, if you wish to appear (medically) certain that the death is from anaphylactic shock, there has to be a sudden change in the patient's condition as soon as the penicillin is introduced. As stated before, the best time to administer the drug would be before invasive treatment of the wound. Given the nature of severe anaphylactic shock, I doubt that Claire would have the opportunity to do anything but life support following onset of the reaction.

With a longer time span, the idea that the penicillin engendered a fatal reaction in Rosamund becomes less supportable, I think, though not out of the question. That's what I was getting at. If you want there to be a question of cause, the scene's timing is good as is—with the exception that the first penicillin injection should have come before the wound care. I do think it's important for her to explain her reasoning in her notes, to justify her unorthodox choices. I don't know if it's necessary to be explicit. There might be an artful way to allude to it without shoveling medical concepts by the bucketload at the reader.

I think that the scene stands well as is, as long as you intend for there to be a question about cause of death. And the way you use the words really fixes the scene in my mind. I feel like I'm looking out through Claire's eyes part of the time, and I can feel the warmth of the communion with her daughter on my skin.

I'm having to fight my wife for OUTLANDER. Shouldn't have said anything about it until I had finished it. Ha!

Have a good one! Alan

Fm: Ellen Mandell 76764,2512
To: Diana Gabaldon 76530,523

Dear Diana,

Made me cry. More later. Ellen

Fm: Jo C. Harmon 103151,655
To: Diana Gabaldon 76530,523

Dear Diana,

I've read your excerpt from THE FIERY CROSS. I'm an RN who worked in the area of internal medicine for a few years. For me, what interrupted the flow of the narrative were the following questions:

Just how is Claire purifying and/or extracting the penicillin from rotted casaba rind?

Where is she getting needles to administer the medication IV?

(My guess is that you've addressed these issues earlier in the book.)

With the patient's manifestations of symptoms which could be indicative of hypersensitivity, why did Claire choose to administer the second dose of the drug . . . given that the state of the patient's illness was, for that time, most assuredly fatal?

Was she gambling that she could knock out the infection before hypersensitivity became life-threatening?

I know she's feeling guilty, but there are other possibilities as to why the patient developed these symptoms, aren't there? Do these other possibilities cross her mind at some point?

Hope this helps. <g>

Jo

Fm: Diana Gabaldon 76530,523
To: Jo C. Harmon 103151,655

Dear Jo—

Thanks! Re your questions:

1. Damned if I know. It ain't going to be _very_ purified, which is of course one of the difficulties with do-it-yourself penicillin. However, all the trouble in getting hold of enough of the stuff, and how, and whether it's effective—i.e., her experimental methods— is dealt with elsewhere. With luck, by the time I write that part, I'll have figured out how (sort of) to do it. _Penicillium_ does _grow_ on rotted melon rind, though, since one of my sources cited a picture of same.

2. Needles are no problem (unless I want them to be <g>)—she had six of them at the end of VOYAGER, and no doubt at least a couple have survived thus far (getting more is going to be one of the later issues to be dealt with; eighteenth century technology would have been adequate; it's just a matter of finding the proper craftsman <g>). Anyway, one of my earlier medical consultants informed me that to do a proper anaphylaxis, it would have to be an IV administration, because penicillin by mouth doesn't do that.

3. Given that the patient's illness was most assuredly fatal anyway—what did she have to lose by trying the penicillin? The urticaria, etc., might _not_ have been symptomatic of hypersensitivity; my earlier consultant tells me they could as easily be symptoms of the septicemia. Or, even if the patient did have a hypersensitivity, there would be at least a chance that a further dose would be survivable—while the infection wasn't.

4. Yes, the other possibilities cross her mind—in this scene, in fact—pulmonary embolism, for one. However—not being a doctor, etc., myself, I'm guessing on this one—I _think_ that a doctor with a good deal of clinical experience (which Claire is, by this time) and a reputation as a diagnostician

(which she has; established in earlier books) would have a very good gut feel for what was happening or had happened, even if he or she couldn't foresee it. I.e., having seen this woman die in front of her, Claire is pretty sure that it was anaphylaxis, even though the dry recital of symptoms might fit other diagnostic scenarios.

Sound plausible?—Diana

Fm: Jo C. Harmon 103151,655
To: Diana Gabaldon 76530,523

Diana:

<< she had six of them at the end of VOYAGER, and no doubt at least a couple have survived thus far >>

Oh. My memory fails me . . . I'd thought she'd lost all of them in the shipwreck. I don't recall her using or mentioning them in DRUMS . . . did she? (Guess I'd better go back and read it one more time—shucks.)

<<one of my earlier medical consultants informed me that to do a proper anaphylaxis, it would have to be an IV administration, because penicillin by mouth doesn't do that.>>

I certainly defer to those who likely have more knowledge and experience than I (and there are plenty); however, my mother had anaphylaxis after IM injection of penicillin. Fortunately, epinephrine was available and on hand. I suspect that the severeness of a reaction would also depend upon the degree of hypersensitivity. (But, I digress.)

As a reader with some medical background, I'd expect if Claire's patient developed anaphylaxis after IV push administration of penicillin, one of the most outstanding symptoms would be respiratory distress . . . in addition to the others that were mentioned.

<< Given that the patient's illness was most assuredly fatal anyway—what did she have to lose by trying the penicillin? >>

That's what I suspected.

<<—I _think_ that a doctor with a good deal of clinical experience (which Claire is, by this time) and a reputation as a diagnostician (which she has; established in earlier books) would have a very good gut feel for what was happening or had happened, even if he or she couldn't foresee it. >>

I agree. As in every part of life—that gut feel is usually truth.

<<having seen this woman die in front of her, Claire is pretty sure that it was anaphylaxis,>>

<<Sound plausible?>>

Yes, it does. I do feel, though, that the symptom of respiratory distress would be present . . . but, again, defer to those who have more knowledge than I.
Jo

Fm: Diana Gabaldon 76530,523
To: Jo C. Harmon 103151,655

Dear Jo—

Well, I thought she'd lost them in the shipwreck, too, but small matters like that are easily adjustable <g>. As long as I didn't flat out _say_ she lost them somewhere, I can always explain them _ex post facto_, one way or the other (ah, what it is to be a godlike Author!).

I'm sorry, I wasn't precise. My informant said it would need to be _injectable_, not necessarily IV. Just my guess that if you had what looked like a systemic septicemia, you'd do IV push.

Hm. You mean, you would expect respiratory distress following the _first_ administration of penicillin? Because Rosamund definitely had respiratory distress following the second. <g>

Do hypersensitive individuals normally show symptoms of allergy following a first exposure, though? I know very little about it, but had the impression that a first exposure might be symptomless, but—having had the effect of sensitizing the patient—the second exposure might have dramatic effects. Very easy to include respiratory distress following the first injection, if it should be there, of course.

Thanks for the help!—Diana

Fm: Jo C. Harmon 103151,655
To: Diana Gabaldon 76530,523

Dear Diana:

<< Do hypersensitive individuals normally show symptoms of allergy following a first exposure, though? I know very little about it, but had the impression that a first exposure might be symptomless, but—having had the effect of sensitizing the patient—the second exposure might have dramatic effects.>>

I think you're right about the probable lack of reaction to the first exposure, of course. Didn't think that one through before my fingers flew across the keys!

<<Blood chemicals are _very_ mysterious!>>

So true—don't know about you, but I have to avoid mushrooms, cheese, and wines or else I get a whopping migraine. (Can't eat too much chocolate, either.) Jo

Fm: Arlene McCrea 73051,2517
To: Diana Gabaldon 76530,523

Diana,

Thought your section PENICILLIN was terrific! Did, however, have something you might consider.

Since the funeral repast was being laid out in the same room as the corpse, I wondered how soon after death did this occur? If the corpse had such a virulent infection, I would think that without embalming, the odor of death would be pervasive.

I wanted to be certain about this before I wrote you, so I phoned my daughter Lisa (who has been a nurse for twenty years) and she agreed with me. Her comment was "You'd better put the corpse in the root cellar right away if you expect to eat in that room!" Even more so since she had the open wound! With the kind of a wound you described the odor would get bad very quickly!

Lisa said in reading the passage she would notice that right away!

Just trying to be helpful! <g>Arlene

Fm: Ellen Mandell 76764,2512
To: Diana Gabaldon 76530,523

Dear Diana,

Let's see, where should I begin? Penicillin, which is what Alex Fleming named the liquid secreted by his mold, isn't toxic. Neither is the mold. Fleming showed this by injecting his mold—full strength—into mice and rabbits without harm. Although large doses of penicillin may cause nausea or diarrhea, you (Claire, rather <g>) won't be able to kill your patient with an overdose.

The big problem in penicillin production was getting a high enough yield of the liquid—I read somewhere that adding brewer's yeast improved the yield—and the key step in purification was freeze-drying. Not much help, I'm afraid.

Certainly exposure to the molds can be sensitizing. I had a positive scratch test to the _Penicillium spp._ mixture, because I'm sensitized to one or more of the molds in the mixture. But if I inhaled raw _Penicillium_, without first snorting some Nasalcrom, I expect that I'd get a runny nose at worst, and I eat Roquefort and other blue cheeses with allergenic impunity.

Molds aren't on the list of substances—mostly proteins—that cause anaphylaxis. And while penicillin most definitely is, the manifestation of human drug allergies depends on the route of administration as well as genetic predisposition and the extent of prior exposure. So while Claire's patient could have an idiosyncratic reaction, I think the chance of allergic anaphylaxis is vanishingly small, unless the stuff was injected, and even then it's hardly likely.

In the big surveillance studies, the rate of anaphylactoid reactions to injected penicillins is less than 1 in 3,000, the vast majority being to semisynthetic penicillins, which are more allergenic than penicillin G. It's estimated there are fewer than 100 annual fatalities attributable to penicillin injections in the U.S., and none to oral penicillins.

Okay . . . Claire would know that toxicity wasn't a problem, so she'd want to get as much of her culture as possible into the patient. She'd know that oral dosing was useless <g>—stomach acid would destroy most of the drug's activity—but she'd have only a little worry about an allergic reaction. Knowing

she _had_ to inject the drug, she'd find a way. Perhaps with a clyster syringe and some sort of deep puncture? The husband would expect such standard therapy as bleeding and clysters, wouldn't he?

Oh yeah, mustn't forget—she might not be allowed to amputate, but she'd try to surgically drain the infected limb. Ellen

Fm: Mira Brown 100425,170
To: Diana Gabaldon 76530,523

Hi Diana,

Arlene is right, and so are you. <g> As I told you before, I've seen it in villages. The smell is pervasive and peculiar. People usually put a lot of, as you say, herbs, but mostly frequently changed fir/pine branches on the floor. As mourners tread on them they bruise the needles and release the smell. It helps, but not a great deal, not even on the first day.

I expect that's why some communities keep the windows open to "help the soul leave" or something like that. But elsewhere, the windows are shut and curtains closed and a lot of people faint, not strictly from emotion.
Mira

Fm: Diana Gabaldon 76530,523
To: Mira Brown 100425,170

Dear Mira—

A good thought, to add aromatic conifer branches on the floor. It wouldn't have been (I don't think) a Scottish custom, they not having a lot of conifers to hand in Scotland—

but there are certainly plenty in North Carolina (or were).—Diana

Fm: Diana Gabaldon 76530,523
To: Arlene McCrea 73051,2517

Dear Arlene—

A very good thought! <g> However, the woman died at dawn; it's now late afternoon of the same day, as Claire is writing up her notes (that should be clear when I add the [date] bits). The body will also have been washed and "laid out" (presumably with the addition of turpentine or vinegar, and aromatic herbs) in the meantime, most likely in Claire's surgery or out in the woodshed. Since it will have taken the men a little while to build the coffin, chances are the newly shrouded corpse was brought into the room only a little time before—and will be taken out by dawn of the next day, for burial after the wake.

Thanks!—Diana

PART SIX

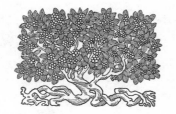

WHERE TITLES COME FROM

———

AND OTHER MATTERS
OF GENERAL INTEREST

The Shag

Honey Tree
and Fruit.

Outlander vs. Cross Stitch

ne of the questions asked most frequently—by people who have looked for my books in the U.K.—is, "Why does your first book have a different title over there?" That is, the book titled *Outlander* here in the States is titled *Cross Stitch* in the U.K. (and the Commonwealth countries, such as Australia and New Zealand).

Well, *Cross Stitch* was my working title for the manuscript. It's not a particularly *good* title; it's a weak play on "a stitch in time," with an (even weaker) reference to Claire's occupation as a healer (doctor-wound-stitch . . . that sort of thing), but it was my first book, after all.

I'd also thought—as the book grew, and I could see something of the shape of the story—that Claire would return to the present at the end of the book (which in fact she didn't do until the end of *Dragonfly*). If she had returned in the first book, though, that would have made the "cross"—crossing back to the past and then forth to the future, which gave me the mental shape of an "X"—which is, of course, the shape of a cross-stitch. And cross-stitch is made up of lots of little things that make an overall interesting pattern, and . . . well, look I *said* it wasn't a good title.

When we sold the book, the American publisher's (tactful) response was, "Well, we can't call it that, or people will think it's about embroidery. Can you think of something else, maybe a little more . . . adventurous?"

Then ensued some eight months of reciprocating title suggestions, ranging from the bland to the ridiculous (*Unicorns and Lions Wild* and *Tartan Temptation* being a couple that I recall—along with every variation ever heard on the word "time").

Along the way, I had suggested *Sassenach,* which I liked, but the general consensus was that this would not be a good title because no one could pronounce it. Coupled with the fact that no one could pronounce the author's name, either, this was thought to be too great a liability.

Thinking along these lines, though, I eventually came up with *Outlander*—which is, of course, what "Sassenach" means in Gaelic (though with a slightly more derogatory implication). This seemed quite suitable, given Claire's situation. Since the book was going to press at any moment, the publisher was enthusiastic.

The result of this was that when the book was published and I began doing signings, a certain number of people would pick up the book, frown at it, and then ask, "Is this the book that Sean Connery movie was based on?" (*Outland* was released in 1981; *Highlander* in 1986—both starring Sean Connery, and neither one having anything whatever to do with my book.)

So.

A year or so after we sold the book to Delacorte Press in the United States, we sold the U.K. rights to a British publisher, Century Random. The British editor said, "*Outlander*? But we can't call it that—to us, an outlander is specifically someone from Australia or South Africa! Do you have any other ideas?" I coughed modestly and said, well, the original title had been *Cross Stitch,* but . . .

"Perfect!" said the British editor, and *Cross Stitch* it was.

The result of this being that for some time, I got letters from readers in the U.K. saying, "You know, there's a funny story about how I found your book. I was browsing through the needlework section in the local bookstore, and . . ."

ROCK-POLISHING AND OTHER PASTIMES FOR AN IDLE HOUR

As for the titles of the other books in the series—well, I have no real standard operating procedure for coming up with titles. Thinking them up is always a good means of procrastination, when you can't think what to begin working on. The real process of titling, though, is essentially like rock-polishing; you drop vaguely interesting lumps of words into the machine, let them roll around banging into all the other stuff in there—and then you pull out a handful and see if they look pretty yet.

The working title for the second book was *Firebringer*. This was a reference to the Prometheus legend (the implication being

that Claire's advance knowledge of the future wasn't an unalloyed blessing, either), and—I thought—made a nice echo of the "er" in *Outlander* (well, look, I never said titles were my strong point, okay?).

Having heard a few doubts expressed as to whether most readers would make the connection with Prometheus (my American editor is a *very* tactful person), I also thought of calling the book *Pretender*. This would be a bit more straightforward—I mean, the book *did* deal with Bonnie Prince Charlie (a.k.a. the Young Pretender)—and would keep the "er" pattern. (See, I knew already that I wanted the third book to be called *Voyager*. That's the only book I've ever written that had an easy title.)

However, as I was working along, with the rock polisher whirring away in the background, someone asked me what had ever happened to the chunk of amber (with dragonfly embedded) that Hugh Munro gave Claire for a wedding present. Actually, I don't know what happened to it (though it's probably in Jenny's jewelry box, back at Lallybroch), but that question did recall the image to my mind.

Now, *Dragonfly in Amber* is a pretty good title, if you ask me. "Dragon" is one of those nice, evocative words that always catches people's attention (similar words being "blood," "moon," "blue," etc. I couldn't tell you *why* "a blue and bloody moon" is more evocative than "newspaper on a beige street," but it is). A dragonfly in amber is a visually arresting image, rather poetic in sound—and it actually had something to do with the book, insofar as notions of fate and inevitability, helplessness in the face of circumstance, references to antiquity, etc., are concerned. Besides, dragonflies are good luck.

The British publisher liked *Dragonfly in Amber,* too, so that was fine. True, I did get science fiction and fantasy fans asking me whether this was part of Roger Zelazny's famous *Amber* series, but nothing's perfect. And, as I say, I already knew the third book was titled *Voyager.*

To me, *Voyager* conjured up not only the superficial meanings of journey and adventure—and the very concrete reference to an ocean voyage—but something a bit more. Growing up in the sixties as I did, I was exposed to the U.S. program of space exploration in a big way, and found the whole notion unspeakably romantic. Of all the different missions, Voyager was one that particularly caught my imagination. This was commitment to the dark unknown, in the search for unimagined knowledge. Courage and daring, in the service of hope. Very suitable, I thought, for a book dealing with dangerous journeys in search of self and soul.

And then, along came the fourth book. The Colonies—New World, whiffs of revolution, lost daughters, gallant quests through time, Native Americans up the gazoo . . . *Next to the Last of the Mohicans? One If by Land, Sick If by Sea? There's a Wet Dog in My Wigwam?*

Well, hey, sometimes it's easier than others. And if all else fails—look back at what you did the last time you got stuck. So . . . sounds like . . . *Dragonfly in Amber.* (whirrrrrrr-clank, whirrrr-clank) Begins with "D." Okay, fine. (whirrrrr . . .) Three words? Awright, if they're short. (whirr . . .) With prepositional phrase? Hmmmm.

Evocative word beginning with "D," having (preferably) something to do with something in this book. Got Indians (in the eighteenth century they were still

called Indians). Got Redcoats. Both got drums. Oh-HO! "Drum" is an evocative word, too. "Drums" is even better. (Slaves used drums occasionally, too, but my husband said he would divorce me if I did any more voodoo scenes.)

Okay, *Drums.* Why *of Autumn?* Well, heck. I needed a prepositional phrase, the second word of which began with "A," and one could make a case that Claire and Jamie were entering the autumn phase of their lives (though it may be a long season, what with more books to go), and it *is* on the eve of the Revolution, i.e., the autumn of British rule in the Colonies, and . . . well, actually, I later decided that *Drums of Eden* would be better, but the publisher had already sent out thousands of catalogs calling it *Drums of Autumn,* and besides, I liked the look of all those "U"s and "M"s—aesthetically pleasing, you know.

Now, pause a moment and ask yourself: Would you rather read a really good book with a strange title, or a mediocre book with a straightforward title? (This is not a trick question; feel free to consult the *New York Times* Bestseller List before answering.) Yes, well, that's what I thought, too.

Okay. The fifth book is called *The Fiery Cross,* and I'm pretty set on that one, like I was with *Voyager.* Since I *am* set on it, I'll explain it.

In the distant past of the Scottish Highlands, it was the custom for a chieftain bent on war to make a cross of two sticks of wood, which he would set on fire. Two clansmen would then carry this cross through the glens and corries, as a signal to the men of the clan to fetch their weapons and come to the gathering place, prepared for battle. (Naturally the cross didn't *stay* on fire. Damp as the Scottish climate is, it probably went out within minutes of the clansmen stepping out into the downpour. However, the charred remains were still referred to as "the fiery cross.")

Now, given that at this point in the story, the American Revolution is looming on the horizon, and the Scottish Highlanders had quite a bit to do with it (though mostly fighting on the wrong side, as usual), this seemed a very good title to me. Warlike foreshadowing aside, the word "cross" implies "double-cross," which is always a good bet when you're dealing with people named MacKenzie, and then there's all the crisscrossing of storylines, too (by this point, there are enough of them to weave a basket). It also has those interesting Christ-like implications of betrayal and burning anguish, about which I will say no more because I haven't finished writing the book yet.

An electronic friend, apprised of this title, objected to it on grounds that it reminded her of the Ku Klux Klan, and she thought a nice book should have a better title.

"Interesting you should mention that," I said. "Er . . . where do you figure the KKK—many of whom just happened to be descendants of the original Scottish settlers in the American South—got the notion?" That *is* where they got it. However, I don't write nice books anyway, so I don't think there's a problem.

I have—for contractual and reference purposes—been calling the final book of the series *King, Farewell.* That title comes from a very moving Jacobite song, in which the singer bids farewell to the Stuart dynasty (and, by implication, all that went with it, like the Highland clans themselves). However, no one seems able to remember it, which is always a Bad Sign. People keep asking me when *Farewell to the King* (or worse, *Farewell to Arms*) will be released. Now, I do get the occasional letter praising my excellent novel *Butterfly in Amber,* or asking when *Drums of August* will be out in some foreign edition, but it's nothing like the confusion over *King, Farewell.*

I must therefore assume a) that *King, Farewell* is probably more memorable if set to music, but book publishing technology has not advanced that far yet, and b) the title of the final book should preferably be one word, to reduce the chances of people mangling it (of course, they call the first book *Highlander* all the time, and *Voyager* is commonly referred to as *Voyageur* [featuring that intrepid French trapper Jamie Frezeliere, and his wife, La Dame Blanche], but still . . .).

So I don't know the title of the last book will be, but as slowly as I write, I figure I've got time to come up with something (no, I don't know how many books there are).

Oh, this book? Well, that title wasn't mine. A longtime electronic friend named Marte Brengle suggested *The Outlandish Companion* many years ago, and I glommed on to it, not being one to pass up a good thing. (Since the U.K. publisher couldn't call the first book *Outlander,* of course they couldn't call this one *The Outlandish Companion.* Instead, it's called *Through the Stones: A Companion to the Novels of Diana Gabaldon.* Very imposing.)

FOREIGN EDITIONS, OR "AUTRES TEMPS, AUTRES MOEURS"

Sometime after the sale of *Outlander* to Delacorte Press, I was surprised to get a call from a pleasant-voiced person who informed me that he was my foreign-rights agent (I didn't know I had one), and that he was delighted to inform me that he had just sold the rights to my book to a Swedish publisher.

"You can *do* that?" I blurted. Evidently so. So far, various of the books have been sold to publishers in Sweden, France, Spain (and Latin America), Italy, Germany, Canada, the U.K., Russia, Korea, and Poland.[1]

While I had realized that naturally books could be published and sold in countries other than the United States, I *hadn't* realized that the author normally got paid for this. I also hadn't realized that there might be differences between the original of a book and a foreign edition—especially one written in the same language.

Sale of the first book to a British publisher led to a number of small changes and complications. At my request (since I'd never been to Scotland), the British publisher obligingly asked Reay Tannahill, a very well-known Scottish historian (and a fine historical novelist herself) to read the manuscript. Reay kindly sent me a

number of notes on small details of the manuscript (such as what colors one could reasonably expect to produce using vegetable dyes, the color of the prevailing granite in Argyllshire, and what Loch Ness really smells like), which were immensely appreciated. The U.S. version of the book had reached galley-proof stage by the time I received Reay's comments. However, I was able to incorporate almost all of them into the American version, with one exception.

Reay told me, "The war (World War II) didn't end as abruptly for us as it did for you in the United States. Rationing and wartime austerity were still in effect for some time after peace was declared—and there are still a number of people alive who remember that. Your story starts in 1945, but the conditions you're describing would be much more believable a year later; the book really should begin in 1946."

"Fine," I said, and called my American publisher.

"We can't do that," they said. "You can make the other changes, as long as they're small, but if you change the beginning date, that will change dates all through the book. We'd have to send the manuscript back through copy-editing, and we're too close to production to do that."

Consequently, *Outlander* begins in 1945, and *Cross Stitch* begins in 1946. This small dichotomy later led to a persistent error in *Dragonfly in Amber* (see "Errata"), which I have never quite figured out how to clear up, other than to explain its existence.

---

[1] *See Appendix VI for a list of foreign editions and publishers.*

ing that this was perhaps slightly too graphic for their intended audience. I was not quite sure why *that* particular scene struck her as more graphic than a number of others in the book, but it was not—as most of the others were—integral to the plot or thematically connected to other parts of the book. Removing it would do no damage to the book as a whole, so I agreed to cut it out.[2,3]

Beyond such minor cosmetic differences, though, the U.S. and U.K. editions are the same, and the texts of the U.S. and U.K. editions of all the other books are completely identical, as the U.K. publisher now prints directly from the U.S. text.

While the books from *Dragonfly* to *Drums* are mostly identical in terms of text between the U.K. and U.S. editions (naturally, the covers are quite different), there are a few small differences between *Outlander* and *Cross Stitch,* beyond the title and dating.

The Americans' response to the book was, "Once she has Jamie, why would Claire even *think* of going back to Frank?" whereas the English editor's response was, "But what about her nice husband back in 1946?!" The British editor felt that Claire didn't spend quite enough time worrying about poor Frank, and might be perceived as coldhearted. Consequently, there are six additional paragraphs scattered through *Cross Stitch* (that aren't in *Outlander*) in which Claire worries about Frank.

Beyond small copy-editing changes, I did alter a bit of geographical description that was incorrect; the sort of readers who go through novels with a map in hand will have noticed (in *Outlander*) that I had Fort William misplaced by a number of miles, and that it is not really feasible to end up in Inverness while on the way to Oxfordshire, no matter how you mean to travel.

The British editor also asked me to excise the brief scene that concludes the chapter titled "Raiders in the Rocks," feel-

---

[2] *There was one other small change; an alteration of one line in a later scene, so that—as the English editor put it—"it looks like they're having **normal** sex."*
[3] *What with one thing and another, I was never sent the galley-proofs for* **Cross Stitch** *(normally, this is the last chance an author has to check for errors, specify small inclusions, or alter the text in any way). I was therefore shocked and dismayed, upon receiving the printed book, to find that the editor had replaced terms such as **skein dhu** with "sock knife," and that someone had—for reasons unknown—massacred the small comic "hedgehog" scene in Chapter 23.*

THE CANNIBAL'S ART

WRITING AND REAL LIFE[1]

I get quite a number of letters and messages from people who are either working at writing or thinking of writing, all asking (in varying tones of desperation) exactly *how* one gets any writing done if one has a family, a job, and/or any pretensions to Real Life?

Well, it's not easy. (Oh, you knew that part already. Well, wait; it gets more interesting as we go on.)

The major difficulty regarding one's family is that until you have sold something you've written, you are not—so far as anyone you know is concerned—a "real" writer. In fact, your family is most likely to regard your writing activities either as subversive in the extreme ("You aren't writing about *me,* are you?!?") or simply as "wasting time" (which might better be spent on them, they think).

Once you *do* sell something, your efforts will get a little more respect (not much, but more). The fact that you are doing exactly the same thing, whether you sell what you write or not, is irrelevant. Money equals respect—and if you aren't writing with the intention of selling your work, what the heck are you wasting your time for? (So they think. Actually, they'll

say it out loud, at least until you start yelling and throwing things.)

This means that until you do sell something, you will have to fight for every second at your keyboard (I've personally found screaming and kicking wastebaskets to be fairly effective in the short term).

After a few months of this kind of struggle, though, it finally occurred to me that the major reason one's family behaves this way is that they are *threatened* by your writing (the writing, of course, is threatened by them, but that's another consideration). Therefore, if you can find a way of assuring your family of your undying affection, they will be much more tolerant of your idiosyncratic hobby.

For example, you can't really blame a husband for disgruntlement if his wife rises from the dinner table, announces that she is going to write, and decamps, leaving him alone with the children and *America's Funniest Home Videos,* not to be seen again until breakfast the next morning. Likewise, children know darn well when they are being abandoned—and will take preventive action, like demanding snacks every ten minutes, staging fistfights with

---

[1]*Originally appeared in Part Eleven in earlier printings.*

their siblings, and grabbing you by the ankle as you try to leave the room.

Much better if the would-be writer watches *AFHV with* the family, reads the kids stories, and tucks them in bed, then retires to the bedroom for a spot of marital R&R. *Then* the writer can rise, tiptoe upstairs, and work without hearing a word of complaint from the family, who are all peacefully asleep, secure in the reassurance of her devotion. Of course, this means the writer doesn't get much sleep, but one has to decide what's important in life.

I do have a short, snappy answer for the question "How do you write with a family, job, etc.,"—said answer being, "I don't sleep, and I don't do housework."

I learned how not to sleep when I had three children in four years (on purpose, no less. It's not as bad as it sounds; they're spaced two years apart); a talent that's stood me in good stead in the years since. While it *is* possible to write while all around you are losing their heads (to say nothing of their car keys, their lunch bags, their homework, and a couple of fire-bellied toads) and blaming it on you, solitude is a really nice thing for a writer to have a little of—worth going short on sleep.

You will likely have to stay up late or get up early (most people can't do both), but even half an hour of listening to nothing but your own thoughts is worthwhile. Once you have a foothold on the day's work, it becomes easier both to keep thinking about the work while going about your daily business, and to return quickly to said work, whenever a moment's opportunity occurs. You won't have a lot of time to write, at least in the beginning; you don't want to waste any of it by sitting there, wondering where to start.

Of course, there's a physical limit to how much sleep you can do without and still write coherently. Catnapping isn't an altogether satisfactory substitute for eight hours of the dreamless, but it's a lot better than nothing. You will quickly learn how to do this, within about forty-eight hours of commencing the stay-up-late or get-up-early strategy. I used to lie down on the floor of my university office and sleep while waiting for phone calls to be returned (I often wonder what I said to the people who called back).

If you can't manage to do without sleep in any appreciable quantity, you'll have to eliminate some other activity in order to use that time writing. In the interests of Preserving the Sanctity of Family Life, I don't recommend eliminating dinner, bedtime stories, or sex. However, I am unaware of any studies linking frequency of vacuuming to frequency of divorce, and while all things are possible, I don't *think* your children will come back as adults and sue you because they've suddenly discovered repressed memories of you not cleaning the refrigerator.

Hire someone to clean the house, or get used to dirt. I do both. A nice person with much higher standards than mine comes and cleans the house three times a week, and the rest of the time, it is a Big Mess.

(There is a third alternative—force your spouse and/or children to do housework. This strategy is effective in the long run, but, at least in the beginning, will eat up a lot more time than it saves.)

Still, no matter what strategies you adopt, Real Life tends to intrude. When it does, the only thing you can do is to shuffle the writing to the back of your mind—but keep thinking about it.

As example and encouragement, following is a letter to friends, written in late 1995, while I was struggling to complete *Drums of Autumn,* and illustrating How a Writer Deals with Real Life. (Bear in mind that I *did* eventually finish the book. The moral is: Don't Give Up!)

Research & Craft
15-Dec-95 12:01:46
Sb: #Making Time to Write
Fm: Diana Gabaldon/SL8 76530,523
To: Alex Keegan 100555,1651 (X)

Dear Alex—

Oh, yes—about being first thing a writer and having it always going in your head. Gets you past the days when Life interferes.

Yesterday was One of THOSE Days, beginning with angst and trauma in the morning, when the little one couldn't find her violin and the middle one was so conked, his father couldn't rouse him and had to call for assistance (I have a secret method; I toss back the covers and get him by the feet, then play This Little Piggy on his toes. This aggravates him enough to get him upright and snarling, at which point he can be levered out of bed and into his closet), and the big one wasn't happy with the way her hair looked.

Having gone down at 3 A.M. the night before, getting up at 7:15 left me a hair short, even on my usual rations of sleep. I also ached in every limb, having fallen off the stair-

case the day before (don't ask; it had to do with the fax machine and the fact that I'd been writing. I was still writing in my mind when I came down to retrieve an incoming fax, and—apparently—reached for it while still on the stairs, not aware that I couldn't levitate. Actually, I apparently *did* levitate for a short distance, as I ended up on knee and elbow some six feet from the foot of the staircase).

I rallied round, though—found the violin (by the simple expedient—which drives everyone in my family completely mad—of asking "Where did you see it last?"), combed the big one's hair into a ponytail (had to make her sit down on the edge of the bath to do it; she's four inches taller than I am), tied the middle one's shoes, and ran upstairs to write notes to two of his teachers (he had the flu, on and off, and missed six days of school, with consequent assignments. Problem is, he's too shy to go up and ask any of his teachers for a list of what's missing).

The boys from next-door-but-one came and knocked—they'd missed their bus, could I take them to school? Loaded up everybody, picked up my purse to get in the car, when the housekeeper beetled out and said we're out of X, Y, Z, especially washing powder.

Dropped the kids—adjuring Sam sternly to be sure to deliver notes to his teachers—went to the drugstore, where I got all the cleaning supplies and checked for the homeopathic flu cure JLM recommended (felt a sore throat coming on). While driving to and fro, kept thinking of snow (no good reason, it's about 85 degrees here). Went home, delivered the window cleaner, washing powder, et al, came upstairs and spent my usual hour having breakfast (diet Coke and Milky Way Dark) and reading/answering messages and e-mail, seeing in the back of my mind footprints dark on the snow, and heaped wet leaves, crusted with ice, the dark furrow in the leaves where someone had been lying, under the shelter of a log.

Set in to work as usual at 10, stoked to the gills with vitamin C and occilococcinum. Read through a half-done scene in progress, added a couple of paragraphs, then was overcome by a new, vivid image—I was following the footprints in the snow, and there was a dead hare, caught in a snare, furred with ice crystals, stiff across the path. Switched screens and started the new scene, to get it under way. Fell into the state of mind in which I walked off the staircase, feeling the worry of the woman following the footprints. Why didn't he stop for the hare? Where is he?

Settled nicely into the first paragraph, when comes the dreaded summons from the foot of my stairs, "*Es un hombre a la puerta!*"

Hombres at the puerta are always an intrusion, but usually brief, as in FedEx or UPS, or now and then the exterminator or the man from the feed store delivering horse pellets (this is a *large* nuisance, as I have to go collect all the dogs and shut them in the garage, then go round and open the big gates into the backyard for the truck to come through).

This time it was an hombre from the phone company, come to fix the fax machine's line (cf. staircase, above). Showed him the miscreant fax, helped him track the phone line—which had been installed by one of my husband's programmer employees back when he had his office in that room— then left him to it.

Reminded of phones, checked for messages (only one phone in the house rings, for reasons I won't go into; this means I normally don't hear it from my office—a Good Thing, on the whole—so I'm in the habit of checking the voice mail once every hour or so). Message from my father, wanting to know when girls are off school so my stepmother (bless her heart) can take them to have their hair cut. Message from person wanting to sell my house for me (ignore). Message from person wanting to come and demonstrate antiburglary system (ignore. Inside dogs have finally quit barking at phone person, but he's gone outside, and outside dogs are now having hysterics. There's a reason we've never had burglars, aside from the fact that we haven't got a lot of stuff anyone would think worth stealing, unless you count SuperNintendo. If anyone wants to come steal my ancient XT clone, they're welcome to it; it's insured). Message from librarian in Salt Lake City, wanting to confirm that I am coming to speak at a conference in Snowbird at end of May, and can I do the dinner speech too, they'll pay me extra.

Minor panic. *Did* I agree to go and talk to people in Utah in May? Rustle through tray of speaking/workshop engagements. Evidently I agreed conditionally (hint: never throw anything away, and when you talk to people on the phone, write down on their letter what it is you told them), provided I didn't have to go to ABA. Think suddenly that I don't *know* whether I have to go to ABA; *Drums* may be out late enough that they're featuring it there.

Telephone editor, who is out, but get her assistant, who promises to find out for me about ABA. Return to work, get as far as lyrical description of shadows lengthening under the trees, turning from vanilla to chilly violet and then cold blue on the snow as the sun goes down. Get up to open balcony door, as it's getting rather warm in office. Phone hombre comes inside to ask where main phone line panel is. Luckily I know this (from earlier phone adventures in this house) and go show him.

Go upstairs. Come downstairs at once, as Airborne Express hombre has arrived with parcel to be signed for. This proves to contain a dust jacket proof for *Drums of Autumn,* causing mingled interest and panic (said book being in a state of severe incompletion upstairs). Set proof on kitchen table and stare at it for a while in attempt to decide whether I like it or not, while feeding bloodworms to fish and newts who live on table. Put fresh seed and water in parakeets' cups (if the dogs don't announce a burglar, the four birds will, noisy things).

Leave cover proof to marinate in my subconscious and go upstairs. Finish sentence about shadows, start worrying about the man out hunting, why hasn't he come back? Is he walking his trapline? Go look at book on animal tracks, find out what hare tracks look like in snow. Take passing note of ferret tracks, various bird prints. Check Roger Tory Peterson field guide (pausing to wonder whether constant exposure to this in my field-work days is where I got the name "Roger." Hope not, as I've met RTP, who at the time was rather a pompous old geek. Now he's dead, RIP) to be sure that kind of bird would be in North Carolina in winter.

Federal Express hombre arrives, bearing mysterious box labeled "Norm's Gourmet Mushroom Garden." Unable to put this aside, open it to discover that my sister has sent me . . . a mushroom garden. For

Christmas. Roughly a foot-square chunk of rot oozing brown liquid inside a plastic bag. I am assured (by the enclosed directions) that if I remove the plastic, spray this object with water, set it in a pan of same atop a chunk of wood, and leave it in a quiet, cool place, where it gets roughly 6–8 hours a day of diffuse light, it will sprout shiitake mushrooms (what I am to do with these, once sprouted, the instructions do not reveal).

Put mushroom garden on downstairs desk, where I will not forget it (next to large pile of bookplates waiting to be signed, which I will make every effort to forget, but the secretary's coming round Monday to make sure I don't), and go upstairs, feeling pleased that I have already ordered an Archie McPhee potato gun for my sister for Christmas.

Sit down and reread the six sentences I have onscreen, sinking back into scene. How long will I/she wait before setting out to look for the missing man? It's dark outside, it's getting colder. She's stoked up the fire, but her hands are still cold. Dinner is cooking, but she doesn't feel hungry, and the scent of food doesn't comfort her. If he's had an accident . . . Phone rings and I hear it, for a wonder. Editorial assistant, informing me that they don't know yet whether I should go to ABA, but they've changed the date and it isn't till mid-June, so I can go to Utah if I want.

Meanwhile, husband arrives downstairs, complaining of acute pain in foot, asking a) did I remember to buy him wart remover, and b) do I want to go and eat a hot dog with him? Answer yes to both, and go to eat Polish sausages with sauerkraut and mustard, while discussing whether I should go to Utah in May. Upon finding out that they're offering me $1,000 to come and talk to them, husband agrees that I should, and remarks casually that he has always wanted to build a kit plane.

Return (in car, I find myself crouched behind a screen of rocks and twigs. There are Indians I don't recognize, passing in single file through the wood a few feet away. Their faces are painted, and they're moving in the direction of the house I just left) to find that another Federal Express hombre has come by, but missed the housekeeper, and instead left a delivery notice on the door. Go upstairs, quickly download and skim messages, then sit, list in hand, and try to organize rest of day. Phone rings; in-laws inviting us to come over for dessert after supper. Phone rings; woman in Alabama wanting to get hold of autographed copy

of *Drums* for Christmas present for sister. Explain politely that it isn't finished yet, suppressing various uncharitable remarks that come to mind when she exclaims, "but why NOT?"

Little one comes home from school. Have five minutes to make her a snack, listen to her report of her day, and sympathize with her teeth (she needs orthodontia, and we've just had the first spacers put in yesterday), then go to collect the older kids from their school.

Discover that son hasn't given teachers their notes. Grasp him metaphorically by ear and drag him off to beard teachers in their dens. Extract lists of missing assignments from two, but find third one has already left for day.

Decant everyone at home, distribute food and drink all round, load up little one, who wants to come with me, and set off for afternoon errands—feed store to buy nose bag and two hundredweight of oats for elderly horse who isn't getting his share of the pellets, Alphagraphics for new shipment of bookplates, and grocery store because we are out of necessities like milk and tuna fish, and because little one is holding a Christmas party next day, at which she and six friends intend to decorate cookies, among other things.

Return home, having discovered in the car that the Indians are indeed sinister, being Mohawk far from their home range, raiding for purposes unknown (has this got anything to do with Father Alexandre, the Jesuit missionary, whose flesh is weak, and whom we'll meet a good deal further on?). Cook dinner, slug down more homeopathic flu remedy and vitamin C, go off to dessert at in-laws.

Return (she's found him, denned up in a cavity under a pile of brush. The Mohawk are being stealthily followed by a small band of Tuscarora Indians that they *do* recognize). Superintend massive homework while baking ten dozen sugar cookies ("You know," remarks my little one, who is [ha-ha] "helping" me bake cookies, "I feel kind of bad." "Your teeth still hurt?" I ask. "No," she says, "but I was just thinking, I'll be in bed in a little while, and you'll still be baking cookies. I feel kind of guilty about that." While feeling gratified at this evidence of developing conscience, I assure her that that's perfectly all right, I *like* baking [I do, but], and dash upstairs to find Sam a black marker with which to prepare visual aids for a presentation on current events).

Oldest daughter comes out to ask whether I can type her constitution for the nation she is designing in school, as she is a very slow typist and overwhelmed with work tonight. Assure her that I can, and take document up to park by computer, where I will not forget it.

Tuck people in bed. Take more anti-flu stuff while listening to husband tell me how exhausted he is. Tuck him in bed, eat a bowl of rice and leftover Chinese beef from dinner, drink more Diet Coke, and go upstairs to work at midnight.

Answer a few messages, play one game of solitaire, discover I am falling asleep, lie down on floor, and nap for an hour. Wake up, but can't stay awake—get a sentence or two down but discover it doesn't make sense. Decide flesh and blood has limits, and stagger downstairs to lock up, check kids and animals, turn off lights, feed rabbits and hamsters, etc. Heading for bedroom when I realize I have not typed Laura's constitution,

which she urgently requires for class next morning.

Unlock office, go upstairs . . . came down again at 2:30, took more vitamin C, and passed out. Net result, writing-wise, being that I have maybe 300 words actually *written,* which would be discouraging (and is) in view of my 2,000-word goal, but I *do* know a heck of a lot more about what's going on than I did in the morning, and in fact, I didn't stop writing all day. And maybe tomorrow I'll post the scene itself.

So I'll get there, eventually. If I don't die first.

—Diana

Book Touring
for Beginners

Interviewers often ask me whether (and how) being a successful author has changed my life. Readers ask me (incessantly) whether/when I will be "touring"[1] in places from Ypsilanti to Timbuktu. Answer being that, yes indeedy, being an author has changed my life in many ways—but book touring is a major and noticeable one. Next time you have a long weekend free, you might want to test it out, just for fun. Try this:

Set your alarm for 4:30 A.M. Don't bother actually packing a bag for this, but have a cab come pick you up and take you to the airport. You don't need to book a flight, so you don't have to go through security, but find a place and sit there for two hours while people surge around you and step on your feet and shout loudly into their cell phones while sitting next to you. Then go and lock yourself in a cubicle in the restroom for three hours—you can take a book and a snack—to simulate flight (business class, no less—consider the seat room!). Go home. Your day as a professional author on tour has just begun!

Now, the next phase will require the assistance of a family member—two or three is best, but just a husband, flatmate, or partner will do, if that's all you have in-house.

His/their job is to take a prepared list of questions ("What did you fix for dinner last night?" "Why did you fix that instead of hot dogs?" "What's your favorite brand of toilet paper?" "Why do you prefer *that* brand?" "How many children do you have?" "Which child is your favorite?" "Why?" "How long have you been married?" "How much did you spend on grocery shopping last week?" "Describe your daily routine") and ask you them. You have to answer every question, every time, and you have to smile while doing so. Witty answers are preferred but not required.

Have a family member repeat this process every half hour for, oh . . . three hours, say. (You can vary it by having them call you on a cell phone instead of doing it in person, though in this case you should shut yourself in the laundry room with the washing machine going, in order to simu-

---

[1] *Many people don't realize that a book tour is a specific event, a movement of the author from city to city (to city, to city . . .) over a period of days or weeks for the specific purpose of publicizing a new book—i.e., you don't just "tour" incessantly. An author can—and usually does—make other appearances, but these are normally single events (lectures/readings, conferences, etc.), arranged by an entity like a library foundation, convention organizer, etc. These can happen anytime but are almost always one-offs.*

late doing interviews in a car driving through traffic. If doing the cell-phone variant, you technically needn't smile, but you should—it shows in your voice.)

Then get in your car and drive around the city for two or three hours. If you live in a large city, you can go to actual bookstores—otherwise, just simulate it by driving to random spots. If you do go to bookstores, go in and ask the clerk if they have *X* (any newly released book by a popular author). When they show you a table piled with copies of said book, thank them, then stand there and pick up each book, open it to the title page, pause for ten seconds (that's about how long it takes to sign one, if you're being legible about it), close the book, and put it back. Drive to the next store and repeat. (It's okay; bookstore personnel are used to nuts. They won't call the police unless you start yelling or throwing things.)

Now it's nearly evening—time to get ready for the evening event. Go home and—no, of course you aren't going to have dinner, what's wrong with you, didn't you eat on the plane?—change into your fanciest clothes, comb (if not style) your hair, and put on full makeup. Go to a public sports event (this being the nearest thing I can think of that supplies the necessary sense of an enthusiastic crowd, plus random applause) and stand in some place where you will not be trampled; there you read aloud the Gettysburg Address, the Declaration of Arbroath, the first two chapters of *Pride and Prejudice,* or any other stirring document that strikes your fancy, as long as it takes about thirty minutes. (If you have a cooperative friend, bring him or her along and have them shout questions at you for another fifteen minutes. This is optional, though.)

Now go home and get an old phone book. (No, you can't change or have dinner yet, you're *working*!) Write your name once or twice on each page—a minimum of three hundred times, but up to a thousand if your fingers are up to it and you live in a large city. A family member will stand in front of you with a cell-phone camera and take your picture as you turn each page; you naturally have to look up and smile broadly as they read randomly from the following list ("Oh, darn, my battery's dead!" "Crap, how does this thing work?" "I have no idea how this works." "Wait, wait, wait . . . no, wait . . ." "Did it go?" "Here, you come do this!" "What's the matter with this thing?" "Did it flash?" "How do you 'save' on this thing?") before returning to your signing.

This is a "signature-only" signing; we needn't bother with doing people's names and inscriptions. ("It's spelled G-E-A-N-N-E-E. And can you put, *To my biggest fan—Jamie likes you best! He says you're better than Claire in the sack!*")

Now you're done! It's midnight. You can get into your pajamas, relax, turn on the TV, get something to eat.[2] But don't forget to set your alarm. Remember, you have to be up at 4:30 A.M. to do it all again!

Try this for three days—same schedule

---

[2] *If the hotel they've booked you into happens to have 24-hour room service, that is. If they don't . . . Well, I normally travel with cheese, cashew nuts, teriyaki beef jerky, and a little chocolate in my bag. I eat that 2–3 nights on a normal tour, owing to late arrivals (if you get to your hotel before the event, you can at least order something and have room service park it in your room while you're gone) and non-late room service.*

every day—and see whether you lose your mind or your temper first. Multiply that by ten and then decide if you would *really* like to be a successful author.

The basic situation here is that there are umpty-million people who read and like my books, and I thank God for you all. But there's only one of me. Finding a way for me to interact in even a semi-personal manner with even a fraction of my readers is . . . difficult. Couldn't manage it at all if it weren't for the Internet. But there's still that desire for face-to-face contact—and I do in fact love to talk to readers. I enjoy their company, I enjoy their opinions (even when wrong-headed and perverse), I enjoy entertaining them. But that personal interaction is a small percentage of the actual time spent in promotion—and the sheer physical logistics of getting to a place where those interactions can occur are staggering.

One question that I'm often asked during appearances is, "When is the next book coming out?" (Or, occasionally, with impatience, "Why isn't the next book out yet?") To which the answer (spoken with varying degrees of cordiality, depending how far into a book tour we are at the moment) is, "Well, you have a choice. You can have the next book sooner—or you can look at me and have me sign your book. [Pause.] Are you looking at me?"

Now, I am not basically a nice person. I *am* snide, arrogant, and short-tempered. I try to overcome these things, and sometimes it works and sometimes it doesn't.

I do love all of you, and am deeply pleased and very grateful that you enjoy the books. But I'd ask you in return to do me the kindness of taking me as a human being and not a goddess with an inexhaustible nuclear power source.

A Brief Disquisition on the Existence of Butt Cooties

(Gentlemen, kindly avert your eyes)

Having lived to my present advanced age, and spent a great deal of time traveling, I've also spent a lot of time in public restrooms. And, having been a scientist in my previous professional incarnation, I can't help observing things and drawing statistical inferences. Which is why I am in a position to inform you that roughly half the female population of the United States suffers from the twin delusions that 1) butt cooties exist, and 2) they will, given half a chance, leap several inches from a toilet seat and burrow into the skin of an unsuspecting buttock, resulting in scrofula, assorted STDs, herpes, and probably leprosy.

I draw these conclusions from the fact that roughly half the time I enter a public-restroom cubicle, I observe that the previous user has peed on the seat. Ladies . . .

I can only guess that at some point in an impressionable youth, these women were told by some female authority figure that One Must Never Sit on a Public Toilet, "because you might catch something." Firmly indoc-trinated with this policy, they do not sit on public toilets. They hover. Ladies, ladies . . .

Look. The skin of the buttocks is actually pretty germ-free, owing to the fact that we normally keep them covered and don't (usually) touch other people, animals, etc., with them. Your butt is much cleaner—microbially speaking—than are your hands.

Various studies of the bacterial content of public restrooms indicate that there are a lot more germs on the door of said restroom than there are on any toilet seat therein. You acquire millions more microbes by shaking hands with someone than you would if our social system involved mutual butt-rubbing. (To say nothing of the teeming worlds of microorganisms you acquire every time you accept change from the counter guy at Burger King. How many of you race to the bathroom and scrub your hands after ordering the meal but before eating it?)

In order actually to catch one of the communicable diseases with which excrement or other bodily fluids are associated, two things would have to occur: 1) the bodily fluid of an infected person would have to be applied to the toilet seat (which would

not happen, if said person would sit her bottom on the potty where it belongs and not spray the thing like a hippopotamus), and 2) an uninfected person's mucous membranes would have to come in contact with said fluids, within the few seconds that most bacteria and virii can survive outside the human body. You don't have mucous membranes on your buttocks.

Now, by and large, urine really doesn't contain all that many bacteria. (Male urine contains almost none, owing to the fact that its exit is, um, less impeded by surrounding tissue. A good many alchemical and medical recipes up through the early nineteenth century require "urine of a newborn male child" as an ingredient—this being the most sterile water available.) Feces . . . well, yes. And I have in fact encountered the Really Nasty evidence that there are not only seat pee-ers but also seat poopers (to say nothing of the occasional person who is so afraid of physically encountering a public toilet that they actually don't hit it at all and leave the evidence of their mental derangement on the floor of the facility), but this is fortunately rare. All right. In periods of heavy traffic, one might possibly encounter a live bacterium or virus present in the urine that some inconsiderate idiot has left on a toilet seat. Not likely, but faintly possible. Are you going to encounter it with your mucous membranes? Not unless your excretory habits are both Highly Athletic and Dang Unusual.

Okay. So if the risk of catching a bacterial or viral disease by sitting on a dry toilet seat is negligible, then plainly the Thing to Fear must be . . . butt cooties!

Traveling as much as I do, I am in a position to collect international data, albeit in an anecdotal and unstandardized manner. On the basis of such casual observation, though, I hypothesize that while butt cooties presently have a fairly wide global distribution, they probably originated in the United States. Speaking generally, at least 50 percent of all public toilets in U.S. airports, convenience stores, museums, and restaurants indicate evidence of infestation (judging from the aversive techniques employed by the patrons). European toilets have a much lower incidence—perhaps 10 to 15 percent.

(Point of etiquette: ought one to meet the eyes of, and/or nod to, a person emerging from a toilet cubicle

that one proposes to enter? Common politeness would argue for such cordial acknowledgment—but if the next few seconds reveal that the departing patron was possessed of butt cooties, this might lead one to think harsh and un-Christian thoughts of said person, and surely it's worse to think un-Christian thoughts [WWJD? I'm pretty sure He wouldn't pee on a public toilet seat, and if He did, He would certainly wipe it off. Ditto the Buddha and doubtless any other religious figure you care to name] about someone whose face is imprinted in your short-term memory than about an unknown quantity.)

In fact, we might hypothesize the geographical origin of butt cooties as having occurred in or near Chicago. On what basis? Well, of all the airports I've been in (and I've been in a lot of airports, from New Zealand to Saskatchewan), only O'Hare International has public toilets equipped with a sliding cylinder of plastic sheeting that encases the seats; you wave your hand in front of a magic button and, voilà, the plastic slides round the seat, and you are presented with a pristine surface on which to park your booty. Such is the prevailing fear of butt cooties, though, that people pee on these toilet seats, too.

Well, there's no arguing with psychological aberration, and thus I make no attempt to persuade Those Who See Butt Cooties away from their convictions. I would, though, urge them—in the most kindly manner—to address the results of their antisocial psychosis, and thus leave them with this classic advice:

*"If you sprinkle when you tinkle—
Please be neat, and wipe the seat."*

THE SHAPE OF THINGS[1]

Writing books is kind of an unusual thing to do. Everybody understands pretty much what it is that an attorney, say (my sister's an attorney), does, or a zookeeper, or even a politician, and how they do it. But most people don't know any novelists personally, and so there's a certain amount of curiosity as to just how the heck you get the contents of your head onto paper—let alone do it in such a way that anybody wants to read the results.

There's not any really *good* way of describing this. You're kind of caught between the purely physical (well, first I type a word. Then I type another one . . . then I get up and wander around my office for a while. Then I go back and delete a word. . . .) and the grandiloquently metaphorical. So let me start with the godlike Act of Creation metaphor:

When you begin, there's nothing but a trackless sea before you, stretching to the horizon. But wait! Out in the distance, an undersea volcano begins to spray smoke and cinders! Then another—and another!

As the lava rolls down the sides of the volcanoes, hissing into the sea, huge clouds of steam rise up, making clouds and temporarily obscuring things. But as the steam and rain begin to clear, you see the islands forming around these volcanoes— atolls, lagoons, islets. . . . The mountains grow taller, the islands enlarge, vegetation grows, animals colonize them—and as the land rises and the water falls away, you begin to see the shape of the continent beneath. The slope of one volcano flows down into the water—and another rises over there . . . so you can deduce what the hidden land between them, under the water, must look like.

When the whole job is done and the new continent floats at last on the waves, you have mountain ranges of conflict and excitement, foothills of plot, and valleys of restful lyricism. Small lakes and bodies of water remain in the hollows—those are the depths where the symbolism, the moral ambiguities, and the themes of the book lie submerged, waiting for someone to dive for them. And when you, the reader, lean over to look into these watery mysteries . . . you should see your own face looking back.

Ahem <cough>. So that's the cool metaphorical way to describe what goes on in my head when I write—but how does it really work in practice?

---

[1] *Originally published in the 20th anniversary edition of* Outlander.

Well, what I need when I sit down to write is a kernel. A kernel can be anything: a vivid image, a line of dialogue, an emotional ambience, the smell of a fart . . . anything at all that I can sense concretely. You get kernels from anywhere and everywhere; everything a writer sees, hears, smells, touches, tastes, thinks, or is told forms the mental compost from which ideas sprout in the dark space under your brain (and here you thought it was just termites down there).

If I come up to my office to work and it's what I call a "cold" day (meaning I knew how to write yesterday but seem to have forgotten how overnight), I usually pick up an inspiration of some kind off my bookshelves. I have thousands of inspirations to hand, ranging from books—mostly books—to toy cannon, silver quaichs full of stones and crystals, a nineteenth-century cobbler's hammer, a medieval chessman, a life-size crystal skull (well, it's plastic resin, but you'd never know, and if you're walking through your imagination, there's no difference at all), the shell of a giant clam (that's its genus, *Tridacna,* giant clam; the shell itself is only about six inches across, though they do get as big as three feet or so [these are the kind of clams reputed to clamp on to an unwary foot and drown the hapless beachcomber, though I don't know as how there are any reliably documented instances of this]), a handful of horse chestnuts picked on Guy Fawkes' Day in the U.K., a bevy of little glass bottles filled with herbs and potions (I have a peppermint one that's meant to clear the sinuses, but by and large you'd do better with a generous blast of wasabi), knives (I love knives; I have lots, ranging from a one-inch penknife that won't offend the TSA to a

Highland dirk that a nice Canadian gentleman made for me), two Jewish "widow's mite" coins from the time of the Crucifixion, and several feather amulets. (Don't ask me why, but almost all authors keep feathers in their offices. It's probably Symbolic, though whether it's urging your spirit to fly through the medium of words—and you'd have to write a whole lot faster than I do even to work up a decent taxiway, let alone achieve takeoff—or is an unsubtle warning not to be a chicken, I can't tell you.)

Once I have my kernel in hand—well, in mind—I sit down and write a line or two describing it, as best I can. As an example, on one cold day, I picked up an old Sotheby's auction catalog of Scottish glass and crystal of the eighteenth century and, thumbing through it, found a photo of a cut-glass goblet, its surface incised with thistles.

"Okay," I said. "That'll do." And wrote something memorable like, *The light fell through the cut-glass goblet.* (I mean, it's bound to, unless it's the dead of night and all the lights are off, and in that case, why would you be looking at a glass goblet? Drinking from it, maybe, but I'm not tasting anything here.)

Well, when I've written my line or two, I sit and stare at it. I take words out. I put words back. I put new words in. I rearrange the clauses, if there are any. And all the while, the underside of my brain is kicking through the compost, looking for mushrooms and muttering questions in my ear: *What time of day is it?* (late afternoon; I can tell by the way the light falls), *What time of year is it?* (it's winter; the light has that blue tinge to it . . . oh, and I must be in a room with a glass window or I couldn't see that—so I know I'm not in a cabin on Fraser's Ridge with an oiled deer-hide over the window), *If it's winter, are you cold?* (yes, my fingers are chilly and the end of my nose is cold, but my feet are warm, so there must be a fire . . . oh, there it is, over there, and there's a dog lying by it; I wonder who that dog is, I've never seen him before. . . .), and the line is meanwhile evolving to *The late-afternoon blue winter light* (too many adjectives, do something about that . . .) *fell through the cut-glass goblet incised with thistles* (thistles are really irrelevant, who cares about the thistles . . . but they're important for some reason, I wonder why?) *and made a pool of light* (no, it's amber light, how odd) . . . *and made a pool of amber light . . . on the polished wood table-top.*

Well, there's awkward for you; let's tidy that up: *The cold blue light of the winter afternoon* (nah, you don't need "cold," 'cuz "winter" gives you that same association), *The blue light of the winter afternoon* (no, I really like "cold blue light," let's ditch "the winter" instead), *The cold blue light of afternoon*—no, *The cold blue light of late afternoon* (because the alliteration of "light" and "late" appeals to me, and it is late, I can tell) *fell through the cut-glass* (cut-glass? Maybe crystal? No, "cut-glass" alliterates with "goblet," and I don't think you can have cut-glass that *isn't* technically crystal, and, even if you can, who cares) *goblet and made* (and made? Making? Yes, "making" is better, gives a sense of movement, and light *does* move, even though you wouldn't think so to look at it, and besides, I want the comma before "making" instead of the "and" before "made," because it will make the sentence look better visually), *goblet, making a pool* (no, that doesn't sound right, sounds like the goblet is taking a whiz on the table . . . "casting a pool"? Yeah, much

better), *casting a pool of* (it's still amber; I wonder why, is it just the color of the wood?) *amber light on the wood* (no, it really is polished wood, not just a plank), *on the polished wood of the tabletop* (well, for heaven's sake, of course it's the top of the table, you don't think the goblet's clinging to the underside, do you? And you have plenty of internal alliteration going on in here already, you don't need more), *of the table.*

The cold blue light of late afternoon fell through the cut-glass goblet, casting a pool of amber light on the polished wood of the table.

Okay, it's still a lot of adjectives, but each one of them is doing a necessary job, so they stay—and I get a nagging feeling of dissonance between the cold light and the amber light, which sounds warm. . . . Still, it's a reasonably graceful sentence, and it is what I'm looking at in my mind's eye, so all righty, then! Now I know where I am: I'm in Jocasta Cameron's parlor, because she's the only person in this book who'd own a crystal goblet incised with thistles (I knew they were important, but that's why they're important—as indicating the cup is owned by a Scot—so we needn't mention them) and filled with whisky! (That's why the pool of light is amber; the glass is full of whisky.)

At this point, my eldest daughter comes in and announces that it's time for soccer practice, so I hastily save my work (so what if it's one sentence? It's MY WORK, and I hate losing it. I never, ever leave my computer without saving what I was working on—and usually saving to a thumb drive, too, just in case).

So I'm driving down the road, listening to my daughter with one ear and thinking about my goblet and the fire and the dog and envisioning Jocasta Cameron, whom I know a bit about. She's an older lady, Scottish, very elegant, aristocratic, long white fingers, and I'm seeing her hand—blue veins under the papery skin—reaching for that goblet full of whisky. And out of wherever this stuff comes from, I see a black man's hand, reaching in from the other side of the table, taking hold of the goblet and moving it just a little, so that Jocasta's fingers will curl naturally around it.

Whereupon I turn to my daughter in great excitement and say, "I've just realized Jocasta Cameron is blind!"

To which my daughter replies, "I don't care. You missed the turnoff to the soccer field!"

Yeah, that's how it mostly works, on the word-by-word level, which—horrifying as it is—is really the only way anything ever gets written. Once I have my kernel, and the words and ideas have begun to flow (well, sometimes they flow; sometimes it's like shoveling rocks uphill), the scene grows slowly, sometimes on from the original kernel, sometimes in the opposite direction, frequently both. Sometimes the original kernel disappears completely (it did in this instance); the kernel is seldom what the scene is about; it's just my foothold on the page—a tiki torch to light my way.

But I go poking and fiddling and kicking my way into the dark, pegging my little tiki torches into the compost, and by the time I've finished a scene, I will have been through it literally hundreds of times. And it will be the best I can do with it at that point. If I know what happens next, I write that. If I don't—and usually I don't, especially at the beginning of a book—then I go look for a kernel somewhere else.

But what happens after you have a lot of words? Well, different things, depending on how your mind works. Personally, I don't work with an outline and I don't work in a *straight* line; tastes differ in this regard. So I tend to have handfuls of scenes that aren't related to one another for a while.

These float around inside a sort of n-dimensional hyperspace in what passes for my mind (it's just above the compost; the rising fumes help with the floating), and as I go on working and doing research (I do the research concurrently with the writing. Research and writing feed off each other, and besides, how would you ever know you'd done *enough* research if you were trying to do it all before beginning to write? [And no, I don't use research assistants. I'd have no idea what to tell them to look for, for one thing]), the bits begin to stick together.

I'll write something and think, *Aha! This is why X happened!* So then I lug that bit over in front of X and have a bigger piece, and, reading through that, I suddenly know that Y *has* to happen next, so I write that and have an even bigger piece . . . and so on and so forth.

Okay. Meanwhile, the research has been giving me not only kernels for inspiration and necessary bits of information and cool historical people—but has also been supplying me with an evolving timeline. When starting a book, I don't have any idea how much time it will cover (let alone where it actually begins or ends). But as I work, I start to pick out the historical events that are most important to this story—"important" in any of various ways: important historically (like the Declaration of Independence), important to one or more of my fictional characters (like the death of General Simon Fraser), important structurally (I need an event that would account for someone doing X or being in Y location), or important thematically (like Paul Revere's Ride), and those form a sort of chronological backbone for the book.

(No, I don't write this down. I don't usually write anything except the text of the book itself; if I make notes, I immediately forget the thing I wrote down, and for my purposes, I kind of need it all to be floating around in that n-dimensional hyperspace.)

Anyway, I make semiconscious decisions about how to use these important events—will we live through the Battle(s) of Saratoga or merely mention them offstage, as it were, to orient the reader while the action is elsewhere? If we *do* live through it/them (there were two) (that's not a royal "we," btw; I just mean me and the people inside my head), whose viewpoint will it be? Will it be Claire's, who's in a position to do exciting things, amputating limbs and sewing up wounds, but who can also be in a position to overhear things from messengers and officers and thus have an overall view of the battle? Or should it be Jamie or Young Ian or William, all of whom will be fighting in the battle, and thus having more visceral and immediate experiences, but would be experiencing different things in different places?

That sort of stuff. Anyway, I go on working in this organic fashion, and eventually I have largish chunks of story—forty to sixty pages or so—and a fairly coherent timeline. So I line the chunks up against that timeline in rough order—and with

luck, at that point, I can see the shape of the story in n dimensions.

All my books have an internal geometric shape that emerges in the course of the work, and once I've seen it, the writing goes much faster. I may have no idea exactly what happens, what's said, etc.—but I do know approximately what the missing pieces look like (e.g., I need a scene *here* that involves these three people, and it has a sense of rising tension and a conclusion that will lead into *that* scene over there . . .).

These internal shapes are normally invisible to the reader—who isn't looking for them in the first place—but if pointed out, the reader can certainly see them.

Outlander, for example, has three slightly overlapping triangles. There are three emotional climaxes to the story (these occurring at the apices of the triangles): when Claire makes her choice at the stones, when she rescues Jamie from Wentworth, and when she saves his soul at the abbey.

Dragonfly in Amber is dumbbell-shaped. You have a small arc of framing story at beginning and end (these would be the nuts or fasteners that hold the weights on), then two larger arcs, one dealing with the political intrigue in France, the other the actual battles and events of the Rising (these are the weights); these two main arcs are connected by a relatively level stretch of peace at Lallybroch.

Now, *Voyager* is shaped like a braided horsetail. It has a triple narrative through the first third of the book, with Jamie's,

Claire's, and Roger's voices taking turns, then falls into a simple linear narrative in Claire's voice through the second two-thirds of the story. I quite liked the structure through the early part: Jamie is telling his story forward as it happens, Claire is telling her story backward (to Roger and Brianna), and Roger's story is set in the present moment and provides a turning point to switch between Jamie's and Claire's.

(Yes, they do get more complicated as we go on. Anybody's life gets more complex as they grow older.)

Drums of Autumn—now, this one's interesting but less easily defined. It's shaped like a curving rose stem, with a budding offshoot (Roger and Brianna's story) and a lot of thorns, ending in a big showy whorl of flower, where all the petals of the plot come together.

The Fiery Cross is shaped like a rainbow. It begins with a description of the events of one Very Long Day—and every single plotline in the book has its roots in that one day. Each one then has an arc through the book that comes down at a different point.

A Breath of Snow and Ashes. You've probably seen that Hokusai print "The Great Wave off Kanagawa." Well, that's what this book is shaped like—only there are *two* great waves in it. Multiple plotlines rising to an overwhelming climax—and the little people in boats in the path of the wave. In the distance, Mount Fuji, standing solid and unmoved by all this watery chaos (Mount Fuji being the love between Jamie and Claire).

(Look, I don't like doing stuff I've done before, okay? Ergo, even though it is an ongoing series about the same people, each book is unique in terms of structure, theme, approach, and style. I've also been adding one major viewpoint character to each book—though, in fact, I didn't realize this consciously until a friend pointed it out to me after *Drums of Autumn*.)

An Echo in the Bone is shaped like a caltrop, and I was very pleased that Random House let me have a caltrop as the cover icon for this book. A caltrop is an ancient military weapon used originally to disable oncoming cavalry. It looks like a four-pronged child's jack, the prongs arranged in a tetrahedron, so that no matter how you toss it, it always lands with three prongs down, one spike pointing straight up. There are four major storylines in this book, all welded together in the nexus of the American Revolution—and every one of them ends in a sharp spike, believe me.

(Now, I haven't yet seen the shape of Book Eight, but I can already tell you that I want an octopus on the cover. . . .)[2]

I began writing a book for practice on March 6, 1988. (I know this because I date my work files, and that's the oldest one I have.) I didn't intend to tell anyone I was

---

[2] *Yes, I do like parentheses.*

writing, let alone show it to anyone—and had no notion at all that it might ever be published. But, you know—Things Happen, and here we all are. . . .

Outlander (originally titled *Cross Stitch*) was the book I wrote for practice. As I say, things happened: People read bits of it, encouraged me to try to get it published, gave me good advice; I found a wonderful literary agent, Perry Knowlton—and when I finally finished the thing and sent the manuscript to Perry, I said to him, "I can tell there's more to this story, but I thought I should stop while I could still lift it."

Further things happened. . . . The book was published in 1991—and as I say, here we all are, and what a long, strange trip it's been . . . but I thank you all for being my companions on the journey!

Since I don't plan the books ahead of time (what fun would *that* be?), I have no idea where the end of the series is. There is an end; I know that much. But it's not yet.

THE GABALDON THEORY
OF TIME TRAVEL

I t's all Claire Beauchamp's fault. If she hadn't refused to shut up and talk like an eighteenth-century woman, these would have been perfectly straightforward historical novels. As it was, though, being too lazy to wrestle with her natural inclinations through a whole book, I found myself instead obliged first, to allow her to be modern (not that I had much of a choice; she's remarkably stubborn), secondly, to figure out how she got there, and thirdly, to conclude what happened *then*.

The stone circles helpfully presented themselves in the course of my research into Scottish geography and settings, so I had a mechanism for the time travel. The actual mechanics and implications of the process, though, required a little time to be worked out—whoever erected the stone circles having not thought to chisel instructions on them.

Since Claire herself had no notion how time travel worked—and was unfortunately deprived of Geilie Duncan's company in Cranesmuir before being able to compare notes—the explication of the process has been slow and halting, developing through the various books, as further bits of information come to light, and as those capable of travel begin to discuss the subject.

A couple of things are obvious: 1) the stone circles mark places of passage, and 2) the ability to pass through time is evidently genetic.

Now, we *don't* yet know whether the stone circles are only markers, meant as ancient warnings of a place of mysterious disappearance, or whether the stones themselves play some active role in the "opening" of a door through the layers of time. I incline to the first idea, myself, but it remains an open question.

So far as the ability being genetic, it's apparent that not everyone can travel through the stones.[1] Of those who can, we know that two (Brianna and Roger) are descended directly from two others (Claire and Geillis Duncan). This suggests that the gene for time travel is dominant; i.e., only one parent need have the gene, and only one copy of the gene need be present in a person in order for the trait to be expressed. It's like the ability to roll one's

---

[1] *In answer to the assorted pleas I get for Jamie Fraser to find some way of traveling forward, because some people think it would be so neat to see him be amazed at microwave ovens and video games . . . sorry, not on your tintype. He's a man of his time, and I have more respect for his dignity than to try to circumvent the ways of nature for the sake of a lame joke.*

tongue into a cylinder; if you don't have the gene for this trait, you simply can't do it at all. If you do, it's perfectly easy and natural.

Genes that control traits of this sort normally occur in alleles, or pairs, one allele being derived from each parent. Each parent, however, will have two alleles—one from each of *that* parent's parents. This means that, for instance, if a person (Brianna Fraser, for example) is descended from a traveler and a nontraveler, then she will have only one time travel gene—but that gene is sufficient to allow the trait to be expressed; that is, to allow her to pass through time-gates. However, it also means that she possesses one travel gene, and one nontravel gene. She will pass only *one* of the alleles on to her offspring, and which one is given to a specific child is purely a matter of random assortment.

If the child's other parent (Roger MacKenzie, for instance) is also a time traveler who is heterozygous for the traveling gene (that is, has travel gene and one nontravel gene), then we have the following possibilities:

ROGER = Tt	BRIANNA = Tt	
	T	t
T	TT	Tt
t	Tt	tt

In other words, on average, if Brianna and Roger have four children, three of them will be time-travelers, and one of them won't. If they have one child (Jeremiah, for instance), the odds are three out of four that he *will* be able to travel—but there's a one-in-four chance that he can't.

However, if Jeremiah's father is *not* a time traveler (Stephen Bonnet, for instance), then the assortment is as follows:

STEPHEN BONNET - tt	BRIANNA = Tt	
	T	t
t	Tt	tt
t	Tt	tt

Which in turn means that Jeremiah may still be able to travel, but the odds are only one-in-two, or fifty/fifty.

On the other hand, we only know Brianna's genotype for sure; Roger *could* have received a traveling gene from *both* parents. If he did, then his genotype is TT, and *all* the children born to him and Brianna will be able to travel.

On the third hand, we don't know for sure that Stephen Bonnet *isn't* a traveler. After all, a person wouldn't find that out until he or she happened to walk through a circle of standing stones—and only at the right time of the year. We can assume from Geilie Duncan's research that this doesn't happen all that often—though it *does* happen.

Geillis Duncan seems to have done a lot of research, and probably knew more than anyone about the ways and means of time travel. Unfortunately, she's dead,[2] so unless she wrote down more of her findings somewhere else along the way, we're just

---

[2]*As my husband once observed, "In your books, you can only be sure somebody's **really** dead if you see them clutch their throat and go 'Gak!' right in front of you."*

going to have to try to work things out by deduction and experiment.

We must also bear in mind that Geillis Duncan may not always have been right in her own deductions, either; for instance, she was originally convinced that a blood sacrifice was required in order to open the time-passage. We know this is not correct, since Claire passed through without any such assistance.

Geillis also thought—presumably on the basis of ancient writings she later discovered[3]—that gemstones offered a means both of controlling the process of time travel (opening passages at times other than the sun feasts and fire feasts, for example) and protecting the traveler. She appears to have been closer the mark in this assumption, since Roger was in fact protected in his journey—first by the garnets on his mother's locket, and then by the diamond given to him by Fiona Graham.

The grimoire that Fiona found and gave to Roger contained Geilie's hypothesis that the time-passages were located at spots where the "ley lines" (lines of magnetic force that pass through the earth's crust) come close enough together that they are drawn into vortices, forming passages that join the layers of time. Evidently the time-passages may indeed be subject to some influence of magnetic force, since they stand widest open on the sun feasts and fire feasts—the times of year when the gravitational pull of the sun is most pronounced with respect to the earth's lines of magnetic force.

Still, these are only hypotheses; the true effect of gemstones remains to be seen.

This is as much as we presently know, concerning the mechanism of time travel. Beyond the simple fact of the phenomenon, though, we can observe and deduce

Presentism

LACK OF PERSPECTIVE *in literature (or in readers) often causes a contemporary condition I've heard referred to as "presentism"; that is, a disposition to judge all literature by the narrow standards of present time and present culture. This leads to peculiar phenomena such as the denunciation of classic novels such as* **Huckleberry Finn,** *on grounds that they deal with issues such as slavery, women's civil rights, etc., in a way not consistent with the present-day notion of political correctness. In essence, this attitude is based on a failure to acknowledge that any time other than the present has actually existed; since that underlying assumption is clearly mistaken, the resultant attitude—that it is reasonable to judge historical times and characters by modern standards—can't possibly be taken seriously. At least by me.*

[3]*We can only speculate as to the nature of these; however, she did, when talking to Claire about gemstones, refer to them as* **bhasmas** *and* **nagina** *stones, which are terms from Ayurvedic texts. All ancient cultures have mysterious sites—and all involve stone.*

various things concerning its effects. In other words, how, when, and why one time-travels is one thing; but what happens to the time-traveler—and to time—on the other side?

PARADOX, PREDESTINATION, AND FREE CHOICE

There are always two choices facing a writer who deals with time travel, whether these are addressed specifically or not: one, the time travel paradox (that is, can the past be changed, and if so, how is the future affected?), and two, the choice between predestination and free choice.

These questions are of course linked through the underlying notions of linearity and causality—naturally, if one declines to accept the hypothesis that time is linear, but one does accept causality (and it is, I think, impossible to write a story in which the notion of causality does not exist. "Experimental fiction," yes—story, no), then paradox not only becomes possible, but must almost certainly become a major focus of the story.

If one accepts the hypothesis that history (that is, the events of the past) can be changed, then one allows the philosophy of free choice on the part of characters. If one rejects the hypothesis that history can be changed, then one is forced to accept the notion of predestination.

If the past *can't* be changed by the actions of time-travelers, then this implies the necessity for predestination (or post-destination, as the case may be)—that is, the basic idea that events are "fated" to occur and thus are outside the abilities of an individual to affect.

Accepting this notion implies that there

is some large order to the universe, much greater in scope than human action. As a philosophical or religious point of view, this is appealing to many people; we would like to think that somebody is in charge who knows what he's doing.

On the other hand, the notion of predestination doesn't do much for either our sense of self-esteem or our sense of possibility—and both are important to the notion of story (we identify with characters, and we keep asking, "And then what happens?"). It leads to a feeling of "Why bother?" that is counterproductive both to endeavor and to absorption in the story. I'll tell you; predestination can work in fiction, but it's much less attractive than the notion of free choice.

The acceptability of a story to a given reader depends primarily on the suspension of disbelief: the reader's acceptance of the reality created by the author, even when this reality runs counter to the reader's own experience. An author has a greater chance of achieving this suspension of disbelief if he or she can keep as much of the story as possible within the reader's frame of reference, altering only those elements that *must* be changed to achieve the desired reality.

Consequently, it's easier for a reader to accept a paradox-story—one involving circularity and predestination—if it is told only in personal terms, detached from any major historical events. Telling a time travel story in which major recognizable events are changed will disturb the reader's suspension of disbelief by setting up cognitive dissonance between what the reader *knows* to have happened, and the created world he or she is trying to enter.

This is why the most successful stories of this type most often involve either a res-

AN EXCEPTION HERE is a type of story that has recently become popular, called "alternative history." In this sort of story, the reader is asked to accept as a beginning premise that some crucial event of history took place differently—the South won the American Civil War, Hitler won World War II, etc.—and the story proceeds on the basis of that assumption. This requires an upfront, conscious suspension of disbelief from the reader.

olution or a process in which the main character ends up as his or her own ancestor and/or descendant. (The two best-known classics of this type are Robert Heinlein's *By His Bootstraps,* and David Gerrold's *The Man Who Folded Himself.*)

For me, stories that involve free choice on the part of the protagonists are more interesting to write, and, I think, much more likely to be attractive to readers. In this particular time and culture, the idea that we do have individual power over our own destinies is not only widely accepted, but highly desirable (the fiction of other times and cultures naturally may—and does—reflect different notions of individual power).

How to deal with these opposing choices, then? That's a decision for an individual writer; for myself, I decided to

have it both ways—to allow free choice, but not to change major historical events (ah, what it is to be a godlike Writer!). The Gabaldon Theory of Time Travel therefore depends on this central postulate:

A time-traveler has free choice and individual power of action; however, he or she has *no more* power of action than is allowed by the traveler's personal circumstances.

A necessary corollary to this postulate does not deal with time travel at all, but only with the observed nature of historical events:

Most notable historical events (those affecting large numbers of people and thus likely to be recorded) are the result of the *collective* actions of many people.

There are exceptions to this corollary, of course: political assassination, which affects a great many people, but can be carried out by a single individual; scientific discovery, geographical exploration, commercial invention, etc. Still, the effects of events such as these depend in large part on the circumstances in which they take place; many scientific discoveries have been made—and lost—a number of times, before reaching general acceptance or social relevance.

Thus, the notion that knowledge is power is not absolutely true—knowledge is power *only* to the extent that circumstances allow that knowledge to be used.

That is, if a time-traveler arrives in a society where he or she is merely a normal citizen, then the traveler has relatively little power to affect social events. Madame X arrives in Paris on the eve of the French Revolution, for instance. If Madame X is in fact merely a time-traveler, and is not taking the place of an extant citizen, then she is not an aristocrat, has no connections among the powers of the revolution, and is thus in no position to affect the overall course of the revolution.

Even if she should somehow gain access to the Petit Trianon, scrape acquaintance with the Queen, and hint that it would be injudicious to make remarks regarding cake . . . the French Revolution was a complex social phenomenon, emerging from the results of years—centuries!—of actions taken and not taken by hundreds and thousands of people. Madame X very likely *cannot* take any individual action that would succeed in preventing the revolution as a whole; that was a social event of such complexity that control of it is simply beyond the scope of any individual.

Madame X does, however, retain the power that any individual *of that time* has; she can warn a friend that it would be wise to leave Paris, for instance. If he listens, she may indeed save his life—and thus change "history" (but not recorded history).

Ergo, a time-traveler can exercise free choice, and can effect small-scale, personal changes in the past—such as advising a friend to plant potatoes, thus averting the consequences of an anticipated famine. However, because large social events are usually the effect of the *cumulative* actions of large numbers of people, the time-traveler most likely cannot make a change in larger, well-documented historical events.

Ergo, from a "story" point of view, we preserve the philosophical and fictional advantages of free choice, without incur-

ring the cognitive dissonance associated with changing "history," as perceived by the reader.

NONSIMULTANEOUSNESS

Two individuals cannot occupy the same physical space; two species cannot occupy the same ecological space, or niche. Ergo, it seems intuitively obvious that two entities cannot occupy the same temporal location. The trick here, of course, is that physical space and ecological niches exist *outside* the individual, while time exists *inside* the individual. Any moment in time— or any longer segment (a lifetime, for instance)—belongs only to an individual.

Therefore, the implication of nonsimultaneousness is clear; two individuals can exist in different spaces at the same time, but an individual cannot exist simultaneously at more than one temporal location.

This leads to one of the interesting basic questions of time travel—so, what if the individual *does* try to exist in more than one time? Is this possible?

In terms of our physical frame of reference, no, it isn't—but the nice thing about fiction is that one isn't limited to the physical frame of reference, by any means. If one assumes nonetheless that it *is* possible for a person to exist in more than one temporal location simultaneously, we get entertaining complexities and possibilities, such as the Heinlein and Gerrold stories mentioned above suggest.

These stories depend on an assumption of duality (or other pluralities) of time and space—that an individual is in fact a *different* individual from one moment of time to another (which is certainly true, in terms of physical and perhaps mental processes). Thus, under this hypothesis, a person is not really a discrete entity, but rather a contiguous chain of identities, all with a great deal of similarity but all slightly different, *and* (this is the basic assumption) that any of these identities can persist physically, if removed from the temporal chain that binds them together.

Naturally, one of the benefits of fiction is that it is a simple matter to remove the temporal linkage; the author merely devises a plausible causality, and declares it to be true. The only drawback to this particular fictional assumption is that if one uses it, it's so obtrusive as to require the device to become the central premise and conflict of the story. Fine, but limiting.

If one assumes instead—on the basis of the natural phenomenon/nonsimultaneousness argument—that it is *not* possible for pluralities to exist, then a different set of intriguing situations and logical evolutions occur. What happens if one *tries* to exist simultaneously in more than one temporal location? How might one avoid the possibility?

The Gabaldon Theory postulates that it is not possible for plural identities of the same character to exist simultaneously. Therefore, a character can exist only *once*, whatever the time period in which that character finds himself. On the assumption of nonsimultaneousness, if a character *tries* to exist in a time in which he or she already exist(s/ed), the result should be disaster or displacement or both.

Ergo, when Roger first enters the stone circle on Craigh na Dun and passes through the cleft stone while thinking of his father, he inadvertently travels *through his own lifeline*—that is, he (involuntarily) tries to exist twice in the same time. Since he can't possibly do that, the result is something like what happens if two atoms try to exist in the same space—an immediate explosion of force that drives them apart.[4]

Had Roger not been wearing gemstones (which presumably absorbed or deflected the force), he would undoubtedly have been killed. Lucky for him (and the story), though, he was.

THE MOEBIUS TWIST OF FATE

What I call a fictional "Moebius twist" effect is a situation in which a character *by the action of free choice* achieves a result that preserves a personal historical reality, which would not be preserved without the character's intervention. Examples of this are (in *Drums of Autumn*) a young man who risks his life to save a baby for humanitarian motives—this child being (unknown to him) his own ancestor; or (in Jack Finney's *Time and Again*), a time-traveler who takes a conscious but trifling step that prevents the conception of a man who will later discover time travel, thus removing a personal risk. This sort of situation of course smacks of predestination—but as I said, we do like to feel sometimes that someone is in charge.[5]

---

[4] *In very simplified terms, this is what happens in a nuclear explosion.*

[5] *In this case, it's the author.*

PART SEVEN

THE VIEW FROM LALLYBROCH

OBJECTS OF VERTUE,

OBJECTS OF USE

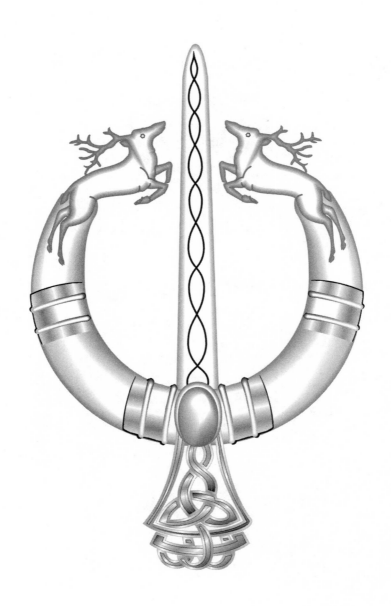

LALLYBROCH

"Big chap," said Frank, frowning in recollection. "And a Scot, in complete Highland rig-out, complete to sporran and the most beautiful running-stag brooch on his plaid. I wanted to ask where he'd got it from, but he was off before I could."

I went to the bureau and poured another drink. "Well, not so unusual an appearance for these parts, surely? I've seen men dressed like that in the village now and then."

"Nooo . . ." Frank sounded doubtful. "No, it wasn't his dress that was odd. But when he pushed past me, I could swear he was close enough that I should have felt him brush my sleeve—but I didn't. And I was intrigued enough to turn round and watch him as he walked away. He walked down the Gereside Road, but when he'd almost reached the corner, he . . . disappeared. That's when I began to feel a bit cold down the backbone."

"Perhaps your attention was distracted for a second, and he just stepped aside into the shadows," I suggested. "There are a lot of trees down near that corner."

"I could swear I didn't take my eyes off him for a moment," muttered Frank. He looked up suddenly. "I know! I remember now why I thought he was so odd, though I didn't realize it at the time."

"What?" I was getting a bit tired of the ghost, and wanted to go on to more interesting matters, such as bed.

"The wind was cutting up like billy-o, but his drapes—his kilts and plaid, you know—they didn't move at all, except to the stir of his walking."

We stared at each other. "Well," I said finally, "that is a bit spooky."

—*Outlander*, chapter 1, "A New Beginning"

"Why, it's a henge!" I said, delighted. "A miniature henge!"

. . . There were no signs of burial in the miniature henge atop the hill. By "miniature," I mean only that the circle of standing stones was smaller than Stonehenge; each stone was still twice my own height, and massive in proportion. . . .

Some of the standing stones were brindled, striped with dim colors. Others were speckled with flakes of mica that caught the morning sun with a cheerful shimmer. All of them were remarkably different from the clumps of native stone that thrust out of the bracken all around. Whoever built the stone circles, and for whatever purpose, thought it important enough to have quarried, shaped, and transported special stone blocks for the erection of their testimonial. Shaped—how? Transported—how, and from what unimaginable distance?

—*Outlander*, chapter 2,
"Standing Stones"

She couldn't go back to sleep after hanging up; restless, she swung her feet out of bed and padded out to the kitchen of the small apartment for a glass of milk. It was only after several minutes of staring blankly into the recesses of the refrigerator that she realized she wasn't seeing ranks of ketchup bottles and half-used cans. She was seeing standing stones, black against a pale dawn sky.

—*Drums of Autumn*, chapter 3,
"The Minister's Cat"

On Midsummer's Eve in Scotland, the sun hangs in the sky with the moon. Summer solstice, the feast of Litha, Alban Eilir. Nearly midnight, and the light was dim and milky white, but light nonetheless.

He could feel the stones long before he saw them. Claire and Geillis had both been right, he thought; the date mattered. They had been eerie on his earlier visits, but silent. Now he could hear them; not with his ears but with his skin—a low buzzing hum like the drone of bagpipes.

—*Drums of Autumn*, chapter 33,
"Midsummer's Eve"

Our guide shrugged and spat into the water.

"Weel, the loch's queer, and no mistake. There's stories, to be sure, of something old and evil that once lived in the depths. Sacrifices were made to it—kine, and sometimes even wee bairns, flung into the water in withy baskets." He spat again. "And some say the loch's bottomless—got a hole in the center deeper than anything else in Scotland. On the other hand"—the guide's crinkled eyes crinkled a bit more—"'twas a family here from Lancashire a few years ago, cam' rushin' to the police station in Invermoriston, screamin' as they'd seen the monster come out o' the water and hide in the bracken. Said 'twas a terrible creature, covered wi' red hair and fearsome horns, and chewin' something, wi' the blood all dripping from its mouth." He held up a hand, stemming my horrified exclamation.

"The constable they sent to see cam' back and said, weel, bar the drippin' blood, 'twas a verra accurate description"—he paused for effect—"of a nice Highland cow, chewin' her cud in the bracken!"

—*Outlander*, chapter 2,
"Standing Stones"

I had seen the cattle disappear, one shaggy beast at a time, down the ditch that led to the hidden postern door, under the expert driving of Rupert and his men. But would they be able to force the cattle through that door, singly or not? And if so, what would they do once inside; half-wild cattle, trapped suddenly in a stone corridor lit with glaring torchlight? Well, perhaps it would work. The corridor itself would be not unlike their stone-floored barn, including torches and the scent of humans. If they got so far, the plan might succeed.

. . . Jamie winced as the spirit stung his torn mouth, but drained the beaker before laying his head down again. His eyes slanted up at me, slightly filmed with pain and whisky, but alight with amusement nonetheless. "Cows?" he asked. "Was it really cows, or was I dreaming?"

—*Outlander,* chapter 36, "MacRannoch"

I had begun "building" a picture of Castle Leoch in the same fashion as Lallybroch; by giving the illustrators both a general description of the castle, and a number of photographs and drawings of buildings of the proper period, noting the elements of each that were "right" for the

vision of the castle that I had in my head. The preliminary drawing looked like that on the left—Castle Leoch, gradually taking solid shape out of the fog of my imagination.

Before we got further with the picture, though, I happened to go to a Highland Games in California. As I was signing books, a couple of people came up to me, holding a scrapbook, and introduced themselves to me: Steven McKenzie and his daughter, Anne, of the local Clan MacKenzie Society. They invited me to become an honorary member of clan MacKenzie, and upon my pleased acceptance,[1] presented me with a T-shirt decorated with the clan badge, and showed me the photographs in their scrapbook— taken at the most recent Gathering of clan MacKenzie, in Scotland. Among the scenes of Highland beauty and massed MacKenzies, were several photographs of the clan seat—Castle Leod.

"You're kidding!" I said, seeing this. "You mean there *is* a place called Leod?"

They were surprised at this, having assumed that I not only knew about Castle Leod, but had seen it, since the description in *Outlander* matched the reality so well.

"Well, I *have* seen it," I said. "But not in a photograph."

Since the reality had so abruptly popped up in front of me, though, it seemed unnecessary to go on constructing the imaginary version, and so I asked the McKenzies' permission—graciously granted—to use their photographs of the Real Thing.

—D.G.

✦ ✦ ✦

---

[1] *I am an honorary Fraser, as well.*

The rest of the journey passed uneventfully, if you consider it uneventful to ride fifteen miles on horseback through rough country at night, frequently without benefit of roads, in company with kilted men armed to the teeth, and sharing a horse with a wounded man. At least we were not set upon by highwaymen, we encountered no wild beasts, and it didn't rain. By the standards I was becoming used to, it was quite dull. . . .

Not surprisingly, it was misting heavily, but there was enough light to show a stone bridge, arching over a small stream that ran past the front of the castle, down to a dully gleaming loch a quarter mile away.

The castle itself was blunt and solid. No fanciful turrets or toothed battlements. This was more like an enormous fortified house, with thick stone walls and high, slitted windows. A number of chimney pots smoked over the slick tiles of the roof, adding to the general impression of greyness.

The gated entrance of the castle was wide enough to accommodate two wagons side by side. I say this without fear of contradiction, because it was doing exactly that as we crossed the bridge. One ox-drawn wagon was loaded with barrels, the other with hay. Our little cavalcade huddled on the bridge, waiting impatiently for the wagons to complete their laborious entry.

I risked a question as the horses picked their way over the slippery stones of the wet courtyard. I hadn't spoken to my escort since hastily re-dressing his shoulder by the roadside. He had been silent, too, aside from an occasional grunt of discomfort when a misstep by the horse jolted him.

"Where are we?" I croaked, my voice hoarse from cold and disuse.

"The keep of Leoch," he answered shortly. Castle Leoch. Well, at least now I knew where I was. When I had known it, Castle Leoch was a picturesque ruin, some thirty miles north of Bargrennan. It was considerably more picturesque now, what with the pigs rooting under the walls of the keep and the pervasive smell of raw sewage. I was beginning to accept the impossible idea that I was, most likely, somewhere in the eighteenth century.

—*Outlander*, chapter 4,
"I Come to the Castle"

But Jamie was not quite finished, it seemed. Ignoring Dougal's fuming, he drew a short string of white beads from his sporran. He stepped forward and fastened the necklace around my neck. Looking down, I could see it was a string of small baroque pearls, those irregularly shaped productions of freshwater mussels, interspersed with tiny pierced-work gold roundels. Smaller pearls dangled from the gold beads.

"They're only Scotch pearls," he said, apologetically, "but they look bonny on you." His fingers lingered a moment on my neck.

"Those were your mother's pearls!" said Dougal, glowering at the necklace.

"Aye," said Jamie calmly, "and now they're my wife's. Shall we go?"

—*Outlander*, chapter 14,
"A Marriage Takes Place"

Brianna put a stop to the outcry simply by standing up. She was as tall as any of the men, and towered over the women. Laoghaire took one quick step back. Every face in the room was turned to her, marked with hostility, sympathy, or merely curiosity.

With a coolness that she didn't feel, Brianna reached for the inner pocket of her coat, the secret pocket she had sewed into the seam only a week before. It seemed like a century.

"My mother's name is Claire," she said, and dropped the necklace on the table.

There was utter silence in the room, save for the soft hissing of the peat fire, burning low on the hearth. The pearl necklace lay gleaming, the spring sun from the window picking out the gold pierced-work roundels like sparks.

It was Jenny who spoke first. Moving like a sleepwalker, she reached out a slender finger and touched one of the pearls. Freshwater pearls, the kind called baroque because of their singular, irregular, unmistakable shapes.

"Oh, my," Jenny said softly.

—*Drums of Autumn*, chapter 34, "Lallybroch"

"And what did you want to buy so much?" I asked suspiciously.

He sighed and hesitated for a moment, then tossed the small package lightly into my lap. "A wedding ring, Sassenach," he said. "I got it from Ewen the armorer; he makes such things in his own time."

"Oh," I said in a small voice.

"Go ahead," he said, a moment later. "Open it. It's yours."

The outlines of the little package blurred under my fingers. I blinked and sniffed, but made no move to open it. "I'm sorry," I said.

"Well, so ye should be, Sassenach," he said, but his voice was no longer angry. Reaching, he took the package from my lap and tore away the wrapping, revealing a wide silver band, decorated in the Highland interlace style, a small and delicate Jacobean thistle bloom carved in the center of each link.

So much I saw, and then my eyes blurred again.

I found a handkerchief thrust into my hand, and did my best to stanch the flow with it. "It's . . . beautiful," I said, clearing my throat and dabbling at my eyes.

"Will ye wear it, Claire?" His voice was gentle now, and his use of my name, mostly reserved for occasions of formality or tenderness, nearly made me break down again. . . .

I couldn't speak, but held out my right hand to him, fingers trembling. The ring slipped cool and bright over my knuckle and rested snug at the base of my finger—a good fit.

—*Outlander*, chapter 23, "Return to Leoch"

"There are words in it," she said wonderingly. "I never realized that he'd . . . Oh, dear God." Her voice broke, and the ring slipped from her fingers, rattling on the table with a tiny metal chime. . . .

Roger stood for a minute, feeling unbearably awkward and out of place. With a terrible feeling that he was violating a privacy that ran deeper than anything he had ever

known, but not knowing what else to do, he lifted the tiny metal circle to the light and read the words inside.

"Da mi basia mille . . ." *But it was Claire's voice that spoke the words, not his.*

> —*Dragonfly in Amber*, chapter 47, "Loose Ends"

"Good as new." Jamie finished polishing the silver ring on his shirttail and held it up, admiring it in the glow of the lantern.

"That is somewhat better than can be said of me," I replied coldly. I lay in a crumpled heap on the deck, which in spite of the placid current, seemed still to be heaving very slightly under me. "You are a grade-A, double-dyed, sadistic fucking bastard, Jamie Fraser!"

> —*Drums of Autumn*, chapter 9, "Two-thirds of a Ghost"

"It was a long time ago," I said softly.

"And a long time," he said. "I am a jealous man, but not a vengeful one. I would take you from him, my Sassenach—but I wouldna take him from you."

He paused a moment, the fire glinting softly from the ring in his hand. "It was your life, no?"

And he asked again, "Do you want it back?"

I held up my hand in answer and he slid the gold ring on my finger, the metal warm from his body.

From F. to C. with love. Always.

> —*Drums of Autumn*, chapter 71, "Circle's Close"

✦ ✦ ✦

I've had any number of inquiries regarding Claire's wedding ring, some simply curious as to whether a real ring of this description exists, some with a more practical application—that is, persons wanting to have a facsimile of it made for their own wedding!

The ring doesn't exist physically, I'm afraid; only inside my head. I wear four rings, myself: two gold ones on the left hand, two silver on the right. On my left ring finger is my own wedding ring, which was a commercial pattern (i.e., it wasn't custom-made for me, but was simply available). The pattern is called (oddly enough, in view of the fact that I was married long before even thinking of writing a Scottish novel) "Brigadoon."

It's made of gold, and is 8 mm (5/16") wide. It has an incised pattern of what I think are fern leaves, interspersed with small, four-petaled flowers, and it's rather pretty. It looks as though the ferns and flowers are incised on a black background, but this is merely a side effect of the fact that I don't bother to scrub it with a toothbrush now and then; it was all gold, originally.

When I began writing *Outlander*, I undertook all kinds of things for research, including going to a Highland Games in Mesa, Arizona. I'd never been to a Highland Games before, and found it fascinating; bagpipes up the gazoo: drums, shortbread, and quite a lot of men in kilts. I came away from this event with two important souvenirs: a Clan Map of Scotland, which is still on my wall, and which has supplied most of the names for minor characters—as well as the odd geographical reference—for all of the books so far—and a silver ring.

This one is 5 mm (3/16") wide, and has a narrow band of plain silver at top and bottom, with a single band of interlace (aka Celtic knotwork) in between. Owing to its origins, I've always thought of it in terms of *Outlander* and things Scottish.

Consequently, when Jamie decided to give Claire a ring (I had no idea that's why he'd gone off right after arrival at the Castle), I was faced with the problem of describing it. Being a practical person, as well as a person of sentiment, I looked at my hands—and gave her a cross between my own two rings.

Claire's ring, therefore, is wide (like my own wedding band), made of silver (because gold jewelry wasn't common in the Scottish Highlands, but silver was), and made with an interlace pattern (which is ancient, thus historically appropriate, and thoroughly Scottish) interspersed with thistle blooms (flowers, like my ring, but thistles for Scottishness).

Now, there are certain elements described in the *Outlander* books that I would not under any circumstances allow to be illustrated—the characters, for instance. (As I say to the occasional person who complains that they want a picture because they can't visualize Claire or Jamie— you now have the option of watching the lovely television series that Starz has made (see photo insert).

At the same time, there's at least a sporting chance of coming up with a reasonable approximation of some of the inanimate objects about which people are curious— and with the aid of a pair of talented illustrators[2] who were willing to take my rough suggestions and give me approximations to fiddle with, we've produced illustrations of some of the principal items of jewelry described in the books: Claire's wedding ring, Ellen's pearls, the boar's-tusk bracelets, and the running-stag brooch worn by the ghost in Iverness.

Oh, my other two rings? Well, they're identical, save for the metal; one's silver, one gold (silver on the right, gold on the left). They're reproductions of fifteenth-century French poesy rings, and were given to me by my husband—one for a birthday gift, the other for an anniversary. Each of them bears the legend *"Vous, et nul autre."*[3]

✦ ✦ ✦

Broch Tuarach means "the north-facing tower." From the side of the mountain above, the broch that gave the small estate its name was no more than another mound of rocks, much like those that lay at the foot of the hills we had been traveling through.

We came down through a narrow, rocky gap between two crags, leading the horse between boulders. Then the going was easier, the land sloping more gently down through the fields and scattered cottages, until at last we struck a small winding road that led to the house.

It was larger than I had expected; a handsome three-story manor of harled white stone, windows outlined in the natural grey stone, a high slate roof with multiple chimneys, and several smaller whitewashed buildings clustered about it, like chicks about a hen. The old stone broch, situated on a small rise to the rear of the house, rose sixty feet above the ground, cone-topped like a witch's hat, girdled with three rows of tiny arrow-slits.

—*Outlander*, chapter 26,
"The Laird's Return"

"Scotland," I sighed, thinking of the cool brown streams and dark pines of Lallybroch, Jamie's estate. "Can we really go home?"

—*Dragonfly in Amber*, chapter 29,
"To Grasp the Nettle"

From this distance, the house seemed completely unchanged. Built of white harled stone, its three stories gleamed immaculately amid its cluster of shabby outbuildings and the spread of stone-dyked brown fields. On the small rise behind the house stood the remains of the ancient broch, the circular stone tower that gave the place its name.

On closer inspection, I could see that the outbuildings had changed a bit; Jamie had told me that the English soldiery had burned the dovecote and the chapel the year after Culloden, and I could see the gaps where they had been. A space where the wall of the kailyard had been broken through had been repaired with stone of a different color, and a new shed built of stone and scrap lumber was evidently serving as a dovecote, judging from the row of plump

feathered bodies lined up on the rooftree, enjoying the late autumn sun.

The rose brier planted by Jamie's mother, Ellen, had grown up into a great, sprawling tangle latticed to the wall of the house, only now losing the last of its leaves.

—*Voyager*, chapter 32,
"The Prodigal's Return"

The peat fire hissed on the hearth behind me, smelling of the Highlands, and the rich scent of cock-a-leekie and baking bread spread through the house, warm and comforting as a blanket.

I could feel the pull of it around me—the house, the family, the place itself. I, who couldn't remember a childhood home, felt the urge to sit down here and stay forever, enmeshed in the thousand strands of daily life, bound securely to this bit of earth. What would it have meant to him, who had lived all his life in the strength of that bond?

—*Voyager*, chapter 37,
"What's in a Name"

Brianna let the reins lie on Brutus's neck, letting him rest after the last climb, and sat still, surveying the small valley below. The big white-harled farmhouse sat serenely in the middle of pale green fields of oats and barley, its windows and chimneys edged in gray stone, the walled kailyard and the numerous outbuildings clustering around it like chicks round a big white hen.

---

[2]*Carlos and Deborah Gonzales, of Running Changes, Inc.*
[3]*You, and no other.*

She had never seen it before, but she was sure. She had heard her mother's descriptions of Lallybroch often enough. And besides, it was the only substantial house for miles; she had seen nothing else in the last three days but the tiny stone-walled crofters' cottages, many deserted and tumbled down, some no more than fire-black ruins.

Smoke was rising from a chimney below; someone was home.

—*Drums of Autumn*, chapter 34, "Lallybroch"

I caught a strange nonmetallic gleam in the depths of the box, and pointed. "What's that?"

"Oh, those," she said, dipping into the box again. "I've never worn them; they don't suit me. But you could wear them—you're tall and queenly, like my mother was. They were hers, ye ken."

They were a pair of bracelets. Each made from the curving, almost-circular tusk of a wild boar, polished to a deep ivory glow, the ends capped with silver tappets, etched with flowered tracery.

"Lord, they're gorgeous! I've never seen anything so . . . so wonderfully barbaric."

Jenny was amused. "Aye, that they are. Someone gave them to Mother as a wedding gift, but she never would say who. My father used to tease her now and then about her admirer, but she wouldna tell him, either, just smiled like a cat that's had cream to its supper. Here, try them."

The ivory was cool and heavy on my arm. I couldn't resist stroking the deep yellow surface, grained with age.

"Aye, they suit ye," Jenny declared. . . .

The bannocks were steaming gently in the cool air, and smelt heavenly. I reached for one, the heavy boar's-tooth bracelets clinking together on my wrist. I saw Murtagh's eyes on them and adjusted them so he could see the engraved silver end pieces.

"Aren't they lovely?" I said. "Jenny said they were her mother's."

Murtagh's eyes dropped to the bowl of parritch that Mrs. Cook had thrust unceremoniously under his nose.

"They suit ye," he mumbled.

—Outlander, chapter 31,
"Quarter Day"

MacRannoch was studying the wizened little man, trying to subtract thirty years from the seamed countenance.

"Aye, I know ye," he said at last. "Or not the name, but you. Ye killed a wounded boar single-handed with a dagger, during the tynchal. A gallant beast too. That's right, the MacKenzie gave ye the tushes—a bonny

set, almost a complete double curve. Lovely work, that, man." A look perilously close to gratification creased Murtagh's pitted cheek momentarily.

I started, remembering the magnificent, barbaric bracelets I had seen at Lallybroch. My mother's, Jenny had said, given to her by an admirer.

—Outlander, chapter 36,
"MacRannoch"

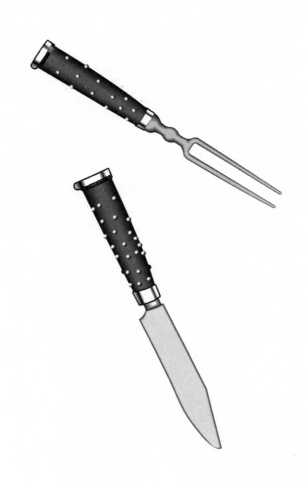

"Arma virumque cano"

Wrapping his hand in the bloodstained cloth, Jamie cautiously pulled the dirk from the fire. He advanced slowly toward the boy, letting the blade fall, as though of its own volition, until it touched the lad's jerkin. There was a strong smell of singed cloth from the handkerchief wrapped around the haft of the knife, which grew stronger as a narrow burnt line traced its way up the front of the jerkin in the dagger's path. The point, darkening as it cooled, stopped just short of the upwardly straining chin. I could see the thin lines of sweat shining in the stretched hollows of the slender neck.

—Dragonfly in Amber, chapter 36, "Prestonpans"

He turned back to the prisoner, busying himself in checking the priming and loading of the pistol. The twelve inches of heart-butted metal gleamed dark, the firelight picking out sparks of silver at trigger and priming pin. "Head or heart?" Jamie asked casually, raising his head at last.

"Eh?" The boy's mouth hung open in blank incomprehension.

"I am going to shoot you," Jamie explained patiently. "Spies are usually hanged, but in consideration of your gallantry, I am willing to give you a quick, clean death. Do ye prefer to take the ball in the head, or the heart?"

—Dragonfly in Amber, chapter 36, "Prestonpans"

The priest would have to take care of himself, he thought. Jamie drew the broadsword as he rose, and with one long step, was within reach. The man was no more than a shape in the darkness, but distinct enough. The merciless blade smashed down with all his strength, and split the man's skull where he stood.

"Highlanders!" The shriek broke from the man's companion, and the second sentry sprang out like a rabbit flushed from a copse, bounding away into the fading dark before Jamie could free his weapon from its gory cleft. He put a foot on the fallen man's

back and jerked, gritting his teeth against the unpleasant sensation of slack flesh and grating bone.

—*Dragonfly in Amber*, chapter 36, "Prestonpans"

There was a faint, wheezing chuckle from Rupert, and another coughing spell.

"Weel, grieve for me and ye will, Dougal," he said, when he'd finished. "And I'm glad for it. But ye canna grieve 'til I be deid, can ye? I would die by your hand, mo caraidh, not in the hands of the strangers."

. . .

"You are my chief, man, and it's your duty," he whispered. "Come now. Do it now. This dying hurts me, Dougal, and I would have it over."

. . .

Dougal's dirk took him under the breastbone, hard and straight. The burly body convulsed, turning to the side with a coughing explosion of air and blood, but the brief sound of agony came from Dougal.

—*Dragonfly in Amber*, chapter 43, "Falkirk"

Fire is a poor illuminator, but it would have taken total darkness to conceal that look on Geilie's face; the sudden realization of what was coming toward her.

She jerked the other pistol from her belt and swung it to bear on me. I saw the round hole of the muzzle clearly—and didn't care. The roar of the discharge caromed through the cave, the echoes sending down showers of rocks and dirt, but by then I had seized the ax from the floor.

I heard a noise behind me, but didn't turn. Reflections of the fire burned red in the pupils of her eyes. The red thing, Jamie had called it. I gave myself to it, he had said.

I didn't need to give myself; it had taken me.

There was no fear, no rage, no doubt. Only the stroke of the swinging ax.

The shock of it echoed up my arm, and I let go, my fingers numbed. I stood quite still, not even moving when she staggered toward me.

Blood in firelight is black, not red.

—*Voyager*, chapter 62, "Abandawe"

"Sometimes I know there's something there, like," Maisri said suddenly, "but I can block it out of my mind, not look. 'Twas like that with his lordship; I knew there was something, but I'd managed not to see it. But then he bade me look, and say the divining spell to make the vision come clear. And I did." The hood of her cloak slipped back as she tilted her head, looking up at the wall of the Priory as it soared above us, ochre and white and red, with the mortar crumbling between its stones. White-streaked black hair spilled down her back, free in the wind.

"He was standing there before the fire, but it was daylight, and clear to see. A man stood behind him, still as a tree, and his face covered in black. And across his lordship's face there fell the shadow of an ax."

—*Dragonfly in Amber*, chapter 41,
"The Seer's Curse"

It was the gralloch prayer he had been taught as a boy, learning to hunt in the Highlands of Scotland. It was old, he had told me; so old that some of the words were no longer in common use, so it sounded unfamiliar. But it must be said for any animal

slain that was larger than a hare, before the throat was cut or the bellyskin split.

Without hesitation, he made a shallow slash across the chest—no need to bleed the carcass; the heart was long since still—and ripped the skin between the legs, so the pale swell of the intestines bulged up from the narrow, black-furred slit, gleaming in the light.

It took both strength and considerable skill to split and peel back the heavy skin without penetrating the mesenteric membrane that held the visceral sac enclosed. I, who had opened softer human bodies, recognized surgical competence when I saw it.

—*Drums of Autumn*, chapter 15,
"Noble Savages"

PART EIGHT

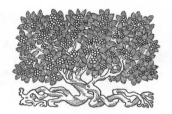

FREQUENTLY
ASKED
QUESTIONS

Q: Is Craigh na Dun a real place?
A: Let's put it this way; if it was . . . would I tell you?

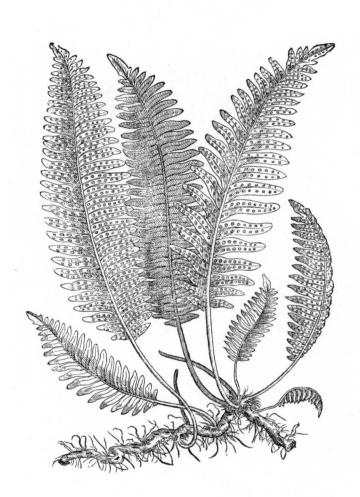

ANSWERS

Q: Who is speaking in the prologues? Claire? Brianna? You?

A: Well, that's a good question. To me, the prologue is essentially the voice of the book speaking, if that makes any sense. All the books are designed to stand individually, as well as to interlock as parts of a whole. Consequently, while I hope the various plot elements, characters, etc., are consistent among the books, each book is meant to be unique in tone, structure, and approach. So, each prologue is meant to convey *something* about the tone and essence of that particular book.

With the exception of *Outlander,* the prologues have been the single most difficult passage to write in each book.[1] It always takes multiple tries to get one right, and I often have to wait for inspiration—in the form of a phrase or vision—to hit.[2] In *Drums,* the prologue was the *last* thing written!

As to the question, though, I prefer to leave the prologues ambiguous. Who is speaking? The book itself (though I do imagine that any given reader may hear the book speaking with the voice of one or another of the characters).

One peculiarity regarding the prologues is that while the ambiguity works fine in written form, the recorded version really has to be a little more certain. That is, the poor actress who does the audiobook recordings (Geraldine James for the abridged Bantam audio versions; Davina Porter for the unabridged versions from Recorded Books (see Appendix VI: "Foreign Editions Audiotapes, and Strange, Strange Covers") is obliged to read the prologues in *someone's* voice.

Evidently, either the abridger or Ms. James decided (they didn't ask me) that the prologues of the first three books should be read in Claire's voice, while the *Drums of Autumn* prologue was read in Brianna's voice.

---

[1] *The* **Outlander** *prologue wasn't actually written* **as** *a prologue; I just began writing a bit of something, and instead of growing into a scene, it stopped. Since I couldn't see where to go with it, I left it alone, and later decided that the reason it wouldn't grow was that it was complete as is. Since the rest of the book was in Claire's voice and this might or might not be, it was obviously the voice of the book talking; ergo, it must be a prologue.*

[2] *A common question to writers is: "Do you write according to a regular routine, or wait for inspiration?" If one waited for inspiration* **all** *the time, there would be very few books written. Most of the time, you write whether you "feel like it" or not—but there are times when you have to wait for Something to speak to you.*

However, the first paragraph of the *Drums* prologue contains this line: "When I look in the mirror, my mother's eyes look back at me. . . ." For what the observation is worth—we've made rather a Big Deal through three books, now, about how much Brianna resembles Jamie Fraser, up to and including the slanted blue cat eyes. Claire's eyes, on the other hand, have been described at no-doubt tedious length in terms of sherry, whisky, and other intoxicant substances of a brownish hue.

And Claire *does* once describe her own mother, while looking at a photograph (in *Voyager*): "Warm brown eyes . . ."

Q: Is there going to be another book about Jamie and Claire?

A: Oh, yes. There will be two more novels—*The Fiery Cross* and (so far) *King, Farewell*—that complete the story of Jamie and Claire. There will also be a prequel volume, dealing with Jamie Fraser's parents, Brian and Ellen, and the 1715 Rising.

That came about rather by accident.[3] A friend asked me whether I would be interested in writing a novella for a four-author anthology she was putting together. "I dunno," I said. "I've never written anything under three hundred thousand words; it would be an interesting technical challenge. Let me check with the publisher, though, and make sure there's no problem."[4]

When I described the invitation to my editor, she said that sounded interesting; what had I thought of doing? I replied that I thought I'd maybe tell the story of Brian and Ellen Fraser's courtship—to which the editor's response was, "Oh, you can't do it

for them, you have to do it for me—I *lust* for that story!"

I pointed out that the publisher doesn't do novellas, to which the editor's response—she's known me a long time—was, "Oh, I'm sure you could make it longer."

The final result was the suggestion of a book that consists of three interlinked novellas; the first tells the story of Colum and Dougal MacKenzie, and how the brothers claimed the leadership of the MacKenzies of Leoch; the second novella is the story of Brian and Ellen's courtship and elopement; the third is Murtagh's story—his friendship with Brian, his love for Ellen, and how it was that he came to stand as godfather to her son.

So let's see—that's six Jamie and Claire novels, one prequel, one companion . . . and I suppose it's possible that we'll have to do a second companion, to catch up with the last two novels (if I do, *that* book will feature a comprehensive index to the whole series). So there will be either eight or nine books in this series, altogether.

Q: Have you written anything else, besides the *Outlander* novels? Are you planning to write any different stories?

A: I've written lots of other things—comic books, radio ads, scholarly articles, com-

---

[3]*Like everything else about these books; I don't know why I should be surprised.*
[4]*Book contracts often give the publisher an "option" on the author's next work; which means that you can't sell another book to someone else until the first publisher decides whether* **they** *want it. This is a simplification of the situation, but that's essentially how it works.*

puter manuals, software reviews, technical articles on the proper way of cleaning a cow's skull—but no other fiction. *Outlander* was my first novel, and I haven't really had time to write anything else besides the Claire and Jamie stories yet.

I do, however, have a contract for two contemporary mystery novels, and I expect (hope) to have the first of these finished soon.

Beyond books, I did in fact produce three pieces of short (well, relatively short) fiction during the last year. I was asked to do a story for an anthology called *Mothers and Daughters,* whose "gimmick" was to have stories written by well-known authors collaborating with either a mother or a daughter.[5] I asked my (then-fifteen-year-old) elder daughter if she'd like to do this, and since she said she would, we did. The story—a romantic fairy tale farce involving a white cat and a copy editor—is titled "Dream a Little Dream for Me."

That experience having proved to be fun for both of us, when another editor asked if I would write a fantasy short story for a German Arthurian anthology, I said I would, if they didn't mind my doing it with my son (I having a son with a major taste for fantastic fiction). They thought that a good idea, so we produced "The Castellan"—the story of a lonely man of mixed blood, a white raven with a sarcastic sense of humor, and a *real* dragon lady, who thinks blood is blood, and it all tastes fine.[6]

I don't know why it should have been such a big year for anthologies, but it was. The editor of *Past Poisons: An Ellis Peters Memorial Anthology of Historical Crime* invited me to contribute a historical crime story. This seemed like an offer I couldn't refuse, so I agreed.

Now, the only historical period I happen to know much about is the eighteenth century, and I didn't think I could take the time to do adequate research on another period for the sake of a short story.[7] So, the eighteenth century it was, and the result was "Hellfire," a story about Lord John Grey,[8] the murder of a red-haired man, and Sir Francis Dashwood's notorious Hell-fire Club at Medmenham Abbey.

Q: When is the next book coming out?

A: I have no idea. It takes me roughly two to three years to write one of the big historical novels, but this span is affected by things like book tours and other promotional activities (to say nothing of family life). Once a manuscript is delivered, the publisher does need time[9] to do the production work, and then the actual publication date is determined by all sorts of factors that aren't in my control and can't be predicted.

I write as fast as possible, consistent with producing a good book, and the publisher nobly tries to get books on the shelves as soon as it can—that's about all

---

[5] *Published by Signet in both hardcover and paperback.*

[6] *The anthology is titled* **Out of Avalon** *(stories set in Arthurian times); to be published in Germany by Droemer, sometime in 1999. So far as I know, the book doesn't yet have an American publisher.*

[7] *Not with people breathing down my neck about where the next novel is, anyway.*

[8] *Yes, the same Lord John who appears in the* **Outlander** *novels. "Hellfire" is set during 1757—a period in his life when he was not interacting with Claire and Jamie, but was tending to his own affairs in London.*

[9] *They'd like a year, but they seldom get it.*

I can tell you. When we do have solid pub dates for books, though, I always post this information on my Web page (www.cco.caltech.edu/~gatti/gabaldon/-gabaldon.html).[10]

Q: Jamie is described as being unable to wink, but in several places in the books, he "opens one eye" to look at Claire. Isn't this the same thing? If he can open one eye at a time, surely he can blink?

A: Well, no, it's not really the same thing. The movements are controlled by different sets of muscles. Try this: Close both eyes, then open one. You should feel a "pull" or movement, in the muscles of your upper eyelid/lower forehead.

Okay. Now, with both eyes open, wink with one eye. Assuming you can do this, you should feel most of the muscle movement in the upper cheek and *lower* eyelid muscles. See?

There was a long discussion on this point in one of the AOL groups, with people trying it both ways. Turns out there are quite a few people out there who can't wink! Some people can wink, but only with one eye. Most were able to open one eye at a time, but some people (who could wink) couldn't open one eye and leave the other closed. Likewise, many people could lift one eyebrow, but not the other. Evidently, there's quite a lot of individual idiosyncrasy in eyelid-muscle coordination.

Q: How do you pronounce your name? What kind of name is it?

A: Gabaldon is a Hispanic name. This means it has two common pronunciations, one English, one Spanish. The most common (English) pronunciation is GAB-uhl-dohn (long "o" in the last syllable; it rhymes with "stone").

The common Spanish pronunciation is gah-vahl-DOHN (still a long "o"). If I meet anyone who pronounces the name correctly in Spanish, I know that they are a) from New Mexico, and b) very likely from the area around Belen, which is where my father came from.[11] (Yes, Gabaldon is my own name, not my husband's).[12]

Q: What happened to Claire's pearls? She pawned them, in *Dragonfly in Amber,* but later on she gives them to Brianna.

A: Well, when I finished the draft of the manuscript, I realized upon reading it through that I had forgotten to get the pearls back. I therefore made a quick note in the margin—"Get pearls!"—but didn't do anything about it until we had reached the galley proof stage.

Since changes in the text are highly undesirable at this stage, whatever I did had to be brief—and it was. On page 672 (U.S. hardcover edition): *"I am a fool,"*

---

[10] *Frankly, you're better off just searching on "Gabaldon."*

[11] *Family legend holds that the first of that name to settle in Belen was one Henrique Gabaldon, who led a small troop of Spanish explorers to New Mexico in the late 1500s. Family legend reports that he was the leader because he was the only one who had a horse. I couldn't say whether this is true, but there have certainly been Gabaldons in New Mexico for a good long time.*

[12] *My husband was mildly put out that I refused to take his name when we got married. I told him, though, that I'd been spelling "Gabaldon" for people for twenty-five years, and I was attached to it.*

Q: Are you Scottish or English?

A: American. Raised in Flagstaff, Arizona.[14] However, my ancestry is both English (with one German branch) and Mexican-American (Latina, Hispanic, Chicana, whatever you want to call it); one of my maternal great-grandfathers emigrated from England (Yorkshire) to Arizona in the late 1800s, and two other branches of my maternal family arrived in New York during the American Revolution,[15] while my father's family is from New Mexico.[16]

Q: Have you ever been to Scotland?

A: I had never been there when I wrote *Outlander*, and did that book entirely from library research (since at the time, I thought the book was purely for practice,

Jamie grumbled, climbing the steep, cobbled streets to the wynd where Alex Randall had his lodgings. "We should have left yesterday, at once, as soon as we got back your pearls from the pawnbroker! D'ye no ken how far it is to Inverness? And we wi' little more than nags to get us there?"

Q: In *Drums of Autumn*, what happened to Willie, after he and Jamie went to the Indian village?

A: I reckon he and Jamie returned to Fraser's Ridge, whereupon he was joyfully reunited with the recovered John Grey, and the two of them went on their merry way to Virginia.

These are long books, but there's only so much room in them, even so; I can't take extra space to explain events that can reasonabiy be taken for granted, or there wouldn't be room to deal with the Truly Interesting Stuff. And while I could certainly have thought of some Interesting Stuff to happen after Willie's return with Jamie, explicating it and tying it in with the overall structure of the story would have made the book substantially longer.[13]

---

[13] *The production people tend to scream loudly and suffer mass coronaries when I turn in a manuscript, as it is.*

[14] *I was actually **born** in Williams, Arizona, a small town some thirty miles from Flagstaff. My family lived in Flagstaff, but the family doctor was having a difference of opinion with the board of the Flagstaff Hospital, and was therefore practicing out of the hospital in Williams—thus causing my twenty-one-year-old parents to drive thirty miles over icy roads in the dead of winter when my mother went into labor. At the age of two days, though, I returned to Flagstaff.*

[15] *Including one Hessian mercenary named Schweitzer (who, judging from the name, must originally have come from a Swiss family).*

[16] *The net result of this interesting heritage is that people most commonly ask me if I am a Cherokee. While I undoubtedly have some small quantity of Native American genes among my DNA, they're most likely Aztec, Maya, or Yaqui, and they come from a looooong way back.*

I hardly thought I could tell my husband I had to go to Scotland to do research). I did take part of the advance money from the sale of *Outlander* and go to Scotland for two weeks, though, while working on *Dragonfly*. It was (luckily!) just as I'd been imagining it. I've been back several times since, for book tours and the like, and would go back like a shot, at the slightest opportunity.

Q: What is your academic background? What did you do professionally before *Outlander* was published?

A: I have an M.S. in marine biology from Scripps Institution of Oceanography, and a B.S. in zoology and Ph.D. in quantitative behavioral ecology (animal behavior with statistics involved) from Northern Arizona University. My thesis was on Nest Site Selection in Pinyon Jays.[17] After getting my last degree, I did two postdoctoral appointments, at the University of Pennsylvania[18] and at UCLA.[19]

I also wrote comic books (freelance) for Walt Disney for a year or two in the late seventies.[20] Then I was a professor at Arizona State for twelve years or so, in the Center for Environmental Studies.

What I actually *did* there, weirdly enough, was to develop an expertise in the brand-new field of scientific computation (the use of computers to do scientific research—in botany, ecology, physiology, meteorology, etc. This is a completely different field from computer science, which is the study of computers and how they work).

As part of this endeavor, I started and ran a scholarly journal called *Science Soft-*

ware for several years. See, I started using computers for scientific analysis in the early eighties, just when microcomputers were getting started. It occurred to me that there should be a venue for other scientists who did what I did (not many, back then) to share their work. The journal took off, and took over—within a year, I was doing virtually nothing else; I ran the journal, did training seminars for scientists wanting to get into computers and lab automation, wrote texts and manuals, and so on.

Essentially, I invented my own specialty. I then called up magazine editors and offered to write about it. That is, I started sending copies of *Science Software* around to the editors of the mainstream computer press (along with one of my Walt Disney comic books, just to be sure they *noticed* my query), asking for assignments—which I got instantly, because at that time, I was one of maybe a dozen people in the world who knew anything about scientific and technical software and could write coherently about it.

In other words, I became established as an "expert" in scientific computation the same way I started writing fiction; I just did it.

I kept doing it, in fact, until I had fin-

---

[17]*Or, as my husband says, "Why Birds Build Nests Where They Do, and Who Cares, Anyway?"*
[18]*This was the job where I butchered seabirds.*
[19]*Torturing boxfish.*
[20]*While holding the postdoc at UCLA. It was very convenient; I lived in Burbank, and could drop off my comic scripts at the Disney studios on my way to UCLA—sometimes also pausing at the NBC studio across the street, where the film technicians were obligingly developing my boxfish movies as a public service.*

ished the draft of *Dragonfly in Amber*. At this point, my university contract came up for renewal, and I decided that it would be nice to see what it was like to sleep for more than four hours at a stretch, so I resigned.

Q: Where did you get the idea for a time travel novel?

A: I had meant *Outlander* to be a straight historical novel, but when I introduced Claire Beauchamp Randall (around the third day of writing—it was the scene where she meets Dougal and the others in the cottage), she wouldn't cooperate. Dougal asked her who she was, and without my stopping to think who she *should* be, she drew herself up, stared belligerently at him, and said "Claire Elizabeth Beauchamp. And who the hell are you?" She promptly took over the story and began telling it herself, making smart-ass modern remarks about everything.

At this point I shrugged and said, "Fine. Nobody's ever going to see this book, so it doesn't matter *what* bizarre thing I do—go ahead and *be* modern, and I'll figure out how you got there later." So the time travel was entirely Claire's fault.

Q: Why did you have *Outlander* start in the 1940s, rather than the present day?

A: Well, three main reasons.

1) I wanted Claire's transition to the past to be as plausible as possible. Thus, coming from both the hardships of postwar Europe and the anthropological travels with her uncle Lamb, her adaptation to Jacobite Scotland would not be as difficult as it might be for a more modern person. It's

difficult for many present-day Americans to realize, but pre-war Britain was really fairly primitive, in terms of the kinds of conveniences—food, travel, refrigeration, plumbing—we take for granted.

2) As I went on working, it was clear to me that at some point Claire would come back to the future, and I had decided that time moves linearly, no matter where you are in it—that is, if you leave from point A, and spend X amount of time living in the past before returning, you will return to A + X. I didn't want to have to go into *my* future in order to write Claire's future—that is, I didn't want to be dealing with the problems both of historical and futuristic novels simultaneously.

3) The third reason turned out not to be of any particular importance, but in the beginning, when I was still playing with the time travel notion, I hypothesized that the time-passage in the stones might be "open" only in or near periods of social violence—warfare, particularly. That would mean time travelers would be likely to "fall in" during times of upheaval, and to travel between periods of violence, when their appearances and disappearances were less likely to be noticed.[21]

I later decided that it made more sense for the time-passages to be geomagnetic in nature, and thus they were affected by the ancient sun feasts (which are related to the gravitational field of the earth and its changing orientation to sun and moon). I

---

[21] *The appearance of time-travelers during such time might also **affect** events of the time, without anyone noticing particularly, owing to the general state of social upheaval.*

Q: Why does Roger not "hear" the stones in North Carolina, when he's fleeing from the Indians and stumbles into the circle?

A: Wrong time of year. If the passage through the stones stands widest open on sun feasts and fire feasts, it is presumably more or less "closed" in the periods between. As Geillis/Gillian's notes indicate, an attempted passage at the wrong time can be fatal.

Q: Why is there a date discrepancy between *Outlander* and *Cross Stitch* with regard to the disappearance of Geillis Duncan into the past?

A: The discrepancy in dates is a mistake—it's a copy-editing error caused by differences between the British edition of the book, which begins in 1946, and the American one, which begins in 1945. The American book was already in galleys when we sold *Outlander* in the U.K., and the publisher's feeling was that since changing the initial date would have required sending the whole manuscript back to the copy editor, it was better to leave it. See "Errata" for a fuller explanation of the error.

Q: Why did you choose Scotland during the Jacobite period as the setting for your books?

A: Well, like almost everything else about these books, it was an accident. I was looking for a time in which to set a historical novel, because I thought that would be the easiest kind of book to write for practice. While pondering, I happened to see a re-run of an ancient *Doctor Who* episode on PBS—one in which the Doctor had a young Scottish sidekick, picked up in 1745. The sidekick was a cute little guy, about seventeen, named Jamie MacCrimmon, and he looked rather nice in his kilt.

I was sitting in church the next day thinking about it, and thought, Well, you've got to start somewhere, and it doesn't really matter where, since no one's ever going to see this—so why not? Scotland, eighteenth century. And that's where I started—no outline, no characters, no plot—just a place and time.

Q: Is there any significance to the title *Dragonfly in Amber?*

A: The dragonfly in amber is something of a symbol of Jamie and Claire's marriage—not only via the token Hugh Munro gives Claire—but as a metaphor; a means of preserving something of great beauty that exists out of its proper time. Also, amber is a rather mystical substance that's been used for magic and protection for thousands of years. (See "Where Titles Come From" for a fuller explanation.)

Q: Which cover(s) do you like best?

A: I like the American hardcover art very much. As for the others . . . well, there are quite a number of different ones, counting all the foreign editions, and some are remarkably beautiful (I particularly like the first edition of the British *Dragonfly* paperback—no longer available, alas). Some are just remarkable.

Let me just state for the record that I really, really, REALLY hate any art that attempts to show the actual features of any of the characters. Since an artist can't possibly imagine what Jamie, Claire, et al really look like, the result is bound to be unsatisfactory to someone who *does* know what they look like. I much prefer such details to be left to the reader's imagination.

Q: Are the books available in audio format?

A: Yes, in various versions. Bantam Audiobooks owns the right to produce abridged commercial versions of all the books, and all four published books have been recorded and are available. The CDs are beautifully produced and beautifully read (the reader for all four books is Geraldine James; a very fine British actress, who does a wonderful job), but they're *very* much abridged; only about one-fifth of each story is on the CDs. These CDs are a good companion to the books, but certainly no substitute.

The unabridged versions of *Outlander* and *Dragonfly in Amber* have been produced commercially by Recorded Books, Inc. (*Voyager* and *Drums* will follow, sometime in 1999).[22] The unabridged version doesn't have music or sound effects, but is beautifully read (by Davina Porter, a terrific Scottish/English actress who sounds a *lot* like Claire), and does include the complete text of the book—on thirty-two-plus hours of CDs per book.

There aren't any U.K. audiobooks available as yet, I'm afraid.

In addition to the commercial CDs, there are two noncommercial recorded versions of the books, produced for print-handicapped readers in the United States. I've been a vol-

unteer at Recording for the Blind for the last seventeen years, and as a special treat, they allowed me to read *Outlander* and *Dragonfly*—normally, I read scientific, medical, and computer texts for them. All books available through RFB are provided free of charge to qualified borrowers, and are read in their entirety. (Perhaps they'll let me read *Voyager* or *Drums,* too, once I've finished the eighth edition of *Biology of Microorganisms.*)

I'm told (I haven't heard them) that all the books are also available from the Library of Congress's Talking Books program, also in unabridged form.

Q: How long does it take you to write a book?

A: It took me eighteen months to finish *Outlander,* about two years each for *Dragonfly in Amber* and *Voyager,* and roughly two and a half years for *Drums of Autumn.* The books got longer, and slightly (ha) more complicated; also, I spent more than four months on the road, doing book tours and promotional appearances for *Voyager,* which tends to cut into the writing time.[23] I'm extremely slow and snail-like, and I rewrite and edit as I go, word by

---

[22]*Recorded Books produces audiobooks mainly for libraries, but does rent or sell books to private readers as well. Call 1-800-638-1304 for details, or check the Recorded Books Web site:www.recordedbk.com.*
[23]*I spent nearly six months, all told, doing promotion for* **Drums of Autumn,** *owing to foreign publishers getting into the act and wanting me to go to Australia and New Zealand and the U.K., etc. It's fun, and I like to meet readers—but I don't get much writing done on the road.*

word, sentence by sentence . . . then go back and change the words again. I average maybe two to three pages a day, except at the very end of the book. At this point, when I know what I'm doing, and where everything goes, I will be writing ten to fifteen pages a day—and sleeping very little.

Q: What kind of research do you do for your books? How do you know when you've done enough research? How long do you research before you begin writing?

A: I know a lot of people do all their research and then begin to write, but that wouldn't work for me—since I never know what's going to happen, I wouldn't know where to stop![24] So I don't—I read and research during all the time I'm writing, and I begin writing immediately.

It's the writing that's important in a book. In terms of research, I often don't know what I need to know until I find it.[25] If something turns out to be wrong, I can change it. If I come to a spot where I really must know something specific before writing it—then I can go and look it up, or I can skip to a different place in the story and leave that spot for later. But nothing counts except words on the page.

I have about two hundred books that belong to the university library (every so often they want one back, which is a traumatic experience), and I also buy books like salted peanuts. I carry a research book around in the car, to read at stoplights or at kids' flute lessons, and I read research material while I work out on an exercise bike or treadmill. Sometimes I do have something specific to look up—like how to extract a tooth, or how many slaves were on the average sugar plantation in North Carolina in 1767, or how much a black bear weighs, but it really doesn't take time to discover a discrete fact—it's the browsing and finding fascinating items like hanged-men's grease (that's historically true, by the way—it was one of the perks of an eighteenth century hangman) that take time. Fortunately, it's also fun.

At one point, I recall coming across a mention of a specific book that seemed, from its title, likely to be important in terms of the research for *Voyager*. The university library didn't have it, and I didn't have time to wait for them to obtain it through interlibrary loan. I called around, and finally located two copies of the book, in a bookstore in New York City. By coincidence, the bookstore was located on the first floor of the building in which my publisher's offices were located. Which is how it happened that my (extremely obliging and forbearant) editor found herself attempting to keep a straight face while asking the bookstore clerk for two copies of *Sodomy and the Pirate Tradition*.[26]

Q: How did you get the Scottish accent right? I am a Scot with a passion for Scottish history, and having heard that you are not Scottish, was frankly expecting the worst. I was pleasantly surprised!

A: Thank you—I'm pleased to hear it! I "got" the Scottish accents from quite a few sources, but the main bases were Scottish

---

[24] *I don't know where to start, either, but that's a different question.*

[25] *See "Research," Part Five.*

[26] *Why two? Well, I have a lot of friends who are writers, and I thought it would make a great Christmas present.*

novels (written by Scots, I mean) and Scottish folk song recordings. Especially in live recordings, groups (like the Corries, for example) will banter with the audience, and you can hear them talk, as well as pick up idiom and vocabulary from the songs themselves.

The "accent" isn't purely an accent, of course—it's my approximation of Scots, which is a real dialect of English. It's not the same thing as Gaelic, which is a completely separate language. Scots is English, but has quite a number of specific words and idioms not found in standard English, and also has its own peculiarly idiosyncratic sentence structures.

Q: Your books are so complex! Do you use an outline?

A: No, I don't use an outline. Of course, I also don't write in a *straight* line; I write in lots of little pieces and then glue them together like a jigsaw puzzle. I'll work forward and back, backward and forward, until a scene is finished—then hop somewhere else and write something different. I don't even have chapters, until just before I print the completed manuscript to send to my editor; breaking the text into chapters and titling them is just about the last thing I do to a book.[27]

And yes, now and then I'll have scenes or fragments that either don't fit or are redundant or extraneous (I'm sure no one thinks I ever edit or cut anything, but I really do. The next-to-next-to-the-last thing I do to a manuscript is a process called "slash and burn"). In most cases, though, those scenes can be recycled into the next book—one of the benefits of writing a series. For example, the brief scene involving Mayer Rothschild,

the traveling numismatist, was originally written for *Dragonfly*. It wasn't that it didn't fit well there—but it wasn't necessary to that story, so I removed it. And lo and behold, it tied in beautifully with the clue of the coins in *Voyager*, where I used it in almost the original version, making only small adjustments for the sake of the plot.

Then there are versions of things that simply don't work—I rewrote the front half of the framing story for *Dragonfly* seven times before I was happy with it—keeping whatever small pieces seemed to work from each iteration.

All writers are different in their approaches to writing, but for me, it's a very organic sort of process, though with its own internal logic—something like growing crystals in the basement.

Q: Do your readers give you ideas?

A: Well, in all honesty, not often. Or rather, they don't give me specific ideas, though often enough, a conversation will trigger a train of thought that eventually results in something—though it may not be at all what the original suggester had in mind! I generally know the shape of the story, if not the specifics, and I know the characters in such a way that I can say that yes they *would* do this, no they *wouldn't* do that, under any circumstances. The only cases I can recall where a suggestion resulted in a specific scene were from a couple of my LitForum (CompuServe) friends—both people I've known for years,

---

[27] *The next-to-last thing I do to a manuscript is to go through and fill in all the little empty square brackets ([ ]), indicating missing pieces of information that I didn't manage to look up yet.*

who've watched the development of the books and characters from the earliest days.

For example, one woman asked me—half-kiddingly—what I thought Jamie would say, think, or do if he came forward in time and saw his daughter in a bikini. Now, there's no way he can travel forward in time, but the question did spark a train of thought that led to that conversation by moonlight in *Voyager,* and Claire's letter to her daughter.

Q: Why is *Outlander* written in the first person point of view?

A: My initial impulse is to say, "Why on earth shouldn't it be?" However, I do get this question quite often at writers conferences, so I'll try to go into a bit more detail.

I like to experiment and try new and interesting things in terms of structure and literary technique (not that writing in the first person is what you'd call madly adventurous). However, the answer is simply that a first person narrative was the easiest and most comfortable for me to use at the

time, and since I was writing the book for practice, I saw no reason to make things complicated.

Now that I know more about writing, there are other good reasons to have done it, but that's why I did it at the time; it felt natural to me. I think I may have felt most comfortable with this (aside from the minor fact that Claire Beauchamp Randall took over and began telling the story herself), because many of my favorite works of literature are first person narratives.

If you look at the classic novels of the English language, roughly half of them are written in the first person, from *Moby-Dick* to *David Copperfield, Swiss Family Robinson, Treasure Island*—even large chunks of the Bible are written in the first person![28]

Which is not to say that there are no drawbacks to using this technique, or that it suits everyone. But if it fits your style and your story, why on earth not?

The framing story of *Dragonfly* is written partly in Claire's first person voice, partly in the third person voice of Roger Wakefield. And, if you look at the first half of *Voyager,* you'll see that it's done in a "braided" technique, telling Jamie's story in third person in a linear chronology, Claire's story in first person backward, in flashback, and using the sections in Roger's voice as the turning points that trigger the other two voices.

---

[28]*I point this out with great regularity to people at conferences who come up to me and demand, "How did you **dare** to write a novel in the first person?" "Easy," I reply. "I just sat down and typed 'I.'"*

Drums, in turn, uses *four* main narrative voices: Claire, Jamie, Roger, and Brianna.[29] Still, Claire's voice is by far the most comfortable for me to use.

Q: What have been the most difficult sections for you to write?

A: Difficult? Goodness, all of them. Well, not really, but writing is hard work, you know, even though a great deal of fun. As for emotional difficulty, which is what I suspect you mean—Claire's farewell letter to Bree, the rape scene in *Outlander,* the farewell scene in *Dragonfly in Amber,* the "Away in a Manger" scene in *Drums,* and a few others that don't come immediately to mind. The ones you'd expect, in other words.

Q: Are all the locations used in the books real?

A: I suppose that depends a bit on what you mean by "real." They're all certainly real to *me.* However, places like Inverness, Loch Ness, and Fort William are real in the map sense as well, as are Paris, Fontainebleau, Cap-Haïtien, etc. If you mean the stone circle at Craigh na Dun . . .

Bear in mind that I had never been to Scotland when I wrote *Outlander.* When I finally did go, I found a stone circle very like the one I had described, at a place called Castlerigg. There is also a place near Inverness called the Clava Cairns, which has a stone circle,[30] and another place called Tomnahurich, which is supposed to be a fairy's hill, but I've never been there, so I don't know how like Craigh na Dun it is. As for Lallybroch . . . well, I do repeat-

edly find things that really exist after I've written them, so I really wouldn't be at all surprised.

Q: How do you develop your characters? Do you keep charts or index cards to keep track of them?

A: I don't keep charts of characters, notes, outlines, anything. I don't write down anything but the text of the book, in part because if I write something down, I forget it.

In the later books, I do occasionally have to count back to see what month of what year it is when a given scene takes place, so I'll know what the weather should be like, but that's about as far as it goes. I don't forget the characters, because I can "see" them. You wouldn't forget what your spouse looks like, or what s/he likes for breakfast, would you? (See "Characters" in Part Two for a fuller description of character development.)

Q: Are you Claire?

A: Well, no. Though of course, I'm *all* the characters; I have to be, after all. But if you are asking whether I based the character of Claire on myself, no, I didn't.

(See "Characters" for a fuller explanation.)

---

[29] *This was not, by the way, a conscious decision. I didn't realize I had done it, until someone wrote to ask me how I'd done it. Oddly—or not—**The Fiery Cross** seems to have five main voices. (The fifth voice is Young Ian's, by the way—for the benefit of readers fearing that I had abandoned him to the Mohawks.)*
[30] *The photo on the back cover of the dust jacket was taken at the Clava Cairns.*

Q: We were trying to figure out the "rules" for the Minister's Cat. Any light you could shed would be helpful.

A: The Minister's Cat is just a simple word game, with no real overall "winner." Each player takes a turn for each letter of the alphabet, trying to pick an adjective that will either baffle or simply amuse his opponent; the person who picks the "best" adjective (one his opponent doesn't know, or just one that's more entertaining) is the winner of that round.

> *The Minister's Cat is an adipose cat.*
> *The Minister's Cat is an adhesive cat.*

Both good, but "adhesive" might be better, since the thought of a sticky cat is funnier than the image of a fat cat.

> *The Minister's cat is a bad cat.*
> *The Minister's cat is a bandkeramik cat.*

("Bandkeramik" is a term used to describe a type of Neolithic pottery, marked with a banded design, i.e., this is a striped cat.) "Bandkeramik" probably wins this round.

The game can vary from the simple to the complex, and is often used to teach vocabulary. I happened on it in a bookstore in Inverness, where I found two small books: *The Minister's Cat,* which showed several alternatives per letter, with amusing illustrations, and *Cat A'Mhinister,* a Gaelic version, which was presented with the suggestion that the game was an effective way of learning Gaelic (Gaidhlig) vocabulary.

Roger and Brianna are, of course, using the game to communicate indirectly with each other, as well as to pass the time on their car trip.

Q: Several of us read and reread the books, discussing them and trying to figure out why Claire and Jamie did what they did or reacted the way they did. We all have one question, though: Why was it so important to Claire to take back Frank's wedding ring at the end of *Drums?* None of us would have taken it back! Can you explain what your thinking was on this point? Even given Claire's history with Frank, her love for Jamie was so great, why would she feel the need to have any ring other than his?

A: I'm tempted to say that this is one of those things that you either see or you don't see—but I'll try to explain. Yes, Claire has history with Frank—a *lot* of history, and very mixed, in terms of joy and pain. He was her first love, her first husband, and when she married him, she did so with the full intention of *being* married to him for life. She is, after all, a very loyal and honest person. For her to have "left" him and chosen to stay with Jamie was an act of betrayal, and she knows it. Frank did nothing wrong; his only "crime" was not to be Jamie. You figure it's fine to forswear your vows and run off with somebody else, just because they're more attractive than the person you married? Claire doesn't.

Granted, the circumstances were extremely pressing, and she had overwhelming reasons—emotional as well as physical—to do what she did, but it *was* betrayal, and the knowledge of it nags at her now and then through the two early books (remember her dreaming of Frank and the miniature portraits?). Her feelings of guilt and her loyalty to Frank are what cause her to press Jamie not to kill Jack Randall, in order to save Frank's life.

Later, when she goes back, pregnant and emotionally shattered, it's Frank who picks up the pieces and glues their life back together. He accepts Brianna fully as his own—which is not something that every man could do; he supports Claire in her decision to become a doctor, appreciating (even as he envies) her sense of destiny. This is pretty much the admirable behavior of an honorable man, and Claire both knows and appreciates it.

Now, in terms of their personal and sexual relationship . . . she abandoned him, and came back only by necessity, carrying the child of a man with whom she obviously remains in love. You figure this was easy for Frank to accept? He's a man with a lot of compassion—but he's very human. He makes repeated efforts at their marriage—and so does Claire—but the simmering rage at her betrayal is still there, underneath. Since he can't or won't admit the truth of her story, they can never discuss it fully, never resolve the situation; Jamie Fraser is always the ghost that haunts their marriage. Small wonder if Frank takes lovers now and then—as either revenge, or simply as refuge.

Okay. So this is a difficult, complex relationship. The difficulties and guilts don't mean that there is nothing of value between them. The love they once had for each other is still there, augmented and supported by their united feelings for Brianna, diminished and eroded by the memory of their betrayals of each other—but still a pillar, standing like a desert rock, twisted and shaped by wind and rain.

If Claire were capable of simply walking away from this sort of history and feeling, abandoning a huge piece of her life and identity, just because she was now in a different place . . . well, she wouldn't be capable of loving Jamie in the whole-hearted way that she does. She wouldn't be a whole person.

As it is, she's now relieved of the guilt of her flawed relationship with Frank, and free to treasure the memory of its good moments. Jamie, being the whole-hearted person *he* is, is aware of this, and wants her to know that he's able to accept the knowledge of what she shared with another man—the one thing Frank *couldn't* do. This has something to do with the nature of love and the concept of obligation as part of love. While Roger is contemplating the issue explicitly (*"Love? Obligation? How the hell could you have love **without** obligation?" he wondered.*), Jamie and Claire are living it implicitly.

For her to refuse Frank's ring, and essentially reject all he was, to deny the value of thirty years of a complex but valuable relationship—well, that would be both dishonest and petty. And neither Claire nor Jamie is small in mind or heart.

Q: I'm confused by Frank's letter at the end of *Drums*—the one Roger tells Jamie about. Did Frank know that Jamie survived, and keep the knowledge from Claire? That's awful!

A: Well, maybe so and maybe no, as Jamie himself is given to saying. That is, it seems clear that at some point Frank *did* find out enough about Jamie to at least suspect a) that Claire's story was true, and b) that Jamie had survived Culloden. However, we don't know *when* Frank found this out, or how convinced he was.

Now look at it from Frank's point of view (I know; readers just don't want to even *think* about Frank, but there he is, nonetheless). You're happily married, then your wife vanishes. You worry, obsess, search, grieve, finally become sort of reconciled . . . and then she comes back, pregnant by another man, and telling wild stories about where she's been.

All right. Being a kind and honorable person—and still loving this woman—you grit your teeth, accept the situation and the oncoming child, and do your best. Your wife is doing her best, too, but it's plain to you that she's still in love with the child's father—whoever that was. Being a professional historian, you have the tools and resources to at least begin to check into her story. It probably takes some time before you get up the resolve to do this, but once you do . . . well, there *was* a guy named Jamie Fraser, and the bits and pieces you can dig up about him do match what your wife told you . . . but do you *really* believe this?

Meanwhile, you have a wonderful daughter, whom you love desperately, and who adores you. You and your wife have some difficulties, but you still do love her very deeply. Losing your wife once was horrible, but you survived; losing both of them now would destroy you.

So what do you do?

IF you assume that the story isn't true, OR that the Jamie Fraser you found is not the one Claire was involved with, then plainly there's nothing you can or should do.

However, IF you assume that the story IS true, and that this IS the correct Jamie Fraser . . . well, then you have a slight moral dilemma.

Do you tell your wife (and by extension, your daughter)? If you do, either of two things may happen: 1) she promptly abandons you *again* and tries to return to Fraser, or 2) she stays with you, but only

out of duty, while plainly longing for another man—which will ruin the fragile web of the marriage you've rebuilt with such pain and difficulty. You'd risk this, on the *supposition* that a wildly unlikely set of circumstances is true, and on small fragments of historical research? (Even if it were all true, you have no way of knowing how long Fraser lived after Culloden.)

If you tell your wife and she does leave, she may well try to take your daughter with her. You might stand your wife's desertion; you can't stand the thought of losing your daughter—or even of losing your daughter's love, which might happen if she learns the truth, whether or not she goes with Claire.

If you tell your wife and she doesn't leave, your marriage will be a hollow shell, and you may still lose your daughter's unquestioning love and acceptance of you as her father. Again, you'd risk your entire life's happiness, on a *chance*? Not bloody likely.

Taking into account only Claire's feelings—if you think her sense of obligation will keep her with you, is it fair or kind to reveal the truth to her? She's made her peace with the loss of the other man, and found some happiness and stability here with you and your daughter. Even if you disregard your own feelings in the matter, and assume the most honorable response from her—is it right to let her be tortured by the knowledge that Fraser survived, to let her agonize over the choice? And once more . . . on only the *chance* that you're right in what you think you know. No.

At the same time, Frank is both a historian *and* an honorable man. He can't, in all conscience, completely ignore what he knows or suspects. IF this is the Jamie Fraser who fathered Brianna, then there is a certain obligation toward Brianna. Frank values the truth; any historian must, even while realizing its limits.

When he learns (as he tells the Reverend) that he has a heart condition, he decides that he must make some gesture. There is a possibility that he might die in the relatively near future. Once he is gone, then the confusing multiplicity of possibilities is reduced. Once dead, he can't be hurt by either Claire's or Brianna's choices—there can be no direct damage to him in their finding out about Jamie Fraser.

At the same time, he can't bear the thought that Brianna might regard him with anger or loathing, once she learns the truth. She may feel this as a betrayal—which it is, but one in which he feels somewhat justified; he *is* Brianna's father, as much or more than the man who sired her, and he will not give up her love for him, or tolerate the thought that she will remember him with scorn.

How then, to impart the truth—safely, after he is dead—and still without letting Claire or Bree know that he had withheld this knowledge from them?

He hits upon the idea of the false gravestone, placed near his own kinsman's. Brianna has always been interested in history, has helped him with his own work, knows about Jack Randall. If she thinks of Frank much after his demise, chances are good that eventually she will go looking for Jack Randall's resting place—as indeed she does. IF she then finds the false grave, and tells her mother . . . well, then it will be up to Claire to tell her daughter the truth. Brianna will learn who her father really is, thus satisfying Frank's feeling of obligation to her and to the truth—and at the same time, will never know that Frank had kept the knowledge from her.

This is not a completely honest method, and Frank knows that; still, it's the most he can bring himself to do, under the circumstances. He does, however, feel the need to confess what he's done—and why—and chooses to tell the Reverend, who he knows will keep his secrets.

So that's what's behind Frank's letter, and why he did what he did. What Roger—and Jamie—choose to do with the knowledge . . . well, that's *their* moral dilemma. It's worth noting, maybe, that Jamie has no hesitation in choosing to tell Claire everything, trusting that the knowledge will not damage her love for him. Frank had no such assurance.

Q: Are any of the fictional characters based on real historical figures?

A: Yes, several of them are. Hard to write about the '45 without mentioning Charles Stuart, after all.

Beyond that—there's a "real" female witch (late sixteenth century) named Geilis Duncane in *Daemonologie,* a treatise on witches by King James of Scotland (later James I of England . . .). The book is about the trial of a coven of witches who James believed tried to assassinate him via black magic (you know how women are always teaming up with the devil to do things like that). I figured anybody up on Scottish witchcraft would know the name, and for anyone who wasn't, it didn't matter.

It is, of course, not *Outlander's* witch's real name—we meet her in *Dragonfly* under (what we suppose is) her original name of Gillian—she took Geillis deliberately as a name because of the original, whom she of course was familiar with, owing to her researches into witchcraft. We'll hear a bit more of this when Roger finds his ancestress's grimoire.

Jack Randall is not real—so far as I know, anyway.

Now, Mother Hildegarde *was* a real historical person, though she lived in the twelfth century, rather than the eighteenth. Likewise, Monsieur Forez, the hangman of *Dragonfly*, was a real public hangman in the Paris of the eighteenth century. Bonnie Prince Charlie and many of the Jacobite lords were naturally real people, as well. (See Part Two, "Characters.")

Q: Who is the ghost in *Outlander*?

A: The ghost is Jamie—but as to exactly how his appearance fits into the story, All Will Be Explained—in the last book of the series.

Q: How is Sassenach pronounced?

A: SASS-uh-nak. It's actually a little guttural on the end, a bit like the German "ach," but not quite so throaty. That's close, though. I asked a kilt salesman I met at a Highland Games, and his pronunciation was later verified by assorted Scots.

Q: Have you ever thought of writing children's books?

A: I included this question because people really do ask it of me quite often, but I haven't the faintest idea why. Do I *look* like someone with a deep-seated urge to write children's books? Does something in what I *do* write suggest to these questioners that I am currently in the wrong line of work?

Whatever the reasons behind the question, though, I'm afraid the answer is no, I can't say I ever *have* had any particular desire to write children's books—though several years ago, one of the neighborhood children down the street asked me if I would someday write a book for *him*. I said dubiously that I supposed I might try, though I couldn't say how long it might take. He asked what the book would be called, whereupon I told him (I can't imagine why; first time a good title has ever popped into my head without prompting) it would be called *The Tree That Ate Small Children*. So if you ever see a book with this title on the shelf in the children's section of the bookstore, you will know I finally got around to it. I have a few other things to do first, though.

Q: When is Jamie's birthday?

A: May 1. I had one reader argue with me about this, insisting that he *had* to be a Leo, but I assure you he isn't. My husband and kids are all Tauruses, and I know what they're like. May 1 it is. (See "Horoscopes," in Part Two.)

Q: Is the story of the Dunbonnet and the laird who hid for seven years true?

A: Leap o' the Cask is real—so is the story of the laird who hid in the cave for seven years, whose tenants called him the Dunbonnet, and his servant, who brought the ale to him in hiding. The laird's name? Ah . . . James Fraser. Really.

Q: Who/what is Master Raymond? What is his significance?

A: He's a prehistoric time-traveler. I think he came from somewhere about 4000 B.C. or perhaps a bit earlier (not technically prehistoric, but they certainly weren't using written records where *he* started out), and the eighteenth century is not his first stop. I think I won't say more about him just now, though—other than to note that we'll tell his story in a later series of novels, after the *Outlander* cycle is complete.

Q: Were Jonathan Randall and the Duke of Sandringham lovers?

A: No, the Duke and Randall weren't lovers, though the Duke certainly understood Randall's psychology, and no doubt used it to control him. The Duke was simply a practicing homosexual, whereas Randall was a sadist of indiscriminate appetites. Given their relative social positions—and the Duke's taste for manipulation and power—Randall couldn't possibly have assumed the necessary psychological dominance over the Duke for a sexual relationship between them to exist, nor would he willingly have submitted to the Duke. And while the Duke might have forced Randall to oblige him, it's not likely; Randall was an effective tool for him, and engaging Randall in a sexual relationship would have destroyed that effectiveness. The Duke might also have found Randall not quite to his taste—which evidently ran to young, handsome, fair-skinned boys, given his early attempt on Jamie's virtue.

"Lovers," as a term, implies a certain emotional equality, which certainly didn't exist in this case.

Q: How is Laoghaire pronounced? Where did the name come from?

A: I got Laoghaire off a map. And no, I had no idea how it was pronounced, though I had a guess. Geraldine James, who does the abridged recordings of the books, pronounces it "Leery," and Davina Porter (who does the unabridged versions) pronounces it "Lee-yur"—and a couple of Scottish correspondents have given me slightly different pronunciations (one person said this was her grandmother's name, and that the grandmother pronounced it "L'heer.").

Q: How is Geillis's name pronounced?

A: I don't know. For what the observation is worth, Geraldine James (on the abridged recording) calls her GAY-liss or GAY-lee, and Davina Porter (unabridged) pronounces it GEE-liss (GEE as in "geese") and GEE-lee. Either or both of them may be right. I recently met a Scot who pronounced it "JILL-is."

Q: Why doesn't Jamie use the endearment *"mo duinne"* in *Voyager* or *Drums*?

A: Er . . . well . . . cough. He doesn't say *"mo duinne"* in *Voyager* because between *Dragonfly in Amber* and *Voyager* I acquired the gracious assistance of a native speaker of Gaelic, one Iain MacKinnon Taylor (who kindly advised on all the Gaelic bits in *Voyager* and *Drums*).[31]

---

[31] *And kindly went beyond the call of duty in constructing the Gaelic pronunciation guide for this book, as well.*

Mr. Taylor informed me that while *"mo duinne"* had the right words for what I meant to convey, it wasn't idiomatically correct—that is, the proper expression would be *"mo nighean donn."* So I used that in the subsequent books, wishing (as always) to be as accurate as possible.

Q: Who were the Paleolithic lovers in *Dragonfly in Amber*? What was their significance?

A: I didn't really have anything specifically in mind about the Paleolithic lovers—they were simply a metaphor for the briefness of life and the importance of love—but then again, often I write something that I intend to be only color, and it turns into something else in later books.

There's that ghost in *Outlander,* for instance. . . .

I got the lovers from the *National Geographic,* as a matter of fact. The original were a couple from Herculaneum (or possibly Pompeii) whose skeletons had been found during the excavation, lying in the manner I described in *Dragonfly*—his arms around her, trying to protect her when the fire came down on them. One of the most touching and dramatic pictures I've ever seen. It's stuck in my mind for years, so it was there when my subconscious needed it as an image of mortality and love.[32]

Q: As a scientist, what do you really think about the Loch Ness Monster?

A: Well, when someone hauls one in, I'll look at it and tell you. Anything else would be hypothesizing without the benefit of data, which is rather unsound, scientifically speaking.

Speaking UNscientifically, my best guess is the one that Claire and Roger come up with in *Voyager*—that there's a time-gate under the loch, and various creatures have come and gone through it over the years, each staying in the present-day loch for varying periods. This accounts for a) the occasionally conflicting descriptions of the creature, and b) the fact that periodic searches by boat and sonar have failed to find any large-bodied creatures (not that this necessarily shows that there is no large creature there; it's impossible, practically speaking, to search a large body of water with any certainty).

Q: What kind of dinosaur is Nessie?

A: The one Claire saw is probably a plesiosaur. I have one of the British Museum models of it on my bookshelf. The model is blue . . . and so is Claire's monster. The small details of appearance are based on a knowledge of basic reptilian anatomy, though.

Q: Where will the story end?

A: I think the *Outlander* books will end in about 1800, in Scotland. If this tells you anything, more power to you.

Q: Will the story have a happy ending?

A: Oh, yes, the last book will have a happy ending, though I confidently expect it to leave the readers in floods of tears, anyway.

---

[32]*And is at least a partial answer to the people who ask, "Where do you get your ideas?" Everywhere.*

Q: What is the one thing you are most proud of accomplishing and why?

A: Being married to the same man for more than forty years. It's so much better than promiscuity or loneliness.

Q: You've said before that your writing style is to write all the scenes and then piece them together in order when you've gotten them all done. Do you only do this for novels or does it apply to your short stories and novellas as well? Why is this method so effective for you and do you ever try writing in a straight line just for the fun of it?

A: What fun would *that* be? <puzzled look> It would take forever to do it that way, since I couldn't start writing until I'd figured out the entire story, and if I'd done that, it wouldn't be fun at all to write it.

Anyway, yes; I write just about everything piecemeal, including nonfiction articles, book reviews, and essays. It's effective because it works; I'm never held up stewing about What Comes Next—I don't *care* what comes *next,* I just care about something I can see happening. The order of the happening has a logic to it (often, more than one), and that will become clear to me as I work.

Q: Who was your favorite author when you were younger and who is your favorite author now? Why?

A: You gotta be kidding. How would I pick *one?*

Q: What is the significance of the letters—Q, E, and D—that Jamie shows Claire in *Voyager?*

A: QED is the abbreviation for a common Latin expression, *"Quod erat demonstrandum"*—"Thus it has been shown."[33] In the olden days (when I went to school), one would do a proof of a theorem, and then write at the bottom of it, next to the result, "QED."[34]

In terms of Jamie and the story, though, he keeps the slugs of lead type as a reminder not to overlook alternative answers to what seem insoluble problems. As you may recall, he tells Claire the story of how an acquaintance was urging him to write something, and he was demurring, saying that it was impossible because of his difficulty with a pen—not realizing, until the acquaintance pointed it out, that he had been setting type with great facility (i.e., "writing") all through the discussion. In other words, "thus it has been shown" that there was another way—and one which he promptly adopted.

Q.E.D.

Q: What does Roger mean by his comment in *Drums*—"Eat your heart out, Tom Wolfe"?

A: Just me being too literarily cute for my own good. He's referring (obliquely) to Thomas Wolfe's (not Tom Wolfe; the ear-

---

[33] *Evidently not nearly as common as I thought, considering how many people ask this question. Don't people take geometry anymore?*
[34] *The Latin equivalent of "SEE?"*

lier one) work, with its reiterated theme of "You can't go home again." I.e., Roger is sardonically recognizing both the truth of that statement—and the contradictory fact that the manse under Fiona's mangement seems just as it did when it *was* his home.

Q: How supportive was your family when you decided to change careers from a solid science-based field to writing fiction?

A: I wasn't crazy enough to tell them. My husband would have tried to stop me—not out of any objection to my writing novels, but out of fear that I'd drop dead of exhaustion. He would have said, "Wait 'til my business is doing better and you can quit one of your jobs, wait 'til the kids are all in school. . . ." And I just knew that if I didn't do it now, I might never do it. So I didn't tell him.

By the time he found out, I'd been at it for eight months or so; it was too late to stop me. I didn't tell my father until after I'd sold *Outlander*. I called him; told him all about it. He said how proud he was of me, how much my mother (who died when I was 19) would have loved it, and so on. We hung up. Thirty seconds later, the phone rings; it's Dad. "Don't quit your job!" he said.

Q: Have the *Outlander* books been translated into other languages? How many countries are they available in?

A: Yes, many of them. As of early 2015, I believe the books have been published in 42 countries (Bulgaria, Latvia, and mainland China having recently joined the gang) and 38 languages (four of the countries in which the books are published being English-speaking).

Q: How did Fergus and his wife get to the New World? They weren't on the boat (that got wrecked by the hurricane) with Claire and Jamie.

A: True. We assume that Jamie sent for Fergus, as soon as they got dried off. The Frasers would have spent a few weeks at Les Perles, waiting for Claire's broken leg to heal, before beginning their trek northward through the Carolinas, and this would allow enough time for a message to reach Fergus in Jamaica, and for him to come and join them. Marsali, of course, stays behind in Jamaica, awaiting the birth of their first child, and joins them later, after they've established the settlement on Fraser's Ridge.

Q: I have a question in regard to the La Dame Blanche story that you refer to in a couple of these novels. Did you invent this story or does it have significant traces in history? The reason that I ask is that I am studying in a Chaucer class here at Bucknell University and I found a reference in one of his poems that reminded me of the "White Woman" story within your books. If this is in fact an historical legend, then I would love to research it a little to find out more about the story.

A: The "white woman" is a well-known figure in Celtic mythology; I'd found brief mentions in several different sources on Celtic folklore and mythology. See the Annotated Bibliography, and the essay "Magic, Medicine and White Ladies" (Part Two), for more details.

Q: Has it ever been revealed who hit Jamie in the head with an ax before he went to the French monastery to recover? Was it Dougal or one of his men?

A: It hasn't yet been revealed, but we may find out, one of these days.

Q: What becomes of young Hamish MacKenzie? Will he come to America?

A: You'll find out a bit about Hamish and the other survivors from Leoch who went into exile, in *An Echo in The Bone*, the seventh book in the series (the synopsis of *Echo* is in *The Outlandish Companion, Volume Two*). For what the observation is worth, though, a good many MacKenzies did settle on Prince Edward Isle and in Nova Scotia—and a regiment of these MacKenzies did come down across the border to fight (on the American side) in the Battle of Saratoga, in 1777.

I know Jamie and Claire are in that battle, because I *have* written about the events that transpired after it.[35] I'd be really surprised if they didn't meet Hamish again, but you never know. A heck of a lot of things happened during that battle.

Q: I read an excerpt on your Web page from *King, Farewell*, in which Jamie writes a letter to Claire, and was distressed that he seemed to have lost his charming Scottish accent. Why is this?

A: Well, it was a letter, rather than dialogue. Most people who *speak* with accents don't *write* with accents, you know. A Southern gentleman, for instance, would probably begin a letter to a female acquaintance as "Dear Mary," rather than, "Hey, darlin'," even if the latter was his common mode of address in person.

Q: I'm confused about one thing; if Geillis went through the stones in 1968, for the first time, how is it that she was there before Claire?

A: We don't yet know everything there is to know about the intricacies of time travel (though I imagine we'll find out more as Claire, Roger, and Brianna put their heads together and compare experiences and make deductions). Remember that Gillian Edgars used a blood sacrifice when going through the door for the first time—it may have been that she was right about this giving her power, and thus traveled farther—or the sacrifice may have been irrelevant, but some other factor was operating.

Q: When Claire, Brianna, and Roger were trying to find out what happened to Jamie at and after Culloden, couldn't they have saved themselves a lot of work by reading Frank's books? I don't recall seeing it mentioned anywhere that anyone actually read his books, and didn't he write of that time period? Had he followed up on Jamie?

A: Claire couldn't bring herself to read the books because—convinced Jamie was dead—she couldn't bear to relive the days of the Rising. Roger is a scholar of the period, though, and Brianna loved and admired her father, and wanted (originally) to follow in Frank's footsteps as a historian. They've almost certainly read

---

[35] *This part of the story was published as a short story, titled "Surgeon's Steel," in **Excalibur**, a fantasy anthology edited by Richard Gilliam, Martin Greenberg, and Edward E. Kramer, and published as a trade paperback in 1995 by Warner Books, Inc.*

the books—and since they didn't mention anything in them connected to Jamie Fraser, there probably was nothing in the published books about him. However, Frank's correspondence with the Reverend Wakefield makes it clear that he not only looked for Jamie Fraser—he found him. Now, *what* he found, and what use he chose to make of the information . . . well, that we may learn in time.

Q: Do you ever have any objections from Scottish readers regarding "appropriation of voice"? That is, do they object to you writing about Scottish characters and issues, when you aren't Scottish?

A: Well, my own opinion is that imagination is its own country. Also, I don't think much of the notion that one can only write about a particular ethnic or geographical group if one happens to have a genetic membership in that group. Still less, the notion that one *can* write well about a given group only *because* one belongs to it.[36]

Fortunately, however, I haven't had any complaints whatever by Scottish readers. The books luckily have been very popular in Scotland; in fact, *Drums of Autumn* came out at number two on the Scottish bestseller list (right under the new *Scottish Parliament's Green Paper,* which was number one) and I regularly get fan letters from Scotland, many of them asking, "How long did you live in the Highlands before moving to Arizona?"[37]

---

[36] *I recall a poet friend once telling me of a heated academic controversy regarding whether another (well-known) poet's work should or should not be regarded as "black poetry." I said that I'd met the poet in question, and . . . um . . . she **is** black, so where did the controversy come in? Evidently, some critics thought her poems did not deal with "The Black Experience"—that is, what **they** thought/said Experience was—as though an entire race, composed of dozens of cultures, was only entitled to one. I said I thought this was silly, and I still do.*

[37] *Which just goes to show that you really can fool all of the people some of the time, and some of the people all of the time, I suppose. It also goes to show that it pays to do research.*

When I did my first book tour in Scotland, I was thrilled to discover my books placed in the "Scottish Fiction" section of each bookstore I went into. Scots being very proud of their literary and cultural heritage, I was more than flattered to find my work placed with that of Robert Louis Stevenson, John Buchan, Lady Antonia Fraser, et al. I said as much to one bookstore manager, who looked at me, raised his eyebrows, and replied, "Well, Guh-BALDun is such an odd name, we thought it might quite well be Scottish!"

In short, far from the Scots objecting to my appropriating their voice—I rather think they've appropriated *me*.

PART NINE

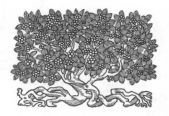

CONTROVERSY

*When I read my mail, I sometimes think I'm not writing novels,
I'm writing Rorschach tests.*

—*David Gerrold,*
fantasy and science fiction novelist
and screenwriter

Communication

Interviewers are often curious as to why I continue to post excerpts of my work in electronic venues such as my Web site and the various CompuServe forums I inhabit. After all, I already have an agent, an editor, a multibook contract; why else would anyone do this?[1]

The answer is that I make small pieces of my work available electronically for one reason, and one reason only—I like people to read them.

All art is an act of communication, and while an artist had better have some appreciation of his or her own work, no work of art is complete until someone else shares it. Some ephemeral forms, such as dance and stage-acting, don't even exist independently of the observer. Writing at least has the advantage of semipermanence; barring disk crashes, viruses, and house fires, the words aren't going anywhere once you've captured them on paper—and the creation not only *can* be done in solitude, but often demands it.

Still, communication requires two parties. Having written something, I feel that some small cosmic circle remains unclosed until that something is read. Given the snail-like speed with which I work, books emerge into the light of day at fairly wide intervals; two or three years is a long time to wait for gratification. At the same time, because I write episodically, small pieces of the work are in fact "finished" (i.e., done as well as I can do them, given my capabilities at the time) a long time before the work as a whole is complete.

I never post more than a fraction of any book—only a few pieces are really appropriate for such independent reading—but being able to share my work periodically gives me great satisfaction, and encourages me to go *on* working. I'm not looking for critique or suggestion when I post something—the work is "finished," as I say—but I do enjoy hearing comments, either on posted excerpts, or on published books, both because that closes the circle for me, and because it's very interesting to see how readers respond to specific incidents and characters.

However, among the enormous quantities of mail I receive (both regular mail and e-mail), is an occasional communication that makes me think that some small cosmic circle has perhaps closed with a Moebius twist.

---

[1] *In fact, I never **did** post work in an attempt to attract agents or editors. Given the way publishing works, random electronic exposure is not really a very effective way to go about it, and was still less so when I began writing novels, many years ago.*

Unless one is writing the sort of book that focuses on major political events—and giving very unusual interpretations of same—historical fiction isn't often a strongly controversial subject. Still, I have noticed a few subjects of controversy in the *Outlander* books; subjects that have formed the basis of heated discussions among groups of readers in online venues, or are the subject of (rare, luckily) complaint by letter writers.

The thing about communications, as I noted above, is that it takes two to tango. This means that while I intended something specific in the writing, the persons reading it will be interpreting it in the light of their own experiences and preconceptions, and may well come to different conclusions than the one I intended. I now and then read a letter with one eye shut (out of disbelief at what I'm seeing), meanwhile thinking, I'm not sure which book you read, but I'm pretty sure it wasn't the one I wrote.

Still, I do make an effort to address any sincerely expressed concern, explaining how and why I have taken a particular step in the writing that has caused concern to my correspondent. In most such cases, the correspondence draws to a mutually cordial and respectful close, as did most of the conversations below.

Red Bird

I don't really like controversy and certainly don't seek to create it—but if one is going to have strong opinions (and I'm afraid one is), one had better be willing to explain or defend them when necessary.

Sex

Every now and then—roughly once every two years—I get a letter from someone objecting to the sexual content of the novels. These letters are invariably polite; their objection is usually based on the theory that Great Literature does not include sex scenes. Since they are kind enough to consider my books as otherwise qualifying for this classification, they feel that the inclusion of sexual encounters lowers the tone of the work, and is thus to my artistic detriment.

While I do appreciate the care for my literary reputation reflected by these letters, I must respectfully disagree on the place of sex in the novels. There are a great many reasons why an author may choose to include explicit depictions of sex; the least worthy is of course to provide titillation to the reader—and I suspect some of my correspondents feel that this is the *only* possible reason for including such material.

It's not, though. Human beings being what they are, an interest in sex is hard-wired into the genetic machinery, and thus lies behind a great deal of human behavior, whether it's explicitly recognized or not.[2]

---

[2]*I was at one point in my checkered career an ethologist—one who specializes not in ethics, but in the study of animal behavior (not that animals are unethical; it's just a concept that doesn't apply).*

Given that one level of the novels is devoted to an exploration of the nature of love and marriage, it seems to me that some reference to sex is likely desirable. That is, there may possibly have been devoted asexual marriages in history, but that isn't how it usually works. And if one is interested in what *does* work between two people, I think that the sexual aspects of their relationship are certainly a legitimate concern.

While I'm happy to hear that these readers think so highly of my efforts otherwise, I really do think the scenes involving sex are a necessity to this particular story, whatever one feels the requirements of Great Literature to be.

To avoid giving a false impression, I should perhaps emphasize here that I get a very small number of controversial letters, overall. So far as I can recall, I've had perhaps three (out of ten thousand or so) objecting to the sexual content. On the other hand, I've had roughly three hundred letters asking for *more* sexual content—but not being either a television network or a politician, I'm afraid I don't respond to preference polls.

FOUL LANGUAGE—"THE F-WORD"

After wife-beating (see p. 411), the most common objection I encounter among letter writers (roughly twenty letters, so far) is to "foul language," or blasphemy—"taking the Lord's name in vain," as my correspondents put it, though in fact they are often concerned with language that is merely vulgar, rather than truly profane.[3]

A nice woman in her seventies (I know how old she was, because she announced that she had been born in 1925) came up to me at a signing once, and after the usual sort of conversation, in which she said how much she enjoyed all the books, confided that she had been just a *little* disappointed in *Drums,* because of my use of "the F-word."

I didn't point out that I had used the same word in *Outlander, Dragonfly,* and *Voyager,* where it evidently hadn't troubled her in the least. I did, however, say that I felt the use of that particular word was appropriate in the spot where I used it—i.e., that a young man of Roger Wakefield's age and background, in the late 1960s, would have been inclined to use that expression in the particularly stressful situation in which he found himself (*Drums,* chapter 18, "Unseemly Lust").

The lady frowned and said that *she* had been born in 1925, and *she* never used such language. I bit the inside of my mouth and politely replied that I'd been born in 1952, and I didn't use that sort of language, either—but Roger does.

In point of fact, as the result of a conservative upbringing, and an early education acquired in a Catholic elementary school, I am completely unable to swear. I might say "Damn!" under extreme provocation, but the F-word has never passed my lips in public hearing. It's therefore quite a relief that Claire has no such inhibitions.

---

[3]*Many people no longer make any distinction between obscenity, vulgarity, and profanity. I spent eight years in a Catholic parochial school, and I do.*

The F-word, however, was not (so far as I can ascertain) nearly so popular in the time in which Claire acquired her habitual colorful expressions as it is now. So while she is given to casual blasphemy ("Jesus H. Roosevelt Christ!"), she tends not to employ the F-word often (though she does use it now and then, under stress).

NB: The following is a representative sample of the sort of correspondence I sometimes get on this subject.[4]

From: Doug Toole
To: 76530.523@CompuServe.COM
Date: Mon, 2 Jun 1997 18:22:41 EDT
Subject: commendation & word question

Dear Diana

The Outlander series is great. I have listened to and read the series several times and find it difficult to wait for you to get another read. Thank you for the series.

Question: The first three books were great without the F-words,[5] is it necessary to use these words? I personally feel that the people of that time did not use that word.[6] I will continue to read and listen to your books but would rather not have to expose my children to the word when I can prevent. Doug Toole

---

[4]*Mr. Toole's messages are reprinted here with his permission.*
[5]*In fact, all four of the novels include the F-word. Apparently it didn't/doesn't trouble people to hear Claire use it, while hearing it from Roger **did** bother them. I couldn't say whether this is because they're accustomed to Claire's fairly casual use of bad language (while Roger is a clean-spoken preacher's boy), or simply because the scene in which Roger uses the word is one of considerable emotional intensity, causing the word to stand out more sharply. Interesting, though.*
[6]*I have now and then had a reader tell me that the F-word was certainly known in the eighteenth century, having been recorded since the fifteenth century, and therefore, it's not likely that Jamie would be unfamiliar with it, in the scene (**Outlander** [page 432]) in which he asks Claire its meaning. It's quite true that the word was in existence in 1743. However, I offer two possibilities in response:*

*1) While the F-word certainly was a well-known **English** expression, it's much less likely that it was commonly employed in the Scottish Highlands (where many—in fact most [but we have made slight adjustments to strict historical accuracy, for the sake both of Claire and the reader]—people spoke no English at all in the eighteenth century). Nor was it likely to have been commonly heard in France, where Jamie fought as a mercenary. Given that he had never been in England at the time, and did not normally associate with English people, it's at least reasonable to assume that he might **not** be familiar with the word.*

*2) It's possible that Jamie **did** know what Claire meant by the word—by context, if not by familiarity. However, examine the effect of his claim of ignorance; it temporarily deflects Claire's anger, and defuses the situation, which hitherto has been Fraught. Do we think that Jamie might possibly be a sufficiently good psychologist as to be claiming ignorance as a means of changing the force and direction of the argument, rather than because he truly **is** ignorant?*

I don't know about you, but I'm inclined to give him credit.

From: Diana Gabaldon
To: Doug Toole
Date: Fri 06 Jun 97 03:11:29 EDT
Subject: commendation & word question

Dear Doug—

If you were reading the books with some attention, you might notice that "the F-word" is _not_ used in "that time" (i.e., by eighteenth century characters). It _was,_ however, used—with what I thought reasonable frequency—both in the 1940s (where Claire learned it, no doubt), and in the 1960s, which is where it occurred in the book Drums of Autumn. Hate to tell you this, but people—especially young men in a rage—did indeed use that there word; I was alive in 1960, and I heard them.<g>[7]

Glad you've enjoyed the books otherwise.—Diana

From: Diana Gabaldon
To: Doug Toole
Date: Fri 06 Jun 97 03:11:30 EDT
Subject: commendation & word question

P.S. It does occur to me to wonder about your comment about "not exposing your children" to the F-word—how old *are* your children? If they're too young to be entirely familiar with that word, I'm afraid they're a *lot* too young to be reading my books, and not (by any means) because of the language.

---

[7] *<g> is what's called—in electronic parlance—an "emoticon." Since facial expressions aren't visible in online conversation, correspondents may now and then include an emoticon for clarification—ensuring, for instance, that their correspondent knows they are smiling or intending a light tone. The <g> (or <G>) emoticon indicates a <grin>.*

From Doug Toole
To: 76530.523@CompuServe.COM
Date: Fri, 6 Jun 1997 07:44:02 EDT
Subject: Re: Commendation & word question

Diana,

Thanks for your prompt response. The children or child now is four and loves books either audio or printed. You are right, too young to be reading your book. But we as a family traveling on trips enjoy listening to books, yours included. As an example we just returned from eleven days driving from Seattle to Needles and back. So we are cognizant of the language popping up. We know she will learn the words but would like to keep her virginal as long as possible. No reply is needed unless you would prefer. Once again we enjoy your books and will continue to look forward to them in the future.

From: Diana Gabaldon
To: Doug Toole
Date: Sun 08 Jun 97 04:43:37 EDT
Subject: commendation & word question

Dear Doug—

Well, I have children myself (11, 13, and 15 at the moment), and we try not to expose them to "bad language," either, in spite of the fact that they all *know* all the words already (there's still some point to insisting that these are not suitable for civilized conversation, after all).

The thing is, though—my books are definitely written (and carefully written at that) for adults. When I *do* use bad language in the books (oddly enough, I never use it, personally; never), it's because it seems to me to be

called for, by the circumstances and character. In the case of the F-word in DRUMS (I did use that same word in all the other books, by the way, though sparingly), it's used by a young man in the grip of angry (and sexually motivated) passion, in the late 1960s. Given *this* character, *this* time period, and *this* set of circumstances, his language seemed entirely appropriate.

Now, one reason for insisting that bad language not be used in everyday discourse is, of course, that it's low-class and offensive. One other reason—equally important, in my opinion—is that such language does have its own legitimate purpose; that is, to express feeling that is *also* beyond the limits of normal civilized discourse. To use such words casually deprives them of their impact.

You can see that, in the scene in question in DRUMS. If Roger normally spoke like that, the reader wouldn't have (what I hope is) the impression of a man driven almost beyond endurance, and holding on to his notions of decent behavior with great effort.

Okay. So, the point is that when I do use strong language, I have a specific reason for doing so. It really doesn't seem reasonable to me to eradicate such language—chosen and used carefully, to a purpose—on the grounds that someone *might* someday wish to listen to a taped version of an adult book in the presence of a small child. Hm?

(By the way, I do hope you read the books themselves; owing to abridgment constraints,

only about one-fifth of each story is on the audio versions.[8])

Cordially,—Diana

From: Doug Toole
To: 76530.523@CompuServe.COM
Date: Sun, 8 Jun 1997 04:58:34 EDT
Subject: Re: commendation & word question

Diana

The fact that you have heard my concerns puts it to rest, thank you for that personal response. My wife and I will continue to be readers and listeners of your works. We hope that you have many rewards and much happiness in your life.

"Taking the Lord's Name in Vain"

The following is a letter I wrote to an early correspondent in reply to her objection to what she perceived as unnecessary blasphemy. As it stated my position fairly clearly and was well received by my correspondent, I've continued to use variants of it in reply to similar complaints, whenever they occur.

December 7, 1993

My dear Mrs. F.:

Thank you so much for your lovely letter. I do try to answer all of my mail[9]—I love to hear from people who read my books—but it often takes me months, since there is rather a

---

[8]*At the time this conversation took place, only the abridged form of the audiobook was available.*
[9]*Well, in 1993 I did.*

lot of mail, and my husband and editor tend to object strongly to my writing letters when they think I ought to be writing books!

Still, I thought I would snatch a moment to respond to your letter, today being slightly less busy than usual.

I'm happy that you appreciate the research and the quantity of detail that goes into these books; it is a great deal of work, but I do enjoy the research very much, as well as the embodiment of detail in the story. And, as I'm sure you've noticed, it is in great part this use of detail that gives the books their sense of immediacy—of the reader "being there," so to speak.

What I would like to observe, though, is that this concern with accuracy and detail extends as much to the language of the characters as it does to the physical details described in the book. I appreciate your concern over the use of profanity and vulgar expressions; I am myself an observant Roman Catholic, and—owing to having been raised in a Catholic home, and gone to parochial school throughout my formative years—I don't use any form of such language myself.

However, I have read a great many documents composed in the eighteenth century—and earlier—comprising correspondence, journalistic accounts, essays, and fiction of the period. I have an extensive collection of dictionaries, dealing with Scots, Gaelic, idiomatic French, and historical English slang, which I consult while writing. Such terms (including what my children refer to as "the s-h word") have been in use—and the common use of them deplored by moral writers—for a very long time indeed. If I could unearth it from the huge piles of material in my study, I would send you an extract from an essay written in the Middle Ages by St. Jerome (of Vulgate Bible fame), in which the writer strongly deplores the common use of profanity and vulgarity, and laments the undoubted corruptive effect of such language upon society.

In addition, owing to the oddness of my previous careers—I was a professional ecologist (I was a university professor for twelve years, prior to the publication of *Dragonfly in Amber*), an "expert" in scientific computation, and a marine biologist—I tended to work in environments where most of my colleagues were men, ages 20 to 45. And the unfortunate truth is that men do talk that way.[10]

The casual use of profanity and vulgarity is much less apparent in mixed situations—and women in groups tend to do it much less frequently—but it is a common pattern of speech in male groups. There seems to be no real intent of disrespect to the Almighty or offense to one's companions; it's simply a common and accepted manner of speech. This is particularly true in military situations, and—so far as I can ascertain from my reading of World War I and World War II documents, as well as the private journals of earlier combatants—it has always been the case.

This being so, I do feel that depicting speech as it is or was commonly practiced is merely part and parcel of the commitment to historical realism that is the job of a historical novelist—not a condonement or encouragement of improper speech, but simply the best approximation possible of what persons in such a situation might actually have said. You will have observed, I hope, that people in mixed groups, in family settings, or in groups of women in my books do *not* use any such

_____

[10]*I have since learned—to my horror—that women often do this, too. Can't imagine what the world is coming to.*

language. But men—particularly on the battle-field or in casual work—definitely do.

In other words, while I hope the existence of such dialogue will not impair your enjoyment of my books, I don't mean to stop doing it. The use of such expressions is not the result of carelessness or of my own personal preference in usage, but a conscious inclusion—as much a meticulous detail as the description of house furnishings or wardrobe.

I am delighted that the books have brought you pleasure in other respects, particularly the relationship between Jamie and Claire. Speaking of the books, I really must go and write some more, so I trust you will excuse my stopping here. Again, thank you so much for writing, and I trust you will enjoy the next two books. And have a good time on your trip to Scotland!

Best wishes, Diana Gabaldon

HOMOSEXUALITY

Among the occasional controversies, I find that the topic of homosexuality arises now and then. A few readers dislike any reference to homosexuality and simply object to the inclusion of any gay character ("I don't want to see Jamie kiss any more men!" as one letter writer sternly adjured me). That is, of course, their personal preference, but really has nothing to do with either the books or the characters.

I do, however, get a few letters objecting to what the reader sees as my "negative portrayal of homosexuals"—usually with reference to the character of Black Jack Randall.

Black Jack Randall

Well, one swallow does not a summer make, and one pervert scarcely condemns an entire segment of the sexual populace. Black Jack Randall is who he is—an individual—and he fulfills his fictional purpose in *Outlander* and *Dragonfly in Amber* without in any way implying a reprehensible view of gay men as a group.

Also, as I point out to the occasional reader who writes me with this concern[11]—the fact is that Jack Randall *isn't* gay; he's a pervert (and no, those really aren't the same thing).

Jack Randall is a sadist; he derives sexual pleasure from hurting people. In *Outlander*, four separate sexual attacks by Randall are described—two on men, two on women (men: Alexander MacGregor and Jamie Fraser; women: Jenny Murray and Claire Fraser). Clearly, he's not all that particular about the gender of the person he's hurting; it's the pain and the act of domination that turns him on.

At the same time, given the society and situation in which he's operating—he's an officer in an occupying army—he's plainly going to have much greater access to males as potential victims. Early in *Outlander*, Frank Randall reports that there were instances of "insult—unspecified," laid to his ancestor's account, and that these resulted in complaints from the populace (*Outlander*, page 30 [U.S. paperback edi-

Horn Snake

---

[11] Six, so far.

tion]). Evidently, going about the countryside attacking women was a risky pastime; abusing male prisoners (or subordinates) in the confines of an English-run prison would be a good deal safer.

Of course, there's the possibility that his sadistic side would be especially gratified by the response of males, since they might suffer additional pain or horror as a result of homosexual attack, but I don't think there's sufficient evidence in the text to adduce that. On the other hand, one *could* reasonably assume that a male held in a prison where no one cares what happens to him might be much more severely abused than might a woman whose welfare was to some degree the responsibility of the community, as well as of her own relatives. So, we might reasonably assume that Randall did indeed prefer males—but as the result of their increased vulnerability, rather than as a result of a homosexual orientation.

Alexander MacGregor

A few of the other complaints I see regarding the treatment of homosexuals (virtually all from readers who have only read the first book of the series) are based simply on misinterpretation. Two or three letter writers urged me to consider the possible ill effects of Alexander MacGregor's suicide on young people struggling with awareness of their sexual orientation— surely I ought not to be suggesting that discovering one is gay is grounds for killing oneself?

Putting aside the larger question of whether it is a novelist's responsibility to address every possible mental response that every possible reader might have, and handle these in such a way as to maximize the (collectively hypothetical) readers' self-

esteem, in the context of Modern Enlightened Thought,[12] the simple fact is that there isn't the slightest indication anywhere in the text that Alexander MacGregor *is* gay.

In other words, he *didn't* hang himself out of shame at discovering his sexual nature—he hung himself for the much more sensible reason that he couldn't stand being raped and tortured. Most people would find this distressing, I daresay, no matter what their proclivities.

The Duke of Sandringham

Now, the Duke of Sandringham actually *is* gay; that's evident from the story that Jamie tells during supper at Castle Leoch (*Outlander*, page 482–487 [U.S. paperback]). Frankly, that scene was an accident, and so was the Duke.

One of my chief reasons for writing *Outlander* was to learn *how* to write. Consequently, I very often tried to write a specific sort of scene, simply because I didn't know how to do it, and wanted to learn. When I wrote this dinner party scene, I had no idea what would be said, or how it might fit into the book at large; it was simply that I had never (at that point) written a dialogue scene involving more than two characters.

Most dialogue scenes in novels do involve only two characters, for good reason; it's very difficult to handle a conversation with several participants without either losing track of who's saying what, or hopelessly confusing the reader. I had written several dialogue scenes in a row, involving two characters—Jamie and Claire—and had begun to find this monotonous. So I

---

[12]*It isn't, in case you were wondering.*

thought I'd try a scene in which a number of people take part in an ongoing conversation, just to learn how to do that. Hence, Colum's dinner table, and the conversation that evolved into Jamie's rather ribald story, inviting comments from his hearers.

The story itself *did* evolve; I didn't plan it. However, in *Outlander,* the Duke is a shadowy character who never appears on-stage; he was simply a prop at that point, and—as the hilarity at Jamie's story makes clear—homosexuality was not regarded with any particular popular revulsion in the eighteenth century.[13] In the social context shown, it was rather simply accepted as one known idiosyncrasy of this particular nobleman. I found no particularly negative attitude toward homosexuality anywhere in the Scottish sources consulted; a rather scornful dismissal of the behavior of James I[14] being about as far as it went.

As I've said elsewhere, I do *not* plan these books out before writing them—I certainly didn't plan the whole series (I couldn't very well, since I didn't know it *was* a series). However, when working on a book, I often do suddenly perceive a good use for elements or characters from a previous book.

So, as I was writing along in *Dragonfly,* and wondering how to make the necessary connections between the Scottish Highlands and the French Court (since these connections did exist and were historically important), I thought of using the Duke. He was, after all, the only member of the nobility appearing in *Outlander,* and as such, he might well have entree to the Court of Louis XV, as well as be associated with the Stuarts.

I had already written the scene (*Dragonfly,* chapter 10, "A Lady, with Brown Hair Curling Luxuriantly") in which Claire first meets Alexander Randall; the Duke's pres-

ence provided both a simple explanation for Alex's presence in France—and a Really Useful connection to the Randall family, thus allowing me to drag Black Jack back into the story without too much standing on my head.

Now, Black Jack being who he is, he seldom appears without some kind of sinister sexual overtone. Still, the Duke himself is not shown engaging in any really discreditable behavior *as a gay man.* He's a major-league political plotter, and thoroughly conscienceless in terms of his goals, but beyond Jamie's story in *Outlander* and the Duke's vague remarks about Jack Randall, we never see him in a sexual context. In other words, his homosexuality is incidental; simply one facet of his character, but not one that particularly affects our perception of him as good or evil.

When he revealed himself (so to speak) as being gay in *Outlander,* I decided to keep him as a sort of grace note in counterpoint to Jack Randall—that is, making it clear that simple homosexuality was neither inherently evil nor regarded as such, whereas Jack Randall's particular perversion was Something Quite Different. Most readers fortunately observed the distinction.

Lord John Grey

I could—as a few readers suggest—have included an admirable homosexual char-

---

[13]It was not, in fact—it was seldom prosecuted in London, where "mollyhouses" and homosexual activity in general were common—though there were periodic "moral" outcries against it in the English public press and the speeches of politicians seeking a moral high ground on which to achieve visibility (cf. "Hellfire").

[14]Commonly referred to as "Queenie," for reasons that needn't be elaborated on here.

acter in the first two books, as "balance" to Black Jack Randall—but that would be perversion of its own sort; distortion of a story for purposes of political correctness—and you already know what I think about *that*. It would also have been overkill; while homosexual people have undoubtedly always been represented in any population, to have a noticeable proportion of the characters in a story be gay is to draw more attention to them than is historically or artistically appropriate—unless the story is focused specifically on a gay community or deals with homosexual issues as a major theme.

However. I mentioned above my habit of looking back and picking up useful characters from earlier books. Having decided that Jamie Fraser was going to be "the Fraser, of the Master of Lovat's regiment" who escaped the slaughter of the Jacobite officers at Culloden, I had the problem of figuring out just *how* he was to escape.

I could have managed it in any of various ways, of course, but looking back, I spotted the young man whom Jamie had met and overpowered on the eve of the battle of Prestonpans (*Dragonfly*, chapter 36, "Prestonpans"). Now, I had intended him to meet that young man again, somewhere down the line, since John William Grey[15] had made such a dramatic parting threat. I had no idea *where* they might meet, though.

At first, I thought the young man himself might rescue Jamie from Culloden. That didn't seem quite right, though; the boy was young and essentially powerless, as well as being physically slight. I knew Jamie was wounded (because all the Jacobite officers in the cottage were), and I didn't think John Grey would be able to

get him away plausibly. Also, I wasn't at all sure that Grey would consider his earlier rescue a debt of honor—he *had* promised to kill Jamie, after all.

An elder brother, though, would see the debt and the honorable necessity of repaying it. So far, so good—and no reason to assume any particular sexual orientation on Lord John's part. But then, it was obviously necessary for Lord John to meet Jamie in person somewhere else, later—and the situation with the prison popped into my head immediately. What better sort of conflict? A man with a profound hatred of another man, put in a position where he holds complete power over his enemy—but is prevented by honor from using that power.

What better sort of conflict? Well, what if the man in the position of power finds his hatred being gradually . . . changed to something else? And then, what if the man to whom he tentatively offered his budding affection could not under any circumstances accept even the thought of it—owing to the secrets of his own traumatic past?

---

[15] *He was originally called William; however, I very much wanted to name Jamie's son Willie, and—with Jamie's older brother having the same name—I thought that would be too many Williams in a small space, so I changed Lord William to Lord John, as unobtrusively as I could.*

Well, heck, I couldn't pass up an opportunity to make things difficult. So we—and Jamie—discover that Lord John is gay, with concomitant complications.

However, Lord John revealed himself as a gay man because he was; i.e., that facet of his personality was key to the part of the story in which he appears—rather than because I felt any need to include a "good" gay character as an antidote to Jack Randall.

On a tangential issue:

Why did Jamie offer himself to Lord John (*Voyager*, chapter 59, "In Which Much Is Revealed")? A few readers (male and female) said the very thought made them ill; many others (male *and* female) said they found the scene (pp. 929–930, U.S. paperback) intensely arousing and emotionally moving. As I said above, novelists really can't be trying to figure out how readers will respond to *anything*, because there's simply no telling.

In answer to the question, though: Jamie feels a deep—and deeply disturbing—sense of obligation to Lord John. Lord John, after all, has saved him from a dangerous fate (being transported was often a death sentence, even for those without acute seasickness) and from permanent separation from his loved ones, given him as much freedom as possible, freely offered his friendship—and made no attempt at all to demand any sort of return.

Now Lord John has revealed that he knows Jamie's secret—that is, Willie's true paternity—and will not only protect the secret, but the boy as well. Knowing that Jamie must leave Willie, Lord John is willing to alter his entire life—even going so far as to marry Isobel Dunsany—in order to safeguard Jamie's son and ensure that Jamie will still have some connection with the boy.

Jamie, in his present position, can offer Lord John nothing at all as a gesture of gratitude or acknowledgment—except himself. His offering this particular gift is both an effort to acknowledge the great debt he feels he owes, and to show his final acceptance of Lord John, as a friend and as a man.

That is, he is aware that his earlier rejection (and the method he chose to implement it) has hurt John deeply. Though it is impossible for him to overcome his repugnance at the thought, he can force himself to the action (Jamie's made himself do quite a lot of things that he didn't want to do, after all), and thus show Lord John that he does not hold Lord John's nature against him—Jamie accepts him as he is.

Still, Lord John is quite aware of Jamie's true feelings, and thus gently refuses the offer—while accepting the gift of Jamie's friendship.

ABORTION

I must say, I had expected to receive quite a bit of comment on the abortion scene in *Drums* (chapter 49, "Choices"), if only because this is a subject on which a great many people hold extremely strong opinions. I've encountered surprisingly

Pole Cat

few comments about it, though (mind you, I'm not looking for any more).

One lawyer generously sent me a four-page treatise on the legal meaning of "murder," presumably in reference to Claire's remark about justifiable homicide committed in self-defense (page 831, U.S. paperback). This is irrelevant (also immaterial) to the book, given that Claire isn't a lawyer, there were no such interpretations in the eighteenth century, and law doesn't apply to personal opinions anyway—but I certainly appreciate the effort this person took to share her knowledge with me.

Beyond that, I've seen only two or three comments (not made directly to me, but seen on electronic services) regarding this scene. One person said that the scene made her uncomfortable (I should certainly hope so), and she wished that Claire had not made the offer to abort the child. Two others said they approved heartily of Claire's actions; they sympathized with Jamie's anguish, but the decision was Brianna's and no one else's. That's what I think, too.

Wife-Beating

This is, by a wide margin, the single biggest topic of controversy about the books. I refer, of course, to the notorious scene in which Jamie, completely fed up with Claire's (he thinks) irresponsible behavior, Takes Steps (*Outlander,* chapter 22, "Reckonings").

Frankly, this is one of my favorite scenes in that particular book. It illustrates perfectly the cultural and personal clashes going on between these two characters— clashes in which each one is absolutely convinced that he or she has the right of it—and they both do!

By Claire's lights, she was behaving with great courage and moral responsibility. She's tearing herself away from Jamie at great personal cost, setting off alone and on foot to return to the stone circle, in an attempt to return to Frank, her first husband, doing violence to her own feelings in an effort to keep faith with a man to whom she's made vows. She couldn't reasonably explain her circumstances to Jamie, with any hope of being believed; to stay with him longer would merely increase his pain when she left. She'd failed with earlier attempts to escape; this looks like not only the best, but perhaps the *only* chance she'll get. By accident, she falls into the hands of Captain Randall, with horrific consequences—but that, she feels, is hardly *her* fault.

From Jamie's point of view, his wife has—for no apparent reason beyond stubbornness—flagrantly disobeyed instructions meant only to keep her safe, and has fatheadedly wandered into a situation endangering not only her and himself, but all the men with him. Beyond that, she's brought him into face-to-face contact with the man he most despises, caused him to reveal himself in a way that will ensure determined pursuit, and worst of all— allowed Jack Randall to assault her sexually.

He's not only annoyed with her for her original thoughtless (he thinks) behavior, he's sexually outraged at its results, and— unable to deal properly with Randall—is strongly inclined to take it out on the available guilty party. Even so, he might not resort to violence, save for two things: his own history of physical discipline, which leads him to consider the punishment he intends inflicting not only reasonable, but quite moderate—and more important, his notions of the rightness of things, (which includes, though less important, the moral pressure of his companions' opinion).

The man is twenty-three years old, and while he's an accomplished warrior, he's very new to this husband business, and anxious to do it right. That means dealing responsibly with his wayward wife, in a manner that will not only keep her safe, by convincing her of the wisdom of obeying his orders, but will redeem her socially.

He therefore declares his intention of taking a strap to her. He isn't seeking personal revenge, or exercising a taste for sadistic violence; he's trying to do justice. Historically and geographically, this was an entirely appropriate thing to do,[16] and Jamie sees nothing even faintly questionable about it.

Claire does. From both a personal and a historical (*her* history) point of view, she sees quite a lot wrong with this proposition. In the end, of course, this clash of viewpoints comes down to the . . . er . . . bottom line—which is that Jamie is nearly a foot taller than she is, and outweighs her by a good eighty pounds. Over the greater span of historical time, might *has* made right.

The public response to this particular scene is fascinating. Most readers find it hilarious, erotic, or simply very entertaining. A few find it absolutely unacceptable—a "good" man, they argue, would *never* beat his wife, no matter what the circumstance!

Well, but he would. Jamie Fraser is arguably a "good man," but he's an *eighteenth-century* good man, and he's acting not only from a completely different perception of the situation, but from a completely different set of assumptions as to what constitutes appropriate behavior.

Those readers who object to this scene seem to respond in one of two ways: a) They simply can't sympathize with a man who resorts to violence, no matter what. Ergo, I should not have allowed him to do so! or b) Even if Jamie's behavior *is* historically appropriate, it's wrong for me to have shown it, because women who are in abusive relationships will read this and conclude that it is okay for their husbands to beat *them*!

It is not the business of a novelist to pursue political agendas. Still less is it the business of a historical novelist to pursue modern political agendas. It deprives the reader of any sense of perspective or notion of social ambiguity, and reinforces a smug, narrow-minded belief in the self-righteousness of modern Western cultural values that is highly detrimental to the evolution of thought *or* values.

(Curiously, no one at all has *ever* complained of the rampant child abuse that takes place in the books. Perfectly okay for Jamie to beat his nephew [*Voyager*, chapter 32, "The Prodigal's Return"] and his foster son [age ten or so] [*Dragonfly*, chapter 14, "Meditations on the Flesh"], and no objections whatever to Jamie's graphic descriptions of his own disciplinary experiences while growing up [*Outlander*, chapter 22, "Reckonings"]—but to see him using vio-

---

[16]cf. **An Illustrated History of the Rod**, *Annotated Bibliography*.

lence on a woman is evidently enough to cause a major reaction in some women.)[17]

Still, people's perceptions will always be colored by experience. Response to some material on the basis of personal experience is entirely understandable and I sympathize with such attitudes, but I can't in good conscience think them relevant to my own work.

MINOR ISSUES

"Minor issues" are those subjects on which I have received obviously sincere letters—but from only one or two people. I respect their opinions, but apparently these fall into the realm of responses that depend on the reader's individual perception and experience. Following are my responses to the letters in question (the content of the original letters being plain from the replies).

Body Image

May 5, 1994

Dear S:

Thanks for your thoughtful letter; I enjoyed it, and your analysis of historical attitudes toward plumpness, which are of course accurate.

However . . . are we possibly overreacting a bit here? Claire has *not* got an eating disorder, nor is there the slightest implication that she has, in any of the three books. She eats rather heartily, whenever food is available (as you note, it often wasn't), appears to enjoy it, judging by her descriptions of aromas and tastes, and there isn't any indication at all of her dieting, obsessing about food, allowing eating to control her behavior, or worrying in the least about her food intake or whether she's getting fat.

I took some pains to make sure she didn't appear as the "standard" heroine in *Outlander,* including the historically accurate (as you note) appreciation for a well-endowed rear. I didn't do so out of any political position on what women ought to look like; merely out of a sense of contrariness (having read way too many novels with eighteen-year-old slender heroines), and an urge to make Claire as believable and human as possible.

I don't know quite what you mean, that "the second book had not a peep about Claire's physical attributes, other than Jamie's continued enjoyment of them." Since she's pregnant through the first half of *Dragonfly,* descriptions of her weight and/or build seemed more or less irrelevant—she describes her heaviness, and "waddling up to take a nap," along with the loosening of joints, breast swelling, etc., which surely ought not to give anybody the notion that she's a slender waif. Jamie certainly continues to be physically attracted to her, pregnant or not, which I would *think* might convey the notion that slenderness is not one of his—or Claire's—criteria. Hardly "not a peep," though; Claire talks about her body and is aware of it throughout the books; whether or not she refers constantly to the size of her bottom seems rather irrelevant.

What seems to bother you is the third book—that Claire would have examined herself in the mirror before going back through the stones, and that she included "don't get fat" in her letter of motherly advice to Brianna.

---

[17] *This particular scene evidently doesn't bother men at all; I've never heard a male reader even mention it.*

As I said before, Claire is (I hope) human and believable. Whether women *should* worry about their looks in sexual situations is irrelevant—they do. Whether men *should* be attracted to women on the basis of their looks is also irrelevant—they are. I'm not pushing propaganda, here; I'm telling a story about two people, as real as I can make them.

Were I going to see a man with whom I had had a passionate physical relationship twenty years ago—with the specific intent of resuming said physical relationship—I would definitely take a good look at myself and wonder what the lover would see, and how it might compare to the way he'd seen me before. This is *not* being obsessed with thinness or "doing the skinny dance," as you put it—it's a sign of very human doubt and insecurity.

You may notice that that scene is phrased almost entirely in terms of muscle tone, not fatness or thinness. The only indication that Claire is reasonably slender is that her waist is "still narrow," seen in back view. She doesn't say exactly what her bottom looks like, but the strong implication is that it's reasonably hefty, though well-toned (no dimples, at least, she thinks, after a long look at it).

So we're left with her adjuration to her daughter not to get fat. Well, let's consider a couple of things. For one, this was 1968, not the 1990s. People didn't even jog back then, and aerobics was a crackpot new fad. Women by and large weren't physically active, and those who weren't careful of their nutrition generally *did* tend to be pudgy, out of shape, unhealthy, and look middle-aged. Coupled with the advice to "stand up straight," and Claire's own apparent levelheaded attitudes toward food and body (which we've seen in both pronounced and subtle ways all through the books), basically, Claire is not telling her daughter to starve, but to stay fit.

For another, let us consider the rhythm of that letter and the scene of which it's a part. We have deep emotion, heart-wrenching, soul-searching explorations of guilt and love. Then, at the end, we have a short, ultramaternal zetz (as one of my Jewish friends put it) to break the tension, restore the tone of the relationship between Claire and Brianna, and—not least—give the reader the feeling of Claire's sense of humor, which is profound and inclined to pop up even in the midst of Sturm und Drang. (This is not an isolated instance, after all; the reader certainly ought to have a good idea of Claire's style by now.)

So yeah, she *could* have said "Eat leafy green vegetables, take calcium supplements, and always wash the pesticides off apples or peel them." Or any number of other accurate, medically informed bits of advice (don't you figure she's told her daughter that kind of stuff all along? I've got kids. You do this kind of brainwashing constantly; you don't save it up for your deathbed or some other dramatic parting). But that wouldn't have had the sudden break in rhythm and the comic effect I was after.

In short, Claire isn't offering Important Advice there; she's reasserting her role as Bree's mother. Readers who mention that letter (I've heard from quite a number of them—though none concerned with Claire's attitude toward eating) have told me that they're awash in tears and throbbing emotion. Then they hit that line, and laugh, with a sudden bittersweetness that makes the whole thing much more affecting than it would had I made the whole letter a straightforward tearjerker. They suddenly see themselves and their own mothers or daughters, which is what I intended.

See, I'm a writer. Not—repeat not—a feminist, a political activist or a spokesperson for some group that perceives itself as entitled to

everyone's attention. My own rather strongly held opinion is that it is not the business of novels to push political agendas of any kind. There are plenty of novels that do this, but I personally don't care for them.

I take such concerns as yours very seriously—if I didn't, I wouldn't have spent two hours I can't afford to answer your letter in such detail. I trust you will take mine with equal seriousness.

Any reader brings his or her own experience to a book, and consequently, perceptions will differ. That being so, I cannot possibly write with the possibility of multiple hypersensitivities in mind. Such an approach—seeking above all to offend no one, or to adhere to some standard of political correctness—results in blandness and mediocrity. I'm a storyteller, and it's my job to tell the story of these people, keeping faith with my characters, to the best of my ability. Nothing more.

Sincerely, Diana Gabaldon

Chinese Sex Fiends

I was rather surprised, a couple of years ago, to receive a fairly lengthy and impassioned letter, denouncing me for "perpetuating negative stereotypes of Asian men as short, English-mangling, alcoholic sex fiends."

This gave me pause, since frankly—as I told my correspondent—I was totally un-aware that there *was* a stereotype of Asian men as alcoholic sex fiends. Now, I realize I have led a rather sheltered life, but still. . . .

Now, for all I know, Chinese men are known far and wide as alcoholic sex fiends, but it isn't a view I'd ever personally been exposed to before hearing from this particular correspondent. I therefore don't really *think* I can be deliberately perpetuating a vile canard by having allowed Mr. Willoughby to drink brandy—particularly given that all the Europeans around him are drinking as much or more—or by allowing him to express his admiration for women in general.

I did consider the other half of this accusation, though. I imagined there *might* be a perception, spread through films and TV, of Asian persons as "English-mangling." However, as I explained to my correspondent, simply noting the fact that a person from one country might not arrive in another with a totally fluent grasp of the unfamiliar language does not really seem to me to be culturally derogatory.

I then descended to particularities, since we were, after all, dealing with an individual, Mr. Willoughby (aka Yi Tien Cho). Given that Mr. Willoughby had arrived in Edinburgh rather precipitously as a stowaway—i.e., without time to bone up on his English before leaving China—had been in Scotland for no more than a year or two, and had spent his time exclusively in the company of wharf rats, prostitutes, and Scottish smugglers, most of whom regarded him as a worm and wouldn't be talking to him at all if they could help it—I thought it would be highly unlikely for him to be speaking grammatically correct King's English.

Now, "short." I did stop to consider this one. Why *did* I depict Mr. Willoughby as short? Was it truly the result of negative cultural stereotyping? (It could be; one doesn't usually recognize one's own biases, and while I *have* seen the Chinese Olympic basketball team on television, I might conceivably have been warped by years of watching Deng Xiaoping smiling into the belt buckles of various American diplomats).

Of course, one would first have to stipulate that shortness is in fact a negative characteristic, which I for one (one who is five feet three—well, all *right;* five feet

two-and-seven-eighths) wouldn't be inclined to do.

However, one prime minister does not a culture make, any more than does a basketball team. Neither does a single fictional character. Yes, Asians come in all sizes; however, a single person, be he fictional or real, can only come in *one* size.[18] If one ranked the eighteenth-century male population of China, in order of size, one would no doubt find individuals of varying heights, said heights occurring in a bell curve distribution (because height is one of those natural characteristics that always *does* occur in a "normal" distribution).

I have no data comparing height distributions for European and Chinese males in the eighteenth century, so I can't say whether there was or was not a difference in mean height. However, this scarcely matters. Mr. Willoughby is the only Chinese character in *Voyager* (or in fact, in the whole series). It isn't possible for a single character in a book to exhibit multiple heights for the purpose of reflecting cultural heterogeneity, I'm sorry. You have to pick one height for a character—how can it be a "stereotype" to pick one from *anywhere* in this distribution? There is a difference

---

[18]*As a direct result of this letter, I took to paying careful attention to fictional representations of Asian men in books I read. Interestingly enough, most contemporary authors make a particular point of identifying Asian characters as "tall," even when height isn't mentioned for most other characters. However, Asians are not universally tall, any more than they are universally short, and while I understand the desire of writers not to offend sensibilities, the unfortunate fact remains that **some** Chinese men really **are** short.*

between a stereotype and a statistical distribution, surely.

So, in the event, the question comes down—as it must, in fictional terms—to the individual. Now, in *Voyager*, the story is told through the eyes of Claire Randall, a time-traveler from the future, who is described throughout the books as being "unusually tall" for the times. The average European woman of the times was quite small—perhaps less than five feet tall, with tiny feet, judging from the clothing and shoes I've seen in museums; Claire, by contrast, is five-feet-six.

Her husband, in even greater contrast, is a six-feet-four-inch Scottish Highlander. Men of this size were certainly known to exist during the eighteenth century, but they were remarkable—George Washington was roughly six-feet-three, and judged an "impressive man."

The point here is that Mr. Willoughby is seen entirely through Claire's eyes and, most often, in close company with her very tall husband. Descriptions of him are given either by her, or by her husband, Jamie. Even if Mr. Willoughby were the same mean height as the average European male of the time, he would likely still seem "short" to either Claire or Jamie, and be described as such.

Now, in terms of novelistic intent, there is a real (if subtle) reason for depicting Yi Tien Cho as "small"—I wished to emphasize his relatively helpless situation in this strange culture, because this is key to the character and motivations of Mr. Willoughby. I.e., while he consciously acknowledges Jamie's friendship and patronage, subconsciously, he greatly resents the dependence imposed upon him by the relationship. It's this resentment—at being deprived of his rightful social position, at being despised by people he considers the lowest of barbarians, at being deprived of even his real name[19]—that causes him inadvertently to betray Jamie (an act he redeems later, by his rescue of Claire—while acknowledging his anger and claiming his independence at the same time).

Mr. Willoughby is an "outsider," and an obvious one, by reason of his strange culture and customs (hence the mention of foot-binding, which underlines the "otherness" of his culture, in the eyes of the Scots and English he associates with). But there are "outsiders" of various kinds all through the book—Jamie, as a Jacobite prisoner, Lord John, as a gay man, Claire, as a time-traveler—the theme of the book is identity, with explorations of how people define themselves: in terms of profession, relationship, place in society, the perceptions of those around them—and most of all, by the ability to name themselves. Mr. Willoughby is merely one more exemplar of the theme.

While I understand that many short people (particularly men) are sensitive about their height, objecting to the portrayal of a single "small" Chinese man as a negative cultural stereotype seems . . .

Well, some people read to expand their experience; others read to confirm their prejudices. I'm writing for the former, I hope.

---

[19] *You may note the play with names that takes place all through* **Voyager***, with Jamie shifting his alias according to need, Claire adjusting her own name (among Beauchamp, Randall, and Fraser), and even Roger noting his original family name.* **Voyager** *is all "about" the search for identity, and the ways in which people define themselves, and the name-shifting is a deliberate part of this overall theme.*

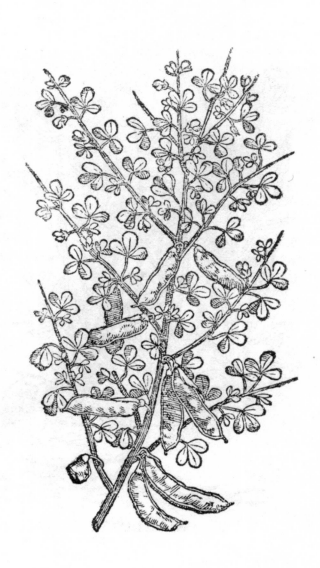

JAMIE AND THE RULE OF THREE

One of my male readers, a book reviewer, recently sent me a message on Twitter, saying that he'd just finished reading *Outlander* and enjoyed it a lot *until the prison chapters*. I tweeted back that I'd be kind of worried about him if he'd *enjoyed* the Wentworth Prison part, to which he said . . . *but why put our hero through such pain and suffering? :),* adding in the next, *I know I'm late to the #Outlander party & you've probably already addressed this, but that was intense emotional, physical pain.*

My first impulse was to reply, *Well, yeah* . . . But it was a serious question and deserved a real answer, which took some thought.

The simple answer is just that that's what I saw happening. That's not really a satisfactory answer for a reader, though. I "see" things happening, because the subconscious part of my mind is digging things out of the compost and shipping them up into my visual cortex. The waybill with the tracking number comes along much later—and only if I look for it.

Let me make a brief distinction here about the components of writing. There's What Happens, and there's How You Get It On The Page. "How" is the craft part of writing: How do I convey a sense of ac-

tion, of tension, of tenderness, of curiosity, of awe? How do I make people turn the page? (An important consideration, if you tend to write books with a lot of pages.) How do I *explain*?

Now, the craft part—the actual putting of words on the page—that's pretty conscious; it has to be. You're making a million (not exaggerating) decisions on every page. Whose viewpoint is this? Where are we? What time of day is it? Who's speaking here? What do they sound like? Does what this person said make sense? That chair over there—should it be a chair? Ought it perhaps to be a low stool? Or a nursing chair? Someone just kicked it—ought it to break when it hits the wall? Did the person who kicked it hurt his foot? What did he say *then*? The chair/stool made a dent in the wall; shall I mention that? No, it will interfere with the person who's laughing at him—are they convulsed with mirth? No, too much; are they going pink in the face with the effort *not* to laugh? Et cetera, et cetera, et cetera, to quote the King of Siam.

But *what* happens is often not conscious at all. I saw a man, obviously exasperated beyond bearing, kick a stool with great force. What exasperated him? Who is the person laughing at him? Are they doing so derisively, or are they supportive of him but can't help being amused by his frustration? Those are all "What happened?" sorts of questions and are largely being answered *as* I write, again by the nonverbal subconscious.

There always *is* a reason why things happen or are necessary in a story, whether I know what those things are while I'm writing or not. So—returning to my reader's question—what were the reasons for the terrible things that happened to Jamie in Wentworth Prison?

In part it's because *Outlander* is a high-stakes story. Almost everybody understands that you have to have *something* at stake for a story to be good. And way too many thrillers and science fiction/fantasy novels assume that nothing less than the Fate of the Known Universe will do, these authors mistaking scale for intensity. No matter what the background may be, a story that focuses on the impact of events on one or two individual *lives* will be—generally speaking—much more engaging and emotionally intense than one where everyone is just rushing around trying to save a planet or get their hands on the fortunium bomb that could Destroy Everything!

So *Outlander* is a high-stakes story—on an individual level—throughout. It's a love story, sure, and it's all about what people will do for the sake of love. Claire, for instance, chooses to abandon the life she knew (and was about to reclaim postwar), the safety of the twentieth century (and she of all people would value that safety, having come through such a war), and the husband she'd loved. She chooses hardship, danger, and emotional pain, in order to be with Jamie.

But love for these two is always reciprocal. It's not about one partner making a sacrifice for the other's sake. Throughout the story, they keep rescuing each other. And the stakes are high. Jamie marries Claire originally in order to save her from Black Jack Randall. Would that be a striking thing to do if Jack Randall was not, in fact, a serious threat? He *is* a serious threat; we learn that from Jamie's backstory. The man's a genuine sadistic psychopath, who has essentially destroyed Jamie's family and seriously injured him, both physically and emotionally. And here's Jamie swearing to give Claire everything he has, the protection of his name and his clan—and the protection of his body—in order to save *her* from this man.

He then does save her, physically and immediately, from Randall, when Randall captures her and assaults her at Fort William—even though by doing so he puts not only himself but everyone with him in serious danger, *and* does so at some emotional as well as physical cost. *"I was tied to that post, tied like an animal, and whipped 'til my blood ran! . . . If I'd not been lucky as the devil this afternoon, that's the least as would have happened to me. . . . And when ye screamed, I went to you, armed wi' nothing but an empty gun and my two hands."* The stakes are higher; the threat to Jamie (and Claire) from Captain Randall is increased.

One, two, three. The Rule of Three. Its one of the important underlying patterns of storytelling: One event can be striking.

The next (related) event creates resonance. But the third brings it home—WHAM. (That is, by the way, why classic fairy tales always involve three brothers, three sisters, three fairies, etc.—and why the most classic form of joke always starts, "A priest, a minister, and a rabbi . . ." The climax of the story, the punch line of the joke, always comes on the third iteration.) The third encounter with Black Jack Randall is the climax, the point where the stakes are highest. Jamie's been captured and seriously hurt, Claire's come to save him, but Randall turns up and takes her captive, threatening her life.

Okay. This *has* to be a credible threat. Ergo, we have to have seen (and heard about) the real damage Randall has done to Jamie thus far; we have to be in no doubt whatever that he'd do real damage to Claire. We can't just say, "Oh, he's *such* a nasty person, you wouldn't believe . . ." We *have* to believe, and therefore appreciate, the enormity of what Jamie is doing when he trades what's left of his life for Claire's.

And because we do believe that, we share both Jamie's despair and Claire's desperation.

Throughout the book, we've seen that love has a real cost. Jamie and Claire have built a relationship through honest struggle, a relationship that's *worth* what it's cost them. This is the final challenge, and Jamie's willing to pay what will apparently be the ultimate cost.

Why would I throw that away? To have him escape rape and torture (he—and we—*know* what's coming) by the skin of his teeth would be to undercut his sacrifice, to make it of little moment. (It would be like someone turning up in Gethsemane and telling Christ, "Hey, buddy, you don't really have to do this. Come with me, I got a secret way outta here. . . .")

So love has a cost, and it's a real one. But they do rescue each other, and Claire saves not only his life but also his soul. (Yes, it is redemption and resurrection, and, yes, there's Christ imagery all through the story—it was my first book, okay?) His soul wouldn't have been in danger had he not been really and truly nearly destroyed by his sacrifice.

I.e., had Claire shown up with reinforcements in the nick of time and saved him before he'd been put through such pain and suffering . . . well, then it would have been a nice, heartwarming story in which Hero and Heroine conquer evil and ride off into the sunset together. But it wouldn't have half the power of a story in which Jamie and Claire truly conquer *real* evil and thus show what real love is. Real love has real costs—and they're worth it.

I've always said all my books have a shape, and *Outlander*'s internal geometry consists of three slightly overlapping triangles. The apex of each triangle is one of the three emotional climaxes of the book: 1) when Claire makes her wrenching choice at the stones, 2) when she saves Jamie from Wentworth, and 3) when she saves his soul at the abbey. It would still be a good story if I'd had only One and Two—but, see above, the Rule of Three. A story that goes one, two, *three,* has a lot more impact than just a one-two punch.

PART TEN

FROM BOOK
TO SCREEN

INTRODUCTION

OR "BRING ME THE HEAD OF
RON D. MOORE."

About two months after Sam Heughan was cast to play the part of Jamie Fraser in the Starz TV production of *Outlander,* when the fans' demonstrations of enthusiasm and creativity online began to be Truly Visible, he e-mailed me and asked, "What will they do when they actually see the show?"

To which I replied, "Either they'll collectively wet their pants, or they'll march down the street waving torches and demanding Ron's head on a pike."

You know, if there's something you want urgently to do in life—do it. The universe will usually come out to meet you. In my case, I knew I was meant to write novels, and when I was thirty-five—about the age Sam Heughan and Caitriona Balfe are now—I took my courage in both hands and wrote a novel. And, among other things, the universe brought me a TV show.

Along with it came the acquaintance—sometimes the friendship—of a lot of magic people. Not only producers Ron and Maril and Terry, not only actors Sam and Cait and Tobias and Graham and Lotte and Gary . . . but all of you who've loved the books for so long and have longed to see them brought to life.

It's your love—all of you: the fans, the producers, the actors, the crew—that's made this happen. All I did was open the door.

So now it's open, and the world can come in. And I can't say more than I did the night of the first premiere in San Diego: "Ladies and gentlemen . . . you've done me proud."

Nice to know that Ron's head is safe, too. . . .

But How on Earth
Did We Get *Here*?

rom a book that couldn't be described, by a writer no one had ever heard of, to a hit TV show, I mean.

It was rather a long road. For years and years and years, people have been saying to me, "Oh, I can't *wait* for there to be a movie of *Outlander*! But I want it to be just the way it is in the book!"

To which my reply was usually, "Yeah? Which forty pages would you like to see?"

Because, you see, your normal feature film runs approximately two hours and is shot from a script that runs about one hundred twenty pages. Now, I was a volunteer reader for Recording for the Blind & Dyslexic for some twenty-seven years, and while my value to that organization lay in my ability to read passages like ". . . producing alga with many free-living species, especially common in crustose tropical lichens: *Coccomyxa*, a common terrestrial alga, occurring in the common green species of *Peltigera* and *Solorina* and the mushroom lichens, *Dictyochloropsis,* common in *Lobaria* and *Pseudocyphellaria* . . ."[1] at two hundred forty words a minute without stumbling, they did occasionally ask me to record one of my own books.[2] And I therefore happen to know that, even at my speed,[3] it takes thirty-two hours to read *Outlander* out loud.

---

[1] *Lichens of North America, by Irwin M. Brodo, Sylvia Duran Sharnoff, and Stephen Sharnoff. Fascinating book; I recommend it highly.*

[2] *RFB&D is a foundation whose mission is to provide educational materials to people who are "print-handicapped." This includes not only people with vision problems or reading difficulties such as dyslexia but also people who suffer from conditions like multiple sclerosis that might make holding a book for long periods difficult. Any person with such a difficulty can request that a particular text be recorded for them at no charge—but this means that only educational materials are recorded. Therefore, something like a novel would only be recorded if a client needed it for a class in literature, for instance—or required it for some other kind of professional development.*

[3] *Normal average reading speed is 120 wpm. The people at RFB&D were sufficiently fascinated that they clocked me, which is how I know that I read aloud at 240 wpm. This is actually an advantage for this particular kind of reading, as people can listen much faster than anyone can talk. This is why a person's mind wanders if a lecturer speaks slowly. The RFB&D clients are given adjustable-speed players, so they can speed up the text they're listening to, and most of them do just that. So a fast reader is a help—particularly when adjusting text that contains errors, as often you have to record a longer passage than what was originally read but fit it into the same time span.*

In other words, there's No Way you're going to be able to cram everything in that book into a two-hour movie. No. Way.

This obvious fact didn't stop people from trying. *Outlander* was first published in 1991, and since then we (my agents and I) have had constant inquiries about the film rights, often two or three a month. It *is* an exciting story, after all.

Now, I must digress for a moment[4] and tell you a bit about how film rights work. It all begins with the option. If a producer or production company is interested in making a film (movie/TV/video, etc.) of your book, they approach you and offer you a (generally) modest amount of money for an option. And what an option is, is a period of time—one year, two, five, whatever you agree upon—during which the production company has the exclusive right to "develop" the film.

"Development" basically means the complicated process of finding someone who's willing to fork over fifty to a hundred million dollars or so for the purpose of making this film and, in the process, also finding a scriptwriter, a director (preferably a well-known one, so he or she will attract "talent" eager to work with him/her), facilities, actors, and so on.

This is, as you might suppose, a freaking hard thing to do, and it's not surprising that most options lapse at the end of their time, without results. When this happens, you—the original author—may renew the option (if you and the option holder both want to), sell the option to another prospective production entity, or . . . just sit on the property until artistic curiosity or penury causes you to consider it again.[5, 6]

Now, there are things to consider when deciding whether to grant an option to someone. While most options lapse, there is the outside chance that this one will succeed—and, that being so, you'd better be sure you're willing to yield control of your book to This Person (or entity). Because, make no mistake about it, the only author to have actually *had* "control" over a movie made of her work is (to the best of my knowledge) J. K. Rowling. Once an option is "exercised"—meaning they actually *buy* the film rights, for a somewhat larger sum than the option fee—they own the property, lock, stock, and barrel;[7] you'll never get it back, and they can do anything

―――――――

[4] *There's a reason why I write long books; it's because I like digressions. . . .*

[5] Most *options lapse without result. Someone along the way told me that of all the books published (in the United States) in a given year, approximately three percent will be optioned for their film rights. Of that three percent, one-tenth of one percent will actually become a film in that same year.*

[6] *Mind you, this isn't always a bad thing. You get to keep the option money, regardless. Sir Anthony Burgess, I'm told, lived on options for* A Clockwork Orange *for some thirty-five years before someone actually got around to making a movie of it. (And, fortunately, it was a good movie.)*

[7] Lock, stock, and barrel *is a* merism *(figure of speech) used predominantly in the United Kingdom and North America, meaning "all," "total," "everything." The effective portions of a* gun *(or more specifically a* rifle*) are the lock (used to hold ready the sparking mechanism), the* stock *(the portion held), and the* barrel *(the aiming guide and conveyor for the explosive-driven ball). Collectively they are the weapon, therefore, everything.—Source: Wikipedia (You want to be careful about using Wikipedia for serious research, but it's fairly good for things like this.)*

they want with it.[8] So how do you decide whether you want to engage in this very risky venture with a given prospect?

Well, first, you'd like someone who's actually *made* a movie before. This requirement will eliminate roughly 95 percent of the people who want to make a movie of your book.

Then you'd like someone who's actually *read* your book. Cross off another four percent; many producers are interested in a book because it's a bestseller and/or the title has a lot of name recognition. They have no intention of filming your story as such; they just want the name.[9]

And finally . . . you'd like to work with someone who understands your book. During one option negotiation, a very nice producer flew out from Los Angeles to have lunch and discuss things with me. We were getting along splendidly, until we reached the matter of casting. This lady was interested in making a four- or six-hour miniseries, possibly for ABC, and was telling me that ABC, like most networks, had a stable of actors that they preferred to use, these being, for the most part, American actors.

"Of course," she said, "Jamie needs to be Scottish [in the script], because of the kilt and the accent, but I don't see why Claire can't be an American."[10]

"Oh, you don't," I said. "Well, in that case, you probably don't see why I won't give you an option."

Given the above considerations, it's likely apparent why we've accepted only four option proposals in the last twenty years. Fortunately, the first three of these lapsed without incident. The fourth option deal that we did was with a gentleman named Jim Kohlberg. Jim had made several small but critically acclaimed movies—he knew what he was doing—and he'd fallen in love with *Outlander*.

He'd read the book four times before coming to talk to me, and in the midst of the negotiations he called to tell me he thought he was channeling Murtagh. ("I was having a difficult day," he said, "dealing with all sorts of problems, and I was

[8] *I once had the privilege of having dinner at John Irving's house—his wife was my Canadian literary agent at the time—and hearing a very vivid exposition on what filmmakers had done with his* A Prayer for Owen Meany *(wonderful book, by the way; one of my all-time favorites). Later, I read the short book* (My Movie Business: A Memoir) *he'd written on the experience of making* The Cider House Rules— *a film for which he wrote the script and was personally involved to a high degree. The process took him fourteen years, during which time four different producers died on him. I mean—be warned. (On the other hand, he did win an Oscar for his script.)*

[9] *As Ron D. Moore said in various interviews (paraphrasing slightly), "Starz said, 'Make the book for the fans.' That's unheard of. Usually they say, 'Throw away the book and write your own story; we just bought it for the cover.'"*

[10] *Caitriona Balfe, the wonderful actress who plays Claire in the Starz television series, is in fact Irish—but does a great English accent. Sam Heughan, who plays Jamie, is fortunately a Scot.*

just sitting there feeling frustrated, when I heard Murtagh saying to Claire, 'For most people, what they want and what they get are no' the same thing. Why should he [Jamie] be any different?' That really helped.")

So we did an option deal with Jim, and he set about the business of getting a script written, finding a director, etc. He went to some lengths to commission scripts from some very well-known scriptwriters (whose names you would recognize, were I indiscreet enough to mention them, which I'm not). And he kindly sent me the scripts to look at, though he wasn't obliged to do so.

I've always thought that it was flat-out impossible to squeeze *Outlander* into a two-hour script and have the result resemble the original in any real way. Let's say I was correct in this assumption, and leave it at that. Jim, however, is a stubborn man and had faith in the project. He renewed his option when it lapsed and renewed it again eighteen months later.

Now, unbeknownst to me, there was a gentleman named Ron D. Moore whom I'd heard of, vaguely, as being the creator of *Battlestar Galactica* (which I'd never watched, or I would have known a lot more about Ron D. Moore than his name). Ron was sitting at dinner one evening with his wife, Terry, and his production partner, Maril Davis. The three of them were discussing what project Ron might want to explore next, as *Battlestar Galactica* had ended.

One of the women said, "What about *Outlander*? It's got all the things you love: historical fiction, a strong central female character—"

The other woman exclaimed, "You've read *Outlander*!" And (according to Ron)

they started talking to each other and generally behaving in the manner that *Outlander* fans who meet each other generally do. "I was just sipping my martini and looking back and forth between them," he said, but finally he asked for a copy of the book and stayed up all night reading it.

"I was struck by the story," he said.[11] "I liked the way it pulled the rug out from under you and went off in a completely unexpected direction. And, more importantly, I could see how to make a TV show out of it."

So Ron and Maril went looking for the rights holder to the property, this being Jim Kohlberg. Jim still wanted to make a two-hour feature film, so Ron said, "Okay, we'll check back." And they did; they called Jim once a year or so, asking, "How's that feature film working out for you, Jim?"[12] And finally Jim said, "I'm beginning to think you're right; maybe it's a TV show."

At this point, *I* heard the name "Ron D. Moore" in a personal context. And thus began more than a year of negotiations, which I won't go into—partly because they're boring, and mostly because I have only the vaguest notion of what was actually going on.[13] The end result was a huge contract establishing a weird five-sided relationship among Jim, Ron, the Sony Corporation (which makes and owns the

---

[11] *These quotes from Ron are not formal quotes from a printed source; they're what he said to dozens of interviewers while I was sitting next to him. While the wording occasionally varied slightly from one interview to the next, the basic story didn't.*

[12] *I, of course, had no idea any of this was going on.*

[13] *This is why you should have a good agent, and fortunately I do.*

show), the Starz cable network (which has the U.S. license to distribute the show), and me.

People have since been praising me for "holding out" for Ron and giving me all sorts of credit for casting the show's actors. In fact, I did none of this and had nothing whatever to say about it. But there is that saying "It's better to be lucky than good." And what's happened with the TV show has been a lot more than lucky.

I was of course pleased at the possibility of a ten-hour TV show[14] rather than a two-hour movie, simply because there'd be more room. But I wasn't (at the time) familiar with Ron's work and had no idea what he might do with the project.

The first thing he did, though, was to talk to me. Ron and Maril came out to my home in Scottsdale and spent two days with me, talking through story lines and characters, asking intelligent questions about backstory and future developments in the novels, sharing their ideas on adaptation[15], and . . . we found that we were much on the same wavelength regarding notions of character, story, and storytelling.

Ron also sent me his projected outline for a ten-part series and showed me his pilot script—the material he was planning to take to pitch to the various cable networks that were potential markets for the show. As I told him after reading the script, "You know, this is the first thing I've ever read based on my books that didn't make me either turn white or burst into flame."

During our discussions, Ron asked me cautiously whether I thought I might like to write a script, assuming the show was picked up. I replied that I didn't think I would. Firstly because I didn't want to

be responsible for screwing up the all-important, vital first season. (I've never written a TV script; I imagined I could learn to do it, but there were no guarantees that I'd do it *well*.) Beyond that, though, I told him that I'm not a team player. I'm a novelist; I'm God. I have total control over characters and story, all of the time.

Contrariwise, I have friends who are scriptwriters and know various writers who've had movies or TV shows made of their work, and I knew from talking to them that the world of filmmaking is completely different from the world of novels. It's a tremendously communal sort of work, with creation happening as the result of dozens—sometimes hundreds—of different people who all have to work together effectively.

Scripts alone may be written by one person to begin with, but they go through dozens of iterations, with notes and comments and input from everyone from the showrunner and director to the other scriptwriters and occasionally the actors. I didn't know if I could do that effectively.

---

[14] *As it was, Starz had sufficient faith in the project that they gave us sixteen episodes to cover the first book, though ten is standard for a cable TV show.*

[15] *At one point, Ron noted that the book begins rather slowly, but you can do that in a book, as the prose will carry people along. In a visual medium (he said), you need to fix the audience's attention instantly or you lose them. "So," he said, "I'd like to do a two-minute visual prologue, where we see Claire in a World War Two military hospital, with blood and severed limbs and that sort of thing, doing what it is she does and being who she is. She's the central figure of the story, and if we know immediately what sort of woman she is—" To all of which I was nodding eagerly and going, "Yeah! Great idea!"*

And there was the minor consideration that filmmaking is very time-consuming and I had books to write. . . . So I said I'd pass for the time being. *If* the show was successful and *if* there were future seasons, I might think again, but for now it was all theirs.

Starz picked up the show, and a great flurry of action began. I wasn't involved in any of this, of course, but heard the echoes. The best news was that the show would be shot in Scotland. A huge new studio with soundstages was built at Cumbernauld, near Glasgow; the Scottish government provided tax incentives and grants and a lot of publicity, the casting was done (see below)—and filming began in October of 2013.[16]

In mid-October, Starz held a fan event in New York, to coincide with New York Comic Con. This was a gathering (with lunch) for two hundred fifty lucky fans, who got to hear Ron and me talk and see fascinating bits of film on "*Outlander*-world," the sets, and "making of" footage.

Before the show started, though, Ron and I were backstage with Carmi Zlotnik, Starz's Head of Production, who was going to introduce the show. Carmi had his laptop with him and asked if I might like to see a bit of the dailies they'd shot so far—

"dailies" being the daily raw footage (though I suppose it should technically be called "pixelage," these days).

"Er . . . yes," I said, trying not to salivate on his shoes. "I'd love to!" So we sat down on the ratty backstage sofa, Carmi to the left of me and Ron to my right, and . . . I saw the first bits of *Outlander* come to life in my lap.

It was riveting. I was seeing scenes of Claire walking through the circle of standing stones, wearing a white dress and a brown/gray tartan shawl. (My first thought? *My God, she walks like a giraffe.* And by that I mean amazingly long-legged and graceful.) The next set of scenes showed Caitriona lying on her back on the shawl (evidently post time travel), eyes closed—and clutching a white hot-water bottle to her chest for dear life. Then someone shouted, "Set!" and a hand reached in and snatched the hot-water bottle away; someone else yelled, "Action," and she opened her eyes.

At this point, I tore my own eyes away from the screen long enough to glance at Ron and was surprised—and moved—to find him moist-eyed. "It's just so great," he said, "to see you see it for the first time."

It really was.

---

[16] *Maril asked me whether there was anything in the story—either in* Outlander *or future books—that would prevent them beginning the story in October, rather than April. I thought about it and said no; the feast of Samhain would work as well as Beltane for the supernatural aspects, and there were relatively few events in the story that were seasonally dependent, the haymaking at Lallybroch being the only one I could think of, and I didn't think that was vital to the story.*

ACTORS AND MAGIC

Do you, um, *know* what it is that an actor does?

No, really. Do you? They do what I do—they make magic happen. They do it with their faces and bodies, while I do it with words, but it's essentially the same thing. They create something that wasn't there before.

Granted, sometimes it helps if you have the rough physical outline for a particular role. A detailed physical resemblance, though, is really not necessary, and for two reasons:

1) Physical appearance is *very* mutable. Hair and eye color are so simple to change that I was amazed anyone was carrying on about what color Mr. Heughan's hair *is*. (For the record, he's blond. Like any other actor, he dyes his hair as needed. It was dark in photos current when he was cast; it could be red within half an hour.)[1]

2) Much more important: beyond very basic things like height and general build, physical aspects are just not that essential, provided that an actor can *act*.

As one of the producers said to me—anent the auditioning process—"We were hoping that somebody would just walk in and *be* Jamie."

I got the word about Sam Heughan[2] while I was driving to Santa Fe with my husband: Ron and Maril were very ex-cited; they thought they'd found Jamie and were sending me the audition videos.

"Great!" I said. "I won't be able to watch them 'til this evening, but what's the guy's name?" They told me, and, naturally, I spent the next hour Googling *Sam Heughan* on my phone.

Now—I think this point may just possibly have escaped a few thousand of you, so let me restate it: Jamie is *twenty-two* in *Outlander*, and a virgin. And as the producers do understand and respect the story very much, they wanted a guy who could believably be a twenty-two-year-old virgin. (Yes, I know half of you are thinking of him as he is in the later books and thus "see" him in his fifties. That doesn't mean the producers should cast someone in his late forties and ask him to play a twenty-two-year-old virgin. Am I right? Yes, I am. Now that *that's* settled . . .)

Mr. Heughan is a remarkably chameleonic actor; he looks completely different

---

[1] *Actually—he told me later—it took seven attempts and twenty-seven hours in a salon chair for the colorist to achieve an acceptable shade of red that wouldn't look either garish or washed-out against the vivid greens of the Scottish landscape.*

[2] *I asked him how to pronounce it: He replied, "'HEW-an' is good, or, if you can, insert the Scottish throat-clearing/spitting sound in the middle—'HewCH-an.' Hard to get right first time without spraying close friends with saliva."*

in every single role. And at the time he was cast, he'd not been in a great many productions. His photographs on IMDb[3] were interesting but sort of blink-worthy.[4]

(Husband approved of the stills from *First Light*, by the way, where Sam is playing a Spitfire pilot in the Battle of Britain. "He looks good beat up," he said. "A good thing for playing Jamie."[5])

Eventually, we got to Santa Fe, let the dogs out, aired the house, went to have dinner . . . and then I sat down at my computer, in a lather of trepidation and excitement, to watch the audition tapes.

For the first five seconds, I was thinking, *But he doesn't look anything like his photos, he looks fine.* . . . Five seconds later, Sam Heughan's GONE, and so am I. It's Jamie Fraser, right *there* in front of me, moving, talking. One of the biggest thrills ever.

And that's what actors do. Good ones. They can "be" someone else, totally.

I saw Sam do two scenes: the confrontation between Jamie and Dougal, after Dougal exposes Jamie's back in a tavern. Ferocious, explosive, a glimpse of the warrior. And he absolutely freaking *exploded*.

And then—the scene in which Jamie explains to Claire exactly why he intends to punish her for disobeying his orders to stay hidden, thus nearly getting them all killed.

This is arguably the most controversial scene in all the books. And I'm not about to go into the scene itself—not the point here. The point is that that's one heck of a complex scene, emotionally, and *could* be read/performed in a lot of different ways. Now, I happen to know exactly how Jamie acted and spoke during that scene . . . and that's exactly what Sam *did*. Thoughtfulness, intimacy, fair-mindedness, annoyance, firmness—and quite a lot of humor.

One of Jamie's hallmarks is the ability to be threatening and funny at the same time—and Sam pulled that off.

Now the necessary physical aspects are all there. Sam's big—my head would hit about the middle of his chest—and very well built, in terms of what Jamie actually looks like. Tall, lean (not burly), rangy (not bulgy), broad-shouldered, muscular (but a young muscular. Young athletes look way different from gnarly middle-aged ones). Face—chiseled, striking, but looks different in every single role.

And the bottom line is simply this: he showed up and he *was* Jamie.

Watching Caitriona's audition—two scenes that she played with Sam—was just as enthralling. They did it in street clothes, no set, costumes, makeup—nothing but their face-to-face personalities, and those just lit up my computer screen. They struck sparks off each other immediately, and as I enthused to one friend, "She has *the* most expressive chin!" (So is the rest of her lovely face, of course—but I'd never seen a chin with that much personality.)

Either Sam or Caitriona alone is wonderful onscreen, but the two of them together are absolutely riveting.

---

[3] *The Internet Movie Database (this includes information on television and video, as well as feature films). While it's a great resource for checking actual data and what you might call historical material— the names of director, cast and crew of* Stagecoach, *for instance—it's rather spotty with regard to newer material and material still in development (which may never actually be made). It can be added to or edited by anyone, and therefore is just about as reliable as Wikipedia, for the same reasons.*

[4] *What I actually said to my husband was, "This man looks grotesque; what can they be* thinking*?"*

[5] *Truer words were never spoken. . . .*

MY BRIEF CAREER AS A
TV ACTOR

PART 1

I posted this blog entry in early February, 2014, while on set in Scotland.

 ou know, I'm not at all surprised that actors have occasional trouble dealing with Real Life. Not that they can't separate the reality of their characters (and believe me, it *is* a reality) from that of their own personae—but if you're a film actor, Real Life doesn't exist for you on the job.

After a read-through of Block 3[1] and a production meeting[2] on Monday, then on Tuesday a huge and fascinating tour of "*Outlander*-world" (and I'll tell you about all these in some detail later; I had four hours' sleep last night, a call for 5:30 A.M. this morning—Thursday, that is—which meant I got up at 4:30, and another Really Full Day), followed by hours of press interviews, I embarked on My Brief Career as a TV Actor on Wednesday morning.

"Call" means the hour at which a car comes to your residence to pick you up and transport you to work. There are five "unit drivers" who work for the *Outlander* production, all vivid personalities in their own right. (You can follow some of them on Twitter, with handles such as @daviehollywood, and give them your opinion of their suggested project of having a "Drivers of *Outlander*" calendar. Davie asked me what I thought of the notion, to which I replied, "I dunno . . . Full Monty or G-strings?" Didn't get an answer to that one yet.)

---

[1] *Episodes are grouped in blocks, each block including two episodes. Each block will have its own director and director of photography (DP), and these offices may change from block to block. This blocking allows the production team to arrange location filming and shooting schedules with maximum efficiency: For example, when scenes from both episodes are shot in a particular distant location, all the scenes can be shot in one trip, rather than having to return for the second episode's scenes.*

[2] *This was fascinating. The production meeting for each block essentially gathers all the heads of departments around a table and they go through the shooting schedule for the new block, asking questions, discussing, and clarifying exactly what may be needed in terms of logistics, equipment, costume, housing, etc.—and handling questions specific to each department. At the meeting I was privileged to witness, the Master of Horse noted that "[Actor X] does not get on with his horse. We'll have to find him a different one, but of course it won't look the same. How are you going to explain that?" After some discussion, it was decided that the actor's original horse could be stolen, making it logical that he'd have another.*

When you leave at night, the production office gives you (any actor, that is) a call sheet for the next day. This tells you when to be picked up, when to report to Hair and Makeup, and the theoretical time at which you'll be on set, along with other arcane information as to whether they think you'll be filming only that day or for several days and, if so, which ones (this all being subject to change).

So Wednesday, my husband (company photojournalist and documentarian) and I were picked up at 6:55 A.M., as per the call sheet, and driven round a few corners to pick up Caitriona Balfe and her younger sister Lorraine, who's working in Costume on the *Outlander* production. Both lovely young women, and as friendly and funny as one can reasonably be expected to *be* at that hour of the morning.

We were all decanted at the back of the lot, where the trailers are. Now, the "artists" (the regular performers with speaking parts, as opposed to the supporting actors, or extras) each have trailer space—in this case, most have half of a large two-person trailer. The trailers have the character names on the doors and are quite cozy inside. There's a tiny bathroom in each trailer half, as well, with a pump toilet, and the living room has a pop-out where the sofa lives. Otherwise, it's sparsely but comfortably furnished with a cozy chair, a coffee table, a tiny refrigerator, and a tray with such amenities as Kleenex, an electric carafe, and Tetley's tea bags.

There are people all over the lot whose job is to keep track of other people—particularly the artists. When you're working, someone knows where you are at every given minute, and you can be found instantly. These minions hand you off to one another like—exactly like—a parcel. (Though a cherished and respected parcel, to be sure.)[3]

All the trailers had very narrow, very steep steps up to the doors—ungodly treacherous to negotiate while wearing an eighteenth-century costume, I tell you, but I luckily managed not to fall off and break my neck (I did break the costume a couple of times, but that's another story). And whenever you're *in* your trailer, people come and knock at the door at frequent intervals, bearing food (breakfast and lunch are not only provided but brought out to you), costumes, or prepared to take you wherever you're meant to be next.

In this instance, someone popped up and instructed me to take off my shirt, don the pink fuzzy hooded bathrobe on the couch, and come with them. I did, and they took me to Hair and Makeup, where Annie McEwan (with a deep interest in—and extensive research on—the hairstyles of the eighteenth century) oversees things. Julie Mutch made me up—very basic makeup, as your average eighteenth-century

---

[3] *After the first day's work, I said to Sam Heughan, "Now I know what your life is like—it's indentured servitude!" He laughed, and agreed. It's true, though; everyone on set works like a dog, with twelve-hour days, five or six days a week.*

respectable woman wouldn't be wearing any; mine essentially just lightened my skin tone, evened it out, and provided a minimally reflective surface for the camera (this augmented by powder, applied roughly every five minutes when the cameras weren't actually running—more on that later, too). And then she fitted my wig. This was . . . um . . . "amazing" is probably the only reasonable word.

Prep for wearing a wig meant they plaited my hair into four tiny braids and crisscrossed these back and forth over my head, anchoring them with flat metal hair clips. This provided a base to which the wig could be attached, with zillions of hoop-shaped hairpins in different calibers.

The wig itself is human hair, carefully dressed and styled, mounted on a "lace" cap. By "lace," they mean the very fine mesh to which the hair is attached. This cap fits over your own hair, and the extensions of the lace fit across the top of your forehead and down in front of your ears. Once they'd got the wig fixed securely, they trimmed the lace to a minimum and then pasted it to my face with some fixative that looked and smelled more or less like pine pitch but probably wasn't. Once pasted, the lace essentially becomes invisible; you can't see it even when standing right next to a person wearing it—unless the fixative has dried unevenly or not quite enough was put on, in which case the lace raises unevenly off the skin, and people are seen to put a hand to their temple and exclaim, "My lace is dimpling!" Whereupon a makeup person materializes magically beside them, alcohol-laden brush at the ready (the alcohol dissolves the fixative, allowing the lace to be lifted clear of the skin, smoothed, and re-fixed).

Someone was waiting for me as I stepped out of the Hair and Makeup trailer and, after asking what I wanted for breakfast (they have all the standard things; I chose bacon, eggs, and toast), took me back to my trailer to startle my husband. ("You look like a geisha in a small Afro," he told me.)

Breakfast showed up promptly—along with the Diet Coke I'd requested; most people on set drink tea or coffee or water all day, but as Ron D. Moore runs on Diet Coke, too, there was always a supply to hand—followed in short order by two ladies from Costume, bearing the pieces of my outfit.

These consisted of a knee-length muslin shift, knee-high dark-green stockings (thick ones), reddish-brown shoes with satin ribbon ties, a set of stays (a corset) that went over the shift, a very heavy canvas petticoat (which they held for me and I sort of dived into, so they could pull it down over the shift and stays), and a bum roll, which is just what it sounds like—wide hips were apparently sexy in the eighteenth century.

Stays. These lace up the back, and it takes considerable effort to get them adequately tightened. As in: if it's done properly, you can't breathe, though you do

acclimate to this. You *really* can't bend over, so my husband had to keep retying the ribbons on my shoes, until he gave up and double-knotted them. Does give you the desired wasp-waisted look, though, I'll say that.

Anyway, once all these layers had been applied, my dressers put on the pièce de résistance, an absolutely gorgeous dress designed especially for me by Terry Moore, head of the Costume Department (and Ron's wife). Crushed blue velvet with hand-painted tartan pattern, gold lace, MacKenzie tartan stomacher and sacque back (a sort of cape that attaches to the shoulders), bag sleeves, and *gorgeous*. Once I was in it, they opened the door and invited in Crawford, one of three male employees of the Costume Department (Terry says the core staff is seventy-five), as Muscle was required to lace up the dress itself over the stays. Also, Crawford himself had made the dress and wanted to see how it looked.[4]

It looked great, but I tell you—once tightened and dressed in all the layers, you really can't do much beyond walk and wave your arms in a circumscribed sort of way. Going to the bathroom is *possible* (just) but no simple undertaking.[5] You can sit down, but you don't lean back—not out of fear of rumpling your clothes, but because you can't. You have great posture, involuntary though it is.

I was then left to wheeze gently and talk to my husband for a bit, having been assured that someone would come get me—and, sure enough, someone did come to escort me to the soundstage where filming was to take place that day. (There are two soundstages; the one I was on was the one where the Great Hall is built—and one impressive set it is, too.)

Now, I do need to sleep a little more tonight (I slept for a few hours, because I had to, but then got up to do a modicum of writing—mostly this post), because while tomorrow's call isn't as ungodly early as Thursday's, I am still working tomorrow.

If I have time after tomorrow's work, though, I'll tell you all about the Gathering, the Great Hall, and how filming really works. Stay tuned!

---

[4] *Fantastic!*

[5] *Just recently, a reenactor told me that the best way to go to the bathroom while attired like this is to sit on the toilet facing backward. I haven't tried this but noted the technique for possible future use.*

My Brief Career as a
TV Actor

Part 2

es, I hear you saying, but what about the actual *acting* part?

Well, good question. *Outlander*-world is HUGE, to start with. They made it from an enormous, disused circuit-board factory, and to walk through it and see how it's been transformed is astonishing. The point about the hugeness, though, is that the place includes two large soundstages—one of which has the set of the Great Hall at Leoch.

They (production team and publicists) wanted me to come do a cameo in this specific episode because a number of press/media people were invited—and they were invited now because of the spectacular nature of the Gathering: dozens of supporting actors (aka SA's, aka extras) in full and glorious costume, stunning set design, and lots of Interesting Stuff.

Now, originally they'd asked if I'd like to be an extra, and I said sure, that might be fun, and the fans could play "Where's Waldo?" when the show was released. But some weeks later, Maril e-mailed me to say that they'd been thinking about this; if I were an extra, I'd have to stand essentially in the same place for three days, as you can't be pulling extras out of carefully composed crowd scenes and screwing up the painstaking configurations that the director and DP (director of photography, and a person of Vital Importance) have worked out. As Maril put it, "The novelty wears off quickly."

They'd therefore come up with a better suggestion: Matt Roberts, the scriptwriter for this particular episode (and a lovely man he is, too, Guy Fawkes beard notwithstanding), would write a tiny scenelet for me. Just a couple of lines of dialogue. They could film that pretty quickly on its own and I'd then be released. "Great!" I said.

So I became the wife of a wealthy merchant, Iona MacTavish by name.[1] The lady in question has come (with her husband; Ron played Mr. MacTavish, though we weren't seen together anywhere. Ron was among the extras on the floor of the hall) to the Gathering, and the scenelet in question takes place in one of the galleries over the Great Hall.

---

[1] They let me choose my own name. "MacTavish" was a nod to Jamie's alias when he meets Claire, and "Iona" was chosen in honor of my Scottish son-in-law's baby niece.

It's One Impressive Set, let's put it that way. Among other things—quite a lot of things—it has torches and candles absolutely everywhere; massive chandeliers with three or four dozen fat wax candles (and they are real wax; Matt mentioned that hot wax not infrequently drips on people underneath—including one who yelped in response to being splattered but was told it was better than being flogged); wall sconces with pairs of tapers; candelabra all over the horizontal surfaces . . . plus two large hearths roaring away (gas flames there and in the torches). LOTS of light—augmented by huge stage lights (which probably have a technical name, but I don't know it) that, equipped with gels, can simulate anything from high noon to moonlight. Add in a thick squirt of the artificial fog/mist they call "Atmos" and you have Real Atmosphere.[2]

The point here is that when everything is lit, it's bloody hot on that set. Add a few dozen people dressed in woolen clothing (all the costumes are using period-authentic fabrics, naturally) and the resultant mass body temperature contributes nearly as much heat as do the lights.

An important point of physics: Heat Rises.

So I'm standing in the gallery, wearing roughly ten pounds of wool and velvet, in the company of a dozen other people similarly attired. And Neville (Neville Kidd, the DP[3]) sets the lights just *so* for spectacular effect and, with the director (Brian Kelly) and camera operators, is setting up a Very Ambitious shot—a really long, looping shot that goes down the hall, up the stairs, through the gallery, and out the other end, requiring the use of a crane, an elevating platform, and a Steadicam.

My husband, who watched all of the technical setting-up—which took hours in itself—told me that the Steadicam was actually the star of the entire episode: "After every run, they hang it up in its frame, pet it, powder its nose, and get it a drink of water. . . ." The necessary equipment to operate this thing—run by a lovely guy named Ossie with dark-red hair (I'm partial to gingers, you know. . . .)—was in itself straight out of Bionic Pinups.

Yes, they really *do* shout, "Action!" when a take begins and "Cut!" when they stop it. Followed, usually, by "Do it again." Even if a take works well, they do multiple takes of a scene for "coverage"—meaning they want enough raw material so that they can pick and choose the footage they want for the final edited cut. And, yes, they do use clapper boards (an Immense one, for this particular run, so everyone in the Great Hall could see it, including the galleries) with the relevant scene/take information.

While the main technical setup had all been done the day before (I didn't see it, as I was being interviewed nonstop, but

---

[2]*You also have incipient black lung. It's like breathing campfire smoke all day; your nasal passages are coated with soot.*

[3]*I encourage you to go look at his own spectacular showreel at https://www.youtube.com/watch?v= VBsONvme3Uw .*

Doug told me all about it), it still takes a long time to reset a shot, especially if the lights need to be adjusted. And a particularly long or ambitious shot requires not only ideal lighting and camera operation—it means that everyone *in* the shot has to do exactly the right thing at the right time. Or you do it again. And again. And again. With fairly long waits in between the "agains." (As a well-known actress who shall be nameless was heard to remark, "Another take—another chance to fuck it up.")

Heat *does* rise. And by the time we'd been at it for three hours, it was about 103 F. in the gallery. (I kid you not; I live in Phoenix, Arizona. I know what 103 F. feels like.) Caitriona, who entered and left the gallery with each shot (I was in place throughout), kindly lent me the fan she was carrying (which had been lent to her by one of the Costume people), and very welcome it was—particularly when one of the SA's standing behind me collapsed from the heat and puddled down in the corner, red in the face and streaming sweat. I whipped the fan out of my sleeve and fanned her madly, though only for a few seconds before a couple of alert minions came racing up to take her downstairs.

At this point, they cleared everyone out of the gallery and opened the doors to let the temperature drop while they reset the next shot. Brian Kelly, the director, came up, too, and in passing said something to me that I understood to be "stay there," so I did. Evidently he'd actually been telling me to go downstairs, because at the door he looked over his shoulder at me, still standing there, and I heard him call to his AD (assistant director—the one who does the shouting), "Davey, come translate for me, will you?" Glaswegian accents are something special. . . .

In the end, it took five hours to get that one shot (when we came back to the loft, fans had been brought up, as well as water, and things were a good bit more tolerable).

Oddly enough, I wasn't really nervous about doing my lines. On Monday, I'd had a lovely meeting with Carol Ann Crawford, the dialect coach, who ran me through the quick version of "How to Speak with a Scottish Accent"—very helpful. And after I'd said it once and got over the oddness of hearing it, I thought I probably wouldn't be so bad as to ruin the shot, so didn't worry about it. Besides, the physical discomfort of being baked to death while standing for hours in high-heeled shoes that throw all your weight onto the balls of your feet and being unable to twist your torso to relieve strain on your lower back kind of overshadowed anything minor like stage fright.

In all honesty, I didn't have anything approaching stage fright. For one thing, I've been talking out loud in front of hundreds of people for some years now, and for another, I was pretty sure that if I did anything horrible, it wouldn't make it into public view. I'd also been watching the dailies for some time and had noticed just how often very good professional actors forget their lines, say the wrong thing, or trip over something.[4]

Now, when you're filming, there are—as noted—long breaks between takes. It's fascinating to watch what happens in these breaks, especially when there are a lot of

_____

[4] *The usual response by an actor when this happens is to shout "Fuck!" (often more than once) and then snap back into character and do the line/scene again.*

actors involved. The instant the AD shouts, "Cut! Do it again," antlike streams of Makeup and Hair people come pouring in and scatter to their assigned actors—powder brushes, combs, and other implements at the ready. The director passes round, giving people instructions, and various specialists, such as the dialect coach and the Gaelic expert (this would be Àdhamh Ó Broin, whom you've seen in the "Speak Outlander" videos—a star in his own right), also zoom in to render aid and advice.

So every time there was a break, someone would pop up in front of me—sometimes two or three of them—to instigate repairs or say, "More of a 'Nyee-EW,' rather than 'new,' and keep the force up all the way through the line."

Really interesting; an extension of the being-passed-along-like-a-parcel feeling.

You're a basically inanimate object most of the time. And "they" (the production people) know exactly where you are at every moment of the day, on set or off, so they can find and produce you instantly. The operation is just too big and too complex to be held up while someone goes to find a missing actor. As one of the cast said to me, "They know when you go to the restroom and exactly how long you're in there." I think this might get on my nerves after a while, but for the two days I did it (I was in another brief shot the next day—that one only took a couple of hours to get, and there were no people downstairs and many fewer candles burning, so much cooler), the whole thing was a lot of fun.

That's the thing about being a writer, though: you'll do *anything* once, just so you can write about it.

Blog: Film Commentary

Adaptation, Logistics, and Testicles

Since book touring is done (thank GOD!) and the show is on hiatus, we have a bit of time to stop, think, and catch up on the e-mail. . . .

So, I thought I might address a few recent comments and questions on Episode 8. Not to refute people's opinions—everyone's entitled to think as they like, and say so—but just to show you a bit about How Things Work.

While most people were riveted—as they should have been; it was a terrific episode—there were a few who were upset at things they perceived to be "missing," these including:

* Scenes of one-on-one dialogue between Jamie and Claire
* More scenes of intimacy
* Claire patching people up and doing healing
* And, specifically, the "waterweed" scene following the Grants' raid.

(One person also thought we should have seen the redcoats stalking Claire, rather than have them pop out abruptly to seize her as she reaches for the stone.)

And there were a number of questions regarding the "deserter" scene—mostly as to whether Claire had actually been raped or not (and if she had, what kind of doofus was Jamie for going off to talk to Dougal instead of tenderly cradling her and soothing her, etc.).

Okay.

As I replied to one such commenter:

Well . . . your comments pinpoint the major difference between Book and Show: time.

ALL the things you wanted to see— one-on-one Jamie and Claire, more scenes of intimacy, relationship building, Claire patching people up, etc.— ALL of them are things that would require extended chunks of time ("extended," in a TV show, is anything that lasts more than sixty seconds). None of these things are "action," none of them move the plot in any direct way.

The show has fifty-two to fifty-five minutes in which to do everything that has to be done. They don't have time to do nice-but-nonessential "Oh, wait while I triage the whole group, bandage Angus's scorched hand, and reset Ned Gowan's tooth," or "Oh, my God, I know we just had sex, but let's do it again. . . ."

In short . . . if you want more of all those things—you can have 'em. In the book.

Now, a successful adaptation is always balancing the needs of the story versus the exigencies of the form. As Andrew Marvell notes in "To His Coy Mistress": Had we but world enough and time, this coyness, lady, were no crime. . . . I have world enough and time in a novel—pretty much all I want. I can shape the story to fit my own notion of pace, rhythm, focus, and climax. So can a showrunner and his gang of writers—but they don't have world enough and time. They have to decide what's essential and then shape the story to the time available and to the necessity for each fifty-five-minute episode to have a satisfying dramatic arc of its own.

So—in reply to the person complaining about the redcoats' abrupt appearance:

But . . . the redcoats came out of "nowhere" in the book, as well, when they pull Claire out of the stream. It isn't that they aren't "there"—it's that in neither case does Claire see them, because she's so totally focused on her goal . . . and we're in her head, so we don't see them, either.

To have shown the soldiers sneaking in from the side while Claire was laboring up the hill, calling for Frank, would have given us a different sort of suspense in the scene—but would have been a distraction from the growing sense of desperate hope between Claire and Frank. And that was the true point of the scene.

See, one of the main tools of good storytelling is focus, getting the reader/viewer to look where you want them to look. And physical reality is really a pretty small part of that. The fact that X must have been there may be logical—but it isn't relevant, so you don't show it. Q.E.D.

Now, the focus of that scene is really what's controlling it and thus dictating changes from the book. Several people expressed disappointment

at not seeing Claire fall into the water and be pulled out by the redcoats. Amusing as that might have been, it's merely a way of interrupting her headlong rush toward the stones and getting her into Captain Randall's clutches. The way it was done instead accomplishes that same plot goal—but also makes a very solid and dramatic point about her longing for Frank and his for her. So the adapted form is not detracting from the original version; in fact, it's adding to it and giving us a really good two-for-one, combining plot and character development/backstory reminder.

When Ron and I met in New York for the first-ever *Outlander* fan event,

we shared a long car ride, during which we talked Book. I told him why the flowers at Craigh na Dun are forget-me-nots and why the ghost is there (and, no, I'm not telling you guys; you'll find out, eventually), and he told me about his vision of that scene with Claire and Frank approaching the stones from either side. I thought that was a great idea and said so.

See, that's something that I couldn't have done in the book, because it's told entirely from Claire's point of view. We can't see what Frank was doing and going through after Claire disappeared. I preserved Claire's worry about/attachment to Frank by having her think about him and grieve for him periodically—but that's all internal; the only way of doing internal monologue in a visual medium is voice-overs, and I think y'all would agree that it's best to keep that technique to a minimum. . . .

But it's simple to change time, place, and viewpoint in a visual medium; one shot and you're there. Also, since you're working in a constrained time-space, the balance of viewpoints is easier to manage.

Technically, it's possible to use multiple viewpoints in a book (in fact, I got a note from one of my editors regarding a chunk of *Written in My Own Heart's Blood* I'd sent him, saying, *Congratulations . . . I think you've just done the literary equivalent of juggling half a dozen chain saws*), but *Outlander* was my first book, written for practice, and I wasn't out to make things too complicated. Had I used flashbacks of Frank's life in the context of a book of that size, they'd either be overwhelming

or trivial distractions. Used in the context of a fifty-five-minute TV episode, they were beautifully balanced against Claire's eighteenth-century life.

In addition, there's a visceral punch to seeing Frank's actions that gives you an instant emotional investment in him and his story. I probably have the chops to do such a thing effectively in print now, but I didn't when I wrote *Outlander* (and, in fact, I wouldn't have thought of doing it; I wanted most of the focus on Jamie and the eighteenth century, both because that's where most of the color and action and story was but also to assist the reader in falling in love with Jamie along with Claire, so that we would understand her later choices. But just as the visual invests the viewers in Frank, it does the same for Jamie—are we in any doubt, following "The Wedding" episode, that Claire is falling in love with him?).

See, a visual medium speeds things up. You don't necessarily need the longer buildup that you have in text, because the images are much more immediate and easier for the audience to absorb in an emotional way.

Moving on to the was-it-rape scene and the aftermath . . .

Well, the people who've read the book (and remember it) know it was attempted rape. Claire grabbed her attacker around the neck while he was fumbling for a, um, connection, pulled him down, and stabbed him in the kidney—but he never did succeed in penetrating her.

The TV-only people probably think he did succeed, because one of the warnings at the beginning was an "R" for "Rape," even though there isn't one in the episode. Now, whether whoever put the warning on thought that's what happened, or whether it's merely a "trigger" warning (i.e., people with a sensitivity to scenes of sexual assault might want to know there is such a scene in this episode), I don't know.

But this is one of those things where stuff from the book actually can't be shown adequately. It's absolutely clear from the book, because we're in Claire's head, and we know what she was perceiving. But the shot can't be under her skirt—and unless they put in a line where Claire tells

Jamie, "Don't worry, he didn't manage to get it in" (which would not only be crude but would grossly undercut her—and the audience's—sense of shock and dislocation), then it's not going to be clear to viewers, who will have to be left to draw their own conclusions.

It's the same case with the "waterweed" scene. This is a scene in the book that occurs between the fight with the Grants and the men instructing Claire next morning in the art of killing people. It's a very vivid scene (sufficiently vivid that the U.K. editor asked me to remove it from her edition of the book, she thinking it "too graphic" for her audience. So this scene is in *Outlander* but not in *Cross Stitch*. The relevant part of the scene is available below, for convenient reference), and extremely memorable to readers, many of whom complained about its omission in the episode.

I didn't discuss the decision to omit this scene with the production team, both because I try not to nitpick them and because I could easily see why it was omitted.

1) It doesn't advance the plot or develop an important bit of character. It reaffirms Jamie and Claire's strong

sense of/need for each other, but there are a lot of other scenes that do that (we see one within the next five minutes). Ergo, it's not necessary. And that consideration is why I reluctantly agreed to remove the scene from the U.K. book. Its removal didn't damage the plot structure or deprive us of anything we really needed. In that respect, it's one of only two scenes in Outlander that aren't structurally attached to something else (the Loch Ness monster scene is the other one).

2) See remarks above about time. Including this scene would have meant leaving out something else, and everything in this episode is necessary to the purpose intended by the writer/production team.

3) The scene wouldn't have been nearly as effective on film as it is on the page—and the reasons have to do with Claire's subjective sensory perceptions. You simply can't show most of what she's experiencing without it

being pornography (and even so, there's no possible way of showing a man's testicles contracting at the moment of orgasm, no matter how professionally accommodating your actor may be). But you can describe it in text, vividly and straightforwardly, without it being gross. Without those subjective bits from Claire's interior point of view, though, the scene doesn't have either the deep sense of intimacy or the intense sensuality that you have in the book version; it's just another sex scene (albeit one admittedly with some fairly funny dialogue). And while some shows would likely use repetitive sex scenes just because people will watch them . . . that's luckily not a technique this show goes for. Every sex scene you see has an emotional point or a plot point to make.

4) And now I really must go and do some work.

#ReadWhileYouWait #OUT-LANDER #RaidersInTheRocks #NoSpoilersInThisOne

[Excerpt from Outlander, *Chapter 18: the rent party has retired for the night, and Jamie and Claire are conversing quietly under their blankets.]*

I rolled over and put my arms about his neck.

"Not as proud as I was. You were wonderful, Jamie. I've never seen anything like that."

He snorted deprecatingly, but I thought he was pleased, nonetheless.

"Only a raid, Sassenach. I've been doin' that since I was fourteen. It's only in fun, ye see; it's different when you're up against someone who really means to kill ye."

"Fun," I said, a little faintly. "Yes, quite."

His arms tightened around me, and one of the stroking hands dipped lower, beginning to inch my skirt upward. Clearly the thrill of the fight was being transmuted into a different kind of excitement.

"Jamie! Not here!" I said, squirming away and pushing my skirt down again.

"Are ye tired, Sassenach?" he asked with concern. "Dinna worry, I won't take long." Now both hands were at it, rucking the heavy fabric up in front.

"No!" I replied, all too mindful of the twenty men lying a few feet away. "I'm not tired, it's just—" I gasped as his groping hand found its way between my legs.

"Lord," he said softly. "It's slippery as waterweed."

"Jamie! There are twenty men sleeping right next to us!" I shouted in a whisper.

"They wilna be sleeping long, if you keep talking." He rolled on top of me, pinning me to the rock. His knee wedged between my thighs and began to work gently back and forth. Despite myself, my legs were beginning to loosen. Twenty-seven years of propriety were no match for several hundred thousand years of instinct. While my mind might object to being taken on a bare rock next to several sleeping soldiers, my body plainly considered itself the spoils of war and was eager to complete the formalities of surrender. He kissed me, long and deep, his tongue sweet and restless in my mouth.

"Jamie," I panted. He pushed his kilt out of the way and pressed my hand against him.

"Bloody Christ," I said, impressed despite myself. My sense of propriety slipped another notch.

"Fighting gives ye a terrible cockstand, after. Ye want me, do ye no?" he said, pulling back a little to look at me. It seemed pointless to deny it, what with all the evidence to hand. He was hard as a brass rod against my bared thigh.

"Er . . . yes . . . but . . ."

He took a firm grip on my shoulders with both hands.

"Be quiet, Sassenach," he said with authority. "It isn't going to take verra long."

It didn't. I began to climax with the first powerful thrust, in long, racking spasms. I dug my fingers hard into his back and held on, biting the fabric of his shirt to muffle any sounds. In less than a dozen strokes, I felt his testicles contract, tight against his body, and the warm flood of his own release. He lowered himself slowly to the side and lay trembling.

The blood was still beating heavily in my ears, echoing the fading pulse between my legs. Jamie's hand lay on my breast, limp and heavy. Turning my head, I could see the dim figure of the sentry, leaning against a rock on the far side of the fire. He had his back tactfully turned. I was mildly shocked to realize that I was not even embarrassed. I wondered rather dimly whether I would be in the morning, and then wondered no more.

Interview for the Unabridged German Edition of *Outlander*

I've had a good many questions asked as to if and how I'm involved in the Starz television production of *Outlander*. As it is, most of them are covered in this interview (done for the new, unabridged German edition of *Outlander,* published by Droemer Knaur), so I thought I'd include portions of it here:

1) As the author of the novel, how closely were you involved in adapting *Outlander* for television?

Not closely, in that I don't write scripts or work directly on the production. But on the other hand very closely, in that the producers have chosen to include me in what they're doing and to ask my opinion on things. (They don't necessarily take my opinions, but they do ask for them.)

2) Have there been changes and modifications the writers had to make in order to adapt the story for the screen?

Of course. You can't film a seven-hundred-page book literally, page by page. It would take years to film, months to show, and very likely be bad television. A book has its own shape and unlimited space in which to achieve the author's in-

tentions. A TV series has a very specific number of fifty-five-minute episodes, and each of those episodes must have its own dramatic shape and thematic content.

I think the *Outlander* production team has done marvels in their adaptation, preserving the essence of the original story and a great deal of the original material (in terms of important scenes and original lines of dialogue). Ron D. Moore has always said that his intent was to "realize" the book, not to change it, and I think he's succeeded wonderfully. Anyone who's read and loved the book will instantly recognize it on-screen—but will also be entranced by the extra dimensions that the visual medium allows.

3) You are one of the producers of the TV series *Outlander*—what tasks and challenges does that job include?

No, I'm actually not a producer; I'm a consultant, that being a fairly flexible term: it can mean nothing or quite a bit. In this case, I've been very fortunate; the production team has been more than courteous in including me in their affairs, showing me scripts and daily footage, and inviting my comments.

My job, essentially, is to make such comments as may be useful—either in terms of historical accuracy or reference or in terms of the original source material. The latter may mean reference to plot or character that will be important later in the season or in later books/seasons—or may have to do with what I know about the books' fans and their particular perceptions and likes.

A couple of brief examples: in one script, Claire wanders away from the rent-collecting party and falls into conversation with some Highland village women. In the original draft (scripts go through multiple iterations and change constantly, right up to—and in many cases during—filming), the village was described like one of the towns in which early scenes had been filmed, with stone cottages, cobbled streets, village shops, and Claire's new-met friends invited her to come sit down and drink tea and play cards with them.

I commented that while the point of the scene—her isolation, with all the men, and her need for some sympathetic connection—was fine, that particular situation wouldn't be appropriate; remote Highland villages were much cruder in aspect: cottages made of laths and thatch, no streets, certainly no shops—and women in such a time and place wouldn't be drinking tea (they didn't have any) or playing cards. Not only were cards considered the work of the devil, such women just wouldn't have time for frivolous pursuits, especially during the daylight hours. Making a living in the harsh conditions of the Highlands required almost everyone to work from dawn to dark. I suggested a few things that the women *could* have been doing, including milking goats, making butter or cheese, carding or spinning wool . . . or "waulking" wool.

This (I noted) is a process unique to the Highlands of Scotland, and fairly picturesque. Several women would sit on either side of a table or floor, with a long roll of freshly woven tartan cloth between them. This would be soaked in hot urine (urine is a mordant, setting the dye fast), and the cloth was then pushed and slapped to and fro for hours, felting the surface and making the fabric reasonably waterproof. To ease the tedium of the process, women would sing traditional "waulking songs."

The production people promptly went and found the Highland Folk Museum at Newtonmore, which has a reproduction village of exactly the sort I'd described and a team of reenactors, including women who know how to waulk wool and know the traditional songs. You'll see them doing it—with Claire—in Episode 5 ("Rent"), where it's a charming bit of atmosphere *and* serves the purpose of the original scene, with Claire welcomed and included.

On another occasion, I saw the rough cut of Episode 2, where Claire mends Jamie's shoulder and he comforts her over the loss of her husband. He takes his leave, telling her that she need not fear him, or anyone else, so long as he's with her.

I'd seen this whole scene shot (many times) in the daily footage, so I knew what it looked like and that the complete scene existed. In the rough cut of the episode, though, that final line had been omitted; the scene stopped about five seconds earlier. I urged the production team to try to include that particular line, telling them that it was one of the iconic lines of the book and that the fans would particularly note its absence. (I also added, "Besides, Jamie looks *great* in that shot, all half-

naked, blood-smeared, and earnest.") And they did listen and did put that line back in—and the fans (of course) loved it.

This is not to say that they always do what I suggest—but they do listen to me, which is a privilege I appreciate very much.

4) The casting of the actors must have been a huge challenge. Was it difficult to find actors who fitted your description of the characters?

Luckily, it wasn't my responsibility. There is a very talented casting director, Suzanne M. Smith, who did the major part of the searching; the executive producers then made the final choices, I believe.

However, they did very kindly share the audition tapes for the people they'd selected for the major roles, expressing a strong hope that I'd share their positive impressions of these actors—as indeed I did!

Interestingly, Sam Heughan (who plays Jamie Fraser; his last name is commonly pronounced "HEW-an") was chosen very early in the process. One of the producers told me, "I thought we'd search for months for Jamie, and then he'd finally turn out to be the UPS man or something," but apparently he turned up after only a few days.

The role of Claire was another matter; they searched high and low for another four months and began to worry that they'd have to push back the start date for filming, because they didn't feel they could settle for anything less than the perfect actress for such a major role. Finally, they went back through tapes that had been discarded early in the process . . . and all of the executives who looked through these came back and said, "There's something about *this* one. . . ." And all of them had chosen Caitriona's self-made audition. So

they called her in, sent Sam to Los Angeles to do an audition with her—and it was instant chemistry. Caitriona simply inhabits Claire's role; it's amazing.

Just a note: Sam is (appropriately) Scottish, and Caitriona is Irish (but does a fine English accent). Tobias Menzies, who plays both Frank Randall and Captain Jack Randall, is English (despite his Scottish surname).

5) Obviously, Scottish nature, Scottish culture, and Scottish history play a great role in the novel. Was it possible to shoot most of the series in Scotland, as well?

Fortunately, it was. Season 1 was shot entirely in Scotland, both on location and at "*Outlander*-world," a massive studio/soundstage installation built in Cumbernauld (a small town near Glasgow).

6) Did you visit the set? How did it feel to see all the characters and settings come to life?

I did! It was tremendously interesting and really impressive to see the thousands of people required to do such a production, the amazing intricacy of everything, and the level of skill required to make it all work. They did a marvelous job in creating the world of the book, in everything from sets and props to costumes, directing, photography (which is stunning!), and, of course, the acting.

7) What reactions to the series did you get from American viewers?

Huge enthusiasm. There are—there always will be—a small number of people who gripe and complain that "It [some small line of dialogue or favorite scene] isn't like it was in the book!" But, as I've told everyone for months, if you watch the show with the book in your hand, you're not going to enjoy either one. Most people are wise enough not to do that, and consequently the show has been instantly popular in the States—and has so far been sold in eighty-seven other countries.

8) Could you already tell us a little bit more about the second season? When will it start and will it cover the entire plotline of Book 2, *Dragonfly in Amber*?

Season 2 will cover *Dragonfly in Amber*. I don't imagine they can fit the *entire* plotline into a television show, even with a very generous number of episodes. (I had breakfast with George R. R. Martin—a friend of mine—soon after we had signed the deal for the Starz series, and he asked me how many episodes we were getting. "Sixteen," I replied. "Sixteen!" he exclaimed. "They only give me *ten*!") Still, I'm sure that they'll do an equally wonderful job in realizing the story on-screen as they have done with *Outlander,* so that fans of the book will recognize it at once and be ecstatic at seeing the story brought to life.

Is It Like You Thought It Would Be?

Ever since clips and trailers and stills of the new Starz *Outlander* TV show were released, people have been eagerly asking me, "So—is it just like you imagined?" "What's it like to see these people who've lived in your head for so long come to life?" "Did you ever imagine it would be like this?"

Frankly, it's a bit like the scene in *Outlander* where, immediately after Claire and Jamie have made love together for the first time (and his first time ever), she asks him, "So was it like you thought it would be?" And, after making her promise not to laugh at him, he confesses, "Almost . . . I didna realize that ye did it face-to-face. I thought ye must do it the back way, like . . . like horses, ye know."

As in, yes, it's a lot like I imagined it ("it" being the show itself) and at the same time quite different. How so?

1. I have friends who are screenwriters, friends who have worked in the film world, and friends who have had films made of their work. Based on everything I'd heard and read, I was expecting to have nothing whatever to do with the production myself. I was familiar with Ron D. Moore's work so had high hopes that it would be good but figured all I could do was cross my fingers.

Instead, I was startled—though very gratified—at the degree of involvement offered me. Ron and his production partner, Maril Davis, came to my house and spent two days with me, talking through ideas, characters, storylines, etc. We were much on the same wavelength, and as the production got under way, they were more than courteous about including me, asking my opinion on things (though they are, of course, under no legal compulsion to take account of it), showing me scripts and footage, inviting me to the set in Scotland, and generally making me feel welcome.

2. I always want to roll my eyes when people say, "Isn't it exciting seeing your characters come to life?" because, as far as I'm concerned, they've always been alive. Still, I know what these people mean, and, yeah—it *is* exciting. Is it like I expected? No, it's much better. . . .

Everyone has a mental image of what Jamie Fraser and Claire Beauchamp Randall look like. I actually know what they look like. Now, plainly, no actor alive will look exactly like anyone's mental image of a character, and I certainly didn't expect the actors chosen for these parts to look "like" my knowledge of Jamie and Claire. And they don't.

See, actors do magic, no less than writers do. And beyond certain minimal physical requirements, it doesn't really matter what they look like—only that they can *be* the character they play. And every single actor in this show can do that.

3. Now, I do understand what "adaptation" means and a bit about how one translates text to a visual medium (I used to write comic-book scripts for Walt Disney and have in fact done a graphic novel—*The Exile*—version of *Outlander*). But what I didn't realize was just how engaging a good adaptation could be.

Ron's adaptation is very faithful to the original story; anyone who's read *Outlander* will recognize it instantly. But there are the small changes—the insertions, the moving of scenes for dramatic cohesion—and, all together, these "different" touches give the show a constant sense of novelty and discovery. I watch footage, knowing what's going on—but wanting to know what happens next.

And you can't ask more of a good story than that.

ANNOTATED

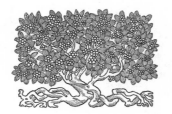

BIBLIOGRAPHY

This bibliography has two purposes. The main purpose, of course, is to allow people with an interest in some topic to find further information on it. The secondary purpose is to give the reader a glimpse of the research and resources behind some elements of the *Outlander* novels—if only to indicate just how tenuous the connection between inspiration and execution sometimes is!

I've done bibliographies before; many of them. I used to be a scientist, after all. However, this present bibliography is rather different from the scholarly version. First off, while I would have read every word (frequently more than once) of each reference in a scholarly bibliography, there are several books in this one that I haven't read at all. There are many more that I've read only in part, others that I've skimmed—and a few that I never intend to read, but keep in case I need to look up some particular bit of information.

A scholarly bibliography would also be complete—or as complete as industrious research could assure. This one isn't, by a long shot. Many books that I consulted in the early days of writing were returned to the library without being recorded anywhere (I didn't realize at the time that I'd have to do this, or I'd have been more careful about it, I assure you). Many others have been consulted and then consigned to my storeroom—and if you think I'm going to go dig around in *there* . . . ! I acquire books constantly, and in fact currently have fifteen hundred books in my core reference collection.

No, this bibliography essentially consists of the books that I used as background and reference while writing the first four books of the series—but isn't a complete listing of those books; it's what's still on my office shelves. This is highly unscholarly, totally idiosyncratic—and has a lot to do with the differences between a scientist and a novelist.

A scientist would refer to a specific citation either in order to support her own work, or to challenge the citation's conclusions. A writer may simply pick up a book, smell it, and sit down to write, without even opening it (my thanks to Anne Bennett, the kind lady who sent me the 1777 edition of Pope's *Iliad*, which I've never read, but which smells great and inspired bits of several scenes in *Voyager*). A writer may read an authoritative reference, and then merrily disregard everything it says.

Looking over the headings in this section, I came to the conclusion that this bibliography ought really to be subtitled "Etc." (This isn't really a proper bibliography; it's a compost heap, and I'm not sure there are any rules for the organization of compost heaps.) As it is, references are grouped according to the main area of interest into which they fall—but since ideas know no bounds, there will undoubtedly be a bit of overlap here and there.

Consequently, while the list of herbal guides—for instance—could certainly be included in the "Natural History (Etc.)" heading, I have instead included them in the "Medicine" section, since virtually all herbal guides deal with the medical aspects of the herbs described. A few books seemed to fall equally into either of two sections; in these cases, I generally included the title in both sections, to make it easier for people to find specifically what they may be looking for.

N.B.: *All references are as complete as possible, which in some cases is not very.*

EIGHTEENTH CENTURY: GENERAL HISTORY, GEOGRAPHY, BACKGROUND, ARTIFACTS, ETC.

Collins Encyclopedia of Antiques. London: Tiger Books International.

Great Britain: A Bantam Travel Guide. New York: Bantam Books.

Alexander, William, and George Henry Mason. Views of 18th Century China: Costumes, History, Customs. London: Studio Editions, 1988.

Allcott, Kenneth. Eighteenth-Century Prose, 1700–1780, Vol. III. Baltimore: Penguin Books, Ltd., 1956.

Andrews, E.W., et al. Journal of a Lady of Quality, 1774–1776. New Haven: Yale University Press, 1939.

Andrews, William. Old Time Punishments. Williamstown, MA.: Corner House Publishers, 1985.

Big Road Atlas Britain: New Computer Mapping. The Automobile Association-Fanum House, Basingstoke, Hampshire RG21 2EA.

Heritage: The British Review, Vol. 28. (June/July 1989).

Historical Atlas of the World. New York: Barnes & Noble Books, 1980.

The House of Parliament, The Palace of Westminster. Hampshire: Pitkin Pictorials, Andover, 1992.

Illustrated Walks in London. Andover, Hants: Pitkin Pictorials, 1990.

Mini Great Britain Road Atlas. A to Z Publications.

Pigot & Co.'s British Atlas: Counties of England. London: Garamond Publishers Ltd., 1990.

Realm: The Magazine of Britain's History and Countryside, vol. 40 (Aug/Sept. 1991).

Scalamandre Guide to Passementerie.

Threads, vol. 33 (Feb/Mar. 1991).

The Wall Chart of World History: From Earliest Times to the Present. Dorset Press, 1988.

Atterbury, Paul and Lars Tharp, eds. The Bulfinch Illustrated Encyclopedia of Antiques. New York: Little, Brown and Co., 1994.

Atton, Henry. The King's Customs, Vols. I and II. New York: A. M. Kelley, 1967.

Baigent, Michael, et al. The Temple and the Lodge. New York: Arcade Publishing, Inc., 1991.

Bamford, Paul Walden. Privilege and Profit: A Business Family in Eighteenth-Century France. Philadelphia: University of Pennsylvania Press, 1998.

Boswell, James. Boswell's London Journal, 1762–1763. London: The Reprint Society, 1952.

Boswell, James. The Life of Samuel Johnson, vols. I and II. New York: The Heritage Press, 1963.

Head, Barclay V. British Museum Dept. of Coins and Medals: Catalogue of the Greek Coins of Phrygia. Bologna: A Forni, 1964.

Brownstone, David and Irene Franck. Timelines of War: A Chronology of Warfare from 100,000 B.C. to the Present. New York: Little, Brown and Co., 1994.

Bruce, George. The Paladin Dictionary of Battles. Edison, N.J.: Hunter Publishing, Inc., 1986.

Burl, Aubrey. Megalithic Brittany. New York: Thames and Hudson, 1985.

Bush, Barbara. Slave Women in Caribbean Society, 1650–1838. Indiana University Press, 1990.

Chittenden, Margaret. Merrymaking in Great Britain. Champaign, Ill.: Garrard Publishing Company, 1974.

Clair, Colin. A History of Printing in Britain. London: Cassell, 1965.

Coke, Thomas. A History of the West Indies, vols. I, II, and III. Miami: Mnemosyne, 1969.

Cooke, Edward William. Sailing Vessels in Authentic Early Nineteenth-Century Illustrations. Mineola, N.Y.: Dover Publications, Inc., 1989.

Copeland, Peter F. Pirates and Buccaneers Coloring Book. Mineola, N.Y.: Dover Publications, Inc., 1977.

Corry, Joseph. Observations upon the Windward Coast of Africa, the Religion, Character, Customs, & c. of the Natives. London: Cass, 1968.

Cottell, P.L., and D. H. Aldcroft. Shipping, Trade and Commerce: Essays in Memory of Ralph Davis. Leicester: University Press, 1981.

Coupland, Lawrence. Living in Bath 200 Years Ago. Bath: Bath City Council, 1986.

Crystal, David. The Cambridge Factfinder. New York: Cambridge University Press, 1993.

Culver, B. Henry. The Book of Old Ships, from Egyptian Galleys to Clipper Ships. Mineola, N.Y.: Dover Publications, Inc., 1992.

Defoe, Daniel. An Account of the Conduct and Proceedings of the Pirate Gow (the Original of Sir Walter Scott's Captain Cleveland). New York: B. Franklin, 1970.

Defoe, Daniel. The History and Remarkable Life of the Truly Honourable Colonel Jack. London: Constable & Company, Ltd., 1923.

Desmond, Kevin. A Timetable of Inventions and Discoveries. New York: M. Evans and Company Inc., 1986.

Duffy, Christopher. The Military Experience in the Age of Reason, 1715–1789. New York: Barnes & Noble Books, Inc., 1987.

Earle, Alice Morse. Curious Punishments of Bygone Days. Applewood Books, Bedford, Ma.: 1995.

Edmunds, John. A Williamsburg Songbook. 1964.

Eggenberger, David. An Encyclopedia of Battles: Accounts of Over 1,560 Battles from 1479 B.C. to the Present. Mineola, N.Y.: Dover Publications, Inc., 1985.

Ellis, Alfred Burdon. The Ewe-Speaking Peoples of the Slave Coast of West Africa, Their Religion, Manners, Laws, Languages. Oosterhous, NB: Anthropological Publications, 1966.

Fajeon, Joseph Jefferson. The Complete Smuggler; A Book About Smuggling in England, America and Elsewhere, Past and Present. Indianapolis: The Bobbs-Merrill Company, 1938.

Fisher, Louise B. An Eighteenth-Century Garland. Williamsburg, Va.: 1951.

Fouchard, Jean. The Haitian Maroons; Liberty or Death. New York: E. W. Blyden Press, 1981.

Fox, Henry Richard. English Merchants: Memoirs in Illustration of the Progress of British Commerce. New York: Kraus Reprint, 1969.

Fraser-Mackintosh, Charles. Antiquarian Notes, Historical, Genealogical, and Social. Inverness: A & W Mackenzie, 1897.

Girard, Jacques. Versailles Gardens: Sculpture and Mythology. New York: The Vendome Press, 1985.

Glass, H. The Servants Directory, Improved; or, House-keepers Companion. Dublin: J. Potts, 1812.

Grun, Bernard. The Timetables of History. A Horizonal Linkage of People and Events. New York: Simon and Schuster, 1982.

Medieval Punishment: Torture and Executions in Europe: 1100–1600, How It Was Done, Why It Was Done. Lifkin, Tx.: The Gutenberg Press, 1994.

Haggard, Andrew. The Real Louis the Fifteenth, vol I. London: Hutchinson, 1907.

Hague, Norma. Antique Pocket Guides: Combs and Hair Accessories. Cincinnati: Seven Hills Books, 1985.

Hansard, T.C. Typographia: An Historical Sketch of the Origin and Progress of the Art of Printing. London: Gregg Press, 1966.

Hastings, Max, Ed. The Oxford Book of Military Anecdotes. New York: Oxford University Press, 1986.

Hoon, Elizabeth Evelynola. The Organization of the English Customs System, 1696–1786. New York and London: D. Appleton-Century Company, Inc., 1938.

Isaac, Peter. Six Centuries of the Provincial Book Trade in Britain. Winchester: St. Paul's Bibliographies, 1990.

Jennett, Sean. Pioneers in Printing: Johannes Gutenburg, William Caxton, William Caslon, John Baskerville, Alois Senefelder, Frederick Koenig, Ottmar Mergenthaler, Tolbert Lanston. London: Routledge & Paul, 1958.

Jordan, Katharine. The Folklore of Ancient Wiltshire. Wiltshire: Wiltshire County Council, Library and Museum Service, 1990.

Kalman, Bobbie. Eighteenth-Century Clothing. New York: Crabtree Publishing Company, 1993.

Kaplan, Steven L. Provisioning Paris: Merchants and Millers in the Grain and Flour Trade During the Eighteenth Century. Ithaca: Cornell University Press, 1984.

Kennedy, Paul E. Stained Glass Windows Coloring Book. Mineola, N.Y.: Dover Publications, Inc., 1972.

Kennedy, Richard. The Dictionary of Beliefs. An Illustrated Guide to World Religions and Beliefs. Sussex: BLA Publishing Limited, 1984.

King, Noel Quinton: African Cosmos: An Introduction to Religion in Africa. Belmont, Ca.: Wadsworth Publishing Co., 1986.

Knowlson, T. Sharper. The Origins of Popular Superstitions and Customs. London: Studio Editions Ltd., 1994.

Laffin, John. Brassey's Dictionary of Battles. New York: Barnes & Noble Books, 1995.

Lagemann, Robert and Albert C. Manucy. The Long Rifle. Eastern Acorn Press, 1993.

Leonard, C.H., A.M., M.D. The Concise Gray's Anatomy. Hertfordshire, England: Omega Books Ltd., 1985.

Leroi-Gourhan, Andre. The Dawn of European Art: An Introduction to Palaeolithic Cave Painting. New York: Cambridge University Press, 1982.

Lockley, R. M., ed. Britain in Colour. London: Batsford Books, 1964.

Loewen, James W. Lies My Teacher Told Me. New York: Simon & Schuster, 1995.

Macdonald, John, with an introduction by Peter Quennell. Memoirs of an Eighteenth-Century Footman. London: Century Hutchinson Ltd., 1985.

MacGibbon, John. Going Abroad. Wellington, New Zealand: Ngaio Press, 1997.

Mackey, Albert. The History of Freemasonry. New York: Gramercy Books, 1996.

Manucy, Albert. Artillery Through the Ages. Washington, D.C.: Division of Publications, National Park Service, U.S. Department of the Interior, 1985.

Marshack, Alexander. The Roots of Civilization; The Cognitive Beginnings of Man's First Art, Symbol, and Notation. New York: McGraw-Hill, 1972.

May, Robin and G.A. Embleton. Men-at-Arms Series: The British Army in North America, 1775–1783. London: Reed International Books Ltd., 1996.

Mbiti, John S. Introduction to African Religion. London: Heinemann Educational, 1975.

McLaren, Angus. Birth Control in Nineteenth-Century England. New York: Holmes & Meire, 1978.

Messadie, Gerald. Great Inventions Through History. New York: W&R Chambers, Ltd., 1991.

Miall, Anton. Xenophobe's guide to the English. West Sussex: Ravette Books Limited, 1994.

Millas, Jose Carlos. Hurricanes of the Caribbean and Adjacent Regions, 1492–1800. Ann Arbor, Mich.: Edwards Brothers Incorporated, 1968.

Mitford, Nancy. Madame de Pompadour. New York: Random House, 1953.

Montgomerie, Norah, ed. This Little Pig Went to Market. London: The Brodley Head Ltd., 1966.

Newton, Norman. The Life and Times of Inverness. Edinburgh: John Donald Publishers Ltd., 1996.

Nicholls, Frederick Francis. The Free Traders. New York: Scribner, 1967.

Nickel, Helmut. Arms and Armor. New York: The Metropolitan Museum of Art, 1991.

Nordhoff, Charles and James Norman Hall. Mutiny on the Bounty Boston: Little, Brown and Co., 1960.

Page, Robin. Weather Forecasting the Country Way. New York: Viking Penguin Inc., 1977.

Paiewonsky, Isidor. Eyewitness Accounts of Slavery in the Danish West Indies. 1987 I. Paiewonsky, St. Thomas VI.

Peacock, John. The Chronicle of Western Costumes: From the Ancient World to the

Late Twentieth Century. London: Thames and Hudson, Ltd. 1996.

Pepper, Elizabeth and John Wilcock. Magical and Mystical Sites: Europe and the British Isles. Grand Rapids, Mich.: Phanes Press, 1993.

Phillipson, David. Smuggling; A History. Newton, Abbot, David & Charles, 1973.

Platt, Richard. Cross-sections: Man-of-War. New York: Dorling Kindersley, 1993.

Porter, Roy. English Society in the Eighteenth Century. New York: Penguin Books, 1984.

Potter, Jonathan. Country Life Book of Antique Maps: An Introduction to the History of Maps and How to Appreciate Them. Secaucus, N.J.: Chartwell Books, 1989.

Prebble, John. The Darien Disaster: A Scots Colony in the New World, 1698–1700. New York: Holt, Rinehart and Winston, Inc., 1968.

Pyne, William H. British Costumes. Hertfordshire: Woodsworth Editions, Ltd., 1989.

Rawley, James A. The Transatlantic Slave Trade: A History. New York: Norton, 1981.

Reid, Stuart, and Paul Chappel. Men-at-Arms Series: King George's Army, 1740–1793. London: Reed International Books Ltd., 1996.

Ribeiro, Aileen. Dress in Eighteenth-Century Europe, 1715–1789. New York: Holmes & Meier Publishers, Inc., 1985.

Roberts, Nancy. Blackbeard and Other Pirates of the Atlantic Coast. Winston-Salem, N.C.: John F. Blair, 1993.

Shaw, P. Carol. Whisky: A Discriminating Guide to Scotch Whiskies. Philadelphia: Running Press, 1994.

Simmons, Eva, ed. Bloomsbury Guides to English Literature: Augustan Literature from 1660 to 1789. London: Bloomsbury Publishing Ltd., 1994.

Smith, A.G. Castles of the World Coloring Book. Mineola, N.Y.: Dover Publications Inc., 1986.

Smith, A.G. Knights and Armour Coloring Book. Mineola, N.Y.: Dover Publications, Inc., 1985.

Sotheby's. English and Continental Silver, Portrait Miniatures and Objects of Vertu. London: Sotheby's, 1989. (Auction catalogue)

Sotheby's. European Works of Art, Arms and Armour, Furniture and Tapestries. London: Sotheby's, 1988. (Auction catalogue)

Sotheby's. Fine Instruments of Science and Technology, 1500–1900. London: Sotheby's, 1989. (Auction catalogue)

Sotheby's. Important English Furniture, Decorations, Ceramics, and Carpets. London: Sotheby's, 1989. (Auction catalogue)

Sotheby's. Important French Furniture and Clocks. London: Sotheby's, 1988. (Auction catalogue)

Sotheby's. Wemyss Ware, Scottish Silver and Jewels, Scottish and Sporting Painting, Drawings and Watercolours. London: Sotheby's, 1988. (Auction catalogue)

Spearing, G.W. The Craft of the Gunsmith. Sterling Publishing Co., Inc., 1986.

Stein, Robert Louis. **The French Sugar Business in the Eighteenth Century.** Baton Rouge: Louisiana State University Press, 1988.

Stone, Norman, ed. **The Times Atlas of World History.** Maplewood, N.J., Hammond Incorporated, 1989.

Stryienski, Casimir. **The Eighteenth Century.** (Crowned by the Académie des Sciences Morales et Politiques.) New York: AMS Press, 1967.

Svensson, Sam, Ed. **The Lore of Ships.** New York: Barnes & Noble Books, 1988.

Swain, John. **The Pleasures of the Torture Chamber.** New York: Dorset Press, 1995.

Swan, June. **Shoemaking.** Buckinghamshire: Shire Publications Ltd., 1997.

Sykes, Christopher Simon. **Black Sheep.** London: Chatto and Windus, 1982.

Tiegnmouth, Baron (Henry Noel Shore). **The Smugglers; Picturesque Chapters in the History of Contraband, vols. I and II.** New York: George H. Doran Company, 1923.

Underhill, Roy. **The Woodwright's Shop: Exploring Traditional Woodcraft.** New York: Fine Communications, 1983.

Van Doren, Charles. **A History of Knowledge: The Pivotal Events, People, and Achievements of World History.** New York: Ballantine Books, 1992.

Waite, Edward Arthur. **A New Encyclopedia of Freemasonry.** New York: Weathervane Books.

Ward, J.R. **British West Indian Slavery, 1750–1834: The Process of Amelioration.** Clarendon Press: Oxford University Press Oxford (Oxfordshire); New York, 1988.

Wilbur, C. Keith, M.D. **Antique Medical Instruments.** Atglen, PA: Schiffer Publishing Ltd., 1987.

Williams, Neville. **Contraband Cargoes: Seven Centuries of Smuggling.** Hamden, CT: Shoe String Press, 1961.

Zeldin, Theodore. **An Intimate History of Humanity.** HarperCollins: 1994.

SCOTLAND: GENERAL HISTORY, GEOGRAPHY, CUSTOMS, CULTURE, LANGUAGE, ETC.

Scotland—Including the Highlands and the Islands. New York: Fodor's Travel Publications, Inc.

"I Am Come Home": Treasures of Prince Charles Edward Stuart. National Museum of Antiquities of Scotland: 1985.

Auld Scots Songs with Music. Newtongrange, Midlothian: Lang Syne Publishers Ltd., 1983.

Edinburgh Street Guide. Edinburgh: John Bartolomew & Son Ltd.

Scottish Battles. Newtongrange, Midlothian: Lang Syne Publishers Ltd., 1985.

Strange Old Scots Customs and Superstitions. Newtongrange, Midlothian: Lang Syne Publishers.

The Swords and the Sorrows. Scotland: The National Trust for Scotland Trading Company Ltd., 1996.

The New Scottish Song Book, Melody Edition. Oxford: Oxford University Press, 1987.

Scottish Fairy Tales. London: Studio Editions Ltd., Princess House, 1993.

Bain, George. Celtic Art: Key Patterns. Glasgow: William Maclellan Ltd., 1982.

Bain, George. Celtic Art: Knotwork Borders. Glasgow: William Maclellan Ltd., 1982.

Bain, George. Celtic Art: The Methods of Construction. Mineola, New York: Dover Publications, Inc., 1973.

Bain, George. Celtic Art: Zoomorphics. Glasgow: William Maclellan Ltd., 1982.

Bain, Robert. The Clans and Tartans of Scotland. Glasgow and London: Fontana/Collins, 1985.

Bell, Brian, ed. Insight Guides: Scotland. APA Publications, 1991.

Bennett, Margaret. Scottish Customs from the Cradle to the Grave. Edinburgh: Polygon, 1996.

Bingham, Caroline. Land of the Scots: A Short History. London: Fontana Paperback, 1983.

Bold, Alan. Bonnie Prince Charlie. Andover, Hants, England: Pitkin Pictorials, 1973.

Bongie, Laurence L. The Love of a Prince: Bonnie Prince Charlie in France, 1744–1748. Vancouver: University of British Columbia Press, 1986.

Broster, D.K. The Jacobite Trilogy. London: Reed Consumer Books, Ltd., 1984.

Brown, Catherine. Broths to Bannocks: Cooking in Scotland 1690 to the Present Day. London: John Murray (Publishers) Ltd., 1991.

Bryden, Mary. Corn Rigs and Barley Rigs: 200 Years of Change on the Scottish Farm. National Museums of Scotland (pamphlet).

Buchan, John. Witch Wood. Edinburgh: Canongate Publishing Ltd., 1988.

Buckland, Raymond. Scottish Witchcraft: The History and Magic of the Picts. St. Paul, Minn.: Llewellyn Publications, 1995.

Burns, Robert. The Complete Illustrated Poems, Songs, and Ballads. Secaucus, N.J.: Chartwell Books, Inc., 1990.

Calder, Jenni. The Story of the Scottish Soldier, 1600–1914. London: National Museums of Scotland.

Caldwell, David H. The Scottish Armoury. Edinburgh: William Blackwood & Sons Ltd., 1979.

Cameron, Sheila MacNiven. The Highlander's Cookbook: Recipes from Scotland. New York: Gramercy Publishing Company.

Campbell, Grant. Scottish Fairy Tales. London: Pan Books Ltd., 1980.

Campbell, John Lorne. Highland Songs of the Forty-five. Edinburgh: Scottish Gaelic Texts Society, 1984.

Campbell, John Gregorson. Superstitions of the Highlands and Islands of Scotland; Collected Entirely from Oral Sources. New York: B. Blom, 1971.

Carmichael, Alexander. Celtic Invocations: Selections from Volume 1 of Carmina Gadelica. Norton, Conn.: Vineyard Books, 1977.

Cherry, Alastair. Princes, Poets and Patrons: The Stuarts of Scotland. Edinburgh: HMSO, 1987.

Chitnis, Anand C. The Scottish Enlightment: A Social History. London: Rowman and Littlefield, 1976.

Cirker, Blanche, ed. The Book of Kells: Selected Plates in Full Color. Mineola, N.Y.: Dover Publications, Inc., 1982.

Conway, Pat, ed. 100 Great Scottish Songs, with Words and Music. Dublin, Waltons Mnf. Ltd., 1986.

Costello, Sean, and Tom Johnstone. Famous Last Words. Edinburgh: Mercat Press, 1996.

Coulton, George Gordon. Scottish Abbeys and Social Life. Cambridge, England: The University Press, 1993.

Craigie, Sir William Alexander. The Scottish Tongue. College Park, Md.: McGrath Publishing Co., 1970.

Crichton, Robert. The Camerons. New York: Warner Paperback Library, 1974.

Crowl, A. Philip. The Intelligent Traveller's Guide to Historic Scotland. Chicago: Congdon & Weed, 1986.

Delaney, Frank. Legends of the Celts. London: HarperCollins Publishers, 1994.

Douglas, Ronald MacDonald. Scottish Lore and Folklore. New York: Bonanza Books, 1990.

Douglas, Sir George Brisbane, ed. Scottish Fairy and Folk Tales. New York: Arno Press, 1977.

Dunkling, Alan Leslie. Scottish Christian Names: An A to Z of First Names. Stirling, Scotland: Johnston and Bacon (Books), Ltd. 1988.

Dunnett, Dorothy and Alastair Dunnett. The Scottish Highlands. Edinburgh: Mainstream Publishing, 1993.

Ellis, Peter Berresford. Macbeth, High King of Scotland, 1040–57. New York: Barnes & Noble Books, 1993.

Fenwick, Hubert. Scottish Baronial Houses. London: R. Hale, 1986.

Fletcher, Inglis. The Scotswoman. New York: The Bobbs-Merrill Company, Inc., 1954.

Forman, James D. The Scottish Dirk. Alexandria Bay, N.Y.: Museum Restoration Service, 1991.

Foster, Sally M. Picts, Gaels and Scots. London: B.T. Bastford Ltd., 1996.

Fraser, Antonia. Scottish Love Poems. New York: Peter Bedrick Books, 1989.

Fraser, Charles Ian of Reelig, M.A. The Clan Fraser of Lovat. Edinburgh and London: Johnston and Bacon, 1979.

Fraser-Mackintosh, Charles. Antiquarian Notes, Historical, Genealogical, and Social. Inverness: A & W Mackenzie, 1897.

Gervin, Joseph. The Celtic Colouring Book. Cork, Ireland: Ossian Publications Ltd., 1995.

Gilbert, Leslie. The Highland Clans. Tokyo, Rutland, Vt.: Charles R. Tuttle, 1972.

Goodchild, Peter. The Raven Tales. Chicago: Chicago Review Press, 1991.

Gordon, Giles, ed. Prevailing Spirits: A Book of Scottish Ghost Stories. London: Grafton Books, 1976.

Gordon, Giles, ed. Scottish Ghost Stories. London: Random House UK Ltd., 1996.

Gorlach, Manfred, ed. Focus on Scotland. Amsterdam, Philadelphia: J. Benjamins Publishing Co., 1985.

Graham, Henry Grey. The Social Life of Scotland in the Eighteenth Century. London: Black, 1937.

Grant, James. Scottish Tartans in Full Color. Mineola, N.Y.: Dover Publications, Inc., 1992.

Grimble, Ian. Scottish Clans and Tartans. New York: Harmony Books, 1989.

Hanley, Cliff. History of Scotland. Greenwich, Conn.: Brompton Books Corp., 1990.

Harris, Paul. A Little Scottish Cookbook. San Francisco: Chronicle Books, 1988.

Herm, Gerhard. The Celts. New York: St. Martin's Press, 1977.

Hook, Michael and Walter Ross. The 'Forty-five: The Last Jacobite Rebellion. Edinburgh: The National Library of Scotland, 1995.

Howlett, Hamilton. Highland Constable; The Life and Times of Rob Roy MacGregor. Edinburgh: Blackwood, 1950.

Hubert, Henri. The History of the Celtic People. London: Bracken Books, 1992.

Hunter, Mollie. A Stranger Came Ashore. New York: HarperCollins Publishers, 1977.

Hunter, Mollie. The Walking Stones. New York: Harcourt Brace & Company, 1996.

Innes, Sir Thomas of Learney. The Scottish Tartans: Histories of the Clans, Chiefs' Arms and Clansmen's Badges Stirling, Scotland: Johnston and Bacon (Books) Ltd., 1984.

James, Simon. The World of the Celts. New York: Thames & Hudson, 1993.

Jenner, Michael. Scotland Through the Ages. New York: Viking Penguin Inc., 1987.

Johnson, Samuel. A Journey to the Western Islands of Scotland. Oxford, New York: Oxford University Press, 1985.

Kennedy, Ludovic. In Bed with an Elephant. London: Transworld Publishers, Ltd., 1996.

Kermack, W.K., ed. A Scots Sampler: An Anthology of Prose and Verse. New York: Barnes & Noble Books, 1993.

Kirkwood, James. A Collection of Highland Rites and Customs. Totowa, N.J.: Rowman and Littlefield for the Folklore Society, 1975.

Knight, Peter. Scottish Country Dancing. New York: HarperCollins Publishers, 1996.

Kybett, Susan MacLean. Bonnie Prince Charlie: A Biography of Charles Edward Stuart. New York: Dodd, Mead & Company, 1988.

Laing, Lloyd, and Jennifer Laing. Art of the Celts. New York: Thames and Hudson, 1992.

Lamont-Brown, Raymond. Scottish Epitaphs. Edinburgh: W & R Chambers Ltd., 1990.

Lauder, Sir Harry. My Best Scotch Stories. Dundee and London: Valentine & Sons, Ltd., 1929.

Leaf, Munro. Wee Gillis. New York: The Trumpet Club, 1988.

Lindsay, Joyce and Maurice Lindsay. The Scottish Quotation Book. New York: Barnes & Noble Books, 1992.

Linklater, Eric. The Prince in the Heather. New York: Harcourt, Brace & World, 1966.

Livingstone, Sheila. Scottish Customs. Edinburgh: Birlinn Limited, 1996.

Lochhead, Marion, ed. Scottish Tales of Magic and Mystery. Stirling, Scotland: Johnston & Bacon Books Limited, 1990.

Love, Dane. Scottish Ghosts. New York: Barnes & Noble Books, 1996.

Luzel, F.M. Celtic Folk-Tales from Armorica. Felinfach: Llanerch Publishers, 1992.

Lyle, Emily, ed. Scottish Ballads. New York: Barnes & Noble Books, 1995.

MacColl, Ewan. Till Doomsday in the Afternoon: The Folklore of a Family of Scots Travellers, the Stewarts of Blairgowrie. Dover, N.H.: Manchester University Press, 1986.

MacDonald, Micheil. The Clans of Scotland: The History and Landscape of the Scottish Clans. London: Brian Trodd Publishing House Limited, 1991.

Macdonald, Ross. Famous Edinburgh Crimes. Newtongrange, Midlothian: Lang Syne Publishers Ltd., 1987.

MacDougall, Carl, ed. The Giant Book of Scottish Short Stories. New York: Peter Bedrick Books, 1989.

Macgregor, Forbes. MacGregor's Mixture. Edinburgh: Gordon Wright, 1979.

MacKay, Charles. The Auld Scots Dictionary. Glasgow: Lang Syne Publishers, Ltd., 1992.

MacKay, Donald. Scotland Farewell: The People of the Hector. Ontario, Canada: McGraw-Hill, 1980.

Mackenzie, Alexander. The Prophecies of the Brahan Seer. Glasgow: Lang Syne Publishers Ltd., 1989.

MacKenzie, Ross. William Wallace: Liberty's in Every Blow. Press and Journal (pamphlet).

Mackenzie, Sir Compton. Prince Charlie and His Ladies. London: Cassell, 1934.

MacKie, Euan Wallace. Scotland: An Archaeological Guide from Earliest Times to the 12th Century. Park Ridge, N.J.: Noyes Press, 1975.

Maclaren, Ian. Graham of Claverhouse. Norwood, MA: The Plimpton Press, 1907.

Maclean, Loraine of Dochgarroch. Discovering Inverness-shire. John Donald Publishers, 1988.

Macleod, Iseabail, Pauline Cairns, Caroline Macafee, and Ruth Martin, eds. The Scots Thesaurus. Aberdeen: Aberdeen University Press, 1990.

MacLeod, John. Highlanders: A History of the Gaels. London: Hodder and Stoughton, 1996.

Manson, W.L. Tunes of Glory: Stories, History, Traditions, Music and Humor of the Highland Bagpipe. Glasgow: Lang Syne Publishers Ltd., 1992.

Marshall, Nancy. Scottish Songs and Ballads. Edinburgh: W & R Chambers Ltd., 1990.

Matthews, Caitlin. Celtic Devotional: Daily Prayers and Blessings. Godsfield Press, 1996.

Matthews, John, and Bob Stewart. Celtic Battle Heroes. New York: Firebird Books Ltd. Sterling Publishing Co., Inc., 1988.

McClure, J. Derrick. Why Scots Matters. Edinburgh: Saltire Society in association with the Scots Language Society, 1988.

McCrumb, Sharyn. Highland Laddie Gone. New York: Ballantine Books, 1991.

McDougall, James. Folk Tales and Fairy Lore in Gaelic and English. New York: Arno Press, 1977.

McDougall, James. Highland Fairy Legends. Totowa, N.J.: Rowman & Littlefield, 1978.

McGonagall, William. Collected Poems. Edinburgh: Birlinn Ltd., 1992.

McIan, R.R. The Clans and Tartans of Scotland. New York: Crescent Books, 1988.

McLaren, Moray. Lord Lovat of the '45. London: Jarrolds Publishers Ltd., 1957.

McLintock, Mrs., with an introduction and glossary by Iseabail Macleod. Mrs. McLintock's Receipts for Cookery and Pastry-Work. Aberdeen: The University Press, 1986. Reprint: original publication 1767.

McNeill, F. Marian. The Scots Kitchen: Its Traditions and Lore with Old-Time Recipes. Edinburgh: The Mercat Press, 1994.

McNie, Alan. Your Clan Heritage: Clan Fraser. Jedburgh, Scotland: Cascade Publishing Company, 1989.

McPherson, Joseph McKenzie. Primitive Beliefs in the North-East of Scotland. New York: Arno Press, 1977.

Meehan, Aidan. Celtic Design: Knotwork, The Secret Method of the Scribes. New York: Thames and Hudson, 1993.

Meyer, Duane. The Highland Scots of North Carolina: 1732–1776. The University of North Carolina Press, 1961.

Miller, Peggy. A Wife for the Pretender. New York: Harcourt, Brace and World, 1966.

Milligan, Jean C. 101 Scottish Country Dances. London: Peterson's Publications, Ltd., 1956.

Mitford, Nancy. Highland Fling. New York: Carroll & Graf Publishers, Inc., 1988.

Murdoch, Alexander. The People Above: Politics and Administration in Mid-Eighteenth-Century Scotland. Edinburgh: J. Donald Publishers, 1980.

Murison, David. Scots Saws. Edinburgh: The Mercat Press, 1981.

Newton, Norman. The Life and Times of Inverness. Edinburgh: John Donald Publishers Ltd., 1996.

O'Connor, Anne, and D.V. Clarke, eds. From the Stone Age to the 'Forty-Five: Studies presented to RBK Stevenson, National Museum of Antiquities of Scotland. Edinburgh: Humanities Press, 1983.

Pearce, Mallory. Celtic Borders on Layout Grids. Mineola, N.Y.: Dover Publications, Inc., 1990.

Pearce, Mallory. Decorative Celtic Alphabets. Mineola, N.Y.: Dover Publications, Inc., 1992.

Phillips, Dave. Celtic Mazes. Mineola, N.Y.: Dover Publications, Inc., 1998.

Phillips, R. Michael. George MacDonald, Scotland's Beloved Storyteller. Minneapolis, MN: Bethany House Publishers, 1987.

Piggot, Stuart. The Druids. New York: Thames and Hudson, 1985.

Porter, Jane. The Scottish Chiefs. Philadelphia: J.B. Lippincott & Co., 1883.

Ramsay, Allan. The Ever Green: A Collection of Scots Poems, vols I, II. Glasgow: Robert Forrester, 1875.

Ratcliffe, Derek. **Highland Flora.** Inverness: Highlands and Islands Development, 1977.

Ravenstone, (Baron). **Scotland Bloody Scotland.** Edinburgh: Canongate Press, 1986.

Reid, J.M., ed. **Classic Scottish Short Stories.** Oxford: Oxford University Press, 1989.

Reid, Stuart. **18th Century Highlanders.** Men-At-Arms Series: London: Osprey Publishing Ltd., 1993.

Rennie, Alan James. **The Scottish People.** Morgantown, W.V.: Scotpress, 1960.

Ritchie, Anna. **Picts.** London: HMSO Publications, 1993.

Ritchie, Anna. **Viking Scotland.** London: B.T. Batsford Ltd., 1994.

Robertson, James, ed. **A Tongue in Yer Heid.** Edinburgh: B & W Publishing, 1994.

Robertson, Willie. **Calum's Way of It.** Scotland: Argyll Publishing.

Robson, Alan. **Grisly Trails and Ghostly Tales.** London: Virgin Books.

Ross, Anne. **Druids, Gods & Heroes from Celtic Mythology.** New York: Peter Bedrick Books, 1986.

Ross, Anne. **The Folklore of the Scottish Highlands.** New York: Barnes and Noble Books, 1993.

Sanderson, William. **Scottish Life and Character.** London: A & C Black, 1914.

Shaw, Carol P. **Famous Scots.** Glasgow: HarperCollins, 1995.

Shaw, Carol P. **Whisky: A Discriminating Guide to Scotch Whiskies.** Philadelphia: Running Press, 1994.

Sierra, Judy. **Celtic Baby Names.** Eugene, Or.: Folkprint, 1997.

Sked, Phil. **Culloden.** Edinburgh: Marketing Services, Division of the National Trust for Scotland, 1990.

Sked, Phil. **Glenfinnan.** Edinburgh: Publications Department of The National Trust for Scotland.

Spinhoven, Co. **Celtic Charted Designs.** Mineola, N.Y.: Dover Publications, Inc., 1987.

Spinhoven, Co. **Celtic Stencil Designs.** Mineola N.Y.: Dover Publications, Inc., 1990.

Starmore, Alice. **Celtic Needlepoint.** North Pomfret, Vt.: Trafalgar Square Publishing, 1994.

Sutherland, Elizabeth. **Ravens and Black Rain.** London: Transworld Publishers Ltd., 1985.

Swire, Otta F. **The Highlands and Their Legends.** Edinburgh: Oliver & Boyd, 1963.

Tabraham, Christopher. **Scottish Castles and Fortifications.** Edinburgh: Historic Buildings and Monuments, Scottish Development Department, 1986.

Thompson, Derick S., ed. **The Companion to Gaelic Scotland.** Oxford: Blackwell Reference, 1983.

Tod, Andrew. **Memoirs of a Highland Lady: Elizabeth Grant of Rothiemurchus.** Canongate Classics, 1988.

Tranter, Nigel. **The MacGregor Trilogy: MacGregor's Gathering, The Clansman, Gold for Prince Charlie.** London: Hodder and Stoughton, 1996.

Troon, Tony. **The Best of the Scotsman Diary.** Edinburgh: Mainstream Publishing Company, 1992.

Van de Weyer, Robert, ed. **Celtic Fire.** New York: Doubleday, 1991.

Warrack, Alexander, ed. **The Concise Scots Dictionary.** New York: Crown Publishers, Inc., 1988.

Webb, Keith. **The Growth of Nationalism in Scotland.** New York: Penguin Books, 1978.

Whittington, G. and I.D. Whyte, eds. **An Historical Geography of Scotland.** London, New York: Academic Press, 1983.

Whyte, Hamish, ed. **The Minister's Cat.** Edinburgh: The Mercat Press, 1993.

Whyte, Hamish, et al, eds. **Cat A' Mhinisteir: The Gaelic Minister's Cat.** Edinburgh: The Mercat Press, 1994.

Wickham-Jones, C.R. **Scotland's First Settlers.** London: B.T. Bastford Ltd., 1996.

Willsher, Betty. **Understanding Scottish Graveyards.** Edinburgh: W & R Chambers Ltd., 1990.

Wilson, Barbara Ker. **Scottish Folk-tales and Legends.** Oxford: Oxford University Press, 1989.

Woods, Nicola. **Scottish Proverbs.** Edinburgh: W & R Chambers, 1989.

COLONIAL NORTH AMERICA AND THE AMERICAN REVOLUTION

Smallpox in Colonial America. New York: Arno Press.

Andrews, Charles M. **The Colonial Period of American History,** Vol. III. New Haven: Yale University Press, 1934.

Andrews, E.W. et al. **Journal of a Lady of Quality, 1774–1776.** New Haven: Yale University Press, 1939.

American Heritage: Truth and Fiction. Des Moines, Iowa: American Heritage Books, 1992.

Heroes of the American Revolution. Santa Barbara, Calif.: Bellerophon Books, 1987.

The Uncommon Soldier of the Revolution: Women and Young People Who Fought for American Independence. Historical Times, Inc., 1986.

Bailyn, Bernard and B. John Hench, eds. **The Press and the American Revolution.** Boston: Northeastern University Press, 1981.

Castiglioni, Luigi. **Luigi Castiglioni's Viaggio: Travels in the United States of North America, 1785–87.** Syracuse: Syracuse University Press, 1983.

Chartrand, Rene and Francis Black. **The French Army in the American War of Independence. Men-at-Arms Series.** London: Osprey Publishing Ltd., 1991.

Cook, Don. **The Long Fuse: How England Lost the American Colonies, 1760–1785.** New York: The Atlantic Monthly Press, 1995.

Copeland, Peter. **American Military Uniforms 1639–1968 Coloring Book.** Mineola, N.Y.: Dover Publications, Inc., 1976.

Copeland, Peter. **Early American Trades Coloring Book.** Mineola, N.Y.: Dover Publications, Inc., 1990.

Copeland, Peter. **Everyday Dress of the American Colonial Period Coloring Book.** Mineola, N.Y.: Dover Publications, Inc., 1975.

Copeland, Peter. **Story of the American Revolution Coloring Book.** Mineola, N.Y.: Dover Publications, Inc., 1988.

Copeland, Peter. **Uniforms of the American Revolution Coloring Book.** Mineola, N.Y.: Dover Publications, Inc., 1974.

Demos, John. The Unredeemed Captive: A Family Story from Early America. New York: Alfred A. Knopf, Inc., 1994.

Duffy, Christopher. The Military Experience in the Age of Reason, 1715–1789. New York: Barnes & Noble Books, 1987.

Fleming, Thomas. 1776: Year of Illusions. New York: Norton, 1975.

Forbes, Esther. Paul Revere and the World He Lived In. Cambridge: The Riverside Press, 1942.

Franklin, Benjamin, ed. L. Jesse Lemisch. The Autobiography of Benjamin Franklin. New York: New American Library, 1961.

Frucht, Richard. Black Society in the New World. New York: Random House, 1971.

Greene, Jack P. and J.R. Pole, eds. Colonial British America: Essays in the New History of the Early Modern Era. Baltimore: The Johns Hopkins University Press, 1984.

Hunter, James. A Dance Called America. Edinburgh: Mainstream Publishing Company, 1994.

Hutchens, Alma R. Indian Herbalogy of North America. Boston: Shambala, 1991.

Johnson, Curt. Battles of the American Revolution. New York: Rand McNally & Company, 1975.

Kalman, Bobbie. Early Family Homes. New York: Crabtree Publishing Company, 1992.

Kalman, Bobbie. Early Health and Medicine. New York: Crabtree Publishing Company, 1991.

Kalman, Bobbie. Eighteenth Century Clothing. New York: Crabtree Publishing Company, 1993.

Kammen, Michael G. Politics and Society in Colonial America: Democracy or Deference? Hinsdale, Ill.: Dryden Press, 1973.

Keane, John. Tom Paine: A Political Life. London: Bloomsbury Publishing, 1995.

Klinger, Robert L. Sketch Book 76: The American Soldier, 1775–1781. Union City Tenn.: Pioneer Press, 1974.

Klinger, Robert L. Sketch Book: A Collection of Notes and Sketches on Women's Dress in America, 1774–1783. Union City, Tenn.: Pioneer Press, 1974.

Langguth, A.J. Patriots: The Men Who Started the American Revolution. New York: Simon & Schuster, Inc., 1988.

Martin, James Kirby. Men in Rebellion; Higher Governmental Leaders and the Coming of the American Revolution. New Brunswick, N.J.: Rutgers University Press, 1973.

May, Robin and G.A. Embleton. Men-at-Arms Series: The British Army in North America, 1775–1783. London: Reed International Books Ltd., 1996.

McGregor, Malcolm. The American Revolution: Military Uniforms and Weaponry. New York: Military Press, 1987.

McLaughlin, Jack. Jefferson and Monticello: The Biography of a Builder. New York: Henry Holt and Company, 1990.

Meyer, Clarence. American Folk Medicine. Publisher, Illinois: Meyerbooks, 1973.

Mitchell, Weir S. Hugh Wynne, Free Quaker. New York: D. Appleton-Century Company, Inc., 1941.

Morris, Richard B. Witnesses at the Creation: Hamilton, Madison, Jay, and the Constitution. New York: New American Library, 1986.

Moseley, Hardwick. **The Romance of North America.** Boston: Houghton Mifflin Company, 1958.

Moss, Kay. **A Backcountry Herbal.** North Carolina: Schiele Museum, 1993.

Oberg, Barbara B. ed. **The Papers of Benjamin Franklin,** Vol. 30. New Haven and London: Yale University Press, 1993.

Oswald, John Clyde. **Benjamin Franklin, Printer.** Ann Arbor, Mich.: Gryphon Books, 1971.

Parry, S. Edwin. **Betsy Ross: Quaker Rebel.** Chicago: The John C. Winston Company, 1932.

Parson, Nels A. **The Compleat Journal of Landon Vickers.** Georgia: Iberian Publishing Company, 1996.

Randall, Sterne Willard. **Benedict Arnold: Patriot and Traitor.** New York: William Morrow, 1990.

Reid, Stuart and Paul Chappel. **Men-at-Arms Series: King George's Army, 1740–1793.** London: Reed International Books Ltd., 1996.

Sachs, William S. **The Enterprising Colonials; Society on the Eve of the Revolution.** Chicago: Argonaut.

Sloane, Eric. **ABC Book of Early Americana.** New York: Wings Books, 1963.

Sloane, Eric. **Eric Sloane's Sketches of America Past.** New York: Promontory Press, 1986.

Smith, A. G. **The American House: Styles of Architecture Coloring Book.** Mineola, N.Y.: Dover Publications, Inc., 1983.

Stevens, F. Peter. **The Mayflower Murderer, and Other Forgotten Firsts in American History.** New York: William Morrow and Company, Inc., 1993.

Taylor, Dale. **The Writer's Guide to Everyday Life in Colonial America from 1607–1783.** Cincinnati: Writer's Digest Books, 1997.

Tharp, Louise Hall. **The Baroness and the General.** Boston: Little, Brown and Company, 1962.

Underhill, Roy. **The Woodwright's Shop: Exploring Traditional Woodcraft.** New York: Fine Communications, 1983.

Vidal, Gore. **Burr.** New York: Ballantine Books, 1993.

Weber, Ralph Edward. **United States Diplomatic Codes and Ciphers, 1775–1938.** Chicago: Precedent Publishing, 1979.

Werstein, Irving. **1776: The Adventure of the American Revolution.** New York: Cooper Square Publishers, Inc., 1965.

Wigginton, Eliot, ed. **The Foxfire Book: Hog Dressing, Log Cabin Building, Mountain Crafts and Foods, Planting by the Signs, Snakelore, Hunting Tales, Faith Healing.** New York: Anchor Books, 1972.

Wiggington, Eliot, and his students, eds. **Foxfire 5: Ironmaking, Blacksmithing, Flintlock Rifles, and Bear Hunting.** New York: Anchor Books, 1979.

Wilbur, C. Keith, M.D. **Home Building and Woodworking in Colonial America.** Old Saybrook, Conn.: The Globe Pequot Press, 1992.

Wilbur, C. Keith, M.D. **The Revolutionary Soldier, 1775–1783.** Old Saybrook, Conn.: The Globe Pequot Press, 1993.

Wilbur, C. Keith, M.D. Revolutionary Medicine, 1700–1800. Chester, Conn.: The Globe Pequot Press, 1980.

Woodward, W.E. George Washington: The Image and the Man. New York: Liveright, 1945.

Wright, Merideth. Everyday Dress of Rural America, 1783–1800. Mineola, N.Y.: Dover Publications, 1992.

MEDICINE
(INCLUDING ALL HERBALS)

The Dictionary of Medicine. Leicester: W. H. Smith Limited, 1989.

Smallpox in Colonial America. New York: Arno Press.

Medicines: The Comprehensive Guide. London: Parragon in arrangement with Bloomsbury Publications.

Arbel, Ilil. Medicinal Plants Coloring Book. Mineola, N.Y.: Dover Publications, 1992.

Aries, Phillippe, and George Duby, eds. A History of Private Life: Revelations of the Medieval World. Cambridge: Harvard University Press, 1988.

Bell, Whitfield (Whitfield Jenks). The Colonial Physician and Other Essays. New York: Science History Publications, 1975.

Beyerl, Paul. The Master Book of Herbalism. Phoenix Publishing Co., 1984.

Bown, Deni. Encyclopedia of Herbs & Their Uses. New York: Dorling Kindersley Publishing Inc., 1995.

Bown, Deni. The Herb Society of America Encyclopedia of Herbs and Their Uses. New York: Dorling Kindersley, 1995.

Bremness, Lesley. Herbs. New York: The Reader's Digest Association, Inc., 1990.

Bricklin, Mark. The Practical Encyclopedia of Natural Healing. New York: Fine Communications, 1983.

Brimer, John Burton. Growing Herbs in Pots. New York: Simon & Schuster, 1976.

Buchman, Dian Dincin. Ancient Healing Secrets. New York: Crescent Books, 1996.

Buckley, Anthony D. Yoruba Medicine. Oxford: Oxford University Press, 1985.

Caleel, Dr. Richard T. Surgeon! A Year in the Life of an Inner City Doctor. New York: St. Martin's Press, 1986.

Cassedy, James H. Medicine in America: A Short History. Baltimore: The Johns Hopkins University Press, 1991.

Chan, Pedro. Finger Acupressure. New York: Ballantine Books, 1975.

Chopra, Deepak, M.D. Alternative Medicine. Fife, Wash.: Future Medicine Publishing, 1994.

Chopra, Deepak, M.D. Perfect Health: The Complete Mind\Body Guide. New York: Harmony Books.

Clendening, Logan, ed. Source Book of Medical History. Mineola, NY: Dover Publications, 1942 (reprinted 1960).

Darwin, Tess. The Scots Herbal: The Plant Lore of Scotland. Edinburgh: The Mercat Press, 1996.

Debus, Allen G. Medicine in Seventeenth-Century England: A Symposium Held at UCLA in Honor of C.D. O'Malley. Berkeley: University of California Press, 1974.

Doane, Nancy Locke. Indian Doctor. Nancy Locke Doane, 1980.

Dougans, Inge, et al. Reflexology: Foot Massage for Total Health. New York: Barnes & Noble Books, 1991.

Evans, Mark. A Guide to Herbal Remedies. The C.W. Daniel Company Ltd., 1990.

Flexner, James Thomas. Doctors on Horseback: Pioneers of American Medicine. New York: Garden City Pub., 1939.

Forey, Pamela, et al. An Instant Guide to Medicinal Plants. New York: Crescent Books, 1991.

Forey, Pamela, et al. An Instant Guide to Edible Plants. New York: Crescent Books, 1989.

Gordon, Maurice Bear. Aesculapius Comes to the Colonies: The Story of the Early Days of Medicine in the Thirteen Original Colonies. Ventnor N.J.: Ventnor Publishers, 1949.

Gordon, Richard. The Alarming History of Medicine. New York: St. Martin's Press, 1993.

Gottlieb, Bill, ed. New Choices in Natural Healing. Emmaus, Penn.: Rodale Press, Inc., 1995.

Grieve, Mrs. M. A Modern Herbal, vols. I and II. Mineola, N.Y.: Dover Publications, 1971.

Griffith, H. Winter, M.D. Complete Guide to Symptoms, Illness & Surgery. Tucson: The Body Press, 1985.

Hayfield, Robin. The Family Homeopath. VT: Healing Arts Press, 1994.

Hill, Madalene, and Gwen Barclay, with Jean Hardy. Southern Herb Growing. Shearer Publishing, 1987.

Hoffman, David. Herbs to Help Relieve Stress. Conn.: Keats Publishing, Inc., 1996.

Hoffman, David, ed. The Information Sourcebook of Herbal Medicine. The Crossing Press, 1994.

Hopkins, Donald R., foreword by George L. Lythcott. Princes and Peasants; Smallpox in History. Chicago: University of Chicago Press, 1983.

Howard, Judy. The Bach Flower Remedies Step by Step. The C.W. Daniel Company Ltd., 1994.

Hutchens, Alma R. A Handbook of Native American Herbs. Boston: Shambala, 1992.

Hutchens, Alma R. Indian Herbalogy of North America. Boston: Shambala, 1991.

Jenner, Edward. Letters of Edward Jenner, and Other Documents Concerning the Early History of Vaccination. Baltimore: John Hopkins University Press, 1983.

Jensen, Bernard. Foods That Heal. Garden City Park, N.Y.: Avery Publishing Group, 1993.

Kalman, Bobbie. Early Health and Medicine. New York: Crabtree Publishing Company, 1991.

Krochmal, Arnold and Connie. A Field Guide to Medicinal Plants. New York: Times Books, 1984.

Launert, Edmund. The Hamlyn Guide to Edible Plants of Britain and Northern Europe, 1989.

Leonard, C.H., A.M., M.D. The Concise Gray's Anatomy. Hertfordshire, England: Omega Books Ltd., 1985.

Leung, Albert Y. Chinese Herbal Remedies. New York: Universe Books, 1984.

Livingston, A.D. and Helen Livingston, Ed.D. **Edible Plants and Animals.** New York: Facts on File, Inc., 1993.

Lockie, Dr. Andrew and Dr. Nicola Gedds. **Homeopathy: The Principles and Practice of Treatment.** New York: Dorling Kindersley, Inc., 1995.

Lust, John. **The Herb Book.** New York: Bantam Books, 1974.

Lyons, M. D., Albert and R. Joseph Petrucelli II, M.D. **Medicine: An Illustrated History.** New York: Abradale Press/Harry N. Abrams, Inc., 1987.

Marion, Robert, M.D. **The Intern Blues.** New York: William Morrow and Company, Inc., 1989.

Martin, Laura C. **The Folklore of Birds.** Old Saybrook, Conn.: The Globe Pequot Press, 1993.

Martin, Laura C. **The Folklore of Trees and Shrubs.** Old Saybrook, Conn.: The Globe Pequot Press, 1992.

Martin, Laura C. **Wildflower Folklore.** Old Saybrook, Conn.: The Globe Pequot Press, 1993.

Martin, Laura C. **Wildlife Folklore.** Old Saybrook, Conn.: The Globe Pequot Press, 1994.

Matossian, Mary Kilbourne. **Poisons of the Past: Molds, Epidemics, and History.** New Haven and London: Yale University Press, 1989.

McGilvery, Carole, Jimi Reed, and Mire Metha. **The Encyclopedia of Aromatherapy Massage and Yoga.** New York: Smithmark Publishers, Inc., 1994.

McLaren, Angus. **Birth Control in Nineteenth-Century England.** New York: Holmes & Meire, 1978.

McNeill, William H. **Plagues and People.** New York: Quality Paperback Book Club, 1993.

Medve, Richard J. **Edible Wild Plants of Pennsylvania and Neighboring States.** University Park, Penn.: Pennsylvania State University Press, 1990.

Meuninck, Jim. **The Basic Essentials of Edible Wild Plants and Useful Herbs.** Indiana: ICS Books, Inc., 1988.

Meyer, Clarence. **American Folk Medicine.** Ill.: Meyerbooks, Publishers, 1973.

Meyer, Clarence. **Herbal Aphrodisiacs, from World Sources.** Ill.: Meyerbooks Publisher, 1986.

Millspaugh, Charles F. **American Medicinal Plants.** Mineola, N.Y.: Dover Publications, 1974.

Moore, Michael. **Medicinal Plants of the Mountain West.** N.M.: Museum of New Mexico Press, 1979.

Moorey, Teresa. **Herbs for Magic and Ritual: A Beginner's Guide.** London: Hodder & Stoughton, 1996.

Morton, Dr. I.K.M. and Dr. J.M. Hall. **Medicines: The Comprehensive Guide.** London: Bloomsbury Publishing, 1997.

Moss, Kay. **A Backcountry Herbal.** N.C.: Schiele Museum, 1993.

Moyers, Bill. **Healing and the Mind.** New York: Bantam Doubleday Dell Publishing Group Inc., 1993.

Myatt, Dr. Dana. **A Physician's Diary.** Virginia Beach, Va.: A.R.E. Press, 1994.

Nagy, Doreen Evenden. **Popular Medicine in Seventeenth-Century England.** Bowling Green Ohio: Bowling Green State University Popular Press, 1988.

Ody, Penelope. **The Complete Medicinal Herbal.** New York: Dorling Kindersley, Inc., 1993.

Ovenden, Denys, et al. **A Handguide to the Wild Animals of Britain and Europe.** Treasure Press, 1989.

Porter, Roy. **Medicine, a History of Healing: Ancient Traditions to Modern Practices.** New York: Marlowe & Company, 1997.

Prevention Magazine Health Books, eds. **The Doctor's Book of Home Remedies.** Emmaus, Penn.: Rodale Press, Inc., 1990.

Prevention Magazine Health Books, eds. **The Prevention How-To Dictionary of Healing Remedies and Techniques.** New York: MJF Books, Fine Communications, 1992.

Puotinen, C.J. **Herbs to Help You Breathe Freely.** New Canaan, Conn.: Keats Publishing, Inc., 1996.

Puotinen, C.J. **Herbs to Improve Digestion.** New Canaan, Conn.: Keats Publications, Inc., 1996.

Ramsey, Matthew. **Professional and Popular Medicine in France, 1770–1830: The Social World of Medical Practice.** Cambridge: Cambridge University Press, 1988.

Razzell, P.E. **Edward Jenner's Cowpox Vaccine: The History of a Medical Myth.** England: Caliban Books, 1977.

Reilly, Harold J., M.D. and Ruth Hagy Brod. **The Edgar Cayce Handbook for Health through Drugless Therapy.** Virginia Beach, Va.: Associations for Research and Enlightenment, 1975.

Riotte, Louise. **Sleeping with a Sunflower.** Pownal, Vt.: Garden Way Publishing Storey Communications, Inc., 1987.

Rosenfeld, Isadore, M.D. **Doctor, What Should I Eat?** New York: Random House, 1995.

Scott, Julian and Susan. **Natural Medicine for Women:** New York: Avon Books, 1991.

Selzer, Richard. **Confessions of a Knife.** New York: Quill, 1979.

Selzer, Richard. **Letters to a Young Doctor.** New York: Simon & Schuster, Inc., 1983.

Shorter, Edward. **Bedside Manners: The Troubled History of Doctors and Patients.** New York: Viking Penguin Inc., 1986.

Siegel, Bernie S., M.D. **Love, Medicine and Miracles.** New York: Harper & Row Publishers, Inc., 1986.

Starr, Douglas. **Blood: An Epic History of Medicine and Commerce.** New York: Alfred A. Knopf, Inc., 1998.

Stone, Lelanie F. **Indian Herbs and Plants.** Cherokee Lady Publications, 1991.

Streep, Peg. **A Gift of Herbs.** New York: Viking Studio Books, 1991.

Sugrue, Thomas. **There Is a River: The Story of Edgar Cayce.** Virginia Beach, Va.: A.R.E. Press, 1994.

Sutcliffe, Dr. Jenny and Nancy Duin. **A History of Medicine.** New York: Barnes & Noble Books, 1992.

Talbot, Charles H. Medicine in Medieval England. London: Oldbourne, 1967.

Tang, Stephen et al. Chinese Herbal Medicine. New York: Berkley Books, 1995.

Tierra, Michael. The Way of Herbs. New York: Pocket Books, 1990.

Vertosick, Frank Jr., M.D. When the Air Hits Your Brain: Tales of Neurosurgery. New York: Ballantine Books, 1996.

Weil, Andrew, M.D. Spontaneous Healing. New York: Alfred A. Knopf, Inc., 1995.

Wilbur, C. Keith, M.D. Antique Medical Instruments. Atglen, Penn.: Schiffer Publishing Ltd., 1987.

Wilbur, C. Keith, M.D. Revolutionary Medicine, 1700–1800. Chester, Conn.: The Globe Pequot Press, 1980.

Wingate, Peter, with Richard Wingate. The Penguin Medical Encyclopedia. New York, London: Penguin Books, 1972.

Youngson, Dr. Robert. Symptoms: A Complete A–Z of Thousands of Symptoms and Signs. London: Bloomsbury Publishing, 1996.

Youngson, Robert M., M.D. with the Diagram Group. The Surgery Book: An Illustrated Guide to 73 of the Most Common Operations. New York: St. Martin's Press, 1993.

African Cultures, Afro-European Relations, and Slavery

Aspinall, Sir Algernon Edward. The Pocket Guide to the West Indies, British Guiana, British Honduras, Bermuda, the Spanish Main, Surinam, and the Panama Canal. London: Sifton, Praed & Co., 1931.

Awolalu, J. Omosade. Yoruba Beliefs and Sacrificial Rites. London: Longman, 1979.

Baumgarten, Dr. Peter, general ed. Baedeker's Caribbean. New York: Prentice Hall Press, 1992.

Buckley, Anthony D. Yoruba Medicine. Oxford: Oxford University Press, 1985.

Bush, Barbara. Slave Women in Caribbean Society, 1650–1838. London: Heinemann Publishers, 1990.

Carrington, Selwyn H.H. The British West Indies During the American Revolution. Dordrecht, Holland: Foris Publications, 1988.

Coke, Thomas. A History of the West Indies, vols. I, II, and III. Miami, Fl.: Mnemosyne, 1969.

Corry, Joseph. Observations Upon the Windward Coast of Africa, the Religion, Character, Customs, & c. of the Natives. London: Cass, 1968.

Ellis, Alfred Burdon. The Ewe-Speaking Peoples of the Slave Coast of West Africa, Their Religion, Manners, Laws, Languages. Oosterhous: Anthropological Publications, 1966.

Fouchard, Jean. The Haitian Maroons: Liberty or Death. New York: E.W. Blyden Press, 1981.

Frucht, Richard. Black Society in the New World. New York: Random House, 1971.

Graham, Alistair and Peter Beard. Eyelids of Morning: The Mingled Destinies of Crocodiles and Men. Greenwich, Conn.: New York Graphic Society Ltd., 1973.

Haskins, Jim. Voodoo and Hoodoo: The Craft as Revealed by Traditional Practitioners. Lanham, Md.: Scarborough House, 1990.

Hurston, Zora Neale. Tell My Horse: Voodoo and Life in Haiti and Jamaica. New York: Perennial Library, 1990.

Idowu, E. Bolaji. African Traditional Religion: A Definition. Maryknoll, N.Y.: Orbis Books, 1973.

King, Noel Quinton. African Cosmos: An Introduction to Religion in Africa. Belmont, Calif.: Wadsworth Publishing Co., 1986.

Mbiti, John S. Introduction to African Religion. London: Heinemann Educational, 1975.

Paiewonsky, Isidor. Eyewitness Accounts of Slavery in the Danish West Indies. St. Thomas: I. Paiewonsky, 1987.

Parrinder, Edward Geoffrey. West African Religion: A Study of the Beliefs and Practices of Akan, Ewe, Yoruba, Ibo, and Kindred People. London: Epworth Press, 1961.

Rawley, James A. The Transatlantic Slave Trade: A History. New York: Norton, 1981.

Ray, Benjamin C. African Religions: Symbol, Ritual, and Community. Englewood Cliffs N.J.: Prentice-Hall, 1976.

Shorter, Aylward. Prayer in the Religious Traditions of Africa. New York: Oxford University Press, 1976.

Ward, J.R. British West Indian Slavery, 1750–1834: The Process of Amelioration. Oxford: Oxford University Press, 1988.

GHOSTS AND GHOST STORIES

Belyk, Robert C. Ghosts: True Stories from British Columbia. Victoria, B.C.: Horsdal & Schubart Publishing Ltd., 1994.

Cavendish, Richard. The World of Ghosts and the Supernatural: The Occult, the Unexplained, and the Mystical Around the Globe. New York: Facts on File, Inc., 1994.

Corliss, William R. Unusual Natural Phenomena. New York: Arlington House, 1977.

Gordon, Giles, ed. Prevailing Spirits: A Book of Scottish Ghost Stories. London: Grafton Books, 1976.

Gordon, Giles, ed. Scottish Ghost Stories. London: Random House UK Ltd., 1996.

Innes, Brian. Ghost Sightings. New York: Barnes & Noble, Inc., 1996.

Lochhead, Marion, ed. Scottish Tales of Magic and Mystery. Stirling, Scotland: Johnston & Bacon Books Limited, 1990.

Love, Dane. Scottish Ghosts. New York: Barnes & Noble Books, 1996.

McNeil, W.K., ed. Ghost Stories from the American South. Little Rock, Ark.: August House, 1985.

Norman, Diana. The Stately Ghosts of England. Dorset Press, 1987.

Preik, Brooks Newton. Haunted Wilmington and the Cape Fear Coast. Wilmington, N.C.: Banks Channel Books, 1995.

Roberts, Nancy. Ghosts and Specters of the Old South. Orangeberg, S.C.: Sandlapper Publishing Co., Inc., 1974.

Roberts, Nancy. The Haunted South, Where Ghosts Still Roam. Columbia, S.C.: University of South Carolina Press, 1995.

Roberts, Nancy. Haunted Houses: Tales from 30 American Homes. Chester, Conn.: The Globe Pequot Press, 1988.

Robson, Alan. Grisly Trails and Ghostly Tales. London: Virgin Books.

Russell, Randy and Janet Barnett. Mountain Ghost Stories and Curious Tales of Western North Carolina. Winston-Salem, N.C.: John F. Blair, Publisher.

USA Weekend, eds. I Never Believed in Ghosts Until . . . : 100 Real-Life Encounters. New York: Barnes & Noble Books, 1994.

Woodyard, Chris. Haunted Ohio, vols. I through IV. Ohio: Kestrel Publications, 1991.

LITERATURE: NOVELS, STORIES, FOLKLORE, POEMS, SONGS, ETC.

The Oxford Dictionary of Quotations. New York: Oxford University Press, 1980.

Allcott, Kenneth, ed. Eighteenth-Century Prose, 1700–1780, Vol. III. Baltimore, Md.: Penguin Books, Ltd., 1956.

Auld Scots Songs with Music. Newtongrange, Midlothian: Lang Syne Publishers Ltd., 1983.

The New Scottish Song Book: Melody Edition. Oxford: Oxford University Press, 1987.

Scottish Fairy Tales. London: Studio Editions Ltd., 1993.

Bartlett, John and Justin Kaplan, ed. Bartlett's Familiar Quotations. Boston: Little, Brown and Company, 1992.

Beaton, M.C. Death of a Gossip. New York: Ballantine Books, 1985.

Beaton, M.C. Death of a Perfect Wife. New York: Ballantine Books, 1990.

Beaton, M.C. Death of an Outsider. New York: Ballantine Books, 1990.

Beaton, M.C. Death of a Hussy. New York: Ballantine Books, 1991.

Beaton, M.C. Death of a Snob. New York: St. Martin's Press, 1991.

Beaton, M.C. Death of a Prankster. New York: Ballantine Books, 1992.

Beaton, M.C. Death of a Charming Man. Mysterious Press, Inc.: 1994.

Beaton, M.C. Death of a Nag. New York: Mysterious Press, 1995.

Beaton, M.C. Death of a Traveling Man. New York: Ballantine Books, 1996.

Beaton, M.C. Death of a Scriptwriter. New York: The Mysterious Press, 1998.

Bennett, Alan. The Madness of King George. New York: Random House, Inc., 1995.

Briggs, Katherine. British Folktales. New York: Dorset Press, 1997.

Brown, Charles Brockden. Wieland and Memoirs of Carwin the Biloquist. New York: Penguin Books, 1991. (Reprint)

Buchan, John. Witch Wood. Edinburgh: Canongate Publishing Ltd., 1988.

Burns, Robert. The Complete Illustrated Poems, Songs, and Ballads. Secaucus, N.J.: Chartwell Books, Inc., 1990.

Busch, Robert. Wolf Songs. San Francisco: Sierra Club Books, 1994.

Cairns, Huntington. The Limits of Art. New York: Pantheon Books, 1948.

Cameron, Kate. Orenda: A Novel of the Iroquois Nation. New York: Ballantine Books, 1991.

Campbell, Grant. Scottish Fairy Tales. London: Pan Books Ltd., 1980.

Campbell, John Lorne. Highland Songs of the Forty-five. Edinburgh: Scottish Gaelic Texts Society, 1984.

Chase, Richard. American Folk Tales and Songs. New York: New American Library.

Cole, Allan, and Chris Bunch. A Daughter of Liberty. New York: Ballantine Books, 1993.

Coleridge, Samuel Taylor. The Rime of The Ancient Mariner and Other Poems. New York: Penguin Books, 1995.

Conway, Pat, ed. 100 Great Scottish Songs, with Words and Music. Dublin: Waltons Mnf. Ltd., 1986.

Crichton, Robert. The Camerons. New York: Warner Paperback Library, 1974.

Daniel Defoe. Robinson Crusoe. New York: Thomas Nelson and Sons Ltd.

Doig, Ivan. Dancing at the Rascal Fair. New York: Atheneum, 1987.

Douglas, Ronald MacDonald. Scottish Lore and Folklore. New York: Random House, 1990.

Douglas, Sir George Brisbane, ed. Scottish Fairy and Folk Tales. New York: Arno Press, 1977.

Durham, Charles. Walk in the Light. New York: Ballatine Books, 1992.

Edmunds, John. A Williamsburg Songbook. 1964.

Farnol, Jeffrey. Adam Penfeather, Buccaneer: His Early Exploits. Garden City, N.Y.: Doubleday, Doran and Co., 1941.

Fletcher, Inglis. The Scotswoman. New York: The Bobbs-Merrill Company, Inc., 1954.

Fowlie, Wallace, ed. French Stories. New York: Bantam Books, 1960.

Fraser, Antonia. Scottish Love Poems. New York: Peter Bedrick Books, 1989.

Garrison, Webb. A Treasury of Carolina Tales: Unusual, Interesting, and Little-Known Stories of North Carolina and South Carolina. Nashville: Rutledge Hill Press, 1988.

Goodchild, Peter. The Raven Tales. Chicago: Chicago Review Press, 1991.

Hunter, Mollie. A Stranger Came Ashore. New York: HarperCollins Publishers, 1977.

Hunter, Mollie. The Walking Stones. New York: Harcourt Brace & Company, 1996.

Keith, Andrew J. The Warrior's Code: For Use with the Doctor Who Role Playing Game. Chicago: FASA Corporation, 1986.

Kingston, Maxine Hong. Tripmaster Monkey: His Fake Book. New York: Random House Inc., 1990.

Lauder, Sir Harry. My Best Scotch Stories. Dundee and London: Valentine & Sons, Ltd., 1929.

Leaf, Munro. Wee Gillis. New York: The Trumpet Club, 1988.

Lochhead, Marion, ed. Scottish Tales of Magic and Mystery. Stirling, Scotland: Johnston & Bacon Books Limited, 1990.

Luzel, F.M. Celtic Folk-Tales from Armorica. Felinfach: Llanerch Publishers, 1992.

Lyle, Emily, ed. Scottish Ballads. New York: Barnes & Noble Books, 1995.

MacColl, Ewan. Till Doomsday in the Afternoon: The Folklore of a Family of Scots Travellers, the Stewarts of Blairgowrie. Dover N.H.: Manchester University Press, 1986.

Macdonald, Donnie, ed. Gaelic Echo: Scottish Bi-lingual Magazine, Autumn 1992.

MacDougall, Carl, ed. The Giant Book of Scottish Short Stories. New York: Peter Bedrick Books, 1989.

MacGregor, Forbes. MacGregor's Mixture. Edinburgh: Gordon Wright, 1979.

Manson, W.L. Tunes of Glory. Stories, History, Traditions, Music, and Humor of the Highland Bagpipe. Glasgow: Lang Syne Publishers Ltd., 1992.

Marshall, Nancy. Scottish Songs and Ballads. Edinburgh: W & R Chambers Ltd., 1990.

Martin, Laura C. The Folklore of Birds. Old Saybrook, Conn.: The Globe Pequot Press, 1993.

Martin, Laura C. The Folklore of Trees and Shrubs. Old Saybrook, Conn.: The Globe Pequot Press, 1992.

Martin, Laura C. Wildlife Folklore. Old Saybrook, Conn.: The Globe Pequot Press, 1994.

Massignon, Genevieve. Folktales of France. Chicago: University of Chicago Press, 1968.

Matthews, Caitlin. Celtic Devotional: Daily Prayers and Blessings. Godsfield Press, 1996.

McCrumb, Sharyn. Highland Laddie Gone. New York: Ballantine Books, 1991.

McDougall, James. Folk Tales and Fairy Lore in Gaelic and English. New York: Arno Press, 1977.

McDougall, James. Highland Fairy Legends. Totowa, N.J.: Rowman & Littlefield, 1978.

McGonagall, William. Collected Poems. Edinburgh: Birlinn Ltd., 1992.

Melling, Orla. The Druid's Tune. Dublin: The O'Brien Press, 1992.

Michaels, Barbara. Wait for What Will Come. New York: Dodd, Mead, 1978.

Miller, Peggy. A Wife for the Pretender. New York: Harcourt, Brace and World, 1966.

Mitford, Nancy. Highland Fling. New York: Carroll & Graf Publishers, Inc., 1988.

Murison, David. Scots Saws. Edinburgh: The Mercat Press, 1981.

Nordhoff, Charles, and James Norman Hall. Mutiny on the Bounty. Boston: Little, Brown and Company, 1960.

Parson, Nels A. The Compleat Journal of Landon Vickers. Georgia: Iberian Publishing Company, 1996.

Peel, John. Doctor Who: The Wheel in Space. Canoga Park, Calif.: New Media Books, Inc., 1986.

Phillips, Michael R. George MacDonald, Scotland's Beloved Storyteller. Minneapolis, Minn.: Bethany House Publishers, 1987.

Pope, Alexander. The Iliad of Homer. London: J. Buckland and T. Longman, 1777.

Porter, Jane. The Scottish Chiefs. Philadelphia: J.B. Lippincott & Co., 1883.

Ramsay, Allan. **The Ever Green: A Collection of Scots Poems**, vols. I and II. Glasgow: Robert Forrester, 1875.

Reid, J.J., ed. **Classic Scottish Short Stories.** Oxford: Oxford University Press, 1989.

Roberts, Moss, (translator and editor): **Chinese Fairy Tales and Fantasies.** New York: Pantheon Books, 1979.

Robertson, James, ed. **A Tongue in Yer Heid.** Edinburgh: B&W Publishing, 1994.

Robertson, Willie. **Calum's Way of It.** Argyll, Penn.: Argyll Publishing.

Ross, Anne. **The Folklore of the Scottish Highlands.** New York: Barnes & Noble Books, 1993.

Ross, Anne, Ph.D. **The Folklore of the Scottish Highlands.** Totowa, N.J.: Rowman and Littlefield, 1976.

Stevenson, Robert Louis. **Kidnapped.** New York: Cassell and Company, Inc., 1909.

Sutcliff, Rosemary. **Flame-Colored Taffeta.** New York: Farrar, Straus, and Giroux, 1987.

Van de Weyer, Robert, ed. **Celtic Fire.** New York: Bantam Doubleday Dell, Inc., 1991.

Vidal, Gore. **Burr.** New York: Ballantine Books, 1993.

Wilson, Barbara Ker. **Scottish Folk-Tales and Legends.** Oxford: Oxford University Press, 1989.

Wiscombe, Martin. **The Old Pig.** London: Robinson Publishing Ltd., 1996.

Wolf, Joan. **Daughter of the Red Deer.** New York: Penguin Books, 1992.

Woods, Nicola. **Scottish Proverbs.** Edinburgh: W&R Chambers, 1989.

LANGUAGE RESOURCES: DICTIONARIES, PHRASE BOOKS, ETYMOLOGY, ETC.

The Oxford Dictionary of Quotations. New York: Oxford University Press, 1980.

Aliadro, Hygino. **Dictionario: Ingles-Portugues:** New York: Pocket Books Inc., 1957.

Aman, Reinhold. **Opus Maledictorum: A Book of Bad Words.** Marlowe & Company, 1996.

Ammer, Christine. **It's Raining Cats and Dogs (and Other Beastly Expressions).** New York: Bantam Doubleday Dell Publishing Group Inc., 1989.

Bartlett, John and Justin Kaplan, ed. **Bartlett's Familiar Quotations.** Boston: Little, Brown and Company, 1992.

Beale, Paul, ed. **Partridge's Concise Dictionary of Slang and Unconventional English (from the Work of Eric Partridge).** New York: Macmillan Publishing Company, 1989.

Berger, Frances de Talavera. **Mierda! The Real Spanish You Were Never Taught in School.** New York: Penguin Books, 1990.

Berlitz Guides Staff, eds. **Engelsk-Svensk Swedish-English Dictionary.** New York: Macmillan Publishing Company, 1981.

Biedermann, Hans (translated by James Hulbert). **Dictionary of Symbolism.** New York: Meridian, 1994.

Bryson, Bill. **The Mother Tongue: English and How It Got That Way.** New York: William Morrow and Company, 1990.

Buchanan-Brown, John, Jennifer Craig, John Crawley, Barbara Galushka, Brendan

McCabe, and Gilman Parsons, eds. Le Mot Juste: A Dictionary of Classical and Foreign Words and Phrases. New York: Vintage Books, a division of Random House, 1981.

Carr, Edwin Hamlin. Putnam's Phrase Book. New York: GP Putnam's Sons, 1923.

Castillo, Carlos, and Otto F. Bond, eds. The University of Chicago Dictionary: Espanol-English, English-Espanol. New York: Washington Square Press Inc., 1968.

Cirlot, J.E. A Dictionary of Symbols. Dorset Press, 1991.

Craigie, Sir William Alexander. The Scottish Tongue. College Park, Md.: McGrath Pub. Co., 1970.

De Vries, Louis. German-English Science Dictionary. New York: McGraw-Hill Book Company, 1959.

Funk, Charles Earle. Heavens to Betsy! and Other Curious Sayings. New York: Harper & Row Publishers, 1986.

Funk, Charles Earle. A Hog on Ice. New York: Harper and Row Publishers, Inc., 1985.

Genevieve. Merde Encore! More of the Real French You Were Never Taught in School. New York: Atheneum, 1986.

Grose, Francis. 1811 Dictionary of the Vulgar Tongue. Northfield, Ill.: Digest Books, 1971.

Grose, Francis. A Classical Dictionary of the Vulgar Tongue. New York: Barnes & Noble Books, 1963. (Reprint; original published 1746)

Grose, Francis. A Provincial Glossary, 1787. Menston, Yorks: Scolar Publishers, 1968.

Hendrickson, Robert. QPB Encyclopedia of Word and Phrase Origins. New York: Quality Paperback Book Club, 1998.

Hill, Robert A. Jr., ed. The Random House Italian Dictionary. New York: Random House, 1992.

Hughes, Charles A. French Phrase Book and Dictionary. New York: Grosset & Dunlap, Inc., 1971.

Kidd, D.A., M.A. Latin Dictionary. Glasgow: HarperCollins Publishers, 1993.

Langenscheidt Staff, eds. German-English English-German Dictionary. New York: Simon & Schuster Inc., 1974.

Lederer, Richard. Anguished English. New York: Bantam Doubleday Dell Publishing Group Inc., 1989.

Macdonald, Donnie, ed. Gaelic Echo Scottish Bi-lingual Magazine (Autumn 1992).

MacKay, Charles. The Auld Scots Dictionary. Glasgow: Lang Syne Publishers, Ltd., 1992.

MacKay, Charles. The Lost Beauties of the English Language: An Appeal to Authors, Poets, Clergymen, and Public Speakers. New York: J.W. Bouton, 1874.

Mackinnon, Roderick. Teach Yourself Gaelic. New York: Random House Inc., 1971.

Maclennan, Malcolm. Gaelic Dictionary: Gaelic-English, English-Gaelic. Great Britain: Acair and Aberdeen University Press, 1979.

Macleod, Iseabail. The Pocket Guide to Scottish Words: Scots-Gaelic. Glasgow: Richard Drew Publishing Ltd., 1986.

Macleod, Iseabail, Pauline Cairns, Caroline Macafee, and Ruth Martin, eds. The Scots

Thesaurus. Aberdeen: Aberdeen University Press, 1990.

Maracle, David Kanatawakhow. One Thousand Useful Mohawk Words. Guilford, Conn.: Audio-Forum, 1992.

Matkins, Marian, ed. Scots Dictionary. Glasgow: HarperCollins, 1995.

McArthur, Tom, ed. The Oxford Companion to the English Language. Oxford University Press, 1992.

McClure, J. Derrick. Why Scots Matters. Edinburgh: Saltire Society in association with the Scots Language Society, 1988.

McCutcheon, Marc. Descriptionary: A Thematic Dictionary. New York: Ballantine Books, 1992.

Moss, Norman. British/American Language Dictionary. Lincolnwood, Ill.: Passport Books, 1988.

Munro, Michael. The Original Patter: A Guide to Current Glasgow Usage. Glasgow: Glasgow City Libraries, 1992.

Partridge, Eric. A Dictionary of Catch Phrases, American & British. Chelsea, Mich.: Scarborough House, 1992.

Partridge, Eric. A Dictionary of Slang and Unconventional English. New York: Macmillan Publishing Company, 1984.

Partridge, Eric, revised and edited by Paul Beale. A Dictionary of Catch Phrases: American and British, from the Sixteenth Century to the Present Day. Lanham, Md.: Scarborough House, 1992.

Reaney, P.H. and R.M. Wilson. A Dictionary of English Surnames. Oxford: Oxford University Press, 1996.

Sheidlower, Jesse, ed. The F Word. New York: Random House, 1995.

Sierra, Judy. Celtic Baby Names. Eugene, Or.: Folkprint, 1997.

Thomson, Derick S. ed. The New English-Gaelic Dictionary. Glasgow, Gairm, 1986.

Warrack, Alexander, ed. The Concise Scots Dictionary. New York: Crescent Books, 1988.

Wright, Elizabeth Mary. Rustic Speech and Folk-Lore. London, New York: Oxford University Press, 1914.

MAGIC: WITCHCRAFT, WICCA, PAGANISM, MYSTICISM, ETC.

The World's Last Mysteries. Pleasantville, N.Y.: The Reader's Digest Association, Inc., 1982.

Anonymous. Edited with an Introduction by "Simon." The Necronomicon. New York: Avon Books, 1977.

Arrowsmith, Nancy, and George Morse. Field Guide to the Little People. New York: Hill and Wang, 1977.

Beyerl, Paul. The Master Book of Herbalism. Phoenix Publishing Co., 1984.

Bonewits, Isaac. Real Magic. York Beach, Maine: Samuel Weiser, Inc., 1993.

Buckland, Raymond. Scottish Witchcraft: The History and Magic of the Picts. St. Paul, Minn.: Llewellyn Publications, 1995.

Cabot, Laurie, with Tom Cowan. Power of the Witch: The Earth, the Moon, and the Magical Path to Enlightenment. New York: Delacorte Press, 1989.

Cavendish, Richard. A History of Magic. New York: Arkana, The Penguin Group, 1990.

Cavendish, Richard. The World of Ghosts and the Supernatural: The Occult, the Unexplained, and the Mystical Around the Globe. New York: Facts on File, Inc., 1994.

Conway, D.J. Celtic Magic. St. Paul, Minn.: Llewellyn Publications, 1990.

Conway, D.J. Norse Magic. St. Paul, Minn.: Llewellyn Publications, 1991.

Fenton, Sasha. Fortune-Telling by Tarot Cards. New York: Sterling Publishing Co., Inc., 1990.

Frazer, Sir James George. The Golden Bough: A Study in Magic and Religion. New York: Collier Books, 1950.

Gordon, Stuart. The Book of Spells, Hexes, and Curses. Secaucus, N.J.: Carol Publishing Group, 1995.

Guiley, Rosemary Ellen. Harper's Encyclopedia of Magical and Paranormal Experience. New York: HarperCollins, 1991.

Gundarsson, Kveldulf. Teutonic Magic: The Magical and Spiritual Practices of the Germanic Peoples. St. Paul, Minn.: Llewellyn Publications, Inc., 1990.

Haskins, Jim. Voodoo and Hoodoo: The Craft as Revealed by Traditional Practitioners. Lanham, Md.: Scarborough House, 1990.

Hewitt, William W. Astrology for Beginners. St. Paul, Minn.: Llewellyn Publications, 1991.

Hurston, Zora Neale. Tell My Horse: Voodoo and Life in Haiti and Jamaica. New York: Perennial Library, 1990.

Jackson, Robert. Mysteries of Witchcraft and the Occult. Secaucus, N.J.: Chartwell Books, 1991.

Kennedy, Richard. The Dictionary of Beliefs: An Illustrated Guide to World Religions and Beliefs. Sussex: BLA Publishing Limited, 1984.

Kieckhefer, Richard. Magic in the Middle Ages. New York: Cambridge University Press, 1989.

Leland, Charles G. Aradia, or Gospel of the Witches. Custer, Wash.: Phoenix Publishing, 1990.

Mathers, S.L. MacGregor et al. Astral Projection, Ritual Magic, and Alchemy. Rochester, Vt.: Destiny Books, 1987.

Monroe, Douglas. The 21 Lessons of Merlyn: A Study in Druid Magic and Lore. St. Paul, Mn.: Llewellyn Publications, 2002.

Moorey, Teresa. Herbs for Magic and Ritual: A Beginner's Guide. London: Hodder & Stoughton, 1996.

Parkinson, Cornelia M. Gem Magic. New York: Ballantine Books, 1988.

Pennick, Nigel. The Pagan Book of Days: A Guide to the Festivals, Traditions, and Sacred Days of the Year. Rochester, Vt.: Destiny Books, 1992.

Pepper, Elizabeth and John Wilcock. Magical and Mystical Sites: Europe and the British Isles. Grand Rapids, Mich.: Phanes Press, 1993.

Piggot, Stuart. The Druids. New York: Thames and Hudson, 1985.

Ryall, Rhiannon. West Country Wicca: A Journal of the Old Religion. Custer, Wash.: Phoenix Publications Inc., 1989.

Seymour, St. John D. Irish Witchcraft and Demonology. New York: Barnes & Noble Books, 1996.

Slade, Paddy. Encyclopedia of White Magic: A Seasonal Guide. New York: Mallard Press, 1990.

Sutherland, Elizabeth. Ravens and Black Rain. London: Corgi Books, 1985.

Weinstein, Marion. Positive Magic: Occult Self-Help. Custer, Wash.: Phoenix Publishing Inc., 1991.

Williams, Charles. Witchcraft. Faber & Faber Ltd., 1941.

NATURAL HISTORY GUIDES AND RESOURCES

Alsop, Fred J. Birds of the Smokies. Gatlinburg, Tenn.: Great Smoky Mountain Natural History Association, 1991.

Amos, William H., and Stephen H. Amos. The Audubon Society Nature Guides: Atlantic and Gulf Coasts New York: Alfred A. Knopf, Inc., 1985.

Brickell, John. The Natural History of North Carolina. New York: Johnson Reprint Corp., 1733 (reprinted 1969).

Condry, William. Woodlands. London: William Collins Sons & Co. Ltd., 1974.

Corliss, William R. Unusual Natural Phenomena. New York: Arlington House, 1977.

Darwin, Tess. The Scots Herbal: The Plant Lore of Scotland. Edinburgh: The Mercat Press, 1996.

Dennis, Jerry. It's Raining Frogs and Fishes. New York: HarperCollins Publishers Inc., 1993.

Dunmire, Marjorie S. Mountain Wildlife. Estes Park, Co.: Pegasus Graphics, 1986.

Forey, Pamela, et al. An Instant Guide to Edible Plants. New York: Crescent Books, 1989.

Hart, Cyril. British Trees in Color. London: Book Club Associates, 1974.

Hill, Madalene, and Gwen Barclay, with Jean Hardy. Southern Herb Growing. Shearer Publishing, 1987.

Launert, Edmund. The Hamlyn Guide to Edible Plants of Britain and Northern Europe. Hamlyn, 1989.

Livingston, A.D., and Helen Livingston, ED.D. Edible Plants and Animals. New York: Facts on File, Inc., 1993.

Lockley, R. M. ed. Britain in Colour. London: A Batsford Book, 1964.

Martin, Laura C. The Folklore of Birds. Old Saybrook, Conn.: The Globe Pequot Press, 1993.

Martin, Laura C. The Folklore of Trees and Shrubs. Old Saybrook, Conn.: The Globe Pequot Press, 1992.

Martin, Laura C. Wildflower Folklore. Old Saybrook, Conn.: The Globe Pequot Press, 1993.

Medve, Richard J. Edible Wild Plants of Pennsylvania and Neighboring States. University Park, Penn.: Pennsylvania State University Press, 1990.

Millas, Jose Carlos. Hurricanes of the Caribbean and Adjacent Regions, 1492–1800. Ann Arbor Mich.: Edwards Brothers Incorporated, 1968.

Ovenden, Denys et al. A Handguide to the Wild Animals of Britain and Europe. Treasure Press, 1989.

Page, Robin. Weather Forecasting the Country Way. New York: Viking Penguin Inc., 1977.

Parkinson, Cornelia M. Gem Magic. New York: Ballantine Books, 1988.

Perrins, Christopher. Collins New Generation Guide: Birds of Britain and Europe. London: Collins, 1987.

Quirk Jr., Thomas C. Reptiles and Amphibians Coloring Book. Mineola N.Y.: Dover Publications, Inc., 1981.

Ratcliffe, Derek. Highland Flora. Inverness: Highlands and Islands Development, 1977.

Riotte, Louise. Sleeping with a Sunflower. Pawnal, Vt.: Garden Way Publishing, 1987.

Sutton, Ann, and Myron Sutton. Audubon Society Nature Guides: Eastern Forests. New York: Alfred A. Knopf, Inc., 1985.

Webster, William David, James F. Parnell, and Walter C. Biggs, Jr. Mammals of the Carolinas, Virginia, and Maryland. Chapel Hill, N.C.: The University of North Carolina Press, 1985.

Wigginton, Eliot, ed. The Foxfire Book: Hog Dressing, Log Cabin Building, Mountain Crafts and Foods, Planting by the Signs, Snakelore, Hunting Tales, Faith Healing. New York: Anchor Books, 1972.

Wigginton, Eliot and his students, eds. Foxfire 5: Ironmaking, Blacksmithing, Flintlock Rifles, and Bear Hunting. New York: Anchor Books, 1979.

NORTH CAROLINA: HISTORY, GEOGRAPHY, NATURAL HISTORY, ETC.

Alsop, Fred J. Birds of the Smokies. Gatlinburg, Tenn.: Great Smoky Mountain Natural History Association, 1991.

Brickell, John. The Natural History of North Carolina. New York: Johnson Reprint Corp., 1733 (reprinted 1969).

Dunmire, Marjorie S. Mountain Wildlife. Estes Park, Colo.: Pegasus Graphics, 1986.

Frucht, Richard. Black Society in the New World. New York: Random House, 1971.

Garrison, Webb. A Treasury of Carolina Tales: Unusual, Interesting and Little-Known Stories of North Carolina and South Carolina. Nashville, Tenn.: Rutledge Hill Press, 1988.

Merrens, Harry Roy. Colonial North Carolina in the Eighteenth Century: A Study in Historical Geography. Chapel Hill N.C.: University of North Carolina Press, 1964.

Meyer, Duane. The Highland Scots of North Carolina, 1732–1776. Chapel Hill, N.C.: The University of North Carolina Press, 1961.

Powell, William S. North Carolina, a History. Chapel Hill, N.C.: The University of North Carolina Press, 1988.

Preik, Brooks Newton. Haunted Wilmington and the Cape Fear Coast. Wilmington, N.C.: Banks Channel Books, 1995.

Ravi, Jennifer. Notable North Carolina Women. Winston-Salem, N.C.: Bandit Books, Inc., 1992.

Roberts, Nancy. Blackbeard and Other Pirates of the Atlantic Coast. Winston-Salem, N.C.: John F. Blair, Publisher, 1993.

Russell, Randy and Janet Barnett. Mountain Ghost Stories and Curious Tales of Western North Carolina. Winston-Salem, N.C.: John F. Blair, Publisher, 1994.

Sheppard, Muriel Earley. Cabins in the Laurel. Chapel Hill, N.C.: The University of North Carolina Press, 1991.

Sutton, Ann, and Myron Sutton. Audubon Society Nature Guides: Eastern Forests. New York: Alfred A. Knopf, Inc., 1985.

Webster, William David, James F. Parnell, and Walter C. Biggs, Jr. Mammals of the Carolinas, Virginia, and Maryland. Chapel Hill: The University of North Carolina Press, 1985.

Wigginton, Eliot, ed. The Foxfire Book: Hog Dressing, Log Cabin Building, Mountain Crafts and Foods, Planting by the Signs, Snakelore, Hunting Tales, Faith Healing. New York: Anchor Books, 1972.

Wigginton, Eliot and his students, eds. Foxfire 5: Ironmaking, Blacksmithing, Flintlock Rifles, and Bear Hunting. New York: Anchor Books, 1979.

FOOD AND COOKERY

Brown, Catherine. Broths to Bannocks: Cooking in Scotland, 1690 to the Present Day. London: John Murray (Publishers) Ltd., 1991.

Cameron, Sheila MacNiven. The Highlander's Cookbook: Recipes from Scotland. New York: Gramercy Publishing Company, 1966.

Duff, Gail. A Loaf of Bread: Bread in History, in the Kitchen, and on the Table. Edison, N.J.: Chartwell Books, 1998.

Harris, Paul. A Little Scottish Cookbook. San Francisco: Chronicle Books, 1988.

Jensen, Bernard. Foods That Heal. Garden City Park, N.Y.: Avery Publishing Group, Inc., 1993.

Kaplan, Steven L. Provisioning Paris: Merchants and Millers in the Grain and Flour Trade During the Eighteenth Century. Ithaca, N.Y.: Cornell University Press, 1984.

Launert, Edmund. The Hamlyn Guide to Edible Plants of Britain and Northern Europe. Hamlyn, 1989.

Livingston, A.D., and Helen Livingston, Ed.D. Edible Plants and Animals. New York: Facts on File, Inc., 1993.

McLintock, Mrs., introduction and glossary by Iseabail Macleod. Mrs. McLintock's Receipts For Cookery and Pastry-Work. Aberdeen: The University Press, 1986.

McNeill, Marian F. The Scots Kitchen: Its Traditions and Lore, with Old-Time Recipes. Edinburgh: The Mercat Press, 1994.

Medve, Richard J. Edible Wild Plants of Pennsylvania and Neighboring States. University Park, Penn.: Pennsylvania State University Press, 1990.

Norman, Jill. Teas and Tisanes. New York: Bantam Books Inc., 1989.

Puotinen, C.J. Herbs to Improve Digestion. New Canaan, Conn.: Keats Publications, Inc., 1996.

Rasmussen, Dean L. How to Live Through a Famine. Bountiful, Utah: Horizon Publishers, 1976.

Shaw, Carol P. Whisky: A Discriminating Guide to Scotch Whiskies. Philadelphia: Running Press, 1994.

Tannahill, Reay. Food in History. New York: Crown Trade Paperbacks, 1989.

Taylor, Dale. The Writer's Guide to Everyday Life in Colonial America from 1607–1783. Cincinnati, Ohio: Writer's Digest Books, 1997.

NATIVE AMERICAN CULTURES AND HISTORY, ETC.

Adams, Spencer Lionel. The Long House of the Iroquois. New York: AMS Press, 1978.

Cameron, Kate. Orenda: A Novel of the Iroquois Nation. New York: Random House, Inc., 1991.

Demos, John. The Unredeemed Captive: A Family Story from Early America. New York: Alfred A. Knopf, Inc., 1994.

Doane, Nancy Locke. Indian Doctor. Nancy Locke Doane, 1980.

Fenton, William Nelson. Contacts Between Iroquois Herbalism and Colonial Medicine. Seattle: Shorey Book Store, 1971.

Goodchild, Peter. The Raven Tales. Chicago: Chicago Review Press, 1991.

Hale, Haraito. The Iroquois Book of Rites. Toronto: University of Toronto Press, 1963.

Hughes, Thomas. History of the Society of Jesus in North America, Colonial and Federal. London: Longmans, Green, and Co., 1907.

Hutchens, Alma R. Indian Herbology of North America. Boston: Shambala, 1991.

Johnson, Elias. Legends, Traditions, and Laws of the Iroquois, or Six Nations, and History of the Tuscarora Indians. New York: AMS Press, 1978.

Kate, Maggie, ed. North American Indian Motifs. Mineola, N.Y.: Dover Publications, Inc., 1996.

Kelsay, Isabel Thompson. Joseph Brant, 1743–1807, Man of Two Worlds. Syracuse, N.Y.: Syracuse University Press, 1984.

Maracle, David Kanatawakhow. One Thousand Useful Mohawk Words. Guilford, Conn.: Audio-Forum, a division of Jeffrey Norton Publishers, 1992.

Morgan, Lewis Henry. League of the Ho-de-no-sau-nee, or Iroquois, Vol. II. New Haven: Reprinted by Human Relations Area Files, 1954.

Schoolcraft, Henry Rowe. Notes on the Iroquois: Or, Contributions to the Statistics, Aboriginal History, Antiquities and General Ethnology of Western New York. New York: Bartlett & Welford, 1846.

Thom, James Alexander. Panther in the Sky. New York: Ballantine Books, 1990.

Van Horn, Elizabeth; Geno Paesano, ed. Iroquois Silver Brooches (as-ne-as-ga) in the Rochester Museum. Rochester, N.Y.: Rochester Museum and Science Center, 1971.

Weaver, Sally M. Medicine and Politics Among the Grand River Iroquois; a Study of the Nonconservatives. Ottawa: National Museums of Canada, 1972.

Wilson, Edmond. Apologies to the Iroquois: With a Study of the Mohawks in High Steel by Joseph Mitchell. New York: Farrar, Straus & Giroux, 1960.

Wolf, Joan. Daughter of the Red Deer. New York: Penguin Books, 1992.

Rather Odd Books

Andrews, William. **Old Time Punishments.** Williamstown, Mass.: Corner House Publishers, 1985.

Cohen, Daniel. **The Encyclopedia of Monsters.** New York: Dorset Press, a division of Marlboro Books Corporation, 1982.

Cooper, William M. **An Illustrated History of the Rod.** Ware, Hertfordshire: Wordsworth Editions, 1988.

Earle, Alice Morse. **Curious Punishments of Bygone Days.** Bedford, Mass.: Applewood Books, 1995.

Medieval Punishment: Torture and Executions in Europe, 1100–1600, How It Was Done, Why It Was Done. Lifkin, Tx.: The Gutenberg Press, 1994.

Rossi, William A. **The Sex Life of the Foot and Shoe.** Hertfordshire, England: Wordsworth Editions Ltd., 1989.

Swain, John. **The Pleasures of the Torture Chamber.** New York: Dorset Press, division of Barnes & Noble, Inc., 1995.

Miscellaneous

The New York Public Library Desk Reference Collection of the Most Frequently Sought Information. New York: The Stonesong Press, Inc.

Atkinson, R.J.C. **Stonehenge.** New York: Penguin Books, 1990.

Boyne, William. **A Manual of Roman Coins; From the Earliest Period of the Extinction of the Empire; with Rarity Guide & 22 Plates.** Chicago: Ammon Press, 1968.

Gallatin, Albert. **Syracusan Dekadrachms of the Euainetos Type.** Cambridge: Harvard University Press, 1930.

Grasse, Pierre P. ed. **Lascaux en Périgord Noir: Environment, Art Parietal et Conservation.** Périgueux: P. Fanlac, 1982.

Hawking, Stephen W. **A Brief History of Time: From the Big Bang to Black Holes.** New York: Bantam Books, 1988.

Hawkins, Gerald S. et al. **Stonehenge Decoded.** New York: Dell Publishing Co., Inc., 1965.

Macvey, John W. **Time Travel.** Chelsea, Mich.: Scarborough House/Publishers, 1990.

APPENDIX I

ERRATA

I shot an error in the air,
It fell to earth I knew not where,
Until some people wrote to tell
Me where on earth my error fell.

A few of them in rage profound
Berated me on my home ground.
While others of a kinder bent
Politely questioned my intent.

But most were fans who wrote to say
They loved my books, though by the way,
That whizzing error split their clout
And I'd be wise to cut it out.

(with thanks to the author,
Dr. Ellen Mandell, and apologies to
Robert Louis Stevenson)

Well, look—nobody's perfect. Not me, not copy editors, not typesetters. Least of all, me. However, it's my name on the front of the book. Some of the following corrections are simply typographical errors, some are not really errors but people think they are—and some really *are* mistakes. I doubt this list is comprehensive; it's the nature of errors to hide and multiply, new ones emerging with each reading of a text. (I think they breed while the book is closed, hatching in the light of day every time you open the covers.)

Forthwith, corrections, explanations, and emendations—page references are to the U.S. paperback editions. My thanks to Elizabeth M. Phillips for her detailed comments, which were of great help.

OUTLANDER

Page 3: "1945"

Beginning date. Now, this is one of those errors that isn't *exactly* an error, but then again . . . When we sold *Outlander* in the United States, it had a starting date of 1945 because when I looked briefly at a summary account of World War II (upon deciding that that's where Claire came from), it gave 1945 as the official end of the war, and since World War II wasn't the primary setting of the book (and since I wasn't intending ever to show the thing to anybody anyway), I didn't look deeply into its chronology. So, a year after selling the book to a U.S. publisher, we sold it in the U.K., whereupon I said (to the U.K. publisher), "For God's sake, have a Scot read it before you publish it; I've never actually been there!"

Reay Tannahill, a Scot, a historian, and a fine historical novelist herself, kindly read the manuscript and sent me a number of small notes and corrections, all of which

I incorporated into the galley proofs of *Outlander*—with one exception.

Reay told me that 1946 would be much more accurate, in terms of the postwar conditions I described, since rationing, etc., was still the norm in Britain in 1945. However, the American publisher didn't want to change the beginning date since this would require re-copyediting the entire manuscript to make sure all the dates were coherent, and publication was imminent. "Besides," they added, "nobody in the States will know the difference." (They were largely, if not entirely, correct in this supposition, by the way.)

However, in the interest of accuracy—and because it later caused another and more significant error in the chronology of *Dragonfly in Amber*—the beginning date should really be 1946, instead of 1945.

Page 6: Claire refers to Frank's "great-great-great-great-grandfather," while Jack Randall is elsewhere mentioned as Frank's "six-times great-grandfather." I would assume that Claire, having little or no interest (at this point) in the finer details of genealogy, is not bothering about precision.

Page 28/29: Frank and the Reverend announce to Claire their finding of "news" regarding Jack Randall, which Claire calculates—from the appearance of the papers on the desk, as dating from "around 1750." If Jack Randall died in 1746, he couldn't have been "harassing the countryside" in 1750. And since he was newly arrived as commander at Ft. William when Jamie was flogged in October 1739, the date Claire gives should probably be 1740. On the other hand, Claire is no antiquarian and has no knowledge of Randall's history—so I would myself think an eyeball estimate with a ten-year standard deviation is pretty good.

Page 62: "lobsterbacks"

This term was indeed used to describe English soldiers—but not in Scotland. It was in common use some years later, during the American Revolution, but probably was not current for the Scottish Highlands in 1743.

Page 105: The Selkirk Grace

The prayer young Hamish speaks is actually a well-known piece, called "The Selkirk Grace." It is an authentic bit of Scottish culture; however, it was written by (or at least attributed to) Robert Burns—who unfortunately wasn't born yet in 1743.

The inclusion of this prayer was something of an ironic accident; I originally came across it in a collection of multicultural children's poetry, where it was titled simply "Scottish prayer" and attributed to our old friend Anonymous. I would likely have recognized it, nonetheless—save that I was assiduously avoiding reading the works of Robert Burns because I knew that he wasn't extant in the time period I was dealing with—and I wanted to avoid accidentally using this material anachronistically. Ironic, as I say.

A year or so ago, I met with Dr. Sheila Brock, curator of the new Museum of Scotland. Hearing that she was about to embark on *Cross Stitch,* I warned her (in some alarm) that there were in fact a few errors here or there (for example, the substitution of the innocuous if silly "sock knife" for the Gaelic term *sgian dhu,* and the Selkirk Grace).

Dr. Brock laughed, and said, "Well, you know, the Selkirk Grace is only *attributed* to

Burns; there's no actual proof he wrote it. I should think your best defense is to claim that Burns might have taken it from an existing bit of folk verse." That seemed good advice to me, so I'm sticking with it.

Page 105: "MacTavish"

This was a bit of clumsy editing (on my part). I had originally had Jamie going under the alias "Jamie MacTavish" when he meets Claire—the Scots not knowing who she was, but strongly suspecting she was a spy of some kind, and unwilling to reveal Jamie's identity. However, the bit in which he was so introduced was cut out when I did the final trimming and splicing of the manuscript—and neither I, the editor, nor the copy editor noticed this reference, which was left hanging in the breeze.

Page 160: "cherries and apricots"

I am reliably informed by horticulturists of my acquaintance that neither cherries nor apricots would have been fruiting at this time of year. Am I a botanist? No.

Page 184: "Je suis prest."

This is one of those things that isn't an error, but people often think is. Yes, I know (as several dozen people have informed me) that the correct French spelling is "Je suis *prêt.*" However, the fact remains that the bloody Fraser motto *is* "Je suis prest." The "prest" is an obsolete French spelling; the "s" was replaced by the diacritical "ê" sometime in the nineteenth or twentieth century—but "prest" it was, and "prest" it is.

Page 196: ". . . his heart's blood staining the same leaves, dyed by the blood of the beast that killed him." Should read ". . . his heart's blood staining the same leaves dyed by the blood of the beast that killed him."

Page 197: "nasturtium syrup"

My botanical expert informs me that the plant Americans normally refer to as "nasturtium" was not found in Scotland in the eighteenth century, being New World in origin. However, another plant (whose name I forget), also known commonly as "nasturtium" in the Old World *was* found in Scotland. However, it's the first kind—*Nasturtium* spp.—from which one makes a remedy for indigestion; I don't think the Old World plant has any medical usages.

Page 218: "cherry tree"

Okay, this is what comes of writing scenes out of order and gluing them together. You get people punching flowering cherry trees, when other people were picking cherries off them a month earlier (even if they shouldn't have been). Damn all cherries, is what I say.

Page 276: "My father was a Fraser, of course; a younger half-brother to the present Master of Lovat."

This should clearly have been *"older* half-brother," since Brian Fraser was considerably older than Simon, Master of Lovat (who is depicted—fairly accurately—as being near Jamie's own age, in *Dragonfly in Amber*).

Page 277: ". . . running side by side from the seacoast."

This one isn't precisely an error, it just sounds wrong. It should have read something like, "running side by side from Inverness." While Inverness *is* on the Firth of Forth (which in turn is an inlet of the sea), no one would really describe it as "on the seacoast."

Page 286: "balcony" should be "gallery."

Page 312: "Brian Dhu" should probably be "Brian Dubh." There is no such thing as "correct" spelling in Gaelic (since it was largely unwritten for a good long time, there was no major attempt to standardize its orthography until the present day), but some forms are more widely seen and accepted than others.

Gaelic spelling is not all that consistent, especially if you look at older documents (well, neither is English spelling, in all fairness), and I have seen "Dhu" used as a nickname, with that spelling. However, my Gaelic expert says it should be "Dubh," and he knows lots better than I do.

Page 313: "mo duinne" should be "mo nighean donn."

This was an attempt on my part to render "my brown one," using a Gaelic dictionary. My Gaelic expert, Iain Taylor (who graciously volunteered for the job after reading the first two books), informs me that the correct form should really be "mo nighean donn" (my brown-haired girl), and so I used that form in the later books.

Page 316: "Lag Cruime"

I don't know that this is exactly an *error,* but it isn't Gaelic, either. I made it up.

Page 337: "Grants, I supposed. Or Campbells."

"Campbells" should be "Chisholms."

Page 366: typo; "chivying" should be "chivvying."

Page 384: typo; "very" should be "every." ("I'm tired of having to watch ye every minute.")

Page 445: "grey" should be changed to "green."

Page 582: "Fergus nic Leodhas" should be changed to "Fergus mac Leodhas"; "nic" is "daughter of," while "mac" is "son of."

Page 584: Young Jamie's date of birth. Jenny tells her brother that her son turned two years old "last August." This being at the end of October 1743, Jamie Murray would have been born in August 1741. However, Jenny also says her son was "conceived six months past the time I last saw . . . Randall." If she last saw Randall in October 1739, when he took Jamie Fraser to Ft. William, then Jamie Murray would have been conceived in April 1740, and born in January 1741, not August. Oooookay. Change "August" to "January," then.

Page 586: "mi dhu" should be changed to "mo nighean dubh," in accordance with correct Gaelic usage. It means "my black-haired one (girl)."

Page 621: missing open quotes—"He looked so funny. . . ."

Page 632: " . . . sat still by the fire hearth." Remove the word *fire*.

Page 637: Change "*ruadh*" to "*ruaidh.*"

Page 644: first "himself" should be "Himself."

Page 691: "The numbers were one, nine, six, and seven." This refers to the year 1967 (see page 692), and should be changed to ". . . one, nine, six, and eight" (1968). See "1945" p. 519; also "Where Titles Come From."

Page 692: change "Nineteen sixty-seven" to "Nineteen sixty-eight."

Page 768: insert comma. "ripping through a soldier's upper arm, leaving a tuft of shredded fabric flapping."

Page 778: "the black robes of a Franciscan"
Well, here again, it might be an error, and it might not. One researcher with a specialty in church history assured me, after reading *Outlander,* that Franciscans wore brown robes. Upon looking into the matter more thoroughly, though, I discovered that there were assorted suborders of Franciscans, who seem to have been wearing robes in all sorts of colors, from brown and black to gray (the last being called "The Dusty Friars," in consequence). So, the probability may be that Father Anselm should have been wearing the *brown* robes of a Franciscan, but then again, maybe he wasn't.

Page 803: "myrrh leaves"; delete "leaves."
The part of the *Commiphora myrrha* plant used as an aromatic essence ("myrrh") is the crystallized sap, not the leaves.

Page 818: typo; change "solid foot" to "solid food."

Page 833: "1745" should be changed to "1746."

Page 834: "The chart—that cursed chart!—had given the date of his marriage, sometime in 1744. And the birth of his son, Frank's five-times-great-grandfather, soon after." In fact, Jack Randall married early in 1746—but surely by this time we all appreciate just how inaccurate historical documents can be?

Page 834: "1744" should be changed to "1745."

Miscellany

I have had some readers inform me that there could not be wolves in Scotland at the time described, or that it is impossible for a woman to kill a full-grown wolf with her bare hands. Well, maybe so—and maybe no.

Wolves have been extinct in Scotland since the mid-eighteenth century; the last (fairly reliable) recorded sighting that I was able to find was in 1749, and sightings were infrequent for some years before that. However, this does mean that wolves *could* still have been extant in 1743, when Claire encounters a small pack outside Wentworth.

Now, the behavior described for these wolves is not that characteristic of a truly wild pack, but it *is* consistent with that of animals driven out of their usual habitat and forced to rely on scraps and carrion, rather than on free hunting. One would expect adverse effects not only on the behavior of such animals, but on nutrition and general health.

Therefore, while it is unlikely—though not impossible—that a woman could overpower and kill a full-grown wolf under normal circumstances, it's rather more likely that a desperate woman *could* overpower a mangy, underfed animal, which might well be suffering from parasitic disease or nutritional deficiencies.

NB: Recent efforts by the Scottish Wildlife Council to reintroduce wolves in Scotland have been fairly successful. On one trip to Scotland in the early 1990s, I saw several posters, all bearing the full-face likeness of a big, yellow-eyed wolf, teeth showing just ever-so-slightly. "Don't tell *him* he's extinct!" read the legend underneath.

DRAGONFLY IN AMBER

Page 23: "**The Flying Scotsman** could have him in Edinburgh in three hours." More like four or five.

Page 30: Brianna's age

All right. I freely admit that I lose track of dates easily, since I usually stick in something approximate while writing, and then try to tidy it up later. However, I *think* Brianna was born in November 1948. If she was, she would have been nineteen in May of 1968, when introduced to Roger Wakefield. And if *that's* so, then Claire ought to have said, "Bree has another year and a half to go" rather than "Bree has another eight months to go" before being legally allowed to drink alcohol.

Page 168: change "Oh no you don't," to "Oh, no, you don't!"

Page 172: "size-nine shoes"

Now, when I wrote this, it didn't occur to me—never having bought shoes in England—that U.K. sizes would be different than those in the U.S. I therefore envisioned a size-nine foot as being fairly large, but not pontoonlike (I wear a U.S. size six, myself, but my elder daughter, who is 5'8", wears size nine).

In fact, only one person has written to note that the sizes—in 1946—would *not* have been similar, and that an English size nine ladies' shoe would have been truly enormous. The situation is complicated by more recent historical developments, in which the U.K. has entered into commercial arrangements with the European community, and there has—evidently—been a shift in sizing. After considerable conversation with online acquaintances in the U.K.,

Israel, Germany, and assorted other places, it appears that *now,* a size-nine shoe sold in England might be only a bit larger than the equivalent size sold in the United States—but according to the testimony of people alive during Claire's World War II era, the sizing then *was* different. Ergo, I *ought* to have given her a size six or the like, in the interests of historical accuracy—but if I had done so, I would have given modern-day readers an inaccurate impression of exactly how big her feet *are.*

The bottom line is that I have no idea whether this ought to be considered an error or not—but Claire's feet measure roughly ten inches, heel to toe. The reader may choose an appropriate shoe size to reflect this, depending on the reader's country of origin, age, and general interest in the matter.

Page 184: insert comma; "You *know* it's not Frank,"

Page 196: "producing a sound wedged somewhere in the crack between E-flat and D-sharp."
This is one of those nonerrors that people feel obliged to call to my attention, pointing out that E-flat and D-sharp are the same note. I am aware of this, having a minor degree in music, and so is Claire; she's exaggerating the discordance of Jamie's voice, in implying that he can hit a note that's so wrong it doesn't even exist. So much for hyperbole!

Page 201: a scene slightly out of place. This scene is ostensibly the first time we've met Annalise de Marillac, but in fact we have already encountered her a few pages earlier. This is what comes of writing in pieces and gluing them together.

Page 205: size-nine shoes again.

Page 283: "middle of one of Madame Elise's salon"—remove the second "of"; should be "middle of one Madame Elise's salon."

Page 349: "Do no harm."
It is a popular misconception that the Hippocratic Oath begins with the phrase "Do no harm." In fact, it doesn't, but the notion that a physician should refrain from making things worse is definitely embodied in the oath (the complete text of the oath itself is given in *Voyager,* page 716) so this appeared to be a reasonable bit of poetic license, and was certainly much more graceful when incorporated into the existing dialogue.

Page 411: "in to" should be "into"; "popped the sausage whole into his mouth."

Page 465: insert hyphen between "coelis" and "et"; "in-coelis-et-in-terra."

Page 479: delete sentence "She accepted Claire's proffered note to Jamie." I have no

idea where this sentence came from. I have no memory of writing it, and it makes no sense in the context of the story. I'm used to the spontaneous generation of typographical errors, but this is the first time I've seen a whole erroneous sentence create itself.

Page 489: insert "in"; "wisps drifting in the languid air."

Page 570: change "*mi dhu*" to "*mo nighean dubh.*"

Page 586: change "*Mo cridh*" to "*Mo chridhe*"

Page 643: insert comma; "grinned up at his commander, . . ."

Page 770: change "mearchin'" to "meachin'." A dialect form of "meaching," this meaning is "obsequious, servile, skulking."

Page 778: "But my hands grew damp at the thought, and I wiped them unobtrusively on my robe." Actually, at this point Claire is still wearing her muddy, salt-stained dress; she doesn't change into Father Fogden's spare robe until page 779. So change "robe" to "skirt," if you will, please.

Page 913: "1968."
This is not an error, *if* the dates in *Outlander* are adjusted from 1945 to 1946, and 1967 to 1968 (see discussion of chronology in "Where Titles Comes From"). On the other hand, if they aren't, it is.

VOYAGER

Page 120: change "chess" to "dice."

Page 145: *a charaid(h)?*

Page 223: punctuation error. Change "married couldn't do enough" to "married. Couldn't do enough."

Page 244: change 1945 to 1946.

Page 258: typo. Change "intstead" to "instead."

Pages 373–374: we have a prostitute named Mollie on one page, and Millie on the next. Take your choice, but it ought to be the same name on both pages.

Page 409: change "I drifted down the street" to "As I drifted down the street."

Page 538: "lang-nebbit" shouldn't be italicized; it's Scots, not Gaidhlig.

Page 636: typo. "stop at Lewes" should be "stop at Lewis."

Page 681: "**His eyes were on Fergus,** who was teasing Marsali with an albatross's feather, holding her by one arm and tickling her beneath the chin as she struggled ineffectually to get away."

Well, this is another of the maybe so/maybe no errors. As a few astute readers have pointed out, Fergus has only one hand, and presumably would find it difficult to hold an albatross's feather with his hook. This is perfectly true; on the other hand, I'm not so sure that he isn't holding Marsali's arm with his hook, and using his hand to wield the feather. Naturally, he couldn't be restraining her very effectively in this fashion—but then, he obviously *isn't,* or she wouldn't be struggling "ineffectually," would she?

Page 699: change "out the realm of Kraken" to "out of the realm of Kraken."

Page 709: "**Gideon and his daughter.**"

Okay, it's a fair cop. Claire's not a Bible scholar, and neither am I. It wasn't Gideon, it was Jephthath (Judges 12).

Page 737: punctuation error. Change "thought he'd killed, lank brown hair" to "thought he'd killed. Lank brown hair."

Page 761: insert comma. Change "kirtling it up above my knees and took" to "kirtling it up above my knees, and took."

Page 822: MacKimmie/Joyce

Okay. I admit it, I temporarily lost track of Laoghaire's husbands. She had two before marrying Jamie—Hugh MacKenzie, one of Colum's tacksmen, and then Simon MacKimmie, who fathered Marsali and Joan and died in prison. Only I hadn't taken proper note of Simon, and so had him in one spot as Simon MacKimmie and in another as Simon Joyce, and when I wrote this particular passage, I hadn't yet made up my mind which was right, so included both names, intending to strike out the extraneous one later. Only I didn't.

Page 848: "**How much blood** did ye tell me a person has in his body?" he asked.
"About eight quarts," I said, bewildered. "Why?"

At this point in the story, Claire is under a fair amount of stress, having been attacked by a pirate and seriously wounded. It's therefore understandable that she should have suffered a slight lapse of attention, since she plainly would know that the human body contains an average of eight *pints* of blood, rather than eight quarts.

Page 894: insert period. "Yes, that was his name. Why?"

Page 897: change "MacIvers" to "MacIver."

Page 1024: the Gaidhlig phrase beginning "A Mhìcheal" should be italicized.

Drums of Autumn

Page 83: At the calling of the clans, I am reliably informed, customary usage dictates that the representative of the MacDonalds should call, "Clan Donald is here," rather than "MacDonald is here." This is reasonable usage, given that "MacDonald" really means "son(s) of Donald;" on the other hand, MacLeod, McKuen, MacLaren, and (to the best of my knowledge) all other "Mac" clans don't do this, but call according to the "Mac" form of the name. On the third hand, nobody says custom has to be consistent, and if Clan Donald wants to call itself that, it's certainly fine by me.

Page 94: The same vigilant horticulturists who objected to the cherry season in Scotland are still on the job regarding the proper season for peaches in the Carolinas. Hmm. Possibly it does not occur to these helpful souls that the weather patterns might have been slightly different in the 1700s than they are now? (Maybe they weren't, too, but I take my defenses where I can find them.)

Page 131: A helpful French-speaking reader wrote to inquire why I had called Fergus's male child "Germaine," this being the strictly female spelling of said name. Well . . . because I don't speak French, and none of my French dictionaries and idiom books included proper names, that's why. Change "Germaine" to "Germain," throughout, please.

Page 139: typo; change "*breois voluptas*" to "*brevis voluptas.*"

Page 139: typo; change "*veneiis*" to "*veneris.*"

Page 225: change "Thou" to "Thee."

Page 229: insert comma. Change "dribbled down staining the blanket" to "dribbled down, staining the blanket."

Pages 333, 336: "Glenmorangie" is one word, not two.

Page 333: "then" should be "hen"; "That's not it, hen, and you know it."

Page 420: Moravians.
This was a matter of some mild confusion to me, since varying sources informed me that the Moravians were a) from Moravia (a likely story), which is in part of modern-day Czechoslovakia (or whatever they're calling it these days), and therefore spoke something like Slovakian, *and* that b) the Moravians who settled in North Carolina spoke German. Since I needed German-speakers (I thought it doubtful that Jamie spoke either Czech or Slovakian, but I did know he could speak German), I opted merely to mention the Moravians in a doubtful tone of voice, and feature the Muellers and Pastor Gottfried as German Lutherans—who were certainly *there,* and who also certainly spoke German.

However, I am now reliably informed that the Moravian settlement at Salem (which may appear in one of the future books) *was* composed of German-speaking people, who were merely called Moravians because the religious movement to which they were attached originated in Moravia. So there, now we've got that straight. Not that it matters, since there aren't actually any Moravians in any of the first four books, but we like to be as accurate as possible anyway.

Page 500: insert comma. Change "Fresh, too—see the sap's not dried" to "Fresh, too—see, the sap's not dried."

Page 520: knitting.

Again, here's one of those maybe so/maybe no bits. I knew there were such things as straight knitting needles in the eighteenth century, but that's about all I knew about them. I therefore asked one of my knowledgeable friends, who is a crafts expert, about the history of knitting needles, wanting to know whether such things as circular knitting needles existed at the time.

She replied with a great deal of useful and valuable information, including a description of something called "knitting sheaths," made of steel wire, and (I gathered) used to hold excess stitches while working on a large garment. This, of course, is what circular knitting needles do, and I promptly made a mental leap, equating the two—and provided Claire with circular knitting needles in her basket, as well as the quadruple double-pointed needles for turning stocking heels.

As I later learned from the experts of the CompuServe Crafts Forum, a knitting sheath is *not* the same thing as a circular needle, and while the double-pointed needles are historically accurate, the circular ones aren't. On the other hand, they all added, they loved the scene, and we are writing fiction here rather than history, aren't we?

Page 528: "the the." Pick one, discard the other.

Page 696: Change "silent for moment." to "silent for a moment."

Page 847: Insert period after "fight"; "It was a fair fight. I said."

Page 1070: Insert comma; "brushing sand from her skirts, and bent."

Now, I don't by any means claim that this listing of errata is complete. I now and then get helpful letters or e-mail pointing out some small inaccuracy (perceived or real), which invariably conclude with the writer kindly assuring me that this is really pretty good, if they've found only one error in umpty-zillion pages! I thank them graciously, and refrain from telling them about the errors they didn't happen to notice.

Appendix II

Gaelic
(Gaidhlig)
Resources

———

A Writer's Short Guide
to Scottish Speech Patterns
Using Scots and Gaelic in Dialogue

I get a number of letters from writers who want to use a Scottish setting in their books, asking me for advice and information on using "Gaelic" in the dialogue of their characters, as they've found my handling of Scottish "brogue" to be effective. I usually write back to tell them that if they really mean to use Gaelic, I'm afraid the effect is not going to be quite what they think.

With the basic disclaimer that I Am Not a Scot:

A good many people are under the misapprehension that Gaelic and Scots are the same thing, and are likewise confused about the difference between a dialect and an accent. In hopes of lending some small clarification to these matters, following is a short (and highly inexpert) observation on Scottish speech patterns:

"Scots" is an honest-to-goodness *dialect* of the English language. By this, I mean that it is basically English (and can be—more or less—understood by an English speaker), but has its own specific and distinguishable idiom, sentence structure, and vocabulary. In its most exaggerated form, it's called "broad Scots," ("braid Scots") which is the highly accented form of the dialect, in which Robbie Burns wrote his poetry ("wee cow'rin', sleekit, timorous beastie," etc.).

Gaelic, on the other hand, is a completely different *language,* spoken (in differing forms) by Scottish Highlanders and the Irish (it is the official language of Ireland, and is taught in the schools—but is not in common use by most of the inhabitants). Both forms of Gaelic are referred to as "Erse" in older reference texts, and the modern Scottish movement prefers to spell their form of the language as "Gaidhlig" (so as to reject English influence), just to make things more confusing.

As a brief example: "My bonny wee lassie"

is a Scots endearment—"*Mo nighean donn*" is the Gaelic equivalent (literally, it means "my brown-haired girl"). Spoken (or sung) Gaelic sounds like nothing you've ever heard before, and definitely wouldn't be understood by an English speaker.

Now, Gaelic in Scotland is spoken only in the Highlands (and is not all that common there, though the Scottish Nationalist movement has spurred new interest in preserving and encouraging the language. [In terms of the *Outlander* books, Gaelic would likely have been fairly common in the 1940s, but still restricted to the Highlands]). Scots is spoken throughout Scotland, but occurs in broad form mostly in the Lowlands—if you've heard Glaswegians, you've heard the broadest—and most idiosyncratic—Scots there is. Highlanders, by contrast, speak fairly pure English, in that there is not a great deal of accent or peculiar vocabulary to their speech, though they do use the Scots idiom and sentence structure.

Now, accent and dialect. As I mentioned above, a dialect has a peculiar idiom, vocabulary, and sentence structure. To illustrate the latter point—

An American hotel clerk will say, "Can I help you?"

An English clerk will say, "May I help you, please?"

A Highland clerk will say, "Can I be helpin' ye at all, then?"

Likewise,

An American will say, "Sorry, I don't remember that."

An Englishman will say, "I'm afraid I don't recall that."

And a Scot *may* say (if he's being old-fashioned about it), "Aye, well, I canna just charge my memory about that, I'm afraid."

In general, the occasional dropping of the terminal "g" ("helpin'," "doin'") is a characteristic of Scots dialect, as is the common insertion of "particle" words at the beginning or end of a sentence—things like "then," "aye," "well," or "man," which aren't necessary to the meaning of the sentence, but give the speech a characteristic rhythm. Example: "Ye canna be doin' that, man!"

By contrast, the slight oddities of pronunciation—"canna" for "cannot," "didna" for "didn't," "ye" for "you" (or however an individual writer chooses to render these expressions)—are *accent* rather than dialect. Consequently, they vary in the strength and frequency of their usage among individuals, and they aren't invariable in either usage or form. That is, a given person may use both "you" and "ye" in a single sentence, and does not *have* to say, "I canna do that," every time. If one is writing Scottish dialect, in some cases, "I cannot" will sound better, and it is perfectly all right to use the unaccented form when it does.

Now, representation of Scots dialect in written form is another question altogether. When writing accented speech, representation is a matter of judgment on the writer's part. You may use "canna," "cannae," "can na" or whatever seems best to you and easiest on the reader's eye and comprehension.

Two general points of advice:

1) "Eye dialect" spellings (strictly phonetic spellings that often involve a lot of apostrophes) are more difficult to read.

2) Accent is best used sparingly when writing dialogue. Too much of it is both jarring to the ear and hard on the eye. It's better to depend more on idiom and sentence structure than on accent to get the "flavor" of speech, without annoying the reader.

It's a common mistake among authors writing Scottish characters to write straight English dialogue, merely substituting "ye" for "you" throughout (the most irritating ones also put "yer" for "your," which is characteristic of some kinds of Irish speech, but not usually of Scots, though lower-class Lowlanders and some people from the northern parts of England do it sometimes). If you listen to Scots speak, they don't invariably say "ye"—sometimes the word sounds like "ye" (especially at the beginnings of sentences) and frequently it's clearly "you," depending on the rhythm of the sentence and the words surrounding the pronoun. Making it "ye" every time makes the sentences read awkwardly, I think, and the rhythms of English and Scots are distinctly different.

If you are writing about the historical Highlands, and you do want to give your Highlander a salting of Gaelic (it's useful for picturesque cursing where you want to make it clear that a person is using dreadful invective[1] by the shocked expression of his companions—without offending your readers or having to try to think up accurate period curses that will still sound like bad language to your readers), you can use the occasional Gaelic phrase or sentence, provided (as with any other foreign-language insertion) that you make the meaning clear—whether you do this through direct translation or merely by context.

As with any writing that involves the British Isles, the language of the characters will be affected by their social class. Lower-class Scots do not speak the same as upper-class Scots, though both may use similar

---

[1] I'm told that Gaidhlig cursing depends much more on colorful expression and imaginative relationships than on "bad language"—i.e., swear words—as such.

expressions, depending on the circumstances of the story. Lower-class characters will tend to use more strongly accented speech; upper-class characters will use fairly clear standard English—though often with the unique Scots sentence structures and idioms. Lower-class characters are likely to show more strongly accented dialect.

Obviously, making effective use of dialect and accent depends on developing a good "ear" for these elements. One thing I've found useful is to listen to tapes of Scottish bands and singers; beyond the lyrics of the songs themselves, the bands in "live" recordings will often banter with the audience between numbers, giving you a chance to hear real Scots talk naturally.

Novels set in Scotland—preferably written by native Scots—are also helpful. One very good reference, which includes several meticulously rendered Scottish accents from different social classes, is Dorothy L. Sayers's *Five Red Herrings* (Sayers wasn't Scottish, but she had a wonderful ear and a painstaking approach to nuances of accent and social class). I'd also recommend *The Big Book of Scottish Stories,* which is composed entirely of stories—both historical and contemporary—by Scottish authors, and gives a wide range of depicted accents and idioms. For more modern depictions of Scottish speech, the novels of Irvine Welsh or Iain Banks are excellent; Welsh uses very idiomatic (and phonetically spelled) Edinburgh patois, while Banks's characters tend to use clear English, with the Scots structures and idioms simply embedded in the dialogue, rather than shown off.

In my own work, I've used several Gaelic dictionaries (listed later in this appendix), but have also been lucky enough to have the invaluable services of one Iain MacKinnon Taylor, an expatriate Scot and native Gaelic speaker from the Isle of Harris.

Mr. Taylor wrote to me, following the publication of *Dragonfly in Amber,* to say that he very much enjoyed my books, particularly seeing Scottish history treated with such accuracy and respect. However, he continued delicately, he did wonder whether perhaps I was getting my Gaelic from a dictionary?

The words, he gave me to understand, were largely correct, but were not used idiomatically (or, likely, grammatically!), as a real Gaelic-speaker would use them. Would I think it presumptuous of him, he asked, if he were to volunteer to assist with the Gaelic translation, in case I intended writing more books?

To this generous offer, my response was, "Mr. Taylor! Where have you *been* all my life?"

So it's Iain Taylor who (now) vets the Gaelic inclusions in my own books for correctness of grammar and idiom. Consequently, there is a lot more Gaelic in the books than there would be if I were doing this on my own. The usual procedure is for me to write out what I want to say in English, then fax it to Mr. Taylor, who returns me the correct Gaelic version—frequently with additional comments as to appropriate usage.

Mr. Taylor's twin brother, Hamish, also obliges now and then with assistance in particularly difficult bits of translation. Hamish Taylor still lives on Harris, where he is a lay-preacher, preaching in Gaelic every Sunday. As his brother Iain says, "When it comes to cursing, you really need a preacher to get it right!"

MANY PEOPLE WRITE TO ME (evidently under the wildly mistaken impression that I am a Gaelic-speaker) for advice or resources in learning Gaelic themselves. A few have asked me to teach them Gaelic. Unfortunately, I'm not equipped to oblige in this way, but I did think it might be helpful to provide a list of

Gaelic books and resources, for those with an interest in this part of Scottish culture.

I'm indebted to several people from the CompuServe Writers Forum for help in compiling the following list of Gaelic resources (all comments regarding the publications, Web sites, etc., are those of the people recommending them, and are marked with the person's name or initials). —D.G.

BOOKS, TAPES, AND OTHER GAELIC (GAIDHLIG) PUBLICATIONS

One that will be recommended to you often in Scotland if you ask is *Speaking Our Language,* based on a TV series on Grampian Television. It consists of tapes and books, which can be used separately and are produced by a company called Cànan, P.O. Box 345, Isle of Skye IV44 8XA, Scotland. —Barbara Schnell

I myself am using the Teach Yourself series, "Gaelic" by Boyd Robertson and Iain Taylor, published by NTC Publishing Group. Comes with two videos of native Scottish Gaelic-speakers and has grammar, structure, etc. Mine was purchased at a Highland Games, fairly reasonable—about $45.00. I highly recommend it. —Tamara Bernard

First things first: Gaelic is Irish. "Gaidhlig" is Scottish Gaelic (or Gaeilge)—there's a big push in the speaking communities to reclaim the original name of the language and to move away from English influences on the syntax. Here is a brief list of resources:

Am Braighe
P.O. Box 170
Mabou, Nova Scotia
B0E 1X0
Canada

A quarterly bilingual paper out of Cape Breton that focuses on events in the Gaidhlig speaking communities of North America. It's $15.95 (American) for a yearly subscription. In the back it always has a list of publications for Scotophiles, including Gaidhlig learning resources, history books, etc. It's a good read generally.—Michelle LaFrance[2]

(The following titles are from D.G.'s bookshelf; this list includes books on Scots dialect, as well as those dealing with the Gaelic language, as many people seem interested in the overall linguistic environment of Scotland.)

The Concise Scots Dictionary compiled by Alexander Warrack, published by Crescent Books, New York.

The Gaelic Dictionary (This is actually a two-way dictionary; Gaelic to English, English to Gaelic.) by Malcolm Maclennan, published jointly by Acair (a Gaelic-language press) and Aberdeen University Press.

The New English-Gaelic Dictionary (This really *is* only from English to Gaelic, which makes it of limited use. It doesn't always agree with the Maclennan dictionary on spelling, either.) by Derick S. Thomson, published by Gairm Publications, Glasgow.

The Original Patter: A Guide to Current Glasgow Usage by Michael Munro, published by Glasgow District Libraries.

Scottish Proverbs compiled by Nicola Wood, published by W&R Chambers Ltd., Edinburgh.

Scottish Love Poems: A Personal Anthology, compiled by Antonia Fraser, published by Peter Bedrick Books, New York.

The Complete Illustrated Poems, Songs, and Ballads of Robert Burns, published by Chartwell Books, Inc., Edison, N.J.

---

[2]NB: for the sake of clarity, I've divided Michelle's very extensive list among the various classifications of the appendix. Her contributions are initialed.

Teach Yourself Gaelic, by Roderick Mackinnon, published by Teach Yourself Books, Hodder & Stoughton, London. I am told this book is now out of print, but there is a new edition by different authors.

The Pocket Guide to Scottish Words: Place Names, Personal Names, Food and Drink (Scots and Gaelic) by Iseabail MacLeod, published by Richard Drew Publishing Limited, Glasgow.

British/American Language Dictionary (Doesn't involve Scots directly, but an interesting book that deals with differences between the British and American dialects of English.) by Norman Moss, published by Passport Books, National Textbook Company, Lincolnwood, Ill.

The Giant Book of Scottish Short Stories, edited by Carl MacDougall, published by Peter Bedrick Books, New York. (Includes many stories written in broad Scots dialect, as well as those containing only occasional Scots or Gaidhlig elements.)

A Tongue in Yer Heid: A Selection of the Best Contemporary Short Stories in Scots, edited by James Robertson, published by B&W Publishing, Edinburgh.

BOOKSTORES AND MAIL-ORDER RESOURCES

For the person who wants to study on their own—I've (MLF) had luck finding rare stuff at these two bookstores:

Sandy Publications/An Crann Corp.
P.O. Box 179
Mabou, NS
Canada B0E 1X0

For $6, plus shipping, they'll send you a lovely and extensive catalog of Gairm publications and other stuff that's near impossible to get in the States. Verb wheels, pronoun flash cards, you name it.

Thistle and Shamrock Books
P.O. Box 42
Alexandria, VA 22313

This is my personal favorite place to get my oddball Gaidhlig supplies, because Rory Mor, the proprietor, really does aim to please. He has fantastic contacts in Scotland and can get anything you want rare or used, if you give him some time to come up with it.

And then there's:

GAIRM
29 Sràid Bhatairliù
Glaschu, G2 6BZ
Alba

(or "Glasgow, Scotland," just in case the Scottish postal system isn't up on its Gaidhlig. —D.G.)

Gairm is the premiere Gaidhlig resource publisher. —Michelle LaFrance

Scottish Images
This is a mail order company specializing in Scottish and Celtic artifacts, music, books, and videos. Email for free catalog, at scotimages@aol.com, or call at 1-800-700-0334.

ASSOCIATIONS AND SOCIAL ORGANIZATIONS

An Comunn Gaidhealach Ameriga (The American Gaelic Learners Association)
P.O. Box 5288
Takoma Park, MD 20913

This is the largest—and I believe the oldest—Gaidhlig association in the States. They offer immersions, classes, private tutoring, and other cultural events. (MLF)

Bay Area Scottish Gaelic Learner's Association
3611 Walnut Street
Lafayette, CA 94549
E-mail: scotgaelic@earthlink.net
They are a great group of teachers and performers. Immersions, classes, etc. (MLF)

Slighe Nan Gaidheal
(The Way of the Gael, Seattle Scottish Gaidhlig Society)
P.O. Box 20667
Seattle, WA 98112
They offer weekly language classes, weekend immersions, Gaidhlig Choir, First Footing, traditional Waulking Parties, a Gaidhlig Poetry Guild, and other performances. (Michelle LaFrance, Slighe Nan Gaidheal)

COLLEGES, SCHOOLS, AND OTHER EDUCATIONAL PROGRAMS

Canan
P.O. Box 345
Isle of Skye
IV44 8XA
Scotland
Immersions, tours, books, classes. Affiliated somehow with Sabhal Mor.

Gaelic Summer School at the Gaelic College
P.O. Box 9
Baddeck, Nova Scotia
BOE 1BO
Canada
They do week-long intensives in the summer (for all levels of students) that are quite reasonable.

Sabhal Mor Ostaig
Teangue, Sleat
Isle of Skye
Scotland, IV44 8RQ
E-mail: oifis@smo.uhi.ac.uk
www.smo.uhi.ac.uk
Sabhal Mor is the Gaelic College on Sleat. They offer business, computer, and management classes all in Gaidhlig, as well as immersions, classes, and other events for the learner. I'd give my eyeteeth to study there for a quarter. Abair Sin! (Michelle LaFrance, Slighe Nan Gaidheal)

SCOTTISH/CELTIC/GAELIC WEB SITES, LISTSERVES, AND E-MAIL ADDRESSES OF INTEREST[3]

www.ceantar.org has links to various Gaelic organizations (Irish, Scottish, Manx) and the North American Assn. of Celtic Language Teachers.

UNC at Chapel Hill: sunsite.unc.edu:80/gaelic.
Six Celtic languages represented. Discussion of language and culture. (Sandra Parshall)

Bay Area Scottish Gaelic Learner's Association: E-mail: scotgaelic@earthlink.net.

Additionally, there are two Internet lists that are pretty good for the learner. You'll see other lists that are more high-profile, but that aren't as accommodating for beginners.

---

[3]Please note that Web sites do change, add links, or disappear now and then; I can't guarantee that these sites will be in existence, or in the form described, by the time this book is published.

Gaidhlig-B

To register, send an e-mail to: LISTSERV @LISTSERV.HEA.IE with "SUBSCRIBE GAIDHLIG-B [full-name]" as the subject header (do not include quotes in header).

GAIDHLIG 4U

Send an e-mail to: Majordomo@lists .sonic.net with "subscribe gaidhlig 4U [e-mail address]" as the subject (do not include quotes). (Michelle LaFrance)

Appendix III

Poems and Quotations

One of the aspects of eighteenth-century literature and letters that I particularly enjoy is the frequent and easy use of quotes and classical allusion. In the eighteenth century, an educated man (or woman; there were not a few) would have been familiar with the best-known of the classical writers, and it was common to employ both specific references and less direct allusion, both as a means of establishing one's social credentials, and—I suspect—for fun.

One of the small advantages of writing historical fiction from a well-documented period is the ability to use elements of the style *of* that period in the narration of the book. When it's well done, this gives the story a pervasive atmosphere that adds to the overall impression of authenticity. (When it's not well done, the less said, the better. This is one of those stylistic tricks that can backfire, if the writer doesn't have a firm grip on it.)

This particular technique is most obvious in books set during the Civil War. I've seldom seen a popular book of this kind that didn't employ some form of the courtly, formal, Bible-cadenced language seen in nineteenth-century documents (My husband calls it the "PBS Voice-over Effect"). In fact, the audience for Civil War material is so used to this style that it would be difficult to produce a popular mainstream book set in this period that did *not* use such language, and have it be well accepted.

Since the *Outlander* books are told primarily from the point of view of Claire Beauchamp Randall, the prevailing idiom is not eighteenth-century Scots, but World War II–vintage British English—articulate, educated, but slangy and humorous, spiced with casual profanity. However, those sections of the later books that are told, for example, from the point of view of Jamie Fraser or Lord John Grey, tend to use the circumlocu-tions and elegant structures of the eighteenth century.

For both the university-educated person of the 1930s and the 1940s,[1] and the mid–eighteenth century, though, wide reading and an easy habit of quotation were natural attributes. It's therefore a natural notion for Jamie to have inscribed in Claire's ring a brief phrase from Catullus—while it's likewise natural for Claire to quote Housman and Coleridge.

Being neither British nor a classics scholar myself, I asked and browsed, in order to come up with appropriate poetry, expressions, etc. Some poems and quotations were sent to me by friends online who knew what I was doing and came across something they thought might suit now and then; some I found in the course of the research for the novels—and some came ready to hand, given that while not a literary scholar, I do read a lot.

I also used frequent Biblical quotation and allusion, because of the common usage of such allusion in the eighteenth-century style, because it was suited to the metaphysical and spiritual concerns of the books—and because it's beautiful.[2]

Now, I'm not sure whether I should feel slighted or not, but I don't get a lot of mail

---

[1] *While not university-educated in the usual sense, Claire has an equivalent cultural background, owing to her unorthodox upbringing and her marriage to an academic.*

[2] *Personally, I'm a hardcore King James version reader; I think the New American Bible is heresy, just on aesthetic grounds, and you don't even want to **know** what I think about gender-neutral scriptures. Don't talk to me about inclusion; I'd rather be referred to as "mankind" than be included in something so clumsily written. St. Jerome and the Vulgate are fine, and the Douay-Rheims version is okay, too—but the King James stands as possibly the only excellent piece of work ever produced by a committee.*

from prisons. You'd think long books would be appealing in that venue, but maybe not.

So far, I believe I've only received three letters from incarcerated persons (not that I'm complaining, mind you). One of these, though, was from a gentleman who requested the entire text of the Catullus poem that Jamie refers to in *Outlander*. He said that the concept struck him as most romantic, and he would like to letter the poem in calligraphy as a present for his wife—adding that she had been through a lot, and he would like to make it up to her.

I couldn't refuse a request like that, so I sent the poem. I've since had many requests for the text of the poem—and some others quoted in the *Outlander* novels—and so have decided to list the sources for poetry and quotations used in the novels,[3] for the benefit of the curious.

In some cases, where copyright (and the author's energy) permits, I've included the whole text of short poems. Where a poem was unavailable or too long to type out in its entirety, only the portion quoted is given.

LATIN POETRY

A working knowledge of Latin and Greek and an appreciation for the major works of the ancient philosophers were hallmarks of a "man of worth"—a gentleman—in the eighteenth century. Jamie, grandson of a noble (even if illegitimate), and nephew of a clan chieftain, has certainly been well educated, and thus well versed in ancient languages and writings. Small wonder that he turns to these both as expressions of his love for Claire, and as tutoring for his beloved nephew Ian.

The Catullus poem referred to in *Outlander* is titled "Lesbia," and was translated in the seventeenth century by Richard Crashaw;[4] both the original Latin and the English translation (with original spelling) are shown here. Both

versions were sent to me originally by Janet McConnaughey, an online friend from the CompuServe Literary Forum, whose knowledge of poetry and lyrics is simply staggering. Having read the scene in which Jamie gives Claire the silver ring, Janet suggested that perhaps *da mi basia mille* would be appropriate as an inscription.

I liked the notion, but wanted to use somewhat more of the poem than would fit inside the average ring. I therefore used small quotations from the poem in the course of the dialogue in *Outlander,* referring to the inscription only later, in *Dragonfly in Amber.*

LESBIA

Vivamus, mea Lesbia, atque amemus,
rumoresque senum severiorum
omnes unius aestimemus assis.
soles occidere et redire possunt:
nobis cum semel occidit brevis lux,
nox est perpetua una dormienda.
da mi basia mille, deinde centum,
dein mille altera, dein secunda centum,
deinde usque altera mille, deinde centum.
dein, cum milia multa fecerimus,
conturbabimus illa, ne sciamus,
aut nequis malus invidere possit,
cum tantum sciat esse basiorum.

—Catullus (84?–54 B.C.)

---

[3]*So far as I can. I don't claim this appendix is absolutely complete; I don't keep track of quotations as I write, so was obliged to cruise back through the novels, picking them out. Consequently, I may well have missed one here or there.*
[4]*Doubtless by a few other people before and since; however, I like Crashaw, and his translation is also out of copyright, which allows me to reprint the entire text.*

Come and let us live my Deare,
Let us love and never feare,
What the sowrest Fathers say:
Brightest **Sol** that dyes to day
Lives againe as blith to morrow,
But if we darke sons of sorrow
Set; o then, how long a Night
Shuts the eye of our short light!
Then let amorous kisses dwell
On our lips, begin and tell
A Thousand, and a Hundred, score
An Hundred, and a Thousand more,
Till another Thousand smother
That, and that wipe of another.
Thus at last when we have numbred
Many a Thousand, many a Hundred;
Wee'l confound the reckoning quite,
And lose our selves in wild delight:
While our joyes so multiply,
As shall mocke the envious eye.

> —translation by Richard Crashaw
> (1612?—1649)

When Jamie is faced with the grave responsibility of training his nephew Ian to be a "man of worth" himself, he turns from the sensual delights of Catullus to the sterner "Vertue" of Plautus:

VERTUE

Virtus praemium est optimum;
virtus omnibus rebus anteit profecto:
libertas salus vita res et parentes, patria et prognati
tutantur, servantur:
virtus omnia in sese habet, omnia adsunt
bona quem penest virtus.

> —from *Amphitryon,* Plautus
> (254?–184 B.C.)

Verily Vertue dothe all thinges excelle.
For if librtie, helthe, lyvyng and substance,
Our country, our parentes and children do well
It hapneth by vertue; she doth all aduance.
Vertue hath all thinges under gouernaunce,
And in whom of vertue is founden great
    plentie,
Any thinge that is good may neuer be deintie.

> —translation by Sir Thomas Elyot
> (1531)

And later still, as stimulus and mental refreshment amid bodily labors, Jamie recites from the "Meditations" of Marcus Aurelius Antonius: (A.D. 121–180)

"'Body, soul, and mind,'" Jamie said, translating as he bent to seize the end of another trimmed log. "'The body for sensation, the soul for the springs of action, the mind for principles. Yet the capacity for sensation belongs also to the stalled ox; there is no wild beast or degenerate but obeys the twitchings of impulse; and even men who deny the gods, or betray their country, or'—careful, man!"

Ian, thus warned, stepped neatly backward over the ax handle, and turned to the left, steering his end of the burden carefully round the corner of the half-built log wall.

"'—or perpetrate all manner of villainy behind locked doors, have minds to guide them to the clear path of duty,'" Jamie resumed Marcus Aurelius's **Meditations.** "'Seeing then'—step up. Aye, good, that's got it—'seeing then that all else is in common heritage of such types, the good man's only singularity lies in his approving welcome to every experience the looms of fate may weave for him, his refusal to soil the divinity seated in his breast or perturb it with disorderly impressions . . .' All right, now, one, and two, and . . . **ergh!**"

> —*Drums of Autumn,* Chapter 20, page 371

By contrast, Claire's Latin is less formal:
"All I remember is *Arma virumque cano.*" I glanced at Ian and translated, grinning. "My arm got bit off by a dog."[5]

GREEK QUOTES

While an educated eighteenth-century gentleman might have been as familiar with the Greek poets and philosophers as with the Romans, I'm not. There's also the minor consideration that original Greek quotations are written in ... ah ... Greek. This is a major pain in the neck for typesetters and copy editors.

Therefore, most of the classical allusions in the novels are Latin. For the sake of accurate representation, though, I did include one brief exchange in Greek, between Jamie and Lord John Grey, during the Incident of the Snake in the Privy (*Drums,* chapter 25, "Enter a Serpent").

The references used here [pp. 481–482] are not literal, but only allusive; Epicharmus *did* say philosophical things about the oracle at Delphi, but the quote attributed to him is only a rough approximation.

CELTIC INVOCATIONS

While Greek and Latin were the languages of an educated eighteenth-century man, Gaidhlig (Gaelic) was the language of the Scottish Highlander. A rich and beautiful language, this Celtic tongue gives voice to prayer and poetry.

During the late part of the nineteenth century, an exciseman and scholar named Alexander Carmichael performed a great service to future generations by collecting a massive amount of traditional Gaelic oral lore: poems, prayers, songs, incantations, charms, and hymns, which were published early in the twentieth century as the *Carmina Gadel-*

ica. This collection has been reprinted in various volumes and forms over the years; the particular volume I used as a source for the *Outlander* books is a small portion of the work, published separately as *Celtic Invocations* (the complete bibliographic citation will be found in the Annotated Bibliography).

I used small bits of several of the invocations and prayers from this huge collection, as seemed appropriate to the occasion. While only parts of the prayers are actually quoted in the novels, I've included the entire text of each prayer as follows.[6]

---

[5]*My husband, who took Latin in school, originally contributed this gem (as well as the information that the quote is from Virgil,* **The Aeneid***). He prefers the variation "My arm was run over by a dog on a motorcycle" (virumque,* **vroom-kay,** *motorcycle ... geddit?)—but since the allusion would be lost on Ian, Claire likely would use the less sophisticated (ahem) form.*

Oh—for the benefit of those who **didn't** *take Latin in school, the quote actually is translated: "Of arms and a man I sing."*

[6]*Both Celtic and English versions are per Carmichael.*

THE BATTLE TO COME
VOLUME 1, PAGE 113

Jesus, Thou Son of Mary, I call on Thy name,
And on the name of John the apostle beloved,
And on the names of all the saints in the red
domain,
To shield me in the battle to come,
  To shield me in the battle to come.

When the mouth shall be closed,
When the eye shall be shut,
When the breath shall cease to rattle,
When the heart shall cease to throb,
  When the heart shall cease to throb.

When the Judge shall take the throne,
And when the cause is fully pleaded,
O Jesu, Son of Mary, shield Thou my soul,
O Michael fair, acknowledge my departure.
  O Jesu, Son of Mary, shield Thou my soul!
  O Michael fair, receive my departure!

Claire begins this prayer, as her blessing to
Jamie when they prepare to part on the
morning of the Battle of Culloden, but is interrupted by the arrival of English soldiers.
[*Outlander*]

SOUL PEACE
VOLUME 1, PAGE 121

Since Thou Christ it was who didst buy
  the soul—
At the time of yielding the life,
At the time of pouring the sweat,
At the time of offering the clay,
At the time of shedding the blood,
At the time of balancing the beam,
At the time of severing the breath,
At the time of delivering the judement,
Be its peace upon Thine own ingathering.
Jesus Christ Son of gentle Mary,
  Be its peace upon Thine own ingathering,
O Jesus! Upon Thine own ingathering.

And may Michael white kindly,
High king of the holy angels,
Take possession of the beloved soul,
And shield it home to the Three of surpassing
  love,
    Oh! To the Three of surpassing love.

(This is the prayer that Jamie recommends to
Young Ian, for use when one has been compelled to kill in battle or in self-defense. Or, if
time is too short to allow for this, he recommends the shorter version, "Soul Leading."
[*Dragonfly*]

THE SOUL LEADING
VOLUME 1, PAGE 117

By this soul on Thine arm, O Christ,
Thou King of the City of Heaven.
  Amen.

Since Thou, O Christ, it was who brought'st
  this soul,
Be its peace on Thine own keeping.
  Amen.

And may the strong Michael, high king of the
  angels,
Be preparing the path before this soul, O God.
  Amen.

Oh! the strong Michael in peace with thee,
  soul,
And preparing for thee the way to the kingdom
  of the Son of God.
  Amen.

HOUSE PROTECTING
VOLUME 1, PAGE 103

God, bless the world and all that is therein.
God, bless my spouse and my children,
God, bless the eye that is in my head,

And bless, O God, the handling of my hand;
What time I rise in the morning early,
What time I lie down late in bed,
    Bless the rising in the morning early,
    And my lying down late in bed.

God, protect the house, and the household,
God, consecrate the children of the motherhood,
God, encompass the flocks and the young;
Be Thou after them and tending them,
What time the flocks ascend hill and wold,
What time I lie down to sleep,
    What time the flocks ascend hill and wold,
    What time I lie down in peace to sleep.

(This is the blessing prayer that Jamie speaks at the laying of the hearthstone on Fraser's Ridge, in *Drums of Autumn*.)

[*Drums*, pp. 368–69]
THE DRIVING
(AN SAODACHADH)
VOLUME IV, PAGE 43

The protection of Odhran the dun be yours,
The protection of Brigit the Nurse be yours,
The protection of Mary the Virgin be yours
    In marshes and in rocky ground,
    In marshes and in rocky ground.

The keeping of Ciaran the swart be yours,
The keeping of Brianan the yellow be yours,
The keeping of Diarmuid the brown be yours,
    A-sauntering the meadows,
    A-sauntering the meadows.

The safeguard of Fionn son of Cumhall be yours,
The safeguard of Cormac the shapely be yours,
The safeguard of Conn and Cumhall be yours
    From wolf and from bird-flock,
    From wolf and from bird-flock.

The sanctuary of Colum Cille be yours,
The sanctuary of Maol Ruibhe be yours,
The sanctuary of the milking Maid be yours,

To seek you and search for you,
To seek you and search for you.

The encircling of Maol Odhrian be yours,
The encircling of Maol Oighe be yours,
The encircling of Maol Domhnaich be yours,
    To protect you and to herd you,
    To protect you and to herd you.

The shield of the King of the Fiann be yours
The shield of the King of the sun be yours
The shield of the King of the stars be yours
    In jeopardy and distress,
    In jeopardy and distress.

The sheltering of the King of Kings be yours,
The sheltering of Jesus Christ be yours,
The sheltering of the Spirit of healing be yours,
    From evil deed and quarrel,
    From evil dog and red dog.

(Duncan Innes uses portions of this incantation for the protection of the stock, while helping to bless the hearthstone at Fraser's Ridge.)

[*Voyager*, p. 954]
THE DEATH BLESSING
VOLUME 1, PAGE 119
"**God, omit not** this woman from Thy covenant, and the many evils that she in the body committed."

—traditional Celtic invocation, from *Carmina Gadelica*

BIBLICAL QUOTES[7]

[*Voyager*, p. 196]
"*O, Lucifer, thou son of the morning . . .*"
    Lord John is paraphrasing slightly; the correct (and complete) quote is: "How art

---

[7]*All Biblical quotes are taken from the King James version.*

thou fallen from heaven, O Lucifer, son of the morning!"

—Isaiah 14:12

[*Voyager,* p. 815]
"**My beloved's arm** is under me, and his hand behind my head. Comfort me with apples, and stay me with flagons, for I am sick of love." (Note that Claire has—as she now and then does—slightly misquoted this; the actual quote is "Stay me with flagons, comfort me with apples: for I am sick of love.")

—Song of Solomon 2:5

[*Drums,* p. 161]
"**Sufficient unto the day** is the evil thereof." Matthew 6:34

Frank's favorite Biblical saying (for good reason), repeated now and then by both Claire and Brianna.

[*Drums,* p. 224]
"**Thy neck is as** *a tower of ivory; thine eyes like the fishpools in Heshbon, by the gate of Bathrabbim: thy nose is as the tower of Lebanon which looketh toward Damascus.*"

Claire and Philip Wylie are trading lines from the Song of Solomon 7:4.

[*Drums,* p. 242]
"**Whither thou goest . . .**"

"And Ruth said, Entreat me not to leave thee, or to return from following after thee: for whither thou goest, I will go: and where thou lodgest, I will lodge: thy people shall be my people, and thy God my God:

"Where thou diest, will I die, and there will I be buried: the Lord do so to me, and more also, if aught but death part thee and me."

—Book of Ruth 1:16

While often used as a reading in wedding ceremonies—and as Claire uses it here, to proclaim attachment to a mate—this very moving declaration of devotion is in fact the words of a woman for her mother-in-law; the words of Ruth for Naomi.

[*Drums,* p. 245]
"**Blessed are the merciful,** for they shall obtain mercy."

—The Beatitudes, the Sermon on the Mount, Matthew, 5:7

Dragonfly, p. 944]
"**Blessed are those** *who have not seen, and yet have believed.*"

—The Gospel According to John 20:29

[*Dragonfly,* p. 503]
"**Remember, man,** *that thou are dust, and unto dust thou shalt return.*"

This is part of the Catholic liturgy, recited during the imposition of ashes on Ash Wednesday, at the beginning of Lent. The

original basis is a line from Genesis: "In the sweat of thy face shalt thou eat bread, till thou return unto the ground; for out of it wast thou taken: for dust thou art, and unto dust shalt thou return."

—Genesis 3:19

Miscellaneous English, Scottish, and American Poetry

[*Outlander*, p. 105]

The Selkirk Grace

Some hae meat that canna eat,
And some could eat that want it.
But we hae meat and we can eat,
And so may God be thankit.

—Robert Burns (1759–1796)
[See note in Appendix I,
"Errata"]

[*Outlander*, p. 121]

Hurley, hurley, round the table,
Eat as muckle as you're able.
Eat muckle, pooch nane,
Hurley, hurley, Amen.

I don't for the life of me remember where I got this, and my usual authority, Jack Whyte, can't place it either, though he says "hurley" sounds like the Aberdeen area. We'll call it folk verse and leave it at that, unless anybody knows better.

[*Dragonfly*, p. 547]
Requiem

Under the wide and starry sky,
Dig the grave and let me lie.
Glad did I live and gladly die,
And I laid me down with a will.

This be the verse you grave for me:
Here he lies where he longed to be;
Home is the sailor, home from the sea,
And the hunter home from the hill.

—Robert Louis Stevenson
(1850–1894)

[*Voyager*, p. 446]
Oh, what a tangled web we weave,
When first we practice to deceive!

—from "Marmion," Sir Walter Scott
(1771–1832)

[*Voyager*, p. 486]
Home is the place where, when you have to go
there,
They have to take you in.

—from "The Death of the Hired Man,"
Robert Frost (1874–1963)

[*Voyager*, p. 763]
Water, water, everywhere . . .
Water, water, everywhere,
and all the boards did shrink.
Water, water, everywhere
Nor any drop to drink.

—from "The Rime of the Ancient Mariner,"
Samuel Coleridge (1772–1834)

I will arise and go now, and go to Innisfree,
And a small cabin build there, of clay and
wattles made:
Nine bean-rows will I have there, a hive for
the honeybee,
And live alone in the bee-loud glade.

—from "The Lake Isle of Innisfree,"
William Butler Yeats (1865–1939)

[*Voyager*, p. 634]
"She moves! She stirs! She seems to feel/The thrill
of life along her keel!"

Claire is here slightly misquoting the
original, which reads:

And see! She stirs!
She starts—she moves—she seems to feel
The thrill of life along her keel.

—from "The Building of the Ship,"
Henry Wadsworth Longfellow
(1807–1882)

[*Voyager*, p. 661]
"The weeping Pleiads wester/And the moon is
under seas."

Claire, always fond of Housman, is here
conflating a couple of lines from different
stanzas. The original first line (from "More
Poems") is from a verse that reads "The
rainy Pleiads wester/Orion plunges prone,/
And midnight strikes and hastens/And I lie
down alone."

Later, she quotes from another poem:

Halt by the headstone naming
The heart no longer stirred,
And say the lad that loved you
Was one that kept his word.

and on p. 904:

Oh, who is that young sinner with the hand-
cuffs on his wrists?
And what has he been after that they groan
and shake their fists?
And wherefore is he wearing such a conscience-
stricken air?
Oh they're taking him to prison for the colour
of his hair.
. . .
'Tis a shame to human nature, such a head of
hair as his;
In the good old time 'twas hanging for the
colour that it is;
Though hanging isn't bad enough and flaying
would be fair
For the nameless and abominable colour of his
hair!

—from "Additional Poems,"
Alfred Edward Housman (1859–1936)

[*Drums*, p. 430]
"Forever wilt thou love, and she be fair!"

—from "Ode on a Grecian Urn,"
John Keats (1795–1821)

[*Drums*, p. 431]
"Make me thy lyre . . ."

—from "Ode to the West Wind,"
Percy Bysshe Shelley
(1792–1822)

[*Drums*, p. 430]
While Claire does not directly quote this
poem in the text, she does mention reciting
Keats's "Sonnet Written in Disgust of Vulgar Superstition":

The church bells toll a melancholy round,
Calling the people to some other prayers,
Some other gloominess, more dreadful cares,

More hearkening to the sermon's horrid sound.
Surely the mind of man is closely bound
    In some black spell; seeing that each one
    tears
    Himself from fireside joys, and Lydian airs,
And converse high of those with glory crown'd.
Still, still they toll, and I should feel a
    damp,—
    A chill as from a tomb, did I not know
That they are dying like an outburnt lamp,
    That 'tis their sighing, wailing ere they go
    Into oblivion;—that fresh flowers will grow,
And many glories of immortal stamp.

[*Drums,* p. 431]
"**Fiend, I defy thee!** with a calm, fixed mind."

—from Shelley,
Prometheus Unbound, Act I

[*Drums,* p. 147]
*Amo, amas, I love a lass,
As cedar tall and slender . . .*

—Anonymous

This particular poem is what's known as a "macaronic"; a type of light verse popular in the eighteenth century[8] and later, in which Latin words or phrases are mixed with English to produce a comic effect, either by reason of Latin false cognates (Latin words that sound like English words, but mean something quite different) or by reference to Latin grammar, as in this example. Popular among the upper classes, as it showed off a person's wit, as well as his (or her) education.

Several members of the Literary Forum discovered or recalled bits of macaronics, which they helpfully quoted to me; this one was both complete, and most apropos, so I chose it for Jamie.

[*Drums,* p. 279]
*How many strawberries grow in the salt sea;
    how many ships sail in the forest?*

—from "The Fause Bride," a medieval Scottish ballad. My friend Jack Whyte (my authority on Scottish ballads)[9] tells me that this particular line rates as perhaps the oldest riddle in Scottish literature, and is from the Northeast of Scotland—"Fraser territory," he says.[10]

[*Drums,* p. 776]
From Ushant to Scilly is thirty-five leagues.

—from a traditional sea-chanty

[*Drums,* p. 778]
Farewell to you all, ye fair Spanish ladies.

—traditional sea-chanty

MISCELLANEOUS QUOTATIONS

[*Voyager,* p. 511]
He created a desert and called it peace.

Though later repeated by one of the Duke of Cumberland's contemporaries, in reference to his "pacification" of the Highlands after Culloden, this quotation is orig-

---

[8]*A "macaroni" was a fop; a person of marked affectation and extreme fashion (often imported from Italy; hence the name).*
[9]*Jack's very helpful reminiscences of his days as a Scottish folk-singer formed the backbone—complete with kilt jokes—of this aspect of Roger MacKenzie's character.*
[10]*"Strawberries," right?*

inally from the Roman historian Tacitus, and reads (in translation), "Where they make a desert, they call it peace."

—"Agricola," Cornelius Tacitus
(A.D. c. 56–c. 120)

[*Voyager,* p. 519]
Hawk from a handsaw . . .

. . .

"I am but mad north-northwest: when the wind is southerly I know a hawk from a handsaw."

—from *Hamlet,*
William Shakespeare (1564–1616)

[*Voyager*]
After a war, first come the corbies, and then the lawyers, to pick the bones.
—Anonymous (which merely means *I* don't know who said it)

[*Voyager,* p. 586]
Law is a bottomless pit.
—Dr. John Arbuthnot (1667–1735)
This is not a quote per se, but rather the title of a book, *Law Is a Bottomless Pit,* published by Dr. Arbuthnot in 1712—and likely well known to Ned Gowan.

[*Drums,* p. 726]
Nobody expects the Spanish Inquisition!
—Monty Python
For trivia buffs: Brianna may be stretching a point slightly; I believe Monty Python's television show began in 1967 or 1968, but

I didn't bother trying to find out precisely when the show that contains the Spanish Inquisition skit aired. We'll just assume she saw it, all right?

[*Voyager,* p. 620]
Fifteen men on a dead man's chest . . .
"*Fifteen men on the Dead Man's Chest—*
Yo-ho-ho, and a bottle of rum!
Drink and the devil had done for the rest—
Yo-ho-ho, and a bottle of rum!

—from *Treasure Island,*
Robert Louis Stevenson (1850–1894)

[*Drums,* p. 429]
How long will a man lie i' the earth ere he rot?

—*Hamlet,* William Shakespeare

MISCELLANEOUS QUOTES AND NOTES

"Romances"

Following the publication of *Voyager,* I had letters from some readers amused by the parallels of Claire's and Jamie's reading matter— that Claire should be reading a modern romance novel (*The Impetuous Pirate*)[11] on pages 255–256, while Jamie was reading what they assumed to be the eighteenth-century equivalent. In fact, what Jamie is reading is *Fanny Hill: Memoir of a Woman of*

---

[11] *A number of readers apparently believed the excerpts to have been taken from an actual book titled* **The Impetuous Pirate,** *and inquired as to the author and publisher of this book, as they wished to read the whole story. Ahem. I'm flattered. I think.*

Pleasure, a fairly notable piece of eighteenth-century pornography by John Cleland, published in 1747.[12] (Jamie does in fact read "romances," too—he recounts stories from *The Adventures of Roderick Random* and *The History of Tom Jones, a Foundling* to his men at Ardsmuir, and later discusses Samuel Richardson's *Pamela* (which is somewhat closer to a modern-day romance, in terms of its subject matter)[13] with Lord John Grey— but he is likely reading *Fanny Hill* for purposes other than mental diversion).

In another place (*Voyager,* pp. 80–81), Jamie is shown reading what appears from the excerpts to be Daniel Defoe's *Robinson Crusoe,* a popular—and in the circumstances, rather prophetic—tale of shipwreck and adventure.

"This violent rain forced me to a new work, viz., to cut a hole through my new fortification, like a sink, to let the water go out, which would else have drowned my cave. After I had been in my cave some time, and found still no more shocks of the earthquake follow, I began to be more composed; and now, to support my spirits, which indeed wanted it very much, I went to my little store and took a small sup of rum, which however, I did then and always very spar-

ingly, knowing I could have no more when that was gone.

"It continued raining all that night, and great part of the next day, so that I could not stir abroad; but my mind being more composed, I began to think. . . ."

—from *Robinson Crusoe,* Daniel Defoe
(1660–1731)

_____

[12]*And still in print, which I suppose goes to show something about the durability of Great Literature.*
[13]*If not its length; Sir Samuel is one of my personal patron saints, his works tending to run about 1500 pages in the unabridged original editions.*

Appendix IV

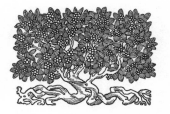

Roots

———

A BRIEF PRIMER ON
GENEALOGICAL RESEARCH

You have four grandparents, eight great-grandparents, sixteen great-great-grandparents, and thirty-two great-great-great-grandparents. With an average of twenty-five years between each generation, this means that during the past five hundred years, there were 1,048,576 people—all contributing to the production of you!

I get a great many letters from people newly interested in their Scottish heritage as a result of reading the *Outlander* novels, and asking either for any information I may have on clan MacLellan, MacLeod, McIver, McEtc., or for advice on beginning an exploration into their own family tree.

I'm really not the person to ask, as I don't have a great deal of information personally on the clans as such. I poke around in the historical records, pick up interesting personalities, and follow entertaining lines of inquiry—but this tends to be at best a random process. Such organization as there is in my inquiries is along historical lines, not clan or family lines; that is, I'm familiar with the major Jacobite figures active during the period of the '45, but those activities are what I'm familiar with—the fact that I know who Lochiel (Donald Cameron of Lochiel) was does not indicate that I know anything else about clan Cameron.

Neither am I a genealogist. Given my circumstances, I am happily able simply to make *up* family trees, rather than being obliged to do tedious research.

I had originally included in this Appendix a number of online resources for genealogical resources—circa 1999. A lot has changed online since then, and most of those references are obsolete, and I've therefore deleted them. There are a huge number of websites that facilitate this sort of research these days, but it's a long way outside my own areas of expertise, so I'll not try to list them here.

I have kept the listings of books, newsletters, and small regional or special groups that may not be easily findable otherwise. (Note, though, that such groups go out of existence, move, or change names, too. I'm not guaranteeing that all these references are still

viable—but here they are, for what assistance they may be.)

Mormon temples and community centers are a valuable source of genealogical information. The Mormon church opens their family history centers to the public as a community service, and most of their data are computerized and readily available for search. Local historical societies are also a valuable resource of reference.

Your local public library likely has the address of every historical society in every county in the country; also many in Europe. See also some of the book and publication listings below.

BOOKS

The following titles were recommended by helpful people in the CompuServe Genealogy Forum as a starting place (complete bibliographic and descriptive information wasn't given for all titles, but is supplied where available).

G. G. Vandagriff. **Voices in Your Blood:**
The Handy Book for Genealogists, by Everton Publishers Staff. Baltimore, Md: Clearfield Company, 1991.

    Includes all the courthouse addresses in the county, very short introductory essays on the resources in each state, prices for services, etc. New editions are published about every five years. It's published by the same people who publish *Genealogical Helper.*

A good world atlas

Guide to Genealogical Research in the National Archives. Washington, D.C.: National Archives and Records Administration, 1985

Eakle, Arlene H. **The Source: A Guidebook of American Genealogy.** Salt Lake City, Utah: Ancestry, 1984.

Ancestry's Redbook: State, County and Town Sources. Alice Eichholz. Salt Lake City, Utah: Ancestry, 1992.

For more in-depth research:

GENEALOGICAL BOOKS IN PRINT

Stratton, Eugene. **Applied Genealogy.**

The Rand McNally Commercial Atlas.
Published as a marketing tool for distribution-oriented businesses—but many genealogy libraries have one, too. A very large book, with one state per page, listing even the tiniest of towns and unincorporated communities. No highways—just railway lines, watercourses, county lines, township lines where they exist. A complete index of town names is included for each state. Much more complete than the Zip Code Directory or the official List of Post Offices. Costs roughly $250 per yearly edition, and weighs about 30 lbs. Check your local library.

Greenwood, Val D. **The Researcher's Guide to American Genealogy.** Baltimore: Genealogical Publishing Co., Inc., 1992.

Rubincam, Milton. **Genealogical Research: Methods and Sources, vols. I and II.**

Kennedy, Imogene Kinard. **Genealogical Records in Texas.**

Szucs, Loretta Dennis. **The Archives: A Guide to the National Archives Field Branches.**

Building an American Pedigree. Author unknown.

Torrey. **New England Marriage Prior to 1700.**

Savage. **Genealogical Dictionary of New England. Vols. I–IV.**

Book Loan Catalog of the New England Historical and Genealogical Society.

Hammond. **The Whole Earth Atlas.**
It has counties for all the United States, as well as counties or provinces for other countries. There is a small gazeteer and topo map next to each map. The book is about 8 inches by 11 inches and weighs a couple of pounds.

MAGAZINES AND OTHER PUBLICATIONS

The Genealogical Helper
The Everton Publishers
P.O. Box 368
Logan, UT 84321
  $17.00/year (6 issues)

Heritage Quest
Drawer 40
Orting, WA 98360-0040
  $25/year ($35 Canadian or foreign)

Genealogical Computing
P.O. Box 476
Salt Lake City, UT 84110
  $25/year (4 issues)

NGS/CIG Digest (National Genealogical Society's Computer Interest Group Digest)
4527 Seventeenth Street
Arlington, VA 22207-2363

$5/year (6 issues), membership in NGS is NOT required (See National Genealogical Society below)

The Genealogical Computer Pioneer
Posey International
P.O. Box 338
Orem, UT 84057
$30/year (6 issues)

Genealogy Digest
P.O. Box 15681
25 North 200 West
Salt Lake City, UT 84115

The Quarterly
National Genealogical Society
4527 Seventeenth Street
Arlington, VA 22207-2363
(The National Genealogical Society also publishes a newsletter and has a separate computer interest group that publishes the **NGS/CIG Digest.**)

The Register
New England Historic Genealogical Society
101 Newberry Street
Boston, MA 02116
(This society also publishes a bimonthly newsletter called **Nexus.**)

The American Genealogist
128 Massasoit Drive
Warwick, RI 02888

The New York Genealogical and Biographical Record
The New York Genealogical and Biographical Society
122 E. 58th Street
New York, NY 10022-1939

Membership is $50/year, which includes the magazine subscription.

The Mayflower Descendant
Massachusetts Society of Mayflower Descendants
101 Newbury Street
Boston, MA 02116

REGIONAL AND SPECIALIST NEWSLETTERS

"Pathways and Passages"
Polish Genealogical Society of Connecticut
c/o Jonathan Shea
8 Lyle Road
New Britain, CT 06053

Journal of the Afro-American Historical and Genealogical Society
Box 13086
T Street Station
Washington, DC 20009
$25.00/year (four issues)

Intercom
Afro-Americans Communicating and Preserving Legacies
P.O. Box 13607
Atlanta, GA 30324-0607

AVOTAYNU
(International Review of Jewish Genealogy)
P.O. Box 1134
Teaneck, NJ 07666

Trails
Birmingham Genealogical Society
Box 2432
Birmingham, AL 35801

Alabama Family History Geneal.
North Central Alabama Genealogical Soc.
P.O. Box 13
Cullman, AL 35056-0013

Bulletin
Alabama Genealogical Society
Box 35
Epes, AL 35460

Arkansas Genealogical Register
Northeast Arkansas Genealogical Association
314 Vine Street
Newport, AR 73112

The Backtracker
Northwest Arkansas Genealogical Society
Box K
Rogers, AR 72756

Copper State Bulletin
Southern Arizona Genealogical Society
Box 6027
Tucson, AZ 85716

Kern-Gen
Kern County Genealogical Society
Box 2214
Bakersfield, GA 93303

Redwood Researcher
Redding Genealogical Society
Box 606
Fortuna, CA 95540

The Searcher
Southern California Genealogical Society
Box 7665
Bixby Knolls Station
Long Beach, CA 90807

Bulletin
California Central Coast Genealogical Society
Box 832
Morro Bay, 93442

Lifeliner
Genealogical Society of Riverside
Box 2664
Riverside, CA 92506

Leaves and Saplings
San Diego Genealogical Society
Studio 30, Spanish Vill.
Balboa Park
San Diego, CA 92101

Colorado Genealogist
7244 S. Platte Canyon Dr.
Littleton, CO 80123

Connecticut Ancestry
Stamford Genealogical Society
Box 249
Stamford, CT 06904

The Virginia Genealogist
Box 4883
Washington, D.C. 20008

The Lost Palatine (bimonthly newsletter)
c/o Gail Breitbard
Route 1 Box 1160
Estero, FL 33928

South Florida Pioneers
Box 166
Fort Ogden, FL 33842

Ancestry
Palm Beach County Genealogical Society
Box 1745
W. Palm Beach, FL 33402

Swedish-American Genealogist
P.O. Box 2186
Winter Park, FL 32790

Georgia Pioneers
Genealogical Magazine
Box 1028
Albany, GA 31702

Family Puzzlers
Heritage Papers
Danielsville, GA 30633

Newsletter:
Genealogical Society of Southern Illinois
c/o Logan College
Carterville, IL 62818

Central Illinois Genealogical
Decatur Genealogical Society
Box 2068
Decatur, IL 62526

Quarterly
Knox County Genealogical Society
Box 13
Galesburg, IL 61404

Happy Hunter
Cumberland County Genealogical Society
Box 676
Greenup, IL 62428

Michiana Roots
225 W. Colfax
South Bend, IN 46626

The Descender
Montgomery County Genealogical Society
Box 444
Coffeyville, KS 67337

The Treesearcher
Kansas Genealogical Society
Box 103
Dodge City, KS 67801

Kansas Kin
Riley County Kansas Genealogical Society
908 Kearney Street
Manhattan, KS 66502

Quarterly
Heritage Genealogical Society
W. A. Rankin Mem. Library
Neodeska, KS 66756

Midwest Genealogical Register
2911 Rivera
Wichita, KS 67611

Bluegrass Roots
Central Kentucky Genealogical Society
Box 153
Frankfort, KY 40601

Kentucky Ancestors
Kentucky Historical Society
Box H
Frankfort, KY 40601

Kentucky Family Records
West-Central Kentucky Family resrch. Asso.
Box 1465
Owensboro, KY 42301

East Kentuckian
Box 107
Stanville, KY 41659

Register
Louisiana Genealogical Society
Box 3454
Baton Rouge, LA 70821

New Orleans Genesis
Genealogical Research Soc. of New Orleans
Box 51791
New Orleans, LA 70151

Western Maryland Genealogy
Catoctin Press
709 East Main Street
Middletown, MD 21769

Maryland and Delaware Genealogist
Box 352
St. Michaels, MD 21663

Downeast Ancestry
P.O. Box 191
Biddeford Pool, ME 04006-0191

Maine Genealogical Enquirer
Box 253
165 Main Street
Oakland, ME 04963

The Second Boat
P.O. Box 398
Machias, ME 04654

Research Magazine
Detroit Society for Genealogical Research
c/o Detroit Pub. Library
5201 Woodward Avenue
Detroit, MI 48202

Eaglet
Polish Genealogical Society of Michigan
c/o Burton Hist. Collect
5201 Woodward Avenue
Detroit, MI 48202

Michigana
Western Michigan Genealogical Society
603 Greenbrier Dr., S.E.
Grand Rapids, MI 49506

Kalamazoo Valley Family Newsletter
315 S. Rose Street
Kalamazoo, MI 49006

Family Trails
Michigan Dept. of Education
State Library
735 E. Michigan Avenue
Lansing, MI 48913

Family Tree Talk
Muskegon County Genealogical Society
3301 Highland
Muskegon Hts, MI 49444

Timbertown Log
Saginaw Genealogical Society
c/o Saginaw Pub. Library
505 Janes Avenue
Saginaw, MI 48607

Northland Newsletter
Range Genealogical Society
Box 726
Buhl, MN 55713

Research
Box 206
Chillicothe, MO 64601

Kansas City Genealogist
The Heart of America Genealogical Society
Kansas City Pub. Library
311 E. 21st Street
Kansas City, MO 64106

The Prairie Gleaner
West Central Missouri Genealogical Society
Box 102A, No. 3
Warrensburg, MO 64093

The Bulletin
Johnson County Historical Society
Warrensburg, MO 64093

Newsletter
North Platte Genealogical Society
820 W. 4th Street
North Platte, NE 69101

The Genealogical Magazine of New Jersey
Genealogical Society of New Jersey
P.O. Box 1291
New Brunswick, NJ 08903
(Membership of $10/year includes the magazine.)

Yesteryears
120 Fern Park Drive
Camillus, NY 13031

Ancestor Hunt
Ashtabula County Genealogical Society
Box 885
Ashtabula, OH 44004

Newsletter
West August Genealogical Society
1510 Prairie Drive
Belpre, OH 45714

Heir Lines
Warren County Genealogical Society
300 E. Silver Street
Lebanon, OH 45036

Tulsa Annals
Tulsa Genealogical Society
Box 585
Tulsa, OK 74101

Rogue Digger
Rogue Valley Genealogical Society
Box 628
Ashland, OR 97520

The Pennsylvania Genealogical Magazine
Genealogical Society of Pennsylvania
1300 Locust Street
Philadelphia, PA 19107
$8.00/year for the magazine only

Keystone Kuzzins
Erie Society of Genealogical Research
YMCA
130 W. 8th Street
Erie, PA 16507

Laurel Messenger
Somerset Genealogical Society
Box 533
Somerset, PA 15501

South Carolina Historical Magazine
South Carolina Historical Society
1500 Old Town Road
Charleston, SC 29407

Georgia Genealogical Magazine
Box 229
Easley, SC 29604

S. Carolina Magazine of Ancestral Rsch.
Box 694
Kingstree, SC 29556

Black Hills Nuggets
Rapid City Society for Genealogical Research
Box 1495
Rapid City, SD 57701

River Counties Magazine
610 Terrace Drive
Columbia, TN 38401

Echoes
East Tennessee Historical Society
Lawson McGhee Library
Knoxville, TN 37902

Stripes
Texas State Genealogical Society
Box 7067
Dallas, TX 75209

Houston Genealogical Forum
5300 Caroline
Houston, TX 77004

The Thorny Trail
Midland Genealogical Society
Box 1191
Midland, TX 79701

Stalkin' Kin
San Angelo Genealogical Society
Box 3453
San Angelo, TX 76901

Our Heritage
San Antonio Genealogical Society
Box 6383
San Antonio, TX 78209

Heart of Texas Records
Central Texas Genealogical Society
1717 Austin Avenue
Waco, TX 76701

The Family Tree
McLennan County Society
1717 Austin Avenue
Waco, TX 76701

Genealogical Journal
Utah Genealogical Association
Box 1144
Salt Lake City, UT 84110

The Virginia Genealogist
Box 4883
Washington, D.C. 20008-0083

Branches and Twigs
Genealogical Society of Vermont
Westminister West
RFD 3
Putney, VT 05346

Bulletin
Tri-City Genealogical Society
Route 1
Box 191
Richland, WA 99352

WEB SITES

**The Society of Genealogists Web site is:
www.cs.ncl.ac.uk/genuki/SoG/**
Their complete book list is published here
and orders can be taken by credit card from
overseas as well. There are a number of
books on tracing Scottish ancestors.
The GENUKI (genealogy of the U.K. and
Ireland) page is the same address, but without the SoG/.
The Baronage Press Web site offers very accurate and detailed information (including

heraldry) on prominent families of the U.K. and Europe:
www.baronage.co.uk

SOCIETIES AND ORGANIZATIONS

Society of Genealogists
14 Charterhouse Buildings
Goswell Road
London EC1M 7BA

Many other society addresses are listed above, in the "Regional and Specialist Newsletter" listings.

Happy hunting!

Appendix V

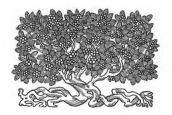

A Brief Discography
of Celtic Music

I first discovered Celtic music while researching speech patterns for *Outlander*. Ballads and other songs gave me a picture of the culture, as well as its speech, and in addition I could listen to the ad lib remarks of the musicians on live recordings, which were very helpful indeed!

Past the point of research, though, I enjoyed Celtic music for its own sake—as do many readers of the *Outlander* series. Following is a (by no means comprehensive) listing of Celtic recordings. Many of these I acquired myself; many were sent to me by kind readers—and many are not in my own collection, but have been recommended to me by fellow enthusiasts. I include the listing merely as a jumping-off point for exploration.

The Alex Sutherland Band and Singers
More Singalong Favourites, Vol. 3.
Fiesta Record Company, Inc.
251 Broadway
Lynbrook, NY 11563

The Alex Sutherland Band and Singers
Music From Scotland, Vol. 2.
Fiesta Record Co., Inc.
251 Broadway
Lynbrook, NY 11563

Baez, Joan (female vocalist)
Joan Baez Ballad Book (cassette)
Vanguard Records
Santa Monica, CA 90401

Battlefield Band (male vocalists)
Across the Borders.
Temple Records (distributed by Rounders
  Records)
One Camp St.
Cambridge, MA 02140

Beat the Drum: (CO)
(multiple musicians)
Songs of Army and Navy Life.
Soundalive Music Ltd.
3 Beckett's Wharf
Lower Teddington Road, Hampton
Wick, Surrey KT1 4ER England

Beaton, Alex
(male vocalist)
*Daft Ditties. A Collection of
Humorous and Tastefully Offensive
Songs.*
Glenfinnan Music Ltd.
21747 Erwin St., Dept. C
Woodland Hills, CA 91367

The Best of Celtic Music
(multiple groups)
AR Productions
36 Avenue Hoche
75008 Paris, France
ARN 55383

**Brown, Tracie, Grace Griffith
and Cathy Palmer**
(female vocalists)
Beyond the Horizon.
Connemara
1710 Bryan Point Rd.
Accokeek, MD 20607

**The Browne Sisters and
George Cavanaugh**
(male and female vocal group)
Castle Dangerous.
Woodenship Records
P.O. Box 1624
Burbank, CA 91507

Capercaillie
(male and female vocal group)
Crosswinds.
Green Linnet Records, Inc.
43 Beaver Brook Rd.
Danbury, CT 06810

Capercaillie *Get Out*
Survival Records Ltd.

Caswell & Carnahan
(USA, male vocalist)
New Leaves on an Old Tree and
Borderlands.
Gargoyle Recordings
Box 1339
Forestville, CA 95436

Celtic Twilight
(multiple groups)
Hearts of Space
P.O. Box 31321
San Francisco, CA 94131

Celtic Twilight I, II, and *III*
(various artists)
Hearts of Space Label

*The Celts Rise Again: Contemporary
and Traditional Music*
(multiple groups)
Green Linnet Records, Inc.
43 Beaver Brook Rd.
Danbury, CT 06819

The Chieftains
The Long Black Veil.
BMG Music
1540 Broadway
New York, NY 10036

The City of Glasgow Police Pipe Band
Scotland's Best, Vol 1.
Fiesta Record Company, Inc.
78 Randall Ave.
Rockville Center, NY 11570

Clannad *Magical Ring*
Tara Records
2 Anne's Lane
Dublin, Ireland

The Corries
(male vocalists)
The Collection.
Lismor Recordings
27-29 Carnoustie Place, Scotland St.
Glasgow G5 8PH

Cross, Mike
(male comedian)
*Best of the Funny Stuff Creme
de la Cross.*
Sugar Hill Records
P.O. Box 55330
Durham, NC 27717-5300
SHC 1010

Dance of the Celts
(various artists)
Narada Label

Enya. *Shepherd Moons*
Reprise Label

Feisty Besoms
(female vocal group)
Auld Flames.
Balnain House
40 Huntley St.
Inverness Scotland 1V3 5HR

Flight of the Green Linnet
(multiple groups)
Celtic Music: The Next Generation.
Green Linnet Records, Inc.
43 Beaver Brook Rd.
Danbury, CT 06810

Fraser, Alasdair
(male, violin)
Dawn Dance.
Culburnie Records UK
P.O. Box 3304
Glasgow, Scotland G66 2BN

P.O. Box 219
Nevada City, NV 95959

Fraser, Alasdair, and Paul Machlis
(male vocalist)
The Road North.
Sona Gaia Productions, Inc.
P.O. Box 2740
Ukiah, CA 95482

Fraser, Alasdair, and Paul Machlis
(male vocalist)
Skyedance
Culburnie Records UK
P.O. Box 3304
Glasgow, Scotland G66 2BN

P.O. Box 219
Nevada City, NV 95959

Gaberlunzie.
Legends of Scotland.
Klub Records Ltd.

The Gathering.
(various artists)
Real World Records Ltd.

Corsham
Wiltshire SN13 8PN, UK

Caroline Records Inc.
104 West 29th St., 4th Floor
New York, NY 10001

Griffith, Grace
(USA, female, guitar)
Every Hue and Shade.
Connemara (Siren Song Distributing
  Celtic Music)
7854 Mayfair Circle
Ellicott City, MD 21043

Griffith, Grace, and Cathy Palmer
(USA, female vocalists)
Connemara Siren Song.
Blix Street Records
11715 Blix St.
N. Hollywood, CA 91607

Hearts of the Gaels
(multiple groups)
Green Linnet Records, Inc.
43 Beaver Brook Rd.
Danbury, CT 06819

Lamond, Mary Jane
(Canadian female vocalist)
Suas e!
Turtle Musik/A&M Records
1345 Denison St.
Markham, Ontario
Canada L3R 5V2

*The Last of the Mohicans: Original
Motion Picture Soundtrack*
Atlantic Records

The McCalmans
(male folk group)
The Very Best of the Corries.
Ross Records
29 Main St.
Turriff, Aberdeenshire, Scotland

McKennitt, Loreena
(Canadian female vocalist)
The Mask and Mirror and *Parallel Dreams.*
Quinlan Road Limited
P.O. Box 933
Stratford, Ontario
Canada N5A 7M3

McKennitt, Loreena
The Visit.
Warner Bros. Records Inc.

McNeil, Keith and Rusty
(songs and history)
Colonial and Revolution Songs with Historical Narration.
WEM Records
16230 Van Buren Blvd.
Riverside, CA 92504

Men of Worth
(male vocal group)
Great Songs of Scotland and Ireland.
Glenfinnan Music Ltd.
21747 Erwin St.
Woodland Hills, CA 91367

Morris, Susan Rode
(female vocalist) *Among the Lasses: Songs of Robert Burns (1759–1796).*
Donsuemor
836 Cragmont Ave.
Berkeley, CA 94708

North Sea Gas
(male group)
Caledonian Connection.
BGS Productions Ltd.
Newton St. Kilsyth
G65 OJX Scotland

Ossian
St. Kilda Wedding.
Iona Records
27-29 Carnoustie Place, Scotland St.
Glasgow G5 8PH

Petteway, Al
Whispering Stones.
Maggie's Music, Inc.
P.O. Box 4144
Annapolis, MD 21403

Redpath, Jean
(female vocalist)
Leaving the Land: A Collection of Songs, Scottish and Western.
Rounder Records Corp.

Rideout, Bonnie
(female, fiddle, viola)
Celtic Circles.
Maggie's Music, Inc.
P.O. Box 4144
Annapolis, MD 21403

Riley, Laurie, Bob McNally, and Friends. *The Flowers of Edinburgh: Celtic Harp Music.*
Handcrafted Recordings
Box 387
Hibernia, NJ 07842

Runrig
(male vocal group)
Amazing Things.
Chrysalis Records, Ltd.

Runrig
(male vocal group, UK)
The Highland Connection.
Ridge Records, Scotland

Runrig
(male vocal group)
Mara.
Chrysalis Music
43 Brook Green
London W6 7EF

Runrig
(male vocal group)
Play Gaelic.
Lismor Recordings
27-29 Carnoustie Place, Scotland St.
Glasgow G5 8PH

Runrig
(male vocal group)
Recovery.
Ridge Records

Scotland's Pipes and Drums.
Maday Inc.
P.O. Box 550
Town of Mount Royal, Quebec
H3P 3C7 Canada

Scotland's Music.
(multiple groups)
Linn Products Limited
Floors Road, Eaglesham
Glasgow, Scotland G76 OEP

The 78th Fraser Highlanders Pipe Band
The Megantic Outlaw Concert.
Lismore Recordings
27-29 Carnoustie Place, Scotland Street
Glasgow G5 8PH

Tempest
(male vocalist)
Turn of the Wheel.
Magna Carta
208 E. 51st St., Suite 1820
New York, NY 10022

This Is Our Scotland.
(multiple groups)
Fiesta Record Company
251 Broadway
Lynbrook, NY 11563

The Voice of Celtic Women
(multiple groups)
There Was a Lady.
Green Linnet Records, Inc.
43 Beaver Brook Rd.
Danbury, CT 06810

Wallace, Edith
(female vocalist)
Standing Naked in the Rain.
Juicy Woman Production, Inc.
35-2561 Runnel Dr.
Coquitlam, BC

Appendix VI

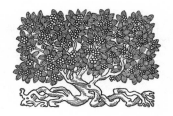

Foreign Editions, Audiotapes, and Strange, Strange Covers

Every now and then, someone asks whether the books are available in one or another foreign language, and if so, how can he obtain a copy thereof?

The answer is that yes, the books are available in a lot of foreign languages, but since the foreign publishers normally send me a few copies of each new translation, I haven't yet had to find any external source for these.

Author's Note: This Appendix is the original, from the 1999 edition of the book. As there are now more than forty publishers—and in some cases, multiple editions of the same book in one language or another.[1] I haven't tried to revise the Appendix to reflect such a large amount of new (and everchanging) material. There will be a fresh Appendix of Publishers in *The Outlandish Companion, Volume Two*, though, which will reflect the situation circa 2015.

I've also supplied a brief description of the publishing history of each title, with a note of varying cover designs, for the use of book collectors. In this regard, I would point out that a) each publisher chooses cover designs according to that publisher's conception both of the book, its market, and national tastes and preferences—all of which may vary quite a bit from publisher to publisher. Also, b) an author usually has nothing at all to say about cover design upfront, unless and until said author establishes a long-term, solid relationship with a domestic publisher. An author generally has nothing at all to say about foreign cover art in advance of publication. It is, therefore, only fair that one can say something about it *ex post facto*.

U.S. EDITIONS

Publisher: Delacorte Press (Dell)
Penguin Random House
1745 Broadway
New York, NY 10019

Outlander
(hardcover)
ISBN 0-385-30230-4

Still in print, still with its original cover art, which I like very much. The excellent artist who does all of the U.S. hardcover designs—Kinuko Craft—actually *reads* the books before implementing her artistry, an attention much appreciated by the author.

Outlander
(paperback, limited low-price edition; out of print)

To facilitate the introduction of new readers to the series, concomitant with the publication of *Drums of Autumn,* Dell issued a limited special edition of the *Outlander* paperback, retailing at $3.99.[2] However, this edition was sold out, and has not been reissued. The cover design (and contents, naturally) are identical with the regularly priced paperback; the only difference is the ISBN and a large "$3.99" in a red starburst superimposed on the cover.

---

[1] *The original German editions of the first three books were heavily abridged and translated by teams of linguists—not an ideal situation. Fortunately, we have a new German publisher who was willing to sponsor fresh, unabridged (and very excellent) translations, done by Barbara Schnell, who has translated all the books since* Drums of Autumn. *I'm thrilled that she's now doing* Outlander, Dragonfly in Amber *and* Voyager.
[2] *This seems to be rather effective. My own editor confesses to feeling like a drug pusher when she gives people* **Outlander.**

Outlander
(paperback)[3]
ISBN 0-440-21256-1

This paperback has had two covers (so far): The first featured some elements of the hardcover design, including the clock, dirk, necklace, and tartan. However, it also featured a Rather Unfortunate stepback cover (an inside cover, visible when the outer cover is opened. This one, though, is visible *through* the outer cover, which has a cutout, allowing a face to leer out through the clock), with drawings purporting to illustrate the story within. Okay, the drawing of Jamie is not bad. It's not quite Jamie, but it's at least a mildly attractive young man with red hair, and he *is* holding a sword of the right period and design. The woman (purporting to be Claire, I suppose) . . . well, she has straight, reddish hair, and she strongly resembles the horse she's holding.[4] The outer cover also featured quite a lot of gold foil.

The next cover was simply a nice adaptation (for smaller size) of the hardcover art, with solid-color bands across top and bottom, carrying the title and author name. Very attractive.

Dragonfly in Amber
(hardcover)
ISBN 0-385-30231-2

I've always particularly liked this cover, both because it's very attractive and because it's the first one I got to say anything about. The artist having done preliminary drawings of the overall scene, the publisher sent these to me, saying that the drawing required a "central object" of some kind, and did I have anything to suggest?

"Well," I said, rubbing my hands together, "it *is* called *Dragonfly in Amber*. You think it would be stretching things too far actually to have a *dragonfly* on the cover?" I promptly faxed them pictures (from my research sources) of several "period" Scottish cups and chalices, and lo and behold . . . a dragonfly, hovering over a cup filled with liquid (it should probably have been red liquid—"Dragon's Blood," as prepared by Master Raymond—but I gather the thinking was that this would merely look like wine, whereas the green liquid portrayed looked more like poison).

Dragonfly in Amber
(paperback)
ISBN 0-440-21562-5

Again, this book has had two covers—or three, counting a sort of intermediary form. The first was a smaller rendition of the hardcover, with a Really Horrible stepback illustration inside. I won't go into all the gory details, save to note that my final request for the illustration—for a red dress on the female figure (i.e., Claire's red ball gown, worn at Versailles)—resulted in a depiction of Lolita in a pumpkin-colored gown with a red cloak.

As for the male figure, who appears to be the illegitimate offspring of Pinocchio and Bob Hope . . .

---

[3] *This paperback has been published with two cover designs, as of 1/98. The original cover design included a stepback illustration, but reprints of this edition do not include the stepback.*
[4] *My father-in-law—a lifelong cowboy—didn't like the horse, either.*

I'm happy to report that the stepback disappeared in the next print run, leaving the book with simply the outer cover.

When *Outlander* was re-covered, both *Dragonfly* and *Voyager* were redone to match, with the original design preserved, but with solid bands across top and bottom for name and title.

Voyager
(hardcover)
ISBN 0-385-30232-0

For this one, the publisher actually *asked* me what I'd like to see on the cover. Always ready, I promptly replied, "A ship and an ocean." I was very pleased with the result—though the initial design featured a pile of roses on the map in the foreground. I said I thought this rather unlikely, on an eighteenth-century sailing ship, and the roses were obligingly replaced—though with a tasteful thistle, rather than the jeweled dagger I suggested.

Voyager
(paperback)
ISBN 0-440-21756-3

Again, the original cover is an adaptation of the hardcover. This time, I succeeded in preventing any attempts to depict literal characters from the book, and while there was a stepback cover for the first printing, it shows only tumbling ocean waves, with review quotes superimposed; a vast improvement. This cover was "refreshed" to match the others, with solid bands top and bottom replacing the original Celtic-themed lettering for title and author name (and covering up the thistle), but the general design was kept intact.

Drums of Autumn
(hardcover)
ISBN 0-385-31140-0

By this time, I trusted the artist implicitly, so merely suggested some sort of outdoor scene, preferably with the "feel" of an eighteenth-century landscape—and sent along a bundle of photocopies of "possible objects," as well as a few samples of paintings that I thought had the correct atmosphere.

This was a very successful cover; in fact, so successful that the Swedish publisher used it intact, and the German publisher used a variant of it.

Drums of Autumn
(paperback)
ISBN 0-440-22325-X

The cover design is an adaptation of the hardcover, with bands top and bottom. The stepback in the first printing shows a tartan background, with review quotes superimposed.

CANADA

Publisher: Doubleday Canada
320 Front Street West
Toronto, ON

Since Doubleday Canada belongs to the same parent company as does the U.S. publisher, there is no separate Canadian edition, per se. Doubleday Canada handles distribution of books within Canada, but uses the same edition (same content, cover, ISBNs, etc.) as the United States.

NB: French translation editions of the books are distributed within Quebec by an affiliate of the French publisher.

FRANCE

Publisher: Les Presses la Cité
12, Avenue d'Italie
75013 Paris

NB: French editions are distributed in Quebec by an associate of the French publisher, rather than by Doubleday Canada, who handles the English editions in that country.

All French titles are published as trade paperback editions rather than hardcover and/or mass market paperback.

Le Chardon et le Tartan
(Outlander)
ISBN 2-258-03984-3

This literally translates to "The Thistle and the Tartan." It's *bright* blue and pink, with a castle in the background and flowering plants in the foreground. It doesn't quite look *Scottish* (possibly owing to the fact that the plants look like azaleas), and the overall tone is pretty gooey, but it does look vaguely historical.

Le Talisman
(Dragonfly in Amber)
ISBN 2-258-03985-1

A talisman is something like a good-luck charm, and one French reader translated the title as "The Lucky Charm." Personally, I wouldn't have thought that's what the dragonfly in amber was, but mine is not to reason why. Possibly "dragonfly" means something obscene in French.

It's a very interesting-looking cover, though it looks more like the novelization of a PBS production of a Henry James novel than anything Scottish. Very French, though. Gray and brown tones, with a street scene, featuring a carriage and a superimposed picture of a young woman in what appears to be a modish velvet hat (à la mode of the early 1900s, that is), looking thoughtful.

Le Voyage
(Voyager)

Again, a quietish sort of cover, echoing the *Talisman* one; this in pale grayish-blue, featuring misty people on a boat and a superimposition of a nice-looking woman in her thirties or forties in the upper right. I really wish they wouldn't put faces on the covers, but no stopping them—and they did at least pick a woman of the proper age, and the right coloring.

ITALY

Publisher: Gruppo Editoriale Fabbri
Bompiani, Sonzogno, Etas S.p.A.
Via Mecenate, 91 - Milano

Ovunque Nel Tempo
(Outlander)
(hardcover, out of print, and a good thing, too)
ISBN 88-454-0510-9

The original cover design wasn't bad; a pair of shadowy female eyes, hovering in the air over Stonehenge. I found the book-club edition objectionable—featuring a raven-haired gypsy wench sprawled on the grass, low-cut gown in disarray—but not as horrifying as the book itself. Both editions were roughly one-quarter the size of the original manuscript.

SPAIN/LATIN AMERICA

Publisher: Emece Editores, S.A.
Alsina 2062 - Buenos Aires, Argentina
Emece Editores Espana, S.A.
Mallorca 237 - 08008 Barcelona

All titles published in trade paperback only; slight differences in cover design between Spanish and Latin American editions, text identical. My guess (judging from the size of the books) is that the text has been cut slightly, and/or the content paraphrased quite a bit.

Forastera[5]
(Outlander) **Latin American edition**
ISBN 950-04-1317-5

Forestera
(Outlander) **Spanish edition**
ISBN 84-7888-193-X

Well, it's orange. Other than that, it's quite nice; a very old-world, misty depiction of a castle, with lots of feathery-looking trees, dripping moss. Not that there happen to be lots of moss-dripping trees around your average Scottish castle, but it's a nice picture anyway.

Attrapado en el tiempo
(Dragonfly in Amber)
ISBN 950-04-1622-0[6]

This means "Trapped in Time," which is at least minimally appropriate.

La Viajera
(Voyager)
ISBN 84-7888-363-0[7]

This title means "The (female) Traveler," which is more or less okay. It features a view (from behind) of two people on a boat, sailing away. Judging from the dress of the people, they're from fifteenth century Spain, rather than eighteenth century Scotland, but you can't see their faces, and one is disposed to be grateful for small mercies. A pale and misty blue in tone.

SWEDEN

Publisher: Bra Bocker
Bokforlaget Bra Böcker AB
5-26380 Hoganas
Sweden
Telephone: 042-39000
FAX: 042-30504

Framlingen
(Outlander)
(hardcover)
ISBN 91-7119-917-9[8]

The early Swedish covers are . . . er . . . well, I *like* them, they're just very strange. *Framlingen* (which I gather means "stranger") has a background done in green and blue swirls, like the peacock endpapers of a very classy book. The title is superimposed on this in

---

[5]*I asked my father (whose first language was Spanish) about the meaning of this title. He laughed and said that while it technically **did** mean "Outlander," the meaning was not so much "Foreigner," or "Stranger," but rather something like "Hick from the Sticks," or "Somebody from waaay out in the weeds."*
[6]*I assume this is the Latin American edition. I don't have an ISBN for the Spanish edition, because the publisher sent me copies of only the Latin American one.*
[7]*They sent me only Spanish copies of this one.*
[8]*These have been published in low-cost book-club editions, but I don't believe they are available in paperback.*

flowing white script, and above the title is inset a really odd painting (it's a real Scottish museum painting, titled—heaven knows why—"Gow leading the Glee Maiden"). It shows a very large brown-bearded Scotsman, wearing a white shirt and a plaid, and carrying a mandolin. A much smaller woman, wearing (no doubt for excellent reasons) a low-cut white chemise and leading a small dog, is attached to the Scotsman's arm and trails after him, head drooping.

Slanda i Bärnsten
(Dragonfly in Amber)
(hardcover)
ISBN 91-7119-923-3

I think this really does mean "Dragonfly in Amber." The cover design is similar to that of *Framlingen;* however, the background is done in a green, pink, and purple plaid, and the inset photo (again, a reproduction of a museum painting), shows a dark and brooding gentleman with a mustache and a gaucho hat, evidently just in from riding the pampas. (I had lunch once with my Swedish editor; he was a very nice man, who certainly *seemed* entirely normal. . . .)

Sjöfararna
(Voyager)
(hardcover, published in two volumes)
Vol. 1: ISBN 91-7119-723-0
Vol. 2: ISBN 91-7119-833-4

I can't say whether it was in response to reader mail or not, but with this book, the Swedish publisher suddenly abandoned their truly unique notions of cover art, and started using the American designs. *Sjöfararna* (which I think does mean "Voyager") has a slight variation on the ship/ocean concept of the American edition.

Sjöfararna
(Voyager)
(paperback)
Vol. 1: ISBN 91-7133-261-8
Vol. 2: ISBN 91-7133-262-6

I believe this is the only one of the Swedish editions published in paperback (more of a trade paper edition than a mass market paperback), but I can't be sure, because of the bewildering multiplicity of book-club editions produced in that country. Same ocean/ship design—on both volumes—as in the hardcover(s).

Trummornas Dan
(Drums of Autumn)
(hardcover) (1997)
ISBN 91-7133-313-4

This book is almost identical (externally) to the American hardcover; the size, cover design and artwork are the same, but with a difference in the typeface used for title and author name. I don't know whether (or why) the publisher decided that the two-volume approach wasn't satisfactory, but they did do this one as a single volume, in spite of the fact that it's longer than *Voyager* (*Sjöfararna*).

GERMANY

Publisher: Blanvalet Verlag GmbH
Neumarkterstrasse 18
W-81664 Munich
Germany

Feuer und Stein
(Outlander)
(hardcover, regular edition)
ISBN 3-7645-0697-0

This title means "Fire and Stone"; adventurous, if not particularly referent. The cover art, oddly, is essentially that of the American edition of *Dragonfly*. (The book-club edition was plainly done as "women's fiction"; a plaid background with an inset of the face and bust of a highly undistinguished-looking girl.)

Feuer und Stein
(Outlander)
(paperback)

Same art as the hardcover. German paperbacks tend to be smaller in dimension than do American ones; the effect of this, given a very long book, is to render the result somewhat cuboidal.

Die Geliehene Zeit
(Dragonfly in Amber)
(hardcover)
ISBN 3-7645-0702-0

This means "The Borrowed Time," which is really rather an appealing title. With (I suppose) perfect logic, this book uses an adaptation of the American *Outlander* art—the clock and tartan motif—though in this version, the ornate French clock has been replaced by a large pocket watch.

Die Geliehene Zeit
(Dragonfly in Amber)
(paperback)

When this paperback arrived, my husband looked at it and said, "When one of your books gets to be as thick as it is wide, do you

get some kind of prize?" If you laminated a few of these things, you could build walls with them.

Ferne Ufer
(Voyager)
(hardcover)

This means "The Far Shore," which is okay, if not inspired. Not yet released in paperback (as of the publication of this Companion, that is).

The art department seems to have caught up with itself; this one uses a variant on the American *Voyager* cover.

Der Ruf Der Trommel
(Drums of Autumn)
(hardcover)

I think this means "The Sound of Drums," which is actually something like the original; rather a change. Like the Swedish edition of *Drums,* this one is almost identical with the American version, save for the dimensions; it's slightly shorter and fatter. (I think this paperback just might win that hypothetical prize.)

UK
(AND COMMONWEALTH COUNTRIES, INCLUDING AUSTRALIA AND NEW ZEALAND, BUT NOT CANADA)

Publisher: Century Random (now Random House UK)
20 Vauxhall Bridge Road
London SW1V 2SA
England

Cross Stitch
(Outlander) (1991)
(hardcover—out of print; may be available in reprint)
ISBN 0-7126-4760-0

This book was originally published in hardcover, but that edition is out of print. However, Random House has indicated an intention to reprint the hardcover (with original cover illustration, which was quite pretty) in a limited quantity, for library consumption. It may be possible to obtain copies of this reprint edition; if not, I have ordered a small quantity for myself, to fill orders from people wanting autographed copies.[9]

Cross Stitch
(paperback)
ISBN 0-09-991170-1

There have been three (wildly) different cover designs for the paperback, so far: The first was truly disgusting, being orange with bouquets of pink roses, tied with MacKenzie tartan ribbons, stuck through with souvenir-stand clan badges. The second was very appealing; it shows a young, quintessentially English-looking couple, standing near a large boulder on a rocky hill. It's a quiet-looking cover (pale yellow in tone), but nice. The third features a full-face, leering portrait of some ghastly female, on a white background. No, it doesn't look like Claire.[10]

(Following prolonged obnoxious complaint from the author, the publisher has announced its intention of reissuing the entire series of paperbacks with Much Improved Covers, which we await with eager anticipation.)

Dragonfly in Amber
(paperback)
ISBN: 0-09-929471-0

Dragonfly **was never** published in hardcover in the U.K.[11] It has had two iterations of the paperback cover; the first being both lovely and suitable, one of my personal favorites[12]—a pointillist-style depiction of a Highland meadow, with a black stone sticking up out of it, and two tiny, faceless figures (tall, red-haired male, shorter bonneted female) crossing through it. The second is/was an iteration of the frightful woman (no offense to the hapless model who posed for it; I'm sure it wasn't *her* fault) on the *Cross Stitch* cover.

Again, there should be a third—much improved—cover for this edition, to be issued simultaneously with this Companion.

---

[9]*Persons wanting autographed copies of books, bookplates (these are free, on request; just send me a stamped, self-addressed envelope to return them in), or anything else, can contact me by mail at P.O. Box 584, Scottsdale, AZ 85252-0584.*

[10]*Adding insult to injury, people all over Australia asked me whether the cover portrait was based on me! No, it wasn't.*

[11]*Owing to the publisher's fear at the time that no one would buy it. The original paperback appeared with "Money-Back Guarantee" stickers—an offer which, I'm pleased to say, no one ever took up.*

[12]*Which is, I supposed, why they decided to do away with it.*

Voyager (1995)
(hardcover)
ISBN 0-7126-6133-6
(paperback)
ISBN 0-09-942851-2

The first *Voyager* paperback cover looks very like the hardback cover—which is a pity. It featured a female figure purporting to be Claire, looking like either a teenybopper or someone who had escaped the house wearing her bathrobe (variations, owing to separate publication in Great Britain and Australia/New Zealand), a redheaded male figure lurking in the background, evidently intended to be a ghost from its spectral shape, and what is presumably Brianna, depicted as an overgrown ten-year-old in a granny dress. It's also a rather nasty purple.

In this case, the reissue—third iteration of the Same Horrible Woman—was actually an improvement, but I'm still looking forward to the newest attempt.

The hardcover *may* be available, but I wouldn't bet on it; U.K. hardcovers are normally done in relatively small print runs, since the main demand for these is from libraries.

Drums of Autumn (1997)
ISBN 0-7126-7623-6

This one was done—and is likely still available—in both hardcover and paperback. The cover design is actually not too bad, save for the presence of a very literal-looking female in the center. This was actually the first appearance of the Lady with Brown Hair; since the book sold quite well, the publisher promptly reissued the other three books with cut-rate versions of the same cover—and the same model, with her hair combed differently.

Stay tuned for the new and much improved cover, *not* featuring female portraits, or so they tell me.

RUSSIA

Well, we did sell rights to the first three books to a company called Centrepolygraph, but I've never seen any of these books, and in fact have no idea whether they ever *were* published in Russia, let alone what they might look like.

HOLLAND

A Dutch publisher, Meulenhoff, has bought rights to the first book, and it should be on the market soon—titled *de Reiziger*. If it does well, presumably they might want the rest.

POLAND AND KOREA

Contracts for *Outlander* have also been signed with publishers in Poland and Korea, but no information is available as yet regarding titles or publication dates.

AUDIO

There are several taped versions of the books (see "Frequently Asked Questions"). The commercially available versions are the (severely) abridged recordings from Bantam, and the (delightfully) unabridged ones from Recorded Books, Inc. Addresses and ISBNs are given below.

Bantam Audio
Penguin Random House LLC
1745 Broadway
New York, NY 10019

Read by Geraldine James, who is a wonderful British actress. Great productions, but owing to the abridgement, these tapes make a good accompaniment to the books—not a substitute for them.

Outlander
(six CDs, six hours)
ISBN 978-0-553-71453-1

Dragonfly in Amber
(5 CDs, six hours)
ISBN 978-0-553-71451-7

Voyager
(5 CDs, six hours)
ISBN 978-0-553-71454-8

Drums of Autumn
(5 CDs, six hours)
ISBN 978-0-553-71452-4

Recorded Books, Inc.
270 Skipjack Road
Prince Frederick, MD 20678
For a free catalog, call 1-800-638-1304

The unabridged series is read by Davina Porter, a terrific actress who does a wonderful job with all the voices, but particularly with Claire's.

Since unabridged recordings are in demand mostly by libraries (being hideously expensive, owing to the length), you may or may not find these versions in your local bookstore (if you do, you'll know it. They aren't inconspicuous). RBI offers a catalog service for rental books, however, available either through their Web site, or by phone.

Outlander (32.5 hours)
ISBN 0-7887-1298-5

Dragonfly in Amber
(39.5 hours)
Part 1 (15 cassettes, 22 hours)
ISBN 0-7887-2170-4
Part 2 (12 cassettes, 17.5 hours)
ISBN 0-7887-2472-X

Both *Voyager* and *Drums* are also in production by RBI, and will be released in 1999.

Appendix VII

The Methadone List

Well, I'm slow. Or at any rate, it definitely takes me longer to write these books than it takes readers to read one. Consequently, a number of people have asked whether there are any other writers who write books like mine, so they will have something to read while waiting for the next in the *Outlander* series.

I'd be hard-pressed to recommend books *like* mine, because I sort of like to think mine are unique.[1] There are, however, quite a few excellent books that are also unique, and that might also appeal to readers who like my books.

I've arranged this listing (roughly) into sections, according to the principal elements or genres of the stories. Those people who are most taken by the time travel premise or the fantastic elements of the *Outlander* novels will be more likely to enjoy books on the Fantasy or Historical Fantasy list, whereas those of you who especially enjoy the historical details might prefer the "straight" Historical list, and might not like some of the others.

Still, I can enthusiastically recommend most of the writers on this list, from my own experience as a reader; a few were added that I haven't yet read myself, but have heard excellent things about. Try them; I hope you'll like them!

HISTORICAL FANTASY

These are books with a skeleton of straight historical fiction, fleshed out in various forms of fantasy.

Judith Merkle Riley
A Vision of Light
In Pursuit of the Green Lion
The Oracle Glass
The Serpent Garden

JMR writes historical fiction (from different periods), with a little romance, a good sense of humor, and excellent research—and she also has a touch of the supernatural or paranormal in all her stories.

Vonda McIntyre
The Moon and the Sun

Vonda McIntyre is a well-known (and award-winning) science fiction/fantasy writer, but this particular book is a really nice mingling of straight historical fiction with fantasy. The Sun King with a captive mermaid at Versailles? Fascinating, intellectually stimulating, and emotionally engaging.

Connie Willis
Doomsday Book

A terrific time travel story, mixing good science fiction and very accurate historical fiction (setting: the Dark Ages in Britain). Very suspenseful, excellent writing.

Tim Powers
The Stress of Her Regard

A truly weird, but very good book, in which the poet Shelley is featured, along with the legend of the lamia. A certain amount of blood and violence, to say nothing of lamias. Set in England and Italy, in the nineteenth century. Great book, but not for the squeamish.

---

[1] *My editor has been known to say on occasion, "These **have** to be word-of-mouth books, because they're too weird to describe to anybody."*

Fantasy

Laurell K. Hamilton
The Anita Blake, Vampire Hunter Series

A unique series (nine books so far), dealing with the adventures of Anita Blake, licensed vampire executioner and working zombie raiser, who—in the course of the series—is courted by a werewolf and a vampire, and battles just about every form of supernatural creature I've ever heard of—and not a few I hadn't. Extremely violent and bloody, but never gratuitously so. Nonstop action, but the most interesting aspect of the series is the increasing complexity of the moral questions asked, as the chief character explores her own powers in greater depth, and begins wondering exactly what the differences are between the humans and the monsters.

Lois McMaster Bujold
Shards of Honor

A story set in the future, but with characters and values instantly recognizable in the here and now. A good adventure, with a strong central love story.

Anne McCaffrey
An excellent storyteller—and prolific writer —who deals with dragons, telepathy, and any number of other adventurous elements.

Raymond Feist
Faerie Tale
The Riftwar Saga (six-book series)

All of Feist's books are good; the six books of the Riftwar Saga are a good recommendation for those who particularly enjoy a mix of fantasy and adventure. *Faerie Tale* is a stand-alone, and—I think—the most interesting of Feist's works, mingling supernatural and sexuality in an intriguing way.

Richard Adams
Watership Down

This book gives you entertainment and adventure, together with the illusion of being completely encompassed by another world—in this case, a rabbit warren.

Historical Fiction

Jack Whyte
Jack Whyte's books (six, so far) deal with pre-Arthurian Britain, and include characters such as Merlyn and Arthur himself—but are straight historical fiction, with no hint of fantasy or magic. As Jack says, "I wanted to figure out how the bloody sword got into the stone—and how the kid pulled it out—without having to invoke magic." He's succeeded, and in the process, gives a detailed and absorbing picture of just what happened in Britain when the Roman Legions folded their tents and went away, leaving the remnants of the Roman settlers to deal with the local Celtic tribes and the struggle to preserve their notion of civilization.

Dorothy Dunnett
The Lymond Chronicles (six books)
The Niccolo Series (eight books)

Dunnett writes big, fat historical novels, rich in plot, character, and detail. The Lymond Chronicles are set in the fifteenth century, the Niccolo books in the fourteenth—both cover a lot of territory, including most of the countries of Europe and the Mediterranean. Dunnett is one of those authors that people either love or hate; little middle ground. The style of writing is rich and the prose often gorgeous—but I sometimes find it oblique.

Jennifer Roberson
Lady of the Forest
Lady of the Glen

Lady of the Forest is a retelling of the Robin Hood legend, told from the point of view of Maid Marian. *Lady of the Glen* is much more straight history; a fictionalized—but quite accurate—account of the Glencoe Massacre.

Nigel Tranter
The MacGregor Trilogy, and others

Tranter is a very popular British author of historical fiction. *The MacGregor Trilogy* deals with the Jacobite era of Scottish history, but he has a great many other interesting titles, dealing with other parts of Britain's past.

Robert Louis Stevenson
An oldie but a goodie. If you haven't read *Treasure Island* or *Kidnapped* recently, treat yourself.

Morgan Llywelyn
Llywelyn's books deal sometimes with characters from legend (e.g., *Red Branch,* which tells the story of Cuchullain) and sometimes with historical persons and events (1916). Her territory is Celtic History, well-researched, and her stories are absorbing.

Charles Palliser
Quincunx

If Charles Dickens had been interested in writing puzzle stories, he would have written this. It's a huge book, with multiple interlacing (and engaging) plots, all written in a very authentic Victorian style. Very evocative and deeply interesting—but it's not light reading (about three pounds, I'd say).

Brian Moore
Black Robe

Set in the late seventeenth century, this is a small book; sparsely written but very evocative—the story of a young French priest, sent to convert and serve among the Huron.

HISTORICAL FICTION SERIES

For those who—having found a good thing—want it to go on and on. These are excellent series, some based on historical events, some merely using historical settings for fictional adventures—but without any fantastic overtones.

Patrick O'Brian
The Aubrey/Maturin series

O'Brian is the most renowned of the seafaring historical novelists. His series (the first book is *Master and Commander*), featuring Captain Jack Aubrey and his friend and ship's surgeon, Dr. Stephen Maturin, is set during the Napoleonic Wars. Great characters, wonderful language, excellent historical detail.

C. S. Forester
The Horatio Hornblower series

Not quite as sophisticated as O'Brian, but still a very good storyteller. The Hornblower series covers the same period and setting—the British Navy in the Napoleonic Wars—as does

O'Brian, but is very different in terms of character and style.

Sharon Kay Penman
Penman writes on significant British (English and Welsh) historical events, using real historical characters as well as fictional ones.

Bernard Cornwell
The Sharpe series

I've read a couple of Cornwell's other books, which I thought were well researched. I haven't read the Sharpe series yet—I'm saving it for a treat, next time I finish a manuscript—but have had it highly recommended to me. PBS did a miniseries based on some of the books, which was well received. The time period is the same as that covered by O'Brian and Forester—the Napoleonic Wars—but Sharpe is a soldier, rather than a sailor, and the stories are mostly land-based.

George MacDonald Fraser
The Flashman series

Flashman is a man you love to hate. A cad, a cheat, a bully, and a bounder, he cavorts through history—with the reader cheering him on. These books are not only remarkably entertaining, they're remarkably researched—with equally entertaining footnotes in each. Flashman's career spans a good part of the nineteenth century, and several continents.

Winston Graham
The Poldark series

Set in Cornwall during the late 1700s. Very good historical soap opera, with extremely engaging characters. PBS had *two* fourteen-week miniseries based on these books.

HISTORICAL MYSTERIES

Anne Perry
Perry has two series, both set in Victorian London. One involves a married couple: Thomas Pitt (a policeman) and his wife, Charlotte. The other series involves Edward Monk, a policeman who wakes up in the first book of his series *(The Face of a Stranger)*, in a hospital, with no memory of who he is or how he got there. Both series are excellent in terms of period detail and social issues; good plotting.

Steven Saylor
Saylor's series features Gordianus the Finder, and is set in Rome during the first century B.C. Written with excellent literary style, and a remarkably colloquial feel for ancient Rome.

Lindsey Davis
A different series set in ancient Rome, featuring Marcus Didius Falco, a fourth-century B.C. gumshoe, and his girlfriend, the Lady Helena Justina. Much lighter than Saylor's books, and a matter of taste; many people like the spoofing modern tone, some don't.

Sharan Newman
The Catherine LeVendeur series (four books so far) is set in medieval France. Engaging characters, with a sense of humor and a strong sense of the times.

Walter Satterthwait
Walter has a contemporary mystery series, which is excellent, but has also written a couple of single title historical mysteries. One of these—*Wilde West*—is unfortunately out of print, but worth looking for; it features Oscar Wilde as detective. Two more recent mysteries, *Escapade* (with Harry Houdini), and

Masquerade, feature Beaumont, a Pinkerton operative.

Dorothy L. Sayers

One of the writers who was an important influence on my own writing. While not originally written as "historical" mysteries—they were contemporary, at the time—the Lord Peter Wimsey mysteries are some of the best, in terms of evocation of social and physical ambiance, rich, three-dimensional characters, engaging plots, and what my husband refers to as Deep Meaning (i.e., moral questions with implications that go beyond the immediate story. "Does this have lots of Deep Meaning?" he asks, when I give him a new excerpt to read).

CONTEMPORARY FICTION

Sharyn McCrumb

The Appalachian series:
If Ever I Return, Pretty Peggy-O
The Hangman's Beautiful Daughter
She Walks These Hills
The Rosewood Casket
The Ballad of Frankie Silver

McCrumb has a series of light contemporary mysteries, which I also like, but I particularly recommend the "ballad" novels, set in modern-day Appalachia, but with strong roots in the past of that region.

Dana Stabenow

Stabenow's mysteries are well plotted, and star a fascinating central character—Kate Shugak, an Aleut investigator, living on her own homestead in Alaska—but are included here because of their skill in showing both the details and the emotions of a different culture.

Reginald Hill

One of the best of the contemporary British crime writers. Hill has two series, and a few single titles; I like them all, but am fondest of his Pascoe and Dalziel books, and his most recent series, starring Joe Sixsmith.

SCOTTISH FICTION

Iain Banks

The Crow Road
Complicity
Feersum Endjinn
The Wasp Factory

Banks's other books are probably good, too—he's one of the most popular modern Scottish writers—but these are the ones I've read so far and can personally recommend. Some of Banks's books are classified as science fiction, others as fiction. He has a wide range of style and character, and is an immensely talented writer.

M. C. Beaton

The series dealing with Hamish Macbeth is *very* light, quick reading, but with considerable charm and a sense of affection for the long, lanky, red-haired Highland policeman who is its hero.

William McIlvanney

At the other end of the literary scale, three of McIlvanney's four books are about a Glasgow policeman, John Laidlaw (the fourth, *The Kiln,* is an autobiographical novel—also very good). Very lyrical, very gritty; not an easy combination to pull off. Very Scottish, too.

John Buchan

John Macnab
Witch Wood

Classic Scottish tales.

D. K. Broster
The Jacobite Trilogy

Three interlinked novels, set in and around the '45.

John Greig
The Return of John Macnab

A new telling of the Buchan tale; that is, a different (contemporary) story, but based on—and exploring some of the same issues as—the original John Macnab.

Irvine Welsh
Trainspotting
Marabou Stork Nightmares
The Acid House
Ecstasy
Filth

Irvine Welsh is not for the weak. These books are simultaneously horrifying and hilarious. Also heart-wrenching. *Trainspotting, Filth* (and parts of *Marabou*), in addition, are written entirely in a heavy Edinburgh dialect, which some readers might find heavy going.

Ian Rankin
Knots and Crosses
Wolfman
Strip Jack
The Black Book
Mortal Causes
Black and Blue
The Hanging Garden

Rankin is sometimes hard to find in the United States, though getting more popular; some of these titles may be U.K. editions. Available through specialist mystery book-

stores and online book services. The books listed above are a series of police procedurals, set in Edinburgh and featuring Detective John Rebus. Tough stories, but beautiful writing and good characterization.

ROMANCE

For those who most enjoy love stories, these are several fine writers of "straight" romance (that is, romance unmixed with any other genre elements).

> *Laura Kinsale*
> *Susan Elizabeth Phillips*
> *Judith McNaught*
> *Nora Roberts*

I haven't listed individual titles, because all of these writers are quite prolific.

STRANGE BOOKS

I couldn't come close to describing these books. All I can say is that they're unique, and I thought they were very interesting.

Jeanette Winterson
Sexing the Cherry

John Berendt
Midnight in the Garden of Good and Evil

Manuel Puig
Kiss of the Spider Woman

Tom Wolfe
A Man in Full

Until the next book—Happy Reading!